SUNRISE AND SOFT MIST

The International Library of Poetry

Alyssa R. Stokes, Editor

Sunrise and Soft Mist

Library of Congress
Cataloging in Publication Data

ISBN 1-58235-121-X

Manufactured in The United States of America by
Watermark Press
One Poetry Plaza
Owings Mills, MD 21117

FOREWORD

Throughout life, we store information collected from experiences and try in some way to make sense of it. When we are not able to fully understand the things that occur in our lives, we often externalize the information. By doing this, we are afforded a different perspective, thus allowing us to think more clearly about difficult or perplexing events and emotions. Art is one of the ways in which people choose to externalize their thoughts.

Within the arts, modes of expression differ, but poetry is a very powerful tool by which people can share sometimes confusing, sometimes perfectly clear concepts and feelings with others. Intentions can run the gamut as well: The artists may simply want to share something that has touched their lives in some way, or they may want to get help to allay anxiety or uncertainty. The poetry within *Sunrise and Soft Mist* is from every point on the spectrum: every topic, every intention, every event or emotion imaginable. Some poems will speak to certain readers more than others, but it is always important to keep in mind that each verse is the voice of a poet, of a mind that needs to make sense of this world, of a heart that feels the effects of every moment in this life, and perhaps of a memory that is striving to surface. Nonetheless, recalling our yesterdays gives birth to our many forms of expression.

Melisa S. Mitchell
Senior Editor

Editor's Note

Every culture has its way of interpreting and attempting to understand its traditions, its system of beliefs, its historical events, and its everyday life. For some, it is through the written word that this interpretation and understanding takes place. Poetry is one of the most profound ways in which people use language to express their feelings and thoughts about their lives, their pasts, and their futures. Through succinct language, diverse stylistic choices, penetrating imagery, and poetic devices, a poet can transport his or her readers to another time or place, into the middle of an event—or to its perimeter—and into the mind and thoughts of a persona. At times, a reader may feel moved by a powerful work on a topic to which he or she has no personal connection—this is what makes a poem great.

One such poem is "Soweto, 6-16-76" (1), which interprets and attempts to understand a historical event using emotion and gripping description. For his skilled use of imagery, language, and temporal shift, and for his successful employment of emotion and drama, the judges have awarded the poem's author, Joshua Rothenberger, the Grand Prize for the contest associated with *SUNRISE AND SOFT MIST*. In his fascinating work, the poet discusses the Soweto riots of 1976, during which South Africans living in the township (short for South West Townships) rebelled against the apartheid government's ruling that Afrikaans be used equally with English in black secondary schools. This decision was impossible to carry out in the townships, where the residents did not know the language. Afrikaans evolved from the Dutch spoken by white employees of the Dutch East India Company who arrived in South Africa in 1652. The white descendants of these colonists speak the language, not the black Africans, who were isolated within the townships by the Group Areas Act of 1950. This act stipulated that the urban and industrial centers were to be reserved for whites, while the outlying areas—the bantustans, or homelands—were to be reserved for blacks. With the passing of the Bantu Homelands Citizenship Act of 1970, all non-whites were made citizens of these homelands—regardless of where they lived—and thus lost South African citizenship and their right to vote. In addition, the rest of the world did not recognize the independence of the bantustans. Thus, denied access to South African passports and forced to travel under those of their homelands, they were usually unable to travel beyond the bounds of their homelands or to seek foreign aid against the bantustan policies.

Despite the homelands' independence, South African law allowed police to strictly control their goings-on. Because of deteriorating conditions in black schools, and because of the regulations delineated in the Bantu Education Act of 1953 requiring the incorporation of Afrikaans into the educational system, black school children in Soweto planned a peaceful protest. As Rothenberger tells us in his poem, they were "up all night and the night before making plans for this day." Surprisingly, the police only caught wind of the protest once it had begun. The authorities moved in immediately, assaulting the demonstrators with "canisters of tear-gas" and "four random bullets." The protestors did not back down, however—they were "somewhat tired, but not wanting to rest never wanting to rest." Instead, they returned the attack not with weapons, but with words: "Morena Boloka Sechaba sa heso!" This is a line from a hymn in seSotho, the language spoken by the BaSotho people from the country of Lesotho, located in the middle of eastern South Africa. This song was originally written by Enoch Sontonga in Xhosa, one of the eleven official languages of the country. It was later translated into many of the other languages, including Zulu, English, Afrikaans, and seSotho. During apartheid, the anthem was sung as an act of defiance against the oppressive government. Though not the official national anthem at the time, "Nkosi Sikelel' iAfrika" was combined later with an Afrikaans anthem, "Die Stem," or "The Call of South Africa," in what is now the National Anthem of South Africa. That this former song of rebellion has been incorporated into the patriotism of post-apartheid South Africa certainly speaks to the desire, as Rothenberger hopes, to "apologize to the bodies of the students / young hearts that never wanted to rest, buried in their school uniforms" and to incorporate the spirit of freedom into the political and emotional landscape of their nation.

While presenting a remarkably accurate account of the riots, the poet balances both the emotional and intellectual aspects of his presentation with historical facts. Perhaps most moving is the struggle that takes place in the third stanza within the persona's mind. While he observes the events that unfold during the struggle, he is shocked—as we all are—by the violence that erupts out of what was meant to be peaceful protest: "in the west we say things like 'you are a human, you can't live like this'." However, the persona realizes, as he helps us to do, that some situations call for behavior that is entirely unlike anything of which we believe ourselves capable:

> *but when you are forced to use one arm to signal "peace"*
> *and the other to carry a young boy called Hector Petersen—who is 13 and covered in blood—from the storm*
> *redemption lies in the burning of a Bantu council office or a jagged piece of the parking lot.*

In retaliation against the attack by South African police, the students destroyed everything they could that belonged to the municipal authority, including the infrastructure and buildings. In the days following the riots, all of the schools in Soweto were closed, and the uprising spread to other townships, particularly to those in Cape Town.

In the above stanza, Rothenberger also eloquently evokes the famous photograph of Hector Petersen being carried away from the riot by a friend, while a young girl cries and raises her hands in horror. This image—etched onto the front of the Hector Petersen Memorial in Soweto—also becomes etched in our minds when we read this work. "Soweto 6-16-76" illustrates in beautiful and disturbing detail, but with very simple language, a shocking historical event that, while beyond our intellectual ken, locks us in the grasp of emotion: confusion, sadness, horror, and shock. Though apartheid has ended and South Africa is now a democratic nation, the aftermath of unemployment, illiteracy, lack of education, and violence remains. The past cannot be undone, and South Africans observe June 16th as a national holiday, to remember this fateful day that marked the beginning of the end of apartheid and to celebrate the roles of the rioters in the struggle for freedom.

Each poem in this anthology presents or attempts to understand some emotion, some idea or thought process, some event—whether personal or historical—that the poet is trying to share or with which the poet is struggling. While reading the many moving and gripping works in *SUNRISE AND SOFT MIST*, please pay special attention to these particularly noteworthy poems: "Nanna's Lap" (12) by Amanda Jo Allen; Michael Handford's "The Quiet English Teacher" (8); "Fragments of Reflections" (13) by Amy Hawkins; Mary Heid's "Valentine Wasteland" (11); "locals" (12), by Susan Lightfoot; "Remembering Mrs. Tanaka" (13), by Lenda Noyes; Courtney

O'Donnell's "Faye" (10); "Requiem" (9), by Aisha Claire Robins; Stacey Starr's "Circus Show" (10); and "Weekly Session" (10), by Jeff Trenner. Congratulations to all the prize-winners, and to everyone featured in this anthology.

I would like to thank the staff members of The National Library of Poetry, without whom this book would not have been possible. Judges, editors, associate editors, customer service representatives, data entry personnel, graphic artists, office administrators and administrative services staff have all made invaluable contributions to this effort. I am *grateful* to them for their contributions and support.

Melisa S. Mitchell
Editor

Cover Art: Jerry Breen

Grand Prize Winner

Joshua Rothenberger / Pittsburgh PA

Second Prize Winners

Amanda Jo Allen / Dublin VA
Michael Handford / Kanagawa, Odawara-Shi JAPAN
Amy Hawkins / Sterling VA
Mary Heid / Oklahoma City OK
Susan Lightfoot / Corning NY

Lenda Noyes / Tooele UT
Courtney O'Donnell / Hull MA
Aisha Claire Robins / Seattle WA
Stacey Starr / Columbia MO
Jeff Trenner / Cold Spring NY

Third Prize Winners

Jean Bell / Ojai CA
Pamela Bentivegna / Phonchatoula LA
Kristie Berry / Anchorage AK
Anna Borders / Anniston AL
Krishna Bose / Balasore, Orissa, INDIA
Vanessa Bracamonte / Tucson AZ
Steven Brita / New York NY
John T. Carney / Castro Valley CA
Teresa Chen / Rockville MD
Catherine B. Cohen / Oakland CA
Joan M. Dahlke / New Market MD
Geoffrey Davis / Tracy's Landing MD
Elaine De Backer / Crescent City CA
Susanna Mason Defever / Anchorville MI
Anindita Devanath / Chesapeake VA
Catherine Fisher / Wayne NJ
Carol Foreman / McHenry IL
bekah k. franick / Akron OH
Angela Garcia / Miami Beach FL
Rebecca Gatian / Ocean Springs MS
Ruth E. Grauert / Jersey City NJ
Elizabeth Hein / Woodstown NJ
Eileen Mary Theresa Heim / Shamokin PA
Michael Hiles / Leesburg FL
Dianne E. Hollingsworth / Cochran GA
Elise House / Bethlehem CT
Misti Huedepohl / Fairfax IA
Susan A. Kaiser / Kalamazoo MI
Kathryn Kelchner / Waldorf MD
Harry S. Kline / Naples FL

Jinny Krohnfeldt / Silver Spring MD
Jon LaBree / Los Angeles CA
Christine Lewandowski / Taylors SC
Sarai Logan / Rochester NY
Robert Mcclellan / Anniston AL
Brian McSherry / Chicago IL
Maria Miller / Atlanta GA
Sangeeta Nair / Brooklyn NY
Linda Kay Nealon / Pelham NY
Elizabeth Oppriecht / Batavia IL
John Peloquin / North Providence RI
Edward Phelan / Lumberton NJ
Shellise Piazza / Woodbridge VA
Suzanne Rindell / Stockton CA
Brett Roberts / Titusville FL
Stephen Roche / Upper Marlboro MD
Kim Ross / Flagstaff AZ
Rashaan A. Saheb / Phoenix AZ
Kathleen Sheldon / Pittsburgh PA
Danel Sitar / Alea HI
Jen Smith / Gainesville FL
Kara Smith (kms) / Hammond LA
Michele Solomon / Lauderhill FL
A. Stefan / Mill Valley CA
Dee Treadway / Clarkdale AZ
Paul Virzi / Piqua OH
Cecil Williams / Jamaica NY
Melinda M. Williams / Chicago IL
Brian Wilson / Jackson MI

Congratulations also to all semi-finalists.

Soweto, 6-16-76

in some pre-tempest testament of social status quo
the winds gathering, thrusting furious against the walls of the black school
where the black students learn
the knobby knees of students knocking ungovernable,
up all night and the night before making plans for this day
somewhat tired, but not wanting to rest never wanting to rest

and when the police arrived to contain the situation
thirsty black men hung chants of "Morena Boloka Sechaba sa heso!" in the skies
words that lit the people afire
words that exploded like canisters of tear-gas
words that pierced the heart like four random bullets shot into the crowd

in the west we say things like "you are a human, you can't live like this"
but when you are forced to use one arm to signal "peace"
and the other to carry a young boy called Hector Petersen—who is 13 and covered in blood—from the storm,
redemption lies in the burning of a Bantu council office or a jagged piece of the parking lot

children made of glass shattered by a camouflage gavel and machine gun bullets
flashes of taxis with back seats of butchered brown youths
riot control vehicles rising like hippos from the sea of asphalt,
one day they will apologize to the bodies of students
young hearts that never wanted to rest, buried in their school uniforms

Joshua Rothenberger

Adolescence

In the days of my sainthood
when I stood on the replete banks
of childhood,
never yet at summer,
who comes late upon the spring
and flourishing,
shaking into my face the damp hair?

Out of the river he came,
unconcerned as a god
with a little smiling to commend him
and over his hand,
his deep hand,
the shadow of an apple . . .
Catherine B. Cohen

Separation

Made love to my husband yesterday
over sushi and miso soup
transparent eyes beheld me
in the mirror
sitting across from me
I'm not as needy anymore
Our bodies did merge
We actually spoke
and laughed and shared our hopes
Pink cheeks, shy glances
Admiration
so much better than ownership
Aware of separation
embarrassing awkwardness regarding our future
Stirring hope and despair, compassion and grief
Your presence touches me
Momentarily letting go
I'm tenderly reminded of my humanness
Through joy and clarity I will grow
Maria Miller

Ojai Nights

My sleep is deep

Here in Ojai
The mountains like musk ox
In a mystic circle
Stand sentinel over the silvery
Empire of the dark
Jean Bell

Augustine

I want to take a trip into you
To taste your blood of iron and lead
To curl into a puddle of your tears
while licking dried salt from your lashes
I want to wrap you in sheets of velvet
black as the midnight sky—with its
moon dripping wax onto the daylight sun
I would whisper sweet sounds of fairylands
and angels—of butterflies that fly into forever
I want to take you there—into forever,
where every word spoken is a promise
and every lie told is never broken
I want to lay you down into the grass
until it feels like feathers beneath your naked back
I would press my fingers on your chest
and burn into you my prints of lost lines
I would sing to you of Augustine sand,
I would feed you waves and rock you to sleep
And I want to fall into all that you have become—
only I would learn that nothing is forever.
Jen Lynn Smith

Artistic Rendezvous

The sky and I had a rendezvous today.
Images and colors were there for the taking.
Clouds were in action creating landscapes never before seen.

Blended sky blue pink was a dominant color
but the palette included angel white, frosted gray,
and multiple blues fit for the royal nature of the sky.

The royal blues looked like a series of tick-tac-toe boards,
white clouds as frames.
There were also hard candy ribbon clouds,
hand-stitched quilt patterns, nerve ganglions,
stepping stones like those at the Mississippi headwaters,
and a Disney parade of teddy bears marching in rank.

The parade ended as the sun set.
The sky, in transition, gave us a submarine,
a Queen Victoria fan, and a vapor trail from a long gone jet.

As the sky was approaching darkness
and before the sun slept,
hundreds of geese soared by in formation,
chattering as they inhaled
energy from our rendezvous.
Jinny Krohnfeldt

Self-Awareness

For Marcina Antoinette Haywood
Within the context of my universe
Grandma's perennial presence
the yellow bus transporting me towards
and away from possibilities my peers, my anger
Who am I?

Hoping to become eleven
struggling to feel okay, maybe even cool
lying, stealing, distorting out of control
disavowing strengths
resorting to wanton behavior.

Love me
your brown and white arms guiding me to your breasts
accept me, notice me, and offer me safety
believe my lies, maybe I will too.

My hugeness makes me small
my anger keeps me alive
experiencing the world in camouflage.

Peel away my disguises
allow me to believe
you'd pay a ransom for me.
Susan A. Kaiser

LAX K-Mart at Christmas

I park under passenger jets landing
full of holiday travelers.
Looking toward the store, I see the sign:
Super K-Mart. Of course.
I see no empty shopping carts outside or
inside, yet still people push them.
They must have brought carts from home.

Right by the door,
I pass gift set sausages and holiday M&Ms.
Toy aisles hit the Richter scale—
maybe CalTech monitors them,
telling the staff when to restock.
Long, crooked lines,
unnaturally happy checkers,
the guy in the back selling
Little Caesar's pizza by the slice—
This carnival comes once a year,
Christmas at K-Mart.
Jon LaBree

Idle Thoughts by a Beach Bum

infant tsunamis parachute earthward
and bathe me in tickles
as an effusion of lemon-yellow sun
DEEP FRIES me

I slowly sip the ephemeral juices
of lassitude toying with each drop
letting it linger on my tastebuds

my razor sharp eyes may slice the WA VES
and cut the CUR RENT
my olfactories may snuff
pinches of salty mists

But I . . . (yawn)
I will listlessly lie here
in my naked thicket with my leaden muscles
coated in the Sandman's hypnotic dust and
lullabied by a mute hoopla of celebration . . .
zzzzzzzzzzzz

Anindita Devanath

Charry Wisdom

An educated man I met in good old Langston Hall,
he had degrees a-plenty and he hanged them on his wall.

He begged that I engage him in a wise and witty chat,
for my degrees were many too, so in his room I sat.

He joked about religion and the superstitious men,
who live by prayers and curses and think God will come again.

And bragged of how his father once donned medals that were blest,
but could not cure the cancer that had laid him to his rest.

Then nudging closer to me in a whisper he did say,
"We learned men of intellect are worthier than they."

But angrily I left my seat and spoke as I arose,
"It seems with each degree you earn, your superstition grows."

He knew not what I said to him, his face was so bereft,
and so I tipped my hat and threw a curse at him and left.

And call it fate or call it chance or curse that did befall,
old Langston Hall went up in flames, a dozen killed in all.

And to that fateful twelve belonged that educated man,
who spoke his mind to me one day but will not speak again.

And now his flesh-made soul is scattered with his burnt degrees,
an educated man I met who put his faith in these.

Paul Virzi

My Father's Hands

Like sausages,
the digits sprung
from meaty
back and palms.

"Shovels," I heard
my uncle say
your hands were like.

More as weapons
I saw them,
always a threat.
In each huge finger
a smack was loaded.

When you died,
white as burnt ash,
I saw that your
hands had shrunken.

Stephen Roche

Ferox

Infidum, capitalist's deus, the Fatuous Pretender, I will not surrender:
Settle for a mundane, mechanical existence,
At the cost of my life;
To be reactive, not proactive,
Silent in my acceptance of artificial strife;
To be prostituted for the minimum pay,
Pacified—deceived—by the promise of the dawn of a new day,
A day destined—designed—to produce no more than yesterday;
Intoxicated and impotent under the capitalist's sway,
An efficacy which perforates the psyche like a knife
And lures the ears with a sound so attractive,
A comely aria flowing mellifluously from Seth's golden fife,
To death, experiencing only a captive's existence.
But to this, to you, I will not surrender.

Rashaan A. Saheb

that last i saw in tears

the bruised yellow-brown ring around the outside edge
the delicate spider's web of red blood stretching inward
the black abyss at the center
these eyes are dead.
these eyes have seen inhuman things
in their schizophrenic existence
and it was too much for them to take.
finally they died.

destroyed by a lot of nightmare hallucinations
(some chemically caused, some not)
phantom images of love and affection
vivid experiences with pain and agony
abuse and neglect burned into the retinas
vision made blurry from confusion and exhaustion
and a long history of tears and regret
these eyes are dead.

Geoffrey Davis

When I in Time Shall Fall Forgotten, Cold

When I in time shall fall forgotten, cold,
And roots of pines are all that fill my chest,
When endless night is all my eyes behold,
Then I shall still consider my days blessed.
No shadow will cover my memory,
Nor dreams of thee find time to dare expire,
But love in all spring fresh for me
And blossom my refreshing, fair desire.
If ever over me thine eyes should cry,
Or winter's breath should turn blue skies to gray,
Think not, in love, that thee for me should die,
But live, my dear, to love and light the way;
Guide my eternal spirit home, set free
From death's enduring corridor to thee.

Michael Hiles

The Widow

you died
underwater
I held my breath
for you
ever since

and the years pass
over me in tides
until I break
and wash away

and I find myself
in waters full
of memories

floating
long enough
to find you
finally too

Kathryn Kelchner

Crawl

You are bipolar aren't you
Sweet newsome pulls me closer 'til I step
Then warns of a crack in the sidewalk I may not see clearly
Because I get blinded by her beauty
She torments me with caution
Then recklessly leads me on into a brick wall
Impatient, she says
I could wait for quite some time is all
Yet I would still wonder what she really wants
Patience
Or restless abandon for her
She could breed either with her words and ways
So, I could crawl back into my work and wait another day
Or ask boldly
Quieting the lack of confidence she said not to display
In so many ways
She is pacing me
And I am racing at a full crawl

Edward Phelan

Figure of Speech

It was a figure of speech;
that's all it was,
with its rounded hips
and voluptuousness.
To make everything bigger
and everything smaller,
and luscious legs longer,
it made men stop and holler.
They stared and they grinned,
then whistled and shouted,
as they started pouring sweat,
turned red and then pouted;
For all that it was, was
a figure of speech,
dirty, uncouth,
and desperate for bleach.

Kristie Berry

Ubi Amor, Ibi Oculus

Ubi amor, ibi oculus

More exists in this air
than what we breathe.
i've ne'er understood your stare
and i will not just believe
that you lock it in your heart
and choose to vault emotion—
i just cannot decode it, nor start
to withdraw any devotion.

two pulses in one, too dense!
or, perhaps, just too rich
for me to comprehend—
just one for each?

you're too complex, love;
a multifoliate rose, from above.

Brett Roberts

O'ersnow'd

Zero visibility. Alberta clipper came south
from the Canadian border
and just into the new year—
A blizzard issued by the weather channel
and wind chill shuddering.
I came to this occasion
and arctic blown, hands deep in the pocket,
only eyes exposed, wondering,
if this was my place of residence,
as drifts surrounded my crest—
More stranded than Odysseus.

Brian McSherry

If I Can Forever

Hold you undissolved
in the flag of my creativity
with the tightness of a hard-nosed businessman
the rivers will run riot
splashing the turned-over fields
of lives dug out from amber pages
of non-negotiable memory.

I will stop a minute or two
on the shoreline of wild woods
at the opening of the spring's pursue
only to solemnly recall in my own drone
the flow of Bhairavi dust like calling from behind
cruising down the boughs of mind.

Maybe I will sly away
from the tearing tears of Tarini
fated to a fallen addict
or ride over the nagging groans
of the massive victims of gas tragedy
and fall into ripples of petal-brushed smiles
even in a haze of sweat in the submarine calm of your arms.

Krishna Bose

A Bohemian Moment on Thoughts of Love

What is the cause of these forgotten kisses
and fond embraces,
this seemingly unheralded lovemaking?
Have we become too intellectual
to say the words that hold the images?
We celebrated in the blackness of the night,
she and I beneath the clearness of the sky,
in a bleak oblivion to obstructed truth.

And we writhed in rhythms with the universe;
we even grooved till the gratification of our souls.
Wise men would call it hypocrisy
to but remember to forget
the meaning of the logic in this chain of events.
And I have spent the entire day trying to rid
myself of unforbidden, erotic passion.

At the risk of sounding too Freudian,
she conceived in my naked arms and I was pleased
to welcome my child into a world that allows
pleasure to be repeated in history.

Cecil Williams

A Span of Position

A streak ran through my face
today. It runs to
my brow and across my temple.
It is lost somewhere
              behind my stringy hair.

I noticed today, high school
was nine years ago.
I see this in the pictures
pulled from the desk where I scraped my name
with a metal quill,
when my span of position was as narrow
              and short as a twig.
I notice the thin skin under my eyes.
It has grown so blue and dark, dropping like
soaking leather, feeling heavy.

And this line.
I feel
its dryness.
It's years. I'm beginning to wonder about
things that once made no sense.

Steven Brita

Ode to Metamorphosis

I opened up my hand today . . .
The palm spot warm from where she sat.
Wrapped within my sheltering cocoon,
She nestled, cried, learned, and taught.

I opened up my hand today . . .
I look inside her soul and see
A woman where the girl used to be.
I struggle to stem the tide.

I opened up my hand today . . .
We turn our backs and seek other vistas:
Mine, her empty room, with lingering memories,
Hers, the world of new discovery.

I opened up my hand today . . .
She has grown to perfection inside her fear.
The time has come to test her wings.
I bring her to my lips and whisper my love.

     Carol Foreman

Behind Stained Glass

I open my eyes and lean over to see Mama cover her bruised
arm as the sun pours out of red stained glass and reveals
a shrunken fly in the corner of the windowsill.

I remember Daddy fighting with her this morning while
she straightened his tie; every Sunday, the same routine.
I helped the twins with their shoes, overheard Daddy's
husk voice, then a faint squeal from Mama.
Glass shattered on the kitchen linoleum. Later, I peeked
and saw red and pink pieces powdered with sugar or maybe flour.

I study the stained windows, slight blues and yellows,
but mostly red like Daddy's bloodshot eyes when he
drinks too much, like the shattered glass on the kitchen floor.

The minister echoes in his palest voice about the greatness
of God's good soul. I close my eyes and wonder
who will clean the kitchen when we get home.

     Christine Lewandowski

BED BUGS

Sometimes at night I feel the bugs bite,
their tongueless faces in my face, drowning in my skin like
bumble bees in a swimming pool.

And as I carelessly scrape their clinging remnants,
the madness of their sour discharge like a cow
lazily swatting flies with her tail,
I watch the tiny pieces fall to my feet like dead weights.

Beneath the scarecrow's shadow overcast I steal sunlight
from ripe oranges ready for juicy dribbles,
my voice the cat's lonely cry
stifled by the crow
Perched.
Screaming echoes of the insects that sting with poisons.

     Melinda M. Williams

Nanny's Cottage

Ravens filled the dusty air
as I bodilessly gazed through the dark screen.
The heavy wood framed the whirling dust,
and my body, too, floated—a mere particle.

Yet, how purposefully ravens browned the picture yard.
So perfect, the lawn a child's square.
I had wondered why they called its trim "monkey grass"
as I once stood a little queen on the oblong, green steps.

Now, I don't notice the green girth of my stage.
The dust and ravens have descended a curtain, a pall,
and the panel's dark, wooden pattern of past "candy bars"
will yield our talking porch to that silent, sinister swoop.

     Dianne E. Hollingsworth

Ode to Ben

Scary,
to think
of all the waves
and debris.

Good thing
Benjamin
is not still inventing,
he might have known
how to filter out the oxygen
so that we'd see
the words and images,
blips and beeps and sounds,
the auto starts, and microwaves,
all the old shows.

Franklin, would Telestar be your guide?
Good thing you're dead!
The sensitive among us should not see
what we walk through.

     Linda Kay Nealon

The Making of the Walking Stick

I hiked out in the woods to find a patch of Aspen trees
It didn't take me long to choose the sapling I would need
It stood proud in all its glory, leaves dancing with the breeze
And as I admired its beauty, I fell down to my knees

I had to say a prayer for the tree that I would take
Thank it for its offering for the walking stick I'd make
And as I sought mere words to thank the tree that I had picked
I thought about my Dad for whom I'd make this walking stick

He's sort of like my Aspen, he can sway both to and fro
A few knots showing here and there, a few scars in his soul
I bent my head and softly sent my prayer up above
A heartfelt thanks for the Aspen tree and for my Father's love

I brought it home and stripped it down, with knife I peeled it bare
Not surprised—I was amazed—at the beauty hidden there
I gave it a coat of satin and buffed it till it shined
Thinking "it" the keeper of the stories in my mind

I placed three stones with love and care for all the world to know
And each one holds a special gift for body, mind, and soul
This walking stick was made and blessed with prayers sent above
A thank you for the memories and for my Father's love

     Kim Ross

Requiem

Peroration. Spy through glass and darkly.
Last bearing on relative compass,
Duet of sanity and mirth.
Till sorrow and grief, turned spectacle in sleep
And joined in dissonance.

A credulous unbeliever I. Castaway
In a universe not susceptible to my logical Examination.
My penitence: to scribe;
To drive and labor my team of quills
Across this stark white fields.

Rediscovering; Infinite surfeit of glory, concentric peals of happiness.
Relearning; The true length of forlorn, mysticism of Belief.
My Virtuosi, of distances untaken,
Taken and Cicatrix covered.

I'm mine own El Cid in the end,
Mine own wave on storm-worn stones.
Look through glass, nights drift black to windows.
Comprehension shifts, glitters, swims.
Stark resonance of self-recrimination.

Requiem

     Danel Sitar

Just a Mom

For my son, Jim Nelson
As I was thinking of the future, the past rose in its stead;
a freckled nose, a toothless grin, a tousled little head.
Grubby hands and torn jeans; questions in a constant stream.
Pockets stuffed with bolts and nails; and wonder of wonders,
an old dried snail.

The cookie jar stands empty; there are mud tracks on the floor.
The towels are wet and soggy; there are handprints on the door.
There's never any quiet; it's chatter all day long.
"What makes the wind blow, Mom? Who gives the birds their song?"

"Why are the clouds so high? Who put the blue up in the sky?
How come the sun shines in the light and the moon only comes out at night?
Why do we have to take a bath? Why don't dogs and horses laugh?
Are there boys like me in other lands? Will I grow up someday to be a man?"

And so it goes, an endless stream;
a small boy's head full of childhood dreams.
Oh! Precious moments swiftly gone yet linger like an old sweet song.
How often I realize, as memories flood my soul,
This little boy's life made mine complete and whole.

　　Elaine De Backer

Melting Snow on a Rug

When I step in from a chilling December day and stomp away the snow
Clinging to my boots, I stand on fragments of history woven in braided patterns

Around and around they travel, leading to the center where
The rug ends mysteriously and starts again retracing the threads of generations

Captured by Grandmother's needle
The dark gray trail is that of my Grandfather's overcoat
I saw it once in a picture
Cleanly covering a tall man, whom I had never met; he was wearing a hat with

Grandmother smiling next to him, pearls and pillbox and lipstick
So beautiful, smooth-faced, and young

She didn't expect to find him dead in the bed next to hers so soon
Or the arthritis that burrowed her joints leaving crooked two fingers
That grip the scissors used to slice the overcoat into even, long strips

Stuffing them with cottony fluff
Some twenty years later, she cleaned his closet

The lapel still holding his scent
She told me that she expected me to use this rug
"It's not a family heirloom, you know," she'd say without looking up

　　Misti Huedepohl

July 22, 1982

She bathes in the hot Sacramento day,
Inviting the rays to seep into her weathered body.
"Today, July 22, 1982 . . ." I heard the man introducing the midday news.

I tried to place the sprinkler just so under my swing
So water drops could dance on my milky white legs, arms, face, and butt.
Perfect placement.

Go, higher, higher, so high I thought my legs would fall off
And I'd fly through space—up to the stars . . .
Reba opened her eyes and laughed.
Her laugh snapped me out of my flying and into my backyard, again.

She smiled at me, and her wrinkles deepened into canyons.
I noticed her weathered face had seen more
Summers, Falls, Winters, and Springs than I could count.
Her grey hair had once been the color of Mom's,
and there were nicely-placed flecks of the Sahara desert
on her chest, arms, and hands.
And then I realized that she has once been my age.

And someday I too
would be a body full of lines and crevices—lying in the sun
like a raisin—wishing to fly again.

　　A. Stefan

Separate Sojourns

Bulging pupils gaze, aghast.
Your head needs to come off,
The dentist said,
So your teeth can sprout.

Bulging blubber in blue bikini
Tans in the shying sun.
Day-star zealots lather,
Lennon's Lucy laughs in the sky.

Bulging baskets, checked cloths, red and white;
Feasters devour eats, like ants and on a dead beatle.
Angus cows sighs in yellow-daisied fields,
Dung puddles drop-plop.

Mirror reflection
An amoeba on a microscope.
Rumpled skin, yellow and fair,
Silver splinters in my head.

　　Pamela Bentivegna

Under the Tree

He sits there with his crooked bones . . .
Hands that can no longer move,
And feet too old to stand.
He sits there with his old eyes
Staring into nowhere.

His mind is still discerning,
Yet his body deceives his frame,
Not allowing him spontaneity to
Run and frolic,
Or to hound his dreams.

In his youth, he stood lofty,
Arms and chest broad. . . .
Hair like a thick carpet,
Legs rooted and hearty.

But now . . . now he only sits,
Letting his mind do its work as it runs and frolics.
He sits with his tortuous bones,
Warming them in the sun.
Under a tree.

　　Rebecca Gatian

herself

blue morning
immense song
dark secrets
bruise the tongue
how wild the wind burns
when summer showers
dry up

　　kms

Pose As Lover

I remember
fated meeting
with faded meaning.
Love me and I'll
keep trying to know
what I should find in you
to love. Hate me
for being selfish when you
need me to be selfless.
I challenge the landscape
for an answer. Maybe
the ocean between us.
I thought I mentioned
I don't want to learn to swim.
Love me for my fear
that I may love you for your desperation.

　　Elizabeth Hein

Jill-in-the-Box

My red, red box is edged in blue,
trimmed with white
shooting, tiny shooting stars.
   I leap above,
      descend from view;
there isn't much to what I do.
But safe I sit and in my turn
   I leap to smiles,
      jump to sighs,
and then again retire
   below,
'til triggered and released.
   I bound above,
      bounce into view,
to nod my painted, staring smile
and rest awhile in my red box
now trimmed in white, but edged
   with blue, stars lost
      from sight. I grow
so lonely in the night.

    Susanna Mason Defever

The War

The window's glass is cold against my skin
from the frigid winter air,
and outside the sunlight on the horizon is pale and soft,
glimmering quietly through the leafless branches.
I sigh knowing that soon this brilliant watercolor sky
will be engulfed by a violent night
coming not so quiet,
forcing the sun to seek shelter
to search for the next day's dawn.
Here I sit in the safety of this room,
out of reach of the war that is being fought.
I undo the buttons on my shirt
one by one and slip it off gently.
I run my hands through my hair,
exhale gently,
and pray that the sun will rise again,
give me the second chance
it's blessed with every morning,
and shine a light on the reason
I rise and fall with it.

    Shellise Piazza

The Martyr Antigone

Adorned sarcophagus
holding with it my life.
Death has not yet
taken its toll on me.
Intricate is the design
which speaks
of what I was.
I am still what I am!
But, languidly,
my past will overcome
my future.
And rid me of my life,
then I will be nothing.
Blessed cord!
cautiously embrace my neck . . .
caress each piece of breath . . .
hold in silence every moment,
of my reality.
Then my life will seep out by my hand . . .
not by yours!

    Vanessa Bracamonte

Nailed

I knew nothing of a spilled salt reflection
But now my back aches where the wings
   were cut
and my heads hurts where the bubbles
   subside
Every last dream played fulfilled
Then awakened to solitude
Loneliness eating away at my inside
And shame stripping its clothes off in my
   mind
I want to matter
I don't want to come close
Then lose you again

    Elizabeth Oppriecht

In Remembrance

The silver was soiled, but Judas,
Hell-bent on his treacherous scheme,
With bargain now made and master betrayed,
Had abandoned the man with a dream.

He joined all those others at table,
Passing sop at that supper repast.
He too would deny, saying, Lord, is it I?
And the man with a dream stood outcast.

Visioning that grande thirty silver
As his eye reflected that gleam,
He sealed with a kiss, has bargain remiss,
As he waylaid the man with a dream.

Boldly now, leading the soldiers,
Still clutching that silvery seem
As his buss was pressed, placed under arrest,
Was the man who still clung to his dream.

Now, with his conscience in terror,
He removed the belated eye beam,
But his was to hold, that 30 as told,
As on trial went the man with a dream.

    Harry S. Kline

Homeless

The sun and the mercury hold hands like old friends,
and ever so gently drop into the darkness.
Huddled in the needless and forgotten refuse,
the narrow runway lands nothing but heartache.
As the daily news slows the persistent wind,
the bitter cold slips straight through the print.
The faceless puppets shield the freezing digits,
as scraps from the bin nurture the rumble.
The soul slowly withers as each night passes,
seemingly drifting inevitably into the hopelessness.
Faith and compassion are the keys to the lock
to the door of their destinies. All is not lost.

    John Peloquin

The Quiet English Teacher

For my wife, Mayu
He wanders to his pleasant work each day.
On entering, he pocketknowledges life
That crisp brief repeating time which never
Seems repetitive, being touched by her
Being. The random passion of his wife
And her coy lovingkindness cannot betray

His frame of tie and suit and shaven face.
He does not seek to hide, nor to replace
His heart, yet neither can he emanate
The openness or rage his love creates.
Like a steadfast shadow of himself he
Works. Then, he strides to what he is to be.

    Michael Handford

Heracles' Tenth Labour

Zeus lay in meditation.

Dreaming, he saw Heracles battling with Helius and Oceanus.
Enraged, Zeus transformed both gods into two pillars,
One facing the other on separate shores.

Yet still the world river kissed the brow of Mother Earth,
And still the fiery sun blazed across the edge of Ocean's end.

Then, in a vision, he beheld Heracles with the Sun Cattle,
Blazing in the heat of day,
As the Hours reclined in the rainbow hall of Aurora.

The heifers formed a circle,
And began to dance with the Hours in twos,
Each wore a golden mask.

Heracles drank from golden goblet,
A draught of golden wine.

Helius was a spinning crown of fire,
Whilst dethroned Semele raced over Earth's rim,
To take Persephone's vacant throne,
Betwixt the fiery stars.

Heracles wore a wreath of golden laurels.
                    John T. Carney

The Newspaper Route

I walk with the dawn;
A cold, white, wet blanket
Slows the padded cat's paw.
Footprints follow a decided
Path to somewhere.
Serene tempest shakes the roof I entered,
To thaw the bitterness
Of a short route.
A newspaper folded and
Waiting in solitude,
For many to follow.
Headlines cut the mornings sleep,
Snoring lines in unmistakable unison.
A sameness pervades the
Doorstep once again.
A microcosm of slush ending
In sleep for the dream
Of a different day.
                    Catherine Fisher

Menlow Park

Kindly remit to ConEdison to keep the lightning in the sky
Candle submit to the god of neon igniting thunder in my eye
Expressions of curious hatred fill my soul with dread
Currents of furious ignorance spit nails to my head

Oh, oh let there be light
To give us some sight
All through the deaf night
Signing off to a test pattern
Hark! My Master's Voice
Darkens the Kathode Ray Lantern
That ushers in Howard Stern

I hear a shrieking gargoyle's comment upon what I am
Hush as the stylus pierces the foil for Mary and her lamb
Filament nerve from the glass spoke in corroded Tungstone
Spooked a baying wolf from the stair of my Brownstone

Cursed the darkness with real aplomb
How far the alchemists have come
Warming chicken soup from Campbell
With a leftover wire from Ma Bell
                    Angela Garcia

In the Ferry Slip

The hungry foam licked the pavement walker,
The park-bred, blue-gray land dove
Floating dead in the bay tide,
Licking the sooted feathers and the callused claws,
Rinsing from the eyes what grass they saw,
Smothering the last land whispers of the city.

What sorrow is there in numbness?
Heaven is the sea for this land-bird thing,
Cleansed and soothed and lullabied.

Billed in the gathered dust on eaves;
Proud strutted on cement, a king;
Gathered homage on the lawn,
The special footsteps of thing bringing corn.
Incarnate tenure, this.

And who will care to mourn?

The foam, the sooted water, the seaward drift
Become this city one to take if off,
As the embrace of new adventure
Becomes any unsensed flesh
That can no longer smile . . .
                    Ruth E. Grauert

Blue in the Night Air

What in the night air
makes breathing so easy?

The stress of work is like graffiti
written plainly on my face.
One stolen moment on a balcony

And the frenzy lags.
Three flags whisper off the railing.
Crickets and tree frogs sing in throaty quartets.
From the surrounding woods and hedges and the pond
there comes a pause—

(Did they plan that?)
—then the lazy summer orchestra.

A sigh escapes me.
The light from the house behind me forms shadow fingers,
which beckon me back to the tasks

Which I'm ignoring for the moment.
The bricks are colored blue in the night air.
Closer to the sliding door and its inevitable hiss,
the impatient light repaints them red.
                    Elise House

Requiem

The image is of a funeral. It is yours.
You are an old man when you die,
the telephone in your hand.

She finds you,
slumped in the chair she gave you
to make you comfortable in her home.

And she cries.
Then she takes the receiver from your hand to call the spirits
of your past to come and mourn.

The names she knows from hours
and hours of hearing your litany of loves—
women who have let you down . . .
your mother and toni and diane and pam and pat and elizabeth and
robin and melissa and and

and she handles
the business of your burial, knowing,
as you would never admit, that she
is not "the one" either; just the last one.
                    Aisha Claire Robins

Faye

She looks so tired and weak
with her ponytail and her
fluorescent attempts at youth, at
better times, at
health.   And the curve of her
mouth is reminiscent of a
porcelain doll half broken,
with her white hands covered in
gold adornments, shaking with
medicinal semi-seizures as she
cautiously lights a cigarette,
careful not to ignite her passion
or her mind
or her soul.

Courtney O'Donnell

Weekly Session

Got this woman on my mind
She lives where my hair used to be
I never see her,
but when I shave
she sighs   gently
So, just to please her
I shave on the hour
twelve strokes at noon
nine with morning coffee (she drinks hers black)
Each time the razor catches
a red gown appears:
time & again
she insists it is hers, slips right into it
What troubles me is—
it fits
& I'm beginning to believe that
possession is nine tenths of the law

Jeff Trenner

Those Geese

A field of geese
Fattening for the cold to come,
Heads bowed
As if in reverence,
Communing with the earth,
Reaching in the grass
For edibles.
Waddling slowly,
Some resting their heavy bodies
Before proceeding,
Occasionally fighting
With their strong beaks.
When alarmed,
They soar as one
And circle around
Looking for the best place
To land again.

Joan M. Dahlke

Six

To Donald, my inspiration, my memory
i sit with you
hoping you'll reach for me
but knowing you won't
and realize how far apart we are
i run my hand over the new grass
each blade reminding me of your gentle touch
i listen to the silence permeating the night around me
and think of your laughter
the wind picks up and i hear your voice carried by the faint breeze
tainted with the soft fragrance of rose petals
i close my eyes and see your face in such wonderfully vivid detail
i reopen them to be sure i am alone
and i am—
fully understanding how far six feet can be

Anna Dawn Borders

Longing

So watch me unfold
like origami swans in your hand.
Let me unfurl, unspooling
the glove on your fingers.
Drag me away, so far
into your soul; I wish
you'd let me go.
The songs of the silent and
the dead awakening the mourners,
carry this heart ripped from my
chest
to the grave and bury.
Even those hairs, like the wind
on wheat, grazing the hand,
the only time
I touch you.
Kiss me in this night,
so starry in these eyes.
Left to the morning,
waves crash the sun.

Brian Wilson

Circus Show

Momma dragged me out of my room
to meet her friends one Sunday.
The four women paused while drinking green tea
from the cups with no handles
as Momma forced me into the kitchen,
pinched the soft flesh of my upper arm,
and whispered clipped instructions:
"Stand tall as a bamboo shoot,
hold arms out, as if playing airplanes.
Smile."
I was a geisha with painted face.
Eight slanted eyes measured my worth.
I was a freak in a side-show.
Had I a tail or webbed fingers,
the clicking of their foreign voices
could be no more disapproving.
The forked-tongue of a she-dragon in a blue dress
spit poisonous verse at me,
and sudden peals of four women's laughter
sent me retreating to my lone cell.

Stacey Starr

Rite of Passage

astride the killing machine
sit the lordling and his lady
mother-may-i ensconced in leather pouch
tribal elders nattered about deadly potential
the boy only laughs
youth and maiden have drunk of the blood
of the "creature"; forbidden communion
to their tender years . . . the creature whispers
"you are the king of your world"

into the night they fly
two-legged deer caught in the merciless glare . . .
screams, squeals
armor crumples; his lady falls
the eye of the beast shatters into
a thousand impotent stars;
the creature only laughs
red blossoms of death spring
thus does the world depose
the pretender to the throne

Kathleen Sheldon

Something about Frost, from the Dead (Who Could Know It Better?)

No unnatural force shows when cold comes,
No oracle sends warnings for everyone's disbelief,
Only the warm cheek's biting message,
Or the mind's eye, seeing the streams turn gelid,
Convinces the wondering mind
Of warmth's impending cessation.

Summer's swarthy child's cheek
Will be seared by coldest flame,
Whose propellant is the northerly wind,
Rustling every rosined limb in dissonant harmony,
And so I send this pale afternoon
In hopes of a dogwood response.

And if I don't receive a fair-weathered reply,
I'll be like an estranged hummingbird
And fly through these sheets like unkempt breezes.
Send me coastal air, warm, with salt,
Like children's most innocent thoughts.

Robert Mcclellan

Still Is

For years the sun's (in morning dawn)
purposed not to shine upon
my path of darkest bends.

For years my path (of darkest bends)
bred my distress and neverending pleas of help to Heaven sending night cries to the sky.

For years my cries (sent to the sky)
fell back to me, unheeded by
His Majesty, His Love Divine,
yet on my knees each prayer I tried
to pray through blackest night.

For years the hours (of blackest night)
lengthened still and dragged in spite
of all my strength and mustered might
to hasten dawning of the light—
yet all in vain, my worthless plight still is,
and I am here.

Teresa Chen

Valentine Wasteland

Must you be female to
understand sensations stemmed
from wandering through
forests of flowers, shading
beaming faces of love,
Your desk
barren.

Each delivery, lie to self,
"It doesn't matter,"
yet pine to claim this bouquet,
Yours.

An empty desk publicly
pricks fruitless hearts
with thorns of disregard.

In anticipation,
I call in
ill.

Mary Heid

Irretrievably Broken

"The marriage is irretrievably broken,"
Those are the words that were spoken
By a stranger who hadn't a notion
Of the infinite sacrifices undertaken.

Fingers, once adorned, bear a ghostly ring,
Pale testaments where symbols of love have been.
Albums, tucked away, lie discretely
Enshrouding dreams that now wait silently.

The court has pronounced judgement of custody
Over the sweetest cherub this life will see,
His body miraculously woven
From the fabric of a misguided passion.

His two little arms provide solace
For a love that will always be effortless.
May he find adequate strength from my embrace
As he stares hopefully into his mother's face.

And may I find a faith so childlike
That will make me forget this past plight
As one who's withstood the dejection
Of a marriage irretrievably broken.

Michele Solomon

the butterfly girl

everything is okay now
until it's not

i measure my time in
music
rows of a blanket
babies' tired cries

when i'm brave
i close my eyes
for a moment unaware

night falls (every night now)
like a backdrop i helped paint

the moon, my soul charger,
slips in my mouth
tongue teasing, throat burning,
self healing; illuminating my pulse to a steady glow

the lonely call of the butterfly girl

i want to believe in something bigger than my own voice

i want to believe in something bigger

bekah k. franick

Surviving

I'm an independent lady
I like the way it feels
I now forgive that lady, "Fate,"
her underhanded deals

She thought her voodoo powers
enough to do me in . . .
Had no reason not to expect
another easy win

Complacently ignoring
her victim's new resolve
paying no attention as a
brand-new me evolved

Used to giving all of me
to share with no disguise
Alone I learned I could endure
much to my surprise

Enlightenment began, time slowed down,
allowing my pace to quicken,
to hear the drums in sync with life,
I pause, its cadence listen

Dee Treadway

Everything I Cannot Say

Everything I cannot say
Could fill novels—libraries, really
Yes, everything I cannot say
Could fill the Library of Congress
Flood the rivers
And still spill over the brim
Of the Grand Canyon
Everything I cannot say
Is infinite
Impossible to study, catalogue, or organize
And yet,
Somehow,
Albeit infinite and bottomless,
Everything I cannot say
Is neatly folded
Like an origami bird
That rests upon my heart
And flutters up from time to time
Only to catch in my throat

Suzanne Rindell

locals

five and dime momma
sinks her last
twenty on the plastic
quasi-yuppie "In Remembrance"
memoriam of the way
We were.
pack of Camels
in the rear pocket
of those
pepto-pink polyester dreams
she always wanted to
put on.
"you're welcome sweetheart" wink
through the eyes mucked
with the cosmetic cesspool
of the corner pharmacy.
you've tried to get
hired there.

some of us have it, and others are lucky.

Susan Lightfoot

Image

There is a small room in her house
A lone bulb hung from atop
The room remains a black veil

I stepped slowly into the room and
was greeted by her bent back
Her silver hair fell past her waist
and her frail hands were clasped in prayer

She sits on the cold cement floor
steel pots and plates by her side
Flowers of red, yellow, and pink
overflow from these steel plates

Her gaze is fixed on the image that sits before her eyes
She picks a flower from the plate, her frail hands shaking
A soft smile breaks on her face
Ah! The picture's adorned with a flower

Her hands caress the deity's face
Her hands roamed—hands, fingers it roamed over
A lone tear slid down her cheeks
and fell on her frail hands
I felt her peace and silently left my own images forming

Sangeeta Nair

Nanna's Lap

The wrinkles of her dress were like a map,
seemingly without direction, and always leading into another,
only to trickle down her legs and disappear into the sticky heat.
As I climbed onto her legs I imagined little fishes in the web
of Nanna's wrinkle streams and wondered if it hurt when I sat on them.
Slowly adjusting my weight, with the fishes in mind,
I leaned into her and she wrapped me in her arms,
a productive barrier from the gnats, the fighter pilots of July.
Nanna's hands were wrinkled like her dress, her fingers rough and twisted.
Clasping my hands, she sighed, and I heaved slightly with her chest,
a boat on a calm sea, rocking with the waves.
Our fingers entwined so that I couldn't tell where one ended
and the other began,
and I peered upon our lattice of fingers and rings, wrinkles and love.
Nanna held me until I got too hot and slid off,
always careful of the fishes.

Amanda Jo Allen

Within

There is Jazz within my lips
Kiss me
And taste the rhythm of a people
The flavor of the moon

There are drums within my hips
Touch me
And feel the pounding of my nature
The heartbeat of a cloud

The Blues are caught within my eyes
See me
And watch the beauty of the origin
The beginning of the light

A symphony is within my mind
Feel me
And hear the Alpha speaking clear
The Truth is in the Sound

Sarai Logan

EXHALE

It's going away,
far . . .
I'm afraid.
Too far for me to find.

Help!
My air is leaving
and it will take
my life.

Susan Hurst

Inspiration

In my heart, I hear
soft whispers, growing louder—
louder, until I see you
guiding me, inspiring.

I move towards you, going
steadily forward, always
doing better in everything
all because you inspired me.

Talking to you, I laugh—
with laughter comes the tears,
tears of confusion.
Why can I talk to you
and not touch you?

I think of days gone by—
words once said,
thoughts never spoken,
and I'm inspired.

Gina Kuniewicz

"Remembering Mrs. Tanaka"

After WWII, released from the Hell that was the Topaz Internment Center in Utah,
You built your little cottage on a foundation of Faith and Hope and Love.
You raised a family and beautiful climbing roses. You grew tulips and daffodils
And violets, and you grew old. Your loving family spirited you away one weekend
And abandoned you to the care of strangers who had never known your gentle heart.
A Nursing Home. Just another kind of Hell to test your will to survive.
He had no chance to say farewell; You were there on Friday, Erased on Monday.
They tore down your dreams and uprooted your weeping cherry trees to construct a
Noisy parking lot for the business next door, paving over peaceful green serenity.
He worked there and came to know you and to share in your love of growing things.
He rescued your garden from the rubble that had been your pride and your life
And transplanted your heart's devotion to his own backyard and into his own heart.
Last week, he learned that you had died as you had lived; with quiet dignity;
But the over-the-fence friendship and your garden will live on.
I thank you for sharing your memories and roses with him and teaching him patience,
For knowing you has made him a more gentle man, a more caring man.
Each year, when spring arrives bearing your memory on delicate flowering
Tendrils that reach toward Heaven, we will think of you and remember
Your remarkable life of courage and grace and survival, and delight in
The fragrant living legacy of your beautiful rambling roses. Sayonara, my friend.

    Lenda Noyes

Zacchaeus and Me

I sat with my August rose pressed into my November Bible,
the scent and beauty long-gone like a sacred quote forgotten,
and the charm of a gospel story faded into fashionable familiarity.

But then there is the enchanting story of Zacchaeus hanging from a tree
like a plump, fresh fig filled and oozing with juice of curiosity,
plucked into eternal preservation,
rolled in the divine fingers of forgiveness.

The story stands at the door of my closed life and knocks,
waiting patiently for an opening, like a mother waits for a birth of her child.
The story of Zacchaeus is good news for me.

Yet why does the lad bad news sit in my memory like a prisoner
being grilled in a interrogation cell?

I need the curiosity to know more of this carpenter passing
through the city of my life. I need the hope that he stop
and invite himself into my home.

But first I must be at home in my own story,
every room and closet and open space revealing the treasures of my memory,
the dreams made known the dreams of my imagination.

    Eileen Mary Theresa Heim

Fragments of Reflections

The sins of the fathers in Catholic families make for lonely pictures at the baptisms.
  She pieces together her past year by year
    and the features of her face from her mother, her mother's mother.
    She cannot find her eyes among the scattered images.
    They belong to no one they have seen.
The ignorant neighbors, sipping drinks from their sweaty glasses around the kitchen table,
    say how she takes after her father: "Her Daddy's face in that little girl?"
And the little girl who knows too much of the truth squirms in her chair, her mother smiles the tight-lipped
    smile—she knows all of the truth—reaches for her glass of water that she isn't thirsty for,
      and just outside of the room, her daddy hears, looks out the window,
   while her mother's maiden name blazes on the birth certificate buried in the file cabinet in the basement,
    the one that hasn't been opened for years.
Mother's smile is tight again as she watches her own shoes that her baby can wear as well as she could.
  She gets in his car, carried away. "So young to be so close to a boy; it isn't love is it?" says Daddy, not
    looking up from the crossword.
   Mother's tight smile fades, she holds the curtain open long after the taillights turn the corner,
    staring at her own reflection in the darkened glass of the windowpane.
   "Yes, she is young."
Too late now to tell her that her inherited traits can't be found in those fuzzy pictures of old.
They were to be found between the sheets, a heart that is too easy to break, a mind too eager to believe.

    Amy Hawkins

The Trains

Clickity-clack, clickity-clack,
The trains are running on the track,
Carrying goods back and forth,
Some to the South and some to the North.
East and West are serviced, too,
Some cars old, some cars new.
Coal and oil, gravel and grain,
On they go, sunshine or rain.
They cut through the night like a knife through bread,
Making noise enough to wake the dead.
Slam, bang, rattle, and rumble—
It's enough to make one grumble.
Business is booming, that's a plus;
Who am I to make a fuss?
Hamlet born, Hamlet bred,
Railroad nurtured, railroad fed.
Husband, father, brothers, too,
Railroad men through and through.
So for my remaining years,
These sounds shall be music to my ears.

Martha S. Pait

Give Me Strength

Lord, give me strength
to see this through
My tears fall in frustration
I don't know what to do
I am praying for guidance and hope
I need courage and peace
Show me the way, show me a release
My heart aches, I cannot sleep
I can only hope when we come
to you in your house of glory
We will be set free
I cannot help but feel death is a tragedy
We seem to forget we are born
to die and come to you
Embrace my loved ones with your love
Keep them safe in your Heaven above

Donna Eckols

Coward

Dedicated to my mother, Georgialle McBean
How am I to describe my faith in thee
When I do not know thee?
My mind says one thing,
Though my heart says another.
Blindly, my mouth speaks falsely.
Unknowingly, I cause thee to accept thy lies.
How I am to escape thee
When I do not run but
Cry to another to care for my worries for me?
What am I to do?
Oh, please tell.

Kateri McBean

Poeting

To Lamer Kyle-Reno (Darling Daughter—DD)
It moves, relentlessly with a power not its own
It moves toward a destiny and a conclusion yet to be revealed.
It moves into realms heretofore unknown to anyone.
Trying to touch, to see, to know, and reveal.
Adding the flavor to history, it goes to the well again and again.
Having done this, it cannot stop, for it is only one of many.
Working with pens that could be needles.
Dedicated to completing the ever-unfolding tapestry of life.

Charles E. Reno

Standing on the Deck of a Boat

Thank you to my loved ones for inspiration
Standing on the deck
with wonder in her eyes
serenity lies
where the water touches the sky
when times are good
when your life is a wreck
there is nothing more precious than life
thought and dreams
where hope comes alive
as sure as birds fly
you'll become nothing if you never try
the sun only shines half of the time
children of God acting as one
born to roam beneath the sun
you can be anything
as long as you try
the sun only shines half of the time
there is nothing more beautiful than life
perhaps only
where the water touches the sky

James Wright

Mother's Prayer

For my mother, Hermine Walters
Dear God, look on my children with loving eyes;
Make them understanding and wise.
Keep them healthy and wealthy,
Meek, kind, and sweet.

Make them gentle and thoughtful, Lord,
To all those who carry a heavy load;
May their faith in You ever grow.
Doubts about thee let them never show.

Lord, please make them patient true and bold,
And give them each a heart of gold;
Teach them daily how to share
Your blessings with those in need of care.

Heavenly Father, please give them hearts loving and tender,
Worthy they to others your love to render;
Make them joyful and happy,
Alive, full of your truth, and never snappy.

Lord, please guide and protect my children,
Walking hand in hand with you;
Grant them daily life anew.
May they ever be a blessing sent from you.

Ina Walters Morrison

Everything

Dedicated to my true love, Richard Paulicelli
Smiling lovingly at you,
though not able to be seen.
Wanting to be beside you,
though many miles lie in between.

I wanna be part of your world,
to be the Queen that rules your land.
I wanna be your everything;
oh, if you could only understand.

You are my sunshine and my rain,
though you are never close enough,
and the nights I spend without you, dear,
are always way too rough.

So come and lie inside my heart,
where the love you gave had grown,
and there you will find unending joy,
a peace you have never known.

Donna J. Griffin

Untitled

There is someone I love with all my heart
And I want him to know I will never part

That special love we have will never dim
My heart will always and forever belong to him

He held me close when things went wrong
Always by my side when days seemed long

I told him my secrets and fears
He softly and gently kissed away my tears

I was there when tears fell from his eyes
Seeing him upset made my emotions rise

Our love helped us forget old fears and tears
It helped us make it through the years

I just want him to know I love him dear
And his heart is safe with mine here

Debbie Linzalone

Untitled

He comes to me with words so sweet and true;
Am I going to be there for him when he is blue?
The answer should be clear as day;
I am here for him in every which way.
I will push you to follow your dreams.
I will encourage you to try new things.
If you should stumble or fall,
I will be there to help mend your broken wing.
Take each word of mine and hold them close until the end of time,
Remembering that each word means something special and sweet.
Now close your eyes and forever will you think of me.

Laura Bay

Untitled

When you smile it fills me
With colors so bright

When you look in my eyes
I see such beautiful light

Your hair
Reminds me of a soft summer breeze

It's like I curl up in happiness
And do nothing but freeze

Your face
Reminds me of beautiful smells in the air

Taking me away
To some place fair

I wonder just how
Your skin might feel

But I can bet
It's enough to heal

Vicki Hart

Holocaust

I am the screams of prisoners as they cry deep into the night,
I can only stand and stare, my eyes . . . filled with fright.
These are the screams that will end never,
These are the screams that will linger in our minds forever.
I am the nightmares of Jews quietly trying to find a place to hide,
Hiding from the Nazis, whose battleground is now vast and wide.
These nightmares change many from being brave,
These nightmares come true and take many to their grave.
I am the lives of victims, who struggling, try to live,
These lives the Germans took, these lives they did not give.
These are the lives that many will forever treasure,
These are the lives that many love and will remember.
I am shattered hearts.

Rachel Day

That's What Love Means to Me

Growing old together, sharing picnics in the park.
Talking to each other, a long heart to heart.
Sharing half-burnt pancakes because you know I tried.
That's what love means to me.

Sharing love forever, and forever there will be
Happiness over heartache, joy over sorrow
Laughter over tears for today and tomorrow.

Long kisses when we're ninety and smiles that are free.
Looks across long hallways between you and me.
Walking barefoot on the shore, walking hand in hand.
Sometimes being like children, making castles in the sand.

Reaching out for you, because our love is true.
Picking you flowers, cuddling by the fire for hours.
Holding hands, walking down a lane.
Laughing as we're dancing in the rain.

That's what love means to me.

Opal Marie Bailey

I Need a Hug

When we began in years past
I knew then that our love would last.
And I knew one day you would say, I need a hug.

With our love our life together grew
making the times we spent apart so blue.
And I knew one day you would say, I need a hug.

In all we did we were a team
even though sometimes we differed, it would seem.
And I knew one day you would say, I need a hug.

In time of deepest trouble and sorrow
you always made things brighter on the morrow.
And I knew one day you would say, I need a hug.

I love the quirks in your silly poses
and then your tears when I give you roses.
And I knew one day you would say, I need a hug.

I wish I could make all things right
so you would enjoy every day bright.
And I knew one day you would say, I need a hug.

So, to remind me that we are one
please always tell me when day is done, I need a hug.

Philip R. Miller

A Love to Call My Own

I knew from the beginning that you were just a flirt,
but yet I fell in love, knowing I'd be hurt.
I thought I could tie you down and make you love just one,
but how can I do something no one else has ever done?
I know you'll never love me and I'm trying not to cry,
so I must find the strength to kiss your tender lips goodbye.
Don't come and look for me; you'll find I won't be there.
I want a love to call my own, not one I have to share.

Stephanie Garcia

Whispering Winds

To sit so still, as still as a cat stalking its prey.
To hear the wind whistling softly into your ear,
Whispering what soon may come your way.
To ignore the prickling sensation
Crawling up and down your spine.
To hear your heartbeat quicken to unknown footsteps.
To know that you too, are prey for the unseen stalker.
As you sit so still,
Listen carefully to the wind,
For it may say more than you hear.

Jessica Perry

My Dad

When I was little, my dad used to be an abusive drinker.
He would keep my mom hostage in the house.
I was scared of him, and I didn't want to be around him at all.
Finally, my mom got out and we went to my grandmother's house.
We were safe there, and we moved to California.
He got in touch with me and my sister,
And he wants to be part of my life again.
But to tell you the truth, I don't want anything to do with him.
But if you think about it, it is nice that he actually
tried to be a new father that I had never had my whole entire life.

Nicole Marie Monpas

One of a Kind

In memory of my loving mother, Beatrice Shawley
My mother was one of a kind
I know in my heart that there
Can never be another to take
The place of my mother.

She was a very special lady
Who always smelled as fresh as a daisy
She never asked for much
And always had a loving touch.

She believed in God
And his holy rod
She always read her bible every night
Praying that she would wake with his morning light.

She would give anyone the shirt off her back
And no that's not a wisecrack
I will always remember her smiling face
Always being so full of grace.

To me my mother was more than
Just a mother she was a friend
Who was always there for me
Up until the very end.

Katrina Shawley

Awkward Knowledge

To Sara Coffey, with love
So now it's awkward.
She knows how I feel and doesn't mind,
is even flattered.
In the halls, we avoid each other,
but not like before—
then because of not knowing each other,
now because we do.
Yet we still don't speak.
We don't try to make things right.
The situation grows more and more strange,
until one day, she will be gone.
Never seeing her again, my love will still grow,
growing and growing until it can grow no more,
and that will be the day that I die.

Lauren Curry

Happiness

Happiness is knowing friends are there for you,
to bring you up when you're feeling blue.
Happiness is family gathered around the Christmas tree,
knowing together forever they'll be.
Happiness is feeling safe and warm,
tight and secure in your lover's arms.
Happiness is when, on your deathbed you lay,
loved ones surrounding you and you can hear them pray.
Happiness is entering the sweet gates above,
knowing you'll soon be filled with warmth and love.

Linden Davis

Helpless

For we are all cursed
For we are all damned
We are kept in boxes
We are forbidden to venture
It's unlawful to love to care or wonder
For only two have braved their master
They found solitude within each other
They were merely broken and despaired
For unlawfulness brought them together again
Nearly broken they flee to become one
They come to know another world together.

Kat

Taking Flight

To Carolyn, for believing in me
Like a young bird in its nest
I begin to emerge from my shell.
As my eyes adjust to the brilliant light
I am able to see a whole new world.
The great mystery of life surrounds me,
Beckoning me to embrace all it has to offer.
As I travel on my journey to self-discovery
I'm encouraged to explore new horizons,
To learn to use my wings, to strengthen them,
To feel the breathtaking gratification of flight!
Anticipating turbulence, I begin uncertainly.
In realizing stormy weather can only cause a delay,
I develop a desire to soar even higher!
The wind begins to swirl all around me
Lifting me to the heights I never dreamed attainable.
You are the wind beneath my delicate, yet capable, wings.

Kathy Rogers

Cry, Cry

Cry, cry, I try not to cry.
But these tears stream down my face
and give me a frown.
I try to keep them hiding but they just
don't stay where I hide them.
I wipe them once, I wipe them twice.
These tears stay upon my face and I will
never let them come down.
They stay here and race upon my face.
Who will win?
We will never know,
Because they hide and hide.
When I try to make them go, one tear comes
and yells out, "No!"
We simply won't as you can see,
we will stay here forever and ever.
One blink of my eye,
I let out a cry and there they go!
What do you know?

Casey Elizabeth Cashman

A Poem of Pam

For my very much-loved Aunt Pam
Pam was a loving, caring,
Perfect person who had everything to live for.
Pam was, and is!
The sweet pain in your side that you never want to fade,
The television show that you can't keep your eyes off,
The scent of the most beautiful rose
That lives forever and never dies,
The perfect pumpkin to carve on a beautiful fall night,
The sweetest story of romance,
The best amusement park known to mankind,
The most important grade in high school to college never failed.

Jaya Johnson

Untitled

A confused little boy with a temper, it all started out
Someone who would always punch and pout.
It must be just a stage that he'll soon grow out.
What would one little boy have to be so mad about?

But as you grew older, the stage didn't go.
It got you in trouble in school and lots of foes.
You should have gotten some help right then and there.
But did you? No.

So as time went on, your problem just kept getting worse.
You never really do much wrong . . .
No rape, no murder, no stealing
From an old lady's purse.

You just had a problem that you could not control.
A temper, an anger deep inside of you that just took control.
Now, you're even older, out of school,
And still all confused and always getting mad.

You need some help like you did the day your problem started out.
You need to realize life is very precious, yet fragile,
And when you strike out in your life, you're out!

Lauren Alexis Berg

The Only One

You are the only one in my dreams, my love.
The only one in the stars above.
The only one I think of at night.
When I think of you, there is no fright.
When I see you, my eyes fill with tears.
That is when I see the fears.
The fear that I'll never see you again.
The fear that this might be the end.
The end of my secret love for you.
The end of the wish that you love me too.
Could this fear possibly come true?
No, it's just my imagination running wild for you.

Samantha Jaskiewicz

My Love for You

I wish to convey my feelings to you,
One of a love so strong and true.
I forever want you at my side,
For there is a love in my heart that I cannot hide.

I feel that we are two parts that make a whole.
Without you, I'm a lost soul.

I want nothing more than you in my life
As my companion, friend, and lover,
But most of all, my wife.

Shawn W. Volkert

Lost Father

To my father, I love you
You don't know how much you meant to me.
Before I knew what was meant to be.
You had always filled my day.
In everything and every way.
I thought you'd be here for long.
But I seem to be wrong.
You said there was a lesson to be taught.
Before I learned your life was bought.
Lesson was, life is unfair.
I wish I had taken the time to care.
For this, I put myself to blame.
Things just aren't the same.
I often cry myself to sleep.
When I think I ask myself why.
How I wish I had the chance to say good bye.

Dessa Boyle

Something She Can Never Have

To my first love, D.M.U.
She walks down the road alone,
Not knowing which way to go.
He looks at her so intense;
There's something between them
They both can sense.
It was lost in time through the shady mist;
She must now realize he doesn't exist.
He came, he faded, he's gone.
She doesn't want to live,
But she must go on.
She's lost without him,
But she'd never found him.
She walks down the road alone,
Not knowing which way to go.
His face is unclear; he was never here.

Robin Hoskins

My Love, Pure Perfection

Even though you think you are one little person,
You are like a massive cathedral to me,
Even though you think your writings don't matter,
I look at them as if they were strips of melted gold,
Just because it's something you told,
You give me this feeling no one has ever given me before,
It's like you are a city full of beautiful, white angels,
You are just pure love and perfection to me,
It's like no matter what you are in my soul,
You are my soul, you make me complete,
Without even trying, you make me happy,
Even if I don't want to be, nothing can be more truthful;
You are my everything. I've never met a soul like you,
I hope your fire never burns out inside me,
Because you, are the mind, body, and soul
That gives me a breath of life.

Carla Menchinella

Hate

When you can't get anything straight
cuz your head is filled with hate
You remember the people who put you there
And you think of a way
to make their lives unfair
You only want to commit suicide
cuz you think the people
you cared about lied
But you know you can't
do that cuz it isn't fair
to the people around you
who love you and really care

Shelly Rofrits

Rainbow

For my mother, Eileen Spadavecchia
A rainbow is as beautiful
as a newborn child.
If you've ever seen rainbow,
it's dazzling and wonderful.

As you watch it glazing
from the far backgrounds,
you wonder and question if
it ever ends or if there really
is a pot of gold on the other end.

So when you see a rainbow dancing
in a waterfall or over your head,
always remember the joy it will bring you
and how its light and design are wonderful,
just like every minute of your life.

Danielle S.

My Own Self

The light shone through the glass window frame
Moonlit dust particles danced before me
Shimmer iridescence, float tame
Softly caressing the wood I see

Sighing, my hand slides across my waist
Embracing serene, calm feelings of mind
Scents outside are sweet and warm to taste
The tool to release, my heart did find

A slow smile envelops my soul
Realizing for once I am now whole

Lori Brennan

What Have We Done?

I shouldn't have fallen in love with you
You shouldn't have fallen in love with me
We shouldn't have met that day
We shouldn't have let our love be.

We shouldn't have gone to your house
We shouldn't have done what we've done
I should have listened to my mind and my heart
But now we have a son.

You said that you were ready
You said that you were sure
But now that I come to think of it
Your love for me was never pure

Now you've left me with all these problems
How am I supposed to handle them?
I have my friends and
I have my heart
That's all I need, Amen.

Teresa Rodriguez

Smoking Is a Bad Habit

Smoking is a bad habit,
but you just got to have it.
So I say to you,
you have better things to do.
Smoking stains your teeth,
it circles your head like a wreath.
Smoking makes your clothes smell bad,
you'll be really sad.
Cancer is not the way to die,
so don't even try.
Don't smoke because you think you're cool,
because all you are is a gullible fool.
Don't fall into peer pressure, it's getting bad,
if you do, you've done been had.
Smoking is a terrible habit,
you don't have to have it.

Amanda Stoltman

Beating the Odds

The story is simple enough, but true
She does what she feels she must do

She's fallen in love, and won't let go
Her parents, well, they don't have to know

Her father tells him to stay away
But he stays with her anyway

They speak of love, life, and marriage
A life her father doesn't want her to carry

But they love each other, and won't give up
So they stay in it together for the victors cup

And in the end, they know where they'll be
It's a place they call "Eternity"

Erin Williams

Hope

Oh, beauteous thing that shines so bright in the midnight sky
Wilt thou grant me my wish to fly, to soar far above the clouds
Where I stood before to see the lovely sight of Heaven's doors
To leave this cruel world and forget who I was
And become a new person with wings so white and grand
Or shall I be condemned to my past sins and never escape
From the power of evil which possess my fate
Am I condemned to this life which has become not worth living
Or do I see it as a chance to change
And become the person that I could be.

Katie Hurst

A Wish Is Like a River

A wish is like an elephant,
So big, it can't come true,
But we can only hope and dream,
Although it may seem,
Impossible to you.

A wish is like a mountain
So high, it's in the clouds,
But we can only climb and climb,
Up the steep incline,
To make us very proud.

A wish is like the wind,
Blowing through our minds,
But we can only fly the kite,
With all our might,
And pray, one day, our wish we will find.

A wish is like a river,
Flowing through our hearts,
A wish will last forever,
And with it we'll never part.

Jessica Pinske

Wondering

Wondering what it would be like being in another's shoes.
Wondering that it might be better.
Wondering why God chose you to be who you are.
Wondering if there really is a God.
Wondering what people really think of you.
Wondering if there is anyone out there for you.
Wondering when he's going to come around.
Wondering if your friends are really your friends.
Wondering what people see in me.
Wondering where I really belong.

Amanda Gallaway

Your Road

Life isn't easy, it's like a crooked road,
A roller coaster of emotions as your destiny unfolds.
You never realize you are lucky,
Until you see someone who's poor.
You never learn that life is precious,
Until you're forced to go to war.
You never believe that you're unhappy,
Until the tears stream down your face.
You never humbly say you're thankful,
'Til you're blessed with some good grace.
You never know that you are frightened,
Until your legs lock at the knee.
You never think that you are blessed,
Until you meet one who can't see.
You never contemplate the future,
Until you lose someone who's near.
You never feel that you are special 'til another says he cares.
These awareness and more time will bring with coming years.
Just remember life is priceless,
Hours, moments, seconds dear.

Aury E. Smyth

You

For Austin and Audrey
You showed the world that you were wise,
You helped me open up my eyes,
You weren't afraid to admit you were wrong,
You helped me find the strength to go on,
You were always ready to share,
No matter what I needed you were always there,
You were strong when I was scared,
You showed me just how much you really cared.

Joselyn Aske

I'll Never Stop Loving You

Every day I see you smile.
I think about you all the time
and now I know that
I'll never stop
loving you.
Your big, big teddy bear hugs
and kisses too
make me say I love you.
You always warm me with love from your heart.
You make me happy when I feel down,
and all I know that I'll never stop
loving you.
My heart skips a beat every day we meet.
I can't explain the feeling; all I know is
I'll never stop loving you.
The day we met, you were so sweet
that until the day I die,
I hope we never part because all I know is
I'll never stop loving you.
In all my hopes and all my dreams,
 I hope to do my best to never stop loving you.

Beverly Campbell

Remember Me

Before you leave, so little time left,
I'll do all I can to make it the best.
Wish you could stay, don't want you to go.
Will you be back? Neither of us know.
Can I get attached in so little time?
I'll find out when you leave from this heart of mine.
Before you go, could you do something please?
All I ask is remember, just remember me.

Very few times we've spent together;
I hope they're enough for you to remember.
Will you miss me after you're gone?
I'll think of you with every sad, lonely song.
Will you forget me or find someone new?
If that happens, to yourself just be true.
I'll be fine, don't worry if you please.
All I ask is remember, just remember me.

Jennifer Robbins

Love

Love is not forever,
Never can it be.
Only if two can work within,
Then love can be.
Only if it's true and if two are true to each other,
Then true love can be.
So look into my eyes, and tell me I love you.
Love is wrapped up in its beauty,
Love shall never fade or die,
Troubled not by hate
Nor blemished by a white lie.
When pierced by love,
Love shall never leak and drain,
The kiss by love shall tell and erase the pain.

Justina Griese

Untitled

I'm in love with five images on my wall
But the thing is they don't know me at all
Two blondes, a brown, and two blacks
Ones eyes are the color of a cat's

They're five of the hottest guys
I hope they're really sweet
And their dance moves can't be beat
'N Sync you're really fine
And hopefully one day you'll be mine

Sandra Toppings

Daffodils and Daisies

Daffodils and daisies,
a child's laughter, an old man's tear
Washed away in the darkness of the night.

I never thought I'd live to see the day you went away
My memories stay so strong, of all the days that you were here.

The windmill points to the east
and you say it's going to rain,
while Grandma's daisies drip tears of pain.

In the garden there grow our childhood days
in the alley, paved on the road,
where our footprints lay.

A life is lived with glory and wonder,
even though now she's gone.

I see the gloom rise in all of our hearts,
yet in her garden, daffodils grow
and the memories just stay inside

When one goes away and says farewell
we must live our life for the tomorrows yet to come
and yesterdays gone by.

Amanda Jean Johnson

Love Is a Beach

Summer love splashes across my brow
as I sit on the sand of time
The boat I sail is not tied to a dock;
it sails its own destined trail
With every step on the sand our feet
feel the heat of the blazing sun
Our love needs no suntan lotion to
protect us from the rays of radiating passion
Every coat is necessary to emerge into the Beach of Love

Candyse J. McDonald

Fears

Dedicated to my large dysfunctional family
I once had a love I thought was true
But he said our time was long overdue
We went our separate ways
I think of him most of my days
I have shed many tears
I think I have too many fears
Loneliness, hate, pain, and suffering
Are some of the things that are hovering
Fears of bad dreams
Keep me awake as I rip at the seams
Was my love for you really true?
It seems I can't get over you
I wonder if you think of me
Did we spend those years together happily?
I don't know if I'll ever go to another
For I have a fear of turning into my mother

Lauren Lubas

The Statue

Brilliance prevailing ours, we are his slaves.
Holy and sacred, he tempts away sin.
Goodness he brings to the home and the land,
Peace is ever present in his realm.
Joyous tidings from afar he sends,
As we kneel in return the worship he demands.
Heads held low, we feel his Heavenly glow.
"Oh, God of ours, we love you so"
He is but a gnome and of trait, made of stone!

Zuzanna Szewczyk

Waking

Once upon a bright and breezy shore,
as the moon cast my shadow down on the floor,
as the wind rolled the misty waves over my feet,
I watched the sad silence, forever more.

I stared up at the shiny stars,
I looked for Venus, and bright red Mars,
I felt the darkness's stunning sleet.
Then I was trapped by slumber's bars.

I drifted into tainted slumber.
Each breath I gave became more nombler.
If I could taste my dreams they would be sweet.
I counted sheep to an endless number.

My next state was rather dear.
Every moment I could exceedingly hear.
Everything was clear, and nothing went too fast.
I felt so confident, I had no fear.

But next was when that thing worried me,
The part where fun ends, and you're welcomed to reality.
This must have been my worst defect.
The light went on and woke yours truly.

Kelly Kermode

Untitled

When I think of you, I think blue and windchimes
I think of hands in mine, hands on my hair, in my hair
Fairy dust with sparkles, anger, disillusionment
I think forgiveness and time ticking of your clock, candy corn
The smell of afternoon, warm sun and cool breezes
I think leaves and you waving goodbye, smiles and tears
I think screaming, thankfulness
I think orange, no yellow vibrations
The motions of life, growing up
Smiling to myself and everyone wondering why
I think of singing out loud because that's me
I think of books and paper, that smell
I think of you

Lindsay Jensen

An Unknown Beauty

To my parents, for inspiring me
As I look down into the water, I wonder how deep it is,
how many living beings are down there,
how many things are down there we don't know about.

Sitting here staring at the waves hitting the side of the ferry,
water very gently splashes onto my face.

I love watching the sun rays beam into the side of the waves;
it looks like a place we've never seen, though we see it every day.

If you look into the water, it looks like a deep hole,
but if you jump in the water it will carry you on the surface.

It looks like a place to get away,
a place to fade away and never return,
a place to forget everything but its beauty.

Jami Willis

Untitled

Love is the world's greatest disease,
but yet it's also the world's greatest pleasure.
How is that?
Well, diseases such as TB or leprosy
can be cured by medicine.
For love, there is no cure, because there are
no substitutes or substances that will cure
loneliness or depression, except for love.
Love will always be the killer and the cure.
There are people who are dying for water,
but millions more are dying for a little love.

Yvonne Banovic

A Black Hero

I'm the man who had a dream;
I wanted everybody to become one team.

I was the one who kept it real,
but the whites and blacks weren't trying to make a deal.

I was a healthy black man
who was taking a stand.

My last name was King;
I even have a song about me you can sing.

Someone in the world had killed me
when it was the world I was trying to build . . . See,

I believed if we stopped the violence,
there would be no noise, just silence.

I tried to feed the poor
and was trying to do something good,
to open up a new door.

I'm in the black history book,
so open it up and take a look.

And now I lie,
so who am I?

Dr. Martin Luther King
Tiffany L. Evans

Reality

I know you are lost my dear;
go away now before you get
trapped here forever.
As you sit, misused, confused,
all I am is concerned for you.
I know we have met before;
I could never forget your face.
All the dead angels live inside of your body;
as for the scars we have that are alike,
can tell it only happens to the best.

I have no more plans for your death and destruction;
you are the biggest threat in my mind.
Now that you have gone and are erased from my head,
I sit awakened from another dream.

Lisa M. Dombrosky

Reach Out to Me

It has been four months since I have heard from you.
Might as well have abandoned us, never call us again.
"What do I care?" is what I try to tell myself,
but the feelings in my head are quite different,
a whole other story.
I'm hurt, confused, and suffering
for no public to see.
Inside I'm reaching out to you.
Why, oh, why, Dad won't you reach out to me?

Danielle Roy

The Pain of Love

For my mom and Mittens
As I lie here on my bed
I think of you.
And even though I try
Hard not to, I feel my days are turning blue.
The days we spent together were so good!
And then I know it's not a dream, but true!
Every time I looked at you my heart melts.
I can't bear the pain any longer;
I loved you, and missed you!
I hugged you, and should have kissed you!
I'm lying here crying now, and it's all because of you!
I may be crazy but I still love you!

Kristina Keeley

Lonesome

Where were you when I needed you most?
But I pray Father, Son, and the Holy Ghost.
Without you in my life, I'd still be up to no good
I don't know where I'd be and don't think I would
Shame shame on me for thinking this way.
My mind doubts my love for you, but I don't obey
Friends and family often tell me that too
But I don't really care, as long as I'm with you.
And even if their words are true.
My heart's left empty, my soul turned blue.
and if thy words came on too strong
Help me by understanding, I haven't loved for so long.

Jena

Shot through the Heart

Everything is screwed up.
(you don't have to cry)
No air, I can't even breathe
And nobody feels my pain.
But I can be strong if I just hold on.
(you don't have to cry)
Feeling like someone shot a hole through your heart.
I'm about to die and there's nothing I can do about it
But lie here and bleed to death.
(you don't have to cry)
I can be strong if I just hold on
and pray, "Dear Lord, I have been shot through my heart
and I need your help to make it. Amen."
(you don't have to cry)
You can be strong if you just hold on.

Carmen Session

Love Is Like a Rose

Love is like a rose, so tender and true,
But nobody knows of all my love for you.
I hold it all inside, so one day you will see
All the love I have for you deep inside of me.

Becky Weigle

Song

A song can drift upon the breeze or rise and fall like water,
It can cry and laugh and scream and always lingers for a time,
A song is like a comrade, a mirage, a butterfly
Song—a nightmare, fantasy, daydream—an ally.
A song can dance amid raindrops, or turn cartwheels over the sun;
Such a being can fall up a mountain and climb right back down,
or glide on the falling leaves
A song can whip through the air on a windy eve,
or float in a quiet, lazy breeze,
Song can be red, yellow, and black, or blue, gray and brown,
Song could have lived an eternity, or only a simple forever;
A song is food for the soul; for the young and for the old.

Amanda Halloway

The Face in the Mirror

The face in the mirror looks just like me.
The face in the mirror sees all I see.
The face in the mirror puts up a good front
when sometimes crying is all that she wants.
When everything is going wrong she pretends
that it doesn't bother her at all.
When she is made fun of, she ignores it
while they crack another whim.
The face in the mirror who is so sad is me.

Gypsy Chamblin

True Love Will Never Cease

For Matthew Jacobs—Amor Vincit Omnia
The passion that burns deep inside.
The hurt that humbles by my side.
The past, I cannot put behind.
The tears that flow, I cannot hide.

The anger and the hate,
Is it true love or is it fate?
How long must I wait?
When it arrives will it be too late?

It was gone without saying good-bye.
It walked away not seeing the tears in my eye.
For me, it is too late to cry.
All my heart wants to do now is die.

Will I find my fountain of youth, to let me live forever?
Will I be able to love again, ever?
Or will my heart decide to sever?
When will I know, now or never?

My heart roars like a wild beast.
It needs much more than a feast.
Someday I will have far more than the least because . . .
True love will never cease.

Melissa Mincoff

Lost Love

You and I have been together for such a long time.
What started one night when you and I combined.
Our love is so strong, but will not go on.
I try so hard to prove my love to you,
but it has left me so blue.
I thought we would be together forever,
but now it seems like never.
You never want to see me, so I just let you be.
I'm so tired of the way I get treated,
I feel like I've just been cheated.
So until I now, I'll just
leave you and I as friends
So maybe our friendship will never end.

Anna Carry

Losing Love

For my first love and heartbreaker
The pain and anger is here to stay;
it comes and haunts me every day.

I thought he was perfect, one of a kind;
but what he did best was play with my mind.

I love you is what he said to me;
but he didn't mean it, how could this be?

I wish we could still be together, holding on;
but all I think about is how he left, he's gone.

I thought everything was meant to be;
what did I miss, what didn't I see?

Noelle Forastiere

Moving Day

It was the day we moved here to Michigan
It was a warm June day
when we got to our house
I thought great wilderness was all around,
I wish I were in Illinois
Man; I missed my old home,
my friends, everything
As we cleaned the house
I thought I can't wait 'til it's done
But it took a long time
As the days passed
I got used to this wilderness
Now I'm happy to be here!

Lisa Krueger

Untitled

Every night I dreamed and wished
of what my life would be.
I fell in love with the perfect man,
the one I wanted to spend the rest of my life with.
My dreams and wishes came true for a short amount of time.
We had the most romantic and intimate moments of our lives.
When we decided to go our separate ways,
I never thought I would get the shock of my life,
knowing I got a second chance to bring
something so beautiful into the world.
Now I know I'm alone and I could never tell anyone
about the precious human being growing inside.
Now the question is what will I do?

Diana Rangel

Why Can't You

Why can't you?
I love you and you love me.
You kiss, hug, hold me,
when we're alone
So you tell me I'm beautiful,
but you never prove it.
Why can't you sing a song,
give me flowers, or poems!
I never met someone as special as you.
Why can't you be sweet?
Kiss me in school, hold my hand, or just tell me that
you love me out of nowhere.
I don't ask for all of this,
but can't you do some?
Why can't you?

Kia Fisher

Confusion

I sit down in my room,
Because I'm in a bad mood.
So many things are going through my head;
Sometimes I wish that I were dead.
Where am I going from here?
There are so many things that are unclear.
Is Heaven only in my imagination,
Or is Heaven a creation?
If I fell, would I go to Hell?
God forgives, I know.
I know because he told me so.
How many times can he forgive me?
That is something I cannot see.
I know what he said in his Word is true,
But is it true for me or for you?
So many times I try to do right,
But from what I see, it's a big fight.
I've been blessed so many times,
But will all that he promised really be mine?
As you can see, I am confused.

Kristina Vargas

My Feeling for You

How can I say exactly,
Why I love you so much?
It could be so many things,
Your smile, your eyes, your burning touch!

Every time we get close,
My heart begins to race.
For if I were to look for Heaven on Earth.
In your arms would definitely be the place!

For your joyful laughs,
Are like a spark that starts a fire
For you know I'll never say no to you
Because you know I'll be a liar.

But it isn't just your laugh and smile;
That makes my day seem bright
You tend to always know what to say,
To make me feel alright!

Well, now you know a little more
Of what I think and feel.
Please don't take my thoughts lightly,
For what I feel for you is real!

Stephanie Croy

Tree

A tree, tall and brisk,
A tree stretching its wooden flesh upward.
Fingers of twigs grasping the sky.
Leaves dancing daintily on their invisible stage.
A tree clutching the side of a hill, roots burrowing deep.
Silhouetted against a knitted blue blanket dusted with glitter,
and flung from the heavens every night.

Jessica S. Hartwick

One Cool Mag

There was a magazine
Fit for every teen
'N SYNC, Leo, Spice Girls, and Hanson
Everything you see, even at a glance'n
Clothes, style, shoes, fashion
Everything of your passion
Some groups are very hot
Even if others are not
Opinion is your choice and mine
Who is thoughtful and who is kind
Do you want to know the name of this magazine?
Believe it or not it is 16!

Nicole Johnston

Weeping Willow

I live beside a tree
That weeps all day and night.
Its head hangs low;
It seems so depressed
As it sways near the ground.
Its beautiful leaves
Turn brown with the coming of winter
And starts dancing with the coming of spring.
It never holds its head high.
It sways back and forth peacefully.
A blue-bell rises from the ground.
That must be a gift from God,
It too, hangs its head low.
I live beside a tree
That weeps all day and night.
Shaded underneath the tree,
A heavenly blue-bell.
Come winter, weeping willow will be there,
As the blue-bell goes to sleep.

Jessica Harvell

Secrets

To my loving family
This little secret is all that we share
that shall never be known, or never be aware;
Not a whisper of the tongue, nor a
whisper of the heart can keep this little secret from falling apart;
This little secret is all that we have
to devote our love from within hand and hand;
No one shall know no one can tell
that this little secret is our hand.

Peaches Jackson

Baby Girl

For Tiffany Gaston, my beloved daughter
I look at my one sweet little baby girl
She's my heart my mind, soul, my whole world

She's growing too fast for me to see
One day she will be gone and will choose to leave me

I'll cherish these years as much as I can
In hopes and prayers she'll be a strong woman

Listen close, baby girl—stay sweet, kind, and pure
Know yourself, your needs, your wants to be sure

I'll always be there when you've run out of friends
The only one to trust through losses and wins

So, baby girl, you say you're ready to go
These thoughts of wisdom I think you should know

Give from the heart, expect nothing in return
Follow your intuition, and be willing to learn.

Tina Gaston

Parents

For my parents, my teacher Mrs. Pearman, and my grandparents
Parents are loveable.
Parents are the people
that put you on this Earth,
so you should be thankful.
Parents help you through
all the phases of life.
They are precious,
so take your time and love them
because they will love you back.
Some people don't have parents,
so you're lucky if you do.
There's just one thing you have to do give them . . . LOVE.

Kristyn L. Ulm

Love Will Make Its Turns

Love will make its turns in life
Why I can't explain
The pain of losing the one you love
Never fades away time and time again
Two people drift apart though deep down inside
They still love each other more than everything in the world

Even though love makes its turns in life
And it doesn't turn out
It's not a reason to shut out the whole world
And forget the ones that really love you
The people that stand by you through the ups and downs of love
The ones that stand by you through thick and thin
Even though you go through good and bad times with your love,
Love there's always friends right beside you
To cheer you up to make you smile laugh and cry happy thoughts

Sometimes in life you think the whole world is against you
But just remember, love will make its turns.

Danielle Shimel

Whisper in the Wind

Yesterday I held you tight
At that time I felt it was all right
Today I pulled away and held your hand
Tomorrow I will walk beside you
We are slowly pulling apart
Fading in the wind
What will the future bring
In the days ahead I will forget you
Soon you'll be a whisper in the wind
Our love is weakening day by day
Our words are often scorned
Lately I forget to care when you come home late
Or when you look the other way and smile at another girl
I know my misery will end
When you finally become a whisper in the wind.

Kim Leach

A Lonely Story

Dedicated to my family and friends
A lonely story is a story with no reason,
a story with unscrupulous meaning,
waiting to be opened and gifted with interest.
A lonely story is a tale of a child with no home,
a war between the East and West, North and South.
A lonely story is a deck of cards
being dealt with no helping hands,
a story of being forced to believe in something
which is not of their belief.
A lonely story is the Earth being suffocated
with litter and toxic disease.
A happy story is something this planet doesn't have—world peace.

Kristin Lort

Why?

Why?
I ask myself this question
over and over again,
I ask myself this,
Why?
It is simple question,
and they have answers,
stupid answers.
I was drunk,
they would say, but the same question remains,
Why?
Why do they kill?
Why do they kidnap?
Why do they steal?
Why do they smoke?
They know they will get punished!
They know they will die!
So the question is why?
And with that, I have one more question,
Why must they?

Jenna Velasquez

Walking Down the Street

To my father, whom I love
When I'm walking down the street, I see people staring at me.
Can't they see I'm just a human being?
I walk down the street looking for a job.
They look at me like someone crazy.
Can't they see that at least I'm not lazy?
Even though they stare at me, I have confidence in being me.
I'll soon have a job, and it'll be them
wandering down the streets like once I was.
I won't stare at them with my eyes so lean.
No, I won't—I'm not that mean.

Beatriz Guzman

I Should Have Listened

As I climb upon my new red bike,
I remember something my mom said I didn't like.
"Put your helmet on!" she screamed,
But I ignored her as I daydreamed.
As I pedaled up the endless hill,
I didn't realize I was going to take a deadly spill.
I grabbed the smooth handles tighter.
I felt like a feather or lighter.
The bitter air smacked my face;
I felt like I were in a race.
As fast as I was going, I smelled no fear.
I changed my bike into second gear.
Then, as I fell down,
I could see in my mind, my mother frown.
I should have listened to what she said;
Because I didn't, I might end up dead.

Nichole Fontana

The Tent

The tent that I took down.
The tent that spread love and joy.
The tent that created laughter.
The tent that inspired me.
The tent that made me think.
The tent that I had dreams in.
The tent where I could spend quality time with my friends.
The tent where we are going to camp with.
The tent with the little ventilation holes.
The tent that has two ugly doors.
The tent that I pulled the wrong string.
The tent that took forever.
The tent that I was first in.
The tent that came with stakes.
The tent that came with two weird gold poles.
The tent that I first got.
The tent that brought me life.
The tent that made adventure much better than I thought.
The tent I always wanted.
My tent.

Debbie Wong

Afterwards

Through a midnight flight
you can hear the sound of wings beating.

The sun rises the sound of wings are still beating.
You realize you must have died,
But how are you flying and where are you going.

A light is seen you can even feel it,
You want to go to it.

You feel soft hands around your face.
You look up and see an angel holding you.

The angel is not beautiful.
Yet it is the most beautiful thing you have ever seen.

Because you can feel the love it gives.
You have now entered Heaven.

Emily McAtee

The Sweater

Love is similar to a pull in a sweater:
If you yank it quick, it gets worse instead of better
If you cut the thread to mend it faster,
Your love is headed for immediate disaster,
But if you take your time,
All can end up fine.
Simply follow the thread wherever it may lead;
Use your heart, and your love will succeed!

Sandy Bravar

Why?

In memory of my Grandma
Why did you have to leave me?
I know you didn't mean it, but I miss you.
Why did you have to leave me hanging,
Standing there alone?
Why didn't you say goodbye?
You saw me looking for you,
But I didn't find you.
Why is this so hard for me?
Why did everything change because you left me?
I know these questions can never be answered,
But why did you leave me?
I'm totally confused.
Why, why, why?

Danielle LaDore

Fear

I'm standing on a beautiful ship, sailing to a place
where fear and anger don't exist.
As we drift closer to shore, the ship breaks apart.
All my dreams, wishes, and hopes float away.
I reach for them, but something pulls me under.
As I sink, my heart slows, the air runs short, and I drown.
As I float to Heaven, an angel tells me
that it was fear that broke the boat,
fear that pulled me down, and fear that killed me.
She said it was fear that caused this, my own fear.
Then she told me this is the place where I wanted to go,
where fear and anger don't exist.
I said then, "I finally made it."

Sarah Carlson

Soulmate

He gazes, staring into my eyes, penetrating my soul;
How can one, with a glance, disarm me so utterly and completely?
I do not look away; I cannot.
His eyes, so deep and dark and intelligent, hold me; capture me.
And yet it does not bother me that I am so easily overcome;
When one loves with all one's heart, there will always be a toll.

I hold my breath, try to regain my composure.
I stare back, hoping to produce a little of that which
He has so embedded in me, but oh, for those eyes!
Those mysterious, intense, sensual eyes. I quickly look down.
Even though I can no longer see them, I feel them;
Like hot irons, boring into the depths of my being.
Is this not a violation of my very soul?

I take his hand in mine, without a word.
What are words, but endless boundaries for that which
Can be spoken by the human heart?
He knows me like no other;
I love him with all my heart, my mind, and my spirit.
He is my soulmate.

Mariah Napier

Rain

From sunrise to sunset,
The weather stays cold and wet.
The droplets fall from the sky
And hit the ground from miles high.
The pitter-patter on the ground
Is a nice, soft, soothing sound.
The rain falls down on the roof
And ruins things that aren't waterproof.
You can hear the water drop,
And very few people want it to stop.
Today is a day in which to snuggle,
To hold your loved ones close and cuddle,
For today is a day in which it rains,
And today is a day when I have no pains.

Whitney Welch

Dad

To Dad, gone too soon

Dad, months ago you passed away.
Today, Dad, I cry more and more each day.
You missed my eighth grade dance, Dad,
And weren't there when I felt true romance.
Now, Dad, I'm in the ninth grade,
And you're not here to help me along the way.
I already went to Homecoming, Dad.
It was great! But you weren't here, Dad, waiting up late.
Mom was, though, Dad. I told her all about it.
I'm hurting more and more, Dad.
My birthday's coming soon, Dad,
And it'll be the first without you.
Dad, why did you leave? I never got to say goodbye, Dad.
The holidays are coming soon,
And they won't be the same without you.
Dad, I just can't believe that someone as great as you
Could be gone like the wind blew.
We all miss you, Dad—me, Mom, and Sis.
We'll never forget you, Dad,
For you'll always be missed.

Dawn Timm

Lost

Do you find yourselves lost with nowhere to go?
As the future seems distant and the past near,
You'll know you will always fear the meaning of being lost.
With a question of where and a thought of your soul,
You'll know you will always be here.
You send out your pain to people close.
But failure again to find your way.
Seeing people of who you used to be has become a nightmare.
But hope remains as your only way.
Hope has become distant now as darkness is taking over light.
There is nowhere to turn.
Breaking free is your only thought.
The world is shutting you out.
Where will I go?
Haven't I been here before?
Yes, I remember, this was my only option to escaping this misery.
Now that I am free, I shall wander.
At last, I have found my future and my past, I shall not be lost.

Sheri Suri

Innocence

Innocence—
It's not the evilness inside the killer.
It's not the wrong-doing of the drug dealer.
It's not like the Death Row prisoner.
Innocence—
It's free from guilt.
It's natural as the blooming rose.
It's sincerity.

Tanya West

Compact Voyager

Naturalistic passenger holding on to the past,
Futuristic rivulet streaming through the states.
Chinese blow fish stare down the heterosexual
Salacious black sheep across the brook into the hills.
Material doves look into the sky
Ready to fly around the world.
Primary colors around the universe
From the Earth to the sunrise,
To the beaming moon, traveling the shiver
To Jupiter's rings to the depths of Pluto.
The sympathy of the real world swallowing
Surprised suspicious warriors,
Vowing to live life to its fullest.

Jessica Moriarity

You and Me

When I look deep in your luminescent eyes,
I see a burning passion, beneath the surface lies,
When I see your gentle smile,
It reminds me of your compassionate style,
I knew with you from the very start,
That I could trust you with my delicate heart,
Holding you I feel everything,
Every moment is like a dream,
I know our relationship will last so long,
Our love is like a soothing song,
You listen to my problems,
I listen to your dreams,
We often talk about life and love,
You understand and trust me it seems,
We will love each other for all eternity,
And I want you to remember,
Without you there is no me.

Ashley Shine

Frogs

Slimy, eww, gooey, gross,
Frogs—aren't they just so cute?
Reds, greens, brown, and grays,
Frogs came in many different assorted ways.
Legend has it if you kiss a frog he will turn into a prince,
But that's not true; I've kissed a few, but still I have no prince.
Maybe one day I'll have the luck
with just one little frog—I'll kiss him on his
slimy head, and then I'll have them all;
All the princes of the land for which the legend will be told
That I was the one, the chosen one, for which they all behold.

Sara Hughes

So Distant, Yet Still in My Heart

We used to be friends
But now we're through
I know it's really my fault
But I've been blaming you.

Every time I see you
I remember how we laughed
But now those hopes and dreams
Are in a box, that's where they're stashed.

I long to be your friend
But I don't know how to say
I will make it up to you
Somewhere, somehow, someday.

Right now you probably hate me
Although you've never really said
My heart and soul will forgive you
Until the day that I am dead.

Jennifer Lynn Allgood

My Grandmother

Like an old bee in the garden,
She flies from place to place.
Her hand touches flower to flower
Like a small bird going branch to branch.
Her world of colors—velvet red,
Sunny yellow, and white of snow,
Getting life from the sun.
They share it with my grandmother.
She holds the garden like she holds her grandchildren.
Sometimes we can see only her sun hat moving
From blossom to blossom, and gliding on.
Nature makes her a curious child.
She feels like a blooming flower in her own outdoors.
She never wears perfume, but always
She carries the fragrance of nature with her.

TuCuong Le

You Are a Waterfall

Dedicated to my special grandmother, for inspiration
To me, you are an amazing waterfall,
You're beautiful no matter where you are or in any form,
Your smile is like the twinkle of the sun reflecting off the water,
Your touch and staring eyes make me feel washed away.
For that is why I can't speak.
You could talk away and I can't answer,
But you can't help it because it's your natural waterfall.

I could never be happier visiting such a wonderful place.
The sun keeps shining on this falls no matter what.
No one could stop this waterfall because it is so strong.
It just keeps going because of its strong will.

But as I watch this waterfall I keep wondering,
How does it feel about me?

Kimberly Whiteman

As I Cry Myself to Sleep

As I cry myself to sleep
I hear, but not a single peep
except my whispers and my fears
I feel my pain, and feel my tears
As the tears roll down my face
I know I am in a safe place
tucked up inside my sheet
As I cover up my feet
I remember I can go to my mother
and tell her anything I think about
She does not leave me when I cry or pout
She loves me dearly,
She has already proved it when I was a child
but now my temper has become mild.
When I get scared
or just need to think
I come to my room
and lie in my bed,
As I cry myself to sleep.

Summer Rhodes

Untitled

To Derek Aaron McGrew from your favorite cousin
I sit here and think of you
Wondering, are you here with me?
I know you had to go somewhere
I never thought you would be.
I hope one day everything
Would be fine, you told me
You were Jesus and that you never would die.
My heart is filled with sadness
Because you're not here with me,
I will always love you, Derek, for eternity.

Daina McGrew

As Time Passes

As time passes through my fingers I am reminded
Reminded of the time when they appeared to be so tiny
Next to yours and I felt safe knowing
I would be completely at ease losing them inside of yours
Or next to yours or with yours
Just as long as they were near yours
But now they are so far
From the fingers that once encompassed them
With a greatness and gentleness
Unsurpassed or reached by any others
And so I watch the time slip
Through the spaces between my fingers
Spaces that should be filled by you.

Sarah Catherine Hayman

Snowflake

Inside a snowflake is the cold winter air.
Inside a snowflake is the water that you cannot bear.
Inside a snowflake you cannot see,
But looking at one, can you see it land on thee?

Cassie Carte

Untitled

On this cold morn' a crisp wind blows;
It wraps around me head to toe,
It takes the breath right out of me;
And clouds my eyes so I cannot see.

By this description you may feel;
To me this wind does not appeal,
That this kind of weather I might shun;
And replace the clouds with sun.

Actually I love the feeling;
To me the wind is quite appealing,
It gives me a little quiet;
When no one dares go out but me,
A time when I can think my thoughts;
In the air my mind flies free.

It goes to places I've never seen;
Or shows me how life might have been,
So on a morning that's cold and brisk;
Give the breeze your cheek to kiss,
Let the air blow your hair;
And wrap around your reddened ears, see what freedom you can get.

Brenna Doyle

One Led to Two, Two Led to Three, and Three Led to Four

There was once a teen that drank to be cool
He always said that he would only have one or two
One led to two, two led to three, and three led to four
Soon he was addicted and wasn't the same as before

The alcohol continued as he grew older
He started going to bars and said he would have only one
One led to two, two led to three, and three led to four
He drank and drank until he couldn't anymore

He got in his car and pushed in the gas
He passed out at the wheel and ran off the road
When he woke up, it was his legs he couldn't feel
Because one led to two, two led to three, and three led to four

When he was released from the hospital, he tried hard to quit
But a few months later, he was at it again
One led to two, two led to three, and three led to four
And again he drank until he couldn't anymore

Once again he got in his car and pushed in the gas
But not long after, he hit another car
A poor, innocent lady coming home from work
Because one led to two, two led to three, and three led to four

Ryan Muench

Untitled

As my brain spins, my thoughts become double-sided;
A world full of many colors tries to be so sweet.
Screaming to hide the wicked and leave the innocent be,
yet innocence is normal and normal cannot be,
for wicked rages within all beings.
My eyes view separate as if they are two windows;
one is dark and sinister,
the other bright and merry.
Catch the stars and make a wish;
catch the stars and burn your hands.
As my brain spins, my thoughts
become double-sided.

Lea Anne Harmon

In Memory of William Cochran

I thought I'd seen you yesterday and I thought I saw you today.
It was just my imagination and you just saying, "Hey."
I was thinking of you today and tomorrow I will too.
I have pictures of you all around me, reminding me of you.
But it's hard when you're not here to see what I go through.

You came into our lives with grace and left everyone in sadness,
But God wanted you, and it was your time to pass us.
Now we can go on with our lives 'til it is time to be with you.
So until then, God bless and we miss you.

Kayla Mauck

Pride

You can stand in our way
You can knock us down
You can spit in our faces
While everyone is around
You can insult us, hit us, and make us cry
But there is one thing you cannot do
And that is take away our pride!

We help to support you
You don't notice we are there
We ask you a favor
And you act as if you don't care
We might get upset but we set it aside
Because there is something better than anger
It's called pride!

Betty Clarett

"A Limerick"

A figurine that was painted
And the artist almost fainted
From the sight, people wanted to fight
For the beautiful picture.

Then, it got so bad,
It became a new fad!
People wearing paintings
All over town,
People went down,
When they discovered that there were clothes
Easier to keep on.
No sliding,
No gliding.
That's how people stopped wearing paintings
And started wearing clothes.

Meghan Upshaw

Hawaii

I've always wanted to go on a cruise on a boat
made of metal and bright, sturdy screws.
A place full of magic in the air, where colorful
sweet-smelling breezes rustle through your hair.
A place where all your dreams come true,
the place where the clear waters keep you from being blue.
White grainy sand wiggles through your toes,
little cream-colored shells lined in rows.
The fragrance of a rainbow of flowers attracts your mind,
a wonderful feeling at these islands you can only find.
Soon a colorful blanket sweeps the land,
Rose, tangerine, and gold fill your hand.

There are places you can go with huge, snowy trees,
a place to visit family.
Only I long for one, the true one,
a place of magic where you're free to run.

Sadly soon I must sit by the shore
and wait, then wave goodbye.
I leave you with one long, loving sigh.

Oh, this magical island.

Patti Goral

To Me

To me you are
like a cute little puppy dog
in a cage, afraid to come out,
afraid of what might happen.

To me you are like the flowers
in the spring, just waiting for the right
moment to blossom.

To me I feel you have a secret to reveal,
a secret of how you should really be to me,

For you are the most
wonderful thing that has ever happened to me,
and to me that is what we both have to share.

Cristy Diane Harris

Ecstasy

The heavens enclosed our mere existence.
Our bodies sparkled with innocence.
Boisterous waves tumbled over our passion.
Moonlight glistened off of our flesh.
Our spirits mingled on the celestial sand.
My heart pounded rapidly,
Our souls danced blissfully.
Everything began anew.

Jodi Kindred

Dreamers

Somebody once told me that dreaming was wrong,
Somebody once told me that dreams just took too long.
Somebody told me to step out of the light,
But what that person told me just simply wasn't right.

Somebody told me that dreams held back life,
Somebody once told me that dreams meant pain and strife.
I can't believe that somebody could live without dreams,
And not know the passion of their sunny gleams.

That same someone told me that I should feel ashamed,
Because some of my hours were spent dreaming in the day.
Somebody told me that I needed to get on,
And that no longer should I sing a dreamers song.

I try, and strive to be all that someone wants me to,
But why should I quit something I love to do?
Why do you have the right to tell me when to dream?
Maybe you don't know as much as it may seem.

I will no longer listen to what someone will say,
Because sometimes it's the dreams that get me through the day.
But no more complaints, and no more words that linger,
Because now I have excepted that I am a dreamer.

Erin L. Shoemaker

Memory

To Ernest Legg, my boyfriend
I can remember the strange, passionate feeling
when I first saw him.
It seemed like I knew him from deep down,
but yet he was a stranger.
I can remember our eyes meeting for the first time,
and something struck me so fast.
Before I knew it, discovered at last
it was love at first sight.
Feeling confused and in a mess,
I stood there speechless.
I can remember the feeling of my heart to melt.
If He only knew how I felt!
I can remember my body feeling like fire
and not able to overcome my desire.

I can remember the sound of an extraordinary voice
ringing in my head:
Go for it, he's the one!

Brenda Hallman

Together

When you are with me,
I soar above the clouds.
Then we fly away together, into the sun.
The powers we have are enormous;
we can push away the darkest cloud.
I live for someone true and sweet,
someone that can sweep me off my feet.
This is the time when I need someone like you.

I have an elaborate dream, a vision,
of you and me down the road of life, together.
Oh, how I felt when I first saw you;
You were a sun to my delicate petals.
Your voice is a symphony of rain to my garden.
We are one, we are together.

Christi Bradshaw

Have You Ever Guessed What an Angel Looks Like

Well ask me, it was the nicest thing on earth
Like the heavens were giving birth.
I didn't know if it was a he or she
But who cares what it could be
It spoke to me in such a kindness
That I started feeling a blindness
Than in a moment right in front of my eyes
It disappeared without any goodbyes.

Michelle Duran

Lost Love

When I first saw you,
I knew what I had to do.
Your smile, your handsome face,
I seemed to be taken to another place.

I need your love more than you'll ever know.
I just want to take it nice and slow.
That way we could spend more time together,
And see if our love could last forever.

I see you, and I smile
For you, I would walk mile after mile
You seem so perfect to me,
Hopefully you will see that we were meant to be.

I need you and only you to hold
You are my love, heart, and soul.
Please come to me and be fair
Just close your eyes and tell me that you care.

I wish I could kiss you
Then that would show if it is true.
Maybe one day, that one fantastic day
I will fall in your arms and be taken away.

Amanda Jennings

Always and Forever

To Kert W.—I love you!
I just wanted to tell you how much I love you,
And only you,
You're always on my mind,
And forever close to my heart.
You bring me joy,
Like no one has before.
I love the way you make me feel,
When you kiss my lips softly,
And gently caress my body.
No matter how far,
Or where you are,
You're always and forever
By my side.

Audrey Ayze

My Bedroom

To Mom and Dad
In my bedroom, I can be myself,
Listening to music and thinking out loud to myself,
Being a normal kid, making friends all in pretend,
Going to school, liking my classes—well, that depends.
At a party, who's playing? My favorite group!
I'm going to dance forever and ever until I drop.
Going home, I say, "Goodnight."
My boyfriend kisses me and says, "Sleep tight."
Smiling dreamily, I walk up the stairs.
My brother runs down, yelling like three bears.
Ignoring him, I walk into my room.
I look around. This is where it all started—
In my bedroom.

Jonalyn A. Albright

Clocks

Ticking away the minutes of each little life;
Always present and dutiful to remind you
Not to waste those precious little moments
In your life, for the span of your life
Is short, and you may regret
Those few seconds wasted.

Laurel E. Grueber

Stand Up for Jesus

To my mom, my dad, and my family
When you see there is no hope
what you have to do is
stand up for Jesus;
He'll make a way for you.
Trust in the Lord;
He will bless you too.
Stand up for Jesus
You have to give Him your heart,
Trusting in God and keeping the faith.
It doesn't make a different if you are young or old;
Give Him your heart before the story can be told.
Stand up for Jesus,
for His message can be told of the remnant,
those who worship God on His Sabbath.
Believe in Jesus, get on your knees and pray.
Stand up for Jesus, He will make a way.
Sometimes it is hard for me to focus on my studies,
but I know God will bless me
where I am weak and make me strong.
With Jesus in my heart, I'll never go wrong.

Auneaka Simmons

My Heart Died without a Sound

I watched you walk out of my life;
it hit me hard, like the stab of a knife.
As you went away, the tears came down;
my heart then died without a sound.
Depressing thoughts instilled my heart;
my soul they over took my mind, began to take control.
I realized and now I see,
your mind and soul are always a part of me.
It hasn't been long, but I miss your touch;
I pray to God to help me through,
but I can't help but cry.
When I think of you alone in my house,
not a soul in the world could feel the pain,
or either watch my thoughts uncurl.
No one understands my sorrow, can feel my pain,
or know my tomorrow, but I know you're there,
possibly thinking of me.
You'll be back someday, then we can have Eternity.

Annie Akootchook

Why?

To my father, Patrick A. Wolf
I wonder why so many people die
In the night or in a fight.
I wonder why they would risk their life,
Dying from drugs they used all their life.
Why do your loved ones die when they can be saved,
But the drug addicts that overdose always survive?
"Why the innocent?" we all ask with sadness.
"What about the guilty?" we say in fright.
I only wonder why? We see it on television day and night—
Murders and burglars all get away, even when they kill.
When it's done on accident, they all say the person should die
Because their loved ones had to.
The families of the people that die say in sadness and tears,
"It's just not fair!" Why can't it be fair? I only wonder why.

Tina Wolf

Pure Emotion

Smelling rose petals ever so near
Heart deepening with extreme sensation
Moonlight piercing twinkling dewdrops in midnight air
dreamy, trance-like state, gripping the soul of eternal fate
fingertips glide along soft, prickling stems
transforming into soft, silky waves
Colorfulness playing to human eyes
deep green jade leaping outwards towards the black-lit sky
Powder yellow circles that smell ever so dear
plummeting into dark uncertainness never to reveal
Roots of angel lit, hope wandering aimlessly in
the night crackling fire flames playing closely to hear
weaving, darting branches collecting atoms of science
shining figures collect patterns creating constellations for life
dashing creatures artistically move gloriously tonight
dreamers see the world as if for the first time
lovers can love in knowledge at mind
truth overcomes every conceivable thought
nature's delights arise, shedding all wonders of hope's questions
through the body's soul letting no more wonders withhold

Debbie Hopson

Untitled

My life is a torment:
The love that we built inside has been torn apart.
My thoughts tremble with the pain that only comes
from dark corners in my heart.
Today I cry; tears are coming from deep inside.
My true love has left my side.
I now feel the true pain when the heart is cold and falling apart.
Time has stopped.
From now on, I can no longer live my life.
He who's left me as cold as stone,
He who hurt me,
Him whom I trusted,
He was the one I loved.

Jessica Pizarro

My Parents

To Daniel and Nancy Xiong
My parents are so special to me,
God gave them to me so let it be.
Down from Heaven like a strike,
He sent my father who I like.
Here comes my mother that shined so bright,
You could even see her through the night.
I love my parents so much,
They make me happy with every touch.
Even though we'll spread apart,
I'll always love them in my heart.

Cheryl Xiong

Remembering Memaw

In memory of Hattie McGraw
As I walked out the door,
I didn't expect much more.
I knew I had shed my last tear,
And cried out my last, "Oh, dear."
I remembered the times you cared
And all the things we've shared.
You may never know just how I love you so.
I have lots of joyful memories
and so many beloved stories.
The memory of things that has happened is coming back
These will only began to fill a sack
Because the memories are like a seesaw
and I'm remembering my Memaw

Jennifer Cole

Heaven Sent

I asked God to send me someone special, nice, kind, and sweet.
I asked God;
I asked God for a special prayer,
for a special thought.
I asked God for a love, a momentarily love.
Each prayer, each look into stars and space,
clouds and sky, I asked God and I received.
Too blind to see, too deaf to hear,
I closed my ears.
I did not see the angel that God had sent to me.
I have had and I have lost selfishly—oh, silly me.

Now when I pray, I look to space and stars,
sky and clouds with tearful eyes and mournful soul.
Please send my angel back;
my eyes are now opened and my ears are listening.
Please send my angel back to me.
I pray and pray because I still have faith
that one day before I lay, my angel will be returned to me!

Nyisha N. Smith

Why Did You Have to Love Me So?

We thought it was forever
and that we would never part.
Now you see that you left me with a broken heart
when we became two parts.

I will start to mend my broken heart.

Many people say we should still be together,
but they don't know what tore us apart.

Well, hopefully we will still be friends
and find someone new to share our hearts with.

Calie Kloppenborg

A Lost Love

In memory of Ella M. Schexneider
Though it's been a year since you have gone
Our love for you still carries on.
When I am sad and begin to cry
I look for your footprints across the sky.
I know you're there in Heaven above
Watching over the ones you love.
And though you're where you want to be,
I still miss having you here with me.
You were our strength, as tough as stone;
Though you're not with us, we're not alone.
You share our laughter, you share our pain.
I feel your tears with each drop of rain.
Even though you've gone and we're apart,
You'll live forever in my heart.
I've written this poem for the world to see
How you're sadly missed by your family.

Lois B. Sonnier

Drinking and Driving

For the McTaggart family
Teens think it's cool to go out and drink,
So they go out and do it before they stop and think.

Drinking may cause accidents and may even cause death,
And drinking is as dangerous as taking drugs like meth.

Drinking and driving, as it's been said,
Will leave people injured and left for the dead,

And for the families the loss will be sad;
That's one of the many things that makes drinking and driving bad.

Drinking and driving will bring out no good;
It's all up to you, but I never would.

Drinking is bad for your heart and your brain;
If you choose to drink and drive, it will leave you in pain.

So next time you want to go drink and then drive,
Think, do you want to be dead or do you want to survive?

Most of you out there would want to be a survivor,
So go out, but make sure you're a designated driver.

Brea Kathol

Untitled

In June flowers bloom,
Bees buzz, and trees sway.
I look out my window to greet another day.
I see hills touched by light;
later they are taken over by night.
That day was in some way just right.

Michelle Bickford

My Love

To Everett Moran—thanks for nothing!
I have this certain love;
He's all that I am thinking of.
When I look into his eyes,
A piece of my heart dies,
For him I cannot trust
'Cause cheat is what he must.
To myself every day I say,
"Maybe he has changed his way,"
But the fear of a broken heart
Makes me think the way for us is apart.
I really wish we could get back together,
But his acts are more then just stormy weather.
As much as I want to be his wife,
I find it hard to keep him in my life.
He will always mean so much to me,
But I have to let him be
'Cause the feelings that love brings
Wouldn't let him do these things.

Jamie Sexton

Mankind

As the night covers me with its jagged wings of darkness,
The world deceives us in many ways.
As we walk among ourselves, fear rises and shows itself.
There is no place to get away, so we run, hide, and stay.
Some are strong enough to stand up and fight;
They scare the world with guns and knives.
We call them gangs, that demon of the night
That taunts our kids and plagues our minds.
The things we do and the things we say
Affect our lives each and every day.
As dawn comes like a magic key that unlocks the door
And sets us free, when we go into the world
Every day, we have many obstacles and things to say.
When you read this poem, don't go astray;
Remember who you are and the role you play.

Melissa Wilborn

Accomplish Your Dream

Whatever I do today
I'll put more effort into it.
I will also do better in the future.
That's when my dream will come true,
that is when I'll understand that it takes hard work
and a lot of effort to accomplish a dream.
I'll understand it takes time.
So follow your dream and accomplish it like I know
I will someday. To accomplish it just think,
"I have to be better than others, smart, responsible,
better than ever, very special, someone with a good mind,
important, very positive, never negative, and
everything I can be.
I have to be all of this to accomplish my dream."
Here's how to accomplish your dream, so now do IT!

Rosa Maria Galvan

Flame of Soul

All my hopes are within this flame
This flame which used to be a torch
But now sputters its plea for life

The curtains flutter their warning
As the breeze enters the room
The coldness wraps this flame
In a blanket of fear and hatred

Why is the world so cruel
That we must struggle
Struggle to stay burning
Struggle against the cold breeze that enters the room

The blanket tightens
It cuts off all of my air
My flame dies
The room grows dark with depression and death

Crystal Dunnington

Stereotypes

I'm tried of living in this man's world
You can't do this or that 'cause you're a girl
Cook, clean is that what I'm supposed to do
Whoever told that lie to you?
It's more like play ball or watch the game
You won't see me in the kitchen cooking a thang
You can't do that, you might break a nail
You think I can't do it 'cause I'm female
Stereotypes, that's what this world's based on
This is the end of my little poem

Rhonda Lee Hood

Words Not Spoken

To whom I cherish
An enchanted moment that seemed inevitable.
Shortness of breath, and emotions going unstable.
I remember when we made eye contact.
My ability to hide my emotions went under attack.
You gave off a smile, and I showed mine.
I can't believe I still feel the same way for you
After all this time.
You slowly walked towards me, so did I.
I wanted to say something, so hard did I try.
I regret that I haven't, I'm so very shy.
The evidence of my feelings went sky high.
As you passed, I didn't say a word.
My pounding heart, I wonder if you heard.
Your rosy blush, your starlit eyes
Keeps me up and awake on those sleepless nights.

Johnson Ancheta

I Didn't Mean To

They were both sitting in front of me, a bad conscience, maybe.
I didn't mean to, you got to believe me!

It was an experiment, I just wanted to see what would be.
I didn't mean to, you got to believe me!

I just put a little of this on a piece of paper,
Then took the other and scratched it on the box.
I fell on my knees in pain.
I didn't mean to, you got to believe me!

I screamed and screamed as the smoke filled the room.
I forgot the baby.
I didn't mean to, you got to believe me!

I ran outside, I fell close to a tree.
I heard sirens and a baby scream; then a man says, "Where is he?"
I didn't mean to, you got to believe me!

I didn't know what would happen, I'm only seven.
You never told me what would happen.
I didn't mean to, you got to believe me!

Now he's dead; you should have been here instead of there.
I didn't mean to, you got to believe me!

You should have taught me.
You should have cared.
Amanda Spores

Angel

Wings like purified milk,
Eyes more beautiful than sparkling crystals,
Lips as red as blood,
Skin as smooth as silk and as white as snow,
Hair more shiny than the sun's rays,
Scent as delicious as roses and rain,
Hands as delicate as a newborn baby,
Breath as sweet as raw sugar,
As the angel scoops you into his or her arms,
The angel soars silently through the clouds,
Wings covering your body so chill won't intrude,
The angel takes you to a mystical place,
Peace fills the air,
Love enters your veins,
Golden trees, golden ponds at every corner,
Laughter fills the ear,
Dreams and wishes come true,
Lips taste more sweetness than ever imagined,
Rainbows take over the skies,
Here, life gives you a second chance.
Jenna Grant

My Angel

Where can this story start?
Only from Heaven could you be a part.
A sweet angel floated down,
With a smile brighter then any clown.
Sent here to dream and watch,
to ease a weary soul with your soft touch.
Your touch is unlike that of any flesh.
Such inner beauty I could not guess.
We share a common thread,
both kicked, beaten and left for dead.
By the world, friends, and even those we trust,
into painful situations we've been thrust,
Yet through all this we live and flourish,
the love in our hearts can nourish.
To feed those who starve for kindness,
yet driven mad by others' blindness,
we both speak from the heart and mind,
only wishing happiness to find.
Someone to care and understand,
to listen, reassure, and just to hold a hand.
Anthony Colquitt

I Long for You

When I am away from you, my heart grows weak;
I am paralyzed and cannot speak.

It is like someone shot me through the heart,
Took it out and ripped it apart.

I long for the moment that I can hold you close to me,
To embrace you in my arms and let my spirit go free.

Just thinking of you makes me light on my toes;
Because of you, the fire in my heart glows.

I wait for you who I want to see;
The passing time takes forever and seems like eternity.

Finally you come and I start saying my million I love you's,
Then you take me to a place of forever and say I love you too.
Diana Wallace

Seventeen

Seventeen guns, all loaded and ready to go
Seventeen dead, what for?
Seventeen roses, red, white, just like you and me
Seventeen, 17 of everything
Seventeen apologies and none accepted
Seventeen prostitutes who were never respected

Seventeen years old all cried out and old
Seventeen friends all fake like most times
Seventeen bunch of lies
Seventeen phone calls none answered
Seventeen mothers who were never concerned

Countdown for me from 1 to 17
Maybe then I'll come down
I'll come down, just give me some time

Seventeen broken hearts
Seventeen ugly work-of-arts
Seventeen words that never made sense
Seventeen unhappy ends
Seventeen of you
Seventeen of me, put it together and it's all 17
Lana Milyavskaya

My Mother's Hands

My mother has such beautiful hands
that talk to you or be in a band.
They sway from side to side
when tell you a story,
or let you know when something is very boring.
But the best thing about my mother's hands
is that they let me in and love me for who I am!
Danielle Middleton

Inspired

Sitting at a window dreaming,
while the dripping rain's gleaming,
I feel inspired.
Reading a book and smelling a spice,
eating chocolate checking it twice,
I feel inspired.
While the Earth spins in space
I stare in a mirror to discover a face,
I feel inspired.
As I walk through the snow I see
Someone approaching me.
Who is this person and what do they want?
Is it something I did, something I forgot?
No, not at all, I tell you now,
it was myself, missing me, my pal.
I stare at myself and see
who is the real person inside of me.
I feel inspired.
Shannon Stanton

Remembering You

As the day goes down in the dreary sky,
I think of you by and by,
When the moon comes up and fill the nightly sky with light,
It fills my soul with gladness, oh, what a sight!
When blue jays, humming birds, cardinals, and more,
Fill your heart with harmony, it's never a bore.
When the tiny baby cries, way up in the skies,
I'll think of you, I'll cheer you up when you're blue.
When you're miserable with boredom, and your days are too long,
Look around and see what you find, sing a joyful song.
I'll always love you no matter what goes wrong,
I'll always love you with endless love,
So look on the bright side, fly graciously as a dove.
Keeping you in my heart always.

Bridget Cox

My Angel in Heaven

For my Aunt Maryann in Heaven
Her hair long and soft
Her eyes as bright as stars in the shining skies
Her smile bright and bold
Her laughter so new but yet so old

That's my Angel in Heaven
Her wings move perfectly
Her gown sways peacefully

That's my Angel in Heaven
She moves about gracefully
That's my Angel in Heaven

She helps everyone in need
Never does she like greed
That's my Angel in Heaven

I often look upon the skies
Hoping to see her bright shining eyes

I often listen to the wind
In hope of hearing her laughter again
And I think to myself
That's my Angel in Heaven!

Amanda Jackson

That's Why I'm Me

I hide from fears, I cry my tears,
I think I should so.
I hide them on a shelf, because I hate myself,
For why I do not know.
I've loved, I've lost, at almost every cost,
Why I should not dare.
I sit alone in my head, sometimes I think I should be dead
Should I even care?
I have love, I have hate, I don't think I should wait,
I'm not very shy, I hate to cry, how can I go on?
You look at me like I'm too fast, maybe like I will not last,
But I'm this way 'til the day ends, I guess.
That's why I'm me.

Talia Hinkley

Sorrow

Oh, the gleaming sky so bright
The sorrows triumph with no fight
The losing battle doesn't quit
But still the candle remains lit
Don't say I die
Don't say it's all a worthless lie inside
Don't say I do not try
Inside of me the sorrow moves
About waiting, waiting, waiting.

Allison Harklerode

My Love

It's been forever
Since I've felt your touch.
I've longed to hold you;
The pain is so much.

But you were gone;
The flowers didn't grow.
I thought you were lost,
But who would know?

You had come back from beyond.
The touch of death kissed you,
But you moved along.
The heartache and pain are finished at last;
I'm here in your arms, finally it's past.

In your arms, I'll be here,
Whether or not you are gone.
I'll always be near,
For death has kissed me as well.

I thought I'd lost you,
For forever and a day,
But now we're together and I'll stay that way.

Sharlee Jorgensen

Untitled

And when the evening comes,
mourning the sun for the loss of beauty and light,
thou shalt understand the meaning of internal darkness.
With deepest remorse and against all odds,
the moon sings his song of sorrow
and loss of his loved one's beauty.
Behold, but within the setting star's grace,
not one but one thousand stars have appeared,
honoring their main beauty,
who shall, in time, rise again when night is done.

Allison Clapp

Double Moons

Double moons, triple moons, four moons high,
Moons are out from behind the clouds,
On this dark cool night.
Whispering to the sun to stay down,
Minutes longer.
As the moon's brightness gets stronger,
And stronger.
Moons high in the dark blue sky.
Floating high, the moons cross the sky,
Triple moons, four moons, five moons high.

Kristy Barnhill

What If

One night as I lay in bed
What if's seeped into my head
What if the sky fell down
What if the world stops turning round
What if I fell at school
What if I wasn't cool
What if I broke my arm
What if I owned a farm
What if I ate strained peas
What if I had fleas
What if I became rich
What if I fell in a ditch
What if my car broke down
What if I weighed a pound
What if this poem stopped
What if my balloon popped
While the what if's sing their song
I guess they'll sing it all day and all night long.

Nina Strickland

Oblivion

A deep lamenting purple
Sprawls out across the skies;
Filling the heart, the soul,
The mind with melancholy sighs.
Cherubs soar like little dreams
Through everlasting love;
Their wings flutter like whispers soft,
To carry them above.
The stars appear as holes
On the darkened curtain of night;
Through the holes in the curtain
Glimmer bits of Heaven's divine white light.
Pinkish hues define eternity,
Dizzying brightness tickles the land;
My dreams are made of angelic love.
Come along, I offer you my hand.

    Kimberly Preston

Change

We are both changing, going our separate way,
the sky is a dusty cloud right now, I can't see your face.
Will we be together through the change,
or will we part and cause everlasting pain?
We are gone and left forever together in peace is where we belong.
Where in our life is there room for change,
yet nothing ever stays the same.
Change will come and go and if you and I love each other
we will see past each other's faults,
then when change suddenly comes to a halt
our new relationship will come apparently clear,
change will bring us closer together
and with it will come a new set of fears,
take your hand in mine and there shall be no tears.
Change can be good or bad often times, it will make people sad.
For us, with more than enough love to spare,
change won't hurt us because you and I both care.
That's what change is for,
to bring people closer and to offer us more.

    Sara A. Negless

Music

Everyone has a different taste in music.
Some choose rap, rock, pop, and so much more.
But in a way, it's all the same.
Each has a beat, a rhythm, and a meaning.
Yet each meaning is different,
whether it's to tell a story,
tell a tale, or to sing a song
of or for someone or something.
And in some way it speaks to you:
maybe if the artist sings about their life,
you envision it, except you put yourself in that situation.
In a way, music takes you places.
So whether you're listening to the radio or just humming a tune,
in a way, music is a wonderful and magical thing!

    Christie Sheridan

Evil

I am evil;
I hide in the back of everybody's mind.
Some think I'm not there but,
I will always be there.
Lurking through darkness and everyone's hearts.
I am there.
My life is twisted.
I have no home but, everyone is a home to me.
My presence is unknown until something bad happens.
I am always blamed for something,
even though it's not my fault.
I never am ashamed of what I have done.
I am evil.

    Lauren Baumer

Daddy's Little Girl

A mother's daughter
A daddy's girl
Mother's diamond
Daddy's pearl
"You are so special,"
Daddy said to me one day.
"You are so much like me, in every little way."
Daddy smiled and hugged me tight;
I hugged him back, with all my might.
Daddy looked to me, and said with great love,
"I'm sorry, I couldn't be with you
With all the hard times you had."
"I Love you, Daddy,
Even when things aren't quite right,"
I said, with tears in my eyes.
And O, what a sight.
"You are my little girl,"
Daddy said with a laugh.
"I hope you know that you are my little pearl."

    Talitha Jo Law

A Dream

At night, when I go to sleep, I have this dream.
This dream is about a girl and me.
We go out at night, and do the things we want to do.
Sometimes, I wish this dream would come true for me.
The girl in the dream is a girl I really care for,
but her name is different in my dream.
Her name is some sort of fantasy.
The girl in the dream in reality ignores me.
That dream was a dream until that dream become reality
this one warm early spring day.
She walked up to me and told me
about the dreams she has been having.
As if turns out, she really cared for me
and she has been having the same dream.
So that was my dream.
Dreams do come true, if you truly believe.

    Tony Negron

Myself

Every morning I look in the mirror,
I wonder why I look this way.
I'm always wondering how to change,
But I am who I am, I am myself.

As I eat breakfast I'm wondering,
"Look at all those round O's."
Why can't I be that way?
Then I think, "I am how God planned,"
I am myself.

I want my little nose, even my pierced ears,
I want my long nails, even my shoulder-length hair.
This is all I want and I want it all.
This is what I am, I am myself.

Though times I realize I can't change how I look,
I can learn things new every day,
I'm learning every day to love myself.

    Trisha Becker

Alone

Alone, alone, always alone.
Nobody but nobody can make it out here alone.
My sweet fingertips rub across your lips.
When you turn the corner, you've got to watch it.
Gun shots whisper through the hills,
People being killed day after day.
So nobody but nobody can make it out here alone.

    Markie Fish

Thoughts before Death

Everything coming to an end,
Wondering how it will feel to end.
Saying goodbye to all things that matter;
Like Mother Earth and loving ones.
Listening to the shouts and cheers of the people,
Seeing the faces of gladness and sadness.
Knowing you are almost there.
You try to foresee where you will go,
Either up or down, Heaven or Hell.
The things you have done wrong,
That you can't take back,
Are the biggest mistakes in life.
All you can do is hope and pray,
And soon the madness will go away.

Amanda Halpin

My Heart Rumbles

When I see you, my heart rumbles with love.
When I think of you, my heart goes thump.
When my heart rumbles and thumps;
I think I'll never leave you, but it's too late.
Why? Why? Why?
Oh, why did I leave you?
Why? Why? Why?
Now I told you, but you don't seem to care.
I told you that I shouldn't have left you,
But you don't seem to care.
You don't seem to care.
Now I see you with your new girlfriend,
And I think that she could be me.
That could be me holding your hand!
That could be me kissing you good night!
But it's not, she could be me.
When I see you my heart rumbles with love,
But sometimes I wish your heart would rumble back.

Priscilla Anderson

My Secret Dollhouse

There's this dollhouse that I know,
A secret place where I can go;
When feeling hopeless, unloved, or just plain sad,
I visit this place where there is no bad;
Sweetest music fills the air,
Little angel's laughter everywhere;
Streets of chocolate, houses of candy,
Children skipping along fine and dandy;
Everyone's beautiful in their own way,
No one shall ever be turned away;
If someone is lost, they're found very quickly,
Good health is replenished to all who are sickly;
This paradise is locked away with a key,
The key is in my heart, and shall always be.

Joan Gorman

Bliss

For Kris, my older sister
Rain beats on the window, me, all snug on the couch.
I lie and listen to the crystal rumble of thunder.
Clutching my pillow, I dream of a castle with beautiful lamps,
and marble floors and gold and silver everywhere.
Porcelain dolls, and doors of dramatic design.
Crack! Lightning strikes and the thunder calls after.
The rain pours down extra hard.
Fighting the urge to run outside,
I drift back to sleep, too cozy, too relaxed to go.
The rain calls fiercely to me,
Tells me everything is good.
No pain, no suffering
Just the casual mumble of the sky.

Tanya Walmsley

Magazine Rack Covergirl

The frigid November air brushed shades
of pink over my face and knuckles.
My feet stopped beside each other
as if they had forgotten where they were once taking me.
My eyes were paralyzed wide open in a steady gaze
about five feet from where you were standing.

You were facing noon traffic from the second shelf
of a magazine rack that I pass by daily.
Carefully painted red lips left just enough space,
inviting my cold lips some warmth from the autumn wind.
Blue shadow fell over your eyes,
overlapped by strings and strands of sandy brown hair.

I pivoted away, shaking you off of my pupils,
and the eternity that had seemingly passed by,
lasted not even the length of a stoplight from green to red.
But I wasn't this warm before.

Jason Camp

Strength

I found the strength to just let go,
Of all my life the high and low,
Of all the memories good and bad,
Of all the times happy and sad.

I found the strength to walk away,
From that year, that month, that day,
From the time I lost it all,
From that dream I just let fall.

I found the strength to realize why,
All my life I've wished to die,
And all this time I've loved then lost,
Now in the end I see the cost.

I found the strength to then look back,
To look at life through holes and cracks,
To see the past and troubles brought,
To see the dreams I never sought.

I found the strength to lay to rest,
Inside this box here, now my nest,
And enter to eternal sleep,
No longer will I laugh or weep.

Shaina L. Race

He Lies above Us

He lies above us in a place we call Heaven.
But is it really Heaven? Is it really a place
where people go when they're not alive?
Why is it so confusing? Why do people die?
Is it because they aren't wanted in the world?

Kara Ketchum

Fork in the Road

There's a fork in the road,
a fork in your life—
One is to happiness,
the other to drugs.
Drugs are like a hole;
You're stuck in it.
Happiness is like the sky,
open and free.
In the hole, opportunities fly over you,
not in your reach.
But in the sky,
opportunities surround you in your reach.
There's a fork in the road,
a fork in your life.

Katie Engmann

Shadow of a Memory

The rain pounds heavily against the window's grain,
As she lies and watches, wallowing in pain.
The wind comes running through the trees,
Stirring the ghosts who live for the breeze.
Delighted with all fanciful fright.
She shudders and holds the blankets tight.
Memories hide in the days darkest cracks,
How she wants her true love back.
Many many moons ago she lost him to a devil's angel.
Though he was never really hers, I know,
Only her dearest friend, I know.
Still she loved him with no return,
Her heart a fire to forever burn.
Suddenly she glances across the misty lane,
To see the shadow of that friend
and she now can't remember his beautiful name.
Blinking hard she looks again,
Only to see rain in the wind.
He was only the shadow of a memory deep within.

Jennifer Buchholz

Sleepless Night

In memory of my father

The moon shines brightly in the dark winter sky
No stars to see, the clouds overshadow them.

As the snow glistens,
A shadow appears.
A sleepless night?

A guilty heart?
Guilt so overwhelming,
Sleep would be impossible.
Waiting for the pain to go away,
But knowing that it never will.

A mourning soul?
Not ready to move on,
Yet forced to let go.
Needing love and support
To take the place of what is now gone forever

Perhaps an unconscious mind,
Searching for the unknown?
Yearning for a need, yet not sure what.
Wanting someone close, but not sure who.

Julie Fiscus

I'd Start Over

It's lonely here without you
My lakes of tears have yet to dry
And I admit to you
I often wonder why

I wonder why you left
It's my fault
If I had a time machine
I'd take back every word I regret

I regret all the cursing
And the rudeness I showed you
You probably won't believe it
But I'm sorry and there's nothing I can do

Believe me, my love,
That if I could
I'd start over my life
I really would

I'd lead a pleasing life
One that would certainly please thee
And hopefully in that new life
You just might love me

Sarah Gaither

Untitled

The perfect way you do things wrong,
The simple way you lead me on,
I can't escape your love,
Even though it isn't there.
Your smile's in my memory,
Imprinted on my brain.
The closeness when you're gone
Is driving me insane.
You expect nothing from me,
And I give nothing back.
But yet you stole my heart.
All I want to do is lie in the sweet embrace
Of your memory,
Because it never leaves me lonely.

Allegra Hope

Wisdom

For my sister and inspiration, Jeralee

Words of wisdom come and go
Lightning flashes like white winter snow
A feather falls to the ground
A child is lost nowhere to be found
Lights flash from high above
You chase around a gray colored dove
With tears in your eyes, you wave goodbye
Knowing someday you will fly away
Angels watch with their bright eyes
Soaring through the peaceful skies
The lightning stops
The child is found
The feather is picked up off the ground
Angels see
Angels hear
We always know that they are near
I'm glad to say that
Words of wisdom are here to stay.

Heidi Kidd

World War III

There is a candle in this world
that just can't wait to be lit,
but if we light this candle,
our lives will never be the same.

Everything will be destroyed,
no one left to save us,
and no time will be left for doing
the things we should have done.

Many candles have been lit,
each before our time.
Now this candle wishes us to be lit;
can we afford to light this candle at all?

I think it best to leave this candle unlit,
because the future of the world
would surely fall from grace—
if this were our last candle to be lit.

Stephanie M. Isley

Friendship

For my mama and papa

Friendship is like a flower they bloom every day.
Friendship is power, power in every way
in every way unspoken in every way unsaid.
I'd rather have friendship than be dead.
To be dead is to be unliving.
Unliving is to be dead.
To be left to death, death in every way
Unspoken in every way unsaid.
Unsaid friendship is like being dead.

Leann Clark

So Many Wonders of the World

Dedicated to my loving family and to God
When it's cold outside and getting ready to snow
And you have nowhere else to go
But to just sit in your bedroom
And wonder what does God look like

What's it like up in that big baby blue sky
Sleeping on fluffy pure white clouds on high
There are many wonders in the heavens
Maybe someday we'll know

But for right now I think I'll just sit
And stare outside my window through the icy air
And wait for the little tiny unique flakes
To come pouring down.

Alexandra Jalili

Flying High

Dedicated to Renee Runquist
She must have been dreaming of flying high.
She must have been thinking of how to die.
She must have been thinking the past will be with her.
She must have been thinking it's right, not wrong.
She must have been thinking of herself, not others.
She must have been dreaming as she flew high, high in the sky.

Lindsay Thompson

My Life

To my family, my friends, and my departed grandmother
I look outside and see the rain fall so grand,
I go outside and I'm not able to stand.

I look from my room, children at play,
And all that my unhappiness is doing is making me lay.

I wish people would sweep my unhappiness away with many brooms.
But all people seem to do is just sit in their rooms.

My soul is dripping, now my heart is ripping.
You could see fire in my eyes, but now it's not there,
And I try to seek it, but I can't find it anywhere.

I look at people and they don't see,
I cry to people, but they don't hear me.

I try to look for hope,
But when I don't seek it, I feel like a dope.

I have a heart strangled by wire,
I'm trying to find my heart that is filled with fire

I want wings to fly to the sun,
But all I seem to do is run.

God knows I don't want to live in vain.

Joanna Oslin

Pray

As I sit at my window,
I look at the world outside
And I think of how it's falling apart.
I feel as though I am alone in a world of deceit and despair.
The new generation will be worse.
I dread seeing January first.
I know, though, if I look unto myself and God, I'll be ok;
I only wish the people outside my window will do the same.
The kids I go to school with always look for someone else to depend on;
They will be the ones who are hurting, all I can do is pray,
Pray for the best,
Pray for the goodness in people.
As I sit at my window,
I look at the world outside and pray!

Trista Faith Woods
Clinchco, VA; U.S.A.

Klutz

Today I ran into the garage door as it was coming down;
I figured I'd try to beat the door but ended up looking like a clown.
I told my dad I'd bruised my nose while shutting the cattle gate;
He smiled at me and knowingly said, "Get your head screwed on straight!"
You see, I left a total mess right upon the floor;
On top of that I didn't even shut that darn garage door.
Then Dad said, "Were you born in a barn?
You need to shut the door."
I quickly ran outside, and then
I fell down to the floor.
Well, once again, I felt like a fool,
But, yes, I was thankful for this:
My clumsiness was confined to my very own home,
And not in front of peers at school—Oh, bliss!

Lindsay Walton

Life

For Odalys, my mom—you're always in my heart!
As I walked through the shadows of life
with my heart in my hand and the feeling
of doom so strong like ice cold mist
through my veins I search for the light
that brings me hope and makes the shadows
and illusions of this harsh world
in my hand, my heart alas, will feel love
in the arms of God.

Alma Quesada

Stranger

For my parents, Kathy and Albert Thomas
As I heard her laughing down the hall,
I thought I also heard my world fall.

But fall to where, to what extent,
To lie beneath the world I meant.

Where was I going, where would I go,
To live the life of someone I know?

To laugh, to cry, to feel of shame
There's only one person that I could blame.

But who was it, who did I choose,
To live the life that I would soon lose?

The life that was meant for me,
I will soon cry myself to sleep.

To lie here beneath my sorrow,
Beneath my pain, beneath my hallow.

She's standing there at my door,
Waiting to knock, waiting for more.

The door slowly closes, she will soon pass,
But the hurt and the sorrow will always last,

So now I end this life of mine
to say goodbye, to say goodnight.

Kathren Thomas

Remember

Do you remember me? Well, you should.
I'm the girl you told me to be.
Now do you remember?
It's not easy being me, everyone yelling and telling
when all you have to do is consider me
for who I am and what I am,
not the way I walk or hey, even the way I talk, but just me.
I represent the color of my skin,
but most of all who I am or maybe even as your friend.
You should remember now.

Ashley Garza

Leaving?

You come to say you're leaving, you come to say goodbye,
I pretend to know why you go, I pretend not to cry.

First you say love me, now you say the end?
If we were still together, what would you say then?

Words to say I love you, there are so many ways,
Words to say I'm leaving, the other always pays.

Why can't you stick with one thing, instead of always changing your mind,
Try and stop now, so the truth you can find.

Why can't we stay together? Why can't you see what is going on?
Why are you leaving? What did I do so wrong?

Or was I blind, not to see what you were doing,
Being with someone new every week, it was my mind I was fooling.

Now to myself the truth, I shouldn't try to hide,
But I can't help it, it's like my heart has died.

I tried to stop our fighting, I tried to be a friend,
I tried to be a lover, I tried until the end.

So go ahead and leave, and even though we are apart,
No matter how you forget me, I will always keep you in my heart.

Katie P. Lawrence

Your Wings of Protection

I hope one day that I will find love.
I have a dream that one day God will touch me from Heaven above.

And when I see His beautiful hand reach down on me,
It reaches for my heart and I know my childhood has set me free.
In the most gracious voice he says, now my child you are ready
I turn to see only a blinding light and a huge hand remarkably steady.
I cry out with questions, "But Father, I have been for years"
He replied, "No, my child, you were much too vulnerable
to take on the pain and tears.
It was not my intent to deprive you I will not lie,
But only to shelter you until you have wings to fly."
"I thank you oh, Heavenly Father above for giving me this gift
That they should call love,
But I should look no further because of your loving display of affection,
That has made me feel warm by your wings of protection
Oh, Heavenly Father above, I think I've found love."

Lyndsey McMahon

Untitled

My future lies within the different paths I choose to take,
but it also lies within the hearts of happiness I break.
The days have not been mine; I don't know where they've gone.
The path I chose to take has done me wrong.
The beauty of Mother Nature's artistic presence surrounds us all
until the burden of reality hits us with a spray-painted picture of a littered land.
My clothes, my suit of armour have been torn from my body.
He's found his way to me. The intrinsic cloth lying beneath me.
Once inherent, now unknown and uncomfortable on my skin.
My heart saddens me, my thoughts jiggle to the twist in my mind.
I wish I possessed the innocence, laughter, and honesty of children.
All words crawl through my skin like a grueling shore in the night.
I just want to get a good night's sleep
wrapped in a blanket of comfort hugging me close.

Anna Domenech

A Fall Rain

The rain, the rain it falls down fast, to the ground it dare not pass.
The leaves, the leaves they fall slow, to the ground they always go.
Slicked down to the ground they will stay, 'til the dawn of the very next day.
When the sun comes out, without a doubt, to dry up the ground,
while the brightly colored leaves go dancing around.
Then a big gust of wind came their way, and blew them all very far away.
But maybe some day, you will see leaves come your way!

Stephanie Myers

This World Today

As I sit under this tree,
I wonder how it would be.
If in this world of fear,
It would all become clear.

Not a bomb bursting in air,
Nor killing the rightful heir,
Only to get their share.

But roses with dew,
And the sky so white and blue.
With people being kind to others,
Not brothers fighting with brothers.

But in this world of sin,
Peace will never win.

Rachel D. Oliver

Love Thy Neighbor,

Thy Self, My Own Family

Love thy neighbor, thy self
Always be on guard
Because for your own respect
Just I'm deeply hurt
Because I love so much
And I will destroy
People that hurt me
And I will with my mind, soul, thoughts
And let the world know
How I feel in my heart
Because we are not free
We are surviving for our love
And for our children
Don't forget that ever
Because I will be hurt forever
Because my love is destroyed
I see before my eyes it hurts so much
Why? Why? God, why my love
Why you hurt him, too many tears
He's mine, forever in my heart

Clara L. Sanders

Potential Love

Bright as the sun,
Blind in light,
It sets,
Permanently,
Gone without a trace,
Black, dull, empty, space.

Courtney Chamberlain

A Fallen Rose

To my mother—thanks, Mom!
A white rose
A blur against the red
It sticks out like a sore thumb
It falls and withers
And is forgotten

Justine Guzman

Friends

To Amy Shephard with love
The night is more night,
And gray is more gray,
And empty is more empty,
When friends go away.

The sun's on the flowers,
The rain's full of song,
When friends are together,
Where true friends belong!

Mary Burden

Sixteen

For my mother and father

I've waited for years for this one special day, counting down the days.

How great it would be, how big it would be when I turn 16!
Now that it is here, it's no special day for me.

Why, the stars are no bigger, the sun is no brighter!
The birds still sing the same old song,
and the world is much crueler to me.

My family is a mess, and I must confess I have much less.
I'm so confused. Oh, how it would be to be a little girl, you see.
It'd be great to have a smile and laugh a good laugh at a silly song,
lay my head down late at night, with my mom and dad to kiss me goodnight,
never to worry or cry a river about stuff that never once mattered—
to say my prayers and wonder if the tooth fairy would visit me that night—
to wake up on Saturday mornings and watch the big black cat struggle
to get the little yellow bird, clenching onto my blanket for hope for the bird—
playing with my dolls and finger-painting the walls . . .
But those days are gone, and I've grown to see,
everyone knows they all have their lows.
People will tell you they love you and then break your heart
or say they will be there, but you find them in the dark.
I'm sixteen now, I hate the thought
because, you see, it's no special time for me!

Nakisha Rigney

I Never Said I Love You to My Mother

Waves from doleful emotions blast the barrage of my heart,
a thousand harrows grub and split my being apart.
Such a dread I have never felt before,
this seclusion, hidden words infringe my soul.

My ungratefulness fills me with penitent memories and pain,
this heart craves to feel your venerable attendance again.
Then I will expend myself from this immense lump in tears,
sharing with you the love obscure in my soul for years.

While I am lying on my cushion, confronting the night so odd and dire,
mighty thunder burns the sky in poignant fire.
Helletic bluster impends my craven body, an outrageous sight,
but an unknown presence from hex and evil is keeping me this night.

It is you who sanctify this moment with your noble grace,
still so dainty and merciful with a heavenly smile on your face.
Mildly you strike a note of hopefulness in me
and verify that never is too late for change, forgiveness, and honesty.

The sky is weeping with me in the dawn of a novel day,
I fall down on my knees, pose my lips, and sprightly pray;
"Forgive me, my glorious angel, for engendering your earth-life sorrowful and unsure,
but now my heart is agape to you; rise, my love, so innocent and so pure."

Jana Arsovska

Racism

I hate people that judge by color of skin;
they try to fight all the blacks with their rebel flags,
but they'll never win.
I think the blacks should do something about it,
but that would probably cause an even bigger riot.

I hate the way they treat them, they're really just like us;
just because you look at them doesn't mean you have to cuss.
If you have a problem with them, you need to keep it in.
When you see a white girl look at them, you think she's committed a sin.

Why do you look at them as if they've done something wrong?
You can't do anything about it because they've been here for so long.
You need to get over what you hear and your state of mind,
and learn to appreciate, accept, and be kind.

I wish all you racist people would grow up and see,
they're just the same as you and me.
It's only their color, they're not any different;
they are here too, and they were God-sent.

Amy Robinson

Dad

I've known you for fifteen years
And I thought I was in Heaven . . .
Because I was your little girl. . . .
You sang me songs
That made me cry
And I don't even know why . . .
But as I got older
We split apart . . .
And that really tore my heart.
Everybody says I'm just like you,
And I really hope that's true,
Because I really love you!

Cassie Falcon

Dreaming of You

As I say my prayers
and lie down in my bed,
I still have thoughts of you
running though my head.

Then I dream
I'm in your arms,
as in my ear you
whisper sweet charms.

Those gorgeous baby blue eyes
are focused on me;
my smiling face
is all they see.

Then I wake up
and tears fall,
for I realized
you weren't there at all.

Maybe someday this dream
will come true, and you'll realize
how much I love you!

Annie Musser

Love Is Blind

Why is it so hard
to look through a man's eyes,
to see his true colors,
his decorative lies?

All his thoughts,
all his secrets
lie between
his strengths
and weaknesses.

Once you find out
he's all a lie,
he's gone;
you're alone,
no chance of goodbye.

Stacy Moore

Love Is Everywhere

Love, love is everywhere
In the air and under your chair
Love is invisible you might say
But I wish I could, I wish I may
See love sometime today.

Love, love is everywhere
You can't see it anyway
And if you did, you wouldn't
Know because love is something
Only your heart knows
Love, love is everywhere

Markia DeClouette

Open Your Mind

Open your mind to a world of possibilities, they say.
You can hold the world in the palm of your hands
if you should expand your mind.
Well, if this is true, I'm telling you to follow your dreams
and reach for the stars, because they are not as far away as you think.
The truth is you don't always get what you want,
but the most important thing is that you tried.
Even though we are different on the outside,
inside we are all as strong as a polar bear,
fast as a cheetah, yet meek as a mouse.
It's okay to let your mind dance sometimes,
but you must always remember common sense.
Sometimes bad things happen, but you can and will go on.
Remember: Life is a battle that you will win,
no matter how long it takes.

Kristen Pepin

I Remember

For my adopted mother, Jill R. Holden
I remember my mom putting a blanket over my head
And picking me up when it was raining.
I remember a kid coming up to me and kissing me on my cheek.
I remember the first time I ate tomato soup; it was so good.
I remember my mom screaming and me tumbling down the stairs.
I remember seeing the tooth fairy with a pink fluffy dress and a wand.
I remember having to live in an apartment with cockroaches.
I remember my cousin breaking a window.
I remember playing with my Barbie doll in the mud puddle.
I remember my cat tried to kill a mouse,
And I washed it down with a hose and my mom
Took it from me and threw it away; it was dead.
I remember me and my brothers getting taken away in a police car.
I remember crying.
I remember my mom saying bye.
I remember coming back to her.
I remember her leaving us at babysitter's and not coming back.
I remember seeing my new family.
I remember crying for my real mom.
I remember my new mom saying it would be ok.

Sarah Torres

The Lonely Past

I felt your loneliness through the trees,
And I knew the peace beyond your blessed leaves,
And knew you were the soft heart that gave my heart life's start.
I've known you to be lonely and sad,
The only thing you knew was what you had.
And the time passed and your life fell before you.
So it cast a spell on your heart but you still couldn't forget the past.
A time when you dared to live on carelessly,
A time when the sky would brighten just for you,
A time before the loneliness,
A time before a broken heart.

Bianca Jamison

Forget Me

To all friends and family
When I die, will you forget me?
Will a single rose die with me?
And will a single tear roll down your cheek?
I am not that big of a deal, but one single wish of you—don't forget me.
That when you need me, all you have to do is call and I will be there.
I will be there when you cry.
You will hear me in the wind saying, "I love you."
But don't forget me because I'm with you.
You can call me your guardian angel.
But don't forget me,
Because I am here with you,
If you like it or not.
So don't forget me.

Tiffany Winburn

Rain

If I go in and dance
will you assign me a small role
in your perfect harmony?
Because I believe you
are not the child of Heaven's misery
but sent to anoint
to heal
the most lacerated wing
or perhaps
to convince every unspoken law to relent
so I might take his hand
with soft lingerings of you
beneath an unremarkable umbrella
of smoky blue

Wei Wei Xiong

Time Is a Treasure

This day could be a treasure
don't let it take its leave.
Your life is traveling moments
the past can't be retrieved.

With a heart full of compassion
and happiness pursued.
Your time's a priceless treasure
watch everything you do.

Remind someone you love them
feel warmth of love renewed.
You'll find that in the doing
that peace will come to you.

This day can be a blessing
a treasure of a sort.
So take each moment as it comes,
be happy in your heart.

Esther Miller

Solitary Rose

A cold room, empty
yet filled with loneliness

An old woman
rocking on her chair
back and forth
back and forth
thinking about the past

A new beginning
An ending

Tears
The emptiness stays in the heart
A solitary rose sits on a headstone

Olivia Obercian

Just a Blue Wave

It's not sea green,
Nor crystal clear.

Just a blue wave
Crashing upon my shore.

Hear the roaring waves
Feel the endless breeze.

The sights and sounds
Surrounding my inner soul.

Refreshing, satisfying, calming
My restless mind.

Over and over,
Waves crashing upon my shore.

Mei-lan Zook

The Real Meaning of Christmas

What is the first thing that comes to mind when someone mentions Christmas?
Is it maybe the gifts, carols, food, family, and the fun,
or is it knowing Jesus Christ was born on this day?
I could see how you might like gifts,
But the real question to you is: Do you like giving or receiving or maybe both?
I could see how it could be carols,
Do you really go to sing carols out in the snow
to make people smile or to get free hot chocolate?
I could see how you would enjoy the food,
Is that why you get together with your family—for the pie or to see your relatives?
I could understand how you would like seeing and being with your family.
Do you really like those family get-togethers,
or do you know that your grandparents give the best gifts?
I could see how you love having fun,
But do you really like laughing with your family or do you like to party?
I could definitely understand how you would like to celebrate the birth of Christ.
No questions asked!
Of course, the gifts, carols, food, family, and fun are extra-added bonuses.
Let us not forget how we got those added bonuses
and that Christ is the reason for the season.

    Melissa Crawford

Letting Go of Us

Now I finally think that I have reached some conclusion.
I think that our time is up and we will pass each other by.
Although I do not control fate, I feel as if I have a part in it.
You have taught me many things about people and myself.
And for that I will cherish you forever.
This has been a relationship for learning and now I must move on.
Although you don't realize,
I grow stronger each day without you by my side.
I feel our door closing almost closing forever.
I now realize that I have not lost in this relationship.
I have given you everything that I had to offer and somehow
I even found more to offer you.
I truly believe that you have always meant well, but some
things always came before me.
What scares me most, is I know that for my benefit I need to let you go.
It's not letting you go that scares me, it's knowing I should.

    Jenna Perline

My Guardian Angel

For my twin sister, Melissa Brueggeman
I know my guardian angel.
I could know her very well, but I don't.
All I know is that she is my sister,
My twin sister.
I wonder what it would be like to have two of me around,
Or if we would look alike in every little way.
Maybe it would be confusing if we did.
A lot of people would know the feeling as having a sister around,
Or maybe they know how I feel.
I love my sister, even though she is not alive.
I trust her with my life to watch after me.
I know she loves me too.
Melissa Marie Brueggeman is my guardian angel, and I know that for a fact.

    Michelle Brueggeman

Insight

Digging deep within her soul, she pulls out her utter frustration,
her fears, her hopes, her dreams . . . as if she were spilling a bottle.
Out comes her known world onto a single sheet of paper . . .
and you can feel it as if the voice were surrounding you . . .
but it is hard to reach deep and unlock those secrets, for anyone.
But for those who can, it is different . . . perspectives are un-numbered,
horizons are un-limited . . . but they're too much to catch every day . . .
or is it just too time-consuming?
You may question . . . and if you do, dig deeper . . . the answer will come,
locked deep within your soul.

    Jacqueline Corey

Untitled

All these feelings, I can't explain,
Sitting alone, out in the rain,
Will I get all these frustrations out,
Will I be at peace, I strongly doubt,
Lying awake in my bed,
A throbbing pain in my head,
Something between us, a giant boulder,
But what I need is a crying shoulder,
Someone who can understand,
Someone willing to lend a hand,
Walking barefoot down the street,
Something hurts, and it's not my feet,
The pain is deep inside of me.
I explain, but they can't see,
How can they all be so blind,
Where are the answers I need to find?

    Alyssa McCaffrey

The Dream

I had a dream at 9:00 a.m.
School just started;
I was asleep.
Mom said,
"Can't walk to school
because all the highways are closed."
I was confused;
I went back to sleep.
Mom woke me up at 8:00 a.m.
I had to go to school.
Not fair!
Nice dream, though.

    Claudia Heye

The Meanings

Life
What does it mean
Why are we here
Were we chosen
Or forced
Are we needed
Or wanted
Questions with no answers
Asked by few
Thought by most
Answers are sought for
But never or rarely found
It's a game
We play it every day
But no one ever wins
We start with life
And finish with death
In the end.

    Jenna Angles

What's Stopping Me

I often think to myself,
is there something more?
My life seems so incomplete.
I know there's much, much more.
I have the feeling of running on,
but I don't move my feet.
Is it I'm afraid of change,
or is it I'm afraid to change?
I feel so trapped, but I'm so free.
The temptation could set me free.
I often wonder if I'm alone,
but soon discover I'm not alone.
There's many more who feel like me.
I want to find what pleases me.

    Krista M. Wall

To the Stars

To the stars of the night where dreams are created, and new lives are born.
This is where the life begins, and the old will eventually die.
And with each new star that is born a new idea of how we are
to live in harmony is resurrected.
Along with these new ideas, there is always a part
of all of us that doesn't want to change.
These new stars represent a little of something in all of us.
The only difference is, we are the people
who will have find it, and eventually understand it.
It could take time to get used
to the changes that will effect our lives forever.
Hard times are surely ahead, but as we show that we all have
just a little bit of humanity left in all of us, I'm sure we will survive.
As time passes, we start to notice the changes
that have now changed us for the better,
and we realize that we either don't want to be alone
or feel the heartaches that love brings.
With each new star that is born a new idea of how we are to live
our lives in harmony is just around the corner,
waiting to give someone happiness just one more time.

Brian Spaulding

Afraid to Love

Waiting to be wanted, needing to be needed, longing to love
Hopes and dreams and immaterial things
And fantasies and flings are what I'm dreaming of
Longing to be close, so very close, close enough to feel his pulse
Afraid to love or give my heart to one I feel so close to
Wanting to push everyone away and out of my own little world
This love and hate at such a rate is paced so fast it's confusing me
And love, oh, love is what I'm dreaming of
And True Love, Dear Love, don't forget my love for you will never end
My love is like the starry night; deep and always ever true
My love is like a ring, which has no end and no beginning
But hopes and dreams and fantasies are crushed
With my words of love from my lips just now gushed
For as I love you, and oh, how I love you!
I'm afraid to love or give my heart to one I feel so close to

Sara Christensen

To Have and Not to Hold

I want you to be mine, but I cannot have you because you belong to another.
You want me to be yours, but first I must be the only one.
I want you to hold me in your arms, but that could never happen for us.
I want to have you back in my life, but I cannot have you.
To hold on to the old memories of you and me,
that is wrong because we are not together anymore.
To have you in my life is to have a dream come true.
To have you back into my life is to have back my best friend.
To have that perfect soulmate, they will always be in your thoughts.
To have that perfect love, no one else can compare to that person.
To hold on to that perfect soulmate, you must never let them go.

Valerie Y. Carty

Heavenly Smiles

In loving memory of Paige Dawson
Can you spare a smile? Ours has suddenly washed away.
We can't seem to find it anywhere,
though we've looked for it night and day.

We think our friend took it with her to her magnificent new home in the sky,
and we caught a glimpse of her grin as we were sadly passing by.

We know it must upset her that she accidentally took ours on her trip.
But wait, we see something falling from the sky with a bounce and a flip.

It has floated straight into our hands as we nervously open them wide,
And a smile comes over our face with care, comfort and pride.

Our friend must have dropped it as she skipped the clouds one by one.
We know she must be happy because a rainbow just emerged from the sun.
So, you can keep your smile but remind others to share theirs with love.
If you happen to lose it one day, Paige will send you one from above.

Katie Wellman

Rose

Rose is red
Rose is pink
Rose does not live under the sink
I see red
I see pink
Rose is red
Rose is pink

Candace Haynes

Eternity

The love so strong
Will hold eternity
When one no longer breathes
The other grieves
And will not last
Slowly dies
Of a broken heart
Meeting in the afterlife
Locking hands
And walking into the sunset

Heather Fabian

Support

Dedicated to Amanda Warden
You brought me up when I was down
You lifted me up off the ground
You were there when I couldn't reach
Great support is what you teach
So when I'm feeling sad and blue
The one thing that makes me happy is you

Scott McGreevy

Life Is A . . .

Life is a circus
Full of laughter and joy
Cotton candy and hay rides
Love and romance
Madness and sadness
Perfect children
And the sight of them growing up
But the worst part of all is leaving it.

Heather Clavey

Butterflies

Butterflies, fluttering,
fluttering, fluttering,
Softly as a whisper.
Moving as gracefully
as leaves falling slowly
to the ground.
Landing on a baby's
soft delicate cheek.
Making it laugh very
happily as its wings
tickle the baby's face.
Tickles that feel like feathers.
Butterflies, fluttering,
fluttering, fluttering.

Cassandra Rose

Zombification

The child of the twentieth century
is alone in a crowd,
dazed, confused, staring blankly
at a roaring TV screen.

Chris Straubhaar

Teenage Girl

I get so lonely, I wonder if anyone cares;
I get upset, they say, "Period's here!"
My parents fight, I end up in tears;
I wonder if I were gone, would they really care?
I end up crying every night, and watch the stars shine so bright
Upon my grandmother's house; I stare and wonder what it's like up there.
I wonder if there is a God, but I do believe there's something;
I wish I could go back through the years, but the future's so becoming.
I try to keep the faith alive and hope that one day, there will be a day
when no tears will be shed and no cries will be heard;
I wish for this day, I wish to be heard!

Emily Irons

Daddy

To my loving father, Randall Boucher
Daddy, I love you, do you love me too?
Daddy, what kind of things did you do?
I know we all make mistakes time and time again,
but we can fix them, we really, really can.
Daddy, all those mistakes you've made are catching up with you now,
and you look at us and say how? How do I change it?
You got yourself in this mix, but we all can help you with the fix.
You think there's no hope and you think you can't get off the dope.
You say to yourself, "My life is done.
I think I have a chance left, but to my memory only one."
Daddy, you've turned your life upside-down right along with that frown.
I'm so proud of you, Daddy, for the accomplishments you've made.
Your life is bright and cheery now, not always in the shade.
Keep up the good work when you come home from where you're at.
I know you can do it let me tell you that.
Good luck, Daddy, I love you and miss you too.
I can't wait too see all the goals you've completed
and just think your imperfect past is deleted.

Jessica Boucher

Always Grandpa's Girl

To Salvatore Depetro, the greatest grandpa ever
Even though your blood didn't run through my veins,
there wasn't one moment in time that you ever
made me feel different from the rest.
In your eyes, I was your princess who could do no wrong.
There you always were for me, no matter what my pain.
If you were alive today, you would probably be upset
that I'm searching for my mother,
but I'm looking for the love
that was so suddenly taken away from me.
Since you're gone, I talk to you every night, but it's not same.
You were made from a different mold.
I just hope and pray when my time comes
that you, my dear grandfather, will be there
to hold me again and help me while you lead the way.
So Grandpa, now I'll let you rest in peace,
but always remember—in heart and soul, I will always be Grandpa's girl.
I'll never stop loving you . . . until we meet again.

Denise T. Orefice-Jones

Flowers of Many Kinds

I shall pick flowers of many colors whose smell is so sweet.
I shall pick roses of red, which look like silky sheets.
I shall pick daisies of golden and white, whose odor brings delight.
I shall pick lilacs when they're in full bloom—
their smell overpowers me in the noon.
I shall pick morning glories, which bloom in the morning
when the sun shines on them.
I shall pick pinks, which please the palate with the odor of cinnamon.
I shall pick buttercups, which make me think of soft-churned butter.
I shall pick lilies of the valley, whose waxen flower smell
brings the sight of spring.
I shall pick all these flowers, whose odors or smells are so sweet.

Stacey Welsh

Alone

Words flow through my mind
Like a raging waterfall
They spill on my paper
And answer my call

I know not what brings
These thoughts to my head
Does it matter to know?
Because soon I'll be dead

My life has been hard
Full of outrage and death
I know the final card
Alone I'll be felt

I feel alone already
Dazed and confused
All I have is sincerity
Is that a lot to lose

Leia Sigler

The Special Rose

Drooping petals fall from afar
I look at it with a broken heart.
Remembering the gift you gave to me
The special rose, I cherished thee.

Then something happened,
You went away,
You came not back
But far away

Your heart was there
Mine here so gray.
Wishing things were another way.

I watch the flower start to fade.
Slowly, painfully, it goes away.
Memories, so many, flooding by,
Hoping, praying, wondering why.

No longer is the flower seen
The one you gave so long to me
The gift of love that was so true
The simple love of me and you.

Amber Elizabeth Logsdon

Quickly

Do you understand my pain
Do you understand my fears
Do you understand my cries
Do you understand my tears
Maybe if you took the time
You would understand
What's going on in my mind
Because I'm screaming as loud as I can
And no one is willing
To lend me a hand

Ashley Thomson

Untitled

Mom, you helped me a lot
The wind is my soul.
The trees are my mind.
Nature is my power.
I float in a river of dreams.
My arms are my wings;
they take me to my future.
I am a goddess and rule the galaxies.
Everybody is in my command.
My only weakness is love.

Jessica Lampe

Homemade Myth

It all started long ago, I was born and so.
Although my myth is made up it starts far beyond a long time ago.
Before life of the dinosaurs, or the cave men.
Even before Adam and Eve, and far beyond Christopher Columbus.
When the world was flat, not a hill rock or mountain in sight.
But when the human race raced into this world,
fighting like crazy and dying like wild,
they did not know what to do with the dead bodies and garbage.
So they dug huge ditches and buried all of it.
Well, these holes turned into hills, which turned into mountains
from all of the cold weather, which made it freeze.
Well, when the loose ridges fell to the ground with a big thud,
that is what made rocks.
Well, over the years, this little system went on and on,
or later it will stop, but I have come to the conclusion that it never will.
So now that you have heard my homemade myth, I will now tell you my moral:
Whenever you are walking, and cold, no matter what,
even if you are starved, you should never ever, ever eat a rock!

Katie Grubham

Nimbus Love

Merriment tells this tale of love
Bonds of truth glow hence whereof
Seek this truth when unmindful challenge to hold
Innermost feelings do forceful stories emerge
Yea yet do unfold

Heartfelt embraces carry me through
Reaching searching can this be thy will
Never more beseech me no nor my joy
Stargazer stargazer ferret thy quandary thy ploy

Centuries have passed glorious feats regaled
Royally refulgent deeds to behold and uphold
Rapture thrust again and again ravished we descend

Herald Hauter cast away thy haze heart and soul
Heed heed we do depend yea we comprehend
Harvest of golden seed hasten to thee be amazed
Harvest of golden seed anoint my soul ablaze

Gossamer love virtue endowed yea not to be worn as a tortured shroud
Once in a lifetime stars engage I beg thee
Believe believe
Nimbus unique love is such as this must be allowed the end

Helen T. Dee Ross

Is There Really a Silence?

Is there a silence?
Is there a quiet sound of taunting in your head?
Maybe of your teacher yelling at you to pay attention,
Or maybe it's of your brother saying mean things to you.
Or even of the ghostly tick tock of the clock as it strikes 2:00.

Is there a silence?
Don't you hear yourself breathing, as you try to fall?
Fall into a world. Your world, a world of happiness and good thoughts.
A world that is enchanting. A world in which only you can go to.
A world which you can only awaken from
when you hear your mom yell for dinner.

Is there a silence? Is there a place of silence?
Can you go there? Is it really as sweet as people say?
Or is it enchanting beyond words?
Or as you fall into a world of thought, can you fall into a world of evil?

Is there a silence? Now you tell me. Is there a silence?
Maybe there is, but maybe it is just thoughts.
Maybe it is sweet. Or could it be enchanting or ghostly?
Now you tell me, is there a silence?

Nicole J. Wellstein

The Little One

Her eyes closed tight,
Her fingers so tiny,
All quietly asleep
In a blanket warm as can be.
Her mother holds her tiny fingers
And kisses her ever so sweetly.

Casey L. Wolfe

The Year

It's the year of love and betrayal,
The feeling of hope and worthlessness.
The mark that anyone can fall in love,
But not everyone can be happy.

Vanessa Mathews

Imagination

Through the clouds
into the sky
with the birds, your mind can fly
Through waterfalls
and into caves
in the ocean
with the waves
Your mind can wander
near or far
With imagination the sky
is only the beginning
of glorious things
with legs or wings
Imagination makes your mind fly.

Lizzy Weiss

Impotent

To my grandma, Barbara Budniewski
The splatter thrashing rigorous
Disgruntled the window,
The mezzanine rivuleting
Every time you gambit,
The television fades to dormant,
Acoustic of the cherub beseeching,
Willows rasping against the flanking
Of the vicarage,
The microburst accelerating,
Extension dwindles azoic,
The door oscillates ope,
In the ingresses,
Then . . . I abscond.

Michelle Budniewski

I Don't Understand

I can't believe it happened.
Why did he have to go?
He was killed by a drunk.
Oh, how I loved him so.

I don't understand it,
why people drink and drive.
They waste their time on Earth,
ruining people's lives.

It is hard to get the picture,
why people drink and drive.
But the thing that gets me most
is when an innocent victim dies.

Why in the world, I ask,
would anyone bother
to take the life
of my one and only father?

Kim Hamby

Untitled

There once was a circle
Made of silver and gold
There once was a circle
That all could have and hold
There once was a circle
That was broken nearly every day
There once was a circle
That then became tarnished in every way
There was once a circle
Once silver and gold, now bronze and sold
There once was a circle
Once bound and bold, now is broken
The story has been told, three little
Words can mend this wound, but three small
Words can be said in so many ways,
I love you, I'm sorry, forever friends,
There once was a circle
Made of silver and gold
There was once a circle forever bold
There once was a circle for friends and lovers, and this circle is forever silver and gold

Katherine McFarland

Untitled

To my first love, Michael C.
I love you more and more
My love for you is as strong as it was before.
I got scared and let you walk out that door
Now my tears are falling onto the wet floor.
My heart has never felt this kind of love before.
Now my heart is weeping because of my love forever more.

You asked me to be yours alone
But I said I want my friends and not you alone.
I wish I had not said, "Not you alone."
Now instead I want to be alone,
Alone in your heart forever more.

You will never know how my love grows.

Your love is in someone else,
Instead of where you fell for me and no one else.
I wish I could turn back time to when you were still mine;
I would hold you until the end of time.

I miss your tender smile,
Which was wide as a mile. Now I have to walk that 100 miles.

I love you and will forever miss you.

My sweet guy who lit up my sky whenever he stopped by, now all I do is cry.

Gabrielle Axelrad

The War

Dedicated to my dad
The war has come, the children run while family goes away.
The war has come—the guns, the bombs, the sirens, and alarms,
Bodies blown to tiny bits just lying in the streets.
Water, land, and sky, the war goes on.
The tears and blood are growing more as the war grows bigger than before.
We've fought for freedom many times, but it's getting out of control.
A little fight turned into a war, and now it's totally out of control.
The more I wish, the more I cry, it doesn't end this war.
We dream of happy times and places, friends and family, smiling faces,
but we see when we awake the tears and blood,
the screams and fear and the losses of our family, friends, men, and kin.
We loved them so, but we see their cold, dead faces asleep forever,
never to wake, we'll never see their smiling faces.
The pain and suffering just go on;
more are hurt and killed each day, but still the pain won't go away.
But hush, little one, try to sleep,
dry your tears and close your eyes
even though you know The War Has Come.

Holly Hamric

A Crack in a Friendship

A crack in a window
is just like a crack in a friendship:
You can tape up the window
and you can tape up your friendship,
but the cold breeze will always be there.
Amber Schuerman

Tunes of Unknown Shadows

I heard your song of peace one day
Such music to my ears
'Cause peace can do away with rain
And challenge all my fears.

Desire struck no chord of mine
'Til your eyes met my own
And fire burned no skin of mine
Your touch is still unknown.

Fantasy made trumpet blasts
My mind could only dream
Of all the man I want
In fact, of all the man I need

Eye to eye we have one thought.
Heart to heart we still don't know
Mouth to mouth we have one kiss
And now with this where do we go

You play the violin so well
I can't help but to listen
But can you make a symphony
With that same tune you kiss in.
Jessica Filomeno

What It Means to Be a Friend

We were put here on this Earth
Not for hate or childbirth
But to help people in need
To improve their self-esteem,
To make them feel loved,
To know they are watched from above,
To teach them that what they are
Or what they will always be is a friend,
A friend to love and support,
Maybe witness in a court,
Never to judge or be mean,
But to help them be keen
And to remember what they are
Or what they will always be is a friend.
Missy Miller

Wishes

It's your face
It's your eyes
That no one can describe
It's your lips
It's your voice
Oh, Lord, I have no choice
It's your touch
It's your gentleness
How can anyone make sense of this
It's your smile
It's your tears
You make my fears disappear
It's your heart
It's your love
It must come from Heaven above
It's your laugh
It's your kisses
You are my only wishes
Brandee Mulac

Glory Days

For anyone who has lost someone
Do you recall
The glorious days with you there
Your comfort, your support
You were right beside me
Like all, we had our ups and downs
But because of our strong bond we always worked it through
We were living our lives to the fullest
Until one cold winter's night, our glorious days ended
You left and went to Heaven
And I was on Earth saddened with dread.
It felt like someone washed me ashore
And took my pearl and left an empty shell of me
With tears and gloom I didn't know what to do
My tears formed a river long and deep
On the other side of the river was hope, I was on the side with grief.
I know I had to reach the other side or my live would be complete Misery
So with work and inspiration I reached the other side.
I knew in Heaven your smile was glowing bright
I miss you still, my friend, and until the day we meet again,
It will be my glory day.

Beth Nigatu

Untitled

As he walked through the halls of the castle
he could feel the ghosts of ancient times walking around him.
He could smell the perfume that the ladies wore
drifting through the walls, and the children's laughter filled his ears.
As he entered the dining room, he could see the dogs
eager for the bones the people readily threw them.
The ghosts in the halls seemed to reach out
and give him their pain, sorrow, and joy;
It flowed through him and caused him to run in fear
and as he exited he looked back,
and saw them staring at him with blank faces
and he ran
never to look back again.

Jennifer Matthews

Love in a Black Cloak

A cloud of darkness, dressed with gray paint covers the sky.
As we rained in little drops, a zigzag of lightening
Cracks the sky screaming, you could have done more.

Being little raindrops, did no good to fight back against the lightening.
Drops go down, not up. Was it the wish of lightening for us to go down?

We glanced at the streak of light and tried to look deep into its soul
Until the part of God within the lightning was revealed.
The lightning's anger wasn't for wrong.
It only made us stronger mentally and showed us the wonder of life, love.

Anicham Kumarasamy

Last Goodbye

Why did this have to happen, why did she have to die?
It all started on the Fourth of July.
Grace went out on the town with a bunch of friends;
some people came up and that was the end.
Some shots were fired—eight, I'm sure;
four hit her boyfriend, the rest hit her.
Another friend called the ambulance;
they could hear sirens and screams.
Their friends shut their eyes, hoping it was a dream.
The ambulance raced to the hospital; everything was a mess.
The nurses called their families; everyone was speechless.
The families came to the hospital, Mom and Dad led,
but it was too late—both of them were dead.
I love you, Grace, Mom and Dad too.
I want you to put us in your heart to go everywhere with you.
I broke my promise today of not to cry, but I know this is my last goodbye.

Lisa Kendhammer

The Game

To my parents for their influence
Up to bat
At the plate
Waiting for the pitch
Across the plate
Through the field it flies
Like a rocket
In the sky
Beyond the fence
Into the crowd
Past roaring fans
Beneath the seats it lies
Around the bases
After scoring the winning run
Toward the dugout
With pride and joy
The game's over

Brandon Steele

Untitled

You whispered softly, "Sorry"
My mind became a blur,
My eyes then became clouded,
My emotions rapidly stirred.

Inside my screams were loud,
But words could not be said,
This was the end of something,
Full of life that now was dead.

There were no tears to cry,
Emptiness filled the air,
Robbed inside to nothing,
Too sad to even care.

My eyes then slowly opened,
Alone I'd start anew,
No place for me to go,
I quickly glanced at you.

You seemed so sad and happy,
If one can seem that way,
You let me go right then,
But in my heart you'd stay.

Renee Mosing

Black Mother Earth

For my mother Gwendolyn, with love
Made by Him, for him
beyond compare
beautiful tones of sable
once majestic, now neglected
infinitely felicific
victim of hate and ignorance
single, priceless
permanent
essential

Chris Dorsey

No One Is Perfect

Don't you know that no one is perfect?
No one can be.
You have to have the perfect walk,
Perfect hair, perfect body!
You have to eat right, sleep right,
Twenty-four hours be right.
Talk great, good rate, even smell great!
So can't you see, no one is perfect,
Not even me, only God!

Samisha Carson-Owens

To My Sweetheart

To Mathew Harrington, my sleeping angel
Corny words and rhyming sentences cannot explain
or interpret what I am about to say.
You have brought me joy with a single touch of your hand.
You have set my heart ablaze with the taste of your sweet lips,
And you have put my soul at ease with the soothing sound of your voice.
My heart has been a prisoner for so long,
And now you've released my soul with a smile and your warm touch.
To fall in love with you is what I fear,
But to lose you would be the death of me and all in which I believe in.
To know that a treasure such as your love was no near by,
And I like a blind fool was still searching in a green ocean
For a love that was never to be found because it was never meant to be.
Now wrapped in your arms is where my treasure lies
and where I intend to stay.
Because being with you is paradise
And your kisses are only a taste of Heaven.

Jananya Paris

Answer to the Past

I can't tell you what I've seen and I can't tell you what I've heard
I can tell you that you don't want to go through the same as I have
The nights were long, the skies were dark, the air was cold
I had to find an answer to my past to live my life longer
What was the answer of my long waiting question the stuff that I must learn
But who could answer me, who could tell me what I need to know
The way that I had to be answered was to go through the halls of hell
The halls were long, dark, and filled with those who failed to pass
Who could tell me, who could answer the question I needed answered,
to pursue my journey and try to discover the answer to my past
As I walked on further a dark figure caught my eye
What is it that you may want to take, my soul, my life, to waste my time,
But no answer did he say just stood there like something had him trapped
Hello, hello what must I say to have you take the pain away
The pain that cannot be revealed or released
The pain that stays buried deep inside.

Kayla Hauck

How I Wanted to Love You

How I wanted you to lie down next to me and hold me close
How I wanted you to hold me and listen to me, tell you how much I love you
And I'm sitting here waiting for you like a fool.

How I wanted to feel your lips and taste your sweet kisses
How I wanted you to kiss me softly, and tell me we would be forever
And still we are not even together.

How I wanted you to walk with me
Through the meadow and listen of my fears and fantasies
How I wanted you to make all of my dreams come true
And here I sit, still so very sad and blue.

Heather Vanderhoff

The Most Beautiful Thing in the World

The most beautiful thing in the world is my mom.
She gives you love, care, food, clothes and a place to live
and helps you when you need it.
She is a mother of three, but she doesn't act like a mom.
She's like one of your friends.
She plays games with you and takes you out to the movies and the mall.
She's always been there through thick and thin.
She'll never turn her back on you.
If she makes a promise, she'll try to keep it,
but if not, somehow she'll make it up to you.
If you ask for presents for Christmas, Easter, or other holidays,
she'll do her best to get it for you.
She's a mom, a friend, a nurse, and other things.

Yolanda Zimmerman

Untitled

I am
longing for a time
ehen the pain goes away
and the wound heals
knowing full well that
a scar will remain
in its place

Tim C. Keith

Without You

You touch me, you tease
You do as you please
We flirt as good friends
Then that is the end
You have a great girl
She makes your head whirl
Now without your touch
I miss it so much
Far apart we grow
With nothing to show
But our tears that fall
Once we had it all
Now we fall apart
Trembling in our hearts
My weakness now shows
My heart is now closed
Now closed to my life
Pain cuts like a knife
What am I to do?
All I want is you

Leah Schulte

Untitled

Ever wonder why?
Think so hard then give a sigh.
Ever wonder why not?
Why even bother to try?
Why?
Why not?
Why?

Melissa Stanley

Love

To Jay-ar Baylon, my boyfriend
Your love is like a river,
Peaceful and deep.
Your soul is like a secret
That I never could keep
When I look into your eyes,
I know that it's true:
God must have spent
A little more time on you.

Christine Helton

Rain

The rain whispers in my ear,
All the words I need to hear.
It has to assure me,
The path I take will be clear.

The cool drops fall down on me,
Washing my eyes so I see.
All truth it has to show,
It reveals all that I'll be.

The clouds start to clear away,
Showing me to seize the day.
So I turn on my heel,
Giving color to all gray.

Stephanie Samens

Women

Born so tiny yet so strong
Many say women's lives don't last very long
Even though we're considered weaker than men
We came up in the world and we'll do it again
Our bitterness can make us powerful at heart
But our sweetness in us was with us from the start
It's funny how we're not considered bold
But we must admit, we're head of our household
Bringing our family closer together every day
Trying to make the loving memories in our house stay
High level queens and as beautiful as we are
We shine with our heads high up, like a beautiful shimmering star
A tiny seed in our mother's stomach was planted
And brought us beautiful women, don't take us for granted
Don't forget that we molded Adam into the man he was in the Garden of Eve
We are the most strongest and caring things on earth
That shouldn't be hard to believe
So I'll end this poem with a "Thank you" to all women young and old
All over the world, or wherever you may be
This inspiring poem should be told

Joy Mullins

Growing Up

They hear me cry, but they don't care;
my life is ending, it's such a scare.
I'm in a place I don't belong,
and no one wants to come along.
It isn't amazing, beautiful, or fun,
and if I had the opportunity, I would run.
It seems like only yesterday, I didn't care about a thing;
It wasn't a choice I could or couldn't bring.
I miss my childhood and all those sunny days;
I miss the times I've laughed and played in my own childish ways.
I can still smell the sweet scent of banana bread my mother always made;
The taste was delicious, it's a taste I'd never trade.
My friends were always there for me, and we'd make up silly rhymes,
but now it seems as if I'm bothering them; they don't have the time.
All those memories seem so far away,
and get fuzzier each and every day.
Though I still remember the carols we sang around the Christmas tree,
but growing up, I never thought it would ever happen to me.

Lana Krajewski

Missing You

Dedicated to my mother, whom I miss

You passed away not too long ago, and my tears just went a-flow.
I miss you and I love you, even though you are so far away,
And we keep getting more distant day by day.
I want you to stay, knowing that one day I'll meet up with you again.
Dad doesn't pay attention to me;
Oh, Mommy dearest, can't you see, I need you here with me?
I was only twelve when God took you away,
And the pain in my heart is here to stay.
I keep everything tucked inside, pretending that you never died.
It's kind of hard to pretend
When all you live with is a bunch of men.
Oh, Mother, why did you have to go?
Please tell me, Mommy—I don't know.
Your hand in life was here dealt;
Oh, dear God, how I felt
When the heart inside my chest was just plain ripped out.
I was so scared watching you take your last breath;
There was a presence in the room claimed by death.
Your forehead oh, so cold when touched upon my lips,
Me knowing that was goodbye, just one last kiss.

Mindie Matuszewski

Dreams

Dreams are dreams,
But many people ask,
"Are dreams, dreams?"

I hope dreams are dreams.
If dreams are not dreams,
Then what's a dream?

Is a bad dream a good dream,
Or is a good dream a bad dream?
What is a dream?

Are dreams, dreams?
Maybe a dream is really not a dream.
What is a dream?

Maybe life is a dream.
If a life is a dream,
then what's a dream?

What is a dream?
Tell me what's a dream;
is life a dream or a dream is dream?

What is a dream?
Please tell me, what is a dream?

Pamela Holbrook

Weeping Willow

For my deceased brother Chad Newbold

Weeping willow dry your tears
The wind is strong and has no fears
There is a bird that has no wing
It makes the sun not want to sing
Weeping willow please be strong
For the stars do no wrong
Weeping willow dry your tears—
For you are strong, have no fears.

Tammy Newbold

Underneath It All

Underneath my exterior,
Underneath my clothes,
Underneath my words,
A special person grows.

I may not be beautiful,
My clothes may not be the best.
My words may not be kind,
But I'm as good as the rest

If you look underneath it all,
You'll know my words are true.
You will see the beauty inside
And understand me too.

Nicky Curtis

Feelings

I must really care for you,
My world used to be so dark and blue,
Until I met you.
I just only wanted to be friends,
But somehow you ended up being my man.
You took me to a distant place,
That I enjoyed our long race.
When I'm feeling down,
You make me feel good,
When no one else could.
You stole my feeling from me,
Which I don't let too many people see.
Please don't destroy them,
With your far away distant realm.

Delshunda L. Ishman

Remembering You

I sit here, all alone,
Remembering our years together.
But now you're gone, and I am nothing,
Barren, nothing.
Your smell still lingers, driving me insane;
You're everywhere, everything, you're part of me.
The closet still disheveled with your things, you never did clean it;
Now you can't, can you?
Why? Why, why did you leave me?
I'm still so young, so eager to continue,
And yet, not willing.
Is that you, behind the shadows?
I think this horribly ominous house might be getting to me, emotionally;
I never wanted it, and only now, I see why you loved it so,
Its vast majority of rooms, the musty smell mixed with my sweet perfume,
I'm not you, I'm not you. Am I?
This house now seems to accept me. Please come back.
Please don't let me live alone.
It was my fault you died.
You died coming home to me.

Kristina Tkach

You Are My Heart, My Soul, My Everything

You are my heart, my soul, my everything.
I never knew that I could ever feel this way,
To see a smile on your face,
Like the first day I saw your friendly face.

The sweetness in your voice, makes me think
Of the times you said pleasant things to me.
You knew what love was,
And I was just waiting for someone like you to come around and teach me.

You are my heart, my soul, my everything.
You gave me your heart, but I didn't take it,
You gave me hope that I could feel love.
My love for you now stands still, hoping you will take it.

The love that you showed for me, I never knew
That someone would or could ever feel that way towards me.
I didn't understand then, but now I do know what true love is.
Maybe you can find it in your heart to, take my love and keep it.

You are my heart, my soul, my everything.
You mean the moon, the stars, the world to me,
Now do you understand why I didn't understand love?
Now maybe we can understand together, what do you say?

Anacaonia Zanikos

Sacrifice

A knight in golden armor with a sword of sharpest death
He fights this day to show the way to glorify God's breath
An army rides against him, without remorse or things to love
This soldier of the purest light, fights more graceful than a dove

The soldier drops to one knee to say a prayer in silence
A battle fought for power is a battle lost to violence
I pray the Lord my soul to keep until the day I turn to dust
My body is a vessel for Your will, there is no one else to trust

He has died this death a thousand times and still he faces fears
To know the grasp of death's hot hand and feel the flaming tears
This death he lives he loves to hate and hates to love the day he dies
He fights so fierce, and rises right to see the world through piercing eyes

A drop of crimson blood is struggling to be heard
Like a fallen angel seeking redemption for a world sin
Calling it a sacrifice cannot do justice to the word
But pain means nothing compared to what it feels like to give in

Although he yearns to do his best and give all that he can give
When his life nears its end, he wishes he could do much more
But will he ever truly know what it means to live
Until he figures out what he is willing to die for

Eric A. Trueblood

Fall Is Here

As the sky is high,
And the ground is low,
The Mother Nature
Looks down and low.
Birds fly by to say
Good-bye.
Those happy faces
Jumping in the leaves
With so much fun,
With so much energy.
The sun is cold and
winds are heavy.
The leaves fall down
And fly away became it's fall.

Yelena Avestisova

Stung in the Face by a Bee

Stung in the face by a bee
While staring at an old oak tree
A bus passes by
I start to cry
Stung in the face by a bee

While staring at an old oak tree
I was stung in the face by a bee
It starts to hail
I start to wail
Stung in the face by a bee

Stung in the face by a bee
While staring at an old oak tree
I see a boy named Bob
I start to sob
Stung in the face by a bee

While staring at an old oak tree
I was stung in the face by a bee
The stars start to shine
I start to whine
Stung in the face by a bee

Jacqueline Partridge

Untitled

Fish swimming,
Frogs jumping,
Birds singing in the wind.
Flowers blooming,
Tadpoles growing,
Little turtles in pond scum.
When it rains,
They all hide long.
Until the sun shines,
They all stay at home,
In the pond.

Garrett Foust

I Would Rather Be Ignorant

I would rather be ignorant
Than know what's going on
I'd rather be a weakling
I don't wish to be strong

I would rather be an idiot
Than be smart as hell
I would rather always fail
Than sometimes do it well

When you're ignorant, you're happy
When you're weak, you're strong
When you're stupid, you don't know
When you're doing it wrong.

Angela Quintana

I Can't Believe Everything

I can't believe everything I've been through
Mostly 'cause of you
In the beginning I shed a lot of tears
But when I look back over the years
I realize that my life for me is ending
I guess I have to face the fact
Or just straighten up my act
Things are going to change now because she wants us to be apart
But you just don't know the pain that I am feeling deep down in my heart
I know that I can do it
I know that I can do anything if I just stand
I know that he will bless me
I know that he will set me free
I know that God will help me in any way that I'm in need
So daddy don't walk away and try and act all tough
Then try to come back in my life and be like wuz up
I'm going to be somebody
You just wait and see
But don't be perpetrating and be like that's my Ke-Ke.

Keisha Elliott

The Key to My Soul

I wear this mask I've so carefully made as my protective guise,
But if you want to see the real me just look into my eyes,
You'll see the twirling thoughts from an imagination gone wild,
And hear the chilling cries of a lonely abandoned child,
You'll see all the wonderful talents that I keep hidden inside,
And hear the growls of the demons from which I run and hide,
And if you're lucky you'll catch a glimpse of my land of make-believe,
Filled with magical characters no other mind could conceive,
Yet still it remains a secret where the key to my soul lies,
'Cause no one has ever taken the time to look into my eyes. . . .

Heather Persico

Angels

Angels looking down from the heavens, showing us the way,
they reach out not wanting us to walk away, protecting our souls from our enemies,
angels wanting to save those who fear death, but not able to do so,
an angel that glows in the dark sky showing you the way home,
when things go wrong or turn upside-down, I sleep my problems away,
even in the world of dreams does the angels come to you and tell you what you must do,
when all the hopes runs out of you, call unto the Creator of all things,
you will see a bright light, a light from the heavens, an angel bringing back your faith,
when the world shakes from underneath you and the walls tumble in,
cry out to the one that knows your pain, angels live forever in our hearts
all we must do is keep the faith and believe,
angels that are always there even though you think different,
you may not see them yet they are there,
all you must do to know where life begins and where it ends,
is by following your heart and call on him, for the angels will come.

Sebrina Mayfield

Pain

Dedicated to the only one, Scott Andrew Moffatt
   I have a pain, a pain in my heart, an aching kind of pain,
The kind that hurt so bad you just want to die,
The kind that rots away for being empty,
The kind that wishes it could be filled with some kind of love.
   I have a pain in my head, the pain that makes you think,
The thinking is torture, knowing what will never be,
Every day praying, hoping, and wishing,
And wondering why, because all these things will never help.
   I have a pain in my arms, the pain from reaching out to him,
Reaching as far as I can but he's too far away,
I don't understand, I yell for him to come back but he just keeps walking,
I must be mute because nobody ever hears what I have to say.
   I have a pain in my legs, the pain from running to him,
But every time I get to him he fades away,
Knowing he won't be there but I just have keep trying,
I guess life is a pain.

Kellie Sparks

Mother Nature

Looking out in the world
I feel nature surround me;
Protecting my innocence,
Shielding me from hatred and harm
I am nature's daughter
And will listen as she speaks
The path that she has chosen
Is the path that I shall seek

Quinta Reed

Waves

Waves rolling in and out
Bursting into raging infernos
Disappearing into nothing
So is life

Waves rolling in and out
As a friend comes and goes
As a flower blooms and wilts
As a candle flames and burns
Proving one point
Everything comes to an end

Waves rolling in and out
Perhaps for better
Signs of remembrance
Lingering in my mind
How life was
How it will be
How it has changed . . . forever

We can never go back
As the waves roll in and out

Nicole Di Chiaro

My Childhood

With the years just passing by
I stop and think, and start to cry
My childhood is gone away
But in my mind it will always stay.
I see a small vision of me
Climbing up a big oak tree.
Days were so easy then,
not hard to find a friend
Careless, fearless, oh, was I
And how the days just seemed to fly
Those days are gone and past
But in my heart, they'll always last.

Jessica Lynne Adams

Goodbye

Why did she have to go?
How could she hurt me so?
Does she know how I cry?
Is she with God in the blue sky?
Should this feeling be so strong?
Will this hurt last that long?
Warm, salty tears down my cheek,
Trembling so hard, I couldn't speak.
Whispers speak into my mind:
Things will heal themselves in time.

Crystal H. Whitehead

Untitled

From the top of the mountains
to the bottom of the sea
When I'm having an adventure
nothing matters to me.

Samantha Marcella

Arabian Knight

On a windless night, she went into the shadows of despair.
Not knowing who she was, what she was, or where she was.
She did not realize the cross over, until completely enfolded.
Her mind was blocked, her heart was stoned.
Little by little, she had crossed over and not once had she realized it.
How could she be so blind. She could not return.
There is no hope of salvation. The innocence has been taken away.
There was no way of return. She will never see the light ever again.
She wept and grieved in silence.
But then in her mind, she saw a light.
It was bright and comforting.
She had never seen such a thing full of love and hope.
She grasped it, she clung to it for life. Neither she nor the light let go.
The light carried her out. Out of the darkness, and into the moonlight.
There she saw him. The Arabian Knight in white.
She realized there was a way out and it was him.
She went away from the darkness with her Arabian Knight
never to return to the dark ever again.

Ruslina Utomo

The Winding Road

Let it be known
That there is a road
A winding, turning road
It is steep and it is lowered
And it falls behind trees so that the sun goes unseen

As you round the corner and come up over the hill
You will find an icy coating and fallen trees in your path
Past and far on there is darkness and danger
And it will seem to you that the road does not end
As the rain falls endlessly soaking
And washing away your dreams
And piercing your last ounce of courage.

But as you turn the last corner afraid and weary,
Feeling helpless and worn
A glimmer catches your eyes
On the horizon there seems to be life
And for the first time in a while you feel of sense of accomplishment
As the darkness fades the sunrises to dry the dampness you turn
Feeling something behind you
And you then realize that hope had been there the whole time.

Stephen Fratello

Untitled

Softly, slowly . . . night unfurls her splendor
Can you sense it? Tremulous and tender,
Feeling is believing, sight alone can be deceiving,
Trust this spell I weave by candlelight.
Join me in the magic of the night,
Come closer, and gaze into my candlelight
In the flame, see what dreams you wish to be,
In the darkness, it's easy to create a dream that can become a reality,
Softly let my silver moon caress you,
Feel it sense it, let it now possess you,
open up your mind, let your fantasies unwind,
As you dream, into my flame of candlelight,
Glowing in the mystery of the night,
Come with me, I'll take you to another world,
Leave all thoughts of the life you live before,
let your soul take you where you long to be,
There you'll know that you belong to me,
Floating, dreaming, sweet intoxication,
Trust me, touch me, savor each sensation,
Now our spell is cast, let all doubts and flares be past.

Samantha Swain

Rain

Our break-up was so simple
then my feelings came
as unexpected as a thunderstorm
but as predictable as the rain.
Rain may cause some damage;
it may create loud sounds.
It will leave its victims heartbroken,
leaving me to drown.
Rain washes out color
that lies within our eyes.
It turns our skin so pale
and works as tears' disguise.
Rain may cause some damage;
it may create loud sounds.
It will leave its victims heartbroken,
leaving me to drown.

Melody Starr

Pain

What is pain?
Is it a headache?
Is it a stomachache?
Could it be
a scrape
or should
it just be
a mistake?

Pain could be all
these things, but
pain is mostly
an ache inside.
Pain is bad
for all who are good,
so pray to God,
so good things
will happen to you!

Kara Ann Hutchinson

Strangers

Though we're distant strangers
we gather hand in hand
we share a common goal
and harvest of the land
As I look from my work
You raise your head too
Then we wipe our brows
under the same sky of blue
And as I lay my head
you also close your eyes
though we sleep in different beds
we wake to the same sunrise
Perhaps some day as we toil
we will look from our task
and our tired eyes will meet
all the questions we would ask
will soon be answered
will we go on with our day
or will our lives be joined
that I cannot say

Lisa Bult

Untitled

Once there was a girl named Shawna,
who didn't know what to do,
because she has four kids,
and is now only twenty-two.
But late one night she meet a guy
she loved so much that she could die.

Lindsay Hill

The Prisoner

These four walls hold me prisoner against my will,
The stone is moss-covered and damp,
Through the iron bars of my window I can hear the birds chirp and trill,
My captors cover the window with a black cloth
and forbid me the light of even a lamp.

A pitcher of water is placed before me along with a piece of bread,
In the corner sits a smattering of hay, over which a blanket I spread,
My face is smeared with dirt, and I am clothed in rags,
Under the weight of each I am here, my spirits sag.

This place reeks of death and tortures untold,
I sometimes hear sobs in the night that make my blood run cold,
The faces of my captors leer at me through the small opening in the door,
Here in my death-room I weave tales of fantasy and forgotten lore.

I dream of the sensation of sun on my face and think that maybe it is real,
But then I awaken to this cold, dark room,
I cannot make sense of all the things that I feel,
In my heart I know someday this place will serve as my tomb.

Leora Clark

The Way the Trees Do

I know that in two weeks things will change, the way the trees change,
losing their leaves, but not forever.
I know how missing my two greatest friends will affect me,
familiarizing myself with the hollow, lonely feeling—
the way the trees feel, until a creature burrows within.
I try to hold back from reaching out to you,
reprimanding my palm from bringing you back,
the way the trees try and gather their apples on the days that they fall from their branches.
You can't gather something that must take its course.
I cry when I think of solitary days and isolated nights.
Hearts break like fragile bones do,
like delicate branches swaying in the wind, snapping.
The way the trees cry for someone to mend them.
I wish I could go, and keep making memories,
but I know you two can withhold that.
When you miss me, laugh and I'm there.
When I miss you, I'll sing and you're here.
Memories are the glue that bonds.
Glue can't be placed, it must be earned.
I wish I were moving too, the way the trees do when they cannot move their roots.

Michael Ann Skizas

That Special Someone

He's the one that brings happiness to my days,
the one that brightens my life with his love rays.

You're that special someone . . . because
you light my life like the sun.

He's the one that makes me smile day in and day out,
the one that could never make me cry or even pout.

You're that special someone . . . because
of all the good things you have done.

He's the one that brings joy when we're together,
the one that holds me tight, no matter what kind of weather.

You're that special someone . . . because you keep our love warm and fun.

He's the one that makes me think about who I am,
the one that makes me sparkle like the shine of a gem.

You're that special someone . . . because you've
changed my life like no one else has done.

Kim Bruno

At the Concert

To my family and 'N Sync
When I saw you up there
dancing to and fro,
I knew when this was over
I wouldn't want to go.

Your sweet voice and gentle lips
that I heard and saw,
I knew that this concert
wouldn't be a bore.

The people all around me
sang and screamed all night,
But I didn't pay any attention to them
but you, at your gorgeous sight.

You showed off all your talent
that I knew you had inside,
The thought that you didn't
never crossed my mind.

But now that it is over
and all the singing is done,
I know that in my heart
you're still number one.

Jen Nusio

Life Is Precious

All these people
that die so young,
when they've never done anything
to harm anyone,

Have been asked to leave
everyone they love
because it's time for them
to go up above.

They leave suddenly,
with no warning at all,
and descend into Heaven
to go have a ball.

And it hurts us down here,
whenever they leave.
All we can do
is cry and grieve.

But I guess that's the way
that life is,
and you never question
who God's going to let live.

Kari Valverde

Rain of Hurt

It seems to fall
As other rain would
Except a bit slower.
When it reaches your lips.
You can taste again
The bitterness.
That you are trying
So very hard
To get rid of.
There is lightning
In your heart and soul.
There is thunder in your mind.
They are both caused by friction,
The friction of hateful words,
Or feelings of sadness,
Thus begins the rain,
The rain of hurt and sorrow.
This rain is called teardrops.

Trisha DeMarrias

The Cry of My Heart

For my dear friend and inspiration, Linda
I told you that I love you,
You just turned and tore my heart, my soul,
Without a blink in your eyes I was nothing
Wishing you could see what you mean to me,
I now know we were not meant to be,
But that does not mean I can't stop loving . ..
Loving you in a place that is warm and dark, in my dreams

You're the one who came and stole my heart away,
And in a flash I'm in darkness once again.

Why can't my heart stop hurting?
For you do not love me,
Therefore I'm not allowed to love you in return,
But now that I'm remembering your touch, your kiss, your warm embrace,
My heart is back where it started,
But now instead of absorbing, it's bleeding for your love.
You are the cry of my heart . . . I still love you!

   Mary Slaven

This Place

To my wonderful mom and dad
This is a place that is not familiar to me
This is somewhere that I am not comfortable
She could spend all her life not going anywhere new
And staying in places that are comfortable to her
But what kind of life would that be for me?
She would become uncomfortable in a place where she once was comfortable
He would never meet her, he would never see her
He would never fall in love, he would never kiss her
She would never fall in love, she would never be held
They would never experience things that I've already known
If only they both knew that one little thing
could forever change their lives
She would never see the look in his eyes when he says I love you
He would never get to see her cry when he proposes
They would never experience love or unite their souls forever
They would never meet, they would never marry
This is a place that is not familiar to me
This is somewhere that I am not comfortable

   Melinda S. Robinson

Fairy Tale

Sitting here in my fairy tale land
Thinking of what could have happened between us
How our lives could have been together forever
How our love could have lasted 'til the last breath

You stole my love with the key to my heart
You broke into my soul with the loving words of a knight in shining armour
You left roses behind the combination of love
Our hearts became one as our lips met under the artificial sun
This, our fairy tale, is loving forever

Our love should have lasted forever
Instead we separated as an earthquake of love
for another tore our hearts in two

Now that you've torn out my heart for another's love
Our fairy tale blew up in smoke
Tumbled off the wall just like Humpty Dumpty's great fall
All the king's men and all the king's horses
couldn't put our hearts together again

You called me your princess, you were my knight
'Til you made me a common girl again and shattered my heart
In your eyes you gave up less than what you had to gain.

   Marriane Howells

Summer

Summer is a bright, beautiful day
playing in the pool.

Summer is the glistening sun
knocking at your door.

Summer is spending a day
reading a book.

Summer is
going to the lake.

Summer is playing
with your friends.

Summer is
taking a vacation.

Summer is a time
to have fun!

   Lindsey Petzold

The Snowflake

A snowflake is a dancer,
Fluttering across the evening sky.
Elegantly twirling in mid-air,
Children let out a joyous cry.

A snowflake is a dancer,
Wearing a gown of white lace.
Glimmering in the moonlight,
The gown gives the snowflake such grace.

A snowflake is a dancer,
Taking a final leap.
Landing on a child's cold nose,
A memory he shall always keep.

   Maria Willbanks

Blue Eyes

Blue eyes like blue skies
Are made of the sweeter things in life

Light blue like sunshiny days
With no clouds to block the rays

Dark blue like the deep blue sea
With exotic specimens for the eye to see

Blue with the tints of other hues
Like bubbles intended to amuse

Blue like the skin of a blueberry
To sweeten the mouth and make you merry

Blue like the eyes of a newborn baby
Cradled in the arms of an elderly lady

Blue like the trueness of a friend
Who'll be beside you until the end

   Bobbi Cook

Titanic

She was a steamboat,
she was a dreamboat.
Many were rich,
many were poor,
many were working door to door.

All people on board,
all people in sea
could see all the wonders,
and many cried with glee.

But now that she is gone,
no one can see
what a beautiful ship
she was supposed to be.

   Bethany Rojanasupya

Untitled

Happiness cries,
Happiness thrives,
Happiness yearns,
Happiness fawns,
Happiness looks,
Happiness seeks
For someone to grow in.

Rachel Lee Kovich

My Dad and I

I wish I'd have a dad
and it makes me sad.

I've often cried
because he died.

I'm glad he didn't have to suffer
that would have made things rougher.

I'm so glad he's in Heaven today.
because that means that there's a way,

For me to see him again someday
in Heaven where I will run and play.

Siobohn Stoltzfus

It's on My Mind

There's something on my mind
I wish I understood.
It's one of a kind
And not very good.

There's something on my mind
If only I knew.
That something I can't find,
I wonder if it's true.

There's something on my mind;
It's affecting me.
I keep trying to find
What it could be.

There's something on my mind;
It's making me tense.
It's all in a bind
And doesn't make sense.

Denise Kidd

Heartaches

She's gone
Gone far, far away
She's gone
I'll have to see her again someday
She's gone my heart is aching
She's gone
Oh, how it's breaking
She's gone and I'll never be the same

Jessica Berke

Only Dream

I love thee
That shall be
My only dream
That you marry me
You shall be
My only love for me
Once we marry
We shall be
A family or a team
But not enemies.

Tina Strahan

Pride

For Yelena and Patrick, my friends
He eliminated my existence,
But I conjured up my own
Little taste of sweet revenge.
I rushed to my pride's
Death bed,
Searching for the right remedy
To prevail and return
From the dark side.
Recuperating took time,
But the long-awaited
Victory
Saw the light of day.
The desirability
He possessed to
Terminate my deepest feelings
Wasn't sufficient.
Extinction is no longer an
Option;
Supremacy is my present state.

Gloribelle Janisse Perez

Untitled

smooth skin,
muscles flexing and relaxing
it's beautiful.
oh, to feel the skin of your back
to feel your spine
trace the outline
of shoulder blades
(shaped like wings, angel's wings)
a little indention of a muscle,
i long to kiss it.

K. Strickler

I Love My Brother Dearly

To my brother, Matthew Lowrance
I love my brother dearly
And now he's gone away
I wish I could have saved him
Maybe he'll be back one day

I love my brother dearly
That's not hard to say
I wish I could be with him
Maybe I will one day

I said something
I did not mean
I love my brother dearly
Oh, why can't that be seen

Why I lost him
I do not know
God came down and got him
I guess it was time to go

Miranda Tela Frost

Afternoon Tea

She stands by herself,
A small girl playing "house."
A rock pile serves as a house,
Tall and sturdy.
An oak tree, massive with age,
Is the tiny girl's shade.
A country girl is she,
With no one her own age.
She serves afternoon tea,
Trying to be a good host
To her guests
Who are never really there.

Shelby L. Fevold

To My Love

To my love I give my heart,
for it is yours to keep.
I give my body to my love,
for you excite it so.
I give my soul to my love,
for it will never leave you.
And to my love I give my love,
For you give me yours,
And you have earned it ten times over.

Patricia Bordeaux

Teardrops in the Night

For my angel of music
When we were five,
You said they were diamonds.
When we were ten,
You said they were stars.
Now they are teardrops
Falling from my eyes.

The pale moonlight
Washes over my crying face.
My tears never make it to the ground;
They just keep falling and falling
'Til they reach the night sky.

I only cry at night.
I watch my teardrops
Mix with your diamonds.
Things have changed
Since you've been gone,
And I miss you.

Celeste Mersenski

Hopes and Dreams

They take you off into a world
Filled with happiness and bliss,
With no deaths and violence,
To be alone with yourself
And your ideas for the future,
Whatever they may be,
Whether drama, singing, or literature,
And they fill you with ambitions
You may or may not fulfill one day,
And you wish and wish,
Until you feel sick,
And then you realize that
You still have years to come,
To start working for
Your hopes and dreams,
And you keep striving for your goals
Until they are achieved.

Amanda Pilley

Day's End

As I stand there in total silence
And stillness and feel unseen,
I look at the distance between me
And the other group of kids.

Gross

My Special Place

I'm going to my special place,
Pretty far away.

Under a tree, as tall as me.
Listening to it sway,
It feels good to get away.
No one knows about my special place,
But I like to know I have my own space.

Amanda Katherine Welsh

Suicide

In this cold world,
There's no way out.
I can't cry, I can't pout.
All my life, I've lived in fear
No one for me, there.
My family has deserted me,
No one even cares.
All the world is empty,
My soul has already died.
There's only one option left:
Attempted suicide.

Iris Chiang

Sarah

You make me laugh
You make me cry
Sometimes I wonder
Why I try
But at the end
it is worth it to me
Because you are my friend for eternity
Sometimes it is weak
And sometimes it is strong
It doesn't matter who is right or wrong
Trust, love, and problems
Will always be around
But hopefully the problems
will never be found
Jealousy and hatred
I wish they were never here
but feeling that again towards you
is something that I fear.

Staci Plikaytis

Kiss

On a bed of roses
A kiss comes easy
But on a bed of snakes
Life comes hard
Remember the night
The kiss came easy
Now remember the day
Kisses to snakes
What a waste of time.

Rebecca Nutick

Snowy Evening

As I look out my window
At the snow-covered ground,
Watching the snowflakes
Move around and around,
I remember winter nights
From a long time ago,
Fresh in my mind
Like the new-fallen snow.

I remember the snow glistening
Under the pale, full moon,
Like a million stars
Filling the room.
With the snow lying peacefully
On the tall, dark trees,
Like a scenic mountain picture
In a magazine.

As I stare out my window
Watching the winter pass by,
I can't help thinking about
The beautiful winter; I cry.

Jessica Rase

Wonders

Our existence on Earth is far too
precious for man to see.
The power and humanity over us
is way out of my league.

We wonder about so many
things in the universe.
It's like we're under someone's
spell or curse.

Where did we come from and
how did we evolve?
These are questions we don't
have the proof to solve.

I believe we should walk
by faith and not by sight.
Then we might understand the
wonders of human light.

Kelly Barber

I Found the One

I found the one that God made
especially for me.
I love him and he loves me,
and that's the way it's gonna be.

Whenever I see him,
My whole world lights up bright,
and I just can't wait
for the next time he holds me tight.

I know the day will finally come
when we won't be able to be together,
and I know I will sit in my room
and cry by myself forever.

Until that day, I guess
that I'll just sit in your warm embrace,
wondering if you'll ever leave me
for another pretty face.

It always seems like people
are constantly breaking my heart.
I can't take it anymore;
I'm already torn apart.

Kristen Koelsch

My Spirit

My spirit is like an eagle
Tall and strong
Flying with might
My wings are long
My throat and chest out
As they look up at me
With good eyesight
I am a eagle I am free

Ashley Joseph

Wishing

Wishing on a star
That you are near
Though you are far
When I wish, I tear
That you have forgotten who we are
When I wish, I fear
Did you have an open ear
When I wished you to be here
You are only a mere
Wish for you to be my dear

Michelle Rutherford

Thank You

To my best friend, my Mother
Thank you for being a friend,
And thank you for taking time to care.
I'll remember you 'til the day I die,
I'll remember how you were always there.

You are a special person in my life,
And I'm thankful for that.
I will always remember you,
No matter where you're at.

Through everything you were there,
You gave me your shoulder to cry on.
When I was angry you calmed me down,
And you never left me alone.

And now that our love has grown,
We are even closer than before.
So I'm writing to thank you for that,
And to thank you for so much more.

Juliana McKenzie

You

I close my eyes, seeing yours,
I hold my hand, feeling yours,
I say my name, hearing yours,
I touch my heart, wanting yours.

Karen Eide

Love

All that is in this heart is gone,
nothing left but an empty hole,
which can be filled with only one thing:
true love,
which is nonexistent, so I sit
here with this cold empty heart
which is filled with only darkness.
It goes on forever and never ends.
That's what the word does and
that word is:
love,
and all I have is a black rose
to remind me of what's inside
this empty, deformed body,,
to remind me of the days past
and gone and the ones ahead.
That love is just a word
that is said, and not meant.

Erin Quackenbush

Outcast

Keep the anger hidden in thee
And no harm will come of thee
Carrying gloom, blink back tears
And no harm will come from me

Difference entwined with rejection
All are mixed in me
Cry and show weakness
But no harm shall come from me

A list of pain
A mirror of reality
A touch of hate
Rational immortality

Words you need not hear
Hence you did
To cover your face
And run amid

But no harm will come from me

Jessica Y. Quintana

Have You Ever . . .

Have you ever dreamed
of a place so beautiful
That you just can't breathe?
Have you ever felt so special
and you suddenly fall apart?
Have you ever loved somebody
so much you cried yourself to sleep?
Have you ever felt the cold
but you sense the warmth?
Have you ever felt the urge
to help someone in trouble?
Have you ever felt the way
I do about you?

Melissa James

Gray

Gray is the clouds
On a rainy day,
Murky and shadowy
And set in their way.

Gray is the sadness
When you sit all alone
It's the color of madness
That wants not to be show.

Gray is the cry,
Of the weeping wind,
Whimpering and whining
Without any friends

But gray is soft
As grandad's hair
It's almost like
An old teddy bear.

Lou Russell

Untitled

Is it intimacy I'm lacking,
When all I have to give is courage,
And all I receive is not what we call
happiness but a mark upon bliss.
With this I take rage to burn within me,
and for passion to rip through me,
Leaving my desire untouched by the
uncuffed freedom I hold in my heart.
A dreamer I may be, but one day
I'll touch the stars, and conquer moons,
with my thoughts I hold in my hands,
and the aggression I keep in my heart.

Amber Yother

The Big Gray Orchard Tree

From far, from eve and morning
And your twelve, winded sky
The stuff of life to knit me
Blew higher, here am I
Here am I under an orchard tree
For here I stay
Eating apples all day long
'Til the sun goes down
I'll be there 'til my life goes on
On and on and on

One day crystals grew upon the tree
For there where ice crystals
It was now winter time
Time for heaters and coats
I was still there under the tree
Cold and hungry I stayed there
I stayed with no heater
I stayed under the big orchard tree

Jennifer Murphy

My Life Your Heart

I'm gazing into the empty blue sky
A bird gliding below the clouds
catches my eye
Your face I can plainly see
up beyond the clouds of eternity
You and me, it's plain to see
that this is a chance of destiny
Love can reach the nearest star
Past the moon, through my heart
Like a love no other can have
you're my life, I'm your heart

Mary E. Wine

Whispers

When I saw his eyes
I guessed he would be the sweetest,
Gentlest guy I've ever met.
As I talked to him
And looked deep in the beautiful eyes
Of the man I began to love
I knew I couldn't pull myself away.
As he would whisper wonderful,
Sweet poems to me,
I wanted to give him
The whole world,
Because he made me so happy.
But I begin to think
Of all the other times
I started liking a guy,
I would get my heart broke,
So I keep backing out.
I'm just afraid
To hear the whispers again.

Alisha Burns

Broken

I was taking a trip down memory lane,
But while I was walking,
the snow became rain.
And suddenly, a door was blown open by
the storm's billowing wind,
and I found out that you'd broken the
one thing the soul can't mend.
So, after that you call yourself a
friend, but you did not know that
the heart you had broken should not bend
I don't forgive you for the love
of the game, for what you have done has
put my soul down to shame.
But I'd like to tell you before I fade,
that nothing can clean the terrible
mess you have made.

Stephanie Amanda Bloss

Sweet Dreams

The sun rises, and a flower blooms.
Far in the distance, lightning strikes.
Darkness glooms, and death looms,
Pain, insane, brain drain.
A boy picks the bloomed flower,
And blood from the sky begins to shower.
For today, children, it's the dark hour,
A green taste, bitter, sour.
Nothing but monsters in the tower.
Love, no skies turn dark above.
Far in the distance, cries a dove.

Dominic Vennera

Did I Do It?

Why are you gone?
Was it because of me?
Did I hurt you,
did I not do enough?
Why oh, why did you leave me?
Is it forever or for a little while?
Is it from me?
Did I do it?

Terrie Phillips

She Is My Friend

When I laugh,
She laughs with me.
When I cry,
She cries with me.
When I sing,
She sings with me.
When I talk,
She talks with me.
When I scream,
She screams with me.
She is My Friend.

Meghan E. Smith

America

I promise to America,
my heart and my soul,
I promise to America,
the red, white, and the blue,
that my Heart and Soul,
will always stay with you.

When we're in war with others,
don't worry,
I'll be there,
I'll fight for you.

In America,
you can see the flowers blooming,
or watch the moon glooming.

America,
America,
You will promise too.

Jillian Peterson

My Angel

Fly away, fly away
My beautiful angel
Fly away, so far away
Through the curtains
And the gates of Heaven
Which we call upon
From the Earth below

Our loss will be forgiven
Our memories will never be forgotten
As we will always know
You will be with us
Even though some may not know

As every day
We may visit your body
Your soul will be protected
By love and peace above all

Crystal A. Choate

Butterflies

Gold, brown, gay colors
fluttering in the sunlight
make me glow inside

Vanessa Gong

Travelling in My Dreams

I have journeyed a million miles
To see a million sights
But never have I seen so much
As I've seen in these few nights

Everything that's happened to me
Has been such a beautiful dream
I'd never thought I'd be so lucky
Or am I as lucky as it seems

I have traveled through land and lands
And from sea to sea
Do you know how I've done this all
Only in my dreams

Your dreams are worth a million trips
Too many different places
To travel to different lands
And to see different faces

In your dreams you're a lot safer
Than anywhere else you can find
So please enjoy your dreams
As long as you possibly can

Sandra Bedore

With You

With you,
I'm like a dove
flying gracefully through the air.

With you,
My dreams are met,
My hopes come true,
and my life is filled . . .
With you.

With you,
I never have to worry
Because you'll always be there
When I need you.

With you,
I always have a shoulder
to cry on, a person
to laugh with,
and someone
to talk to.

Tina Kilpatrick

Ode to Grandpa Riedel

We have been wondering why
Grandpa had to die.
There isn't much you can say
On this very sad day,
But there is one thing
That we can sing.
He has gone to a special place,
And we won't forget his face.
God has take him away
To Heaven, we must say.
We are sad,
Maybe even mad.
He couldn't help it,
So don't have a fit.
We must say goodbye,
So it's okay to cry.
We all might,
For this is a sad night
For us all,
Because we got that one call.

Amy Wessel

Thanks for Being My Parents

Thanks for getting mad
When I deserved it.
Thanks for letting me
Explore and have fun.
Thanks for working to keep
A roof over my head.
Thanks for being my parents.

Thanks for all of the
Happiness you've given me.
Thanks for teaching me when
To be brave and when not to.
Thanks for teaching me
Between right and wrong.
Thanks for being my parents.

Thanks for giving me
A room of my own.
Thanks for everything I have.
Thanks for being you.
Thanks for being my parents.

Breanne Walker

Conquering Your Fears

You're in a dark room.
No light, no way out.
You feel scared and helpless.
You start to feel the wall,
for a light switch or window,
still nothing.
You start to overcome
your fear of being alone.
The room starts to get brighter,
finally you can see a door.
You have conquered your fear.

Nicole Chenoweth

Hatred

For my best friend, Stephanie
Hatred fills the heart,
just like the filling in a tart.
How can one consume so much of this?
Is it like a simple kiss?
Just like the thrust of a sword,
can it become a reward?
Does anyone know this feeling,
inside it must be sealing!
Hurt, can it be,
just between you and me!
Is it because of the world around us,
does it have to be such a fuss?
Hatred is not a reward;
it's just like a stabbing sword.
It hurts you and me,
but can we let it be?

Jennifer Natali

My Imagination

That Turned into a Dream!

Nick, though I may never see
except through posters!

I feel as though angels
have picked me up!

Then I wake up and find
that it was only
and simply an imagination
that turned into a dream!

Shanna Buechler

The Listener

I'm someone you can trust,
Someone you can confide in.
I'll always be able to help,
And I'll always keep your secrets.

I'm not very talkative,
And I'm not too forward.
I'm full of quietness,
And I'm very shy.

But I won't laugh
When you tell me your troubles,
And I won't make rude comments
If you tell me your problems.

I'll sit by your side
In your times of great need,
And I'll always be there for you,
For I am a listener.

Karrianne Foy

Where You Are

We shall live in peace and love
That of which is like the dove,
Beauty and heart is what you are,
I shall love you near or far,
My dear, my heart is where you are.

Kellijo Norton

Star

I am looked upon every night.
No one can resist me;
My beauty is awing.
I amaze even the youngest minds.
Though you have never really known me,
You will never forget me.
Even after I burn out, my light
Will shine for years to come . . .
For I am a star.

Lauren Adams

Without You

To my parents, whom I love
Without you I can't live
Without you I can't think
You're always on my mind
Day and night
I sometimes go to sleep
I sometimes stay awake
But you are always in my head
I try to forget you
But you never leave
I try to regret you
But I just can't
You're always there
And you always care.
So I'll forget you
And how much I love you
Because without you
I just can't live.

Minerva Galvan

Fall

Fall is colorful and cool.
It is a sign that winter is coming.

The trees and ground are filled with
red, green, yellow, and brown leaves.

Fall is cool, fall is nice,
The ground turns into ice.

Jodi Cremens

Addicted to Dreams

For Mom and Dad, dream weavers
Sometimes I find myself wandering
Through a place
I've never been,
On this lonely road
I've always known.

Uncharted territory
Untouchable

Rain falls
Freezing cold

From hazel skies
Bleeding a thousand words
Painting a picture of despair
Displayed to public criticism
Expected
Accepted
In stride

Content with unhappiness
Addicted to dreams
Loving the pain . . .

It's a lyrical passion.
        Robert Sizemore

So Scared

To my mom, Denise, and Chrissy
I'm scared, I don't want to die
Even though I have no time to cry
I'm so young
My life has just begun
I have no choice
It's as if I have no voice
I can't deny it
Even when I try it
I have to live my life right now
'Cause when it's gone I won't know how
I'll live my life to its fullest
It's not my choice, I have to do this
It's not my fault
It's the way I am
If I had a chance I'd change everything
So much has happened
I don't know why
Whenever I think of it I cry
But there's nothing I can do!
        Sarah Belay

Outside My Window

Outside my window I see
The sun fading in the West.
I see the moon blooming in the East.
The stars are shining in the sky.
I know the day has gone by,
And a new day is dawning.
Now I see the moon fading in the West.
I see the sun rising in the East.
Now I wake up and go to school.
        Katie Carroll

Stars

So many stars.
What do they mean?
I mean the stars for me.
Amy, yes, do I have a star to?
Maybe we can go to our star someday.
No, we can only imagine it.
Okay.
        Josh Marshall

The Maze of Guilt

You hit her;
She falls.

You say, "I am sorry."
She says, "So long."

You come back;
She says, "Hello."

You hit her;
She gets bruised.

She says, "So long."
You say, "I am sorry."

When will it end?
You've trapped her in your maze;
She can't break free.

It's all a joke.
You hit her;
She falls.

You say, "I am sorry."
She says, "So long."
        Christina Grady

Stars

I notice those stars
up in the sky,
I see them there
I'm not sure why.

It's like a million cars
turn on their brights,
Oh, how I love those little lights.

And every day I pray for night
Just to see that beautiful sight.
Not mountains, not hills,
Not people with scars
could take my eyes
away from the stars.

However this magic
only happen, at night
accompanied by,
the pale moonlight,

While I watch those stars so bright,
I'm thinking I might
stay up all night.
        Dominique Wessler

Autumn Walk

To Sandy—a nature lover
In my forest cathedral
With altar of leaves
The choir's the birds that sing.
If there is a prayer
That says how I care
To this the world I would bring.

It was then that I saw
A doe . . . and twin fawns
Cavorting like colts in the stream.
No camera to prove it
No one to dispute it
But I knew it wasn't a dream.

The gulls and the looms
Now gone from their nests
I'll miss their most haunting moan.
But the hawk and the crow
Talk to me as I go
To tell me I'm not alone.
        Lorraine Foss Hartmann

My Angel

For my mom and dad
I have an Angel with wings
of silk and a crown of gold.
It looks down on us all
from up above
where the sun shines bright.
It watches over
me day in and day out.
When I have tears in my eyes,
soon I'm filled with joy;
that's one way it watches out
for me and my soul.
My angel makes me happy
and gets me up when I'm down.
I will always love it so,
and never let it go.
        Patrycja Baran

Angel

You're my sweet angel,
my Heaven-sent.
With your paper thin wings
all torn and bent.

You're my sender of hope,
my silver lining.
With your halo rusty,
but still shining.

You're my Heavenly host,
my gift from above.
With your broken harp,
and heart full of love.

You're a dream come true,
that's why I thank God
each and every day
for bringing me to you.
        Amber Whiteman

Heaven

There is a place,
Only in a dream.
I wish I were there,
For then I'd be free.

There is a place,
Behind all the clouds.
The air is clean,
And angels are found.

There is a place,
Higher than the rest.
Nothing can surpass it,
For I know it's the best.

There is a place,
Only in a dream.
I wish I were there,
For then I'd be free.
        Crystal Ultican

Sisterly Love

I know you love me
And love you I do
Some differences come between us
The same would be so blue
Over little stuff that's stupid
Over big stuff that's dumb
Still we love each other
That's sisterly love.
        Elizabeth Rojas

Peace

Peace, a baby's laugh.
A shadow of a child's dream.
A whisper an angel gives.
Something magic or science can't make.
A place we have inside.
A story waiting to be told.
Something we bring with love.
A wish that should come true.
A prayer that needs to be answered.
Something we give to one another.
This is peace.

Jennifer J. Duva

Pleasure and Pain

I was looking out the window
And along came the black widow
That is reality
So harsh to me
Will I ever understand
How pleasure and pain go hand in hand
Reality is no longer
Dreams become fonder
While living in space
Covered in white lace
With a blue satin sash
Kept in a secret stash
With my other dreams
Ripping at their seams.

Amanda Powell

Keeping Secrets

From the bottom of my soul,
My emotions run free,
From the bottom of my soul,
I just want to be me.

In the corner of my eye,
I see evil and pain,
In the corner of my eye,
I see lots I can gain.

From the top of my heart,
There is misled trust,
From the top of my heart,
There is sorrow and lust.

My conclusion is this,
It's simple, it's small,
To strangers say lots,
But do not tell all.

Zhanna Tarshik

Goddess Angel

A psychedelic experiment
A soft, shimmery scream
Life's fashion
Electric red love
Imagine white dreams
Glorious junk
Which creates live angels
Deep in pink
They perform gracefully to purple music
Sense absurd green passion
Approach blue harmony
Dance to champagne rhythm
Celebrate sweet joy
A masterpiece
A goddess angel

Desiree Nichole Jiron

This Manic State

Goading off insecurity
I protect my purity
Never had this clarity
Writing for posterity
I'm feeling fresh as a daisy
Just think, used to be crazy
Loving it, being this way
Hope it lasts another day
Enjoy this quite music trip
Composing, biting my lip
Out of my mind does this song flow
Really fast, not very slow
Enjoying this manic state
Feeling high, feeling great
Feeling buzzed and feeling love
This is the state I speak of
Want to shout from the rooftop
Never ever want to stop
Please, God, help me to keep this, stay
Love the way you let me play

Alexandra Bomhoff

Peace of Mind

As I walk through this city
I look around and see
Old buildings, streets, and houses
filled with poverty

Crowded is this city
Noises a-blare
Automobiles and factories
Polluting the air

It isn't safe in this city
By day or night
It hasn't enough police
To solve all its strife

So I'm going to the mountains
To be safe and free
And hope I am dead
When the city reaches me

But if I'm alive
When the city I see
I'm afraid my mind shall wander
Into eternal insanity

Deanna Hohrman

Imprints

The painter starts
With strokes of grace.
An image forms,
A perfect face.

He walks away,
Already alone.
His heart, once warm,
Has turned to stone.

The picture blurs.
The colors swarm.
The vibrance fades.
New images form.

From warm to cold,
From cruel to kind,
Each one brought,
Forth from his mind.

The day turns to night.
The color fades.
But the canvas remembers,
Every beautiful shade.

Katy Bernock

Starving

Starving for excitement,
Not boredom.
Wanting more.
Knowing you can't get it.
Seeing, hearing
But not fearing.
Starving for a friend,
Not an enemy.
Not knowing what to do.
Confusing, starving.

Sarah Mae Holbrook

Loving Him

Your heart melts
When you look into his eyes.
Your heart burns
When your lips touch him
Because you know
He's falling in love with you!
You can see
The love in his eyes.
You can feel
The love in his touch.
You can sense
The love in his movements,
His everyday actions,
And through his work,
And you know
You can love him
That much as well.

Tina Pirtle

This Is Me

This is me.
This is the way I am.
Don't try to change me.
I refuse to be like you
You think you can.
You can't.
I'll never be like you.
I'll never want to be like you,
But were still alike.
We're both human.
I'm not clay.
You can't shape me.
You can't make me fit your style.
You never can, you never will.
I'm different and I like it.
I'm going to do my thing, not yours.
You may think you can boss me around.
You may think you can change me.
You can't.
You won't.
What I say goes!

Crystal Lowe

Believe

For William Shannahan III
A glance of fear
A shock of pain
A destiny through the rain
A lamenting pink sprays the skies
Endless love fills their eyes
Scared of life, diversions still
Believe emotions they are real
Adore the moment
Life goes on
Love and courage growing strong
Doubtful meaning, no more lies
Breaking feeling, happy cries

Taleah Navarne

Untitled

The word "No"
Must be learned.
Willingness
Is all they know.

The theory of lies and trickery
Has to be seen.
Without a picture
Only the truth will come.

Crime and discrimination
Must be taught,
For there is only innocence
In a child's heart.

If everyone
Had stopped their wicked ways,
Only good would be seen
In the children today.

Jana Muller

Love

Hearts are broken,
Souls are taken,
Wills are bent,
Spirits stolen,
All thanks to a woed
Thing called love.

Serianna Eggen

Sea of Velvet

A pulchritudinous sea of roses
their colorant lustrous, but outfitted
with thorns protruding from stems.
You behold all the velvet petals
beaming back.
Beneath unnoticed pains await,
and for your softness to be touched.
Ahead is the crystalline sky
without a puff of white; instead
colors are streaked like in a dream.
Some will pass without shedding
their tears or blood.
Some will pass then topple,
feel the dirt bite their wounds,
not fathom such beauty given.
To behold and cherish
some will relish all that is given,
not noticing the pain that attaches
to beauty.

Elizabeth Schneider

Outcast

Little white lies come back to you,
In the time you've lived and died.
You never knew what you did to deserve it.
All they've done is cheated and lied.
But then when they've died,
What do you care?
Why should you cry?
They did nothing for you.
They showed you pain.
You didn't deserve it.
What did you gain?
Just a bad name for some mocked fame.
But no one's ever been there for you.
So you just sit alone.
Just you and you.

Tara Gross

As I Sit Here

As I sit here
Late one night
I think of you
With each tear I cry

As I sit here
I fill my heart being ripped in two
This is what goes on
When I'm not with you.

As I sit here,
I feel you inhabiting my heart,
Maybe that's why
My life's falling apart

As I sit here
Looking at the sky,
Wishing for you,
I almost hope to die

As I sit here
I lean back and smile
Nah, I'll just think about
Us for a while

Stephanie Rose Elllson

Snow Dance

For Jeremy, who loves the snow as much as I do
All day the sun
Has been reluctant
To show his face.
The dark clouds brood
As the children leave.
I straighten the desks.

Throughout the evening
The windows reflect
Visions of small faces.
Jumping and twirling,
In a flurry of motion,
Each dances to his own tune.

While my children sleep,
I gaze out the window.
Snowflakes drift
Through the branches,
Pirouette in the moonlight,
Adorn the ground.

Dana Meredith

My Best Gift to Posterity

From now to eternity
There isn't much time for me
To enjoy life
And to write poetry.

Let aside all worries,
Go visiting here and there
Drive my car carefully
On freeways and thoroughfares.

Try meals at different restaurants:
French, Chinese, Italian, Mexican . . .
Drink beer of any kind;
So I enjoy a good time.

Do something useful at home:
Mowing, mopping, cooking, gardening . . .
And when inspired, in my studio
Take a pen for poetic writing.

Little by little, perform my poetry,
Have it published sooner or later;
So I share it with my readers
And leave behind my best gift to posterity.

Nha X. Nguyen

The Loving Scarf

For Paul and Margaret Marzell
I feel your scarf against my skin
You chase the frost, I'm warm within

Your loving arms my throat enfold
You make the chill not seem so cold

You cross my heart then hold me tight
And keep me safe through winter's night

You gave me life so long ago
And love me always as I did grow

You nurtured me when I was small
I delighted in you as I grew tall

This loving scarf I plainly see
Is Mom and Dad embracing me

Lawrence V. Stefanile

The Rugged Irish Oak

Still standing, down in Wicklow,
Not far from Glendalough,
There's a giant gnarled Oak tree,
For a thousand years, somehow.
It sheltered Strongbow's Normans,
Who fought with bow and sword.
They overran the island green,
And set-up their own lord.
It still commands a perfect view,
Of the round tower and the stones;
Left by those who strove to civilize;
It stands guardian of their bones.
Its tortured shape and broken limbs,
Only part of the story tell;
Of a thousand winters, fierce and cold
But of a thousand springs, as well.
It reminds us when we're gnarled,
And weathered like that tree,
There is still His Springtime Promise,
Which sustains us, you and me.

Donald H. Clinton

A Widow's Lament

Why did he leave me such a mess?
I don't know where I should begin.
He took with him my happiness,
And now my head begins to spin.

He never taught me our affairs,
With business dealings I can't cope;
I'm left with oh, so many cares,
Alone I can't see any hope.

No needed records can I find,
His files are such a mystery;
Why did he leave me in a bind?
I'm mad at what he did to me.

But oh, Dear Lord, please treat him well,
His love did bring me happiness;
My anger I find hard to quell,
Confused in all my loneliness.

Sol Finkelman

Type Cast

If you factor in that
My type is one of those
B-Negatives,
You will understand why
My blood runs pessimistic
And my heart beats tentative.

Kimberly Taylor Carmo

Whispering Willows

In a far, far place,
Away from the city,
Far from the pollution that lingers
In the air and the noisy crowds
That fill those small streets,
Is a whole new world waiting to be discovered,

A nice and quiet place,
Where you can rest,
And think,
And wait,

This is where the deer runs free,
Where birds sing,
And if you listen closely enough,
You can hear the trees whispering.

You may say it's just the wind,
"Big deal," you may say,
But I know it's not just the wind,
I know the Willow Tree is whispering to me.

Ashley Helmrich

Grandpa

To my father, James R. Tarantino
Grandpa, Grandpa how I wanted to meet you
You seem interesting and very sweet too.

The way you cooked, the way you glowed.
Grandpa, Grandpa how they hated to see you go.

In high school you met your future wife Joyce
who then gave birth to your five wonderful kids.

You were a janitor who worked hard to support your family.
When your wife and children needed you
you were always there to see them through.

When I was a baby, you were holding me in your comforting arms.
I knew you were my grandpa so loving, so charmed.

I don't remember you even if I tried my hardest to
I knew you existed but now you're only a blurry memory.

Grandpa, Grandpa if only you were here to see the time change,
every time I see your picture in that frame I come to see that I am
something like you and you were something like me.

Grandpa, Grandpa I see a lot of you in my dad,
and your special talent too—
Cooking, and that same great attitude!

Jennifer Tarantino

I Forgive You

In memory of Gary L. Stern Jr.
A life was taken by an inconsiderate man
he used bad judgement; why I can't understand
March 8th will always be a figment in my mind
that's when I got to see you for one last time

It was extremely hard to say goodbye
out of all people, why did you have to die?
you had so many opportunities going for you
and so many things in your life you didn't get a chance to do

To the man that took your short life from you
what are his family and friends supposed to do?
I hope you're satisfied and I hope you're pleased
his family has so much pain and hurt that everyone can see

I can't say I hate you or even go to Hell
because I don't know you, at least not that well
so many people can learn from their mistakes
possibly even you but I speak for myself
and part of my family that I Forgive You

Michelle Coward

Ever Wonder

You might see two or three people,
If you take a walk down my street.
They might be as empty as you,
Like a hole from their head to their feet.

They might be ready to die,
They might be on the verge of a long cry.
Even terrified of the thunder,
But did you ever take the time to wonder?

Often I ask myself,
If anyone around me really cares.
If I were to get really sick,
Would any of them hold back my hair?

I might be ready to die,
Or on the verge of along cry.
They might be pulling me under,
But did you ever take the time to wonder?

Kristen Rutherford

Lies

Why do people have to lie?
It hurts so bad and makes me cry.
You have to know how much I care.
Sometimes it is more than I can bear.

You were thought of as a friend.
Do you really want this friendship to end?
I'd like to know so I don't look like a fool.
If yes or if no, it will all be cool.

Take it for granted or what you will
We could always laugh. We had the skill.
Life was good and always fun.
I thought for once that maybe I had won.

I was wrong. What else is new?
I guess I didn't have a clue.
Sorry if I have ever been a pain.
It must have been me raising Cain.

Please forgive and forget. It would mean a lot.
Let's try again. Give it another shot.
Let's start over. Fresh and brand new.
We need to tell no lies. Always be true.

Jami Hopper

Aftermath

The calm after the storm, the cold beneath the warm
The dark cloud that covers the blue sky
The silence that comes after the battle is won
The pain that cuts you up inside
The fear that stalks you, the eyes that saw you
When you fell apart, the building pressure
That makes you unsure of what you were from the start
The logic of life and the pleasure of dreams
Cut into your heart until nothing is as it seems
And when the monotony of the day doesn't want to go away
And bitter sweet dreams are the only things
to keep me from being lonely
I close my eyes and drift away from the gallows
of darkness that followed me through the day
I go to a place far away where the turquoise sea sparkles
And my nightmares are at bay where the sun is so bright
it burns my eyes and the sand beneath my toes
is the closest thing to life where I can't hear voices
telling me what to do, telling me all of my mistakes
And I can't feel hands pulling me and shaking me 'til I awake

Jessica Osbourne

When I Ask You

To my dad, Paul Frank Jameson
When I ask you to leave, do just that;
don't stay and ask why am I mad.
When I ask you to call me, don't set it aside;
leave me to cry, then say you tried.
When I ask you to love me, do just that
'cause if you asked me to love you, I'd give it a chance.
When I ask you to hate me, do what I say;
don't say that you love me—just turn and walk away.
When I ask you to do things for me that I would do for you,
do them please; I don't ask a lot of you.

Jessica Lackner

God's Words

The word of God is hard to hear
When you are being loud
So quiet your mouth
Open your ears
Open your heart to hear
God's wonderful, magnificent, beautiful words

Tristan E. Voskuhl

Connect

Let me get out in the hills again
I and myself alone
Out through the wind and the lash of rain
To find who we really are
Under the stars while a campfire dies
Let me sit and look myself in the eyes
Connect continued . . .
Let me get out in the hills again
I and myself alone
Out through the cold and rash of pain
To find who we really are
Under the night sky while a campfire dies
Let me sit and stare myself in the eyes until I die.

Michelle Ilene Coats

Imagine

Imagine for a moment
that I bend down on my knee.
I have a little black box in my hand,
and when I open it up, you gasp.
It is a diamond ring in a princess cut
with gold enclosing it.
I see it in your sparkling eyes,
that you know what I am thinking.
You put your right hand on my beating heart,
while you wait patiently for a word from me.
I open my mouth and start to speak,
words out of my heart.
The words coming out make you cry
because you know it is a question
that will change both our lives forever.
You kneel down beside me
and kiss me like you never have before,
then you finally make me the happiest man in the world:
You say, "Yes" to a question of
companionship forever.

Megan M. Lenz

My Valentine

I have a little Valentine.
I put it on my face, and when I take it out,
it's a smile in its place.

Lindsey Hedrick

Untitled

A baby is an angel from Heaven above,
a gift for you to cherish and love.
You'll love her, you'll love her 'til the day you die.
You'll love her forever and not know why.
She'll make you happy, she'll make you sad;
she'll make you mean, she'll make you mad.
Then she grows up and gives you hell;
she's really lost and just can't tell
what she wants or her lifelong dream.
She thinks life sucks and lets off steam.
Later on, she becomes a mom,
and it all begins again,
until the very end.

Michelle Dye

See What I See

Sometimes I wish they would see.
Themselves through the eyes of me.
I see their problems day to day.
Will they leave or will they stay.
Would it be easier if they where me?
If they knew the things I know.
Think of all the good to sow.
If they could see through a different perspective,
Maybe their problems would seem more corrective.
Will they open their eyes?
Open your eyes see what I see.
What harm could their be?
I'm sorry you no longer want to be.
If only you would listen to me.
Now close your eyes feel your pain
open your eyes to a higher power.
Feel his presents for he has forgiven you this very hour.

Charity Strange

You Talk about Leaving

To my boyfriend Greg
I've gotten so attached to you being there
Every day you bounce around the corner
and let us all know you are here
But now you talk about leaving
and you've made us both so sad
We understand that you are hurt
and still upset about your dad
It's been about a year now
I can see it in your eyes
yours and his, the heartbreak
and loneliness you both still feel
Doing things to try to cover up all the pain
is only making things worse
because now he has quit his game
and you are now talking about leaving too
Please don't go
It's hard to make it through the day without you

Stephanie Thompson

I Am a Rose

I am not what I eat
nor the clothes that I wear
I am not worth just the shoes on my feet
nor am I just what I fear
I am a Rose with thorns of pain and tears
with petals that are rich and fine
with leaves as my omniscient ears
with my stem as my very spine
A simple rose like all the rest
but never to be duplicated
for I am my own best

Amanda M. Beerman

Locked Away

Suddenly cold, feeling alone for some reason I feel
I don't belong. I shake it off and walk the other way;
the feeling's still there, it won't go away.

Entering a room, looking around, suddenly realizing
that I'm locked inside. I try to escape and I try to climb;
it's just no use, there's no getting through these doors.

The room is cold and I feel its despair yet,
I long to feel enchantment, I long to feel excited
but most of all, I long to simply belong.

I hear voices outside the room. I shout and yell aloud,
Please, won't someone let me out! Nothing, nothing at all.
Still persist I punch and pound, but nothing, nothing at all.

Exhausted, from all the commotion.
I give in and, lie down on the cold, gray ground.
I surrender myself to my own sorrow
and accept the fact I'd been locked in this bleak room.

Now I feel nothing, I'm just hollow.
I've lost track of the days, months, years . . .
I'm just locked inside, inside my lonely mind.

Lacey Fultz

My Friend

In memory of Marylee Loggins
In my mind, I see the faces of those I've called friends,
Who have done nothing except lie and hurt me in the end.
There are some though who have come through,
to be kind and to care and to be true.
One of these friends, I can neither see nor touch,
Yet there is no other whom I could ever love so much.
When I'm lonely, he's a friend, in darkness, he's a light.
I would like to introduce you to my best friend, Jesus Christ.
He has carried me through bad times and been beside me for the best.
You see, Jesus is my comfort and my rest.
My prayer is for you to see that no better friend,
I have than He, who cared enough to die for me.
You see, my friend, Jesus did something for you.
My friend Jesus, also died for you.
Everyone has a choice to accept or say no,
But that decision tells you where for eternity you'll go.
To accept Him means life, full, rich and pure,
But to say no means damnation, for which there is no cure.
The time is this moment, the place is where you are,
To ask your Savior for forgiveness and to live within your heart.

Jennifer Davis

The Cost of Drunk Driving

Carelessly driving down the road that night,
Two teenagers didn't see that truck in sight.
At the last moment, they swerved the wheel
and ended up in quite an ordeal.

Red, blue lights flashed against the sky;
the ambulance went rushing by.
At the scene they were pronounced dead;
the windshield had gone right through their head.

Police searched around the car and found
two beer bottles lying innocently on the ground.
"It's a shame it had to be this way,
"If it weren't for those bottles they'd live to see another day."

The parents were later told,
and down their cheeks the tears rolled.
They realized their kids would be gone forever,
they would see them again never.

So make the right choice it's up to you,
your fate depends on what you do.
Take the keys away from a drunk friend,
or you might never see them again.

Kristina A. Kern

Is the Feeling Love?

There is a feeling in my heart
It's something I can't describe
One day it came . . . it stayed
But is there something of it made?

Do I really love him, or is it just obsession
All I know is that, I don't feel depression
When I see him through my heart
Once a week or even twice

My heart burns with desire
There is a hot, hot fire
And as long the feeling's still here
I know it's really love.

Iza Wileczek

The Boss Experience

When you first apply,
You think it's a good job.
You were hired as a secretary.
Months later, things were changing.
You were getting paid every two weeks;
It was changed to the middle and last day of the month.
He would say something today,
Then tomorrow he says something different to confuse you.
After a year, things got worse.
He would cheat out on your paycheck.
Then two years have gone by;
One of the employees left after receiving the paycheck.
Now, he wants to change the pay system, again.
The employees are very upset.
It's not fair; he can't punish them for someone's actions.
His kids were very sick.
He took his frustration on his employees.
It's not their fault;
People get sick whether we like it or not.
This is not a normal business.

Shirley Acosta

Playground of Love

The birds are singing their lovely song.
The bees are making their nectar of rum.
The kids are playing in a nearly field.
Oh, how they play and enjoy themselves.
They run, play, and jump rope.
They forget about their differences.
They wash away their sorrows.
They play in the field of life.
They learn how to cherish their lives
And love the lives of others.
They do the things many grown-ups can't seem to do.
They look past race, religion, and color.
They look at the inside as well as the out.
They can make this world a special place.
And with their help, we can change the planet for the better.

Penny Brachman

Mistle Toe

To Stephanie and Trey Bauer
Mistle Toe, you should know,
was a girl who loved to kiss.
And every year, under her tree,
a boy would steal her heart,
and she would steal his.
They kissed so much, she was so sweet,
Family called her down, but she wouldn't come to eat.
They searched, girl had disappeared without a sound.
Where could she have gone? Nobody knows.
Then her love interest found something at his toes.
"What's this?" he'd ask, pick it up, and say, "Neat!"
"This flower smells like Mistle, cute and sweet!"

Suny Bauer

Smile

Dedicated to Kristin Freeman Lowry . . . hold on.
You should smile through the tears,
You should smile through all of the hardships,
Over the years.
You should smile because,
Through the tears, the pain, and the sorrow,
You will become stronger,
For the hardships of tomorrow.

Tabatha Reph

Paradise

For my mother, my special inspiration
On a sunny day,
One beautiful may
the grasses are green
and the robins would preen.

Some place else where,
the ants would dance,
the bees sip tea
A place of peace, and a sheep with the golden fleece.

In magical mystical world,
There ferocious lightning would not be hurled
Where the breezes soft as a sigh
And where no one would could lie.
A dream come true and it welcomes you.

Kailie Gannon

Angry

Sometimes when the day is bad
and someone made me very mad
or I've been given angry stares,
I go behind the front porch stairs.
There curled up with chin on knee,
I like to be alone with me and listen
to the people talk and hurry by me on the walk.
There I sit without a sound and draw stick pictures on the ground.
If I should tire of it all, I throw some pebbles at the wall.
After I've been there a while and find that I can almost smile,
I brush me off and count to ten and try to start the day again.

Tracey Gross

Life

There is so much more to life than being alive . . .
All those memories,
Some that make us cry,
Some that are forever anchored in our hearts,
Those that will haunt us.
Those that will remain silent . . .
Those dreams you couldn't figure out . . .
The saddest thing is to see that
Everything is left in a tomb . . .
Forever silent.

Rebecca Flores

Lonely

I waited by the phone to hear your sweet voice say
I'll be there in two minutes, get ready I'm on my way
Instead your words were silent when I asked you to drop by
You told me you were busy that you hadn't any time
My heart keeps being broken by those simple words you say
But I love you way too much to ever go away
I understand your feelings, I take every one to heart
But I can't stand this feeling
That we're being drawn apart
You've told me time and time again
That it will be okay but how can I be so sure of that
When you're always gone away

Amber Tucker

Why Does My Life Have to Be This Way?

Why does my life have to be this way,
Always getting upset for what people say.
I said I wouldn't let it get to me,
It's hard to keep something inside you never see.
I'm always mugging people because of the way I feel,
Some don't understand but most of them will.
It all started when I lost my first love,
I cried and prayed to the Heaven above.
I've always had one thing on my mind,
Why did he leave me at such a bad time?
I thought he said he love me and I said the same,
But now I know that this was just a game.
I will never express my feelings for my fear of getting hurt,
Like taking my heart and stomping it in dirt.
The people who I thought were really my friends,
Believe it or not they are enemies within.
I send love from the bottom of my heart,
So why did it have to break us apart?
My life is not easy to express each day . . .
But why does my life have to be this way?

Tamika L. Wright

On My Own

Sometimes I feel so lonely,
Like no one understands what I care about,
Like no one understands what I feel inside,
And then I realize it's because I'm really just on my own.

Sometimes I feel so helpless,
Like no one wants to listen to me,
Like no one wants to love or care for me,
And then I realize it's because I'm just on my own.

Sometimes I feel so useless,
Like no one needs me here with them,
Like no one needs my help,
And then I realize it's because I'm still on my own.

Sometimes I feel so trapped,
Like the thoughts in my mind won't let me escape,
Like the people in my life won't let me live life for myself,
Like the love in my heart will never let go,
And then I realize that I'm on my own.

I'm on my own in this world that I can no longer bear to be in,
So I sleep and dream of the thing that I long for:
To no longer be, on my own.

Nicole Brown

Movie Star

There once was a movie star named Eve.
Everyone wanted her to leave,
One day Eve opened a package she had received.

On the package there was a note.
In the package a brown leather coat,
And in the note something strange was wrote!

Dear Eve, please go away.
You were only movie star of the day.
So please Eve go away, today!

Jessica Hamm

Why I Care

I see the flower in the garden
not knowing why it's there.
I lift myself out of the chair
to see the reason why I care.
The smell tells me it's as beautiful as your hair.
The fresh air lets me know
the reason why I care.
The beauty of its petals makes me
aware of the reason why it resembles you.

Jennifer Weinmeister

Untitled

Dedicated to everyone I love
How do you know the truth?
What if they tell you a lie?
Could you tell?
Would you want to know?
Smell.
Taste.
See.
Hear.
Touch.
Know.
Maybe?
Sweet lies
Tell me these falsifications to numb life's pains
Free my sow to the ocean of "dreams"
Let me fly so high I reach the stars
Tell me I make up the sparkle in your eye
Bring me to heights I've never been before in these fibs
The hopes stay in store

Robin Bristol

True Love

I'll love you until the end,
for this I can depend.
Every day when I see you,
you make me smile.
I've always loved you,
I've just never told you.
To see you take another love
would break my heart.
I'd cry, I'd suffer, but my love would never part.
The angels above
make my heart soar like a dove.
For you I'd do anything,
because you're my true love.

Amanda Johnson

Evil Love

Hated the way you treated me,
but loved the things you did to me.

The great feeling I got when you held me
in your arms like a baby.

Yet I remember the horrible thoughts that
sometimes haunt me,
because of the abuse you afflicted upon me.

"Angel in disguise" is the phrase to describe your
mysterious, devilish ways.

So afraid to stop loving you because your love was all I knew,
too blind to see that sinning now became a part of me.
Evil love is what's in store for me.

Tawana Harvey

Two Seconds

Just this second, someone died
Just this second, someone cried
Just this second, someone drowned
Just this second, someone frowned
Just this second, someone starved

In one more second, someone will smile
In one more second, someone will laugh awhile
In one more second, someone will give
In one more second, more people will live

In the last two seconds a lot has changed
The next two seconds could be a surprise
So for just this second, be glad you are alive

Lindsay Jackson

Memory

Dedicated to Lance Bass of 'N Sync
My feelings were hurt, my heart was broken
And few were the words that were often spoken

I wanted you to know just how I felt
And how every time I looked at you, you made my heart melt

My life isn't complete now that you've moved on
Even though my love for you was never really shown

I don't really know why I liked you so much
Maybe it was the sound of your voice, or the softness of your touch
I guess I need to move on and listen to my friends
But the love I have for you is the kind that never ends.
I would wait on you forever, but you'll never like me
So I have to put you in the back of my mind and make you a memory.

Kelly Horn

A Caring Family

I have so many things that go through my mind,
but there is one thing I think of all the time.
It is that I could never have a better mother,
father, or sister so sweet and so kind.
They have always helped me through thick and thin.
I don't think I could ever have
a loving and Christian family like them.
I sometimes have girl problems,
so I always go to my sister or mother.
My Dad loves to take me fishing and hunting,
and that's the great thing about
having a loving family: they always care.

Haley Dillard

Who?

As I leave my school of horror and walk down the path
closer and closer to my realm of unhappiness
I feel all my giggles and faith leave me
sucking my soul dry and bare naked
I feel a draft hit my bare soul
I shiver but it means nothing
I slumber up my dreary steps
and walk down the everlasting hall
As I reach my room I am not comforted
and I think could my life get any worse
but only air leaves my mouth and I think until I realize
my life has no meaning, I am jut a cowering animal
crouching with fear as I am shown off like an animal in the zoo
and I realize what life truly is and I shudder
I am just what other people want me to be
brilliant, charming, optimistic, funny
just what my parents want, what my friends want
what I thought I wanted, and finally it occurs to me
Who am I?

Alyssa Wegner

Tear from a Rose

The tear from a rose is much like mine,
The painful truth will come out in time,
Everyone loves the way it looks,
Enwrapped in the innocence of beauty you only read about in books,
Yet if you come close enough to touch,
Close enough to feel,
You'll hate the rose's touch,
You'll hate its thorns so much.
You won't even wait for the wound to heal
before you steal a tear from the rose
and easily forget its innocent beauty,
but you'll never forget its sinful thorn,
that once caused you to mourn.

Jayme Raichert

Hidden Love

Not being with you I'm falling apart
'Cause I don't know how to get your heart
Of all those nights when I sat and cried
All I can do is run and hide
I always dream of your gentle touch
If only you knew I felt this much
Every time I look at your beautiful face
I know it could never be replaced
The love I feel grows stronger each moment
It feels so good, don't it?
But then again you wouldn't know
Because you refuse me so
You try and avoid the feelings I have,
Sometimes you just make me so sad
You are my hearts forbidden desire
You make my heart sing like a choir
I hold you dear in my heart
And I miss you when we're apart.
My love is there, why can't you see?
I'm hopeful that one day you will love me.

Kristina Magallanes

Rosie

How I love my little Rosie. I shall love her forever,
When she's young or when she's old,
For she is my Rosie my little Rosie.
She's of brown, white, dark orange, and even black.
While we run in the fields of yellow wheat,
She licks my face and I kiss her back.
We have adventures of fun.
I wonder if it will last forever,
But I know it won't last forever.
Soon life will pass on for both of us,
But when it happens,
When night falls or even when the sun grows dead,
No one really knows—not even God himself knows.
But for now we're just fine, not a worry in the world.
It's just me and Rosie.
I love her and she loves me and that's all that matters.
Rosie is my little dog.

Jessica Arendas

Wishing upon a Shooting Star

Every night I see a shooting star,
and I wish upon the shooting star
to someday find out where you are.
I wait. I wait for my wish to come true,
but someone told me that there is a wishing fairy,
and a buck a wish it will come true,
but when the wish came true
the buck a wish didn't buy enough time with him!

Stacy Minchew

Father of Mine

Father of mine, do you hear my cry?
I want to give your love one more try.

I wish you could share these moments with me,
But that's the way it has to be.

Even though we're apart,
I want my heart to never part
with all the love I feel inside.

I loved, adored, and admired you from the start.

When I was sick, you made me feel better.
You were even there when nothing was wrong.
So now I sit here singing this song.

I love you forever more,
Father of mine!

Martina Hawkins

Hello to Stay

Hello, goodbye, it's what we always say
Why can't we say hello to stay
I want to be together
Not just for now, but forever
My friends are so wrong
We'll be sweethearts life-long
They keep saying that you're such a cheat
But only if you and they could meet
Maybe they would understand
If they could see you hold my hand
I really understand you
I know you will always be true
The promises, songs, sweet love, and kisses that were so kind
They seem to be always on my mind
It feels like you're here beside me every day
I wish it could really be that way
Maybe some really close day
We can say hello to stay

Melanie Susan Naylor

As I Look at You

As I look at you I sit and think,
when you smile, and how you think.
As I look at you, I see someone sweet,
night and day, no one can compete.
As I look at you, I start to cry,
but then I wonder . . . why?
As I look at you, I sit and think,
how this ever happened between you and me,
no more thinking, no more pain,
a day gone by my mind is blank,
and then I walk away!

Jamie Arwine

Grandfather

As I gaze down the old, dusty, dirt road,
I try to remember the good times we had.
Looking up at the setting sun,
As though you are here I feel the warmth.
Like Boyz-II-Men said,
"It's so hard to say goodbye to yesterday."

Even though you're gone,
I will always remember you.
Not only were you a grandfather,
You were my companion and best friend.
Now the only way we can talk is in prayer,
For you are now my guardian angel and will be forever more.

At times I wish you were here,
But I now know that is not possible.
I will always love and remember you.
Because I know when times are tough,
You will be watching over me.

Janelle Kerby

My Loneliness

Loneliness is the worst feeling in the world.
It brings out anger and sadness, guilt and shame.
It makes you realize how little they care,
As you sit alone in a broken chair
That rocks you to sleep
As it falls to the floor.
Loneliness tears you apart.
You scream your questions, whisper your pleas.
They don't hear.
Loneliness picks out the bad things,
Pushes them in your face.
You dwell, dwell, dwell, until you have no sun.
The razor tore it all off.

Deborah Potisek

Friends for Life

For Meghan Dirkes and Elizabeth Young
Sadness shows inside and out,
When you aren't spending time with the people you care most about,
Missing my friends in another town,
I miss hearing their voices,
Their laughter and other precious sounds,
I miss being with them to make memorable moments,
Sharing our deepest secrets,
Confessing our major crush,
Looking them in the eye and telling them they are the greatest,
Seeing a smile spread across their delicate face,
I miss my friends,
The time we spent together,
Laughing,
Talking,
Having fun.

    Stefanie L. Frater

Dolphins

Dolphins are blue and sometimes they're gray;
Whatever they are, I will love them today.

They live in the oceans and travel in schools.
Whatever they do, they will always be cool.

I love them so much I would live in the sea
to be with the dolphins as much as can be.

    Lilly Moss

A Person Missed So Much

Strong and brave yet sometimes blue
We always knew he would be true.
Sweet and kind never mean
We always knew what he had seen,
Scared yet happy as he'd always be
Never knew he wouldn't be with us for eternity,
Worked for all never refused
Yet he knew he'd sometimes be used.
Fixed the cars interior so pretty
Everyone had so much pity.
On him,
On the world,
So it suddenly seemed
Just as if he were a delightful dream.

    Cynthia Gomez

Johnny Brave

For Anthony Wilson, the best teacher ever
Once there was a bitter man
whose name was Johnny Brave.
He sailed in all the seven seas
because he was a slave.
Johnny Brave knew in his heart
he was just as good as white.
He would not give up equality
without a solid fight.
He dreamed that night he'd died
and gone to Heaven, he was blessed.
God told him to be himself
It's he who does it best.
He told the white men
what he thought was right and what was wrong.
They killed him in an instant
not caring he was gone.
Johnny went to Heaven
and God told him one thing:
He is an equal man and indeed
he is his name.

    Amy Pratt

In Your Eyes

You saw us as always together,
I saw us as friends forever.
You saw us as a couple until the end,
I saw us as just good friends.

You saw me as your future wife,
I saw you as a friend for life.
You saw me as your soul mate,
I never even saw you as a date.

You saw me as someone to love,
I saw you as a friend sent from above.
You saw me as someone who would love you,
I saw you as just a good friend to talk to.

    Ashley Hutchinson

The Sunrise

The sunrise falls of the cliffs of the deserted beach.
Orange and pink colors fill the awakening sky.
Soon the ocean brings in the morning's tide.

I sit upon the shore with my feet in the blue-green waters.
I take a deep breath and smell the salty sea air.
The breeze lifts the gulls as they fly over the jagged rocks.

The waves are crashing in the background.
I think to myself, this makes life worth living.
In sky I see white clouds moving gracefully above me.

I stand up with my pale blue dress flowing at my ankles.
I walk across the sandy beach to the house.
When arriving, I turn and reflect the sunrise.

His soft gentle hand touches my shoulder.
I then sigh at the breathtaking view.
He pulls me toward him.

I turn to look at him.
He smiles a warm smile to comfort me.
Together we enter the house.

My hand in his and a tear in my eye.
My pain is gone.

    Candess Zona

Untitled

To Joseph, whom I love
Waiting all week, just to see your face.
Listening all week, just to hear your voice.
Thinking of you, just to imagine you
Having you, but not holding you
Wanting you here instead of there
Always wondering what you're thinking.
There is no one in the world I love
More than you, I love you.

    Melissa D. Torres

Ocean

Funny things happen in the ocean,
The animals make such a commotion.
Dolphins will dance and whales will sing,
It is the most amazing thing.
Schools of fish swim in a rainbow of color.
A little crab runs and then comes another.
Within the current, seaweed sways,
It is so fascinating you could watch for days.
Coral stands proudly, without fail,
Crawling around is a little snail.
Seahorse swim cautiously, forever beware.
A shark comes confidently, ready to scare.
These seem like wonderful things for the viewer,
But if we do not take care, they will be gone all the sooner.

    Shanna Prol

My Angel

My Angel came in the strangest form,
But he always makes me feel nice and warm.
Even though he doesn't have much hair,
I'll always know he'll care.
Looking at me with those bright blue eyes,
He can make me laugh, even when someone dies.
Although Angels are visible to few
My Angel is my nephew.

Beverly Wilson

Every Tear

Though I know you're no longer here,
I see your smile with every tear.

And every night without a star I know that
death is where you are.

Though the world was against us, but we were free,
and you died with the highest dignity.

Defending your love from which was wrong.
Though the years passed the pain goes on.

Your trips you showed me every place.
Your sudden kiss across my face.

You showed me passion,
and romance and how my eyes began to dance.

And when the night begins to rise.
It casts a sadness in my eyes.

And though I'll have my every fear.
I'll have to accept with every tear.

Brandi A. Demmons

Inner Beauty

Just be yourself, don't listen to lies.
Let it all out, let out your cries.
The insults are there:
"You're ugly," "You're fat."
The truth is you're you,
And that's that.
You may feel down about your looks.
You're not a model or a picture in a book.
But everyone's beautiful in their own special way.
Be sure to repeat this every day.

Jessica R. Detton

Sundae

The light hits the ice cream,
glistening before my eyes.
The chocolate trickling
from the jar slowly,
but with ease.
Whipped cream soars from the can,
delicately falling on the chocolate,
covering the ground with snow.
Maraschino
red and juicy,
stares at me from its peak,
on top of my mountain of sparkling ice cream,
sinking deeper into the snow.
The spoon gravitates towards the ice cream,
attacking the snow and the chocolate,
digging into the ice cream.
It rose at an angle, soaring into my mouth.
I close,
surrounding the spoon with my tongue,
dissolving the ice cream.

Marnina Cherkin

Words

I don't always want to be the one
who suffers while he has his childish fun.

The words he says really make me hurt inside;
I don't understand why I'm always the one who has to be kind.

Every time I see him I prepare for the worst,
hoping, just maybe he won't put me down.

The expression on my face is always a frown;
he never lays a hand on me in any harming way,
but my emotions are beaten down every day.

I wish he'd understand that I'm hurting all the time.
I hope one day he'll have a change of heart
and suddenly realize these feelings of mine.

Sheana Whitmarsh

Love

Love, pointing you to desolate paths,
deep treads to all sides, never ceasing in length,
no gain ever seen, heartbreak at every turn,

Each corner shows loves lost,
winding by one, then the next,
finally that one face,
the one you know you love,
the one that got away,

Longing for his attention,
knowing you will never receive it,
understanding your eyes will never meet again,
you continue, always looking back into the abyss.

Nicole I. Hansen-Solum

Because the World Goes 'Round

The sun starts to fade and the moon is in sight.
The day is now over, there soon will be night.

The sky turns orange, pink, purple, and blue.
When they all fade away the stars take their cue.

The sun slowly melts and goes far out of sight.
The moon comes to play, now it is night!

The sky is so black as the stars twinkle bright.
The crescent moon shines through the darkness called night.

Children all sleep, snug in their beds.
While fantasies and dreams float 'round in their heads.

Some dream of kind things, fairies, castles, and knights.
While others include monsters, witches, and frights.

The moon will soon fade and the stars start to hide.
Then the colors return with beauty and pride.

The cycle repeats, day after day.
Here, there, and far, far away.

The stars shall return and the sun will be found.
The moon will come back because the world goes 'round.

Jessica Eson

Bliss

I feel bliss in the midst of a Sunday afternoon
All my problems are solved, or so it seems.
As a gentle breeze sends chills over me.
Dark clouds gather,
Rain begins to sprinkle on my head,
It's so dark, it's like I'm dead.
Then you come along and gentle winds blow the clouds away.
And again I am blissful.

Heather Thompson

Love

Love is powerful,
Love is strong.
Love is what I want all day long,
Whether it's from you or someone else.
All I want is you to love me for myself.
I won't break your heart if you won't break mine.
I just want to know, will you be my Valentine?

Megan Long

New Conflagrations

Excitement runs through my veins
Like the way blood flows,
Extinguishing the fiery beasts
That torture the pure land.
I tread through the ash-covered hills
As the soot gathers in reunion upon my face.
Gushing winds charcoal my throat
As I inhale a thick cloud of smoke.

Walking steadily as the sparkling embers
Are unable to touch my skin,
I spray a midst of foamy water,
Blanketing the ashen ground.
As I look up I behold the dancing flames
Escalating upon branches close by,
I smother the blazing fires
With a great river of foam.

As the final flames diminished,
I endured the opaque acreage that surrounded me—
Nothing but a dusk sky and an ebony field
To accompany the scattered coals.

Michelle Gamache

Claudia

The twisted ways of others
Snag you into their interwoven
and complicated spider web.
The cold sun blackens your once tender soul.
Your stagnant mind is like a fish with no water: dead.
Your personality is a colorless rainbow.
What you see is not what you get.
You're the plastered portrait of something you're not.
For an instant it looks as though
everyone is deceived by your flawless ways.
But we must remember:
Looks are deceiving!

Marcie Samples

Hidden Child

There she is every day,
I watch her.
She sits under a tree, her sanctuary,
Untouched by the outside world.
The girl has a peaceful gaze about her,
Sheltered from the hatred that has consumed
So many people.
She is always in a hushed solitude
As if quietly waiting for someone.
Some days she reads,
Soaking up all the knowledge the world has to offer,
But today the girl stares off into the horizon,
Deep in thought, unmoving.
After some time she stirs and rises to leave,
In a solemn, yet satisfied manner.
And I wonder,
Who is she, so hidden from the rest of the world?
I wonder if I will ever discover the secrets
Of the lonely child.

Rachel Golden

Love

Love is a feeling you hold in you
Love is something you share
Love can hurt you
Love can make you happy
To share love you must find someone
That makes you happy
To keep love in and not share love can hurt you
So, love is wonderful, love is peaceful
and love is a feeling that needs to be shared.
So I want to share this love I have
with you 'cause I have found
Someone that makes me happy
and that someone is you.

Terri-Lei L. Paulo

Reaching

You're so close,
yet so far.
My hand tries to stretch for yours,
but I keep getting lost in the fog.
I strain to find you again;
the forest floor holds me down.
I sigh your name into the wind,
thinking the gentle voice will reach you.
You turn and search but cannot see,
so you continue on.
With no luck,
I go around in circles,
getting dizzy,
falling fast.
Come get me in this horrible hell.
Take my hand lead me out,
reaching for my heart.

Ashley MacLaren

Not the Right One

Although I saw you in my dreams
you were not the right one for me.

I fantasize about you when you're not there
but I will not forgive you for your love affair.

I thought I loved you once
but when I saw you flirting with another girl
I got over my stupid crush.

This is the end of my love for you.
Maybe now you'll realize who's the real fool.

Marissa Garza

My Sun?

To my mother whom I love
You are the man that I always wanted to know,
the man I so longed to love.
When I was a child you were praised
like the sun up above.

You truly let me down,
you were nothing but a dog.
I was left betrayed and abandoned
left fatherless in my life's epilogue.

All my life I've been naïve,
wanting you there in the portrayal of my life,
Now time has passed and things have changed.
Your reminiscence only brings back strife.

I ached for you once and hope I forget,
all the pain and rigor that I once wept.
You're not my bright sun and you'll never be,
I live in the darkness where I can safely be kept.

Diana Guido

Mademoiselle, Helene Robart

Mademoiselle stands behind
the old oak chair that no one sits at anymore.
Alone in a mournful deep thought,
She remembers his thick dusty brown hair
And his large protective hands.
As she glances at the pile of folded,
Handwritten letters that lay on the desktop,
He is gone,
Gone to some place more pleasant,
And she stands wondering where to go.
Will she find someone new, or will she stay in her own world
where her heart and his soul will stay bonded together forever?

Amy Marie Flaherty

My Race

My race color is black
You ask me why I'm blue
I tell you that I'm tired
Of you beating on my people
And telling them what to do.
I try to help you understand
About my race but you see nothing
But the brown skin upon my face
As a tear runs down my cheek
I tell you of things that have happened to me;
You tell me things you've done.
I look at you in discouragement
And say our victory will be won,
For we have fought the battle twice or more
But we still got the police at our door saying
We got to go downtown round and round,
But you still ask me why I'm blue
It's all because of you,
My race color is black
Why should I be judged?

Bridgette Grimes

Only in My Dreams

Come to me in my dreams, and then by day I will be well again.
The night will pay for the hopeless longing of the day.

My dreams will enchant the memory of you,
and walk me through the endless day.

Throughout the day of loneliness,
I have the thought of you that I hold against my heart.

Sandy Jacobovitch

You're the Only One Who Makes Me Happy

You give me a new outlook
On my everyday life
You give me reasons to go on
Even through times of strife
You fill my heart with joy
Whenever you are near
You make sure I'm happy
So I don't break a tear
You are concerned
I can tell by what you do
You're always there for me
Even when you don't want to
I love to see you smile
I know you feel the same
'Cause when I do something wrong
You give me shame
You're there for me when I'm sad
You pick me up when I'm down
You make me very happy
You're the one who gives me a smile from a frown.

Dawn Parmentier

Dying

As she slowly wilts away,
like that gorgeous rose I once saw.

Will she always be there?
I fear not.

What will I become,
What's going to happen, God?

You are the one who knows,
why can't I?

I feel so loved and alone all at once,
don't die on me now.

When that day comes when I lay that gorgeous rose above her head,
I will wonder, how could you?

Morgan Miles

Why

Why was her life cut so short of time
Why was it time for her to die
She was so young, and yet
She leaves this world a daughter, wife, and mother.
We try to turn back the hands of time
But in reality it is already too late.
Family and friends gather around
Tears of grief and sorrow start to flow
My mother and best friend is placed forever below.
Her passing is felt everywhere
It's hard to explain the grief and hurt I feel
It's just not fair
At night I pray down on my knees
I pray for her . . . Oh, God don't take her please!
And still I wake another day
Another night I dream and pray
Don't make me hurt, don't make me cry
It's just too hard to say goodbye
To a mother I never knew.

Jennifer Lindgreen

With You

To Steven M. Stamper
Your hair, your beautiful blue eyes
Just send chills down my spine.
The sight of you makes me weak;
My hands shiver, and it's hard to speak.
My heart melts when you look at me that way;
I don't know how, I just can't say.
As I see your delicate face,
In my mind is your place.
I anticipate the days to come;
I want to spend my life with you, the only one.
I can see us in a few years,
Crying only those happy tears.
With each other is where we'll be;
That's a good enough reason for me.

Samantha Waller

Wanting You

Every night as I lie awake
I think of you.
Every day a longing, a burning for you.
I do these little things
To take my mind off you.
But every night I long to touch you.
You seem so close but so far away.
I long for you every day,
A longing, a burning, a dream unfulfilled,
A breath for every waking moment of wanting you still.

Michelle Burch

I Can't Live with or without You

As I look at you I desire so much to be with you again.
But then I think how it might be the same way.
When I'm lying in my bed I think about
Every little memory we had together.
As friends and as togetherness.
And I wonder if at that split second
You're thinking about me too.
But then I wonder if you're really over me
And I'm just lying to myself
I often think if I should of ended it,
I don't think it's because I'm still hurting.
I just feel the same way.
So then again I think that I am better off.
But I think I'm really not.
I put so much effort out toward you.
And it was not easy, and I tell you how I feel.
Now what more should I do.
I'm leaving the rest up to you.
I will not beg you back but I find it often weird,
Because I know I can't live with or without you.

Danielle Robbins

Yesterday

Yesterday I held your hand,
It seems like I moved across the land.
You said you'd love me forever,
Now I just want us to be together.

Yesterday you held me tight,
You said everything would be all right.
Then I had to leave your soul,
Now in my heart there is a hole.

Yesterday we hugged goodbye,
It hurt so bad I wanted to die.
I still sit at home sometimes and cry,
Wishing and praying you were still my guy.

Staci Ranae Bratcher

Utopia

My utopia of thoughts blends
into my magical and mystical world,
being united with the ice-cool breeze.
The summer wind, the foggy mist all have a wonderful twist.
Enlightened day, a darkened moon.
Living in the same world together.
A dark red rose dripping dew in the morning.
A silver blade and a rusted nail,
The yellow sun with the silver hail.
Living a day in my magical mystical world
Is just another utopia of thoughts.

Anna Champ

Tear

As the girl waited for her date
She wondered, "Why do I have to wait?"
Two hours later she got a phone call
From a guy named Slater

She hung up the phone
To hear a tone
And as you watch, a blotch
Came on her heart

Ten years later she remembered while looking outside
That the drizzle sparkled like the tear on her cheek

Then she noticed something bleak
Hoping it was Slater
Then a little later
No Slater

Jessica McKinney

Political Satire

There was a leader named George Bush
Who gave this country one big push.
Into war we did go,
Shooting bombs to and fro.
We did our job and won the war,
But boy were the Iraqis really sore!
Then this country shouted with glee,
And Bush said, "I still won't eat my Broccoli."

Andrea Cunningham

First Day, Second Night

First day, second night,
People are but just a fright.
See the world night and day;
Don't be thrilled, because it won't stay.
If it were for us,
Why would we fuss?
It's here for us all,
Summer, Spring, Winter, and Fall.
For people, creatures, and living things,
Eat food, wear clothes and diamond rings.
Play at the park,
In the light and the dark.
We are what we are,
Maybe someday, even a star.
Going to school doesn't always rule.
We may not like it, but don't throw a fit.

Rachel Dreveniak

Loneliness

To anyone who has felt lonely
Loneliness is feeling apart from others,
like you're not really mentally there.
Things around you continue to go,
and feeling that people don't seem to care.
All you want, is to be normal,
and live a life of constant happiness.
But for some reason, it doesn't turn out,
you end up dealing with times of sadness.
There's times you feel all by yourself,
many times come to mind.
You end up thinking about so much stuff,
and always feel like you're in a bind.
Crying always gets things out,
it usually helps for a little bit.
But later on, the feeling comes back,
so it helps if you have something to hit.
Loneliness—you can't really help it,
it's just this feeling you get inside.
Hopefully it will pass, but who really knows,
it might just be with you for the rest of your life.

Nicole Cain Fivis

To Look into Your Eyes

To look into your eyes
reminds me of just how much
you and I are in love.

To look into your eyes proves
to thee just how much you mean to me.

To look into your eyes,
it makes me feel, that what you
and I have couldn't be more real.

To look into your eyes and feel your embrace
lets me know that you, no one could ever replace.

To look into your eyes each day,
after day tells me that you're here to stay.

Kelly Dolan

Am I Perfect Yet?

I look in the mirror and what do I see?
A big, fat, ugly girl looking back at me
Ashley's so pretty, and Brooke's so great
And Jamie, well, she wears a size eight

Well, the diet didn't work, nor the exercise
I have to think of something to slim down my size
If I don't eat, I can't gain any weight
This has got to work—there is no debate

It has been a month, I am looking much thinner
I know very soon that I will be a winner
Mom's getting worried, I tell her I'm okay
She says, "Then eat," I can't pull away

I purge it up, it can't stay in me
I have to be skinny, I have to be free
Why is the room spinning out of control?
Everything is black, it has taken its toll

The doctor says I am sick, and I almost died
It made me so scared, I cried and cried
It will take me a long time to get well, I am ready for it
I know now that I was always perfect

Jessica Fatland

Fragile

My heart is in this little box . . . with your name on top
But this time I'm not so quick to give it back to you.
But the day that I do . . .

My heart you hold again . . . but if you are not careful,
and you drop that box . . . and you break my heart again!
That I can't replace! It was my heart to start,
And it was yours with time . . . just remember this:

That time heals the best of wounds! And it can heal my heart . . .
Your name may fade away . . . and it will be my heart again!

But this time your name it does not hold . . .
And if this ever becomes to be "true."
I will defend to say.
This has come to be . . . The End.

Kelly Cacciamani

Nature

Red, yellow, orange, and green.
Those are the colors of nature.
Nature takes over your mind,
While the colors rewind.
Nature is magic, nothing can replace it.
But nature is in danger, by all mankind.
Nature is our home, it's like a big throne,
Nature is our king.

Annabelle Eicke

The Child I Am

I was six years old and fast-lane victim,
Tattered jeans and pigtails.
Going to self-destruct,
I'm gonna kill you for what you put me through.
The lack of self-respect reveals my hopes
And fears of a lost little girl,
Molestation, incest.
Let me go, no, there's no hope.
Don't get me from school 'cause I want be there.
Exploited, cheated, and angry is the way I feel.
Where were you as I grew up?
Tortured by my past,
Out of control and numb
Is the child that I am.

Candice Farley Buyers

Friends

Friends come in packages big and small.
Some are short, some are tall.
They make you happy, they share your pain.
They can be wacky, they drive you insane.
Friends give you a shoulder to cry on.
Friends are people you can always rely on.
Friends will always lend an ear,
When you think that no one will hear.
They'll cheer you up with a smile,
And tell you what's in and out of style.
Friends talk about that special guy
Who makes you laugh and makes you cry.
Sometimes friends really can bug you,
But you know they'll always hug you.
Friends are friends forever.
Don't stop making friends, never ever.

Stephanie Breed

Dear Mommy

Hi, Mommy! I'm sitting here thinking about you.
Why must you go, Mommy? Why did you say your time is through?
Who will take care of me, Mommy, when my temperature is high?
Who will love me unconditionally, with an understanding heart?
Who will scorn me, Mommy, when I do something wrong?
Who will praise me, Mommy, when I make the Honor Roll?
Who will explain to Daddy why I think he's unfair?
Who will fill the house with flowers and pictures in a frame?
I wish I could take the pain away, Mommy, but only God can.
What's taking him so long, Mommy? We don't have time to spare.
Time is going on, Mommy, and by the look on your face,
It's a struggle for you to face another day.
Rest your head now, Mommy, and try to get sleep.
It will be okay, Mommy; have faith and believe.
I can't say goodbye, Mommy, because they say that's forever,
and I need you Mommy, I won't understand.
Life without you will bring a lot of pain.
I can't stop the tears, Mommy, from rolling down my face.
Good night, Mommy. I love you always.

Promise Sills

Untitled

Thanks to my family
I hear them howling in the trees,
calling, asking to come with them,
once, twice, thrice times they swoop down
to catch me in their net of spiders' webs.
White and eerie, spooky, scary
And I like a fly in their tangled web.

Ashley Hoeprich

Forever Changing

Forever changing are the trees,
of brown, yellow and red,
their branches swaying in the breeze,
the ground becoming an autumn bed,

Forever changing are the trees,
of pink blossoms in the sun,
and returning are the leaves,
which in fall had gave us so much fun.

Forever changing are the trees,
of nuts and berries that are sweet,
the air is full of pollen dust,
the ground is full of tall and golden wheat,

Forever changing are the trees,
with sparkling snow caps in the night,
Here begins the winter freeze,
And the birds begin their Southward flight.

Ariel Hudnall

Summer Time

It's 2:55, you hear the final bell.
It's going to be a fun and interesting summer, you can already tell.
No more school books, said goodbye to the teachers,
Got rid of the homework, no more sitting on the bleachers.
It's going to the mall, having guys to see,
Friends to call, and places to be.
When you think about it for a while, it brings to your face a smile.
You're out of school for ten long weeks.
Time for vacation, parties, and friend-to-friend links.
The bell has rung, the fun is near;
It's easy to tell that summer is here!

Leah Lack

Untitled

I loved this boy once. I know he loved me back.
He always lit up when he saw me,
And I was always cheered up by him.
Every time I was down, he would literally try to cheer me up.
Even when I wasn't down, he still cheered me up.
He made me laugh a lot.
We never did go out, though.
I wish we did go out, but we didn't.
I'll always remember how he used to stare at me
And how I would stare at him.
Although he almost hugged me once 'cause I was crying,
But he always seem to follow me around.
He scared off most of the guys, I guess.
They used to mess with me, but they didn't after he spoke to them.
I guess he really did care,
But I don't think I'll ever see him again.
Anyway, I really did care.
Now I'm just trying not to think about him anymore,
But sometimes it's hard.

Jeanette Wade

My Best Friend

Let me tell you about my best friend,
She is there whether I lose or win,
Her ears are like a wishing well,
Whatever I want it is she I tell,
Her personality is like a star in the sky,
Both guide me in whatever I try,
Her mouth is always curved in a smile,
For her I would go the extra mile,
My friend is always there that's a fact,
That's because my best friend is my cat.

La Donna Daniel

Friends

Friends are such great people,
don't you know,
I wonder what it's like to be all alone.
Some care about everything you do;
others worry about who you all talk to.
Why do we need them at such great times?
All mean so many different things
to us and everyone that they run into.
Soon someday we will all part,
and not one will forget from the start
what great times we had so many years ago.
Then on the day we reunite,
we'll probably cry and then say goodbye
all over again. We'll say we'll write
almost every night, but really we'll be too busy.
Why does that always happen to us, my friends?
Yet we will still all be good friends
until the very end.

Brandy Hoffman

Looking Back

The light has faded away,
Just like the love we shared left day by day.
You said it would last forever.
You left my heart broken,
My hopes shattered.

The hurt you brought will stay.
I should have learned from the past
That our love was never meant to last.

I look back at some of the happy memories we shared.
I take it day by day,
Hoping it will all end,
But I know it has just begun.

Jennifer Wheatley

Untitled

Here I go again . . .
Hurting myself and the others around me.
Making excuses,
Truthful reasons,
But unacceptable.
Things shall continue to make leaps and bounds
          DO
             WN
                HI
                   LL
Quicker than a cheetah's pounce,
My life continues to fall.
Things are black and gray now.
No vibrance.
No ray of hope.
My smile?
A sign of something untrue.
A hidden message;
That no one,
No one, will ever understand.

Sarah von Wellsheim

A Day at the Beach

It sounds like fun
the sand, the water, and the sun.

She was so innocent young and sweet;
she had the world right at her feet.

Who would have known she would die,
leaving everyone she loved to grieve and to cry?

Into the water she swam so fast;
she didn't know today would be her last.

The current came up too fast for sight,
but she didn't give up without a fight.

The funeral was the saddest day of my life;
reality cut through me like a knife.
In another place, in another time,
her life no longer a part of mine.

Heather Griep

The Sunset

In the evening, just before night strikes,
an extraordinary sunset will be a sight.
Wonderful colors, orange, yellow, pink,
will come across the sky, just with instinct.
The colors up there so high,
we wonder what happened to our bright blue sky.
It will happen just for a while,
then the darkness and shining bright stars
will show their style.

Diandra Marshall

Momma

In memory of my mother Breyce Brantley
Why did you leave me,
in this world alone?
I never wanna come back,
knowing you won't be there to greet me home.

All my life loneliness will
be what I feel.
I know I have more family,
but they don't seem real.

You haven't watched me
play baseball,
And we haven't got our chance,
to go to the mall.

Who's gonna cheer me up
and make me smile,
Especially when the road
is more than a mile?

I loved you then even when
we made each other mad,
And I'd bring back those days,
but they're over and had.
　　Jessica Brantley

Untitled

All my life I have been looking for a start,
staring through windows that have led to my heart.
I have looked deep into my mind
and found things to believe in
and to live for . . . suddenly and slowly
opened a door, a door leading to hope
and light and I'll try my hardest
to keep them within my sight.
If they get lost they will be found
without a sound without a trace
I will have solved the case,
Unknown hands reached a part of me
I never knew was there,
they pulled out the real me and took an endless stare!
　　Jennifer Wells

Untitled

I hear the whisper of the wind as I stand
in the grass and remember exactly how it was
to feel as though the thoughts in my head
are not my own but someone else's
placed in my undeserving mind for a reason
undisclosed and then I feel the wind
lift my hair with the gentlest fingers imaginable
and I feel the swirl of everything wonderful
in this world wrap me in a garment of her finest
silky perfumed breeze and I want it to take me to
wherever it is going in this hurry that leaves me
wanting more.
　　Sarah Weidinger

Love Is the Only Thing That Is Real

To my good friend, Angela Hess
Love is the only thing that is real,
Because love always helps me feel.
Feel the happiness that's within,
Within my heart and soul, but I'll always feel what's in,
All of what's in my entire heart,
They're all together, and not at all apart, together as one,
But as it real, it will never be done.
It will always go on forever,
And as long with does, it will end never.
　　Jeff Goble

Hopelessly Lost

Dedicated to those who've suffered from divorce
Questions roam through her mind
All the answers she may never find
This emotional ladder she continues to climb
Wanting to live a normal life seems to be a crime

Everything is pointing at her
This pain she can no longer endure
Searching in the darkness for a key
Her spirit longs to be free
　　April Melvin

Fading Happiness

To Tim, whom I love . . .
The scent of you on your clothes is beginning to fade
but I'll never forget how I felt your strong love inside of me
though now I can only remember the happiness that we once made
because now in the arms of the one I love is just a memory

Pictures of you that will always hold my stare
love letters and poetry that I'll read over and over again
your smiling face that I will never see again and
your sweet voice that I can no longer hear
how sad to know I've lost my life, my love and my best friend

The image of you in my dreams
is how your warm lips used to kiss me awake and
how your soft touch used to cradle me to sleep at night
but how cruel life seems
to take away a love that felt so right

The only love that I could ever know
the only one that could ever make me happy
but slowly as the tears begin to flow
I know that you'll always be alive in this heart inside of me.
　　Amanda Martin

My Stallion

He is like the coming dawn,
racing through field of green,
up and down hills he goes
wandering through the darkness of night.
He is like the rain, when it begins to fall,
always a sight to see.
He never goes off into the woods,
for fear of the watchers in the deep.
Never have you seen a face,
of more loyalty and hope,
like a small boy, wishing to catch a fish.
Never will you find another, as fine and beautiful,
as my stallion.
　　Kirren Dolan

Untitled

As the water and grass are wet, so are my tears I weep for you,
For you have fallen in to be the everlasting night.
Now that you are gone, I must move on, but I will not forget you,
For you had made my life complete.
I know we must part in different worlds now.
As I say goodbye, my tears flow faster than before.
As I say I will miss you, my friend,
I know you will never leave me in soul but in sight.
So as say I will see you in another day,
you kiss my cheek and float away.
As I will miss you, my friend, I know
you will never leave me in soul but in sight.
So as say I see will you in another day,
you kiss my cheek and float away.
As you float away, you say I will love you.
The last tears fall to the ground in sadness.
　　Linda Rice

Friendship

Friendship is a very special thing.
It is rare to find—
That true kind of friendship.
You can find that fair weather friendship anywhere
Many people think
That true kind of friendship
Is so easy to find. . . .
That may or may not be true, but—
It took me until I was ten
To find out what a true friend is.
I am now fifteen, and we are still like sisters.
Friendship is indeed a very special thing.

Melissa Ramsden

My Star, My Love

You were like my star, my one and only love.
You told me that you love me,
You told me that you cared.
You lied to me about that,
and all that we have shared.
I told you all my secrets,
all I had to bare.
Then you weren't around and told them,
how could you ever dare?
You told me I was special,
and made me feel like someone,
then you turned it all around,
and made me feel like no one.
You were like my star, my one and only love.

Amber Ellison

The End

I see complete chaos.
Fire and brimstone shower the land.
All you hear is the screaming of man.

As the flood pours in,
chunks of earth sink into the sea.
Dear Lord! What will the world come to be?

Babies crying . . . people dying.
Natural disasters come in a hurry,
all examples of nature's fury.

People begin to drop like flies
as plagues begin spreading far and wide
from Earth's end to the other side.

Demon and saint fight to the death,
but God will conquer and spirits will rise.
Then, once again, peace will reside.

There will be no more pain,
no more hunger, and no more fear.
Once again, paradise will be here.

Jennifer J. Passmore

The Rose

There was a seed planted when we first met.
Over the years we would not let the youngness
of the flower hold it down.
While tragedy and calamity lurked all around.
Nothing could stop it, not even storms.
All it needed was care and warmth.
Through all this is continued to be
a magnificent sight for all to see.
Was it destined to happen?
Nobody knows.
All that is seen now is a

Tyler Seth Kazee

Not Welcome Here

I see you every now and then,
every time with a new "friend."
We never talk, we never touch,
I guess to you I don't mean that much.
You tell me you love me, then say goodbye,
And it seems you don't care whenever I cry.
My life with you is full of one night stands,
Why don't you face the truth and be a man.
I can't go on with your stories and lies,
Now it's my turn to say goodbye.
This time I mean it, am I being clear?
After tonight you're not welcome here.
It's my turn to live the life I want to live,
And this time the heartache is mine to glue.
It's my turn to talk and your turn to listen,
And tonight when you sleep it's the pillow you'll be kissin'.
'Cause it's my turn to give the heartache and pain,
To take away your sun and live you with rain.
So tonight when you're alone and want someone near,
Just remember, you're not welcome here.

Tonya M. Bragdon

Mommies

Mommies are sweet.
Mommies are nice.
Mommies cook things with sugar and spice.
Mommies love and adore.
Mommies give love more and more.
Mommies tell what's good and bad.
Mommies give love I've never had.
Mommies give love from far away.
Mommy's arms is where I'll stay.

Virtré Sterling

Untitled

Something so strange, so tender,
feelings so hard to explain,
Emotions no man can hinder,
In no way simple or plain.

Sitting here wondering and worrying,
With ups and downs like a mountain,
And every day I'm learning,
Feelings spill out like a fountain.

Not knowing where to begin,
But wanting to get it out,
Knowing there isn't an end.
Trying to hold my voice, so I don't shout

Everybody is filled with these,
Pain you feel but nobody sees

Juton Sorrells

Grandma

I still see it clearly in my mind,
The day you told me not to cry.
You said, "Sweetie, soon I will be gone,
But for your mother, please stay strong
And each day, move a little further on."

I remember it like it was yesterday,
The day they told me you had passed away.
So many tears and so much sorrow,
With people hoping for a better tomorrow.

You were so sick, but had so much pride;
The sicker you got, the more you tried.
And I will remember that about you,
Until the day comes when I must go
And leave all the people
That loved me as much as "I love you."

Cristina M. Stanley

Untitled

You said you'd always be there.
You said you were my friend,
We were inseparable, best friends until the end.
But then I suppose you changed your mind
Because you weren't always there and
You left me stranded alone when I needed you to care.
I wish you could see what you've done to me,
My life an emotional roller coaster.
My heart aches from all the pain you caused.
Sure it still aches but I will grow stronger
and I will feel better.
For I now have a new friend,
and we are inseparable, best friends until the end.

Alyssa Prete

Untitled

What happened to our love,
it was so strong
I miss what we used to share
the times when we would sit and stare
You always said that we would be together forever
Whatever happened to our forever
In my vision our forever is gone
If to only exist
Was our love
I would be so happy
When you left it scared me
Our love used to flow
Like a river so deep and peaceful
When I see you my heart melts
I wish everything could flow
Smoothly again
I wish we were a couple
My heart is so empty
Would you please help me fill it?

Kheonna Corene Treon

Deep Inside of Me

You might say inside of me are blood and guts,
but inside of me is my heart.
My heart is big and pumping hard.
I don't know if I can keep up with it, it's so fast.
Deep and dark they lurk inside,
the feelings of love and comfort,
here they come urging to come out from their hiding place.
Yes, I have bones, muscle, and skin,
but I often talk to my helpful friend,
he lives deep inside of me.
My conscience is shy and keeps to himself.
He never comes out of his little house.
When I have a problem I dig deep inside
because I hope to find a friend that can help.
My heart, my conscience, and my feelings too
Always can tell me what to do.

Shannon N. Stephens

Dreams

Dreams—what are dreams?
Are they what you won't ever get
But would love to have?
Are they the things
You picture in your mind while sleeping?
Are you a dreamer?
Am I dreamer?
No matter how you look at it,
We all are dreamers!
In one way or another, we all will dream!
So go ahead and dream!

Bobbie R. Taylor

Fantasm

I never saw the fantasm or the glory in your greatness
fight through love's song
all the while hating us
soon enough was too late
now missing what we never really had
to miss out on the shining
in forever's end
bestow the beauty on trusting
that love finds an empty soul
never fill the black
with someone else's colors
we never meant to let go
but we never really had
so tomorrow's sight is glory
I'm living in the fantasm

Carissa McCabe

Memories

Days pass, things will change.
Nothing ever stays the same.
People come and people go,
Like the summer sun and the winter snow,
Born, are we, into this world
many things happen if our fates unfurled
There will be people to break our hearts,
Tear up our souls and rip dreams apart.
Then there are some who carry us when
Our lives fall apart and our hearts won't mend.
They hold and care and love us until
Our hearts are full and our lives are still.
I stop to look back and see you there.
I know you're with me, I know you care.
There are my footprints, stable and true,
Stretching back to the horizon, but where are you?
You've become a thought kept safe in my dreams,
I see you now in the sunshine and beams,
Your face in my prints, clear and sublime.
Memories are footprints in the sands of time.

Karen Mickschl

Untitled

You're my knight in shining armor
The hero of my world
When you smile at me I see a true fire burn
I feel magic each time we touch
Just like Bonnie belonged to Clyde
You can stay prepared I won't let you die
In the heat of the night
Our lips will touch
And our world will become one.

Jenn Braun

The Clouds

Turn away from our reflections
Look past our troubles and sorrows
Are our actions intended,
Or do we act upon our "dreams" of tomorrow?
Let me rest for one more dream
I want just one more kiss from our skies
So I can see through the seams
That lie within all our diversified eyes
Do we hide behind our own subterfuge,
or are we so misled we cannot see the difference?
That changes our lies into truth,
and ruins our intelligence.
Life does become our inner self
To one may not yet be known
Until the day when one discovers
Ourselves are not our own.

Michelle Wisdom

Shades of Our Love

Dreams are made for dreamers;
Stars are made to shine.
You weren't made for Heaven;
You were made to be all mine.
Our love will last forever,
And our memories will never fade.
There is no color to describe us
Because we blend a brand-new shade.

The white is for eternity,
Blue is for the sea.
The black will be the emptiness
If you should ever leave me.
Yellow is for our happiness,
Pink just for me,
And a little bit of that color red
For all the feeling and words left unsaid.

Can you not see, we were meant to be,
Because memories never fade,
And like no one else,
Only we blend a new shade.

Christy Lawson

Goodbye

It's hard to say goodbye to all the things held inside,
But to my heart I must be true,
And it's telling me to let go of you.
The pain and suffering you gave me,
Oh, please somebody save me.
My love I gave to you from my soul,
But's been my heart that you've stole.
For years we've been together,
I can't imagine life if we were apart.
But I must say goodbye,
I realize now, you've never treated me right.
If you would have I'd stay by your side.
It's hard to say farewell to the one thing that was so sacred to me.
But I've made my choice to finally go.
So goodbye, I love you—no.
Maybe one day you'll be sorry.
Maybe one day we'll see,
But now you need to stay away from me.
Love for you I have no more
So goodbye, farewell, forever more.

Patricia Perez

Dream

To my mom, I love you through good and bad
Two eyes looking at me,
as I look back.
This great and wonderful feeling I
feel all over my body.
My soul is free,
as my heart slowly stops pumping.
I daze off into a sky so dark
with stars so bright,

I'm floating,
no one can see me,
no one can hurt me,
but then a loud pounding sound
from below strikes me,
and right then and there I wake up,
I do not see those two beautiful eyes staring at me,
it was all a dream,
and I'm back into this world,
with a broken heart . . .
I wish I could go back to that place in the sky,
where I felt so good with no pain.

Rebecca Tautimer

Nightmare

Dark and stormy I open my eyes and you're not there
I remember what happened, I feel all the pain
In remember the crash, I remember the rain
After the dance you said you wanted our love to last
We started driving away, we couldn't see it all happened too fast
The ambulance, the police, and you right beside me
But now where are you, where could you be
What the doctor said couldn't be true
It had to be a mistake, it couldn't be you
My whole life flashed before my eyes
I remember all the hellos but no goodbyes
I remember the way you held me tight
All through the day and all through the night
It must have been a nightmare
'Cause I can still smell the sweet scent of your hair
Its brushing across my cheek always made me knees go weak
Helping people and smiling all the time
I thanked God you were all mine
You always told the truth never a lie
Why were you the one to die

Mellissa Pettyjohn

Dreaming and Nightmares

Dreaming is a nice thing in our heads.
Nightmares are a thing that we dread.
Both may happen day or night.
One is nice while the other's a fright.
Dreaming is a nice thing in our heads.
Nightmares are a thing that we dread.
I like one while I hate the other.
I dream about a soon-to-be lover.
I scream about a nightmare about killing my brothers.
Dreaming is a nice thing in our heads.
Nightmares are a thing that we dread.

Amanda Hoerner

Shadow

A shadow appears over a lake.
A shadow so familiar
of a man from the past.
Haunting my room.
Why can't my feelings pass?
A shadow of memories follows me
when I look out the door.
Sitting next to the shadow
As I looked up at the stars.
Wondering if the shadow is looking at them afar.

Walking towards the water
makes me remember the night on the dock.
The world was ours as we talked 'til it was time to stop.
He then walked me to the door of my room.
I didn't know that was the end
but the shadow does not leave,
and still follows me to the end.

Jen Adas

Dance with the Angels

Dance into the darkness with the angels and I,
Listen to their whispers and follow me to the sky.
Grasp my hand and follow me straight through,
I'll bring you to a world you never knew.
I'm addicted to your love, please hold on tight,
Don't ever let go, as we dance into the night.
Kiss me and hold me like you never did before,
I look into your eyes and realize there's nothing I want more.
Let's forgive each other for everything we've done wrong,
And let's dance with the angels to their never-ending song.

Jessica Rosen

Keep Away

Keep yourself far away from me;
Keep your words to yourself.
Keep your discussion too;
Keep your breath.
Keep all your charms away.

Keep your expectations to yourself;
Keep your photographs.
Keep the stars and the moon;
Keep your autographs.
Keep your heart from abounding into mine.

Keep your hands far far away;
Keep your lips from touching mine.
Keep your cry's and tears from upsetting me;
Keep your fears from scaring me.
Keep your eyes from looking into mine;
I do not want to fall into your arms again.
So don't speak to me; I don't want to love you anymore.

Margaret Heggan

Life

What is greater than a breath
of life from a single infant on this Earth?
It is the tree that gives the oxygen
chopped into kindling for the hearth.

Jessica Champion

Standing on Perfection

In which we stand together as a whole or
a thought or a perfect sphere
as if we were merged together
for survival and we were,
but the world has fallen
and now we stand as one.
Some struggle in packs or couples.
They strive to be pulled out
of the burning flames of life.
We have been forsaken and we are too far
to repent and too emotional to open your soul.
So with that we must forgive the unforgivable
and forget the unforgettable
and that would probably be the beginning
of a more perfect mankind.

Hope Woodworth

A Metaphor

A whiplash to my head,
as my heart feels dead.

Yet I feel so alive,
I know is can also revive.

A spell is cast upon my soul,
I know no remedy can ever pull.

Yet it is a wonder,
all I could do without it is blunder.

It has such grace,
like that of a loving face.

My mind can float,
as if love was a river and my heart a boat.

This boat I call home,
it is so free it just lets me roam.

Until that day when I see him face to face,
then must use the anchor and call upon all my grace.

Our hearts will merge,
peace, love, and happiness will suddenly surge.

Megan Reinke

Free

I feel I am on a leash.
To see all the free things around me.
To see the wind whipping through the bare, fragile trees.
To see the water run through the hard, cold Earth.
The leash is getting tighter.
To see the children in the park. So carefree.
The leash is intolerable now. Choking.
To see the eagle soar through the grey skies.
I am not free.
But wait.
The trees nor wind are free.
The leash is getting looser.
The children and eagles are no more free as I.
The leash is getting looser still.
We are all the same, really.
I am now
free.

Jennifer Stacy

Untitled

I love someone who doesn't love thee
that I know loves someone but me

He loves a close friend but to me
if he doesn't love thee then it's the end

On my own I think of him and every time
in my mind it seems he loves thee
but when I wake up it's just in my dreams

Thinking of him makes me sad
When I see him with another it makes me mad

But I know he's happy so I'm fine
but still I wish that he was mine

Forever I love him and forever he's fine
but until the time I will make do
without a true love that is mine

As I dream again
I wonder if the dream will come soon
'cause if it does I will wait 'til noon
when I see my true love
my only man in the world and sit there hopin'
that he will come soon

Rachael Klein

River of Motherhood

A translucent river
That only the blessed may see,
A God-given gift
That's just for me.

A blessing so phenomenally miraculous,
Yet so clearly in evidence.
A priceless token of eternal love
And years of passing reminiscence.

Something that is more fragile than glass,
A keepsake that will always be mine.
A little piece of perfection
Within nine months' time.

God has managed to make a new life
Inside my spiritless body of squander.
But why he gave me the greatest gift,
In my heart—I will always ponder.

To be part of the river of motherhood,
Which is only for the chosen few,
And to swirl in its waves of glory,
Is the best thing any woman could do!

Charlene Rose

I Wonder

I wonder if he ever thinks . . .
   about our times gone past.
I wonder if he ever wishes . . .
   that we would be again.
I wonder if he has lonely nights . . .
   like I've had since then.
I wonder if he cries sometimes . . .
   over thoughts of our loss.
I wonder if he misses what we had . . .
   the beginning of a new life.
I wonder if he knows how he made me feel . . .
   the overwhelming joy when his voice met mine.
I wonder if he ever ponders . . .
   of what would happened "this" time.
I wonder if I meant everything to him . . .
   as he was my everything.
I wonder if he ever thinks . . .
   about our time we had.
I wonder if he wonders of the future . . .
   and what we could have had.

   Doreen Moore

Priceless

Roses are red violets are blue;
you are my sweetheart and I will always love you.
As the sun goes down our love
will wither away like a rose gone bad;
you will no longer be mine
for God will take you with him.
Save a kiss for me, for I will be there.
I feel you, cold as my heart, as I hear your voice;
don't cry, my love, for one day we will be together.
Your love is priceless, so is the last kiss we shared.
take this to Heaven, my love.
God will know that you are my guardian angel.

   Chenika Hurt

The Way of Our Time

For my family
Homeless old people living in the streets
while in dark, dreary corners, abused children weep.
Whores and their mongers passing fatal disease,
The young running wild, doing as they please.

Homosexuals no longer bear any shame,
as they fill their quest of sexual gain.
Rich TV evangelist tell us not to sin;
how many hearts wax cold all because of them?

Men of our government committing their crimes,
cling to the dread in their hearts of the skeletons we'll find.
Adult secrets lay twisted in innocent minds,
as good adult morals fade with the times.

Today we call this the human race.
We have forgotten the judgment our souls will face.
As woe fills my heart, and tears blind my sight,
will God ever forgive the wrongs never made right?

   Serena L. Sizemore

Spring

For Mom and Dad
The flowers are rising from their willowness
And are getting warmed in the sunlight.
When they are in a group together,
They look like a field of dreams.
Every day it happens,
But it starts to get colder and they go back to being willow
And covered with leaves and snow.

   Krystal Huston

God Is Always There

I felt as if no one was there, and I was falling fast,
until I got some caring advice, that I should not live in the past.
How I ever thought there was no God I'll never know,
when his whole point up there is to make his love show.
I figured out he was always there
and that it was my love that wouldn't share.
When you turn your back on God, he never leaves you alone;
he has no reason to give a reward so his love is not shown.
So next time you feel there's no God around,
seek him and he will be found.
Many people have gone through stuff,
and we sometimes don't realize it's so tough.
One thing goes wrong in our perfect lives,
and we all seem to reach for the knives,
which I have realized has no point;
instead, Jesus' feet is what we should anoint.
He has done so much for us,
and all we ever seem to do is fuss
on how our life is so unfair,
when people who have it worse, always seem to share.

   Jennifer Foster

You Hold My Heart

Dedicated to Gabriel Mario Cornejo with love
Night and day I think of you,
Oh, darling if you only knew.
There's a special place in my heart,
that only you could break apart.
I pray that you hold it close,
I hope you cherish it the most.
Every beat is meant for you
and it begins to race when I'm with you.
What I feel,
I know it's real.
It's not a game or make-believe,
please don't be one to deceive.
Every moment that passes by
I can't help, but to have you on my mind.
Give me a sign show me you care,
let me know you'll always be there.
For in your hands you hold my heart,
the piece of which you will always be a part.

   Judy Acevedo

A Song of Praise

I entered into this realm of life
With an able body, a survivor,
Fighting through this vale of tears,
Distraught by my own doubts and
Spiritual chaos filling my soul
With confusion of whom I am.

As the pieces of my life fit together,
One by one, I realize that iniquity
And humility will enlighten and
Strengthen me, bringing me closer
To you, my Lord, my God.

The trinity as a whole has one purpose,
Enlightening my soul to reality.
A new reality, not of my younger years;
Clearing my conscience to truth deceiving
Not the true means of peace to my soul.

Praise thee, Dear Lord, for the Holy Spirit
Has touched my inner vessel, introducing
Your great love and light, life-everlasting.

   Jeri Klausner

Why

You promised to be here
You promised to stay
And they wonder why I was so surprised
When you went away.
I was shot in the heart when you took your last breath
I didn't know it was you,
I didn't know it was your death
An innocent soul lost someone so pure
Why couldn't they have found a cure now it's too late
And you've already died
I just want to run away and hide
You were the one who brightened my day,
Why did you have to leave and go so far away
I'll love you forever and in my heart
We will always be together

Nicole Sullivan

Dance

The light, the grace,
the feeling of flying.

It's hard, but when you give it your all,
you rise to your full height,
the sight to see is a beautiful one.

You point your toe
and stand up tall,
for those to look up to:
Mikhail Baryshnikov and Agnes de Mille.

The confidence comes from you,
the freedom it gives,
and all the sore muscles and all the strife.

With thanks to those there for you,
who push you to the max.

It's a dancer's paradise.
It's ballet.

Lee Ann Frye

A Leader

The wind hits me hard in the face,
and makes my lips bitter and tense,
yet I keep pushing, harder and harder.
My legs are being pounded with hammers
and sore badly but I keep walking forward.
I stop and regain my consciousness, that I never lost.
Fists are banging at my back
and keep going until I take the wrong step and fall,
with hope, forever.

Mira Kohl

Artistic Dream

To my beloved father Dennis
The ocean is calm,
The breeze caresses my hair.
I mount on the thick piles of sand,
And dream the afternoon away.

I picture kids laughing and playing,
Dogs barking, then I hear you.

Your voice seems to flow in the wind.
As the breeze passes me I hear it once more.
Remember, remember.

I then close my eyes
And start to dream about before.
While the tide roles in and runs,
Over the tips of my toes.

Shannon Orr

Promises

To Jeff Wright, my love always
Promises were made to be broken,
But not all end up that way.
What you know you can't keep should never be spoken,
Especially the words, I'll always stay.
When the going got tough, you left me alone,
With only hate and fear to call my own.
You promised you loved me, but I've heard that one before,
This time it was different, I thought I was so sure.
So sure that you were different from everyone else,
I wanted my heart to believe,
Believe that you loved me and that you would never leave.
The words you said were so sweetly spoken
But like I said, promises were made to be broken.

Samantha Brierley

Eternal Remembrance

Dedicated to the memory of Tupac Shakur
Think of the sun,
We never saw set.
Dream of the love,
You'll probably forget.
Remember the days,
When nothing mattered more.
And if our last words have been spoken
Know my heart is forever broken.
But not surprised for the these are the days of our lives.
Never promised a prize, so I'll dry my eyes.
But still I can't forget it,
Although I thought it would never end.
And I know you will protect it,
'Cause it has no other friend.
So it's safe inside, others do not know.
But we do,
And they did
But ashes don't disappear, even in the wind.

Kristina Bartolo

President

George Washington, Bill Clinton, and all the ones between;
they are all a part of our country's special team.
They all led to great extents;
now the new will follow in their prints.
They lead us through all the wars,
and open up our future's doors.
They are Presidents old and new,
leading for the red, white, and blue.

Heather Whitt

It Shouldn't Be True

Sitting here thinking of you
Wishing yesterday wasn't true
You didn't deserve the pain
For you did nothing wrong
You were the sweetest kid around
You loved to play and joke around
You're in my prayers and thoughts all day
If only I can see you again someday
Christopher, my brother, if only you were here
I wouldn't be shedding so many tears
You're up in Heaven happily
Flying around with so much glee
You're safe and sound, I wish I could be around
To tell you how much you mean to me
Thoughts of you are on my mind,
If only mom could say everything is fine
I don't understand why it had to be you
You were only ten with a life ahead of you
This poem is especially for you
Because yesterday isn't supposed to be true

Teagin Tracey

Untitled

As a proud, wild stallion breaks loose from all that binds him,
The braided ropes and heavy chains tumbling from his broad back,
Slithering and winding down his slender legs like snakes,
Before his mighty hooves trample them
and leave in the dust as he takes off,
His long, black mane a rippling in the wind, his flanks
Begot of fluid grace, exquisite harmony and steel,
His skin a tapestry of gleaming dark decadent song
Himself without a care to all the world for he is free . . .
So lovely did her golden laughter sound.

Liza Strakhov

Sunset

I walk along the shore
Gazing at the sunsetting sky
And wonder to myself,
What, where, when, and why?

What exactly is a sunset,
Other then the sun setting?
Where is the sun going to—
France, or settling in the meadow's bedding?

When does it go down
At 6:30, does it disappear?
Why does it call to the night
Every day, every year?

These are a mere few
Of the questions in my head
That I try to find the answers for,
Until I decide to just look instead.

Purple, red, orange, and yellow
Are the colors of the sky.
And as I gaze at them, I wonder,
What, where, when, and why?

Amy Baughman

What Is a Mountain Morning in My Eye

A silvery stream trickling by,
A newborn bird learning to fly.
The mist on a field of wheat,
The scent of the wildflowers, so sweet,
The ears of a fox, strolling through the field,
The wise old duck, he knows when to yield.
As I cut a slice of pie,
I am able to say, "This is a mountain morning in my eye."

Linsay Lemke

Loving Hate

My anger boils up inside me.
I can feel my soul
fading to a new evil.
I'd been scared before,
but those were childish fears.
They pale in comparison
to the fear I now have inside.
My soul is crying,
thirsty for one ounce
of a forgotten love from the man
who invokes a whirlwind
of anger, pain, hate, love and depression.
I hate him with as much passion
as I love him.
The lights a deep and ferocious fire
somewhere within my heart.
I can't stop it,
and I don't know that I want to.

Tiffany Lovisone

The Small Child's Cry

To the people I love
The glittering dew of a mid-summer's night
Is often the cause of many a fright.

The dew is set back, looks up to the night sky.
The tears, they rush down, the small baby cries.

The trembling, shaking of the earth's rocky cover,
The crying is heard—in rushes its mother.

The cracks, the dents of nature's great quake.
The child is held, but still does it shake.

The dew still set back looks up to the stars.
The baby settles down, but now, it is scared.

Kellie Gleeson

Lisa Lynn

Love has never meant as much as it does now with you.
Introspection now reveals what I have always known as truth.
Sacred is your love to me, my heart once wild now tame.
And life for me with you not there could never be the same. . . .
Looking back in retrospect, our love was meant to be.
You needed me, I needed you—it's just so plain to see.
Naked is my soul to you, my walls came tumbling down.
Nirvana's what I'm feeling 'cause my queen now wears her crown.

Olander G. Jones

Me

Caught in the voice of my silence
There's no words I can speak,
My heart is very lonely
knowing there's better out there to seek.

My life is very miserable
I haven't found point in it yet,
Looking to find better
Than just take what you can get.

I am treated very different
But among them I'm the same,
Not treated like the family
But like if I was insane.

They think I may be crazy
And maybe a little dumb,
Because they can't see I'm hurting
Not wanting to go on.

I've tried explaining how I feel
But still I can't make them see,
That all I need is someone
Who will come and set me free.

Amelia Gonzalez

You Do

Another's lips can touch my face
Or hold me in their sweet embrace,
But no one can charm me with their style and grace
Like you do.

Another's arms can hold me tight
And keep me safe all through the night,
But no one knows how to hold me just right
Like you do.

I can't explain it,
But my heart can tell
If it's you there
Or someone else.

No one can warm me with their touch
Or help me when I need a crutch
Or even love me just as much
As you do.

Kodi Green

True Love

For my loving mom
Love is life and happiness but sometimes it's farewell
for you have lost a loved one or gone on the carousel.
I've never been in true love before;
they say it will knock down my door.
I don't try to search and search
because true love is no more.
The love you feel inside yourself,
ignore with all your might;
if you get married, I guarantee a fight.
I've lived through them all through my life;
it even once involved a knife.
When I get married someday to come,
I will find a person who doesn't drink or use a gun.
I want a man who's not that dumb.

Nina D. Gutierrez

To the Children of the World

To Lauren Sarah Doherty, my niece
The world is in the palm of your hands,
Grab hold of it, and do all you can.
Make it a better place,
With more love, peace and faith.
Faith in others and yourselves.
Forget that nonsense about power and wealth.
Together my children we can achieve more.
Don't ever be afraid to let your dreams and aspirations soar.

Sarah Hann

Autumn

As the green trees turn to a dark red brown
I take one last look at the emerald green ground,
As I gaze around me at the deep blue sky
I pick out figures that I know will not lie.
As I close my eyes and dream of what I want to be
I take a moment's pause to think of all
The wonderful things around me.
To remember that this moment will always be,
A moment in the back of my head known only to me,
As an ordinary autumn day.

Nichole Deppe

Angels among Us

There are some who believe that there are Angels among us
Guardian Angels who take our hand to guide us
Who come to us in our darkest hour
Who enfold us in their wings to protect or comfort us.

There once was a time when I was skeptic
A "Doubting Thomas"
A non-believer.
My reality was limited by my mind and eyesight
Like blinders on a trotter.

I could not see perfection in a child.
I could not see the Divinity that dwells in each of us.

I saw no haloes.
I saw no wings.
Thus, I saw no Angels.

That was a time before I met you.
The scales have since been lifted from my eyes.

I now see with my heart.
And it sees the brilliance of you that shines
Not from a halo but from your very soul.
And it sees unbeknownst to you that you are my Angel.

Roger A. Nowadzky

A Young Boy and His Dad

As Mark McGwire rounded the bases,
Hitting home run No. 61,
His young son, Matthew was waiting, at home plate.
What a lift of joy he received.

This happened labor Day, September 7, 1998.
Matthew flew from California,
To St. Louis, to watch his Dad,
Play ball for the St. Louis Cardinals.

He was also at the Ball Park,
Tuesday, September 8, 1998,
When his Dad Mark McGwire hit,
Home run No. 62.
Memorial days for young Matthew.

What excitement, flash bulbs going off, like fireflies.
Hugs, love sign, compassion, ovations,
Heartfelt sensations across the country.
It was neat how he missed tagging first base,
Went back, stepped on it.

Connie James

Happiness

Happiness! Happiness! Where is it? How do you find it?
One thing is certain: whether you know it or not,
Happiness can be found in glorified rot.

Happiness is not limited to here nor there,
A little bird perched on a limb,
Happiness can be found by him.

Happiness! Happiness! What is it? How is it?
Whatever it's not limited to here.
Happiness can be found in distant Rome;
It can also be found in the home.

Happiness! Happiness! You can't see nor smell it.
Happiness, I'm thankful, we can feel.
Happiness, though intangible, it is real.

Success in finding happiness and rest
Can be found after we've past a solemn test
And gone to rest on Jesus' breast.

Rev. Theodore Walker

Birthday

Mom, you are a special friend, one I love and treasure
You are always there to help, caring is a pleasure

You comforted my sorrow and took away my pain
Through all the tears and laughter, in sunshine and in rain

I know that I've not always shown how much I care for you
But as the years keep passing, more clearly is it true

That mothers are a special breed, they're good and pure and kind
I love my mother dearly in my heart, my soul, and mind

So happy birthday, Mother, I hope that you can tell
How much I miss and love you, how much you mean as well

Although I know it's never too late
I hope you know I think you're great

Deborah J. Webb

Shimmering Winter

Sharp icicles shimmering in the moonlight skylight.
Cool ice that is fresh as a snowflake.
Chilly penguins in search of food.
Wintry snowflakes gleam in the moonlight starlight.
Warm polar bears drink icy water to keep them cool.
Freezing ice cubes melt in the sunlight.

Thomas Hoffa

Up on the Mountain with God

To Debbie, Danny, Michael, and Vanessa
I love to go up on the mountain away up high
And watch the clouds of the Heaven go sailing by
It seems that I'm so close to God I could reach out and touch His hand
As I breathe in the fragrance of evergreens so grand.
Although I may not touch Him actually I feel so much at peace
And all around I see the proof that His love will never cease.
I get a glimpse of Heaven when I'm up on the mountain so high,
At least the Heaven that I'd want with its beautiful azure sky.
Nothing could be more beautiful than a towering forest so green.
Oh, what a yearning touches my heart when I survey such a scene.
God must really love the world to give us beauty so rare.
How could anyone ever doubt that He could really care?
Well, anyway, the way I feel when I'm up on the mountain with Him,
He makes me feel so very good that I'm filled with vigor and vim.
I want to shout to all the world, "God created this beauty for you.
He wanted to show us all what it's like to live in peace so true.
Oh, won't you come and view it, this beauty, oh, so rare.
In all this Earth there's nothing finer for you and I to share."
The evening falls, the stars come out and my head begins to nod.
Oh, what soothing peace divine when I'm up on the mountain with God.

    Ethel M. Pocius

Back in Time

How to travel back in time is ever eluding man and
the why of this seems strange to me for I go oft as I can.
The constant tinkling of the chimes can always cast a spell,
from there I go just any place where I may choose to dwell.

No need to rush, as time for me is standing very still.
I can come and go for free and always at my will.
No ticket to buy no flight to catch, nothing for me to lose,
no bags to pack no room to hold just a place for me to choose.

In a flash I'm back in time and walking at my own pace,
with all the ones that lived right there and meeting them face to face.
A fear have I of going back home where everyone I knew,
for if by chance I met myself, whatever would I do?

To switch a twilight time of life for one of an early day,
would ever tempt us humans so, we might just want to stay.
Some from the present would choose life in the past,
and some back there would be here ever so fast.

And since our world is burdened in these fast moving times,
it's best not to add more trouble, more strife and more crimes.
So for the sake of all mankind, I'll never reveal the key,
as traveling back in time it seems, could cost too great a fee.

    Lela L. Carter

The New Year

This is the new year of 1999.
I know not what will happen, but I trust everything will be fine.
Whether or not the weather is dim or bright, each day will come,
Filled with surprise or the same old humdrum.
Living eighty plus years, many experiences I've had,
Whether young or old, I am no nomad.
I've used oil lamps, then electricity, the telephone, and radio, too,
As a child to the neighbors' I went,
listening to radio programs, only a few.
Now, we have televisions in several of our rooms,
And the programs we watch, the joy everyone assumes.
To top it all off, computers are in vogue.
Some meet a mate, it matters not which brogue.
Traveling has become a matter of a race.
Whether to the moon, or Mars, they may be in space.
As I look back on my very long life,
Experiences I've had, were mostly free from strife.
I've looked to God, and He has surely directed me.
Every morning, noon, or night, His answers I do see.

    Evelyn Wright

Sage Advice

Silver sage
Shows its age
When it whispers
Wise warnings
To the wind.

Wildflowers—
Newly bloomed—
Bend and sway
In errant breezes,
Oblivious to the
Sage advice.

Naive,
They embrace
The possibilities of
Spring—
Ignorant
That Winter
Waits
Stealthily
Just over the horizon.

    Kimberly Taylor Carmo

Wells of Living Waters

From my wells of living waters,
I drew my bucket up,
and through a heart of kindness,
I gave each one a cup.

The nourishment of living waters,
It's not ours to keep.
It's to quench the thirsty pilgrims,
Wherever we chance to meet.

There are many thirsty children,
along this road we trod.
Let your wells be flourishing,
and let them drink from the word of God.

There are many rivers of water,
and streams that overflow,
but there's nothing like the wells,
within-us so let the living waters flow.

If we satisfy the needy,
the hungry and appressed,
Your wells of living waters,
I'm sure will do the rest.

    Gladys Reed

My Heavenly Favorite

Luscious white chocolate
So rich, so smooth
Luscious white chocolate
I desire you
One taste of you
makes me crave for more
Luscious white chocolate
How I adore
Your smooth creamy texture
Melt in your mouth pleasure
Such heavenly flavor within
Luscious white chocolate
So tempting, so sweet
My desire for you
is so innate
Luscious white chocolate
So rich, so smooth
Luscious white chocolate
I desire you

    Eileen Linda Williams

Inner Conflict

Battle between good and evil, I try to do what's right,
but here's Satan weaseling his way into my life.

There is a constant inner war,
no one keeps score of who's winning,
but the ultimate sacrifice is your soul.
See our flesh is slave to sinning,
but the mind has control.

It may be difficult to comprehend, but listen to the message I send.
The conflict within is because we were born in sin.
The law of God is spiritual and can overcome
all the things that you feel compelled to do
when you know they aren't good for you.

Snorting a line, smoking a joint, or having a drink or two.
That ain't cool, The Lord has bigger plans for you.

He can remove the weakness of the flesh
and fill your heart with pure happiness.
All He wants you to do is confess
that you believe in Him and you will be blessed.

Then the inner conflict will cease and you will be released
from the slavery of sin and begin to feel an inner peace.

Metokie E. Brim

Mother

It would be wonderful if everyone could have a mother like mine
She gives unconditional love and is there for you all of the time
She is not only your mother, she is your best friend
No one could ask for a better blend

Whenever I was sick I always called for my mother
She always got up for me, my sister or a brother
It didn't matter what time of the day or night
She stayed with you until you were feeling all right

My mother has a great sense of humour, likes to laugh and have fun
She used to take us to the beach when we were kids to play in the sun
She had five of us to watch over and that must have been quite a chore
But she would take us again the next day so we would play on the shore

Growing up there wasn't anything that you could do
That would change her love and understanding for you
She always believed in letting you learn from a mistake
Even though she knew it was wrong, and hard for her to take

My mother is a sweetheart with a heart of gold
Whenever you think of her you never feel cold
She is like a ray of sunshine on a cloudy day
I love my mother more than words can say

Darlene Billett

Angel on Your Shoulder

An angel, on your shoulder sits, your angel, it is the one you've sought.
Like a beacon in the sky, lighting a path for you as your days go by.
Your angel keeps you safe, through and through,
and ever prosperous in all you do.
In making your life bright each day and night,
your angel helps you hold love for all that's in sight.
Holding you near, as you do others, beautiful it is, as it is clear,
and especially for you, those who are dear.
Your family, your friends, everyone else in your presence,
their angel for them, yours for you . . .
All wishes come true, not just for the moment,
but for your entire year through.
Like a sunny day, full of spring air, and just as spring flowers,
having arisen from their sleepy winter beds, your angel keeps you safe,
healthy too, and devotedly watches over you in everything you do.
Helping you enjoy what life has to give,
on your shoulder your angel will sit, until the end of time.
With beauty, grace, and a smile on your face,
true joy in your heart and generosity you embrace,
you'll make the lives of others better, and this world a good place.

Marco Giampetruzzi

Eternity Awaits

Remember, earthly pilgrim,
Eternity awaits
And beckons
And my summon you
Any second.

Depending on whether
You lived well
Or miserably,
Virtuously or sinfully,
You will be compelled,
Inexorably and inevitably,
To finally dwell
Either ecstatic in Heaven
Or tormented in Hell
Forever and ever—endlessly.

Frank Kareiva

Forgiveness

If someone were to ask of me
"What is the greatest sin of all?"
I would say, "It's when your man
takes a sudden fall."

As King David in the Bible
Found another love
Their union wasn't sanctioned
By God from up above

And when you find them out
It hurts without a doubt
Hold steadfast to your course
As the pain in you does mount

And when it is over
Was but a fleeting thing
Your husband comes back to you
You must forgive them both
And peace to you
This will bring

Mary Rozanna Allensworth

Cardinal in the Snow

When winter's snow begins to fall,
Covering leaves grass and all,
Plants and nuts still in the shell;
Beckon a Cardinal come
And dine quite well;
His brilliant red feathers
Against a background of white,
Create a portrait of beauty
Lasting well into night.

Marry Kennington

Rhyme and Haiku Medley

Bold rooster, strutting in the sun
I would love to stroke you, shining one!

O lofty cedar, enduring tree
You symbolize eternity!

Fog bank lifting, storm clouds shifting
No play, boys, 'til chores are done!

Horse fly, loud with wrath on window pane
You must learn to land more softly.

What impulse brought you down
Old eagle, soaring high?
Aloft again too soon
We thrilled to hear your cry!

Dorothy Robinson Sharples

H.I.V.

Over hundreds or thousands of years,
the H.I.V. virus impregnated some West African chimpanzees.
Be it at birth, spread by wounds, scratching, sexual contact, biting, or territorial fights.
Our primates given the advantage to combat this infestation, by bio- or genetic-processes.
Contaminated blood getting into food chain,
because chimpanzees, butchered for meat, quelled human appetites.

As Derek Budell (Director, National AIDS Trust)
stated alarmingly, the vast potential suspected.
Horrific, 16,000 H.I.V. daily new cases,
and worldly, 34 million global confirmed infected.

Has the AIDS virus adapted to the species, or species to the virus AIDS?
The virus remains dormant in chimpanzees now,
urgency beckons, investigate and check by mass screen.
A most recent exciting discovery into AIDS research for the last couple of decades!
Mankind's fragile survival rests upon how to create
a permanent, preventative, or curable vaccine.

Joseph Dobson

Bright Star

Stars are twinkling in the night, lighting the sky above.
Some are shooting across the sky while others are steady light.
The beauty of a clear night sky as with diamonds shining so bright.
Many a traveler has followed the stars mapping our history on their way.
Hours are spent gazing at the sky.
Many a wish has been made on the first star of the night.
Dreams are dreamed with each wish.
I can look into a night sky to find the brightest star.
Better still is to hold a bright star in my arms.
To feel her touch and curling fingers, to plant a kiss on her cheek.
For my bright star is my smallest granddaughter, Maddie!
With star dust falling day and night.

Sophia Simmons Borger

My Dog

Give her one more chance, that's all she needed but maybe not,
She had suffered so long.

She was part of the family since baby up,
And she meant as much.
She may have looked mean that she was as gentle as a kitten.

One the third stroke of illness it seemed so helpless.
All I needed was a little more time.
More time caused suffering and it seemed only right to end it soon.

With just one quick trip to the pound it was ended.
Eight happy years were put to everlasting sleep.
I have never forgotten her yet and I doubt I ever will.
She was the best dog around.

Maybe someday we'll get another and to the rest it will seem just as good,
But I know to me, it will seem a lot different.
Nothing new can take her place. She was the best dog around.

Mary Shoumaker

The Genius

The genius runs and hides from society,
and knowing his own inability to protect himself,
he depends on the most unlikely
and unsuspecting to bring him food.
Unable to relate to his own kind or to any other kind,
the genius is more despised than a Russian soldier wearing
a black fur hat, shiny brass buttons
and clicking, polished, laced, and knotted shiny black boots.
He is sneered at more than a Mexican lad doing
a sombrero hat dance in a steamy, sultry,
muddy tobacco field transplanted into mid-North America.

The genius gifted with everything becomes the object of every sleepy joke
and falls, praying, on the floor at the bottom of the ladder.

Patricia Carolyn Miller

To My Husband

You came out of nowhere,
but stole my heart away.
The kindness in you,
could not be found in another.
You listen to my problems,
help me with my fears,
and wipe away my tears.
You are something I always looked for,
but thought I'd never find.
Now you're here,
standing right in front of me,
lying beside me in bed,
walking with me,
down these once lonely streets.
I hope and I pray,
that you never go away.
But I plead with you,
Please never take your love away.

Lynetta M. Johnson

Island Love

When you first came into my sight
Visions of Mauna Kea I see
A kiss hello invites
A gentle breeze in the feverish sun

My island love
When you speak to me
Only the pounding waves
Of the North shore I hear

And
Your eyes

Hypnotizes me
Ah paradise, Hawaiian style
My soul races through the island chain
Like the great Iniki's wind

Unpredictable, unknown journey
To the ends of the rainbow
Bittersweet aloha

Only
Kuha'o (to stand alone)
Once more

Marion Lacad

A Love That Never Ends

A love that never ends a dream or me
To find a love that never ends
I searched everywhere
But still I could not find
That love that never ends

Then one day a friend showed me
A love that never ends
That love was there for me
A love that never ends
Jesus is that love that never ends
Even though I was a sinner He loved me so

I was told that Jesus
Would love me forever
I found that love never ends

Now that I've accepted Jesus
I have that love that never ends

Jesus loves me, and I Him
I know He will never leave me
He will always love me
Jesus love will never end.

Robert A. Misch

'Tis to Laugh

Nobody listens to the brain damaged
You're talked at instead of to
As for what you say
Nobody really ever believes you

When you do say something true
They wonder where you got it from
It's a miracle anything intelligent
Could form in your brain and come out your tongue

Some people try to examine you
Like you're a specimen under a glass
When you act the least bit different
You're seen as weird, crazy and you wish they'd just kiss your backside

So they tell you that you need help
You must see somebody who has your problem as a specialty
You've discovered however that usually people who are the closest
to a problem are the ones who can't see

Like that shrink everyone wants you to see
The last one I saw was a quack
No one ever believes you when you're disabled
Laugh in their face behind their back

Peter Terry

Brothers

To my very good friend, my brother, may I lend a hand?
Tell me true, are our heads buried in the sand

Years ago, watching sun and cloud, we thought we knew
The secrets of living, only to become bewildered by our own fear.
Steadfast was the rally.

My very good friend, my brother, listen to me, can we be
true to ourselves, and relinquish nothing worth saving.
Old days have gone wherever they belong, but we must go on.

To my very good friend, my brother, listen to me and harken to my plea.
Without change, you may not be free to choose, but changing is difficult.
Fail it and death is quick.
Listen to your spirit and speak with the angels who guide your route.
They guard well for they have been chosen with care.
If you deny this path you may kill yourself and the love I have for you.

As I think of saying goodbye, my heart cries at the loss.
I love you too deeply to let you go.
I beg of you not to destroy yourself,
You need me now, I may need you later.
Let me help you and with God's love we will make a go of it together.

Jean Howard Webster and Michael J. Webster

My Love

When daylight comes and I awake secure and safe and warm,
I feel your body next to mine sheltering from the storm
Of life that boundless breaks in fury over my head,
I count among my blessings your nearness in my bed.

And when the morning sun shines down to quietly erase
The terrifying storm of night, I thankfully embrace
Your strength, the comfort of your arms that sheared from night its dread,
As I awaked this morning to find you shared my bed.

And through the lovely afternoon, the pleasures of the day
Will be more great, because of you the terrors of the play
That threatens all our parts of life will lessen all the while
For through the clouds the sun shines down each time I see you smile.

My love, my heart is in your hands and I am confident
When time has left the tree of life its branches broke and bent,
Still in my heart and soul will be those branches ever new,
For through the sorrow, fear, or pain, your love will see me through.

Carol K. Stolz

Dreamers

Come and dream along with me
He has something for us to see
The windows of Heaven are open wide
Come let us go and look inside
The "Son" lights up that Heavenly place
So bright there's light in every space
The beautiful flowers always in bloom
There are bouquets in every room
Their aroma sweetens all of the air
The colors are as the rainbows flair
The streets of gold all polished bright
Their brilliance adds to the eyes delight
When I am asleep I can see these things
because my God gives me my dreams
And allows me to see this Heavenly sight
And fills my life with great delight

Wilford Robert Godwin

Pixies

In my dreams is where I see
Little pixies flying free
Tiny wings and pointed ears
How I wish that you were here
Little people taking flight
What a joyful magic sight
They live in all the hollow trees
Their clothes are made from autumn leaves
Flower angels from head to toe
They help to make the gardens grow
Trails of stardust left behind
In the morning dew you'll find
Fairytales or fantasy
Such a mystic majesty
What I wouldn't give to see
Little pixies flying free

Jeanine Bowman

The Lie

Their meaning is lost
These words, "I love you"
Tossed about without care
My heart is the cost
Of believing you, too
It's the lie I can't bear

They meant everything
They mean nothing

As the winds do blow
The clouds far away
My faith says, "Goodbye"
To the dreams I did know
I discovered this day
Remains only the lie

Love is the fantasy
Pain is the reality

Rochelle Sharapan

Was I the one
to see you there
standing by that old chair
looking out at the world outside
watching life just fly on bye
not knowing what to do
just standing there
you sat on down
and cried into that chair
worried about a life
that wasn't there

Derrick Buron

David

My heart is yours, for always and forever.
My love is strong and true, and for you alone.
Our friendship is priceless, trust and honesty, is strong between us.
Communication gets messed up, but we love each other,
therefore we make up.
You are my knight in shining armor.
you mean everything to me.
You are my life, my heart, my soul.
I love you, forever.

Susan Rondeau

One Magical Day

When I was all alone without a love to call my own
Without someone there to welcome me home
how did I gain the strength to go on
and endure this meager existence I call my life alone.

There was no one to whisper those special words I long to hear,
I love you my darling, how was your day, I'm glad you're here.

I was so downhearted to be depressed as I was day after day
but until I could meet someone to love, there seemed to be no other way.

I went to work each lonely day, without a goodbye, have a nice day.
No one to think of, to ease the pain the loneliness made.
No one to love, no one to phone,
how to go on facing the drudgery, again to spend a night alone.

I wanted so badly to fall in love.
I dreamt each night of one magical day, the day I meet an angel
to love and for her to love my cares away.

Then one day so brimming with magic,
I felt the love so strong in the air.
She was sitting there with the birds in the park
and the cool mist from the fountain spraying her hair.
Feeling alone and sad, waiting with all her love to share.

Frank Yaccarino

Trapping of the Soul

Trapped in my little,
yet large world of misunderstanding.
Feeling as though no one could understand
the pain and sorrow I have buried deep down inside my soul.
If only they could step inside my corpse, my universe,
the vortex I was so carefully tucked behind.

If only the passion and coldness were locked away in its own silent hell,
within the very depths of their minds.

Heather Long

A Sound of Such a Magniloquent Magnitude

To the stimulant
When I listen, I am floating in a magical dinghy made of snowy white clouds.
Every sweet potato pie harmony is mouth-watering.
As the fun time blossoms, I stop and think back of my first welcoming.
Please stargaze me.
I want to escape.
Your words are streams of happy faces.
Your beats are the nourishment for starvelings.
Ascend me.
Descend me.
Antihistamine me.
Devour me.
I submit to you.
Take me to your leader.
You are my Novocain.
You are my morphine.
Each melodious movement is the benevolence to my multitude of influences.
Thank you, calcium-filled orange juice.
Your explosion reduces my cancerous stress by 100%.

Marty King

Father Damian

He lived among them,
In service to his God,
And service to mankind,
He aided the untouchables,
Passing ships threw them,
Into the surf of the island,
The good Father rescued them,
Made them welcome,
And saw to their needs,
His life was dedicated,
To their comforts,
While they lived their short lives,
Only a few remain, they will live there,
Until their call to Heaven,
The good Father was called,
He contracted their disease,
He lived among them, in service to his God,
On the island of Molokai,
There is a white church,
Dedicated to and named for Father Damian.

Mattie M. Stewart

A Touch of Heaven

God took an angel and blessed it
With his precious love.
He sent this angel to me
Straight from Heaven above.
Her face are as rays of sun shine,
Her eyes are heavenly blue,
Her smiles the sweetest smiles on Earth
Her love so precious too.
To hear her footsteps in the hall
Her little handprints on the wall
Oh, her voice, it sounds so sweet
I thank you God, my life is complete.

Helen L. Link

Lord What You Mean to Me

Lord you are my joy
Lord you are my everything
Lord you are my shepherd
Lord you are my doctor
Lord you are my lawyer
Lord you are my very best friend
Lord you are my everything
Thank you Jesus
Lord you are my minister
Lord you are my listener
Lord I can tell you my secrets
Lord you are my counselor
Lord you hear and answer my prayers
Lord you are still working miracles
Lord you may not come when I call;
But you are always on time
Thank you for being my God
Thank you for never leaving me alone
Lord thank you for always being on time
For being an on time God

Sylvia L. Wilborns

Tears

Tears fall as rain
with sorrow and pain.
But you, oh, Lord
can wipe my tears away.

I just called your name
and to my side you came.
You held me tight
all through the night
and wiped my tears away.

Amanda Parker

NYC 101

For Valerio—for showing me how naive I really was
I needed something more than small town life, but I didn't know where to look.

Accidentally, I found you and the destination that would be mine.

Instead of taking your words with a grain of salt, I absorbed them as Gospel.
Idiot.

You introduced me to the city I had dreamed of—more beautiful than I could've imagined.

But only an outer shell, covering the filth that lies below—
Deception, Greed, and a lack of honesty or compassion.

I gave you my trust, my friendship, and my love—unconditionally—
only to have you laugh in my face at what a fool I was.

You told me I was your best friend and nothing would ever come between us—
but my small town values and your New York Attitude tore us apart.

Never have I seen such a heartless place where people are so cold and uncaring.

Poor, naive girl from Ohio—Welcome to the bright lights of the Big City.

Ramona Miller

The Way West

Young people, old people, always on the move.
By wagon or horseback or walking hand in hand.
By the heat of the day or the light of the moon they're always on the move.
Searching here or searching there for a perfect place to call home.
Fighting Indians or Banditos and never giving up on their dreams.

Jessica Anderson

True Love

Having an incredible feeling about a special someone.
Being able to express your feelings on a higher level of understanding.
Knowing that your true love is someone whose smart,
compassionate and thoughtful.
Knowing incredible things about your true love
people couldn't begin to understand.
Your true love is someone that's unlike another.
A man who can make you feel so incredible unlike any one else.
A special someone who you could love forever.
Someone that makes you feel so good inside
when you're around him. You can feel he's the one.
A special someone you feel could love you like no one else could.
A love that can touch your heart on that
spiritual and physical level.
A love that turns so true, and that's
Your true love!

Renita A. Anderson

Untitled

We have yet to find the years gone by made wrong by life's injustice.
Even I cannot believe the fervence with which I have tried to overcome.

The roses, oh so velvety and soft with scent so sweet,
as if to right the wrongs with which he approached me.
The sweet nights we sat upon the bench and spoke of our love;
yet he could not fully understand his own words, his own thoughts
with which he tried to override his deepest hurt inside.

The child we bore he loved so much, who wept with tears
passed on by the same sorrow he could not correct.
Today we stand together this child and I,
just as we did many years ago,
even as an infant in my arms and cry;
why could not he, as we, declare our love, our hurt, our agony.

I give praise to God for what He gave to me.
Our minds, our spirits yet not broken.
We have overcome.
It lies in the now and the future, if only we allow ourselves.

Mary Ann Sino

Love Letters

My muse is not visiting today,
I'm visiting him if I may!
I'm pleading with him
Not to say nay
But of course
I'll not leave you at bay.
I hope he'll say!

Barbara J. Watson

Passion Met

To my passion pleaser
Morning teaser
Passion pleaser
Passionate kiss
Real bliss
Limbs entwined
Oh, sublime
Tension mounts
Seconds count
Time stand still
For us it will
This we feel
Senses reel
Our love it takes
Our world it shakes
Words can't define
Ecstasy mine
Toes curled
Rocked my world
Passion spent
Heaven sent

Ruth E. Fogleman

No Escape

If turn out the light in the dark of night
Thoughts come creeping,
And scratch at the door of my mind,
Worries and fears I try to shut out
And leave far behind.

I'd like to go to deep in that dark
Where all seems safe and warm,
I wish for a lock on that treacherous door
To shut out fear and alarm.

Not for myself do worries creep in
But for those I treasure and love
Many prayers I start on the way
To the master up above

Old Satan must catch them in fiendish glee
Before they reach that gate
Or, so it seems, when trials go on and on
And I wonder, and cry at fate.

Grace Helton

The Creator and His Creation

Look up!
See the light against the dark,
A beautiful galaxy is out tonight,
Amid time and space,
Man explores alone.
Within orbits
Ye find splendour, queries, wonder,
Alongside art, science, and philosophies,
Each moving along
Seemingly advancing towards nowhere.
Man's deep thoughts masquerade as beliefs,
Resisting the truth to "why,"
Look up!
For your answer, He draws nigh.

Maria Dass

You Feed and Nourish My Soul

Without any effort at all, you feed and nourish my soul.
Like a gentle stream, or a voracious waterfall continuously poured into anew.
Like the brightest stars, clusters and clusters in the heavens,
on a clear night.
Shining, like diamonds against blue velvet, just daring you,
to touch and feel their brilliance if you can?
You mimic their twinkling lure, you recharge me and invite me to dance.
You feed and nourish my soul.
Like a walk on a crisp autumn day.
Like the first breaths of spring, freshly cut grass,
and hints of lilacs just beyond your grasp.
You are every sunrise, and sunset,
filled with palettes of indescribable hues.
You are a rhapsody of beauty such as cannot be felt,
Or contained in one lifetime. You feed and nourish my soul.
You bring to me serenity and peace.
You bring me communion with the world, communion with myself,
And communion with our Lord!

Susanne E. Bauccio

Low Flying Eagle

Hey, mighty eagle. Yes! I'm talking to you.
Why do you fly among the pigeons,
when you should be flying so high you're out of reach.
You make your nest on the treetops
but your destiny calls you high above the mountain tops.

Do you know who you are?
You've been told that you'll never fly like your peers.
Dejected and disrespected, you chose to embrace the lie over the years.

Spread your glorious wings and fly.
What you are is inside of you and wants to be released.
No longer accept mediocrity, that old is now deceased.

Soar, mighty eagle! Soar, mighty eagle! Yes! You, mighty eagle.

Robert Thomas

True Love

You looked upon a mound of dirt and saw an emerald beach
While everyone else saw a monster you saw the face beneath
The tears that I would cry in fear would turn to diamonds in your hand
When all I could hear was laughter and jeers your words were a heavenly band
If I felt isolated and without a love one touch by you could clear my mind
I want to let you know right now you are my love for all of time

Laura Burton

Grandma-to-Be

For my first grandchild, Alexa Marie

A dazzling, dancing twinkle in his eye. A precious feeling in her heart.
Before anyone announced the date of your birth, whether a baby girl or boy!
There was nothing on this Earth more precious to me;
that could fill my heart with such feelings of pride and JOY.

The sonogram report showed a half pound of baby growing in her womb.
Now before anyone sees the color of your eyes, your hair!
The shape of your nose, fingers, or tiny toes!
God only knows how my heart's beating,
pounding, leaping, running, and jumping for JOY.

Grandma-to-be reminisces; amazed how time flies.
Will your baby's first cry, smile, warm skin touched,
peach fuzz-like hair be as soft as yours was?
Remembering becoming a parent!
Those first moments holding your child in your arms.
My eyes can't help but fill with tears of love; sheer JOY.

As your parents, grandparents each lullaby and rock you,
Singing their own sweet, soft song in your ear.
As we whisper for the first time your chosen name, I know my heart and soul!
You will be the nearest, dearest child. My first grandchild!
My forever and ever pride; my most heartfelt JOY.

Eleanore E. Anderson

The Book

An old green book
Carelessly kept on the side
Hidden by its fellows
Its spine time-torn
Mildewed and musty too

A well-traveled book
Ancient water-marked pages
Not quite torn
Almost hanging by a thread
Thumb-marked and scribbled
The paper scuffed and browned

In its pages
A much-loved story
Of times past
Of places forgotten

An old green book
On that shelf
On its side
Biding its time.

Ursula Swamy

Our President

To President Clinton and family

Our President is a man
Leadership is his game
He makes decisions with aim
Only to find out he is the blame

Our President is a child of God
He will not be spared by the rod
His actions to him seem to be right
But only God can bring them to the light

Our President is a man of stone
This impeachment process hurts to the bone
He is a man that so many trace
But only God can give him grace

Our President is only a mere man
As sin does it will follow his name
When this nation looks to Jesus as the man
Only his blood can cleanse the stain

Our President fate is in man's hand
For them to carry out their plan
What a job for them to do
Only God's grace will see them through

Vivian S. Drakeford

For My Daddy

To my daddy, Peter A. Young

My daddy works very hard
At his job at Vollers,
He works many hours
But I don't just love him for that.

My daddy is always fixing stuff
Bikes, cars, trucks,
And rototillers and more,
But I don't just love him for that.

I really love when my daddy
Makes time to play with me,
Or just having time to spend
By just going to say, Wal-Mart.

What I meant is that
I appreciate all those things,
But what I really, really love,
Is just hearing you say,
I love you.

Sarah Young

Me, Mama, and the Angel

Late one storming night, I sat here all alone.
I sat here by my window side, just waiting for Mama to come home.
My daddy is in Saudi Arabia fighting in the war,
And you see, my Mama just went down the street to a little store
While I sat here in the candlelight.

I heard a crash outside.
When I looked out my door, all I saw was people in my sight.
An old man came to me and said, "My dear daughter, don't be afraid,
But your Mama was in a crash today, and it took her life away."
I said, "My Dear God, oh, why did she have to go?
You see, today is my Mama's birthday, and God, I still love her so."
I went to the graveyard with just a little rose, and said to her,
"Dear Mama, why did you have to go?"
I lie here on her grave site, with tears in my eyes,
And said, "Dear God, would you take me and let me be by my Mama's side?"
An angel came from Heaven in a beautiful colored light
And said, "Dear daughter, don't be afraid, I'm here to take you home tonight."
With open arms, she came to me and wrapped her wings around me,
And now I am here with Mama and God, watching you.

Cynthia Atkinson

Faith Friends

For my faith friend, Tony Nowak
We've just met,
Yet I've known you all my life.
People, places, experiences,
Good times and strife
All replay themselves in my very being,
Through your knowing eyes.

Childhood chums, a puppy, a confidant,
Friends for life
All epitomized in one conscious moment
Of recognition, identification, acknowledgment of you.

Excitement, anticipation, energy
All stem from the desire to know you,
Like a flower in bloom, an answer to my prayer,
Oh, to discover our coincidences and lift each other up.

Our paths have not crossed by chance.
We find God and ourselves by touching the souls of others.
I find renewed strength, peace, joy and understanding just by knowing you.

Where will this path lead us?
I do not know

Let us walk it together, giving thanks, my Faith Friend.

Gloria J. Bass

Montrose

We have come from the North, we have come from the South,
And even the East and the West.
We are here to enjoy our retirement years
With new friends who ventured to Montrose to rest.

Rest we have not—there is so much to do!
The weather is great to ski or snowshoe.
The golf courses call us to come out and play;
There is no time to work in the land of hay.

The cattle are restless—they like to roam;
To the mountains they go—it's their second home.
Out in the open it's so cool and breezy;
With all of the wild flowers, we get kinda sneezy.

Oh, what a sight on those ol' back woods trails
Where it's so much fun to go climbing or biking;
Get those boots out, we're going hiking.

By nightfall we are tired from all the sightseeing,
But the mountains are up there always a-peeking.
The sun is just about ready to set and there are still so many folks yet to be met.
Plenty of time left to enjoy your golden years,
To Montrose, Colorado, we give our three cheers.

Beverly A. Bumgarner

Susan McDougal

Susan
We strive to comprehend
Moments of madness, sadness
Loneliness
Bearing a heavy yoke
Steadfast, resolute
Persecuted prosecutions
Jail, prison
The human spirit
Caring martyr
History is alive.
We ally with you Susan
Your hurt is our hurt
Tears we share alike
The bond is reinforced
It bodes well for posterity
The status quo will pass
Engineering a wiser time
Blessings on thee Susan McDougal
Ye are indeed the Joan of Arkansas.

Gene Garrett

In Memory of Nancy

God sent an angel with His love
To dwell with us on earth.
The time too short, for her return,
From the moment of her birth.

Her helping hands were everywhere,
Her laughter and her mirth.
She gave to all who came her way;
Fulfillment was her worth.

She had a knack of knowing how
To mend a broken heart;
To fill the world with beauty;
To bake a tasty tart.

God called her home, He needed her.
Her task was now complete.
She snuggled down upon the bed
And closed her eyes in sleep.

It is for us to carry on,
To bear the cross she bore.
Then we will be together
Upon that distant shore!

Dorothy A. Paulson

My Mother's Arms

I stood beside my mother's coffin
Looking down in disbelief;
My tears were falling slowly
After years of pain and grief.

I think of all the times you hurt me,
The times I went to bed in tears;
You never loved me, my dear mother,
This I lived with all my years.

Standing here, looking down upon you,
Knowing there is no soul to mourn,
Your slender arms are folded neatly,
Ne'er to bring me no more harm.

Many things you said to hurt me,
Many times you made me cry.
You made me feel so unwanted;
Many times I wished to die.

Dear Mama, if you go to Heaven,
May you find a little girl like me.
Place your slender arms around her;
Somehow pretend that I am she. . . .

Alice D. Stermer

Reflections

To Jeffrey J. Lawhorn, my grandson
Where were you?
On that beautiful summer night,
when the curtains softly blew, from the breeze.
Where were you?
When I lit a candle in the night, just to see a flicker of warm light.
Where were you?
When I came through the meadow with the cool green grass,
beneath my bare feet.
Where were you?
When I soared like an eagle and looked back and laughed.
Where were you?
When I took and held the small body, at last, held the little hand
and kissed the little face and then laid him beneath the grass.
Where were you?
When I picked up the glass, to only see the lonely reflections of the past.
Where were you?
When I took back my life at last.

    Drema Traicoff

Untitled

While looking into the sun, I found myself.
The soft golden beams of truth enlighten me to the new day.
The warmth encloses me within myself to view my soul.
Awareness has committed itself in the asylum of rebirth.
My new flesh feels vulnerable under the rays of truth.
A spiritual union on the plateau of existence.
Captivate, ravish, take over me, smother me in the flames of passion.
Awaken me to the vision that will save my soul from captivity.

    Tracy Burns

A Moment

Today, I took a moment to capture more than a glance;
Something we all should do whenever we might have the chance.

I heard the music of nature, I felt the wind's steady breeze,
As all of God's natural beauty swayed along with the trees.

I saw some furry little kittens, so glad they were not alone,
They shared an innocent playfulness no human has ever known.

I admired the strength I saw in a pair of horses so proud and tall,
Exhibiting both style and grace with more dignity than us all.

I noticed a colorful butterfly expressing choice and freedom at its best;
And the dew of a cloud shiny wet rainbow put my spirit and soul to rest.

Then I thanked God for Heaven, Earth, the way, the truth, and the light,
Because only His love and blessing can make my life all right.

    Connie L. Gray

Untitled

Sometimes we love someone so dear, it tears our hearts apart.
And when we lose them, and they are gone, it hurts an awful lot.
We try to be strong, and bear with them the pain.
But even ourselves in perfect health, are weakened by the strain.
We pray, we cry, we weep, we mourn. We asked for their life spared.
We try to encourage them often, to let them know we cared.
How sad it is to watch a friend die, slowly drifting away.
We try to hold on to them, encouraging them to stay.
But if it is not meant to be, they must answer to His call.
For it does not help them in their pain, to hold on and try to stall.
Oh, how it hurts to know one day they'll be gone and life for them no more.
But we'd hurt less if we truly understood what God has for them in store.
A place of beauty and of rest, a wonderful Heavenly home.
No longer will they have to lay helplessly and moan.
Wrapped in His arms, they smile, content and free.
And in their hands, to their palace, they proudly hold the key.
And Jesus speaks softly in their ears, welcome home, my child.
I've brought you home to me because it was past time for you to smile.
And then He'll speak again to them, in a voice so very low . . .
I'll protect you now as I did before, and let you go.

    Miracle M. Wynn

Tragically Twisted

Another story,
so dark and twisted
Another story for those
the guilty cannot see
Through truths to them come lies
Shall they ever be more heartless
they're words
cutting into my soul
another Romeo and Juliet
I say but my words go unnoticed
by these confused souls
They know not what they do,
but they have changed
what was once straight
turned the phoenix dark
made the sun fade
to a corrupt starlight night
shall the dark phoenix rise again
just like the story goes but twisted.
into what they feared. . . .

    James M. Parker Jr.

When You Can Love You!

There is a place
where healing beings
and the process of loving
comes from within.

It's time that you realize
your best friend is you.
It's not about what you run from,
but what you run to.

I know too well the feeling
of lost and alone.
Despair, it won't leave you
when all else is gone.

Do you know what you're saying?
I'm not sure that you do.
How can all be departed,
when you still have you?

As for life and its questions,
only one thing holds true!
It's only called living,
when you can love you!

    Bobby L. Holbrooks

The Plaque

Someone had it for a year,
then gave it away without a tear.
It had been in the family,
I was told repeatedly.

Later, then I found out
that there were stories told about
a piece of oval and of wood,
words carved so deep that out they stood.

An old piece from a walnut tree,
very nice saying, not hard to see,
I had it for my married life.
It was my gift when becoming a wife.

The plaque remained all those years,
and even when I shed my tears.

It has a saying true to me,
nobody will understand or see.
For all the quarter of my life,
I am entitled to it because I strived
to be a good wife and a mother,
let no one try to tell me other.

    Ingrid Buch

Untitled

To Jenny, I love you
You are the wind beneath my wings,
You are the shoulder when I cry,
You are the answer to my problems,
You are the reason why,

You are the warmth when I am cold,
You are the truth when others lie,
You are the shelter when it rains,
You are the sunlight through gray skies,

You are the beginning when I was at the end,
The breath that made my heart beat again,
You are the beauty that opened my blind eyes,
The touch that brought back feeling to my cold dead skin,

I want so bad to tell you how much you mean to me,
In my darkest hour your light shined and helped me see,
When I am alone at night you are always there it seems,
I thank God for granting me the gift of seeing you in my dreams,

You've given my life meaning when I thought that nothing mattered,
You put the pieces back together when I thought my world had shattered,
Sometimes I have to touch you because I can't believe it's true,
Day by day I realize even more that a part of me is you.

Brian R. Story

My World Within

I have a world all to myself within me.
I have a home that has an open door.
I have a friend who's always there to answer prayer because I care.
I have winding river flowing through me.
I have a lake and store my treasure there.
I have a ship that sails a sea—inside of me, my world within.

I climb the highest mountain, I sail the deepest sea.
I mine the richest treasure, right here inside of me.
I have a place to go when I am lonely;
I have a well to quench my thirsty soul.
I have a heart that listens so I want to know, my world within.

I have a Captain that I trust within me.
He takes the helm when I don't know the way.
He brings me through and keeps me true and makes the truth as bright as day.
He fills me full of light and intuition.
I seem to know before I know I know,
the answers come and then the sum—that makes my understanding grow.

When things outside seem hazy, and nothing makes much sense,
I till the earth within me, where there is recompense.
"Yes," I retreat into my world within.

Earlene Lewis

I Miss You

When I wake up in the morning, I slide my hand across the bed
so that I may touch you to feel your warmth but all that I feel
is the icy coldness of the bed where you should be,
where I wish you to be, I miss you

I dream that we are together, I dream that you hold me close,
it feels so good to feel you against me, holding me,
I dream that you hold me so tight, so tight as I hope
that you will never let me go, I dream of you,
your beautiful smiling face, the way that it lights up when you're happy,
I dream of your eyes, eyes that I lose myself in with just one glance,
I dream of your perfect body, the special part about you,
that part makes every man wish that you were his to love, I miss you

As I sit here, staring off into space, I wonder what the future holds,
I think about you here alone in this dorm,
I wish that I could be here always to brighten your day,
to save you from the void that loneliness brings, I miss you

I dream that my future holds you
I dream I will hold you forever, does your future hold me?
I love you, I miss you

Lindsay Flick

RENEWED ASSURANCE

The storms once raged about me,
I thought I could not cope,
then with Your arms
You sheltered me
and brought me to new hope
You brought me through the hardships
and gave me peace within,
and though I knew no answers,
at times it seemed so hard,
I only had to trust You
on You I could depend.
You brought renewing to my soul
and sweet assurance too!
I look back now
and I can see Your hand has
been on me,
and now the sweet assurance
is sweeping over me,
and I can see new meaning
in my life with thee!

Dorothy Sannes

Inspiration

A voice says to me,
"You should write poetry."
Days go by.
I do not try.

That voice still says to me,
"You should write poetry."
Weeks go by.
I still don't try.

Again my husband urges.
And thus, this verse emerges.
As days go by,
Again I'll try.

Ruby Flowers Washburn

Go with the Angels

Go with the angels,
were the last words that you said,
to comfort a daughter
as you went on ahead.

In the heavens with
God you begin to renew,
seeking strength and knowledge,
as we knew you would do.

Softly in the dark,
in silence I begin to cry,
and you see me somehow,
for I feel your hand,
softly stroking my brow,
though you were always
close in life, you are closer, now.

Nancy L. Wilson

Runner

Just the Earth beneath his feet
on paths that lead to his desire.

No walls to encompass him
or goals impossible to achieve.

So runner breathe more deeply
and run more swiftly knowing

You're suddenly past the pain
and finally free.

Joan Lamporte

We Thank You, Sun

In tribute to William Wordsworth
"We walked along, while bright and red, uprose the morning sun."
Let us pray, we thank you sun for giving us the sunlight warmth
since our birth and everything that followed.
We thank you sun for the warmth today
and we will pray for your sunlight again tomorrow.
We thank you sun for the love of our life and being our friend,
we made a promise and we will love you until the very end.
We thank you sun for your sunlight guidance because that's all that counts
and show us the path as we walk to our house.
We thank you sun for a dream that came true to your light
and we ask you to bless everybody on this Earth tonight.
We don't always do the right thing and we ask you to forgive us
because we need you here with us.
Without you in our life, it's empty;
we used to think back how the moonlit night was our enemy,
but we pray for you that is our remedy,
we ask you to watch over us. In God we trust,
and we thank you for the love that you have given to us.
So let your warmth in our heart go hand in hand, but for long as we can,
as long as your warmth permits us, please give us the sunlight we need to live, bear
with us. Amen.

Isaac Brooks

You Only Know What You Touch

For Esther Marks
Weren't you the one to choose life where there was none before?
You look into your daughter's eyes, and you're not so sure.
You said you'd never pull the plug, if they hit the floor?
You look into your mother's eyes, you have to think some more.

Wrong and right, it seems so black and white, because you knew so much.
It only went to show, you only know what you can touch.

Weren't you the one who'd drop the bomb on the enemy?
As you look into your son's eye, you think, "Who the hell are we?"
You say you understand Vietnam and the Holocaust,
But you weren't there; you can't know the fear, or what was lost.

The radios and talk show host made it crystal clear.
They sold their soap, and fed upon what you thought was dear.
They waste my time and tell me it's political;
It's times like this, I find it all so comical.

Did I stand for right even though it might be wrong?
I should have said, you'll know the truth when it comes along
Wrong and right, it seemed so black and white, because you knew so much.
It only went to show, you only know what you could touch.

Harold Davis

Wonderment of a Child

For my blessed grandchildren
Wondering about so many new things to learn,
to share and to care not get gooey things in your hair.
Wondering where the sun went all warm and glowing, and the moon,
a soft round light flowing smiling face as you squint your eyes.
Wondering about stars that look like eyes,
winking and blinking, I wonder what they are thinking.
Wondering about God . . . there is this feeling inside that He is near
and He can hear, and knows when you have a tear,
and makes you feel all warm and glowing.
Wondering about white fluffy things in the sky, and wonder why they don't
fall, and where they came from and where they are going.
Then they turn dark and start to cry, I wonder why?
Wondering about birds high up in the sky,
they can fly, I wonder why can't I
Wondering about creatures different than I,
some bite or sting and some are just plain mean.
Wondering . . . caterpillar all fuzzy and gray as it inches its way,
as soon will unfold a mystery of a different kind of being.
Wondering why? Why am I a child, such as I?

Linda Behrens McBroom

Candle

As this lights the way
it goes down and down and down
as a singer sings and says
it is in the wind

It comes big and small
shaped tall and short
as it is in the church and
it is in a holder in a court

As we light for a person
in some stores, we always buy
it in a pack and some people believe
when it goes out, someone dies.

Jaime Humberto Rochet Jr.

Untitled

I'm surrounded by people
But yet I'm alone
I'm part of my surrounding
But yet I'm never noticed
I'm in the middle of a crowd
But yet no one sees me
I'm here for you
But yet you're never to be found
Being a part of everything
But not being seen is hard
Why does life deliver an uneven hand
There is nothing I can do
But live and go on
Do I want to
Only tomorrow can tell

Sandy I. House

The Train

For my Honeybear, Halle
I awake to the whitest light,
Shining through a windowpane,
Finally on the road to my delight,
Going down the tracks in this train.

The journey will be long and hard,
I will complete it just the same.
I carry in my hand this card,
Showing the conductor from where I came.

The conductor's voice is steady,
not showing his exceptional fame.
For my last journey I am ready,
My emotions seem unselfishly tame.

The smile runs from my face,
Unknown in this pleasure of my pain.
This journey has no common place,
For I am on a very distinctive train.

Bryan S. Hines

Life of a Cow

If I were a cow,
I would moo all day.
I'd give milk to the farmers,
eat grass and hay.

When I get old,
and my backs about to break.
My feet become glue,
my body becomes steak.

Now I'm on your plate,
staring up at you.
If I could say anything,
I would probably say moo.

Jesse A. Walton

Good Morning, Lord

Every day that I wake up seeing sunshine,
And look out at the glossy, glistening dew,
I can't help realize what beauty greets my eyes,
And I say a good "Good morning, Lord" to You.

Every day that I wake up to the raindrops,
I know, beyond a doubt, that it is true;
If it weren't for all the showers, would we have the trees and flowers?
And, again, I say, "Good morning, Lord" to You.

I saw another wonder through my window pane last night;
A full moon set the sky aglow, with a mellow golden light;
And as I gazed at all the twinkling stars so far away,
I marveled at the treasured gifts You send to me each day.

So, any day that I wake up feeling lonely,
I know at once, what I must quickly do;
Just lie right back and rest, as I count the ways I'm blessed.
Then I say a good "Good morning, Lord" to You.

Joyce Pardee

Black Christmas

Dedicated to my beloved daughter, Kim
Abundantly glistening ornaments of Tiffany,
garnets kaleidoscopically coalescing,
inescapable carols barging their tinsel eclipsing the mirrors
sparkling within the pupils of my eyes bathed in the famine of disguise.

Arctic chills incredulous to perceive gouge glacial stakes
heart-wrenchingly hewing abysmally within,
a harbinger to the silent murmur
mimicking its demise.

Enigmatic is the dinosaur raking my flesh while the soot of black
snowflakes suffocate all trace, shadows of nativity left behind
nevermore to be retrieved,
nevermore in your embrace,
dangling from cold edges of empty space.

Rebecca Rosado Bloomfield

Men

For Kenneth, Sylvester, Clifton, and Jr.
The man (God) created the Heaven and the Earth.
God gives public man knowledge and wisdom
Our whole being depends on God's provisions for us.

Man has a lot of choices to do the things that he wants to do.
Hopefully he will make the right choices,
Men should use his strength and energy for good causes.
Man and his life can be complicated but rewarding.
Having a goal, trying, working, and caring for others in the best activity.

Sarah Brown

Ghost

Perfect
A ghost that walks out the door
Long before the light of day
Discarding counterfeit bills on the table of a stabbed and bleeding soul

Slamming out the door with no look back
Satisfied with snatches of love
In dark alleys, behind foreign corners
Love is found with the prick of a needle under the skin
Growing euphoria but dissipating, oh, so soon

As the door slams, the reverberations echo back
A reminder of the flimsy sensations
Hanging by a painted fingernail
She rolls over and looks to the window for one last sight
Of the unproductive innocence that she bartered
For a few bills wafting in the breeze
Hardly enough to bribe the devil for her soul

Sara Roth

Cherry

As bitter, yet sweet,
And rosy, like your cheeks,
Quite a cherry you were,
Like I remember before.

How I remember us
When your memory haunts me
Every now and then,
The pain just won't end.

How much I've been missing you,
Yet, I'd rather forget you.
Such a bother you can be,
When you're not here with me.

Why I deserted you,
And why you deserted me
Why did this have to happen
To you and me?

As much as I'd like
To turn back time
You'll be a withering cherry,
In my mind.

Joanne J. Tamayo

Indian Dog

Indian dog with blue eyes
You are so fine to me;
Indian dog with blue eyes
You are a Siberian husky;
Indian dog with blue eyes
You're from the wolf family;
Indian dog with blue eyes
Your real name is "Kodi"

Pam Myers

A Broken Heart

From year to year I often wonder
When time will come that will save my heart
From the scar—everlasting marker
Of thy absence that tore me apart.

Where is the sun that brightened my days
Which light was to last forever more
At least your smile has not faded away
As I often walk along the shore,

Recalling the magic of the past
The missing moments we shared in spring
The hope for love stolen from me fast
The delight you brought that made me swing

I feel lonely among betrayers
And lost in the whirls of endless winters.

Celia Din

Untitled

Caught in a dream,
Going nowhere it seems
devastated from the past
how long will this last
the deprivation, demoralization
filled with gloom and despair
oh, the past is in the past.
How long shall it last
Christ, he paid the price
what value do they place on life
Oh, God they call
but it is not his work
but the people believe such sorts
How long shall this last
A question we all ask!

Stephanie Green

The Prisoner

He paced nervously up and down his cell,
He heard the monotonous ticking of the clock,
He looked and saw the beauty of the world without,
But within, he knew the end had come without a doubt.

Suddenly, in the distance he heard the sounds of approaching steps,
Nearer and nearer they seemed to come,
Until he saw two men standing before his cell.
For he was anxiously awaiting the news they had to tell.

"I'm sorry, Jones," said the warden.
"The governor would not hear of it, although I think he knew."
"Be brave my son," said the Father,
"And take is as an act of God,
although I know he believes your innocence, too."

A faint smile could be seen on the prisoner's lips,
He looked for the last time at the beauty of the world without,
Then, with his head bent, he slowly bowed and without raising it, he said,
"All right Warden, I'm ready now!"

Harriet Bregman

The Chess Game of Life

Pawn to Pawn; Knight to Rook
Dressed in black and white; two enemies stood

Hello, white side. Tell me, what's your plan? Whatever shall you do?
I've got your kind within my challenged view

Head to head to play the game; eye to eye, glaring strange animosity
Give to me the man in the moon's blackened knight
A Bishop stole in the withered Queen

Pain knocks upon my soul once more; I am turning sad sorrow away
Sometimes life is white; sometimes it's black
Upon the chess board of life my soul does play

You've stolen my Knights; you've captured my Rooks
I've surrendered to you most of my pride
There still remains just one serious Pawn left to fend for his King
I will make this Pawn battle; to the end for me she'll fight.

Inch by inch; sly move by move
My peasant Pawn transcends into a headstrong Queen
Checkmate my friend, I have won this game once more
Goodbye, pain and misery.

Mi Wha M. Barker

Remembering

For Lise, Mom, Dad, Eileen, and Cathleen
I never felt I fit so I started with a grit.
Then there was the alcohol that led me to my hardest fall
I would go and park down roads that were very dark
I could not see the light 'cause I didn't know what was right
The alcohol would call and lead me to another fall
I started doing drugs and forgot about the hugs
I always felt so far away and used to ask is this really ray
I always felt apart especially in my heart
Another year went by time just seemed to fly
I could not bear to see what I had done to me.
All I wanted to do was fit. I thank God for never letting me quit.
The Lord has shown me what is right so that I could stand and fight
The Lord has revealed the way to grow, sometimes the path seems very slow
The Lord has showed me my close friends in order that I make amends
With the help of God I never forget that would be the day
To surely regret there once was alcohol that took me to my knees
until I cried Lord please.
I thank God for the thorns that made the rose
By the grace of God in the name of Jesus Christ
Our Lord and Saviour one day at a time.

Raymond C. Jackson

Love

Love is so precious, so soft
Why would anyone want to break your heart?
People say, "I love you"
Do they really mean it?
How do we know if they do?
Are people afraid of the truth?
Why do people hate each other?
If I knew the answers to these questions
I would love to tell people
Maybe people don't really know what love is
Maybe they don't until they are married
I know that one true case of love is
Sue and George

Patricia J. Gray

Not to See My Love

Times are so great when I'm with my love
or just to call her on the phone
to let her know it's her I'm thinking of
and how I feel so all alone.

Sharing our love has been so bliss
to see her once to enjoy her kiss.

But when my love is far away
the sky so blue has turned to gray
and all the flowers have lost their bloom
my lonely life is filled with gloom.

But the birds all know I love her so
and start to sing their song
they sing to me as if to say
she won't be gone from you too long.

Not to see the one I love
could be the end of me
I need to kiss her warm sweet lips
to love and hold her tight to me.

For she's the best thing that happen to me
I'll always love her tenderly.

Frank Yaccarino

The Advent

When God touches souls,
Seeds quicken in utero;
Elizabeth knew.

Robert E. L. Nesbitt Jr., M.D.

Symphony

Now the subtle sounds of Spring
are growing clear,
As from the woods and waters
every nesting birds and rushing stream
makes melody its own . . .
The quickened pulse of Nature
brings a faster beat,
And all the earth responds to it
with urgency—
Ponds and marshes feel the tempo,
mirror the emerging life,
While sweeping winds, crescendo-like,
Blow fresh across the reeds
and willows . . .
All creation seems to sing,
and from the hills come echoes
of its harmony;
For, in this joyous moment, now—
all of One, all is Music,
All is Spring!

Ellen Ward Surdo

The Sand Dollar

To Diane Crowder Rolla, my A.B.E. instructor
The sand dollar plainly shows us the baptism, crucifixion, and the new life
we now have in *Yashua*, the Messiah, before the creation of man.
The sand dollar (sea creature) created the fifth day of creation—Gen. 1:20–23.
(The doves, fowl that fly above the Earth).
There are four inside and the imprint of the fifth is on top back-side,
was also created the fifth day of creation—Gen. 1:20–23.
Man was created on the sixth day of creation—Gen. 1:26–28.
Noah sent forth a raven and three doves after the flood—Gen. 8:7–12.
Also, the Almighty sent forth His Holy Spirit in the form of a dove
when *Yashua* was baptized—Matt. 3:16, Mk. 1:10, Lk. 3:22.
On the back-side of the sand dollar you can see where the Romans
nailed His hands and feet to the tree—Acts 10:39, 13:29, I Peter 2:24.
The fifth wound is where the Romans pierced His side with a spear—John 19:34.
The imprint of the dunce cap under His feet implies that Satan, death,
and darkness are now past—Ps. 8:6, Ps 18:9, Rom. 6:6, I Cor. 15:26, Heb. 2:14, I John 2:8.
The front side shows us that He is free of the wounds—Luke 24:39,40.
He now sits on the right hand of the Almighty *Elohim Yahweh*—Col. 3:1,
Heb. 1:3, Heb. 8:1, Heb. 10:12, I Peter 3:22, Eph. 1:20–22.
You can see His is the bright and morning star—Rev. 22:16,
the Lily of the Valley—Song of Solomon 2:1, the true light now shineth—John 2:8. Hallelujah.

Donald Walters

The Perfect Opening Day

To my mother, for her encouragement
They sit very still looking into the sky, they sit so quietly not even a sigh.
They wait patiently listening for the sound,
the sound of a honk or quack, they're ready for the attack.

They're ready to give up, they've sat for an hour,
but wait, shh, what's that noise?
Look up boys, it's a flock of birds, two or three hundred for sure!
They search for their lanyards, their calls are ready.
They hold their guns against their shoulders tightly and steady.
One whispers, "Here they come, let's hear your song."
"Be ready my friends or they're sure to be gone."

The Labradors are heeled and ready for action.
All are excited and they feel the attraction.
The birds are circling and preparing to land.
The men raise their guns the time is at hand.
They begin to fire their weapons, certainly to hit two or three,
But look they've hit more. Wow! Do you see?

The dogs are sent out to retrieve the game.
Proudly they come running back, thankful that their jobs are still intact.

The men are finally able to breath, they cheer and shout,
their voices ring out! What a wonderful day! The perfect opening day!

Kimberly Ruetz

First and Last Time Skiing

To Donna Laraia and the Nancys
I was already doing 90, I had just left the top.
What better time to realize . . . I don't know how to stop.
I tried plowing and I zig-zagged, I was leaning to the right . . .
I whipped around the corner and I hugged it rather tight.
There it was before me, I screamed . . . GET OUT OF THE WAY!
A lovely group of pine trees and they were there to stay.
I do not like this ride I'm on, nor do I like this town.
The only way to save my life was throw my body down,
So I tumbled and I flipped like I never knew I could.
My body was a rag-doll, yet it snapped and cracked like wood.
Lost my mittens, they went flying and my hat, it was fleece,
But there was something I didn't lose . . . the skis did not release.
The surgery went well, the ligaments were sewn.
I questioned why the skis stayed on, the answer is now known.
The ski release setting has to do with your weight . . .
Oh, sure! Someone told me . . . they just told me it too late.
I filled out a form when I rented the skis.
It asked me some questions and listed the fees.
Not knowing how important those questions were back then . . .
Where they asked me for my weight . . . I lied and put 110.

Karin Kneitel

The Baby

Baby! Baby! Shining proud.
Gift of God, all allowed.
What human will struck your spark,
And gave your life its special mark?

In what wisdom basks your soul?
What your plan? What your goal?
What's your hope upon this earth?
What's the measure of your worth?

With what force took you your stand?
By what embers were you fanned?
What searing glow hurled you on?
Far from darkness, toward the dawn.

Oh, sweet baby, what your charm?
What divine is in your karm?
Will you show us how to live?
Will you take or will you give?

Will you love in gentle way?
Never give your light away?
May you steer your ship aright,
Stay the path, preserve the right.

Glen V. Koch

Mindless Imagination

You look as soft as a bunny
Beautiful and nice
you tickle my fancy,
I always look twice
Your make-up, your hair,
your dress attire
Looking so good, you could set me on fire
I'm hot to trot
From this my lazy old dream
I surely could use, a swirl of ice cream
Vanilla's my flavor
Your sweetness I'll savor
To a song sung
From a voice, all your own
Elegance drawing finesse
From your tender, loving tone
Mindless imagination
Fulfilling a heartfelt duty
Is a gentleman, admiring
Your endless beauty

William M. Hoppe

Your Friendly Heart

Your friendly heart's a treasure,
Surpassing riches of the world,
From it blossoms friendship
With it my heart you've whirled.

Is your heart sweet like candy?
Time to time there's a starburst
extracting gold from your heart,
On your smiles it's seen first.

You must be a magician
With a trick up your sleeve,
For when I think about you
The smiles just won't leave.

I would like to call you friend,
as friendless you show,
By kind things you do and say
That have set hearts aglow.

For your life's quest I'll say a prayer,
God's love will rest on you,
Lightening your heart to show the way
Each day your whole life through.

Joseph G. Schelling

That Remains Indifference

His silence screamed of wayside whistling careless
and unadmittedly incomplete;
of crumpled sorrow matted into the mawkish corner
where tenderness trespassed

Of course she wished (she asked) to see everything there was to see,
and twirl it round, him looking on or "together"
a sort of metaphorical possibility

And something about a plan for serendipitous failure
somehow (seemingly) nonsensical
like absence or falling leaves in mid-air
almost maddening as the fate of Sisyphus

After all, they had already pretended
to be butterflies with wings; he had tasted her words.
They had tumbled through time and awkwardness together on a platform,

Itself symbolic of space shared,
defined by experience vulnerability those glimpses
of a guarded world no one else will ever see.

Jen Dwyer

I Am . . .

I am a funny girl who likes to laugh.
I hear voices coming from unknown places.
I feel satisfaction of being able to follow my dreams.
I touch the bottom of the ocean and feel the sand run through my fingers.
I am a funny girl who likes to laugh.

I worry about the destruction of mankind.
I cry for all those with incurable diseases.
I understand the longing for something new.
I hope that I will fulfill all of my life's dreams.
I am a funny girl who likes to laugh.

I smile at the sunrise bringing me a new day.
I taste the sweetness of a sunset on a summer's eve.
I look and see the dolphins dancing at midnight.
I pray that the moon and stars will shine forever.
I am a funny girl who likes to laugh.

I remember times with my deceased great-grandpa Sam.
I wish that sometimes the world could just revolve around me.
I believe that family helps you through thick and thin.
I can always do my best if I believe in myself.
I am a funny girl who likes to laugh.

Britt Ellis

The Wrong Answer (Just Have Another Drink)

For Paul and others needing answers
I've escaped a thousand times from this cell I'm in
for the world keeps closing in on me. So much pressure,
so much stress but I know the answer: Just have another drink.

Now things will be alright, but only for a while
for I am sensitive, things bother me, and this world
is not a kind nor gentle place. Again and again
my turmoil begins, old ghosts of the past
keep coming back, but I know the answer, what I need
to calm me down, to feel all right: I'll just have another drink.

Internally I tense, but outwardly I put on a show,
a suit of muscle, a tough exterior, don't let them
know my pain, be cool, relax, don't worry.
I've got the answer: Just have another drink.

I fear my world will crumble, a loss of face,
a backward falling, and again my anxiety starts. If I could
just stop thinking, and again the same answer: Just have another drink.

As I look in the mirror, I see the results of my thousand escapes.
I'm much older than my years, what went wrong? What happened
to my life? But I know the answer: I'll just have another drink.

Philip DeSena

When Diamonds Are a Girl's Best Friend

When diamonds are a girl's best friend
Baseball is on her mind
Get her a glove, a bat, and ball
And with her spend some time

If you don't make a hit
And she strikes you out
Her company you'll still have
That's much to rave about

She'd rather have your friendship
Than diamonds sparkling bright
That bring upon her face a smile
Joy to her heart's delight.

Joseph G. Schelling

Autumn

My ancestors are chariots in he sky
the clouds are moving by
of rainbow colors . . .
I am closing the clouds in a circle
and I aim for the celestial spaces
the past could be only a twinkle away

The night and the day might be one
the seasons would cease to live
blossoms fall tearless on the ground
my past is melting like wax
I shall ride a chariot in the sky

Mariana Zavati Gardner

Journeys

How far is our journey?
How long must we walk?

Seeking safe passage
On a ledge in the dark?

The light is our savior,
And to reach it our goal

But the passage is narrow
And yet we strive on . . .

Heaven is the light
And the walk is our life

And the paths that we choose
Are the bad or the right

The short cuts seem many
And so easy to choose

But the wrong path is Hell
Pick it and you lose

Ronnie L. Clay

God Sent an Angel Named Jory

Roses are red,
Tulips are pink,
You're so adorable,
We really do think,
Grandma and Grandpa,
Love you a lot,
Since you were a tiny wee little tot,
Now you're a big girl,
Everyone's joy,
Just like a cute little cuddly toy,
You're so full of love,
And your cute little ways,
Just seeing your smile,
Really makes my days.

Sylvia E. Lasher

Single Burning Flame

The wild child walks among the entities of the land,
Never giving thought to anything but listening to his favorite band.
Laws get broken and rules are destroyed,
He walks his own way, never following anyone, the leaders get annoyed.

He sees the nights we try to live and die . . .
People watch him, listen to him, want to walk with him . . .
but instead just let out a sigh.
He talks in a manner that everyone yearns to understand,
But they're stuck in this spell that makes their life vacant of glam.

Once in a great while,
One gets to see a wild child, walking before his last mile.
Because once his spirit is set free,
No one will learn anymore from me
or get a chance to see across the sea.

Kristoffer Park

Flint Hills Beauty

Early morning in the Flint Hills, oh, what an awesome scene!
The trees, the creeks, the cattle, and hills all covered with green.

The rocks upon the hillside, shine like diamonds in the night,
When the sun shines brightly on them, what a heavenly, sparkling sight.

The birds are singing sweetly, as they flit from post to post,
They search for food and twigs, for their nests they love the most.

The cattle are out grazing, on the pastures all so lush,
There's peace and serenity, in a simple world of hush.

Why there's even several camels, out searching for their food,
They saunter about so gracefully, in a lazy springtime mood.

Away off in the distance, I see an old windmill,
As the wheel is slowly turning, pulling water from the hill.

The red-bud trees have blossomed, and the rest are leafing out,
Here and there the wild flowers blooming, adding color all about.

There's a haze off in the distance, as the fog hugs to the ground,
In the air the warmth of springtime, is snuggled all around.

The cowboys on their horses, are out checking every day,
Making sure the cattle are safe out there, and none have strayed away.

Yes, the Flint Hills out in Kansas, are a gift from God above,
I'm so thankful that he gave it all, for us to share and love.

Donna Lanter

Know Me

Dedicated to 365 days of summer
I stand in the crowded room of life, but yet completely alone.
Almost invisible, if you will, only but an outer core to justify my own.
Slowly I move through this void, patting egos as I go, looking, hoping, and always searching
high and low for someone to think and speak the words of inner-serenity I long to hear,
to carry me through each day and last throughout the years.
I hear a voice say, "I love you" with a heart of no meaning,
and a soul say, "I need you" only trying to fool me with momentary feeling.
For no one seems to realize these aren't the words I choose
to help me bond with myself and so in turn bond with you.
Will these words ever come so I can move on and grow,
or will I die with no one ever knowing the depths of my soul?
At the moment I fear all is lost, and I prepare to settle for the void,
when I see a light, one I had seen as young boy.
I turn towards the light and see you moving close,
fading to back the other souls of the void so it's just you, the light, and me.
Different from the souls long since past, I can see you know and care and see the difference in me.
You say the words I long to hear, in passing just to me.
Whispering softly, "I understand you" setting my soul free and then you walk away.
My heart begins to race as do the tears dampening my face.
A surge of feeling ignited now, but I turn to see you gone again as quickly as you appeared.
I yell, "Come back and tell me more of what you said!"

Toby Williams

Silent Splendor

To my loving husband, Jerry
Majestic grandeur
  calming winds.
Calling quietly.

Cool, clear lakes
  robin egg blue sky
    Saturated colors.

Capturing the soul
Altering the spirit
  never to be same again.

Ageless, still maturing
  yet—
demanding respect.
Never to be exploited.

Silence.

Splendor.

Awakening the heart.

Rocky Mountains
  truly
God's Country.

Sally E. Mechels

Even John Wayne

For my mother, Eva
Even John Wayne was not a cowboy.
He never worked on a ranch
and didn't care much for horses.
Cattle were foreign to him.

With time, the Duke grew fat
and was forgotten, eating handfuls
of doughnuts in public; in depression.
Alcohol numbed his senses.
The greatest of American heroes
was labeled a racist and a bigot,
by some. I wouldn't believe it, but
I was ashamed of his judgments.

Even so, I will always be addicted
to the swagger and the speech
of the Legend on the screen.
He was my father,
In a flawed state of desperation.
True Grit kept him going.
Cancer killed him.
Even John Wayne was just a man.

J. Grice

Memorial for Your Precious Son

Your son has gone, so brief his stay!
He will not play his baby games
upon this earth we've come to know,
but since he left for his new home
his soul lives on beyond the reach
of mortal kin and friends who preach
the goodness of His Holiness.

So dry your tears, and clasp your hands,
and pray as if there was no sand
to mark the passing of the time
through hour glasses tipped on end

Rejoice! Your lad's in Heaven's hands!
His soul's at peace within God's plan!
Who watches him? Ethereal
angels will bring him up among
his many baby friends! Praise God!
He will not want for anything!

Richard E. Smith

True Destiny

Behold the brave souls who seek true destiny!
It's a matter of focused determination to thread
Through a maze of life's drudgery and complexities.
It's a matter of real desires in one's deepest recesses of the heart.

It's a matter of balancing one's faith in their own
power to create destiny and faith in power beyond that help create it.

It's a matter of fortitude in creating one's true path
by taking the actions required.

It's a matter of Darhma sought in restless pursuit
to embrace one's birthright of joy and love.

Yes! Bless the brave souls who find their true destiny.

Mary Louise Merrill

The Wolf

I have been blessed with the spirit of the wolf; by the grace of God.
I am an animal of God, just as the wolf.
I am sensitive to changes in my environment, just as the wolf.
I only take what I need, just as the wolf.
I only hurt others when I feel threatened;
I only hurt others to protect myself or my family.
I only hurt to defend myself, I only hurt when I am hurt, just as the wolf.
I trust very few others except for my family, just as the wolf.
My heart and soul are pure, just as the wolf.
I am cunning and wise, just as the wolf.
I am feared by many, I am adored by millions,
I am loved by several, and I am respected by few, just as the wolf.
I have many children, just as the wolf.
I only have one mate;
if she dies or goes away, I die of loneliness and starvation, just as the wolf.
I am the spirit wolf.
I am strong, I am a survivor, just like the wolf.
I have the spirit of the wolf,
I am the spirit wolf.

David W. Brown

A Dream Come True

With every breath he takes,
his massive, well-built chest tells of his strength.
Every step he takes, it excites and fascinates the mind.
His power and capability are wanted by all.
The rippling of muscles under skin truly shows his beauty.
A coat as gold as a new copper penny could leave even the best to shame.
His mane and tail of snow white that blow in the wind like feathers.
The feeling of excitement racing through even the most skeptical
when they're taken on the ride of their life.
Thinking this is only a dream, it can't be real.
Their eyes say no, but the feel, the touch
sends their head a-spinning like a tilt-a-whirl.
Now they know such a creature exists—a gift from God.
That's the only way to explain it: a rare but captivating beauty.
A dream come true.

Jennifer A. Dauch

My Passion

For my snuggles

My passion for you is like a loving desire that never stops.
I don't know what you did or if it's just your soothing voice,
but every time I think of you I just want you more and more.
Every word you speak is like a wondrous world added onto my own.
You take me by surprise with every invigorating breath
that you let seep into your body.
Your sweetness makes me yearn
for your ever so perfect and gentle touch,
which I long for every night.
And our first touch and all that will follow will leave me breathless
every moment that we're together and apart.
And our dreams are wondrous worlds where our love can grow.
And as it grows all of our moments will be absolutely beautiful.

Rebecca Keebler

Walk of Love

In tribute to William Wordsworth

"We walked along, while bright and red
Uprose the morning sun;"
All time of separation
became dim memory.

The years apart
vanished in the
morning mist, and we
were hand in hand again.

We strolled beneath
that radiant sky
of early morning and
felt the joy of living.

No more tears,
sadness or great
distance between us
as we walked in eternal love.

Kimberly Wasson

Shine

To my brass ring, Michelle

Lightning bugs soaring
In the tapestry of night
A living shooting star
To a child's wondrous sight

The smallest of shooting stars
In silence they do sing
Bound not to the heavens
As lightning bugs take wing

No everlasting beacon
Would ever look so bright
As the dance of tiny dreams
Which fly into the night

Floating through the darkness
Falling upward summer's snow
Where ends their life's desires
Even lightning bugs won't know

For each one has its moments
A simple chance to shine
Searching for one another
And the day to call them "Mine"

Mark E. Johnson

Somebody to Believe

A little girl against the glass,
her breath obscures the view.
She gently wipes away the fog
to watch the chosen few.

Her ribs ache, crying out for food.
Their hollow, rumbling roar
drowns out the sound of cars and trucks
as she moves near the door.

The patrons look right through her smile
as they brush past her face.
Her threadbare coat is stark against
their dinner gloves of lace.

She turns and finally heads for home,
for she knows that she needs
an angel sent to guide her way;
somebody to believe.

Oh, little one, what treasure you
will someday find. You'll see
how great your own bestowal
as a woman who believes.

Susan Kelly

Musicmaker

Here I am again musicmaker, silent before your stilled voice.
All quiet gears, unmoving wheels, electric devices as yet mute and powerless.
Once again I set needle to groove, waiting a still beat before the curtains rise.
But I would rather this than to dance the pulse,
the disharmonious beat which throbs and pumps the land.

I would you take me to the sounds of Master's hands,
where known and new visions have inscribed their symphonies.
I would rather you bespeak of operas as yet new to me,
where men in design have scratched their memoried sound on black circles.
In light and in signals where the design is found.

I cannot call forth such beauty from or strings,
my hands make music which is unwritten,
new with every search, yet I wish to remain forever near those places
where such awesome power in vision, resounds.
To stay forever close to the lofts in which such spirits dwell.

Thus here I am again musicmaker, with a switch . . . and mercy,
you will take me to where the colorless purity sounds, to worlds in other minds.
Though yours in the intermediary, you and I to the musicmaker will be found.

Raoul Peter Mongilardi

Remember Thee

In a lonely place . . . time after time . . .
The wind cometh . . . leaveth . . . returneth . . . time and again . . .

Sometimes . . . when the wind comes . . . restored the daylong . . .
Are you there . . . son . . . ?
Are you here . . . son . . . ?
Are you returned . . . son . . . ?
For he is in the wind . . . restored wishfully . . .
And I remember thee . . . my son . . . respectfully the lifelong . . .
Always . . . I hold thee dear . . . my son . . .
It hurts son . . . if you are not here . . . sometimes . . .
It hurts son . . . if you are not returned again . . .
It still hurts the same . . . your loss . . .

Wait a moment . . . the wind is coming . . . from faraway . . .
Maybe he is not gone forever . . . essentially . . . after all . . .
Still . . . wait . . . and still wonder . . . all in all . . .
And yet . . . our energies are down . . . until the wind returns . . .
For you will find . . . when you return . . . our minds . . . blind . . .
As you travel . . . to faraway spaces . . . places . . .
Remember our memory . . . as your path retraces . . .
Pass by wind . . . son . . . so that we can remember thee . . .

Ann D'Alessandro

In Loving Memoriam

For all my patients, enriching inspirations
A time to be born, time to live, time to die.
Although the thought is heartwrenching, time has come for her
to go home to a beautiful world above, beyond
where there's no more pain, suffering—only sheer happiness and peace.

Though she isn't here with you,
she's watching, guiding you through each, every day—
emotionally, spiritually, she'll always be here with you.

Each time you want to give up, just think of her,
her courageous strength that she must have had,
which pulled her through as far as it did

There was nothing that could be done to prevent the inevitable;
a higher power than anyone had decided that it was time for her to leave,
get on with the next life which she'll enjoy to fullest
each, every time she looks down upon you
with a smile on her face, sheer glow in her heart,
you'll feel an overwhelming power of warmth like never before,
it's at this time that you know she'll always be with you
burning deep within your heart with so much love and adoration
where no one can ever put out the flame that will burn forever,
guiding you through the rest of your life with sheer strength, energy!

Linda Berry

God's Special Gift

It starts with a pencil
Sharpened to the finest point.
To be able to put down on paper
The movements of the muscles and joints.
The artist's hands to her
Are as precious as gold,
Because they are capable of drawing
What the heart can hold.
The eyes watch patiently
As the hands move swift,
Watching the lines and colors
Come from God's special gift.
Satisfaction and happiness
Are all that is required
When the mind, eyes,
And arms become tired.
At last standing back,
And looking at her art.
Knowing in her mind
That it was straight from the heart.

Kerensa Lee Zamora

Seasons

Seasons come and season go, but . . .
What do they teach us, do you know?
My friend the chameleon knows . . .
Change is good . . .
Because when you adapt you also . . .
Overcome!

Donald R. Jones

Waiting on the Muse

I sit upon this comfy chair
my pencil sharp, my mind still bare.
The page all blank before me lies
reflecting what's behind my eyes.
I hope I will see wonders, or
a sight propelling me to soar
above this room, this time and space,
the snowflake's pattern I would trace
on windows clean and clear and cold
a star within my cloak I'd fold
and carry it back into this room
to help me think of something soon!

Kenneth D. Williams

Be There to Serve Him

I don't know what the others thought,
I was tried as I could be.
I could see water to drink and hay to eat.
The stable looked good to me.

It was just becoming quiet
When I heard a baby cry.
I just took a little look.
I didn't mean to pry.

Things just settled down again
When the shepherds and wise men came.
They gathered around the manger.
They even knew His name.

When they said He was the son of God
I realized what I had done.
I had been the transport
Of Jesus Christ His Son.

I guess you don't have to be important
For you to do your part.
Just be there to serve Him
And have a willing heart.

Edward Schwarzer

Mother's Hands

To my mother, Dezzie Birmingham Meggs
Large, gentle hands;
Hands that could soothe a baby's crying,
lower a fever, comfort a broken heart;
Hands worn from many labors: peeling peaches,
stringing beans, shucking corn;
Hands sifting flour and kneading dough
for the biscuits she made twice a day;
Hands rolling out the dumplings, the pie crusts, beating the egg whites
until they formed the perfect peak;
Hands putting on her bonnet or hat in the summer and coat and scarf
in the winter to go feed and milk the cows;
Hands that cared for the sick and disabled: Grandpa Birmingham,
Grandmother Meggs, Papa when he had typhus fever and later the brain tumor;
Hands brushing and combing her long black hair, then pulling it up and
twisting it into a ball on the back of her head;
Hands scarred from getting caught in that first electric washing machine;
Hands clapping for joy when her son, Fordham, returned from World War II;
Hands covering her pain and tears when life became too much for her;
Hands that finally weakened and stiffened, but still held her teddy bear with
that gentle, loving touch that she had held her eleven babies.

Janis Meggs Carroll

Papa

I love you Papa! Your granddaughter, Elizabeth
Oh, my papa, my wonderful papa, Papa is what we called him.

When I was little, he taught me how to hang from a limb.
But I will tell you things I remember.

Like the way he worked on the farm,
And the tattoo on his arm.

And the way he laughed and giggled,
Or the whiskers on his face,
And how he put wheels back in their place.

But the best thing I like, is how he would always fix my bike.
He would fix everything so neat, and when it was finished
He would handle it so sweet.

But now he is gone in the sky up above.
God takes us when he wants us.
And he takes us with love.

No more seeing him was his hands at the sink.
And no more seeing him take the bull for a nice cool drink,
But I know that he is here and there and everywhere.

I know he is not here today, but let me say, even though we are apart.
He'll always stay with me deep in my heart.

Elizabeth Johnson

Free Spirit

"A free spirit you are," the child of ten years thinks
as he holds the four-legged creature close.
You are mine, we are one.
I will groom, feed and care for you; you are my special friend and partner.
The two look as one when galloping down the pasture in the distance.
The child stands on a hillside of luscious green color.
He watches as the chestnut colored creature runs his tail flying to the wind,
His free spirit sends him flying across the meadow.
He is as free as an eagle with wide-spread wings.
Three-and-a-half years go by the lovely creature is joined by a mate with a beauty of her own,
a beauty as amazing as a sunset on a clear summer day.
The child, now a youth of fourteen years, has two beauties of nature to tend to.
In a few months, sadness befalls the youth as he watches
his first lovely, free-spirited creature pain with a long illness.
The monster of death takes him to his Free-Spirited Ancestors of the past.
His free spirit remains in the youth's heart as he keeps on.
For he has the strong, proud, spirited mate to care for and love.
The youth thinks as he looks down at the grave,
"Ride on my friend, tail flying in the wind, a free spirit you are.
You will always be a part of my spirit, my heart!"

Rejeanne Fortin

Gone Yet Cherished

To my wonderful son, Larry Moreland
As you stop and ponder
The days gone by,
I'll be there.

When you sit by the tree
Under the shining sun,
I'll be there.

As the moon caresses
The stars at night,
I'll be there.

And while asleep
To dream your dreams,
I'll call out "quietly,"
For still, I'll be there.

Brenda S. Howrey

My Love

I could love you with all of my heart
With a love so true we'll never ever part

I could love you with a love so warm
No one could break it with all the charm

I could love you with a love so bold
It would be worth much more than gold

I could love you with a love so fine
My love so deep is one of a kind

But . . . if nature says to you
She's not worth your time

We shall shut the doors of love
Never to combine.

Roslyn C. Alabi

Our Friendship

Our Friendship is priceless
something I will never trade
Not even all the money in the world
We're best of friends that we have made

You've touched my heart so many times
And you mean a lot to me
I will never forget you and your smile
In my heart is forever you will be

I miss you so much
So much I even cried
I wish I could be with you, together,
sitting next to each other, side by side

Every day and every night
I've been thinking a lot about you
Because I really miss you
And truly do Love You

Edmund Field

Forever

Forever sad. Forever blue.
Forever not knowing what I thought I knew.
Forever guilty for something I didn't do.
Forever empty, forever feeling nothing
I hear is really true.
Forever crying, forever faking a smile.
Forever pretending to be alive,
but slowly, quietly, dying.
Forever with a broken soul,
Forever with a broken heart.
Forever seeing my whole world
slowly falling apart.

Francie Simpson

Our Shadows

In Memoriam: Warren Miles Jr. (November 24, 1921–August 1, 1997)
In the beginning, as my eyes cracked open for the first time,
cold, naked, and afraid, I stared upward at the bright lights crying.
Suddenly the lights were blocked from my eyes by a shadow and a warm, smiling face.
He appeared with a dream in his eyes, a heart filled with warmth, and huge, strong hands.
He carried me through life with those massive hands.
He taught me right from wrong with his eyes and gave me strength from his heart.
For many years, I lived in his shadow, learning and living all of his experiences
and trying always to be just half the man he was,
never succeeding in my eyes, but always in his.
Throughout my life, his shadow blocked the glaring lights
and allowed me to see clearly and remain focused.
Some men will say it is not a good thing to live someone else's shadow,
and I would agree, until you become the man whose job it is to cast that shadow.
As I stand with my back to the east and face toward his grave,
I cast a shadow on a stone that reads, "Beloved Husband and Father"
and realize the dark outlined shadow on the grass and stone before me is my father,
and I take comfort in knowing that he will walk with me forever,
and someday, I will be that shadow for my sons.

Happy Birthday Pop
—Your loving son,
     Bud
     Bud Miles

Children of the 20th Century

Born as children in the 20th Century
As Americans in a great land and free.
Awakening to each new and unknown day,
We looked to see what merries life would bring our way.
Day in, day out, we all went about
Writing life's stories without a doubt
Our history on pages in Nature's Big Book,
Our deeds for others someday, they'll look.
And yes, the sun came up and went down
The moon arose and set on ocean shores, birds flew and we all grew,
Finding out things in life that seemingly were new.

And before long it was all gone . . . no, not the sun, nor the moon,
nor the ocean shores, not the flying birds, or our growth, or fun;
Just the 20th Century, it was all done!
For as we slept in the middle of the night,
The 20th Century left without even a fight
Quietly, without words or even a goodbye!

Ah, but at last, had come our future: the 21st Century had risen,
Untouched, untaunted, without things of old.
There, just waiting for the lives of the 20th Century children to unfold.
     Linda C. Riley

Untitled

"Please make her well," is all that could be heard
Trying to comfort the child with soft-spoken words.

And as sick as she was, it was others she thought if instead
Her mother, father, brother, and sister
Sitting so closed to her bed.

"I'm ready to go," they heard her say
"For my wings are ready and God needs me today."

And as the day passed on, everyone had tears in their eyes
But when they went outside, they noticed the skies.

For it was clear and sunny with a bright shining star
So now everyone would know, that she hadn't gone far.

And when they go bed tonight, she will not be there,
But as they walk outside each day, it'll be the child that they hear.

For the angels, at last, will again be singing,
The clouds will be rumbling and the Heaven's will be ringing.

God has spoken for no more suffering alone,
For He has called His angel to finally come home.
     Michelle McGee

A New Vision

My eyes are seeing
Life with a new vision

Clear and shimmery
like the sun smiling on the snow

I had almost gone
blind with dependence
consuming me

I didn't see what he was doing
to me until he disposed of me
like filthy trash
Now I'm not the only one
     Karen McCoy Buckley

Life to Me

Born without a care,
Thoughts as clear as air,
This is life, this is life.

Sometimes are good, some are bad,
Some are happy, but mostly sad,
This is life, this is life.

Soon you're on your own,
And you feel you're all alone,
This is life, this is life.

Friends they come and go,
And you're judged by what you know,
This is life, this is life.

Your loved ones pass away,
But you still must start your day,
This is life, this is life.

Now your life has passed you by,
No one to hear you cry,
That was life, that was life.
     James Burdett Jr.

Circles

Here I am,
missing you again
Always on my mind,
deep within my heart.
Loving you all the time,
even when you're not here.
You'll never know,
how much I really care.
My life keeps going back to you.
It won't stop until,
I'm dead and through.
My heart gets chills,
I keep loving you.
Going around in circles,
My memories of you.
     James William Henderson Jr.

Untitled

We say
Freedom
And we test it
And change occurs
And quality changes
And the envelope
Expands
And I notice that
I feel further apart
From myself
Like a balloon
Ready to burst
     Roger Scot Kopet

The Whisper of the Wind

The wind has many voices during the four seasons.
In the winter it can blow the rain and snow.
It can rattle a tin roof, break tree limbs, and chill
you to the bone and then lay as if it was never there.
Only a whisper.

In the spring the wind seems to change somewhat.
It can carry new blooms off of a tree to the ground.
Lift kites into the sky and make them fly.
Blow warm rain into your face and take the umbrella
from your hand and then lay.
Only a whisper.

When the summer comes there are many days
the wind doesn't seem to blow at all.
Then it gets hot and storms develop with clouds and rain.
The wind moves the clouds hurriedly across the sky
and when the storm is over and the wind lays.
Only a whisper.

Then comes the fall with the flowers still blooming until the frost.
The wind saves the flowers many nights by blowing.
Then the wind lays and the flowers die from the chill.
You can feel the whisper of the wind.

Florence G. Bowyer

Forty Hours a Week

Have there been too many twists and turns over the years
to find my way back to myself? It seems I got lost along the way.
I'm not even sure where to begin to search for the remains of me.
I suspect there are pieces to be found along many a different path.
This tattered, weathered shell which exists now
bears little resemblance of the me I recall with such clarity,
at times with such disparity. The me I used to be.
It's been so long since I've seen that young, sensitive child who answered to my name.
The face is so difficult to see. It's like a good friend you've lost touch with
for years after moving away whose familiar smile fades with each passing day.
I never saw myself settling for this expression of life,
expressionless, mundane and methodical, clocking in physically,
checking out emotionally, intellectually.
I'm like a good worker bee droning on, mindlessly going through the motions.
Competent but impotent, never to enjoy an audience with the queen.
I'm playing a supporting part in someone else's feature.

Erick L. Stickney

The Porpoise of Education

The purpose of this poem is plain as it can be.
It describes the educated dolphin and how he got his aquatic degree.

These creatures are quite amazing, we humans love them so.
While at recess they play in the ocean, they frolic and put on a show.

They dislike the subject called English,
dangling participles just don't look right.
But dangle a fish or squid, and the whole darn school starts to fight.

Young dolphins have math lessons,
they count with their fins and bottle nose.
One fish, two fish, three fish, good fish.
They eat each day's lesson, so the story goes.

Because of physical education they can swim and amaze us so.
The school achieves in aquatics, they often have swim meets you know.

They attend physical science classes, the law of gravity they must defy.
So when they perform at Sea World they'll be able to jump real high.

Every quarter they get a report card, each student gets grade average A.
We know every dolphins in Beta, it was reported in the news today.

Each student completes his assignment and turns it in on time.
These creatures help each other study.
They read the Ancient Mariner in rhyme.

Laura Susan Minchew

Storage

I shall fold my dreams and pack them away
In the cupboard called "Never-to-be."
There to remain 'til someday when
I'll come and turn the key
And shake them out to see how they
Have fared since put away.

Perhaps compare their brightness
To the light of a new day.
They may not be as shiny-bright,
They may not seem as fair,

They may not mean a thing at all
To the one who put them there.

Barbara Lawrence

Expiration

One unguarded moment with the stranger
        makes dreams echo in my mind,

Dreams that leave traces of longing
        and whispers of mysticism,

Dreams that intensify the nature
        and reveal the hidden heart,

Dreams that tangle the senses
        and strew glitter on life.

But a dream is intangible.

You can't catch one.

You can't wear one

        in your hair.

And sooner

        or later,

a dream

    always

        dies

Rachel Hilliard Roberts

Connections

Gaze into my eyes
what do you see
a future, a past, a present

It's like a cord of light
between you and me
that grows bigger and brighter

As you find yourself wondering
what was it like
what will it be like
to feel, to touch, to kiss

If you were to feel
a whisper in the ear
you might find yourself
picturing a wish

To be one with whom you see
convince yourself
that there is only one

Aware you become of a bond
so everlasting
Never will it let go

Juan F. Culajay

Untitled

I sit on my peak and look down the jagged slope
that sometimes is made of real solid rock
and other times of the fiberglass cement pretend rock amusements parks have.
Some days I can see all the way to the bottom of my mountain
and the healthy wild grass and green icy flowers of Ireland in
the twentieth century B.C. when no one lived there.
Other days I see down all the way past the base.
I see the air and clouds underneath my mountain
on the days when there is nothing more than it.
But always the blood is pouring warm and sticky
unlike anything else out of my wrists and the warm flannels turn hard and cold.
At first my skin was warm and wet in it
like in a hot bath after lifting boulders onto rusted Datsuns.
But now my tanned skin is grey and cold underneath the drying blood.
My legs and arms are cold and empty painful.
I always curl up tighter when the cold comes and as my body freezes
more and more in my diaphragm my selfish vitals struggle to stay warm.
They do stay warm, but not enough because I still hurt beyond straight thinking.

Jeb Burt

How I Feel Today

Sometimes I feel pain deep within my soul, and my heart throbs so . . .
Look into my eyes, what have I done?
You label me. Maybe it's the way I dress
Sometimes people pick at me and call me names, like retard and slow,
just because I'm on medicine.
I want to be me, but I'm afraid people won't accept me for how I am.
I'm not bad, I'm just misjudged all the time!!

Josh M.

Dirt

An endless path covered in dirt,
where does it go where does is begin?
The dust floats as you begin to clear the path.

You can see how the air stirs
as the sunlight dances off of each fleck of dirt.
Continuing on the dust rises higher,
invading your nostrils one atom after another.
A sensation overcomes you and before you can resist
you expel every ounce of air from your lungs in a fraction of a second.

The air has stirred again and the sunlight's dance has changed.
You continue on, the path must be cleared.
A cloud trails you as if you were traveling at an excessive rate,
yet time is as still as the path is long.

The atomized dirt still dances in the energy of the sunlight.
The path must be cleared.
It does not end so you must continue.
Your progress is marked by the cloud you're in
and the settling dust behind you.

The dance between dust and light continues
though its luster begins to fade.

Mark Moore

John

One of the immortal few
Your music will forever shine through.
I did not live in your days
But I do see your shadow cover everything, in all directions, always.
All I know of you is your music
as well as the words history does speak.
But none of it seems able to capture you
It all falls short, just too weak.
You invited people to imagine no God? No Heaven or Hell?
No world powers? No religion as well.
And in the end you hoped people would learn.
You created such genius, yet you spoke in such simple terms.
You seem too great to be represented by symbols that are
the remnants of a powerful time, now gone.
You planted the seeds for all the music I now know
And I can only wish I could have met you, John.

Ben Hugues

Snow White Party

When Santa comes to town
Snow is falling to town.

When Santa comes to town
Whole world becomes white.

When snow is falling to town
Stars are sparkling, twinkle, twinkle.

When the moon is shining to town
Birds are singing and sleeping.

When Santa comes to town
Snow is dancing, stars are sparkling.

When Santa comes to town
Snow is sparkling, moon is shining.

Whole world is singing.
Jingle Bells. Jingle Bells.

Merry Christmas.
Happy New Year.

Kyung Yang

Final Truth

The days are days
The nights are nights
Death is a death
You fight for life
You wish to be born
You wish to die
In death there is truth
Is alive just a lie?

David A. Zumbrink

Untitled

The setting sun glistens on the water
as the waves lap along the bank.
The animals scurry through the underbrush
and the birds sing their songs.
A single duck glides along
its destination downstream.
As the trees reach out over the water,
offering a place to go,
a cool breeze rustles the leaves
of the trees standing tall.
And driftwood
floats along on its
journey to the unknown.
A fish jumps
to catch a bug
perched upon the glassy water.
And from across the distant sky
Peace extends its arms.

Danette M. Schaaf

In My Mind

In my mind,
holds a shadow of despair.
In my mind,
holds a flare of hope.
In my mind,
holds life and love.
In my mind,
holds death and fear.
In my mind,
holds painful memories.
In my mind,
holds happy memories.
In my mind,
holds a thought of what's to come.

Nam Ho

The Greatest Gift of All

So many have forgotten who gave us with this land, it wasn't given by just
a simple man, he also chose the color of my skin, for this you have fought,
but could never win.

I have watched as you displayed your racial animosities and
discriminations, don't you know that this is where I get more
determination? My color was not given my choice, but it is mine now and I
shall defend it with a very loud and out spoken voice.

I was given this gift by the touch of his hand, some of you forgot this
wonderful man, this beautiful color he blessed and gave to me, this is the
greatest gift, he placed it on the outside for the whole world to see.

You have wasted enough energy on hatred, jealousy and so much mistrust,
but you have forgotten that God gave this gift to all of us.

Be proud of your color red, yellow, black or white, we are of one and we must all unite
you are fighting and you know you will lose, this gift came from God, and he alone will choose.

We all must learn to live and work together,
no one man can say he is better, very few still believe that it all came from God.

And to those of you who have different beliefs,
you are entitled to your own little worlds.

Agnes L. Turner

Precious Name

To the Myles family
To the one whose name is so sweet and precious
The name of "Mother Dear" is given,
For with her name she brings joy and love,
And when we cry she comes running to see what's wrong or right,
Then she kisses our bruises and calms our cries with sweet cheers
And so with hugs and kisses in time.
She hears our prayers at night,
But oh, what joy it brings to hear us say, "Goodnight Mother,"
For to her name she brings a luster light that's pure bright,
And gives her face a lustrous glow,
But to you and me she gives all her love to hold and store.
No one could be so sweet and pure; I call her Mother, some call her Friend,
But to me she was Mother and Friend indeed.
And so, my Friend, as time goes by from year to year
And with my search from sea to sea, one thing that's all but clear to me:
This lady and our mother is sweet to me, but one day and soon I know
And oh, but this I know and time will come when all honor is given to this
Dear One, all honor I say to you Dear One,
just you my Mother and my Friend.

Dolorita Scott

I Love You

For my daughter, Stacy
"I love you." What does mortal man know of these things?
What web awaits?

"I love you." Is it the desert in springtime, wondrous, vibrant, then quickly turning to
scorching sands,
the abode of poisonous serpents seeking the slightest provocation?

"I love you." Is it the delicate blossom of midsummer, waiting for the warmth
of golden beams to gently unfold its velvet petals?
Forever waiting.

"I love you." Is it the large oak tree at rivers edge, gnarled, bent,
shielded by thick, weathered bark that beckons and pleads, "Touch me—caress me"?
Its long tendrils are steadfast, unyielding, rooted true to its cause,
Nourished by decaying matter it itself gave up.
Its boughs offer shelter, foliage to shade at midday.
It is victorious over the storms of frailties, triumphant over fragmented dreams.
Flourishing, thriving, it bursts forth with like seed,
Summoning the Earth to embosom its young.

"I love you." What does mortal man know of these things?
What web awaits? Time—unconquerable Time, insatiable.
Time is the revealer of "I love you."

Madelyn Hendry

My Mother's Arms

In loving memory of Eleanor Mutka
Once a baby in your arms,
So warm and comforting
I seem to recall,
Now an adult, I still need
The warmth and comfort,
But those arms are cold
And cannot reach out!
A memory I hold,
Because that's all I have
Of the arms that held me
Whenever I ran to them.
I remember how soft and smooth
Those arms did feel,
Those arms now cold
Can't help me heal!
But in the dark,
When I reach out
I feel again the warmth
Of your arms!

Constance Mutka Hill

O! Child

O! child you're so lovely
Eyes like night
Hair like raven
Skin so right

O! child you're so lovely
Eyes like sky blue
Hair like gold
Skin so true

O! child you're so lovely
Eyes like honey
Hair like earth
Skin so sunny

O! children you're so lovely
I've come to tell you so
To tell you what a "jewel"
That on earth has been sowed

O! children you're so lovely
May you stay that way today and tomorrow
Time will tell your true colors
I hope there is happiness and not sorrow

Yolanda Paredes Bastani

Untitled

In tribute to William Wordsworth
"We walked along, while bright and red
uprose the morning sun"
Dew sparkled on the morning grass
A new day had begun.

The flower petals gently swayed
In the warming breeze
Bright colors and aromas
Reached out to hungry bees.

Wondrous sights were waiting there
For us along the way
A silken web a spider made
A bird with feathers gray.

Chatter of squirrels in the trees
Filled the clean fresh air
And down below the army ants
Carried crumbs to share.

As we walked along the path
With nature all unfurled
We felt a sense of peacefulness
In the beauty of our world.

Darlene O'Donnell

Hand in Hand

She was beautiful and tall.
I was pudgy and small.
She was older than me,
yet, we shared a special kind of love
as we walked hand in hand
through the woods and meadow lands.

She explained to me why blue-backed swallows
flew low to the ground for food.

How a buttercup could reflect its color to your hand
and how to play the "She loves me, loves me not" game.
I always suspected her a cheating in the game,
for when she plucked the last daisy pedal,
it was always "she loves me."
When Autumn came, we went to other lands in search of sphagnum moss,
princess pine, and other of nature's gifts for our holiday decorations.
She taught me how to make these things.
So went the days, months, and then the years.
When last I saw her, I held her hand,
so different from the hand of the meadow lands.
Our eyes met, each brimming with tears,
and my memory went back through the years
to that wonderful woman who held my hand.

James E. McFarland

The Rock

How many seasons has it stood so scared, so worn, so bare.
It must be ageless for it looks as though 'twas forever there.
Scorched by the sun, swept by the wind and
lapped by the dripping rains,
a landmark for some and a lookout, too
endless miles upon miles unrolled on the plains.
Some weary beings, its refuge they sought
in its shallow cave down under.
Some used it too, to nurse back their ill
and bad men to hide their plunder.
Some left their loved ones in eternal rest,
their final farewell, they gave the one thing left:
the huge, worn rock to mark their lonesome grave.
In this place, too, a start of life brought forth amid childbirth pains,
swaddled and fed by mother and wife
then going forth once again.
Oh, if the sobbing winds that blow
could eulogize the sound,
that would be a mingling of joy and despair
in a chorus for miles around.

Virginia Dennis

Praise unto the Day

For David, Andrew, Katelyn, Jordan, and Kylee
"We walked along, while bright and red uprose the morning sun"
filling the sky with majesty, beauty, and awe.
Life exists but with the ball of burning flames.
Bringing forth warmth to the heart and soul.
Left behind are past yesterdays
with only the promise of a present new today.
Nature continues its timely ritual course.
Instinct will surely guide the daily paths
of all that became by the very breath of God.
We wet our feet upon the delicate slender blades of grass with dew drops
glistening as dazzling diamonds upon the vast carpet of green.
A flower dares to unfold arching its neck less the touch of golden rays.
My heart filled with song upon hearing the birds in the air.
An orchestra performing the blended sounds of the creeping
and crawling creatures of many who posses this grand and glorious theater.
The sun to rule by day suddenly takes over
by the stars and moon of the night.
Both giving great light.
Invasive to this greatness we suddenly may feel.
Alone is he who does great wonders.

Mary Kate Groh

Intelligent Event

Frequent predicament
Incompetent acknowledgment
Diligent experiment
Pertinent development
Implement measurement
Underwent accident
Magnificent enlightenment
Subsequent comment:
Prevent relent!

Excellent accomplishment . . .
Content temperament.

Faye L. Covert

My Sister

To Jo, my love forever
I have my sister
I call her Sally Sue
She will love me forever
No matter what I say or do
And that is who I would
Like to be just for you
She cries with me
She tells me when I am wrong
I don't know I will survive
Whenever she is gone
I will lean on you
And you can lean on me
Between the two of us
We will find out who we can be
She is my sister
Sometimes my best friend
Whenever I need her
She is also my mother
I would never trade her for another

Virginia Freeman

Tears of Love

The tears fall gentle upon this page,
the words turn blurry and begin to age.

Tears of sadness, tears of love,
tears that were created from the one above.

The tears that fall like morning dew,
are tears of having so much love for you.

So when you see a falling tear,
you will always know, I love you, dear.

Charlene Peterson

Winter Grace

To Wynter Grace Williams
Behold this night
a wondrous place
With tiny flakes
of frosted lace
The air so still
only angels race
What could it be
this heaven's space

The snow
it falls at steady pace
The gentle cold
upon my face
Earth's colors fade
without a trace
Behold this night
of "Winter Grace"

Carol M. Chartrand

Untitled

In years to come, I'll hold on to you in the silence of our room,
kiss you softly on your cheek.
And you'll turn to me, smiling.
I will have all the meaning in the world beside me.
In years to come, we'll walk together on a sunny day in the park,
our newly placed rings shining magnificently in the sun.
And we'll look to each other for our happiness.
In years to come, the rain will fall only for us as we watch it
collect into puddles.
And we'll race outside to steal that ever wonderful kiss in the rain.
In years to come, we'll look back on all the years we thought
would never come and laugh about how fast time flies.
Our portrait of an endless love finally pieced together,
we'll hold each other tight.
And we say that we would do it all again.
In years to come, we will be one, you and I.
And we will be beautiful.

Terry Naylor

Untitled

Seasons greetings . . . come ye, come all . . . to Southern California
where the surf meets the turf while the ground is rocking and rolling
and with its little tornadoes here and there
to watch people running around with their hands in the air
not knowing what to do . . . meanwhile sit back and enjoy
the softness of the park lawn grass only to discover
those mean little pesky fire ants out on the prowl,
and before you realize what had bitten you . . .
you jump up off of the ground on fire . . .
and then somewhere in the trees are lurking those killer bees
just waiting for their chance to come
zooming in on you when you least expect it.

Yes, come to California and experience the best action of the west
where carjackings take place and road rage out on the open highway
for your best vacation ever!
Make your dream come true . . . so see you soon!

Anita Fritz

Instructions for Closure

Hesitant fingers, don't open the book sealed tightly a long time ago.
(Eloquent words, once written, fade fast in the afterglow).
Thumb not through moldering chapters, lest you fail to understand
The message on turned back pages crumbling in faltering hands.

If you must, salvage all of the pieces.
Preserve them from further wear,
(For treasure so ancient and lovely dissolves with the soft puff of air).
At the end, store it high on your bookshelf, there to forever remain.
Then vow to never re-open the book that is sealed shut again.

Jeri Stepan

I Wish the Best for You

To Alexandria, and all that I meet
No matter how many times I have scolded or scorned you.
I wish the best for you.
No matter how many times I wasn't there when you needed to talk.
I know that your hearts are in the right places they're just clouded by so
many things that you don't need in your life.
I still wish the best for you.

I wish you joy when you are sad.
I wish you friendship when you're alone.
I wish you guidance when you've lost your way.
I wish the best for you.

I wish you knowledge when you don't know the answers.
I wish you faith when you're struggling between right and wrong.
In all things that you want and your little heart's desire.
I wish the best for you!

Nina Y. Appiah

What's in a Name?

What do you want from this life?
To change? To feel the same?
To know who you are?
To be left in the dark?
A special brand of dark emotion,
lost in your own sad devotion.
Lost in all we tried to say.
Lost in all the games we play.
Will the real martyr please stand?
How about the loser who lost it all
and died quietly without remorse
in the backseat of a station wagon?
Grievous errors make us human,
humiliation makes us pure.
Dying living all the same.
When you're burned beyond recognition,
what's in a name?

Brandon Walker

A Loving Tribute

Thirty-six years of tears and joy
Two little girls and one little boy.
Through sunshine, rain, and stormy weather
We and our brother stood together.

We had our ups, we had our downs,
Now, he's gone to wait his crown;
We'll bid our time 'til the morning is here
When God shall join us to our dear.

He'll wait for us as he's always done
Until this Christian race, we've won.
Then, together we'll stand our test,
And together God will grant us
Eternal rest.

Flossie M. Washington

Autumn

Autumn is here at last
The cool wind a-blowing
As it has in the past

The leaves on the trees
With orange, red, and green
The brown of the branches
Standing out so lean.

The colors of the mountains
Against the big blue sky
As I sit and watch it all
It makes me want to cry.

The colors all together
And the beauty that they cast
Will always remind me
That autumn is here at last.

Sue Pruitt

Eyes Made of China

Look at me with those eyes made of China
Show me the things I don't wanna see
Unlock the door with your stained glass key
Throw your questions in the sky
Let me give you another lie
The ground beneath us is falling
Kill yourself for fascination
Kill yourself imagination
Catch the teardrop on the windowpane
We're too young to fall asleep
You're standing in your white dress
Words are coming all in a mess
Look at me with those eyes made of China

Christopher Cockrum

Coaches

A bitter cold wind blows across the field, hampered only
by a small storage shed and a wooden outbuilding
that would soon hold concessions and extra ice packs.
It is "first come, first serve," so the coach grabs for a duffel bag
and begins to stuff bats, balls, and bases, all the while,
searching for decent catchers' gloves and a mask
and chest protector that might actually last the whole season.
With numb fingers and damp sneakers, he walks back to his truck.
His mind wanders. With the wind still blowing and cold,
the boys show up for their first practice. A menagerie of sorts.
Some of the names have changed, but the ball caps, gloves,
and cleats are strangely familiar. Rusty from a long winter,
the boys go through the motions as balls pass through their legs
and over their heads respectively. The coach rolls his eyes and wonders.
Spring finally arrives, signaling the start of a new season.
Sporting brand new uniforms and sheepish grins, the boys take the field.
Would they remember lessons learned? What did he forget to tell them?
Six innings pass without major mishap and as the boys congratulate
the other team, he packs up the duffel bag and smiles.
With the passing of each game come joy and disappointment.

Doug Clare

Darkness

To Cancer survivors in search of true healing

Perhaps . . . I needed to look back, I needed to reflect upon things
that were pounding as a second heart, things that were there on the back of it all.
Dark secrets, morbid acts, neglected truths, violated rights, not only to others,
but to my own dignity. There had to be a reason for such madness.
No one can deny the horrifying effects so well manifested.
Nevertheless, there was mystery and darkness in my own recollection of facts.
There were so many lies that had been built. So well established in my falling identity.
That was the worst to admit, that I had created a character of faulty traits,
and it was falling slowly falling, layer by layer without integrity,
revealing a soul that had been trapped, that wanted to be free.
The illness . . . yes, that cancer, it was so devastating . . . a fatal blow.
It was there to remind me how little importance my worldly pursuits had,
how meaningless everything had been. Its silent statement was:
Wake up you fool! It was telling me to dispel the violent and cruel atmosphere
that is causing the imbalance rooted in my soul.
It was time to take time . . . no more rushing into frivolous pursuits.
My soul was been cleansed and liberated from the confused shouting of a distorted mind.
It wanted to soar higher and higher . . . into the clear skies of tranquility and forgiveness.

Marjorie R. Firmin

What If?

What if the world was the size of a peanut?
What would be of us?
Every night I lay in bed wondering what if?
The questions haunt me because I cannot answer them.
What if the Earth was not even here? Where would we be?
Mars, Jupiter, the sun? Or maybe nowhere!
If I was to fly to Africa . . . what would I learn?
Would I find a fossil or just those poor people?
What if you were not as lucky, remember you have things others may not.
What if? What if? That question will always haunt me
because what if, what if becomes why did this happen?
So just remember always have faith in yourself so in case
a bad what if becomes true you will always live inside it.
What if the world was black and the skies were orange?
Would you want to live there?
What if you were the only soul living? Could you live?
I would not know because I'm not. That's the trouble of what if's!
You think but cannot answer your thoughts
Everyone sometimes has a bad what if but not everyone gets haunted!

Stephanie Roop

I Am a Cancer Survivor

To my wonderful husband, Edward

I was diagnosed with cancer,
and my life changed.
I encountered losses
that most will never understand.
I gained a new perspective on life
that few have experienced.
I learned that I have this one day
to utilize to the fullest.
And although I may get down
and worried at times,
I forge ahead each day
and take better care of myself
that I ever have.
I am a fighter. I am strong.
I am a cancer survivor.

Kellie Medeiros

Mom

Mom, you are my touchstone,
you make my world go round.
A thought of you fills my heart,
when I cannot be home.

You brought me in, and brought me up
in this crazy world, I thank you
for the love you've shown,
but most of all, the support you gave
as you've watched as I have grown.

I love you, Mom, and hope you know
how much you mean to me,
and one day soon, I'll pay you back
for everything you've done
to make me all that I am and will ever be.

No one or thing could ever change
the way I feel towards you.
The love we've built will ever last,
until our lives are through.

Kristy Permisohn

Number 22

Hers is a beauty,
like that of a rose.
Gentle caresses,
soft contours,
like rose petals kissed by the dew.
The blush,
of supple cheeks,
the colour of a rose in full bloom.
She captivates,
like the lingering scent,
of a fresh bouquet.
She is truly special
quite mystic.
She is like the perfection of the rose.
They both have beauty,
given by nature,
yet cared for by humankind.

Jeremy Haygood

The Wind

I used to know a Fairyland
Of Fairy Meadows running to the sea
The Old Oak winked at his grave pine friend
As the Fairy Willow danced for him to see
But they didn't know that I was the wind
I was the Fairy Wind
And she danced with me.

Louise Kelley

"Untitled 101"

Miles of dusty road pave the road to an ending, here:
Where the stores close at sundown, and the lemonade stand's no more.
The little boy who runs it has left to let the sign grow old;
Too faded to read; too silent to ignore;
Dusted by hushed memories, billowing from the quiet fields:
Voiceless and immaterial.

A Salvation Army veteran sits in front of the five and dime store.
He rings a little bell, like Christmas time, waiting for the hours to leave spare change.
He never lost a limb in battle, all he lost was one battered soul,
Battling the demons in the kitchen sink, and the angels between his ears.
Air fractures as the bell and clock toll one; Voiceless and immaterial.

Clouds find themselves nonexistent in the scorching western sky.
Cattle move to pasture, sometimes raising dumb heads to Heaven:
To Vegas where the cowboys go, following their cowgirls to Hollywood.
I sit in front of the barbershop, where the old men got stubble shaved.
I'm waiting for the next bus to Tucson, to take me far from this place.
For everyone's left this town but me, the Hari-Krishna, and the five and dime.
Without thought, I leave quick, for the realm of street gods and empty men;
Calling the voiceless in songs of empty wonder, or worlds, immaterial.

Laura Germine

Lost Hopes

A child's life far from gone dreams too far too see,
Waiting for the one true love to come and ever be,
Dreams and secrets are at loss in a world full of fright.
He waits all eternity for the dying light.
A soulless past far too great, only wishing to erase the hate,
Soon redemption day will come.
And ever true the world shall see the power that it brings.

Sean Van Den Boom

Just Friends

To my lady friend, Pamela D. Mosley
I heard our song today. "What are you doing here?" I asked myself.
Believe, I'm glad you are. Our friendship is a love song. Write it across the sky.
Would we dare? If, perhaps, not belonging to another.
Why is it I sleep, think, talk, eat, and drink . . . You? The chemistry, too potent to analyze.
Feels so good, so dangerous too. "Why here, why now, why you and why me?" I asked myself.
I just smile again when I think about it. My heart was warmed when you called.
I'll work with what that which I can have. This portion of the gift of love to me.
But how long, though? No such question to be asked.
But we really, truly love each other. Don't deny it, it will only judge you.
Don't run from it, it'll only walk you down.
Don't suppress it, it'll only grow . . . bigger than you can handle.
You love me, and you're angry about it. Just don't get even.
Yet, it is heard in our conversations, it is felt in the laughter and sorrow we share,
our eyes tell it all when of each other we behold. I really love you.
Did I say that? You heard right in your left ear, because it's closer to the heart.
The emptiness, filled and the coldness is melting. My heart is revived when you're around.
The hurt, fear have disappeared. I can love me again because of you.
As the ring of gold is a circle complete, so now am I. Truly, I am.
With this ring of the heart, we do thee wed. Friends for life.
Diagnose the science of the magic of love. The formula written as musical notes across the sky.

Matthew Mosley

Nature's Children

Stand within a field of beautifully grown flowers.
Pick out the empty opening where one has been torn from its roots.
Should it not be the strong, taller stems protecting the developing seeds?
Misdirection and misfortune of the young are so often overlooked.
Or is it that the flourishing do not always see?

Sit beneath the trees amidst a blowing forest.
Watch for the leave as it is carried away by the changing winds.
Should it not be the powerful, plenitude trunks sacrificing their strength?
A new leaf among a world of mature nature is so often disregarded.
Or is it the roots which absorb most of the water,
that do not always care?

Cheryl A. Szurgot

Streetlight

The football goes flying past you
As you just awoke to shine
For many years they fly by
Just before the children are called inside
No one wants to end the game
As another day is done
Both sides had so many scores
Who really cares or knows who won

I kissed my first love in your shadows
The innocence flowing between us both
After talking for hours and hours
Only you knew the trials of love
Had just begun
All WE knew was having fun
At that moment
Each of US was the one
Now both sides have so many scars
Who really cares or knows who won.
With all your brilliance, how 'bout it?
Any clue?

Theodore Menz

Silence

Silence can be comforting
Like the silence of old friends.
Or silence can bring friendship
To the bitterest of ends.

Silence can be listening
To restore a soul to life
Or silence can be wounding
Like the cutting of a knife.

Silence can be searching
For an answer boldly sought.
Or silence can be giving up
Without the slightest thought.

Silence can be loving
When words are not needed.
Or silence can be deadly
When feelings go unheeded.

Choose carefully your silence
For silence is a choice.
Even though it is unspoken
It is deafening with its voice.

Marilyn Healey

God's Gift of Love

There was a little songbird,
he sang a song for me

He sang of hope and happiness,
and the future that's to be

He told me that his chirping,
told of things to come

As he bids farewell to the day,
and descending sun.

He sang a song of beautiful dreams,
that only comes to light

As he is nestled in the tree top,
holding on to the night

And with the day's first dawning,
he sings again for me

Of the gift of love God's granted,
that will always be.

Mary Y. Gonzalez

Peace

The world at peace—
Is it a dream?
It is a thought that soothes me
Like a clear mountain stream.

We have to learn to live
With other's differences and faults.
Life should not be a slamdance;
It should be more of a waltz.

We need to learn to get along
And show each other we care.
We need to learn what is right
And how important it is to share.

We have to work as a team
In order to survive.
This world is all we have;
We need to keep it alive.

William A. Hlas

The Porch

The sun is hot
But here it's cool
And peaceful

Alone
My cup held in two hands
I sip and listen to the birds sing

The chime bell tinkles
And on the highway, the traffic hums

While mine are neglected
The working world pursues its goals

I pay no mind
They can do without me today
My mind's at rest
And my soul heals

Anita Bradley

Is It War or Is It Love?

To my mom
War is not the way to love.
It doesn't come from up above.
When your heart is feeling tired and torn
And your mind is feeling tired and worn,
Maybe then you'll see the way
And know we need a brand new day.
War is not the way, you see.
It never finds the love in me.
So when your heart is torn apart
From the stuff that you start,
Maybe then you'll understand
And see the love inside this man.
Maybe then you'll leave the love shine on,
Until all your aches and pains are gone.
Maybe then you're born again,
And maybe then you'll find a friend.
Make the change and then you'll see
All the love inside of me.

Michael P. Crosby

Untitled

A heart is a place of love and care
and each time you say goodbye
it overflows with grief and sadness
so hug me tight and never leave.
For my heart shall break if you do.
For my heart and soul
belong to you forever will the end of time

Ashley N. Ball

Those Blinking Lights

To my daughter, Shannon Crystal Krajcovic
They caution and flash.
To slow us down
And remind us all
There's children in town.

While most do slow.
There is those few.
Who ignore their warning,
And speed right through.

I'm tell you now.
Do watch and slow.
This zone say's a lot,
And finally I know.

As I look back.
I now truly see.
What those blinking lights.
Really meant to me.

Yesterday it's kindergarten.
Now a senior today,
And tomorrow will come,
And take her away.

Peter Krajcovic

Haiku View

Splintering splendor
seasons through a window pane
pirouette divine

Vernal-showered bones
sculpt lean in flowing meadows
cleansed of all sorrow

Remnants sunbleached white
in Summer moonbeam's spotlight
decorate the night

Halloween delights
with frosty fingers spooking
goblins on the run

Rib cage and legs jut
deer knives slice through winter dunes
the patterns of sleep

K. E. Lawrence

Warm Breeze

It is about to rain or about to snow,
the wind is cold but life is raw.
The sun will shine that we know,
so gather up your thoughts,
and strength will follow.

Nicholas Morina

Lush

Send me with kisses,
And I feel.
You
Breathing into me.
Can this be real.
Trust
Shouldn't have given,
This I can crush.
Me
Fading above you.
Loving the
Lush.

Justin D. E. Williams

The Morning After the Storm

The sky is dark,
The sky is light.
The blue. The pink.
The gray. The white.
The black scares me so.
Suddenly a long, piercing white streak,
It lights up the night sky.
I jump up; then I lie back down.
I cover my head in fear.
What did I hear?
The thunder claps through the cloudy sky.
Now the storm is gone.
No more does it clash and clap.
The birds chirp outside,
And a puddle stands near the step.
The sky is now calm and peaceful.
Now I have nothing to fear.
It is the morning after.

David Ray Leary II

Beyond one's Smile

Smile......
Is what makes our day
where a feeling of happiness lives.
But beyond our smile,
a mystery surrounds.
Fear, Anger, Hatred.
Where only smile can hide,
these feelings from reality.
But once alone, a door opens
for these to destroy our minds.
But then we tend to smile
and then these feelings are jailed,
where in reality nothing happened.
Still, agony and pain exist.
Unless conquered by ourselves,
real things become real,
our smile becomes true.

Seurinane Sean borra-Española

Dedcated to my mother, Mary H. Lee
CAN WE BEAR-2-LOVE
without tha risk of pain?
Will tha differences between,
Black on Black;
Black and White; ever change?
My people's pain, souly real.
What'z constantly felt,
Their passion; and ZEAL.
4-FREEDOM, and Will;
2-B-treated as Human beings.
How pure is that thought?
How real is tha dream?
All people-R-created equal,
but feel-2-show, different;
In how they act.
Such pain-2-feel,
Being under attack.
My prayer, Factz; not Fiction.
Lord please, help us all.
4-we long, 4-your;
"Attention."

AGAINST ALL ODDZ

Poet

To Sr. Michael Francis, O.S.U.
Bare winter trees stand
Flaunting white frosted webs 'gainst
The black evening sky

Renee N. LaFountain

In His Image

When I was created
He breathed in me.
I am made in His image.

I smile whenever I see
A happy child.
I am made in His image.

I give my best to
Those I love.
I am made in His image.

I live my life so
All will know
I am made in His image.

When I am alone
Will the mirror reflect that
I am made in His image?

Gwendolyn Ferguson

Memory

To my daughter, Elizabeth
There's a special place of memory
I often long to be
Where I can meet with those I love
Whom others cannot see.

When shadows fall and night time comes
I close my eyes and see
The sunlight on her golden hair
Where darkness used to be.

When I awake and fear returns
I come again to be
In that safe place I love so much
Of silent memory.

Elizabeth A. Steege

To Be You

I woke up this morning
Wanting to be you,
To be inside your head,
Thinking your thoughts
About me.
I woke up
Wanting to know, without doubt,
If you love me.
I wanted to be your eyes
And see
What you see
When you look at me.
I yearned to be your body
When it held me
And know if you feel
Warm sensations
At the touch of me
As I feel
At the touch of you.

A. Perry Adams

Listening

You were always there to listen
to what I had to say.
I always had the fear of you not
being there one day listening.
There isn't a person anywhere
that could do it the way you did it,
in a mother's loving way.
Who is listening?

Sally Lamberson

Did You Ever Wonder

Do angels never shed a tear?
They see much joy and sadness
They saw the savior born that night
They saw Him on that cross
They saw Him cry at Lazarus' tomb
They saw Him with the children.

They see our sins, they see our joy
Is there no reaction?

God's helpers these, to do their job
Must only see His will.

M. Therese Ensworth

Because in My Head

It's No Longer Just Me

They came in uninvited
Walked around my mind
Trudged in the deepest caverns
Where the darkest secrets lie
They turned on the light
Which made the secrets vulnerable
They got in my head
Walked around and around
They left footprints
In the untouched ground
They touched things that were untouchable
To me it felt like rape
They invaded my space
Left an empty hole
Now my head is open wide
For the whole world to see
I no longer feel safe
Because in my head it's no longer just me.

Jillian True

Untitled

To Waffles, Biscuits, Bud, and Presley
Pretty lights in the street
Look at all the people's feet
Slippery ice on the ground
Snowflakes blowing all around.

Hannah Allen

Winter's Walk

In tribute to William Wordsworth
"We walked along, while bright and red
uprose the morning sun . . ."
This day will not be gloomy
With the coming of the sun.

The frozen snow, upon the earth,
Reflects the morning light
It soon will be a sparkling day
In which we can delight.

Jack Frost has painted windows
With strange and starry shapes
That the morning sun, by afternoon,
Will probably erase.

A snowbird sits on a barren branch
And sings a winter song.
He's telling Mother Nature that
We should not tarry long.

Gloomy days are liked by some
For what might be the reason
But we like days when the sun is out
For that, we find it pleasin'!

Joan Worth Holmes

A Knee's Length

How far is it to Heaven,
That home beyond the blue?
The distance to be measured
Is a knee's length from you.

The way to reach that Heavenly home
With all its splendid hue?
The way up is the way down,
Just a knee's length from you.

Good works and man made theories
Will never never do
To span the distance to that home,
Just a knee's length from you.

The key is found in God's own Son
Whose love has proven true;
He alone unlocks the door
That's a knee's length from you.

Read Acts seven verse forty-nine
Then kneel when you are through
And you will find Heaven's "Welcome Mat"
Was just a knee's length from you.

Dorothea E. Blue

Take My Heart

To my beloved, Julie
Every corner of my existence
has finally surrendered
to the silent scent
of your mysterious bearing.
It's not just the pictures
on the walls, the candles
or the memory box;
my breath longs for you
every minute that goes by.

Your heart keeps me going,
even when you're afar . . .

In the solitude of my nights,
I thank God
for blessing my days
with the light
that emerges from your eyes.
How can I not love you
the way I do,
if one of your kisses
brightens my weary heart?

Oswaldo Estrada Jr.

Soft Breezes Bring You Near

Soft breezes blow, removing the snow.
Soft breezes bring freshness and spring,
Soft breezes try
Forming images of you passing by.
Soft breezes springtime makes,
But your absence means heartbreak.
Soft breezes continue in summer,
The empty heart calmer.
Soft breezes comfort my pillow,
Like the smooth flowing willow.
Soft breezes warm and best
Bring needed peace and rest.
Soft breezes blow up memories,
That haunt and enchant my reveries.
Soft breezes cause sounds
Where bold echoes of you abound.
Soft breezes bring you near
Always near, always near.
Soft breezes the fall of the year,
When you, dear one, were last here

Barbara L. Nelson

Snow

Silently it flies
White flakes whirling all around
Landing softly down

Soft sparkling carpet
Blemish free, it envelops
In quiet stillness

Slowly it abates
Fewer flakes flutter about
The wind runs away

And we awaken
To the sound of perfect calm
To the sight of snow
    Brooke L. Davis

Why?

For Woolfie, a friend forever
Why does man strive for immortality?
Could it be a form of irrationality,
Or could it be an escape from the reality
That all humanity achieves fatality?
    Pamelot

Heights of a Fireman's Mind

Fear: I fear not.
Overpowering, unsure,
eyes showing.

Fear: I fear not.
Climbing high, entering
into a cloudy sky.
Fear: I fear not.
Uncertainties, wandering, searching;
Of course I must climb,
never seeing what's in store.

Fear: I fear not.
My face is blinded,
no one will help.
The clouds seem to thicken;
my mind quickens.

Fear: I fear not.
Doing my duty, scary as such.
The heights of my mind will always be.

Fear: I fear not.
Tranquility and peace at last.
    Jonet Caplan

Brothers and Friends,
Dallas and Doyle Hagg

Two fine doctors working hard
Making their way,
One became a surgeon, the other
a family physician.
Both well-set in their position,
Working day and night serving
their patients' needs,
God smiled down on both doing
their good deeds.
Now, Dr. Doyle is left on to trod;
And Dr. Dallas is gone home
to be with God.
They worked saving their patients' lives,
Of children, husbands, and wives
Someday they will be together again,
Brothers—Best friends.
    Lula Ethington

Untitled

Oh, to be in love
Yes, that is what I want to be
To hold your hand, to feel your touch
To see your smile, to hear your voice
To make you laugh, to stop your cries
To fill your wants, to answer your needs
Oh, to be in love
Yes, that is what I want to be
    Scott Martin

We Are but a Whisper

We are but a whisper
a part of
the wind upon the storm

A breath, a breath
carried to where
we do not know

In our time
to reach a hand
to change some harm

We are but a whisper
a part of, in the heart of
the wind upon the storm
    Janice Kilburn

You

If your ego should rise
By knocking others down in size

Think, when you do
You look smaller, too
    Naomi Lucas

Snowflakes

Little snowflakes in the air
Skittering, scattering, everywhere
People walking down the street
Snowflakes falling on their cheeks!
Children playing in the snow
Building forts and snowmen too!

Snowflakes big and small
Falling softly to the ground
While people are hurrying by
Home to the firelight bright!
To be with loved ones through the night!
    Henrietta A. Perry

Breaking a Dreary Blue

There was a rare light that night,
a beam all its own.
I saw it for a second,
it seemed like an hour, before it was gone
and I felt so alone.
Why light that night?
Then, there, anywhere?
If it were day
who would have noticed, known, or cared?
Before the light, the dark
It was so dark it hit you in the face,
the chest, everywhere!
So dark you could feel it.
So, why light that night?
Breaking a dreary blue,
Out suddenly, quickly, then gone.
Come back rare light,
just for a second and make it an hour!
Rare light!
    John B. Harvey

Love

To my love, Elizabeth
Love is how I feel
A love so true and real
A love that will listen
A love that will heal
A love for you
And everything you do

This love will never leave you
This love will never hurt you
It will always be there
It will always be fair

Love is patient
Love is kind
My love will always have the time
To lift up when you are down
Or put your feet back on the ground

So when you think that no one cares
Sit back and prepare
For a love so true
As the love I have for you
    Wendell Maine

A Wonderful Castle

They gather the sand to make a mound.
Pushing and pulling all that's found.
Making the towers and turrets too,
Doing everything they found do.

Making the windows and the doors.
Making it taller as they add more.
They added the water to the moat.
They made some shells into a boat.

Now their castle is complete.
They take a picture 'cause it's neat.
But what the children didn't know,
Soon their castle would have to go.

The waves came up to the bay,
And swept the castle all away.
The towers cracked, the windows broke.
Through the castle mighty waves poke.

As the sun peeks into the morning sky,
So do birds chirping as they fly.
The moon begins to fade away,
A memory is all that's on the bay.
    Jackie Gerbus

What Lies Within

I loved you once, I loved you twice,
Don't ask again, it's just not nice.

You took my heart, you took my soul.
Honey, I just gotta know.

What made you change to the evil side?
The darkness soon became alive.

I then got scared and did not know,
Who you were or where to go.

I ran to hide, to pray, to find the
answers that might lie inside.

But soon I found my hands were tied.
the answers are for you to find.

The evil lied within yourself.
Not in me, I cannot help.

So darling pray for God to find the evil
that might lark inside.
    Susan Bastyr

Wrong Love

You're at your house and
The air makes you choke
You feel that nobody loves you
And trust is a joke

You want to get out
You don't know what to fight for
You think everyone hates you
And it hurts to the core

You don't have anyone
Until someone comes along
You think you're in love
And you hope it's not wrong!

Jessica Nicks

Untitled

My beautiful swan in that great blue lake.
My great shiny star in that clear sky.
My little Angel fallen from Heaven.
My colorful butterfly that is in
that great garden full of roses.
My mermaid coming out of those
salty waters of the sea.
You are everything to me.
You are my reason why I still breathe
that air every day and in all those nights.

Gustavo Picazo

God's Masterpiece

A tiger lies on dirt bedding,
So gentle, so kind.
It is hard to imagine
Such a sweet thing
Grows up to be
An astonishing killer of prey
That lurks the forest floor.
But wait, could it be?
Is there a bit of kindness
In the cold-blooded killer?
And is it so,
It can be kind and gentle?
Yes, for it has a cub of its own
To love and nourish,
To teach its killer skills,
And to guard it with the tiger's life.
And so now you see
Why a tiger is God's
Masterpiece.

Cara Byrne

Untitled

How far traveled are you?
Can you still see the sun?
I have walked a step towards home
And you a step in a different goal.

I've balanced the time spent in my head
And relieve each perfect kiss.
The sweet touch cuddled on couch,
The noise of each our silence.

A wanted laughter, a needed hug
A smile that burns in my days
Unlike the candle that greets me at my door
Extinguished in our departure.

How far traveled are you?
Is the sun replaced by stars?
For I made a wish and sent to you
Through the moon a kiss goodnight.

Brendan Bartlett

A Word from the Blind

I never knew there would be thirst
Until I came upon this earth
I have no eyes
I have no sight
For only God holds the light.

Our days are dark
Our life is short
So we lean on our blessed Lord

Days have passed and we sat down
Not knowing where that we might land.

We only know that Jesus cares
Lord lead us to a brighter land.

Montie Ruth Bailey

He Will Never Forsake Me

To Steve Lewis and Chi Megwitch
Though I shed my tears,
I stand tall
Through these trials and tribulations
I will grow and be strong
Many try to break my spirit
But to no avail
My spirit and will
Are strong and free
Like the eagle
Who soars high
This good red road is not easy
But it is the road
I choose to follow
For the creator is with me
And will never forsake me as others do
He stands by my side
And carries me through it all
Never misleading me, never judging me
He always loves me and forgives me
For I am only human

Diane Marie McDonald

I Am with You

I have traveled with man
Through time and back again
I have walked in the shadow
Of the tired and weary
I have enjoyed the gaiety of life
And the joy of fulfillment
And I am always with you.

I have felt the pangs
Of hurt and hatred
I have known the ecstasy
Of love and compassion
I have witnessed the fright
Of loneliness and despair
And through it all, I am with you.

Ross E. Morrison

Children

Mischief sparkles in your eyes,
A smile plays upon your lips,
You view the world as a surprise
Of candy canes and chocolate chips.

You love adventurous fairy tales;
You just can't wait to be told
Of far-off lands and ships with sails,
Of following rainbows to pots of gold.

At night you dream of far-off places,
Of making homeruns, of Cheshire cats;
And as we watch your sleeping faces,
We wish we could be more like that.

Rebecca Perry

Room for Me

I don't remember how I know,
But I was loved long ago.
I was born into this love,
And it had room for me.

I don't remember fearing that
I'd turn around and be alone.
I went my way and wandered back,
In love, secure and free.

It can't be said I knew my place
Or worked to earn some favor.
I didn't know, I didn't work.
Love just bid me be.

Tonight I want again to be
That careless child of grace.
I want to tumble mindlessly
Into love's broad embrace.

I want to rest my soul from fear
Against my Father's knee,
And reclaim my inheritance and my identity
For love has room for me.

Mary Boyle

The Rose

I discovered,
While at work this morn,
That we behold the rose,
But seldom the thorn.

The dew on the leaves,
The sun on the petals,
Who would think the rose
Has thorns as nettles?

I inhale its scent,
The fresh-burst bud,
As I see its beauty,
Against the mud.

I stretch out my hand,
To hold this bud,
As my hand closes around it,
Emotions like a flood.

It was then I discovered,
While at work this morn,
That when I held the rose,
I found a thorn.

Matthew B. Splittgerber

This Heart to Thee

To Larry, whom I love
This heart of mine I
Send to thee, tread
Upon it carefully.

The strength and courage
You will find, are within
Me and are mine

But I will share them
With thee, since you are
All that matters to me.

So when you're feeling alone
And blue, search the walls
That surround you.

Search your heart and you
Will find, my love for
All lifetime.

Shelly Holmes

Untitled

To Amanda and Nathan—Love, Auntie
Like the passion for an echo
 So sought our souls
Like serendipitous synchronicity
 Our hearts danced with destiny
Like sweet sovereignty
 Came the embrace of divinity . . .
 Darlene Swanson

The Girl That Used to Be

When I look into a mirror,
And the image that I see,
Is just a faint reminder,
Of the girl I used to be.

My boobs have dropped down to my waist,
A waist no longer there,
The hips and thighs have also spread,
The tummy's everywhere.

Oh, yes, I've lost an inch or two,
Which I could ill afford to do.
Knuckled fingers, crooked toes,
Along with my other woes.

The more I look, the more I see.
Could this old hag, be really me?

But thank you Lord,
For my good health,
And also for my limited wealth.

And underneath this sad old frame,
I know that really I'm the same,
THE GIRL I USED TO BE.
 Kathryn J. Lentz

Hula Dancer

Queenly statuesque posture
Clothed in aqua blue-green
Trimmed in bursting yellow
Touches eyes that smile and gleam

Gentle story-telling gestures
Flow with each careful step
Hips signature the ancient grace
Of Hawaiian spirit in song-filled depth

Hands, hips, feet sway
In rhythmic enticing waves
Leaving viewers longing
Lingering in constant gaze

Heartfelt face
Expresses pride
Her indigenous radiance
From a history none can hide
 Marcelle A. Mendez

Wishing They Knew

Laughter is an expression
Which comes through my joyous soul
Without this feeling
I am not whole

Smile, someone else will see
Then they'll smile too.
It's a big circle
Wishing they all knew.

For we walk by faith, not by sight
and I will love not by fight.
Off yet only I will.
 Nathan Harrington

Red Barn

The red barn sits quietly beckoning
Those who seem bent on reckoning
Search inside its dusty, well worn walls
Adventure always seems to call
Dark, hidden places or bright hayloft
Entering voices loud or soft
Excitement jumping off bright golden hay
Hidden meetings rather than carefree play
Bright summer day, cold wintry night
Pleasures galore, hair-raising fright
Time tho' passes day by day
Quickly or slowly some might say
Those who ventured in forever may find
Memories never quite leave the mind
Leaving brings smiles and tears to sight
The red barn still sits waiting to invite.
 Kathy Wahlberg

Special Friend

A special person is a special friend.
When you're with them,
You know your laughter will never end.
We all have lots of other friends, too,
But my most special friend is really you!
 Ariana Bannister

The Day Star

What hope is there in the midst of darkness
When no light is in my view,
When the dark clouds seem to gather
Blocking out the hope for new,
Worldly trials seem to burden
Is this hopelessness my due?

Then the day dawns bright and shining
And the day star comes to you,
Bringing joy and hope renewing
That our Lord will come in view.
With His presence comes the dawning
Flooding the whole world with His light,
No more doubting, no more darkness,
When our day star ends the night.
 Betty Jane Smith Seay

The Gift

It's not a gift to look upon
It's not a gift to see,
It's the message from the one who loves
Who died for you and me

He died for you, that you might live
Won't you listen to His call?
He desires that you come to him.
To be your all in all

He desires that you hear from him
This message that brings life
It's the story of God's kingdom
and his son, Jesus Christ

He's calling out to you today
can you hear from deep within
He's saying come to me, dear one
And you can be born again.

He wants to give you life so full
So full you can't contain,
This is God's kingdom in your heart.
And life eternal again.
 Adelina Robles

I'm Lost Again!

I wish I'd find the way to go.
I find it then it's lost.
I know it's somewhere, not too far,
the instructions just got lost.

So many ways to choose from,
all seeming to be right;
I chose the one I think's correct, and
I'm lost again!
 Jennifer Hale

An Apple for the Teacher

Dedicated to my daughter, Dayna
An apple for the teacher
is very sweet and dear.
But with a couple bites of it,
it soon will disappear.
And so I thought I'd make you one
To hang upon your wall,
So every time you look at it
You may somehow recall
That I was in your room one year,
And as the years go by,
You will always be the teacher
Who is the apple of my eye.
 Shirley M. Schmitt

Changes

In tribute to William Wordsworth
"We walked along while bright and red
Uprose the morning sun"
The dew kissed leaves by the road bed
Glistened in crisp unison
The melodies of birds in trees
Broke the silence of my thoughts
Reflecting all these memories
And changes life has brought.

Little shoulders I once held tight
Are now so strong and wide
Little fingers I taught to write
Has filled my heart with pride
I turn my head so he can't see
The mist forming in my eyes
Is this my little boy how can it be
My how the time just flies

A boy left home yesterday
But I'm taking this man fishing today.
 Rayona Roszell

I Wish

In memory of Joseph G. Weilks
I wish for truth
I wish for peace
but so much more
I wish that wars may cease

I wish for clean air
clean water, clean land
I wish this soon
could be achieved by man

I wish for good health
good friendship, good fun
I wish that victory over cancer
soon could be won

I wish for so much
I know but you see
through great faith in God
I know it shall be
 Roland Creson Jr.

Dreams

My dreams are my visions
I hope to fulfill in life
They can all come true
If the decisions I make are right

I have to learn for myself
Everyone makes mistakes
And for me to get to my dreams
I'll need to know when one has taken place

I want to make something of myself
Be useful in my life
Be acknowledged for what I did
And not be criticized

I want people to look up to me
For whatever it is I do
So I can teach them something
Even if it's just believe in you

Finally in closing
I have one thing to say
Follow all your dreams
And let nothing stand in your way.

LayKisha Hawkins

Eye and the Sea

An enormous blue sea
waves crash over me
twisting and turning
confusing me so
the dark center of the sea
stares right at me
digs into my heart
please don't fall apart
with its strong cold stare
just isn't fair
a rush of emotions
fly rapidly
back and forth
between I and the sea
captured by love
we give up the fight
we've had enough.
The wide-eyed blue sea
has fallen for me
and I he.

Theresa Kirchner

Silence

Silence speaks to me,
sometimes taunting,
sometimes haunting.

It forces me to think,
sometimes wild-like,
sometimes child-like.

Is it friend or foe?
Sometimes yes,
sometimes no.

Darlane Lambert

Apples

Red and shiny
Some are tiny
Swinging on a tree
They are red as can be
The trees are in a bed
The sun makes the apples red
They are juicy and sweet
Apples make a good treat.

Miriam Gruenwald

By the Sea

The waves crash in
I stand at the shore

Gray sea, green weeds, white sand
The foam churns up
The bubbles burst

The clouds march in
I stand at the shore

Hard rain, wet face, damp clothes
The sand becomes hard
I can't move

Blue sky explodes above
I stand at the shore

Mighty winds, sand blowing, clouds moving
The sky and sea meet
The sun looks out
I turn and walk away

Trenda Staudenmier

To Understand Life

Friend,
bye for a life for a while
for you do not understand
the life I have mentioned.
Life is like a poetry
that some of the times wanders away.
Like the way our heart feels
and how to accept our world in faults.
I'd like to show you
how life is to me
and how this gift should be handled.
To understand life
you have to understand yourself
and other feelings
in order for yourself to understand you.
Bye for a life for a while
for you do not understand
the life I have mentioned.

Cris S. Feliciano

All My Love

Could I live without your smile?
Could I live without you by my side?
Could I live without your arms around me?
Would I live without your love?
Not I, my love, not I!

Patricia Lee

Untitled

A pensioner had numbered his friends
Smiles on his account
'Til none was closer to him than death.
Entranced by steam
It seemed decades before it last took him
His lips hugged his coffee
In the night He walked
The streets he princely kept
And thought In his character
He had neglected
To feel the street without feeling the high
Foreign the morning passed
Bundled up still naked in the street
Clouds in his head grown like rust
On a neglected rake
He closed his eyes and willed silence
And reconciliation between the living
And the dead.

Mark Cooper

Words of Wisdom

They say that things happen for a reason,
I'd like to think that's true.
And in each life there is a season,
We are rewarded or pay for what we do.

Life goes on, so they say,
And that I've found is true.
You can choose to go or stay,
Time and events will continue.

There's time when one wants to give up.
You could lie down and say, "Why?"
Or get on your feet and take a stand.
Go take that stand, give it a try.

Look forward to each new day,
New people you're going to meet.
And choose your words wisely
When you have something to say.

Words can make someone happy,
Or forever torture a soul.
Kind words are always the best.
On that, your life will be blessed.

Gilbert P. Tafoya

Afraid of How I Feel

When I look into your eyes
I'm afraid of what I see.
I'm afraid of how I feel
When you look at me.

I'd been alone so long
Just trying to get by,
Alone with my thoughts,
Sometimes at night I'd cry.

You came back into my life,
A vision from my past
And I began to think
That I'd be happy at last.

Do I dare open up
Or just give you a smile
And know this interlude
Is for just a little while?

It's the safest way to go
So I am going to try
To enjoy you for a day
And be ready for goodbye.

Gloria Haywood

A Penitent's Prayer

Holy Father, Saviour Divine
Look upon this heart of mine
Forgive and cleanse me now from sin
That perfect peace may enter in.

I know thou hast turned thy face from me
Because thy will I've failed to see.
But hear me, Saviour, hear me now
While at thy feet I humbly bow.

My life has been so useless, Lord
Because I've turned against thy word,
But now, O God, my fault I see
Forgive, I pray, and set me free.

O take my life and use it, Lord,
I now repent and trust in thee.
Thou art the Saviour of the world,
Oh, save my soul and set me free.

I thank thee, Lord, for thy matchless love
Which lifts the soul from deep despair.
For now I feel a radiant joy
And know 'tis answered prayer.

Evelyn Lea Starks

Need for Mommies

Your face has lines of time
Your hands are firm and gentle
You wept at the horrid crime
For you the pain was mental
But for us it is too late

Your eyes are filled with tears
And you felt our pain.
You wished to calm our fears
And I know your name
We would have called you Mommy

Peter wanted to be your son
Wondered where you were
Would you ever come?
But before you knew
He was gone.

A tear rolled down your face
To help the helpless child
In your home to make a place
The telephone must be dialed
It's time to make the call

Jeanne Henrick

Forever Blue

Everything you were to me
A single man of mystery
A gentle heart that no one knew
No other could have been so true

To hear your voice is like a dream
It's on your gentle breast I lean
And in those moments so sublime
I feel as one, for you are mine

I'm wrapped within a safety zone
It's where I call your love my own
But where the dream must fade to blue
I wake and search the world for you

It's such a treasure no one knows
For as the wistful story goes
I'm with a love I once held true
No longer mine, forever blue

Suzanne Lynn Dillingham

Life

This poem is about life
and to stand proud,
and when you really think of it,
it's just a confusing crowd.

If we ever lose each other
or fall part,
I want you to remember me
always in your heart.

When the wind blows
from behind a tree,
Will you be thinking?
Thinking of me?

Death, what do we think of?
What do we go through?
I know I couldn't do it without looking
at what I've been through.

But just remember
let yourself be free,
I've learned this the hard way
that I can only be me!

Kristen Penwell

The Warrior Spirit

For Edith, my wife and inspiration
A carefree, almost careless and reckless
Abandoned outlook at life;

A masculinity that makes most men
Wonder in awe;

And yet, an almost feminine ability
To care, understand and sympathize;

Is what attracts most women
To me and my way of life;

And yet, when after a time
Of sincere effort to tame that spirit;

Unable to alter that ego that makes
This man in the first place;

The same traits that attract;
Eventually drive that woman away.

Wayne R. Foate

Me

Things people say
Can make our day.
Some are bad,
And some are good.
Depending on the situation,
We all want to be understood.
If you see me feeling down,
Please see what you can do.
Remember, one day it might be you.
Everyone wants at least one good friend,
Someone who'll be there until the end.
A simple hello and smile would do.
Remember, "Do unto others
As you want done unto you."

Nadia M. Brooks

Destiny

Wondering what life has to offer
Keeps you guessing how it will be
Hoping and praying that you can see
Wonders that are in store for you and me
Taking the good and the bad
Things that would make you happy or sad
This is life full of expectancy
Road are rough but the seed is their
Our ancestors and parents do care
All in all it's a wonderful world
To be alive and to be free.

Frances Vidergar

I, the Sand

I am the sand by the oceanside.
You are the beautiful, rolling tide.

Once your soft, warm touch ceased to be,
You no longer met with me.

You, the tide, went out one day.
I, the sand, was left at bay.

Then one morning bright with sun,
I saw that your journey had begun.

By evening the tide had reached the sand.
Their oneness destined to expand.

I, the sand, and you, the tide,
Now mingle forever by the oceanside.

Misty Pugsley

Life Goes On

The morning comes with utter certainty
As the sun appears to rise like a
giant ball over the hills.

Light filters across the earth
Carrying beams of life
And the day moves on like melted
wax on a candle

As day turns to night, darkness
gently comes, a caring friend
And life goes on.

Cynthia Blair

My Daddy

When I was a little girl,
No bigger than you;
I used to sit and swing,
On my daddy's shoe.

When I grew bigger,
Like your sister there;
I used to sit and talk,
On the arm of my daddy's chair.

When I was older,
And had children of my own;
I stood by my daddy's side;
To watch him play with all of you,
Like he did me, when I was a child.

Now that I've gone far away,
And my children have gone too;
My daddy is left with only mom,
To sit and wait for us to call and say;
"Daddy, I love you!"

Gloria J. Clifford

I Prayed

Last night I prayed
For you and me,
I prayed for all the lost souls
I have and haven't seen,
I prayed for the sick to get well, and
for God to stop all from going to hell.

I prayed for war, not peace
Because it seems to be the only way
We know how to communicate.

I prayed for all who hate and
Praised all that love.

I prayed for the outcast,
Gods people at heart,
I prayed for the unholy, victim or not.

Put it all together and you will see,
I not only prayed for you,
I prayed also for me.

Chrysstina M. Koegler

The Illusion

It is an illusion
The shadow of a cloud;
Foreboding and darkness,
Distorting the land.
But not far from the vision
Are glorious rays!
As winds sweep the skyline
And illumine the scape,
The sun, in immensity,
Retains his control.

Sharon Semmler

Falling

To Shelby and my mother
Falling . . . falling . . . falling
Into a deep hole
Filled with blackness
And sorrow
Everything seems hopeless
Without any resolve
The littlest things hurt
And the biggest things numb
Somehow nothing matters
And nothing will help
But not try
You give me a hand
But I wouldn't grasp it
You give me a rope
But I wouldn't tie it
You give me a parachute
But I won't open it
When it seems you had nothing left
You give me your love
And that stopped my fall.

Chris Piearce

Those Little Blessings

To my family
Many times we overlook,
That simple little brook,
Nestled between the trees.
And covered over with leaves.

We miss out on gorgeous flowers.
Whose marvelous fragrance empowers,
By gracefully refreshing our air,
We seem to not care.

Children seem to get in our way,
They only want to hear us say,
How much we love them,
And that life is not dim.

We have no quality time,
Sometimes being very unkind,
Shunning our children,
A helping hand we can't lend.

Just look carefully around,
Can we see what's abound?
Or are we truly missing,
Those magnificent little blessings.

Bettye J. G. Canada

The Lights of Home

To my mother—gone but not forgotten
Is that the lights of Home, Mama,
I see in yonder sky?
I can hardly wait to see you, Mama;
It's been so long since you said good-bye.

I miss your loving arms, Mama,
And your gentle smile so sweet.
Will Daddy be there, too, Mama,
So that I may kiss his cheek?

I remember all the times, Mama,
You wiped my tears away;
When I was but a child, Mama,
Then you would kneel and pray.

The lights are growing dim, Mama;
I cannot find my way.
Will the angels come to meet me, Mama,
On this bright and glorious day?

Marian McMillioan

The Key

I have a secret,
You may not feel the same,
But I can no longer keep it,
It is driving me insane.

To speak your name,
Knowing that you are so fine,
Urges me to claim
That someday you will be mine.

I dream of you all the time,
You seem to have this overwhelming power.
I constantly picture you in my mind,
And think of you every hour.

I even sing about you in the shower,
Hoping that you have feelings for me.
You are more lovely than a flower,
The most beautiful woman that there can be.

And I know that
This has all happened suddenly,
But only you can open the door to my love,
Only you have the key.

Aaron Da'Mar Henderson

Keeper of the Stars

For my soulmate, lover, and friend
We did not meet by chance that night
This heart that touched my soul
For it was God that saw to it
Two hearts that would unfold
He walked with us to help us see
The wonder of his love
He's held our hands through troubled times
Watching from above
God knows that we're in darkness now
We cannot see the light
Yet I believe in you and me
This feeling still feels right
So in God's hands I've placed our hearts
I wait for answers true
I know he holds the hands my love
That may lead me back to you
Please take my hand and walk with me
The hand I know you trust
God will hold our hearts my dear
He'll leave the rest to us.

Becki Guillory

The Heart of Common Man

In the heart of the common man
There lies simplicity,
Greatness in its truest form,
Born of humility.
Though great works or grand designs
May never there reside,
A life of service and of faith
In his heart abides.
Courage to stand for right remains
Through all of life's trials
And lights the darkness of each hour
With shining faith the while.
Fortune and fame may never shine
Upon his weary heart
But faith in God and goodness
From Him will ne'er depart.

Mary Jo Hemken

So Long but Not Goodbye

They've said, "So long" so often,
More times than stars above,
They knew there'd be another time,
Theirs was that kind of love.

They laughed and talked for hours,
And cried when they heard their song.
Each moment meant so very much,
For soon they would say, "So long."

They met and kissed in happiness,
Trying to keep each moment gay,
Knowing soon they had to part,
And go their separate way.

Yes! All could see a tender touch,
Or a glance held a little too long,
But who can hear a breaking heart
When lovers say, "So long."

They'll meet again, I know,
A love like theirs is strong.
They'll wait and pray for another day
When they don't have to say, "So long."

Florence E. Dempsey

Century Song

Ties that bind in '99
Will hold us all together.
And lead the way to Y2K
In spite of treacherous weather.
We cannot know what future blows
Our destiny will deliver.
But we will last
As long as these
Old bods will
Hang together!

Aletha Nichols

Untitled

To my husband, Richard
Today I saw a leaf float by
And wished just for one day
That I could be that leaf I saw
So I could float your way

Today I watched the sun beam down
And wished just for this ray
That I could be that sun I watched
So I could light your day

Tonight I spied a star shoot by
And wished just for this glance
That I could be that star I spied
So I could o'er you dance

Melinda Cloobeck

Dreamland Stars

To my sister, Tayler Lynn McCain
Fly away to a tall deep tree
upon a mountain, above a sea
In a land so far away
the sun can shine every day
the stars we see are not like yours
they come right up to our doors
they tap real light and then again
for we are asleep and can't let them in
But there they are in our sky
watching us close our eyes
for when we sleep you can see
Dreamland stars watching me

Heather McCain

Cindi Marie

I met a girl a year and a half ago
During a time my life was at a low
We got to know each other
And she soon was my best friend
It wasn't long and our relationship began

I fell in love with her
With all my heart and soul
I couldn't imagine being without her
I couldn't imagine letting her go

Then our problems started
And everything started falling apart
I was losing her
And it was breaking my heart

Love is what love is
But is love what it's supposed to be?

All I know is
I'm in love with Cindi Marie
But Cindi is no longer with me

Did Cindi Marie ever really love me?
Will my Cindi Marie come home to me?

Tina Black

Symbolic Butterfly

God gave us butterflies,
lovely little creatures,
That mean so much to me
because in them I see features,
Reminding me of parallels to our lives.
On this earth we learn to crawl
soon after we arrive.
Here we are in the caterpillar stage,
Limited by gravity
and by disabilities of age.
At the end of this life
we may be enshrined in a tomb
Similar to a caterpillar
wrapped in a cocoon.
At our resurrection,
we, too, will live anew,
Will burst forth in heavenly bodies,
no more to bid adieu.
Freed at last to fly,
similar to the beautiful butterfly.

Lena P. Mahone

Untitled

You left me all alone
You left me here to cry
I gave you all my heart
But you let me die.
I feel all numb inside
Lying here so cold
In this grave alive
I hear the lies you told.
I focus on the pain
The only thing that's real
I try to close my heart
To the pain that will not heal.
I lie awake at night
Wishing you were here
I want to hold you tight
I wipe away a tear.
I've got to let you go
Because you let me down
I can't hold on anymore,
In this sea of pain I drown.

Ginger Foster

DOWNSIZING

DOWNSIZING

DOWNSIZING

downsizing

down

ow

o

Osvaldo Néstor Feinstein

Memories

Swirling clouds of dust
Like distant thoughts appear
The past encased in rust
Deaf unto my ear.

Through silent misty days
And squalid nights I pray
Lift my eyes unto the haze
Of this forgotten day.

See the silent memory unfold
The old gnarled tree
Where once the story was told
For all who cared to see.

On land where the seed
Of lonely wheat was sown
Now lies the choking weed
In the past overgrown.

The tiny twisting stream
Blood of the hungry land
Fooled by a false dream
Touched by half a hand.

Jeanette Nelte

Sleep

You let ice glaze
Your watch, days break,
Caught dawn's night kindled hand to
count
Your seconds, and to make
Your spring,
Because you were awake.

I dreamt I gripped
Your stealing hand,
To sear it, and to keep
Your spring, until you gave me back
My love
To let me sleep.

Erica Levin

The Journey of Life

Life's a journey with many roads
Some you'll walk
And some you won't
Some roads can bring you wealth
And some roads can bring you pain
Some roads can bring you happiness
And others can drive you insane
But no matter what road you take
Or where the road may lead
Just have hope and never give up
And in life you will succeed

Matt Hertzberg

My Mommy

My mommy loves me,
My mommy loves you,
My mommy loves everyone,
including you!

Ida Rose Hodson

See

To my children, Patricia, Joseph, and Julie
If one could only see the birds
within the trees
If one could only see the colors
of the trees
If one could only see the mist
in early morning Spring
If one could only see the sun
that shines so bright
If one could only see the gifts
that we all share
if one could only see the
wonders of this earth
Perhaps then one may really
see the special things
that day by day are here
For you and me to see.

Hortense M. Murphy

Take a Look Around

To God's children
Peace, love, and happiness
God's son and child
War, hate, and sadness
Man lost in sorrow

Lost in a state of confusion
In a world of disillusions
What does tomorrow bring
What's tomorrow for
The answers we ignore
Take a look around

What do you see
Amazing wonders
We can't believe

Diamonds and gold
And all the precious little stones
Beautiful people
Like the colors of the rainbow
Take a look around

Hear Him calling out your name
Don't be afraid

Barbara M. Lecey

Work It Out

For my brother, Johnny with love
When I dream
I think of being a team
When I go to work
Sometimes I feel like a jerk
When I don't fit in
I think it's a sin
When all fails
It feels like everyone bails
When I cry
Sometimes I just want to die
When things go wrong
That's when I feel strong
But most of all
Life is a ball after it all

Jeanne Watkins

It

We walked along the river's bend.
He told me "it" would never end.
For what is this it?
The river or our love.

As the current traveled passed
Our happiness was not going to last.
We were drifting away,
Just like the river with its vessel.

There were so many things we shared.
Now I wonder if he ever cared,
For we were that vessel
And now there are two.

The river splits into two different streams
I wished and hoped they were just dreams,
But they weren't, we were our own vessel
And we went our different ways.

A tear filled my eye as we drifted away
I wanted to cry out for him to come and stay,
To fight the current
And love me again.

     Mary Saffrin

A Cotton Pickin' Story

Some cotton pickin' day I know, I won't be pickin' cotton.
The sun is always far too hot, the pay is always rotten.
I'd rather pick an ear of corn
And lie down in the shade, and dream of all the things I'd buy
If ever I got paid.
I'd eat my corn and slumber
In a hay stack 'neath the sun, and hurry home at sundown
Just as fast as I could run.
My mamma had baked cornbread
And made rice and okra too.
We all said thanks, and ate our fill
As all good children do.
When I grew up I did become
A cotton farmer though.
I had some cotton pickin' hands
That made my old old farm grow,
Into a "Cotton Company"
And now, I'm rich indeed,
And all the folks that work for me
Are plantin' cotton seed.

     Helen E. Baird

The Oak Tree and the Squirrel

From little acorn gathered sure and pressed into the ground
By tiny paws of busy squirrel who makes his treasure sound,
A mighty oak with spreading crown is launched toward the sky
To take its place with giant spires that soar and catch the eye.

To store away a future meal is just the squirrel's intent;
To raise a lofty forest king isn't what he really meant;
But his determined efforts to squirrel those nuts away
Have for him and the oak tree a rich reward to pay.

The oak tree's offspring will arise in open, sunlit field
And not beneath their parents' cloaking, choking, shady shield.
The offspring of the bushytail will someday reap the prize
From off the trees their furry forebear planted well and wise.

To lure this lively vagabond and keep him close at hand,
The oak tree uses sly techniques that are at its command.
Its leaves stay fluffy, dry, and crisp, just right to make a bed,
And hang upon the tree long after others' leaves have fled.

Old oaks contain the nicest holes to make oneself a home,
So that the bright-eyed bushytail no longer needs to roam.
Thus, in a hole with stash of nuts and leaves on which to curl,
We find the two inseparable, the oak tree and the squirrel.

     Henry M. Ditman

Morning Sun with Love

To Kathleen Stewart, you're the freshness of space
(In tribute to William Wordsworth)
"We walked along while bright and red
Uprose the morning sun"
The oak trees swayed in to and fro
Her hair by reasons of the wind became undone

She looked at me with bright green eyes
Then motioned she would fix it in the bye and byes
I held her hand so very tight
In fear the wind would use us as a kite

We stopped to watch a flock of geese fly south
Up high so very high
And with a smile she waved away
The honest of goodbye

With searching eyes I looked at her so deep
Then silently inside of me I said
In you there is a special kind of ecstasy
Now in crystal clear you I truly keep

The morning sun still on bright and red
Brought up to her the love I fed
Upending all existing fears
In ever this to be the finest of our years

     Claudio R. Diaz

My Dream

There were years of such loneliness and brokenness
inside this life of mine so wrong.
But yet I had a dream so deep inside, hidden in my heart,
a dream of a life filled with happiness,
of such peace and joy,
of being loved and to love.

But would this dream ever come true?
Or would this life of mine go unfulfilled,
living in loneliness, and oh, so blue?

But, yes!
My dream did come to pass on a chilly October day in 1977.
My dream is you, my darling husband, when God sent me you.

And so you and I have been blessed
by living my dream for twenty-one wonderful years.
And in honor of you, I write this poem to you:
My dream.

     Peggy J. Hart

More Than Just Words

More than just words, our love I care.
Our love is greater than the air.
More than just words, I like what you wear.
More than words, I love you, and know what to do.
Flowers always says in a big way,
We are in love and it is to stay.
I think about this every day.

     Stephen Berbes

Life!

What is it with us people, when all is said and done?
We're getting a much needed rain but wishing for the sun.
And when the sun is shining bright,
It's much too hot and nothings right

We don't like this, we don't like that.
We're much too thin or else too fat.
We'll still get by it's not too bad
Think of the future not what we had
The flowers still bloom and birds still sing
The skies are blue and bells still ring.
So just sit back and wait and see.
The good and bad are meant to be.

     Irma A. Moody

Brother Louie

To Louie, my great brother
My brother Louie is a great guy
He helped me out when my son died
I was in deep sorrow
he came to me to see the light
and comfort me to make me feel right
He helped me in every way
My brother Louie helps all if you in trouble
or in sorrow he will help all beyond tomorrow
That's why he is a fabulous guy,
just call him, and you will see why
   Loretta Galland

Paratroopers Do Cry

I am a paratrooper, my country's very best
I wear the emblem of courage on my chest
I have conquered God's open space
I have reached out and touched His soft face

I heed the jumpmaster's command and I go
I have jumped when others said it best no
I have shook from fears' stinging cold
I have said, "Follow me," and be bold

I am brave they say the bravest of men
I have prayed to do some things never again
I want no more to battle, just a quiet peace
I want my heart and soul to be at ease

Please God forgive me for what I have done
I did not want or mean to hurt no one
So when you see me tear and ask why
Just remember paratroopers do cry

They cry from the deepest regions of their soul
They cry the purest of tears untold
They cry for those who are at their final home
They cry because they are afraid to be alone
   Lt. Col. Robert K. Doss
   USAF (Ret.)

Suspended

In tribute to William Wordsworth
"We walked along, while bright and red,
Uprose the morning sun"
Behind us, sand filled the tracks
On the trail over which we'd come.
Just ahead, past rocky shores, lay the emerald sea.
Its awesome power and peacefulness
Beckoning to you, to me.
Poised on the sands, suspended, between the old and new
Do we go back over shifting sands
Or set sail, on uncharted blue?
   D. J. Collison-Jones

One View

In blind view within the sun's darkened light.
I reach forth to grasp fading sunsets that remain within my sight.

The energy sets my desire ablaze, emancipating my dreams,
The truth comes from what I am, not merely what I seem.

I can do what it is that I most want to try.
To be who I want to be and always be alive.

I come to this point by following a long and winding road.
A road that leads to nowhere, but never let's me go.

I long to find where it is that I begin to disappear.
So I wake in a different world, where my view is completely clear.
It's hard to imagine, a place such as this.
But never the less, this place really does exist.

It exists between Heaven and Earth, in the midst of our minds.
Where we can grasp fading sunsets and our view is always fine.
   Carson Davis

Chrissy

To my friend, Chrissy Mendola
If God had given me a sister,
I would ask "Him" for a sister like her.
There's is no doubt in my mind;
She would be exactly like her.
One in a million my sister would be,
So beautiful and so full of love.

A face of a goddess so beautiful and so fair,
Her golden hair so long and shining like
the sun that shines so bright.
Her beautiful eyes would sparkle like diamonds,
And her luscious lips are like rubies
so red and so beautiful.

Her beautiful smile is warm and genuine
that makes you feel so good.
Her heart is as gentle as her touch is;
Her hands are so soft and warm.

A wonderful wife and mother she is, so loyal and true.
Her love and her loving are so gentle and kind.
If God had given me a sister, I hope she would
have turned out to be exactly like her.
   William J. Franks

You Learn

As time passes, you learn the subtle difference
Between holding a hand and charming a soul
And you learn that love doesn't mean learning
And company doesn't mean security
And you learn that kisses aren't contracts
And presents aren't promises
And you learn to accept your defeats
With your head up and your eyes open
With the grace of a woman, not the grief of a child.

And you learn to build your own roads on today
Because tomorrow's ground is too uncertain
And futures have a way of falling down in mid flight
After a while you learn that even
Sunshine burns if you get too much
So plant your own garden
And decorate your own soul instead of . . .
Waiting for someone to bring your flowers.

And you learn that you really are strong
And you do have worth and you learn
And you learn with every goodbye . . . You Learn
   Jarret Quinn Hlady

50th Golden Juneies Glenn and Patricia Buck

To my blessed and loving husband, Glenn Buck
   A Shakespearean English Sonnet consists of three quatrains
   (with the first and third lines, second and fourth lines rhyming)
   followed by a rhymed couplet.

1947 was indeed a banner year
Minnesota and Iowa close at hand
America slowly getting back in gear
Time to seal with a wedding band

Soon set stage for family now
Residing in Florida and working American Express
Miracle of life, "God we bow"
Benefits abound providing us fine finesse

Home, music, golf our hobby priority
Our grandchildren and great-grands
Vacations and fun in our seniority
Truly are the ties that stands

Lord, thank you for cherished birth
Through our parents on this earth
   Patricia Buck

World of Destruction

The world is being destroyed in just a wink,
One day the water will be unfit to drink.
With the farmland gone there is not enough food to eat,
Animals are sick, so there is no kind of meat.
The rain forest is being ruined with acid rain,
Every living creature feels the utmost pain.
Nuclear chemicals will be used in the next war,
Wearing gas masks to breathe, enduring how much more.
Covering each inch of our skin as the sun will burn,
This will affect everyone, not just those who are concerned.
Think about what will happen to all the living creatures,
We need to learn what could happen from the best teachers.
Can we ever stop this world of destruction before it's too late?

Linda Deibler

Long Lost One

At times like these with saddened soul
Our longing heart an empty hole

A loved one's gone, it's so unfair
Their love, their joy, no more to share

But in ourselves there lies the key
To keep their lives eternally

So think not of their final days
Our thoughts, our dreams, is where they'll stay

Now looking down from clouds on high
A better place above the sky

I know they care and still love us
This life at times seems so unjust

But one day soon when our time's done
We'll meet again our long lost one

Peter D. Schwotzer

Brush with Death

She was an ebony beauty
Who made love with her eyes
With her wings of wisdom
She whispered to me the torch of truth
And told me no lies

When I was cold, bitter, and hungry
Her dark blue halo of blue satisfied
When her pure bright blue light
Warmed my cold body she whispered
You shall never be denied

With a false prophet giving me my last rites
As a wounded tadpole
Even the top doctor thought I should have died
But giving me her crown of thorns I somehow survived
Then kissing me softly off to Heaven she flied
Yes part of me flew with her but I never cried

Brad Coyote Martens

Number Four

We just heard the news today, that makes our hearts soar,
Spring of 1999 is bringing grandchild number four,
Our son and his wife have given us grandchildren one and three,
And, when sharing this news with us, their joy was plain to see,

When most news we hear today, is riddled with pain and strife,
How refreshing to see this family preparing to celebrate life,
As grandparents, we know it's not our job to worry, fret, or toil,
Instead, when grandchildren visit, we enjoy, reward and spoil,

Although it's not yet known if this child is a girl or boy,
I guarantee, we all pray first for a Healthy bundle of joy,
So, come on grandchild number four, join this clan of ours,
I know you'll enrich our lives for hours and hours and hours,
Hello baby Deimling!

Rita Deimling

My Mom's Best Friend

She was taking care of his stricken wife when they met.
His wife died in her arms with him by his wife's bed.
He was a tall old man with a cheerful smile and wit.
He lived his life in an auto factory and retired gracefully.
He became a shoulder to her as she did him.
He made her happy and was there when she needed to talk,
She was there when the past caught up with him, so he could talk.
They took walks every day for an hour or so,
Talking about everything and anything or just being together.
They both never really had any enemies except people who would talk.
Sometimes they did things to turn the talking eyes,
Just to make each other laugh.
She really didn't have many friends,
And I'm getting more like her.
Life caught up with him and her, started his graceful leave.
She visited him a couple of times as he slowly shut down.
She wouldn't see the end this time.
Remembering him as he was, my mom's best friend.

Michael E. Compton

In the Eyes of My Son's Teddy Bear

In loving memory of Chris Knodel
In the eyes of my son's teddy bear
With reflections his past we both share
Though you're tattered and worn
With his birth you were born
Every part of his life you were there

Bubba's gone to his eternal home
Receiving love that transcends from God's throne
While you're still needed here
Keeping my son real near
As he lives in your eyes, teddy bear

As you're perched on the shelf by my bed
Sharing each of my prayers as they're said
While this mother laments
Over the messages sent
From my son through your eyes, teddy bear

There is so much I wanted to say
Before God went and took you away
In the days that's to come
We will talk much, my son
Through the eyes of your worn teddy bear

Joyce L. Knodel

The Abyss of Love

You are my light, the fragrant breeze,
The strength to fill my day.
You keep my thoughts, my ever move,
With you along life's way.

I miss your touch, your smiling face,
Your words with love and cheer.
My world is empty, lonely too,
Without you being near!

I dream of you both night and day,
Wishing you were here with me.
I only hope this dream comes true,
Making you "my reality."

I need you in my arms again,
To feel your gentle touch,
Then, I can whisper to you, sweet and clear,
"I love you very much!"

Defeated Love! A dream you are!
A dozen years fading into reality.
Though none can ever two shattered hearts unlock,
While another still holds the key!

Doris Lee Gribble

Blanket Wrestling

To Charles Kirk for his love
I get so cold at night,
my nose turns red and bright.
Then I turn my electric blanket up high,
I pull my quilts and blanket tight.

All through the night I feel warm,
my sleep is undisturbed by the cold monster.
Toes no longer tingle or red and bright,
I dream of being warm 'til morn.

Suddenly I feel a foot creeping my way,
cold as mine used to be.
Then a body followed like a snake,
now the warm bed became crowded.

He told me before I bought my electric blanket,
"Never will I turn my side on.
I don't get cold," he said with a smirk.
I proceed to tell him about the person that
crawled under my blanket last night.

Jeanette Kirk

Hoping

Many times I've wondered on a Monday late in the day
why the river runs so clear and yet so fast
I've also wondered briefly on a Tuesday as I lay
if the ripples of the water will always last
I've wondered on a Wednesday in the PM
on a scorching summer night that's hot and dry
how the clear and rapid river runs so freely
as I watch the blue cold water pass me by
I've wondered on a Thursday after noontime,
if someday the lovely river will be gone
and the children and the people of the future
will never know this river . . . but I hope I'm wrong
I've thought about the river on a Friday after three,
and the beauty that Mother Nature has let us share
It's a gift that we can't take for granted,
one that's really way beyond compare.
On a Saturday before I've had my dinner
I give thanks for the beauty of the river
and I pray that it will always be around
and I hope that in a hundred years someone sits where I am now,
on a Sunday afternoon and cares about the river that I've found.

David L. Mack

Could It Be?

As Christmas approached long ago, one glad season,
And children praised God for the holiday season,
Families gathered around tables full-laden and pleasing,
Toasty warmth comforting in temperatures freezing.

There appeared just one blotch in the spiritual realm,
As in envy, the enemy, saw God, at the helm,
Had provided to all Jesus Christ, who could quell
Evil forces of darkness seeking them to overwhelm.

Satan fumed and sputtered in hot, angry dismay
As he sought for a means, without a delay
To draw people's attention, celebrating the day,
From God's son to himself some ulterior way.

Then he chortled in delight with a devilish grin.
How simple it was! He'd just take that old 'n
From the end of his name and toss it right in
The middle of things where he'd soon be again.

Feigning God, who knows all, the father of lies had no problem
Devotees deluding he'd deliver, without hobbling,
To all homes, in one night, just some cookies gobbling,
Their presents, down chimneys, with not one a wobbling.

Nadia Adamiak

Summit Mississippi . . . Iss, Iss, Ippi!

For Thomas Young and Easter Johnson
84 miles of Jackson, short of the sky.

Top of the hill, green grass all around
Hidden in beauty and very small town
M.I.S.S.I.S.S.I.P.P.I.

Well past the trees and dark as the night,
Mississippi, my S.S.I.S.S. takes flight.

Onto Chicago that welcomes the foe.
Struggling past skeltons and knocks on the door.

Exploring the world for his personal pleasure.
Finding and conquering God's hidden treasure.
M.I.S.S.I.S.S.I.P.P.I.

More than the highest love to achieve.
I have found in this man, on earth, I believe.
Ipp, Iss, Iss, my love.

Michelle Grant DeNye

Savior and Deliverer

For my loving mother, Verneida McCray
God is our savior, who watches over thee . . .
God is our deliverer,
He sent His only begotten Son to set us free.

He's there for us during our time of need.
He's a loving and forgiving God, yes indeed.

God is our security, strength, stability to move on.
He's our companion, friend, someone to lean on.

He's our guardian, who watches over us
Through strong winds and trouble storms.

God has an answer for every problem,
And only the Almighty can solve them.

He's there when things gets us down.
He picks us up and turns us around
And places our feet on solid ground.

He sets us in the righteous path
And fills us with happiness.

He lifts our spirits and soul
Makes us feel more alive than old.

He removes evil from our hearts and lives.
Just have faith in God and you will survive.

Natasha Y. Brooks

No Tomorrow

The sun never comes up, it never goes down
The world is just spinning around and around
The changes are endless, 'cause time never sleeps
And even the friendless are playing for keeps

'Cause nothing stops, no one stays
Tomorrows turn to yesterdays
And yesterdays are nothing more
Than days we called today—before

You can live a life of crime
Holding back the hands of time
Soon you'll have to pay the price
A victim of your own device

Me I'd rather heed the call
Do my best and give my all
Deep inside I know somehow
All we've got is here, and now

No tomorrow—we gotta make this moment last
Life does not exist within the future or the past
No tomorrow—we gotta live our lives today
Like there's no tomorrow.

Mark Alan Segers

New Year's Eve

Those dreams dissolved, implausible,
And I knew I'd been betrayed by my own memories.
A lifetime of fear melted into forgottenness when I exploded,
The unmendable fool of charm's deceit.
I repeated my prayer for solace
In this flightless, haphazard world,
But the comfort you offered was meaningless now.
I'd dream my lies elsewhere.

I cradled my heart, unnobled,
As the passage of hours found us once more
Breathless as the night itself.
The stars purred.
We clung one to another in the moonlight
And danced long after the music had stopped playing
As the half light of late December
Merged with the newest days of January.

We detoured those eternal roads
And clasped the intensity of the few moments still guaranteed.
Without promises they still were ours,
And we'd have been content to never have seen tomorrow.

Christia Hayward

The Battle Is the Lord's

Have we done our very best than the battle is the Lord's.
Have we been betrayed by those we trust
Than the battle is the Lord's.

Are we battle scarred and weary and no longer
Very cheery—than the battle is the Lord's.

Have we lost our home and heart and feel
Abandoned on this Earth—the battle is the Lord's.

Has our health gone down the drain and were
Often rocked with pain—the battle is the Lord's.

When the gales of heartbreaks surround us, and our
Loved ones die away, when we feel a deep
Down sorrow and have no strength to
Face tomorrow—the battle is the Lord's.

Remember my dear friends with the spirit of God
Within us we will never be defeated
As we come through each new trial
God will give us the sure knowledge
Even if we haven't been to college—
The battle is the Lord's.

Margaret Fleureton

Untitled

For a wonderful mother, my strength
Sometimes things happen and we all wonder why.
To lose someone very special and you can't say goodbye.
They have taught us so many meaningful things.
Now it's their time to move on and spread their wings.
You gave us life and have taught us well.
To forgive and love and not to dwell.
Your words of wisdom will forever remain.
In our memories always, our lives not the same.
You taught us believe and we could have it all.
Always there to guide us, when you thought we may fall.
You were our eyes when we were too blind to see.
Your love in our hearts will forever be.
Dedication, devotion, and love for us all.
Has made us so very proud and to always stand tall.
Your laughter and your wonderful smile we will all miss.
That special feeling of our mothers kiss.
A mother's band will always beat in our hearts.
Even though we may be so far apart.
The sun will always be shining on you.
A life that's beginning, a life that is new.

Danielle M. Catanzaro

A Plea for One Entity

"'Tis time his heart should be unmoved,
Since others it hath ceased to move:
Yet, though I cannot be loved,
Still let me love!"
Let me love though the other
may lack thereof upon me.
One hopes as the days go longer.
One fears as the time grows near.
One wonders will there ever be a time,
where all I have to do is Rhyme.
Rhyme the reason, find the treason,
It's all going to boil down to whether
or not I will fight for love,
need for love, hurt for love.
I am okay with the desperate yearn
for the deep pit of despair—
one not loving me back with the love I have for them.
But please one begs of you, just once, let me love.

Chandra Cooks

The Eyes of God

To my special husband, Ray
Who can fathom the eyes of God
The deep, rich, spearing eyes that
Look into a person's soul and
Searches his innermost thoughts.

The eyes of God see love or hatred,
Joy or sorrow. They shine with love,
Compassion, peace and joy.

His eyes look at a world torn apart
By war, children that are starving and hatred.
He also sees when we praise Him,
Give food to the hungry and lend a helping hand to those in need.

If only we could look into the eyes of God
And see His love and compassion,
And His hope that all men could live in peace.

Charlotte Dillard

Winter Fantasy

To my beloved husband and children
Sparkling, spiraling ever so high
my dreams of ice castles in clear winter skies

Towering over the small world below
who's blanket is new fallen powdery snow

Crystal and crisp is the steed I would ride
his wings of white feathers, lay draped by his side

My drawbridge, a cloud, to my castle so high
a wondrous fantasia beheld by my eye

An ice castle fit for a king, I might say
In my dreams I will visit, on another cold day

Telsa Michelle Crone

Castles

A castle so beautiful with its peaks so high
A person has to look up way in the sky.
Behold that some castles are very old
They've created ones that you can hold.
They come in very old rock formation
And then the color of pastel creation.
You put them in your hand to be held,
For the great beauty of a castle in pastel.
Is the only beauty certain people can tell
This is the story of it in rock and pastel.

Doris Marie Grillo

Open the Door

As I sat in the chair, while staring into space, if
I'm going to forget my troubles, I've got to get out of this place.

But I could not get up and open the door!
As I heard my wife say, "If you want to get ahead in life
you've got to get up and go somewhere. Get up and get out of here!"

But I could not get up and open the door!
If I got out of this house, I know that it would be best,
I could began to get this burden off my chest.

But I could not get up and open the door!
So what is it out there I think I may regret? Nothing I
could think of, so I'll not set here and sweat.
I'm going to get a move on, of this you sure can bet.

But I could not get up and open the door!
I'm tired of sitting, so I'm going to take a stance,
now that opportunity's knocking, I'm going to take a chance.

But I could not get up and open the door!
Another missed opportunity to heed the advice of my wife.
But I still won't . . .
Get up and open the door to life!

Kenneth McCain

If Only Time Could Continue On

Continued on the next page; that is
where you'll find my heart

Yes, that is exactly right; even
though you left me broken-hearted
and I haven't had a moment peace
since you've been gone, I'm missing you.

Your kiss always left me speechless,
your touch, and smile it is a thing
of the past. Thinking back to the
showers we took together, dripping
wet you were so beautiful. I always
lusted for your body.

Thinking of you is a picture
that has never been seen or can
be imagined, unless one has loved one as I love you.

Again thinking back of your touch
I feel a warmth, I close my eyes and
can see a glow, I'm melting like a
burning candle, dripping from head to toe.
Yes, it's over; but only if it could continue on the next page . . .

Henry Grantham

My Life

As I sit in the corner of a New York street.
Lying in a cardboard box,
I am considered the rat of civilization.
My clothes are tattered and ratty,
Like yesterday's trash.
This is how I live my life.

As I wake up in a cold deep sweat,
I run to the alley to wash my body.
My stomach growls as I yearn for food.
I am a bear awakening from hibernation.
I walk up and down the street as
Kids yell names at me all the time.

My body aches as the cold of the night
Encloses me and takes me prisoner.
I lie on the cold dark ground
Trying to get very comfortable
My cardboard box hugs me like my mother used to.
I'll fall asleep now and pray I don't wake up.

Brett E. Killian

The Anchoring Advisor

My emotions were in a frenzy
I felt pain, anger, and fear
At times, I felt I would lose control
It seemed too much to bear
But through that day, you gave me strength
When in doubt, I knew you were near
Unknowingly, with a few simple words
You gave me the fortitude I would need
For, in myself, I needed to believe
As fate would have it, you're here again
Giving me strength beyond the call
Your kindness, compassion and wisdom
I genuinely appreciate it all
You've given me courage outside the courtroom
Outside the boundaries of your service
The anguish, heartbreak, and duration
Have finally given my life meaning and direction
The journey has been long
Seems this process has taken forever
Your contribution to this, will not be forgotten—Never

Tina M. Cape

Us

Countless nights of endless fights.
So much pain, with nothing to gain.
Has it come to this,
I thought our love was bliss.
I reach inside, and try not to hide,
my feelings true I have for you,
Moments we shared, was it love in the air?
Or were we confused, in how love was used.
To share your life with someone else,
You accept them as you would yourself.
Take not for granted what comes your way,
Be generous in everything you say.
Tell them you love them with honesty and heart,
Make sure you are true right from the start.
After all of this has been said and done
Does it really matter who has won?
If it comes to an end, you know it's near,
Be a friend, be a pal, but most of all, be sincere.

John W. Hepa

The Reunion

I sit here so lonely, sad, and blue
My dear parents, thinking of you.
Since you've gone there has been many tears and pain,
My goal is to live for God so I can see you again.
We'll walk the streets of glory hand in hand,
As you introduce me to your angel friends.
I'll get to meet my grandparents I've never seen,
We'll play with the twins, what a glorious thing.
I'll get to hold my little baby I lost,
I plan to make this reunion no matter what the cost.
There's also two grandchildren I long to see,
So will you all gather together and wait for me?

Martha A. Swanner

Class

Sitting here listening to my teacher and writing
Wondering where the day will take me.
Will it take me here?
Or there?
Near?
Or far?
Will it even take me anywhere at all
Or will it leave me in this boring class?
This is what I wonder while I write in class.

Jacinda Rochet

The Kiss of the Evening Sun

To Dr. Joan M. Watkins
There's no enjoyment like being at home,
And I am grateful for my humble space.
Though far and near I often roam,
My little back porch is the coolest place.

On my little porch I feel a refreshing breeze,
And on film I captured a breath-taking view,
To drink in this scene is bound to please,
Gladly I paint word-pictures to bring this to you.

From the song, "O what a beautiful morning"
Are words of rich color worth repeating,
"There's a bright, golden haze on the meadow,
There's a bright, golden haze on the meadow."

The sun's soft glow a message was sending,
Autumn was coming, with decreasing light,
The harvest is past, the summer is ending,
The evening sun glows with scenes of delight.

Time and again you can enjoy God's great outdoors
I borrow words from a great poet, and say, "Day is done,"
Look often for the golden beauty that is yours
And remember that I saw, the kiss of evening sun.

Curtis D. Watkins

Moment of Truth

For Tonia, my beloved daughter
You sat across the table
where I could take delight
in watching mercurial expressions, like reflected light,
dance across your face.

A visit, like many others,
times of talking and exchanging news and views,
we'd even argue some.
But not for long.

Harsh words would soon melt
in the warmth of understanding,
knowing what we felt.
It was a time like other times.

This time I looked for one moment
into the midnight of your eyes.
Time stopped, not for you, but for me.
All else receded, then I knew.

The girl was gone.
A woman, full grown, appraised me.
I was a child, seeking approval,
You the mother, assuring tenderly.

Georgie Brooke

Red-Eyed Basset-Hound

Felicity Basset-hound, where is your white pebble,
You used to rattle against your canine teeth?
What have you done? Oh, no! It's indigestible,
Why's your belly feeling so hard? Good grief!

The whites of your eyes are turning red,
And your routine habit of poohing, very remote.
A visit to the vet you frequently dread;
Where's your chewed leash, my car, and coat?

Vet's advice, to avoid an operation he assumes,
Has suggested an injection to relax tense stomach,
Given to cows that are calving, relaxes wombs.
White pebble shot out with such a crack.

Leaving a dent on vet's consulting room wall,
Forget pebbles, here's a brand-new rubber ball!

Joseph Dobson

Divine Spiritual Enlightenment

To have let one's inner spirit flow constantly throughout the day,
Reaching an acquiescent, peaceful divine, accordance.

Heavenly upliftment of one's terrigenous soul,
Rising through, and above cirrus clouds,
Reaching one's zenith, ultramundane far below.

The umbra of earth as the glowing aurora
Of the sun sends out brilliant rays in glorious abundance.

Tenuous worldly umbilical cord, straining to be severed,
Where light and tranquility beckon,
Angelic chants at full crescendo.

Joseph Dobson

I Am Here

I can hear a whisper in a crowd
No need to pray out loud
I have caught a tear in the rain
and knew from whom it came

My love is unending
this is the message I am sending
When you feel most alone
You are never far from home

I am with you through it all
I hear you when you call
I hear your hope and fears
I am here

I am the moon I am the stars
I am with you wherever you are
The wind that tousled your hair out of place
was simply my robe that brushed your face

Christine L. Moraca

Modern Ideas

Confusing morality with liberties,
what is right with what is tolerable;
Confusing nutritionist with abortionist.
The life-sustaining impulse
with the comedy of gays;
Confusing men with women
and women with men;
Confusing the saint with the rogue,
the selfless with the selfish;
Confusing good with evil,
ends with means;
Confusing solving problems with expediency,
justice with retribution;
Confusing the rights of mankind with
the selfish interest of men;
Confusing the message with the messenger.
Confusing the truth with repetition of lies;
Confusing God with ourselves. . . .

Joseph Tuccillo

Finding You

Waiting for you so very long,
I find you standing in a field of meadow beauty.
Around you sweet fragrances
Linger as willow larks sing their song.

A faint rainbow surrounds
you as if it was your canopy.
The smile upon your face was all I needed
To give me a peace of mind;
You were such a beauty for me to see.

As I touched your hand, tingling
found its way through me
As I had never had before,
leaving all worries behind.
You were and are the rainbow in my dreams.

Johnny L. Espenschied

The Tree and Me

We have a secret, the tree and me.
I lay and dream among the leaves.
In the winter, when the leaves are gone,
The barren branches carry on.

I lay and make plans for the day,
Or dream of things, as my mind strays.
At times the tree just stands and waits,
Holding thoughts, that time creates.

We play hide and seek, the tree and me.
My vision strays, you disappear.
Off in the clouds, my dreams hold on;
You are gone.

In deep thought, I shut out the tree.
Like an anchor, it comforts me.
The great old tree never lets me down.
With a blink of an eye, you have come and gone.

Martha Mason

Secret Shelter

I'm pondering some thoughts of hiding once again,
of going to a place that only I have been.

It's a shelter I created for myself in the past.
A room that I could go to and take off my heavy mask.

Once inside these solid walls I could be who I truly am,
and I could close the door behind me
so that no one could get in.

The place of which I'm speaking is only inside me.
I built the walls free of charge,
and I pay no monthly fee.

I'm angry with myself for ever coming out.
Who cares about the outside world
and what it's all about?

So whenever I go out there I wear a happy face,
but someday soon the mask will break,
and my smile will be erased.

And when that moment comes, my job on Earth is through.
I made a difference while I was here . . .

. . . But now it's up to you.
Good luck whoever you are.

Michelle D. Hooper

Surrender, Accept, Desire

Surrender to your inner fears
The ones you've held these long past years
Surrender to your endless doubts
That your future is to do without
Surrender to your countless lows
The ones that keep you from your goals

Accept your future as a time to learn
That tomorrow can truly be your turn
Accept today as a time to realize
That happiness need not be denied
Accept all those that still are there
To offer gifts of love they need to share
Accept the bond that cannot be severed
From the one you call a friend forever

Desire blissful memories that you have known
They can be yours again to call your own
Desire past days and nights of pleasure
Know they can again be part of forever.
Desire the peace of better yesterdays
Embrace that serenity as part of today.

Mel Spector

I Wonder if You Noticed

For Eric Young and Papa Monks—you'd be proud, I miss you
Every moment I have to myself
Just to sit and relax
Your face never leaves my mind
Not knowing who you are
Knowing I'll never know
I wish I could touch your innocent complexion
I thought once you noticed me
Everyone likes to look around though
On the days I don't see you
I wonder if you'll ever get to see me
I wonder if you did notice
The last time do you wonder too
If I have that sense
Will you show it to me the next time you notice.

Georgeann Carasotti

To Clinton's Inquisitors

The Republicans have shown themselves to be
As asinine as the laws they pass.
May this final showdown reverberate unto them,
And these ways and means be their last.
Though they stick to their stories hard and fast,
Mortals they be, and cut down as easily as grass.
And to all of us if outraged that is our task!

So Clinton drank from an immortal flask,
But overall, more true to us than any politic mask,
And to his credit, allow him to bask,
And grant him the forgiveness of which
He does but ask, that we may get on
With the important, pressing tasks
Of running our country at long, long last!

Rhea C. Farkas

The Dirty Dish Thing

For Janet Lee
I hate the dishes in my sink,
Someday they'll send me to the brink.
Over the edge and down the hill,
Past all reason, the urge to kill.

A blight of ugly in my home,
They seem to breed, I know they clone.
Why can't they learn to disappear?
Become invisible when I am near.

I don't care if they return to be,
When I leave and I can't see.
Their dirty faces, piled in heap,
They talk about me in my sleep.

I wish the spoon would leave with the knife,
I want them gone, away, out of my life.
They'll drive me to a living hell,
I'm becoming more fond of Taco Bell.

Dennis M. Jones

Who Saw It!

Who saw the bone fly in the air?
"I," said the dog, "But nobody cares!"
Who saw the mouse sit in a trap?
"I," said the cat with a hissy snap!
Who saw the crow land on a tree?
"I," said the scarecrow, "Nobody but me!"
Who saw the snake crawling in the grass.
"I," said the hawk, "Flying, oh, so fast!"
Who saw the wolf howling through the trees?
"Hoooooooooot!" said the owl, "No one's here but me."

Jory Andrew Barker

Soul Mates

My body knows things that I cannot speak,
This is not a language my tongue can easily translate.
My spirit floats free and then, oh, so silently,
Converses and directs my intuition.
Revealing a wisdom and an intimacy with my mind.
A powerful energy contained inside.
I wonder . . .
Can others hear the words unspoken on my lips
As they tumble forth silently from my eyes?
Is there anyone who can decipher them?
My body knows things that I will never speak.
This joining requires no introduction.
Our spirits will fuse.
We will need no conversation, Why should we?
We have known each other intimately, for eons.

Mary J. Cronin

Love Is

Love is a word that you can't define in a one-word quote.
Love is a face that greets you with a warm smile or hug
or with a handshake, saying God bless you.
Love is someone giving you a comforting word when it is needed.
Love is wisdom that you have spread and taught us
through the years we had with you.
Love is the spirit and memories of you
that we will cherish in the years to come.
Love is what you have instilled in us
to love one another as Christians should do.
Love is the confidence and obedience
when you spoke of the Lord and Savior Jesus Christ.
Love is the crown you are wearing with peace within.
Love is only three words for St. John Baptist Church family to say.

Mary Gibson

Gleaming

Gleaming, you are as flameful as one seen in vision;
you are wet light, the pride of form aglow;
gleaming, you are as curved as an act of passion.

Gleaming, you are vermilion like the gloam in Mexico,
earthic orbing erotic, your lightning flesh tawny intensity;
gleaming, you are deep fruitfulness . . . and flow

Like autumn amorous in electricity.
Gleaming, you have starful surfaces, cinnamon oceans,
waving seeing skies glistening holy nudity—

And amidst the long withdrawing twilight reflections,
I feel your infinity foaming turbulence:
fulsome, subtle, warm, angelic unfolding motions

Casting off your daylight chrysalis innocence,
and become a woman, again, in immanence.

Ernest L. Davis

Childhood

As the wind flows by them and wraps around
them like a suit of armor, they yell in
excitement or to be pushed harder,
I wonder about my childhood.
Did I ever do that?
Did I ever run around and scream or yell?
Did I ever swing so high that I did a back-flip onto the ground?
I did, but I could never recall;
because I've been told to grow-up so fast,
that there's a hole in my life
where my memories of childhood once were.
Or, just the reality that I don't remember or don't want to.
That's probably why I act so childish now even though I'm older.
To probably relive those memories of long forgotten
that I once shared, I'll never know,
but eventually I'll figure it out.

Robert Sanders

Defy, Derive, Deny

Devise the plot to bewilder thee.
The blatant enigma is a staggering key.
Shiver from the grave flurry
That creates the illusion of dishonesty.

Hopeless emotions turn into glassy stares.
Dispassionate thoughts emanate from the air.
The delusions spread from here to there.
The minute flame turns into immense flares.

Entrust no one to avoid ruin.
Don't gaze into their eyes or they may view in.
An unfavorable condition to be in.
Encourage the emotion to enable the end.

Animosity of their outlandish creed
Withholds the spite of the villainous deed.
Caution you now, so please take heed
Turn away from the crypt that makes you bleed.

Troy Higginbotham

A Tribute to Mark McGwire

America loves baseball
And though I can't say why
For Mark McGwire it might be
The excitement of watching that ball on the fly!

The pitcher checks his signals
Then throws with all his might
"Big Mac" swings; the ball grows wings
And flies momentarily out of sight!

As it falls back down to earth
The ball is nearly caught
But it's a run that's sixty-one!
The fans stand up to cheer and shout!

To break the home-run record
Mark McGwire did strive
The baseball flew for sixty-two
By season's end he hit seventy-five!

Baseball is not logical
It makes no sense at all
McGwire runs around and the bases
If while at bat he hits that ball

Brenda Appleby

The Computer

Computer! activate your master mind!
Answers to these puzzles I must find!
Flash them on your screen in a luminous light
Show me your power! Make solutions right!

Answer: How does a tree make blossoms appear?
How does it know that spring is near?
Why are daffodils yellow and violets blue?
Explain the meaning of "I love you"
Why some people are generous or reluctant to give?
Analyze for me what it means to live . . .

Mysteries haunted us times ago
Now we have your brain! We demand to know!

Why are people in love? What happens when I die?
Write, tell me who am I?

I do not compute. Programme again
I do not compute: "I have a brain" . . .

I do not compute "why?"
Feed more data! YOU must try!

I do not compute "To be to be"
Give data, data to my memory!

Hana Gerzanicova

Teddy

My special buddy, with fluffy ears and crooked nose,
I unwrapped him Christmas morning 30 years ago,
and he's been with me ever since,
always there to listen to my every thought.

Looking up at me with his loving eyes and smile,
I felt secure telling him anything.
Teddy cheered me up when I was feeling down,
and also shared my joys and happiness.

One terrible day, I found my dog chewing on Teddy.
As I sobbed, Mom carefully sewed his arm back on.
So long ago, yet it seemed like yesterday;
now married, the bear has been sitting on my pillow.

This afternoon, I came across a precious moment—
My daughter, curled up on the bed, sleeping, hugging Teddy,
not caring he was ragged and worn. A bond was formed,
a new generation of love for an old friend!

Chris Hare

Your Loving Sister Always

Your loving sister always
A sister is always caring
She can listen and talk to you
Never makes you feel bad or left out
Always lends advice, shares secrets
And even the same mother and father
A sister grows up and goes her own way
But she never forgets the love she had
Shared in her family or with her sister
Different interests can make us
Individuals. But home always brings us
Back to one another. You never forget
Where you come from. Your loving sister always

Marie Hilley

Women

Such beauty that leaves others in pain.

Just show respect and love
even when she's wrong
and she'll make a man very strong.

God and women worship is life's best stuff
love her with all your heart and soul, it's not that tough.

They're so sensitive and loving, sometimes misunderstood.
Love of women is God's gift to man
No one can love you like a woman can!

Richard Henrich

All Things

My friend when I was lonely, you were there,
The way you stood beside me, your tender loving care,
As my doctor you healed me, soul body and mind,
Through the darkness you led me when my way I could not find.

As my teacher you taught me the things I should know,
The knowledge you give me makes my faith grow,
I love you, for me you've been all things,
I thank you, for me you've been all things.

Let the light, the light of your glory, let it shine wherever I be,
Your right hand has upheld me,
Your gentleness has made me great,
There's no other power by which I could have been saved.

I'm a wonder unto many, but not unto you,
In times of uncertainty, you're my strong refuge,
My hero and my king, the Savior of my life,
The source of all my dreams, Creator of all mankind.

For me you've been all things.

Linda Jean Wegman

Men

Differential, diffident, filled with yin, yang sometimes—yen.
The X/Y contained there in a quintessential blend.
Y Chromos play the determinate genetic part with X
or double the latter to a new start
The flex—split—flow, electrical pulse,
Flesh and blood man does grow
Ripples, earth liquids, rapid loud, steady proud,
or trickling slow
Viscosity gauges, measures ancient current
forces past go
Like snowflakes and raindrops chemically same
Different temperate flow
Our sphere's ponds and oceans, salty, fresh
or brackish may be
Connect with every cell, single, complex,
Manual insect or tree
Human temples em body blood sinew and bone
Ultimate function for mind central's atone
Salubrious, sanative, how many men are?
If you find punctum caecum-transpirea gone far retooling

Kristine H. Smith

Pink Elephants and Blue Kangaroos

Have you heard of pink elephants and blue kangaroos?
And if you saw one, what would you do?
Would you run and hide, or stay and play?
And if you did, would your mom say, "Okay!"?
Sit and ponder about what you'd do,
If you saw a pink elephant or a blue kangaroo!

Angie Fink

Halloween

Halloween sure is scary,
Just ask my little neighbor Mary.
The stores are glad the candy is sold,
It's fun for all—young and old.
Lollipops and gumdrops are sweet,
But be there first and get the good treat.
The little kids' costumes are really cute,
But mess with the big kids, you'll have a dispute.
Ghosts and goblins are everywhere,
It's enough to turn your hair.
This is the day of All Hallows Eve,
So be careful won't you, please!

Erin Colley

Whisper in the Wind

There was a whisper in the wind that came from above,
I heard it say to me, "I am love."
The whisper in the wind took me back to a time
when it felt to me all the world was mine.

My world had been taken from me
by something that I had never seen,
My life was suddenly shattered and full of lost dreams.
To that the whisper in the wind said, "Please do not give in,
for that indeed would be a sin."

The whisper that I heard began to open up my heart;
The whisper in the wind gave me a brand new start.
I often wondered why I did not listen to it years before,
when I sometimes felt it whispering at my heart's door.

The whisper in the wind said, "You have always known me;
look to your heart and you will finally see."
That was when I knew that what I heard was meant to be.

The whisper seemed to speak of where in life I had been.
But how was I to know that the whisper
I heard was always my spirit within?

Maria A. Smith

Retirement

When you're all alone with naught for yourself
But a bed in the guest room, a chest or a shelf
To hold your treasures of a lifetime spent
In caring for others, and now the twig's bent
And you're stripped near bare.
Gone are the frills, not even the chair
That you sought each eve at the end of each day
Resting your bones that toiled without pay
With housework and love, with childwork and care
With worry and loving and many a prayer.
Gone tangible things, behind a closed door
Sitting and listening to grandchildren, more—
Stereo roaring, the vacuum grinding
Away at the dirt, the baby not minding.
Fine for a while, even nice now and then
But wanderlust calls every now and again.

My wallet is full, good health, I trust;
Gone are the geegaws I don't have to dust!
I smile.

Dorothy Carswell

Hidden Spirit

To the lost souls who search
Quiet is the spirit, deep inside
whispering thoughts of lives left behind
Only through the water may the torch be set on fire.
The journey of awakening
brings the flame to my success

Bring me forth to life from the voice inside.
Secret knowledge refused be ego's pride.
Precious gifts await for the price of seeking.
Heavenly bliss if you can only find a way of listening
Only the hidden spirit is your true identity.
Only the hidden spirit holds your destined path
Only the hidden spirit brings you to eternal life.
Only the hidden spirit becomes a part of being life . . .

Gil Hidalgo

The Destiny

Moonlight falls on the mind like the sun blinds the dawn.
The reflection of the light is fate.
To go to the brightness or into the shadows,
That will determine the destiny.
Light or dark?

Lauren J. Perona

Heaven Can Wait

*Based on my true story of going to college with a dime in my pocket,
but the drive to succeed!*
One day in College I was climbing a hill:
Owed my tuition and couldn't pay my bills.
I said to Keith and Lowrey as they called me in:
"The plight I am in is worse than sin.
I've made every possible move—then some,
And now I guess I will be going home."
Keith said, "Freshman, let's get on our knees,"
And they prayed for their frosh in a money-squeeze.
Then Keith with a threatening belt in his hand*
Said, "Stop that whining and be a man!
Just hang in there, I'll see you through;
And if I can't, President Dutchy will do
Whatever is necessary—he'll see you through;
For you know Dutchy, you know that's true.
So hit the books and pray some, too;
Others have had it as hard as you."
And on that day, I joyfully tell,
Von Hagen saved me from my private hell!

*he didn't use it.

Dr. Ray Francis Dykes (90 year-old retired clergyman)

Sting

A bee landed on my waist I was afraid;
but I did not move away.
A bee placed himself on my hand;
I wanted to move away, I let the bee stay.
A bee grazed my shirt, just above my heart;
I trembled I frighteningly let him stay,
to my surprise the bee did not sting me.
My love took hold of my hand, I thought he would squeeze too hard;
I did not move away I held on.
My love put his arm around my waist to dance
I did not know the song; so I followed his lead.
I didn't move away
My love placed his love over my heart;
In panic I wanted to flee, His love was too strong
I did not run, I gave my heart.
Unlike the bee
My love did sting.

Romica Gantt

Heroin

This evil drug has made me sick.
the heroin feels like it's going to kill.
The cold turkey when coming down.
The pain and addiction never found.
The hurt inside buried deep beyond.
The grief and pain of a life once come and gone.
I am coming down rather fast the pain just seems to last and last.
I say just a little more here and a little more there.
My addiction never goes away.
Now I am pregnant nowhere to go.
selling my body my heart my soul.
My baby is born an addict like me.
I have stolen a life that should have been filled with glory.

Megan Wright

One Day

One day, you come into this world, all new, wide-eyed, and fresh.
One day, you find newfound friends, new adventures, new ideas.
One day, you wake up and find yourself striving to succeed
and wanting more out of life.

One day, you find a job, and you find newfound friends,
new adventures, and lots of new ideas.
One day, you wake up and find that you are older,
maybe more wiser, and wonder where you have been,
where you might go, and ponder what will be.

One day, you find that you are alone in the ground,
and wonder what just happened,
but are hoping that what you have done and what ideas you had
might make a difference in this world.
One day we will all be there.
Enjoy life while you can,
and don't worry about the what if's or the might be's.
Just do.

Glenda L. Gamble

Missing You

When I got the news I could date you no more,
I ran in my room and locked the door.
All I can do was remember your sweet little ways.
Now I am isolated from you for days.
I will not listen to them, no matter what.
It's because of them we are apart.
I sit here in the dark room while listening to the rain,
While all my heart can do is feel the pain.
I am hoping one day that we can back together,
But no matter, whatever happens, I will love you forever.

Cindy Glensky

Is There an Echo?

A tree falls in the forest and hits the ground,
And no one was there to hear it . . . "Did it make a sound?"
Although you and I were not there
In the forest were the birds, deer, and the grizzly bear.
'Twas God's wish that the old tree should come down,
To make way for young seedlings pushing through the ground.
"I heard the tree fall," said Mother Earth,
As she measured the land by width and by girth.
And it was time for the old tree to uproot and fall,
Since its roots had rooted and all its leaves were gone.
And was taking up space and blocking the sun.
"I had orders from the Almighty," said Mother Earth.
As she wrote down her notes on by width and by girth.
That the old tree should come down.
So . . . when a tree falls to Earth it's by God's hand alone!
"Since no one was there to hear it did it make a sound?"
Yes, it does make a sound, as it cries out to its creator.
Returning to the ground for rewards far greater.
Because this death is not final, as it passes into the ground.
For a far greater fate is ensured by the new seedlings which abound!

Marghuerita Turner

Untitled

Courage is the strength to stand up
When it's easier to fall down and lose hold.
It is the conviction to explore new horizon
When it's easier to believe what we've been told.

Courage is the desire to maintain our integrity
When it's easier to look the other way.
It is feeling happy and alive, and moving forward
When it's easier to feel sorry for ourselves and stay.

Courage is the will to shape the world.
When it's easier to let someone else do it for us.
It is the recognition that none of us perfect
When it is easier to criticize others and fuss.

Courage is the power to step forward and lead,
When it's easier to follow the crowd, their thoughts resound.
It is the spirit that places you on top of the mountain
When it is easier to never leave the ground.

The foundation of courage is solid,
The rock that doesn't roll.
Courage is the freedom
Of our mind, body, and soul!

Yaakov Ganz

The Music of Yesteryear

How I wish that I could ever hear,
The beautiful music of yesteryear.
Music that would lift the soul with just a melody,
a lovely ballad or maybe a rhapsody.

After the trials of a hard day,
During which others our tempers fray;
We'd sit and listen in ecstasy,
To the soothing strings of Mantovani.

Or, if you preferred a good love song,
Nothing could ever be wrong,
with listening to a standard or two,
by crooners who sang just for you.

For those who chose classical music,
Chopin or Beethoven could weave some magic.
There was music that lulled you into a dream;
Songs in which singers did not shout or scream.

To older folk this was a golden age,
Music was beauty, not an expression of rage.
This, young people should appreciate;
Not seek to condemn or denigrate.

Cynthia Hinkson

Sea of Strength

As indecision fills my mind I wonder what lies ahead,
So many issues to consider, what are the options to choose instead?

I look in front and observe the sea, how calm it looks today
But underneath the curling waves, a fury waits astray.

A seagull dives in, hopes to find his meal on the ocean's floor,
Taking a risk that it's safe and he will surface again once more.

The jellyfish float on top, no worry in their life
Harmless looking at first but a sting as sharp as a knife.

What is going on underneath, is it quiet on the ocean's floor?
What lies ahead is a mystery, not knowing what's in store.

Yet the chance one must consider to feel the ocean's breeze
To swim among the fishes and to fulfill one's life and needs.

So as I gaze out to the ocean, as powerful as it can be
I hope it finds the mercy to guide and strengthen me.

Rebecca Sardella

A Bumpy Road to Success

The road to success can be a bumpy ride.
If you don't have these books.
English, math and science by your side.

Do not ignore what your teacher will have to say.
Come to school prepared each and every day.

Strive to become the very best.
After graduation, then you can rest.

Believe me, applying for the best job is no fun.
So, spend your time cramming for examinations,
under the solar and the sun.

So, please don't forget.
Learn all you can about web-sites and the Internet.

Maxine Atkinson

Heartfelt

Herein lie two beautiful people, my mom and my dad
Such a glorious life with them I had
For them I am so thankful and, oh, so glad
As they gave to me a childhood that not many have had
Two beautiful people, they left me so soon
That life took a turn for the worst of doom
Two beautiful people who gave with no end
All my heartfelt emptiness will truly never mend
Yet cherished memories will keep them alive
And moreso their faith will empower me to survive
Two beautiful people, they were my best friends
Their love lives on even after life ends
Two beautiful people, my mom and my dad
Forever loved and forever respected by their daughter

Shelley Williams Sanders

Starlight

I express my love for Thee this night,
With words that rhyme and songs of the time.
The stars of the Milky Way bow in humble abode.
They find Thy beauty a sight to behold
As they wrap Thee in a blanket of silky white,
To keep Thee safe for me this night.
Upon the breeze, a fragrant nectar is dancing,
So sweet and, oh, so rare
As the moonbeams dance
Upon the highlights of your silvering hair.
My heart sings a love song
That dances with the trees to the stars above.
As I look upon the stars,
I softly whisper my love for Thee.

Rosemarie Anthony

I Do

To Kevin, you're my eternal love
When we first met, the distances we had to travel
To be with each other seemed endless
I often wondered if it was all just fun and games
And would fade away as time passed on, or
Could there be eternal life for us together
The distance kept us apart for days, sometimes weeks
After some time this was too much
For my delicate heart to handle
Tears fell from my eyes when I knew my pain had taken over
And I decided to end our journey together
You must have known, for that very same day
There was a knock at my door
As I opened up the door and gazed through the bright sunlight
There you stood wanting to know if I had room for one more
Many days have passed since then and
I now know that we share eternal life together
We have stood before God and spoken our vows to one another
That bonds us together forever, when we both said . . .
"I do"

Gina Marie Speck

Weep For

Weep for the smile too soon lost
The emptiness it left is an awful cost
Weep for the child too soon grown
Weep for the love no longer at home.
Weep for the parent too busy to live
And for those who always take yet never give
Weep for the tear covering the eye
Or the given truth that was really a lie.
Weep for the anger dispensed without end
And the lover and loved one that will never be friends
Weep for the footprint lost in the dust
Weep for the person unable to trust.
Weep for the soul lost in a maze
Or the person that will never give praise
And the preacher not knowing of the words he does speak
Or strength taken down to a spot on the street.

John Koch

Leaves

Softly they drift down through the air.
Some even landing in my hair.
Their colors of reds, yellows and brown,
Gently cover the entire ground.
Mother nature, putting her babies to bed,
For some, even pillows for their heads.
Blankets for all, covered up light,
Getting them ready for the winters long night.
There they go, skipping here and there,
The wind just blowing them everywhere.
An array of colors to greet the sight,
From early dawn to the edge of night.
God in His Heaven smiles down with delight.

Pauline B. Kuhn

God's Love to Me

When I think of the wonders of God
how he made everything and has given us so much.
I'm sitting here looking out my window
drinking coffee, looking at the trees
so bare in winter months and so pretty in spring
when buds start to come on them
and summer when they are full of leaves
and fall when they turn colors so beautiful to the eyes.
What a wonderful God we have to love
and I give Him thanks for everything
and wonderful people in my life because of Him.

Jeanette Sczygielski

Promises Broken

A long time ago, you made a promise
to always take care of me.

You haven't kept that promise.

A long time ago, we made a promise
to each other to love and cherish until
death do us part.

That promise has been broken.

Because we chose to keep too many secrets,
secrets that are not meant to be in a marriage.

Our rings once symbolized our love and
commitment now they lay in our
jewelry boxes not on our fingers.

Our promises have been broken and our patience has run thin.

To no longer love one another is one thing,
but to have promises broken hurts too much.

Take care of yourself,
for I will always love you.

But don't make any more promises to me.

Sarah Grey

Wishing upon a Star

For my children, Paul and Ann Marie
Did you ever find yourself,
wishing upon a star.
feeling lost and lonely,
it's because you really don't know who you are.

Take precious moments,
when you have nothing else to do.
Think of all you have and what you hold inside,
this special person, all along you knew.

You must get to like yourself,
inside and out and no matter where you are.
You will find out you have a lot to offer,
and to yourself, you are a glowing star.

Do not ever let anyone interfere with your spirit,
because you are, who you are.
Appreciate the things you have and hold,
and you'll find out you can certainly go far.

Always wear a smile,
and try to write your feelings down every day.
Then once a month, take out to read them,
and you'll find that you'll always have something good to say.

Mary Ann Zmuda

World of Hurt

I wish I could just start again,
and be real smart, and not give in.

All my friends said it was cool,
but now they're gone, and say I'm a fool.

I started to party a few years ago,
so I could be hip, wherever I'd go.

But after a while, things started to change:
school was boring, and my friends were all pains.

I partied all day, and at night to escape
all the pain that the world seemed to create.

But now as I sit in this hospital room,
I pray that my brother wakes up really soon.

He's been in a coma for almost a week;
He took my drugs from under the sink.

Patricia Ann Watkins

The Hidden Stars

It's the happy smile of a small child
It's walking on alone dirt road
Wind whispering through the woods
It's black clouds bellowing day like night would
It's a pleasant tear joining warm hearts,
It's because our cabin began love at the start
It's hair that's not too fancy
It's unquestionable love
'N teeth not too prancy
It's that ol' time smell of pine
lighter when it's freezing cold
It's a chimney so very old
It's inside thick and caked
Unusually black and sooty
It's plainly all 'round our hearts
It's pure simple beauty our hearts.

A. J. Baronne

Untitled

The shadows of night blanket my mind
walking me on to another place
of hallowed lamps and cobblestone streets another time.

Life is quiet as waves of gray roll in
silence prevails beyond crying doors
and strangers pass without words
nights of love, nights of crime, nights of sin.

The dampness shrouds the night
footsteps that never were steal through your mind
shapes fade together, tricks played unto one's sight.

A cat screams, silent wind, never moving cursed fog,
droplets form over sullen windows
firelight groans over deadened logs

And still we watch the night.

Robert Voelker

"They"

They won't let you be who you are
as they watch you die behind a metal bar
They won't let you act how you wanna act
these are my feelings all compact
They won't let you have a freedom of speech
even though you know you have a lot to teach
They won't let you live how you wanna live
as my life slowly drains through an empty sieve
They won't let you be who you can be
I don't know why they just can't see
They won't let you offer what you have to offer
they think inside your a whole lot softer
They won't let other people experience your pain
this is all because they know I'm insane

Christina Chubbs

The Wind in My Sail

The fog is now lifting; I'm beginning to see
The age-old promises made to me.
Joy everlasting as Love takes its stance;
Passionately drawn, I rejoice in Life's Dance.

Most Heavenly Father, this game we've created
is completely fulfilling, yet not satiated.
I'm hungry for more and you lovingly whisper,
"Run child, grab hold, dig deeper and deeper."

"Oh, the dreams you want most are the ones I placed there.
Push forward, desire more than you ever would dare.
For I am the wind that is filling your sail;
And together, sweet child, we never shall fail!"

Ravani Jewett Leffler

G.L.T.

As I walk through the halls of this wonderful place
I glance to the right
I see her smiling face
I glance to the left
I see him sitting there
Just sitting and waiting for someone to care.
In their minds they're sitting, completely alone
Just waiting for someone to visit from home

These wonderful people, I want you to know
Are your mom and dad, uncles and aunts
So, please take some time and come into our home
A smile, a touch, a hug and a kiss
is all that they ask for, to give their life bliss

Now remember someday
You might be sitting there
thinking you're all alone in that corner chair
And suddenly someone appears with a smile
a hug and a kiss to make your life worthwhile

Barbara Collins

Blistering Tears

Seeping from this pool of passion
I let my childhood innocence prevail
In forthright splendour my soul flowed
I sang the song of the forgotten years
In the dance of yesterday, I reveled
In my soul I yearn
In my heart, a pain

Blinded by the fury of this onslaught
But like the foe of a mighty army I fell
Face downwards I fell and was trampled
My spirit longs like love fettered by distance
My eyes burn with the acid of their waters
Yet in my soul I yearn
And in my heart, a pain

How long should my soul pray unheeded
Yet my soul would pray with ceaseless hope
Even if my bones should jut out their flesh
And my saliva should dry in its throat
My soul would still yearn
But in my heart I feel a pain

Zubie Okolo

Sunday Dinner

I was raised in the small town of Kermit
That's a town you've never heard of, I bet
My husband, he calls it the armpit of Texas
I, myself, call it my home away from home in West Texas

That's because I recall the good times of my childhood
I remember all the fellowship and food
As we would file out from church
My father for a friend, he would search

We'd head home to a roast in the oven
And to many a friend our door would be open
As we would sit around and visit
The children didn't even want to miss it

Sometimes we could see the tumbleweed bend
As it would pass our window blowing in the wind
And certainly on the West Texas plains, the sand would blow
But the chatter in the house would continue even though

Nothing could stop us from enjoying ourselves
As different people would pull books from the shelves
But before long, our visit would end and we would say goodbye
Knowing that the love of our friends on our hearts still lie

Peggy Collier

At Owode

Their eyes threatening
Through my heart searing
I made a u-turn.

I saw Kelebe, beaming;
Beaming as if reluctantly;
I forced one back
He caught it; a deal struck.

Like a lightning,
On two wheels
The threatening eyes vanquished.
And to the Gendarmes my occiput for conversation.

At the other end
Kelebe's face waved its gratitude, not without
Fingers worming the result into pocket—
—fresh delicacy from the mint.

I forced another one.
A brightened face-the message from Kelebe
And the journey began.

'Tunji Kazeem Adebiyi

How Our Father Cried

Dedicated to my mother, Agnes S. Fancher
How the father must have cried,
When his son was crucified;
How the tears rained down from
Heaven to earth that day.
How the lightning ripped and tore,
Hurling down from Heaven's door;
As they killed his son on a hill so far away.

How the father must have cried,
When his son was so despised;
As they laid the crown of thorns
On Jesus' blessed head.
Did he think about the day,
His boy in the manger lay;
And like a father long to take the blame instead.

Chorus:
And how he must have anguished,
When his son said, "Father, take this cup from me.
But not my will but thine be done,
Father, take my hand, Lord, I understand."

Jayne Reich

A Salute

With tribute to William Wordsworth
"We walked along, while bright and red,
Uprose the morning sun,"
On the beach lay the dead.

Throughout the night, in your pain the troops cried,
For world-wide freedom, you fought and you died.

You fought the enemy with your hands and your knives,
You sacrificed yourselves, to keep others alive.

Without food or water, you continued the struggle,
You conquered the elements, the cliffs, and the jungle.

On the sea, in the air, and on the land you gave,
Unselfish and brave, so that we would be saved.

Without your courage, freedom would be lost,
And to you we owe our lives, and at that enormous cost.

It was your service with honor, that makes you kings among men,
And I walk humbly in your shadow, now, as I did then.

To those who passed with honor and to you who live with pain,
Thank you for protecting us, for to you we owe all gain.

Catlyn Kalyvas

Enjoy Life While You Can

Feel it all now while you can.
Enjoy the chirping sounds of the birds.
Listen to the rain as it sweetly hits the ground.
Don't take anything for granted.
Enjoy it all now while you can,
Fall in love with the different sounds of the wind.
Glorify the beauty of Mother Nature,
And the ocean, fall in love with the calmness, peace,
And tranquility of the ocean.
Feel and enjoy it all now while you can.
Admire smells, all kinds of smells,
They give and create memories.
Feel and enjoy it all now while you can,
Love, hate, pain, sorrow, and beauty.
Learn to live and live as much as you can.
Enjoy life while you can because it's short
And you never know when death is going to arrive.

Melissa R. Mixon

She Is

She is the trees of all kinds all colors
She is the sea the ocean, rivers, and streams
She is the mountains, foothills, and all
She is the sun, the sky, the air I breathe
She is the one and only one I will ever love.
She is my love, my life my dreams,
my reality, my everything.

She is the stars, the universe
She is the moons, planets and here and afar
She is the day and the night
She is the Creator, the Giver of life
She is the one who does so much for me.

She is all this and so very much more,
That I will forever see
Will forever touch, will forever know
and only I will forever love.

Michael Bridges

Thank You

From up above, you've been there for me in a special way.
Touching my soul, blessings my heart, each and every day.
The strong need to kill, I no longer feel.
My mind is at peace, I have begun to heal.

Thank you Lord for the strength I've found.
The joy of life and my children keep my body above ground.

You opened my eyes to see what just wasn't meant to be.
Thank you Lord for protecting me.

The pain is gone and removed from my heart.
Thank you Lord for a fresh new start.

Antoinette Moore

My Elvis to Me

I can't explain to anyone, just why I love him so.
Some people claim that he's been dead for twenty years, they say;
now, to me that's a whole twelve years
before the year that I was born!

But I know for sure, since I was three,
that he has totally fascinated me.
Most girls my age decorate their rooms
with Barbie, or Disney, or other cartoons.
But all of that stuff was just never me;
Mine is decorated with Elvis, The King.

But even after all these years, to me, he's still alive.
So whether or not he died that year, it truly doesn't matter.
Because I keep him in my heart, where, for me,
my Elvis will always live forever.

Loma Watkins

Chosen One

Step out and take a look at yourself
For everyone you have put your heart on a shelf
Thinking of everyone but yourself
Step outside your mind one time
You'd be amazed at what you might find
Peace love harmony
All those things that set you free
Look deeply at what you are to be
Look deeply and you'll see
The reflection of me
Step back into your soul
Return again where you feel whole
Only then your time will come
Your time to be the chosen one

Michelle Kelley

Just Because

Just because I like you, it doesn't mean I want you. And,
Just because I want you, it doesn't mean I need you. And,
Just because I need you, it doesn't mean I love you.
But:
Because I love you, I like, want, and need you. And,
Just because I love you, I want you to love me too. And,
Knowing that if you love me, you'll like, want, and need me.
And
Just because you love me, you'll want me to love you too.

Odis W. Kenton Sr.

Just Five Minutes

Five minutes to myself is all I ask,
Just five minutes alone; then I'll do the task.
Close the door and keep everyone at bay,
Please listen to me and hear what I say.
It doesn't amount to a whole heck of a lot,
But believe me it's wonderful when it's all you got.
Having time to yourself is pretty scarce around here,
So every minute you have, you hold very dear.
So stop the clocks and hold the presses!
Because I'm gonna hide while everyone dresses.
Each second ticks by becoming a minute,
I think I see a room with no one in it.
I'll sit for a minute or maybe two,
Living around here feels like a zoo.
My minutes are over; my time is done,
Show me the tasks that were never begun.

Janice J. Smith

sweet words

not many letters involved
only eight to be exact
one letter stands alone
four letters stick together
the last three form the final team
three simple words working together
to make someone special smile
words which need not be spoken
to be known and understood
these words can be heard in many ways
when these words are true
the eyes say it with a sparkle and gleam
the hands become soft and gentle
the arms hold ever so tightly
the ears listen intently
when these words are true
the voice never has to be used
because the heart and body say it all
the special words, sweet words
i love you . . . the sweetest words one will ever hear

Lorie Michelle Brannom

Love

I know what strength is,
Patience too.
That with faith and hope, dreams come true.
I've felt distance, want with need,
Have patience to wait, perseverance to hold.
I've known acceptance's warmth and rejection's cold.
I've feared time; our future so unsure,
And to close the distance between us seems the only cure.
I know what love is,
Trust to.
And if we just hold on, that we'll make it through.
When reassurance was needed, because we were both unsure,
I felt your pain, dried your tears
As you held me close, eased my fears.
And in the end, whatever may be,
You'll be in my thoughts, held in my heart,
Always near and forever dear.

Heather Parker

Thoughts

I write to you this little story,
And hope that you do not worry.
About all the things that I do think,
That go through my head in one single blink,
My thoughts about love, my thoughts about hate,
I hope that they could only wait.
Until my thoughts get sorted in my head,
But by that time I will be dead.

Bruno Mazzotta

Poem for a Midnight Caller

You've always got me so confused,
Lost in my own mind, not understanding yours.
You make me think: not very common.
You screw up my mind and then say good night.
But, in all this,
You are my light in a dark place,
In my hour of the least understanding,
On the day I wander off the right path,
In my moment of floating with the clouds,
You bring me back to Earth.
When I cover my eyes and deny the truth,
You are there to make me accept.
You tell me things I've never heard.
You show me things I've never seen,
You help me through hurting me,
I hate you for that.
And I love you for this,
You have faith in me.

Kaylen Kelley

Untitled

Let's start the new year out right,
Let's promise each other not to fight.
Let's look forward to future ways,
Let's leave behind us the ugly days.

Life is to short for things to go bad,
Life is to be happy, not to be sad.
Life is something we all must go through,
Life is me the world and you.

Come on love let's start anew,
Come on love just me and you,
Come on love we will see it through,
Come on love my heart is true.

This year is ours and no one can change it,
This year is what we want, so we will make it.
This year I give to you from me,
This year is ours, you wait and see.

Julie A. Wendt

Destiny's Road!

I walked through a doorway, to a world that's unknown;
My heart feels so deserted, and I'm carrying too heavy a load.
How did I seem to manage, to make it this far along;
If I'm not mistaken, I'm traveling up destiny's road.
In the distance reflects a sign, your name in thick gold;
Second chance in a lifetime, to forever love and to hold.
I'll love you even more, and make up the time before;
My heart is on the line, a highway titled Destiny's Road.

Many moons have come; just as fast they're all gone;
I'm out looking for love, and my heart says you're the one.
Been traveling so far, I'm tired, weary, and torn;
To be where you are, on a journey down destiny's road.
I kept a photo in mind, as it's you I aim to hold;
All in a matter of time, this love will guide me home.
Through sleet, snow, or rain, I'm sheltered by a heart so warm;
That will ease all the pain, at the end of destiny's road.

A journey with agony and hurt, in a world as we all know;
A highway made my dirt, for all who travels destiny's road.

M. LaValley

Happy Cake

This recipe starts with a morning smile.
Kind words blended make the day worthwhile.
Mix the deeds, friendly and nice.
Together with a dash of happiness and spice.

Shift out the thoughts that are ugly and mean.
Just waste!
Add laughter and sweetness to better the taste.

Stir and stir,
Take your time don't make haste.
Anger-bubbles out you see.
Make it raise just right for you and me.

Make this cake a "Must!"
For each day of the year.
You can't eat too much! So have no fear!

It's good for the short, the fat or the thin.
Cook a "Happy Cake," success you will win.
Bake it in the oven, full of love from the heart.
Give it to your loved ones and they will not part.

Let this Happy Cake be part of your day.
Of all that you do and all that you say.

Ruth Thomas

Our Child

As we wait, and anticipate!
Wondering what it'll be,
Just have to wait and see!

Pray that it'll be healthy,
And happy more than wealthy!
May it know the difference between wrong from right,
And have God's guidance and insight!

May it live by the Golden Rule,
And be an honor student in school!
May its hardships through life not be overbearing,
May it be gentle, kind, and caring!

May its thoughts and words always be positive,
And may its time always be constructive!
May its imagination always be vivid,
And to the fullest, may life it live!

May compassion take its hand,
And teach it how to understand!
That it may conquer any task,
And give to life, all that is asked!

Nancy Bullinger

Goodness

When goodness shakes her floral head
Lazy flowers flit down to bed
When goodness loses colored lazy leaves
she stands as tall as a barren oak tree
Frills and comforts are not what she seeks
But a barren life quiet and meek
She works so hard to sprout flower and fruit
Pulling water from the ground to give green shoots
Green for growth and prosperity
Brown for the earthy humility
That's what goodness seems to be
rest and sleep
ascetic and meek
in a cycle all its own
perfect when grown.

Stephanie Arbour

DOG

Four-legged animal, Furry creature,
Mammal related to wolves, foxes, and jackals
Animal that barks, woofs, bites,
Brown, black, white, grey, tan, spotted,
Boxers, Chows, Pitbulls, Poodles,

DOG

Man's best friend, hunter, protector, kid's playmate,
cat chaser . . .

DOG

A man (HUSBAND) who cheats on his wife,
skirt chaser . . .

J. Fearrington

Two Sides of the Same Coin

He and I have been and will always be, forever,
He is tails, the dark side of the coin.
That bone-chilling cold on a black starless night,
The shadow that you just can't seem to lose,
The fear of the unknown.
He is darkness eternal, he is evil.
I, I am the sunrise, the sunset, a warm summer's breeze
And the hope of a brighter tomorrow.
I am his balance, his equal.
Without him I am not complete, as he is incomplete without me.
We are as different as night and day,
But unable to exist without the other.

Michelle Thompson

Windows

My window sees a six year-old curlyhead
choosing a dress for her mother who is dead.
My daddy is crying, he said
she died in her sleep and now she is dead.
Only God knows why he needed her today.
Maybe all the gifts she has left me are part of the play of my life.
To be nurtured along my path by the most unique
and unexpected travelers as my map of life unfolds
with each player giving me a precious life skill.
I feel every moment the miracle God has created in me
and this part of the play never fails to amaze me.
My boundaries are invisible and her presence strong,
do what is needed. It is right.
My instincts know and they will never hurt me.
She is here guiding my hands with an overflow
of love as only a mother can.
To help her little girl be the best she can.

Ellen Bouvier

Untitled

I've broken your heart, I know.
I see your pain, fear, emptiness, and sorrow.
You don't show it much,
but I see it in your eyes.
A child, trembling, next to a fire
the fire burns with everlasting sadness.
The fire, strong, never flickering or dimming.
The child is crying and screaming for help.
I hold him close,
telling him,
"Don't cry, sweet child, I am here,
to protect and care for you.
Never will I leave you."

Ashley Mudrinich

A Little Girl Play

When I was just a little girl.
I liked to run and play.
And then I played the hiding game.
To see who I could catch.
I ran and ran, and took a stand,
and did not get a one.
But, then I got tired,
and stopped to rest instead.
And along came my brother, to go fishing at the creek.
We fished, and fished, and had some fun.
But, soon it came to an end.
You see my mother, called us in to eat our supper then.
After it was over, we went out to play again.
This time we played some jump-rope,
and had the greatest time, tugging as we jumped in.
We did the pick up, we did the double, and then we did the hop.
I heard my mother, calling it's time to come in.
As I get ready to go to bed.
I think of the good things I did today.
But, this is the ending of a little girl's play.

Corrie M. White

Gone but Not Forgotten

When I awoke this morning,
I moved my hand to touch you,
But you were not over there.
It was then I really missed you.
I'll miss your loving arms around me;
Your kisses are gone too.
It was then I realized how very much
I had loved you, missed you,
And wanted to be with you.
Yyou are a part of me
For the rest of my life, until we meet again.

Kathrine M. Hood

A Mouse Needs a House

To anyone who likes to laugh and play guitar country
No one like a mouse, 'cause he's dirty as a louse,
But when it gets cold at night, he even needs a house,
He try to find himself some food,
Even if it's on the floor,
He try to find anything that you have in store,
I don't like mice myself, but they're around our town,
If he gets hungry enough, he'll gnaw your house down,
He'll try to find your kitchen, or some bread crumbs on the floor,
Even if he has to, he'll gnaw down your door,
I see him in the woods, running up and down a log,
Something might catch him, an owl or a dog,
The dirty little pest, just seems to survive,
He gnaws on every little thing, even wood to keep alive,
Folks spend millions, trying to kill him,
He's a dirty little louse, but I guess the truth is,
A mouse needs a house.

Robert L. Elkin

Life in the Fast Lane

Are you really contented living in the fast lane,
With money, cars, jewelry, and slayings?
I see you feel so high and mighty,
Now that you are living so materialistically.

You are lacking love in your heart for Jah Almighty,
All because you are selfish and greedy.
You've claimed that you are so full,
Yet, you are starving from the lack of wisdom.

You have given up the Holy Chapters,
In exchange for killing and robbing your brothers.
All of your life your mother knew you as Raieem,
Now to Babylon, you are A.K.A. Zero, Five, Seventeen.

Locked behind steel bars each day and night,
Charged with larceny, murder, and leaving the scene of a crime.
Now you are spending twenty-five to life,
You're still asking yourself, "Why?"
And "Yes," Your dear mother still cries.

Erna Assent

Falling Stars

To my beautiful family
Fire-flakes, flints; The same old stars
Still fiery in the unredemptive sky.
The silvery and hopeless midnight sky
that feels like home from here to Mars,
Then gradually grows foreign into stars
We hardly recognize, that fill the eye
With lofty cleanings we ineptly cry
By framing legends of unending wars.
There is some comfort in the way they sprawl,
Their vast composure in the cold
and careless spaces that absorb them as they fall.

Peter Proctor

Fight, You Can Win!

For the younger people of Calvary Tabernacle in Hempstead, NY
Look up!
Start up!
Stop! Burying
Your head in the drain

Weeping may come
That's life, it comes with pain
Don't let the terror of the nights
Affects your daily fights

This world is full of trickery and
People are in disguised
But don't be fooled by those who are masters of lies.

Instead fight the good fight of faith
Don't give up now 'cause it's not too late

Now is the time to take back
Your God given dignity
Your exuberant appeal
Your character and zeal.

Fay Burnett

What Once Was

Once there was a haven, a paradise I could go to.
Once there was support, something I could hold on to.
Once there was pride something I would defend to the death.
But now . . .
What once was happiness, is now sorrow and pain.
What once was my paradise, is now my hell.
What once was my support, is now my downfall.
What once was my pride, is now my embarrassment.
What once was my everything, is now my nothing.
What once was my life, is now my death.

Monica Navarrete

My Heart Is Slowing Down

To my mother, inspiration to all
I wake up and it's cold again.
Inside and out my heart is still amiss.
My life was lost when you were taken, I can't function without you.
I need you close, I need you now.
Can't you see I'm dying without you, my heart is slowing down.
I walk outside and start the car, I don't know where to go.
I feel you close but I'm without your touch, I'm starting to panic.
I'm losing control.
Will I ever be normal? Will I ever start again?
Light turns to darkness and I'm still in my car,
there's not a clear road ahead.
I'm crying, the road is still wet and I can't see it drying.
In time it may get easier but I don't know how,
I can't see past tomorrow.
I turn back time to see your smile and to hear you say you love me.
It's getting cold again, darkness is setting in.
My life was lost when you were taken.
Can't you see I'm dying, my heart is slowing down.

Daniel Willman

The Sounds of Summer

The sounds of summer still ring in my ears;
The incessant rustle of leaves as rain shower nears.
Low bird conversations at morning's first light,
And the happy laughter of children, ever a delight.
The slow creak of a porch swing on a hot afternoon;
And a chorus of crickets from a field soft-lit by the moon.
Farm country has a chorale of animal sounds,
Far different from those hear in busy small towns
Where there's beckoning music from an ice cream cart,
And rhythmic band music from the shady town park.
There's cries of delight from children bike-racing down hill;
And the flapping of sails left to the wind's fickle will.
How I love the sound of church bells on a bright Sunday morn,
And those precious old hymns sung by Christians new-born.
If I could package all these in a glass water ball,
Have each lovely scene at my beck and call,
I would have beauty enough to last all winter long.
But without the warmth and delight of each summer song,
The beauty would be lacking, need something more
Complete only, with summer's unique musical score.

Helen M. Ott

Journey

As I walk alone on an Autumn's day,
Wondering, how long will it take to mend my way.

The sky seems cloudy, and the sun seems set,
My way is far, my way is far yet.

As I pass house after house on my way,
The day gets darker, towards the end of an Autumn's day.

Although my way is not known and my journey is unclear,
I have a certain path to travel, and it's guided by ear.

My feet knows not where my destination ends,
And I only know where my journey begins.

My place of rest will be under the skies,
The earth will be my pillow the stars will be my eyes.

When I lie down to rest on this Autumn's Night,
The pillows of the earth will hold me tight.

The stars in the sky will watch over me,
As I fall into a somber sleep.

My protection will come from the only one who knows,
My reason for this Journey to me is still unknown.

When I wake I'll walk in the labors of the light,
Of a brand new day, of another Autumn's night . . .

J. A. C. Butler

Fears

Fears surround me
With them comes my tears
I have finally found the one of my dreams
So why have I all these fears that turn to tears?
I can't believe how I'm coming apart
Was I wise to open my eyes and let him in my heart
Or will this heart be "torn apart"?

Kay Kopplin

Not Promised the Next Day

This is a world of unbelief. Looking for peace;
But instead gets nothing but grief.
A man has lost his way,
A woman has gone astray;
And they're not promised the next day.
Murders and suicides, a man arrested.
People are restless and children molested.
Looking for answers for AIDS and cancer;
But when will the day come
That we can stop running from
The man named Jesus
The one who loves us
Who died for our sin
That we may be born again.
The hour is now. The day is at hand
This is a message for every woman, child, and living man.
Take time to think before your life is snuffed away,
Because it's too late to cry and too late to pray.
If you fast, you'll last, if you stop, you'll drop,
If you pray, you'll stay, 'cause we're not promised the next day.

Marcus Armstrong

Too Late

As the years pass by and the days get shorter,
You wonder where the time has gone
But it's too late
It's time you move on yet,
memories hold you back
As you close your eyes a smile
comes to your face but it's
just a memory you've drifted too far
As you dream and look for the love that was lost,
you lose time and fade away
'Cause it's too late
While looking for the answers in
life you realize the questions are forgotten
You want to be free and live for today,
But it's too late
You've wasted the years
in trying and crying
It's too late.

Elizabeth McGuinness

Elburn Lions Park

In memory of Mallisia Wackerlin
Come stand under the tall trees
Just relax and feel the breeze
You can get here with great ease
It's a place that's meant to please
That's okay if you sneeze
The pretty flowers just want to tease
Most people can walk if they need
The park is here for you and me
Once you've been here then you will see
It was built to help people who can't see to read
But the members come to help with your needs
You can tell by their great deeds.

George L. Wacherlin
"Georgie Boy"

The Color of Emotions

For the true inspiration, God
Love is a blushing red heart in motion,
Sustaining the life of the deepest emotion,
Living within as part of our soul.

Hate is the night's black ocean,
Bringing forth unknown tales of destruction,
Seeping through crevices to empty our hearts.

Joy is the shiny yellow sun above,
Giving us light to go a step beyond,
Spreading warmth throughout our days.

Sorrow is a blue day without tomorrow,
Taking treasures from our hands
as our hearts turn slowly bland.

Hope is a morning's green forest,
Sharing peace and tranquility,
Stretching throughout the vast fields of dreams,
Keeping alive the need to believe.

Laughter is the glistening snow
as I go through the soft surroundings
I am often reminded of days long ago
When I would play and run in the frosty white snow.

> *Miriam P. Garcia*

Happy Mother's Day

You are my mother by chance,
You are my friend by choice.
You'll be my mother 'til I die,
In my heart you mean the most.

You stayed up late to help me with my projects,
You cheered for me at my games.
Though I've gone through a lot of changes,
You've always stayed the same.

I know I sometimes lied
And didn't tell the truth,
But you always stood by my side
Since I was a little 'til now that I am a youth.

You always knew my dreams,
And I knew your expectations.
Whenever I had a question I came to you.
You always were full of explanations.

I love you, my dear mother,
And I'm going to show in every way,
How much you really mean to me.
Happy Mother's Day.

> *Emily Poxson*

Grandpa

In memory of Dudley Justice
Grandpa was someone of tender heart, soul, and mind.
Someone who was so very kind.
Kind to one and all, big or small,
everyone he knew, or just saw.

Grandpa was loved and will be missed by so many.
He meant more to me than any.
He was the best grandpa to me
and one day soon, I'll see him again, in Heaven.

But now he's happy and pain-free.
I can just see my papa;
with that big red truck in the sky,
sitting up there by Jesus' side,
watching over me and all the ones he loved so much.

> *Elizabeth Osburn*

It Was You:

The Spoiled Child Version the Boundary of Love

I shall hide my love within the moon on a spring night
After I have dared to reveal my love for you.
You're my heart's desire.
I cherish every moment with you like it was my last.
Sometimes I fall asleep thinking of you,
Knowing the meaning of everlasting love,
Someone who will be there with me through thick and thin,
A person who will love me until the end.
'Til death do us part, that's what you say,
But our love goes beyond the grave.
I know you get lonely, but these words will be here to comfort you.
All these things came true the day I met you.

> *Maurice L. Brown*

Nobody Important

When the phone rings and you're on the line,
My friends ask who it is all the time.
And my response is nobody important.
When I come home late, hair all wild,
My roommates be asking, who you been with child?
And I always say oh, nobody important.
When I get a page and look down to check the number,
My boyfriend looks at me and I know what he wonders.
I just say, baby, it ain't nobody.
When I call you and your cell, and she's in the room,
I can hear you say it's nobody, I'll be to bed soon.
So we creep and we hide,
Keep each other on the side,
Don't know how many times we've lied
About nobody important.

> *Anika Francis*

Essence

The essence of the wolf inhabits my body.
It guides me, strengthens me.
The wolf within helps my pathetic human body.

By lending its soul to me, I am strong
I have heightened senses.
I am faster, swifter, smarter than an ordinary human.

I am the wolf as it guides me.
I am now and always will be the predator.
This essence makes me whole.
I am the wolf!

> *Chris Andrews*

Midnight Operations

Midnight operations taking place at night,
Midnight operations no need to be uptight.
Nurses at their stations, surgeons in their gowns,
Ready for provocations from accidents on the town.
Suddenly without warning, screaming through the door,
Comes a hyper medic, cargo bleeding on the floor.

Interns wandering, hopelessly about,
Apparently pondering probably in doubt.
No need for worry, no cause for concern,
They are only in a hurry to prevent a fateful return.
Sit back relax and let the professionals take care,
Soon you will feel the ax, when they cancel your medicare.

Midnight operations taking place all right,
Boy have you been taken, driving late at night.
So throw away that bottle, disregard that jay,
Ease up on that throttle, and live another day.

For midnight operations are a painful sight,
Don't risk death and annihilations showing off your might.

> *David L. Boles*

Thoughts

I see you love me in your face,
I feel the thought of your embrace.
Alone in a thought of you holding me,
I just close my eyes and your face is all I see.
My heart beats faster as I get lost in thought,
I am holding on to your love and the joy it brought.
I fought to love you without any limit,
I made sure my all was in it.
Before there was you my heart was in a box,
I kept it always closed and chained with many locks.
But then you came and opened me up from inside,
Having you to love you took my heart with pride.
I now am not held down by chains,
My heart runs with yours no worries no pains.
Roaming about with you by my side,
I am grateful you love me I don't have to hide.
By opening my heart you took the risk of getting turned away,
But you took it as it came and never settled for a day.
You showed me you love me and always stayed true,
And now your reward is that I love you.

Deanna Julbe

My Sister, My Friend

To my little sister Kimberly
Helping me through all the years,
Making me laugh, drying my tears.
Borrowing my clothes, fixing my hair,
Showing me how much you care.

Telling me secrets, calming my fears,
Being my friend, through all these years.
Thanking you once, and I'll thank you again,
For being my sister, for being my friend.

Marie Fischer

Untitled

Narrow path, wide path, which one will you take
Be careful, for the one you choose will prove your fate

It could lead you to the gate of Heaven or the gates of Hell
It could lead you to a life of misery and torture
or a life peaceful and well

It could lead you to a place of glory and everlasting riches
or a place of hate with bodies in ditches

It could lead you to a place of love and wonderful dreams
Or a place full of fire, with unmerciful screams

It could lead you to a place where people care,
a place you could forever call home
Or a place where demons beat you and you could forever be alone

All this comes down to one question, the question of your fate
Narrow path, wide path, which one will you take?

Pete Gonzales

My Window

As I gaze from my window, the first thing I see
Is the fluttering leaves on our huge willow tree.
The long slender branches wave slow in the breeze;
And the old wooden swing is squeaking with ease.
Then the first glint of sunrays catches my eye
As the pinks and the golds brighten the sky.
The sunrise is glorious as the first morning glow,
Glistens and dances on the mountain-top snow.
I sadden a little as I see from my pane,
A flock of grey geese flying south once again.
The sky is now brilliant as the morning glow
Bursts into full view on the fresh-fallen snow.
I shudder a little and I'm glad once again
For the warmth of a fire and the stillness within.

Vicky M. Lowder

Her Delicacy and Her Charm

She's statuesque and dexterous
She walks in supple step so light,
Fableistic to the tooth
I mark her every night.

Reverent in her slightest turn
My eyes she stuns them so,
Goddess of nature's offspring
She charms from head to toe.

Her fashion like-sophistication
Black velvet soft and kind,
Conspicuous her every swing
Just boggles drunk, my mind.

Her movements move so draft yet creeping
Her narrowness so fine,
I've encountered many but unlike she
This lady is divine.

Her hair is silky a somewhat satin—darkness is its hue
long and soft—
It runs aloft,
Like she there's very few.

Eduardo Perez

Fear of the Boogieman

He stealthily enters your head
After your parents are dreaming in their bed.

He doesn't want to slit your throat or poke out your eye.
He only wants to make you cry.

Your closet starts to creak open; it's a sign.
You pull your rags of sheets up and start to whine.

The shadowy figure only you can see creeps out.
It's all you can do not to shout.

You try to look for and find.
The courage to survive your own mind.

This dark shadowy figure of the night.
The source of all your fright.

Is not standing here, high over your bed.
But it's all in your head.

Then when you wake up and think it's all not true.
Until the next night when your parents say goodnight to you.

Jake Collar

My Father's Bet

To my dad, Jerry Smith, Am-6445
Price of a life is punishment in the hole
Price of sins are paid with your soul

Verdict of guilty no longer are you free
Twenty to life all twelve would agree

Now wear their clothes and sleep in their bed
All you have left are the thoughts in your head

Given numbers to replace your name
This week or next they're all the same

What's this life about? Figure it out on your own
Sounds are everywhere but you're all alone

Steel doors are locked and windows are barred
Her dreams are shattered and hearts grow hard

Break a rule and they'll lock you away
It all depends on how well you play

Cheating to win is considered a crime
Your debt is not money you pay with time

Forget what you know for you do it their way
Your life is the bet if you decide to play.

Carrie J. Smith

Taffy Cat, Taffy Cat

For pet lovers everywhere
Taffy cat, Taffy cat, where you at,
Somewhere in a window taking a nap.
Taffy cat, Taffy cat chasing a bug,
Someone wants to give you a hug.
You run away, run away, spitting and hissing.
She just don't like all that kissing.
Taffy cat, Taffy cat you purr for a pat,
Then you turn and swat, you crazy cat.
Taffy cat, Taffy cat you're gone for now,
But, while you were here, you were the cat's meow.

Darlene Smith

A Valentine's Day Poem

Valentine's Day
It's a day of love
For the special one you are thinking of.

Be it your wife, your girl, or just a dear friend
It's a day to reflect on the best times that you've spent.

It's a day to be happy, no time to be sad
To remember the good days
And forget all the bad.

For love is strong
It comes deep from within
For one to share and one to take in.

Valentine's Day
It's a day of love
For the special one you are thinking of.

David G. Stepke

Can There Be Love after Love

The feeling you get
when you fall in love is one not many will feel

All others that may be so fortunate
as to have this treasure will never know if it is real.
Can there be love after love.

When a homely man like myself embarks
upon a chance for true
and firm love he must not pass it up.

At the very moment
he sees his maiden
he will know the answer
to the age-old question
and then he will be able to reply
with a simple yes,
there is love after love.

Patrick Kinney

The Batter

The batter steps up to the plate
As the pitcher waits.
The batter looks at the coach to get his signs
And the crowd wonders what's in his mind.

Then all of a sudden he's in the box ready
And the pitcher rocks backs steady.
He releases the ball fast with heat.
Crack! The ball and bat meet.

The batter and fans watch the ball
And think it's over the wall.
Just to be safe they listen for the umpire's call.
He said back, back, going, going, gone!

And the batter touches 1st, 2nd, 3rd
And finally rounds the bases and touches home!

John Cory Russ

Searching

My mind still cannot comprehend what went on;
I still do not believe you are gone.
I expect you to come through our door,
Drop your bag, and talk to me more.
But now that door is not yours, it's mine,
And quite frankly I'm doing more than fine.
You did not break me, but it was near,
Because being alone is what I fear.
Yet the silence in my room is doing me good.
I moved the bed over the spots where you stood.
I look at the phone, and think to call,
But that's not my job, not at all.
You left me, so you make the move.
If you want my friendship, you have to prove
That I can still count on you as I did before,
And heartbreak and crying are no longer in store.
It makes me sad to think we are done;
In the past year or so we had so much fun.
But you have moved on and left me behind,
And the friend that I knew, I can no longer find.

Alexandra Brodsky

The Cold Realities of January

October through December cast a warm and special glow;
Their aromas are so sweet and the ground's covered up with snow,
But you always must remember and be so very wary
That what's coming to you soon are the cold realities of January.

All your worries and your problems always seem so small
When the season goes and changes to the brilliant shades of fall,
So you go round with feelings that are lighthearted and quite merry
'Til suddenly you have reached the cold realities of January.

By December you have pushed all your problems way behind;
You find that you are being very thoughtful and too kind,
Then the first of the year has come and you're sad and very contrary
'Cause now you must really face the cold realities of January.

Sherry L. Wilson

"A Mistake"

I may have made a big mistake trying to write poetry,
but I had to see what I could do and put together this entry.

I know I am an amateur and may have lost my mind,
but I love to put words on paper and try to make them rhyme.

It's nice to write a story too if you can make it fit,
but what's important is to try and see if you can do it.

I honor those who are the pros and admire what they can do;
one day I hope the time will come when someone says, "That's you!"

Joe Scafidi

You Talk to Me

For Tupac Shakur, working spirit brother
May my heart carry all of your burdens that you share with me.
Shall God give me the heart to then still care for you.

The secrets of some friends will surely determine
whether or not you can remain friends.

Faced with my truth, how then will I be able to judge you?
So the spirit that brought you into life
also carries you during your journey, so that you are not alone.

Then the time comes for me to see you again,
my heart pounding with the same anticipation
to listen to your stories about
how the day was just hell.

Now your stories have become a part of my life;
I miss embracing your style of communication.

Waiting to hear from you as soon as the Heavens see I need you too.

Paulus Chapman

On Growing Old

To my Mother
I'm growing old, and Lord, I'm frightened.
Not of death,
But of dreaded entombment in institutions for the living dead.
Instead of roses,
The smothering stench of regression to infancy.
Instead of loved ones,
Aged specters whose images smolder in the brain.
Instead of laughter,
Inane mutterings from withering shells denied blessed release.
Not for me, I pray, not for me.

I'm growing old. Please, Lord, put not on those I birthed
The anguish of my commitment,
The crushing guilt of wishing me gone for my sake.
Instead of remorse,
Tears of honest grief when sprinkling ashes on my bier.
Instead of reproach,
Beautiful memories as the fruition of my having once been.
Instead of earthly purgatory,
Not one hour past productivity for the price extracted.
For me, I pray, for me.

Kate R. Catloth

I Didn't Understand

For Grandmother Leng, David, and Leslie
Many, many years ago,
Think about it and you will know.
You carried me on a boat
You didn't ask me, if I could swim,
or if I could float
You just put me on your big, big boat.
You tied me up, to others like me,
But you didn't even introduce me.
I didn't understand!

Once I got to where you wanted me to be
You really didn't want me to see
For you had big plans for me.
Sell me here trade me there
Work me everywhere
I didn't understand, I didn't understand!

I didn't speak your language.
I couldn't read your books.
but it didn't matter, I just watched and looked, 'cause
I didn't understand!
I didn't understand!

Beverly Hill

Life Is Forever

My hand in waters pure and blessed
Vivifies your spirit and does your life renew.
You are God's. He sought you.

In my hand is sustenance, a banquet, a feast.
Let it replenish your humanity unceasingly.
You are God's. You are His counterpart.

Join your hands with mine.
Each pair of hands bears the imprints
Of sacrifice and sacrament.
Unselfish affection, unwearying devotion,
Compassionate support for each other's betterment.
The embodiment of mind, intellect, will, spirit and soul
Reflect perpetually the communion of life
With Christ and His church.
You are God's. You are now wholly one.

Feel the warmth of my hand against thy chilling cheek.
May it bring a healing for the infirmities you bear,
And offer you strength in knowing
You fulfilled His will in deed and in prayer.
You are God's. You are His earthenware.

Audrey Amerski

Life

For my lovely rose, my mother
The light of the day is the light of your way.
To carry your mind in so many ways.
To carry your heart, body and soul,
become a person to be well known,
To leave your strength and wisdom behind
your love, your laughter linger in time,
Memories you leave when you go away
How we are blessed to still feel your way,
To carry your love through the light of the day.

Amy G. Luna

Our Family Car

Do you want to go for a ride, in our family car,
can't guarantee if we'll make it or go too far.
The muffler is off, and it sounds just like a plane,
Our windshield wipers don't even work, so pray it don't rain.
If it's cold out, you'd better bring a blanket or a quilt,
that's another luxury of our car that's out of kilt.
Keep watching for police cars as we drive along the way,
For our inspection stamp is past due, it expired in May.
The family car is really a menace, to the road,
we must have been blind, to buy such a load.
Don't worry you'll hear us about twenty blocks away,
one thing in our favor, the radio works okay.
Were going to have to junk it in a month or two,
so when you buy a car, don't let them fool you.
Our family car has really seen its last day,
I wish we never bought it, is all I've got to say.

Alice Wamsley

A Mother's Love

To Dan—Love is eternal
His mother's love fades too soon
With solace sought by her son so young.
Life proceeds abundantly,
But he doesn't feel that he has won.

He leaps into books and piles of raked leaves,
And runs from 1st to Home.
A mother's touch he misses much,
But he knows he must go it alone.

Dad's always there in his easy chair
To take care of the sticks and stones,
But his mother's caress and her wrinkled housedress
Are what he yearns to atone.

Looking back at the memories that used to be,
And still are to this day,
Her son feels the love that she could not hide
For she'd have it no other way.

Cheryl Soden Moreland

The Angel

In this poem, I tell of a beauty on the Earth's ground
A story of a girl who speaks beauty all around
A girl who's sweet and lovable straight from the heart
Which can be seen easily from the very start.

With pretty blonde hair, the color of the sun
When you see her, you shall know she's the one
With soft warm skin, which feels so right
She is bright and amazing like a star in the night.

For her dazzling eyes and wonderful warm smile
Make thinking of her every day, all worthwhile
Now that you see and know from these things
She is but a beautiful Angel only with no wings.

So, as I tell of this girl to you from me
This beautiful Angel from Heaven is named, Anna Marie.

Deloyed Charles Landreth

Faithful Mom

Of all the moms in the world, you're the best
All those days and nights you never got much rest.

You cared when no one else did
All my nightmares you have tried to rid.

You gave and gave all of the days
And never once turned you head the other way.

You prayed many prayers from your heart
Hoping one day they would impart.

You shoulder has been there year after year
Ready to catch the many cried tears.

You always give your love unconditionally
No matter how draining emotionally.

The care you've given and the sorrow you've had
Is not always noticed and that is so sad.

All the ugliness you have endured
Will one day be rewarded that's for sure.

Because of you I've never been alone
To live in my past and not go on.

If not for the great Lord above
I'd never have known a true mother's love.

Dyann Blankenship

Juliet's Disaster

A great feud divides our families.
Marriage to Paris, my father decrees,
For Paris I care not, 'tis Romeo I love.
I pray for the help of the Gods above,
To bring me and Romeo together,
And together we will stay forever.
Our love is unwilling to die,
Or in a burial tomb we shall both lie.
For our threatened love we will both die.
Romeo's banishment is for which I cry.
I'll drink a potion to make me seem dead.
The nurse thinks me dead as I lie in my bed.
Later Romeo hears news of my death,
"Romeo!" I cry with my waking breath,
Then enters the friar after I awaken,
Friar Lawrence thinks I should be come a nun
I find both him and Paris dead at my tomb.
Our love has been filled with nothing but gloom.
Because Romeo's life has been taken,
Mine shall also be forsaken!

Angela Danson

Mudtracks

For Andrew and Minna Gottesman
The sticky brown goo of melted snow and constant rain
slows me down to where I feel no gain.

Though dull and gray outside, I must keep up the pace
else it seems that *all* will go to waste.

No sun to stir my body, no kids laughing outside the house,
nor do I hear any bird calling for its spouse.

Very lonely it can be without the summer warmth and light,
where day surely triumphs over night.

I will take heed to that still, small voice within—
which always leads me right—through thick and thin

It speaks of blessing this time, also known
when spring harvests shall be sown.

Winter's blues go away, 'cause seasons come to show
how change truly help God's creations grow.

Steven J. Gottesman

Perfect

No one in this world is always perfect
Not me, not you.
Everyone has their imperfect ways
Their little tricks and games to play
Pranks we pull
Ways that fail
No one in this world can ever be perfect
Not me, not you
We will try and try forever to be
The most perfect person there could be
The harder we try
The more we fail
No one will ever become the most perfect person in this world
Not me, not you
We can never be

Laura Jankowski

Unnamed

In a fleeting moment believe this
speak it, mean it, scream it, repeat it
watch it grow, resounding from the walls
stronger with every echo, seeking the deepest recesses
acquiring depth in the darkest places
riding cold winds over mountains
soft plume wispfully rising with grace-ethereal
a star seed exploding in the deepest violet, tauntingly peripheral
child of the mouth, as Athena of the mind
the speaker's nervous agitation grows, knows it's beyond control
the voice of its birth was not of gods
but the verse was a mind of its own
a prophesy his perception received vacantly
and could not comprehend
a thought-child growing in ghastly brilliance
somewhere at the spectrum's end

Wesley Williams

Song of the Wind

Now if you want to hear a song of the wind
Just start each day with a smile from within
Listen to those who are unhappy trying to win
Praying to Jesus to take away their sin

There is no tomorrow without some sadness
Only those who pray and search for happiness
Will ever find their way to something new
Remember that person could be you
I walked a very lonely road
Trying to find a friend to talk to unload
My sadness was just a test
I just had to ask Jesus to let me rest

Emily M. Scott

A Tribute to Mary Louise Bollman (1909–1998)

The world has suffered a great, great loss.
For without you, it will be lost.
But through Earth's loss, Heaven gained.
You will be there, to praise Jesus' name.
An hour with you, worth more than gold.
For all the memories, that you hold.
The sky lit up, when your face you shown.
How bright it must be, around the throne.
For all of us left here, in despair.
There is no other, who can compare.
Though your love and kindness, are just a start.
You'll always be here in our heart.
For all who have known you, throughout the years
May God bless you with each of our tears.
'Til in Heaven we meet, on that glorious day.
May your love be with us, each step of the way.

John Cabler

My Lover Moon

Where are you tonight, my love?
I search the skies above,
But you hide behind clouds dark and drear.
How I wish you were here and near.

One night you tease and play among your clouds.
Another, you bring me rain to kiss away my tears of love.

Then you take pity on me and shine,
And bathe me with your reciprocating affection.
And linger slowly across your heavens
'Til your true love, the sun,
Steals you from me,
To break my heart again for another day.

June M. Carlson

Recovering

You might strip me of my pride,
or steal away my identity.
You could take back all the treasures I hide.
Corrode my serenity.
You can lead me to a tempting end,
But you cannot have my spirit.
For it is mine, and only mine, my friend.

Paula Lampman Geiser

Hope

The moon sets. A dark night ends.
The sun rises. A new day begins.
You must always look forward, not back in the past,
see the new fresh day, and hope it will last.
A new way of life, a new friend to play,
but sometimes, the sun sets on a sad end to the day.
The loss of a friend, so sudden, untold;
You just didn't realize, your friend had grown old.
One day will be gone, the sunset of a life,
then a new sun will rise, and bring a new life.
A new friend to play with, to love and to hold
When your old friend leaves you, in sadness and cold.
A new day will rise, bring a new warmth of love;
The sun may have set, but it will come back up.
You loose one old friend, and gain a new one,
just like when the moon sets, up comes the sun.
You never know how to cope, with a loss;
But never forget, the sun won't stay set.
It will rise again, you'll find a new friend;
Your hope must not end.

Jenny Freeborn

The Birthday Wish

I give this gift to Sandra Roseman,
The little girl that's now a grown woman,
I write this poem of what was once home,
To sit down and reflect when you are alone,
The gift I give of this Birthday wish,
Is the best wish that I could wish,
I write this wish of your hometown childhood days,
For you to reflect and remember in all the various ways,
Times of youth on Autumn days,
When you laughed and played on long lost days,
Innocent times and innocent days,
All brought back in their different ways,
Shades of memories of the past,
Refreshed and remembered at last,
Memories of sacred and cherished things,
Of which I hope this present brings,
Published in this book of memories of sacred and cherished things,
To have and to hold when the days are long old,
For you to know as the days of life unfold,
That you have touched a heart as I am growing old.

Kenneth K. Stoudt
Hollyhall

The Mourning

For my beloved father, Thomas Nicholas
There is a vision to my early loss,
A pale face at a high window,
Damp dark laughter forced yet feral.
The gentle heartstrings of my Father's violin
Crying out the sorrow of a life's loss
A tall shadow in the moon's light grows longer.

Ella Chill

Mom

For my loved mom, Penny Lee
Mom, you're as sweet
as a New Zealand apple,
the kind I love the best.
Mom, I know you are there
to help me with projects
hard and easy.
Mom, the warmth and softness of your voice flow
through me like a gentle breeze or wave.
Mom, when you talk to me,
your voice is like a high surf.
Whatever the level,
it's always the best.
The only Mom I want is you!

Leonard Lee

Be Afraid

Don't be afraid of my deep dark skin
Don't be afraid of my wide revealing grin

Don't be afraid of my long winded stare
Don't be afraid of the curiosity in my glare

Don't be afraid of my strong stern tones
Don't be afraid of my strength clenched fists and healthy bones

Don't be afraid of my suppressed anger
Don't be afraid because I don't represent danger

But . . . Be afraid of people of all kinds
I want you to be very afraid of all the knowledge in the minds

Be afraid of my expanding intellectuality
Be afraid because this is no virtual reality

Be afraid of my cleverness and creativity together as they rise
Be afraid, be very afraid as I struggle
And reach the top of the executive skies!

Shakila Stephens

Eulogy

We sat with bowed heads out of habit or force
As they said those nice things at the funeral of Alice;
Having known her so well, a decade or two, her moods
And her plots, we thought without malice
That this was no person that we ever knew
Whom we're laying to rest from the church where she served,
And we later agreed with our heads no more bowed
That for us no such hi-jinks would e'er be allowed.

Did you think I was handsome and daring and dashing?
The thought is what counts; don't announce it,
You may have assumed I was loving and caring?
So I was, you assume; don't pronounce it.
Or, the truth laid aside, you possibly thought
I was homely, a boor, I was there to be bought;
Well, think your own thoughts of what you might say,
But keep your lips sealed as they lay me away.
The good that men do, the bad that they hide
Need scarcely be told near that last solemn ride.
And must it be solemn? Not really, I pray;
Sympathy's due the survivors, such words for the dead do not say.

Orren Beaty Jr.

The North Carolina Lighthouse

For my son, Hal Rhodes Jr
There you stand upon the sand
Dressed in a black and white striped band

Ships have seen your beaming light
As they pass on a long stormy night

Millions come to play in the sun
And praise the work you have done

But father time has took its toll
And now dear lighthouse you are growing old

The grains of sand are washing away
Little by little day by day

We will miss you oh, so much
Because of all the lives you touch

Way out on the outer banks
We pause and give you thanks

Of all the friendships you have made
Our memories of you will never fade

God has given us many treasures
Our lighthouse is one that will linger forever

Sue Rhodes

Sister

For Carolyn, my inspiration always
It's difficult to think about, much less put into words . . .
Scary, how anything that even remotely reminds me of her
Can make me feel so raw, so hurt.
This is an old pain.
Shaped by childhood stares in church,
And in the store,
And on the street.
My friend and enemy,
Blessing and curse,
Love and hate
Are all wound up together in this,
My old, familiar pain.
Jagged memories of crying,
Screaming, pleading, praying—
Looks in eyes I cannot forget;
Words and deeds which haunt me still.
And always, the gnawing suspicious hope
That perhaps if I am good enough
And if I hurt enough,
Maybe she won't.

Laurel A. Sydlansky

The Diet That Never Worked

To my ex-coworkers at Farmer's Insurance
They went on a diet trying to lose their fat,
I walked in the cafeteria and there they all sat.
Stuffing their faces with cookies and chips and anything else
they could get past their lips.

They swear they are going to be small,
I wonder how, when they're eating it all.
They rave about how they want to lose weight,
yet they keep right on eating and drinking on every date.
They are as broad as they are tall and built close to the ground,
when they walk, their fat, dances all around.

They tell me I need to go on a diet, I say is that a fact,
You don't see all those calories in my lunch sack.
So, I just go on my merry way,
eating whatever I want from day to day.
And every morning I hear them say,
oh, I almost forgot to weigh.

Shirley G. Kassler

The Lowest

To Cheyenne and Matthew Bleck
A child is made in a one night affair
The mother doesn't want it and the father doesn't care
So the mother decides on how to make her life easy
Even if the thought makes her a little queasy
She makes an appointment for Thursday afternoon
And Wednesday night she prays to God as she stares up at the moon
She rubs her belly and asks for forgiveness
And thinks back to her one night of bliss
Her friends have left her, now she feels alone
And her mother has thrown her out of her home
She feels betrayed and let down
And all God can do is shake his head and frown
She thinks it's her only way out
And she hopes she's right as she begins to pout
If only someone could help her understand
That this isn't God's way to reprimand
If he didn't want her to have a child
He wouldn't have blessed her with a gift so mild
I see it as the lowest blow
To strike a child when it has nowhere to go

Serena Marie Grubb

Dad Will Soon Be Home

At home the fire is warming, within those snow-capped walls
The mistletoe is hanging 'neath the lantern in the hall
The tree is trimmed and waiting that sainted, whiskered man
Who'll split the air at midnight, bringing all he can

The kids are softly dreaming of waking in the morn
Mom is somewhere praying God will lift the storm
For Dad is on the highway, his diesel smoking black
He'll run the night wide open to try to make it back

Then down the way she hears a bell come tinkling from afar
As in the east the clouds are rising, she sees Christ's shining star
She lifts her face toward Heaven for the snow has stopped and gone
And Christmas will be Christmas, for Dad will soon be home

Jack A. Hamilton

Fair Breaks

Here I am alone once more,
With nothing to see but these walls and a door.
Thinking of how I'm considered guilty from the start,
But knowing I'm innocent to the heart.

So now I sit and think all day long,
About how I tried so hard and still come out wrong.
It seems to me no matter how hard I try,
In the end, I'm still the bad guy.

Don't they know or can't they see,
That a man who wants more is what I want to be.
Now I've learned life gives and life takes,
But I ask you, "Lord," are there any fair breaks?

Jeffrey Perry

Thanksgiving Day

We're at the dinner table, we bow our heads in prayer,
We thank the Lord for giving, this day for us to share,
But first we must remember the Pilgrims once did say,
We thank you Lord for giving us this Thanksgiving Day.

Now look at Mr. Turkey dressed up for you and I,
He smiles at Giblet Gravy and winks at Pumpkin Pie,
He waves to Mrs. Dressing and butters Mr. Corn,
And says dear friends you know we soon will all be gone.

He looks at our faces, he's ready and prepared,
He knows we all are waiting to carve with extra care,
So he decides the hour has come for him to say,
Please join us at the table, this is Thanksgiving Day.

Elizabeth G. Chaves

The Gift of Love

Love is a gift that is pure and true
In times of need it will help you through
It gives you strength when you are weak
Love is blind yet so unique

Love is trusting the one you love
Working out problems with a kiss and a hug
Helping a stranger when they're in a jam
Living each day without a plan

Love is being together as we grow old
Most of all a hand to hold
Someone to help share my life
When I'm feeling confused can give me advice

Love is never jealous, it is always free
It may take a while for you to see
Just open your eyes and open your heart
Let's give our love a brand new start

Lisa Childers

Wind in the Wing

Dedicated to the continued progress of I.L.O.P.
One fine day in the middle of the night
Man Mountain Dean was all swiftness in flight
Fleet of foot fully a big man's delight
Only the moon really put up a fight
Together they raced wolves full through the bight

Swooped down through town flying whisker to chin
Nare man dast moving nor feeling to sin
Fourteen fairest fine ladies fainted dead
Four or five wet women drooled nearly red
Fewer small children dared peek out or in
Zero prey animals were found within

Down though the glen they ran fleet wild again
Rivers of flowers flowing with their wind
Creeping up the night the forelight of dawn
For claiming the day holding ev'ry pawn
To Sweet Mona Dean raced favors to win

Only whose grace fair deified beauty
And 'crost sheer fragrance there laid the booty

Mick Bride

Divine Glory

Divine Glory I beseech,
Glowing lamplin holy seat,
You are the creator of all
Whose presence was given Divine call.
I bless the ground you walk on,
Day in and day out.
Sermons christen life is beckoned,
Angels crest upon your holy feet.
Dancing with bells that declare your Divine seat,
We call upon you night and day,
With scriptures of the lay.
The warm glow pronounced in the clouds,
Speaks of Heavenly bodies all in a row.
Glorious rainbow amongst the clouds,
Depicts, the Father, the Son, the Holy Spirit endowed.
Your presence sings beyond the peaks,
Hue, mountain, valleys, clouds of whom we seek.
God Bless You Who Sits on The Divine Seat.

Diane M. Newman-Gregerson

Ode to the Sun

Bright, yellow, light. A great star shining in the sky.
Reigning over the world by day like a noble queen.
She is a lamp to the world. She makes me happy in the summer,
And in the winter she gives me hope for the spring.
She gives off a warmth of love with each refreshing ray.
The sun is like a good friend drying up the tears of the sky when it rains.
She is like the mother of nature; nurturing,
Helping the flowers, and the grass, and the trees to grow.
Her brilliant rays of light make me feel healthy and new.
She is like a magnificent jewel
That is shared by the rich and the poor alike.
When it's dark, the jewel must run from the robber of the night.
The robber is the moon, they fight a courageous battle,
but the sun always wins because she is strong.
Then she marches over the horizon, like a valiant soldier,
Bringing with her the prize of morning to share with all the world.
Her dawn is like a victorious cry,
Singing, "The day is new, and I have returned home!
Come bask in my glory!"

Kathleen Kenwin

One Day

As long as the sun rises and the moon shines bright,
I will always be thinking of her,
Her soft, shiny hair, and her smooth, warm skin,
And the sound of her voice, as gracious as a bird's song.

We're two lost souls,
Searching for love in an endless journey through loneliness.
Heartbreak and grief have taken control,
Every moment my soul grows weaker,
Crying out for you, yearning for us to unite as one.

Fate speaks, yet we do not hear the words,
A symphony of passions sounds, yet we do not hear the music,
The fire burning inside grows fiercely yet we do not feel the heat,
Destiny struggles to bring us together, yet we are held back by fear.

But alas, on our journey for love, we pass one another along the way,
Knowing that time cannot be reversed, we must move on,
Hoping one day we'll meet again.

Maurice Hargrove

Emotions

What are emotions?
Are emotions that feelings that make
your heart cry?

Are emotions what you feel when
you have to say goodbye?

Are emotions that cramp in
your stomach that twists and turn.

Are emotions that red hot feeling of
tears that tend to burn?

Are emotions that feeling that
make you lose control and shout?

Are emotions that feeling of sitting
in a corner trying not to pout?

There is one good thing I can say
about these emotions.

They are a gift from God,
sort of a magic potion
They show how you really feel inside

There world be less tears to bear if these
emotions were shared with someone who cared.

Casey Yeager

Show Me the One . . .

In memory of Sadie Ryan, pal of my cradle days
Who has laughed often, loved much,
and played the game of life by the rules of God,
who has appreciated and expressed the wonders of nature's beauty,
who has earned the respect of decent women,
the admiration of intelligent men, and the love of little children.

Show me the one
Who has stood tall while answering the drums of tragedy,
who would do without so others might partake,
who has left this world a better place whether by a lovely song,
a rescued soul, or an act of kindness to a stranger,
whose destiny is Heaven.

Show me the one
Who shares the joys and hides the sorrows,
who believes in honor and would cast no shame on mankind in the name of the Father,
who the blind call beautiful.

Show me the one
Whose life has been an inspiration, whose memory a benediction, and
I'll show you the meaning of Mother.

Peter Ryan

The Wings of a Young Woman

To Dad—thanks for my wings.
There were broken dreams and broken hearts, lasting with her fist marks.
For it to stop was my only wish, always hoping the pain and fear would diminish.
The questions still linger, and the tears are still there.
A question of why hangs forever in the air.
I knew I could fly. I knew I could do it.
I knew I could fly, and knew I'd beat it.
Once my wings were tattered and broken, as a child my fear hidden and unspoken.
Her cruel words were spoken in hate. Her apologies were always too late.
I was once a cowering and beaten child. I am now a woman, strong and proud.
I will fly, I know I can do it. I will fly, the sky is no limit.
My wings might still be healing, while a dull ache is still lingering.
I am no longer afraid to stand tall, no longer do I feel my back is against the wall.
When I'm at ease, I soar high; through a storm I'm not afraid to fly.
My wings cannot tear, I can stand tall. I open my eyes, not afraid to fall.
I can fly. Oh, yes I can. I can l fly, as a triumphant woman.

Melanie S. Harper

Heritage

In my past I was a Native American living freely on the plains.
There were no fences to create boundaries,
no white man to tell me any wrongs of my ways.

There was no pollution, the water was sweet and the air was clean.
Now drinking from a river can kill and autos cause a choking smoke screen.

We worshipped the buffalo, it is the main food source for my kin.
Now the whites come with guns and slaughter them just for their skin.

Enough with this invasion, we protest these strangers coming onto our land
The whites says if we sign a treaty peace they will abide to our demand.

We sign our names on paper and they promise to stay off of our land.
But with greed for metals they break the treaty,
a hit in the face with the back of their hand.

The land of my people was taken, its value to get an estimate.
Now white people pay for the land and our pictographs they desecrate.

They think they are the settlers of the land
we have been on for countless years.
They cut down massive trees, just for fires to sit around and drink beers.

They make up lies and say we are cannibals.
But they are the most evil, for mere they kill our sacred animals.

They finally decide to get rid of us after all these years.
We are marched toward a far-off reservation, via the Trail of Tears.

Over a hundred years later they quietly asked to be forgiven.
But we cannot forgive you, for the past has already been written.

Michael C. Riggs

Heartbroken

A little bird with a broken wing
Who can fly no more
He just sits on the ground
And wonders what tomorrow holds in store
Just a couple of weeks ago
He was flying with his mate
But now he's all alone
And she has flown away
He longs for her to come back
He whistles for her each day
Hoping she will hear him
But she's too far away
One day she flies back
And when she looks down
There is her mate
Laying dead on the ground
If she had come back sooner
And gave him her love
They would still be together
But now it's only one turtle dove

Ronald Frye

Storm Ambrosia

Fly within the wind?
Or fall within the rain.
Hear the somber whistling of the Gods.
Know the tears that only they can weep.
Listen to the voices.
True, silent, deep
Thunder's clap is hollow.
Lightning's flash is bleak.
Cloudy or clear means nothing
To those who drink its mead,
For knowledge is the bait,
And it's everything they need.

Max Neuwerth

To Our Mother Isabella

The day we were born
You became our mother
In all of our lives
There will be no other

In good times and bad times
Many happy, some sad
We have two great parents
Our mother and dad

From young age until old age
From brown hair to gray
We're so proud to have known you
'Til your dying day

You were there for our beginning
We're here for your end
We're not losing our mother
We're losing a great friend

Isabella Walsh

Sleep Tight

Hound
      Paw
    Turn
go wail
Bed bugle for the forest
      Echo
    Kiss
sing
night lover
A blood thirst lullaby

Danny Blaho

Moments

We want to thank you so much for the love you gave to us.
Living in a Christian home with parents we could trust.
All the support and example we saw,
you gave to each other and were there when we called.
The times you gave it all
when there was nothing left for you,
never with a second thought,
and how we never knew.
On and on we could go
but time will not permit,
but you can count on this
in our hearts the moments live.
Our prayer today is simply this,
that after years and years of bliss
and through the sunshine and the rain
our kids will one day feel the same.
Remember, moments aren't just pictures on shelves.
So, we thank you for the greatest gift you could have given us, yourselves!

Stephanie Files Angel

I Thank God for You

She doesn't need words to say she loves me
It is all in her eyes when she looks at me.
I find comfort is her presence just a touch and I feel secure
I know that through it all her love will endure.
In my eyes she is ageless, her heart and her soul will never grow old.
A mother's love lasts forever or so I am told.

Jerry Hunwardsen

Life View through a Noose

The path he walked was dark and cold,
There was a man on each side, his arms to hold.
They dragged him down his life's last road,
His sorrow-filled heart was his only load.

He no longer had the worldly things he had taken so wrongly,
All he wanted was to live, he prayed so strongly.
A step away from death, his life now inched away,
His life was passing like the sun, tonight it's gone though here today.

As he neared the noose of death, he gazed once more at the world,
The spectators consisted of young and old,
with dark hair and locks of pearl.
He thought of the things that have value in life,
and what has value in death.
When a man comes into the world he has nothing,
and when he leaves the worldly things are left.

Sara McColl

moments of isolation

to emily, my true inspiration
the howling winds and driven rain penetrate my innermost consciousness.
slowly inhaling on a cigarette while the vapors of memory clear.
in my granite tower i feel safe, but that safety comes with a price.
i can remember placing every stone but i failed to build a way out.
so i sit in melancholy with only myself as entertainment
and there are only so many tales you can tell yourself before you hear
them all. and then you go insane from the sounds of silence.
every noise becomes a bomb dropped on the children
and every breeze becomes the shock wave of that bomb
and every whisper becomes the screaming of the butterflies
dying in my head. alone inside my fortifications i am mad.
i smile at the death and carnage around me
and the silent screams of horror never end.
welcome to my madness. welcome to my insanity.
welcome to my world.
won't you join me for supper?
won't you stay with me until my insanity destroys me?
don't worry, it won't be long now.

Joseph Lamont

The Shoebox

Shoebox,
torn and tattered,
worn and old,
full of broken-hearted memories.

The abandoned wreckage
of a lost and lonely love
lives deep and buried
beneath the love letters
that once spoke of their endearment.

A withered rose lay upon
dusty memories,
growing old and broken
inside the dark and dreary
tomb of lost and wandering love.

Shoebox,
dusty and hidden,
dark and lost,
full of broken-hearted memories.

Kristy Lynn Smith

My Mother

For my mother, Mrs. Margaret Akinro
Who starts and watches my infant head
When sleeping on my cradle bed,
And cries and sheds affection's tears?
My mother.

Francis Akinro

A Gift

If you live your life,
The best that you can.
Live each day with your hand in his hand.
If you take each day that comes from above.
And do what you can
To show others his love.
If the reason you're living
Is revealed in your giving.
You have surpassed expectations,
And his declarations,
That in him will abound
All the love to be found,
And in peace you can rest
For you have done your best.

Martie Kinsey

A Trip to a Dream

For my wife of 50 years
Ever night about this time
I take my little sky word climb
We always meet up in the sky,
We kiss and let the time go by.
We take our little evening stroll,
Mr. Moon so shyly says hello,
As we go passing on to Mars,
We get many winks from spying stars

There are no worries nor troubles there.
For time nor money we never care.
Life is so simple gay and free,
I have you and you have me.

Menno L. Buller

Haiku for Type B Personality

To Gayle, my type B—not!
We would not be born
If in the womb there was room
for TV and toys!

Debra Neal

Childhood

She looked like a giant. So tall, dark, and strong.
There she was again at the tetherball court, beating everyone within a few seconds.
Dare I stand in line again?

Teasing me every day on the bus did not satisfy her.
She continued her torture during recess.
The names, the insults, the hate could be seen in her fiery red eyes.
How hard it was to ignore.

Well, I'm up next. My turn to get slaughtered by her.
One by one, each day we all stand in this line hoping for fun, hoping to get to play.
Yet we are merely a herd of cows awaiting the final blow.

Drop by drop, day by day, the tears would fall on that tetherball court.
So many souls hurt, so many egos crushed.
All because of that dark giant that took control over the orange ball.

Sunlight? Is it so? How it was not noticed when the giant stood in its way.
She is not here today!
The laughter, the joy, the smiles and brightness
of the children on the tetherball court overwhelmed me.

It was like falling into a rainbow—bright, wonderful, beautiful, and happy.
Suddenly being a kid was fun. The giant was gone!
No more victims, no more herds of cows, only children were seen.

Miro Rusnak

The New York Subway Train

To Kamilah Evans, "Anything is possible once you try"
You're just another face in the everyday crush.
Everybody jostling in the never-ending rush.
They look everywhere except directly at you.
At times I know they wonder if you are looking at them too.
They sometimes dress outrageously, casual, or business attire.
Even though it's morning, some look as if they are ready for the evening to retire.

We see familiar faces, many new ones too.
We smile and nod hello in greeting which is only the right thing to do.
Those who are already sitting don't have to fight as much.
As those who are standing do, to avoid having to touch.

Once those doors open everyone decides they have to get on.
Because their bosses face, no one else has this morn to look upon.
They shove, push, and mumble saying bad words too.
Because they feel in that tiny space, you who weighs 160 pounds should be able to fit into.

No one can avoid it I guess.
All that morning and evening rush hour distress.
We all have somewhere to go, so what can you do?
Just bite your tongue, hold your bag tight, and fight to get on that train too.
So even if they look at you bad and try to make a fuss,
Just close your eyes, pretend you don't hear, and be glad you don't have to ride the bus!

Ione Evans

Dear Mommy and Daddy

For Patty and David Miranda

You never got to see me smile, or run around and play.
You never got to hear me cry, or learn along the way.

You never got to see me play, with all my little toys.
You never got to hear me laugh, at all the little boys.

But God has something else in mind, for me in Heaven above.
To watch over you from time to time, when you most need my love.

So when you're feeling down and blue, and feel there's nothing you can do,
You'll realize that I am near, a little Angel with no fear.

I'll guide you in your time of need; I'll take your hand so I can lead.
I'll show the way to get you through, and you'll no longer feel so blue.

And when the time comes for you to rest,
when you're no longer taking breaths,
I'll be at Heaven's pearly gates, I promise you with love, have faith.

Glenda J. Reyna

Memories

To my beloved son, David
I look upon your smiling face,
A picture now to take its place,
The memories that I hold dear
No longer do I have you near.

To hold in my arms,
To hear your voice, sweet as a song.
'Twas God that took my babe from me.

No longer will my anger be,
My questions not to wonder why,
The answers far beyond the sky
With him I know where angels fly.

Bernice Lewis

Music to Me

Her lips, play rhythm
Her eyes, radiate a tone
Her smile, reveals a song
Her voice, reflects a melody
Her hands, touch every note
Her mind, responds in harmony

Michael J. Stewart Jr.

So Many

So many things building up within
So many times with love and pain
So many days you thought you could win
So many tears you never wanted to gain

So many memories left in your heart
So many good and bad
So many you want to part
So many wonder why you're sad

So many times you go insane
So many questions of why
So many don't understand the pain
So many laugh when you cry

So many times you wanted to die
So many ways you wanted to live
So many reasons you had to try
So many so many why do we care

Why are we touched by so many things
Why why so many
Only God knows why,
Up there.

Nikolina Davis

A Day with You

Morning comes so softly
Bringing silence, wet with dew.
Then, basking in its beauty,
My thoughts begin with you.

Soon that eastern flame, the sun,
has run its course over skies of blue,
and still I find that all my thoughts
are only thoughts of you.

Now sun has set, the night is still,
another day is through.
Visions fill a weary mind,
my dreams are filled with you.

But when the morning sun has risen
and day begins anew,
The thoughts I treasure most, my love,
will be my thoughts of you.

Phillip A. Smith

One and the Same

Can you see the hatred protruding
through your precious adoring eyes?

Spellbinding is the mocking sediment
of the devil sending a message of love.

Everyone imaging the peace lies
within grasp as a blooming red rose.

Completely ignorant of the piercing pain
of the thorn ripping through soft tender flesh.

The annoyance is our closed lives,
just a contingent garden of weeds.

Suffering is the happiness within,
loss is the only gain, good is the dark evil.

Wretched beauties of hypocrisy
make the world tolerable or is it ghastly.

Controlling instinct is the only way
for a blissful conclusion unreachable.

Grasp the ideals of others,
to accept without question is the dream.

The judgmental, uncontrolled mind is the honest disheartening reality.
If only I could see the hatred protruding from my precious adoring eyes.

Kip Millard

The Poetry of History

When you say the pledge of allegiance or sing of the rocket's red glare,
Do you ever think of a lady sewing in a rocking chair?
Try to think of what I mean.
In a history book she will be seen.
I'm talking of Betsy Ross, who helped America, the best she could.
When asked for her help, she said that she would.
George Washington came with a sketch in hand,
They needed a flag for this great land.
Some changes were made six pointed stars became five.
Betsy felt that her flag would keep hope alive.
On a background of blue shone thirteen white stars,
The rest was completed with red and white bars.
Our flag she has changed as the country grew.
Stars were added, as states were new.
And to this day our flag still stands.
Betsy's simple gift a wonderful land.
So close your eyes and go back with me,
Let's always remember this "sew-er" of Liberty.
Betsy Ross made a difference so why can't I,
Show respect for the flag, wherever it may fly.

Jessica De Martino

Hats Off to the Black Man!

Black man! Black man! I'm proud of you!
In spite of the systematic plan to destroy and eliminate you,
You have proven that determination and will have worked,
As powerful tools for you.
Stolen from African shores, sold, stripped, strapped,
And at times beaten to death, lynched, degraded, castrated,
Ignored, labeled, mis-educated and underestimated you just kept rising,
refusing to give up or die.
You wrapped yourself in who you were and only let those close
To you see your tears and frustrations.
Revealing to them your heart of fears and dreams.
What heavy burdens, you carried, trying to be a man in
a world where everyone denied your existence.
Called names too ugly to repeat, you chose to keep on striving,
Pushing, believing that truth would win.
Black man! Black man! Walk, with pride, you have carried the torch,
You have kept your race alive.
By God's grace and power, you will continue to rise
from the dust of racism and prejudice, clothed in the garment
of dignity that shall always survive!

Catherine L. Thomas

Corruption

Wonders of the world
wonders of the day
dark nights
starless skies
shades of gray
See the sun and moon
in the same hour
stop in the fields
smell the dead flower
The world's been turned
upside down
the new light has been found
Society's dark, dark as night
though said to be wrong
it is viewed as right
In this confused world
of crazy dreams
nothing is really
The way it seems.

Jonathan R. Gray

Sacred Moments

I love the smell
Of collected time
Brewed in dark places
Memories to bind

Lingering in your thoughts
Smells of the past
Picture brought to mind
By forgotten shadows cast

The soft touches of time
Printed upon your mind
The youth of your past
Memories that bind

Wasted on the young
Now too old to care
Fleeting moments lost
Forever we must bear

I love the smell
Of collected time
Brewed in dark places
Memories to bind

Doralene Blakeney

Your Special Gifts

To my husband, Larry—love forever

I love the way you look at me
just before we make love,
the way you touch every inch of my skin
with feather caresses of a dove.
Although you never realize
the special gifts you give,
you keep me always wanting more
Knowing without it, I'll never live.
The way you hold me close to you
While we're soaring to the stars,
Knowing I am safe with you
While descending, time is ours.
I love to hear your every word
Softly lulling me to sleep,
and while we dream our endless dreams,
as does our love grow endlessly deep.
And now my love you've seen a glimpse
of love's perfect fitting glove,
it is you my love, my life,
My everlasting love.

Donna Page

Can't You Hear the Music

To my savior, Jesus Christ
Can't you hear the music in your everyday life.
As you walk along, the way on a cool summer night.
The music in God's creation as he spoke his mighty words
"Let there be" and the music is what I heard.

Birds sing to your master that put your wings in flight.
Sing a song of love, joy, hope, and heavenly delights.
A song about salvation, a word of wisdom that will last.
A song that break yokes, and cast down demons in my path.

The wind blow Gabriel trumpet as the seasons begin to change.
Blow for the down hearted, the sick, the homeless, and the mentally insane.
Wind sing a song of healing, a song of delivering, a song of great cheer.
Then whisper in God's children ear about the Heaven-gates that are near.

Oh! River of old rush to the mighty ocean rush to the mighty mind.
Of men of all nations sing a song of your time.
Sing of strength and sing of power, sing of grace and beauty.
Sing a song as the sun rise and set according to its appointed hour.

Can't you hear the music in your everyday life.
As you walk along, the way on a cool summer night.
The music in God's creation as he spoke his mighty word.
"Let there be" and the music is what I heard.

Gloria Ivery-Lucas

To My E.T.

Dedicated to Rufus Vestito of Indian Creek High in Winterville, Ohio
Hello to you, Hutnik, my E.T. from beyond the Deep blue Azure sky
Unfold the Stars' own Game of Football-of-Flight across Heaven's Gridiron High,
Three Varsities of Reds and Whites and Blues united Spacedom's Fielded Flag
Heaven will call us so, O Varsity Blues, do shed the lows that make us sag.
Into their setting Suns Earth's Kingdoms in decline: Varsity Reds, seek now
Kin's Zenith Sway, Sol's sovereignty among the stars, God's Throne, His regal brow.
So rules The Holy One; His Universe The High Creek Redskins know so well!
"Holed" Empires crumbling to the Dust, Red Dragon's too, his Rise shall end to swell!
Eternity's Decisive Change, Millennium's End, Varsity Whites above,
Destine Three Kings Triumvirate of Red, of White, of Blue, descends the Dove!
Sic Ius . . . coronae tres: three crowns triune—*Res Publica's* Stars' Way.
Construe *Astrorum Rerum Omnium* that Thing: Galactic Stellar Sway
As Sovereignty within the whole 'tis wholly One by God the Holy One.
Perfecting to Earth's End of TIME: *Volet Pila Pedalis per Terros*, Dear Son!
Through all sky, space in aerodynamicity, the Football Flies way on.
Immense! *Ex Regno Entis*, Oh! *Ad Nebulam!* Life's Realm to Death's beyond.
View now the Football of the Sky: Crab Nebula's 1054's Pale Light!
I see your Face, thy skin's so white, slanted fingers, your eyes so black yet bright.
To yearn Freedom's High State, seek God, Hutnik, my E.T. Friend, to set you Free.
Yes, see! No Handcuffs now! Do meet to Greet, to play th' Game with me, we'll see!

Albert Kundrat

Untitled

If you dream of someday living in a world where peace is everywhere,
If you dream someday there will be no hungry children, or no pollution in the air,
If you dream that someday all the leaders
of the nations will work together as a team,
If you dream someday you'll love again,
Then, you know, we share a dream.
If you dream of a world where sickness is no more,
Where families stay together, no soldiers going off to war,
Where hate and fear are no place to be seen,
If you ever thought what it would be like,
Then we share a dream.
Have you ever dreamed that you found happiness
And in your life nothing was going wrong,
For every day was filled with laughter,
and in your heart there was a song?
Have you ever dreamed that you could start all over
And just wipe the chalkboard clean?
If you believe there's life after a divorce,
Then you and I, we share a dream.

Larry W. Cruson

What Am I?

What am I supposed to be?
Will anybody, anywhere please tell me?
Am I the colors of the rainbow
Or am I just rain?
Am I the television station,
Or am I just a station?
Who put me in this situation?
Am I the happiness or am I the joy
Or am I just acute little toy?
Am I a thief,
Am I a crook,
Am I a robber?
What am I? Just look;
None of these are me.
All of these things are just so mean.
What if I'm mean?
Am I the stars in the sky shining bright
Or am I just a glamorous sight?
Am I supposed to die?
Please tell me, who am I?

LaTarsha Whitaker

Take the Time to Pray

Sometimes I feel so lonely,
Sometimes I feel so sad.
Sometimes I feel life's not worth living,
When everything seems to be going bad.

But when I'm at my lowest,
And there's nowhere left to go.
I stop and look around me,
And it's then I start to grow.

For I know it's time to change,
And so I bow my head in prayer.
It's time to face the reality,
That life is not always fair.

But deep prayer can do so much,
And strong faith can pave the way.
And the road seems not so long,
Toward a better and brighter day.

For God is all around us,
He's never very far away.
He's ready to lend a helping hand,
If we would just take the time to pray.

Joanie LeCoq Bishop

In Quiet Moments

What did I have then
What did you want

Do I still have
Do you still want

Where were we heading
Did we get there yet

Was something lost
And has yet to be found

Let's take off the shades
We have no blinders now

The sun is going to set
But there is still time

The road is in front of us
We can't change what is past

What do we want
What will we find

In quiet moments
What do we have

Valerie Wade

Mobeta No More

A lifeless morning
Not a human voice is heard nor car passing
Wind gently swaying
Leaves channeling, rushing a hollowing swish.

Not a human voice is heard nor car passing
Taken with its absence, its reflection reflects wrong side up
Lying branches crack under some pressure, unseen from grassy fields.

The sky, darkening a grayish-blue, weeps a greenish cool color
Minutes before, bolts of light split the sky, cracking the speed of light
Its head held high by its circulation strength
Departed with a thunderous yelp, quieting its strength

Kneeling at its side
Red soaking red clay
Nature watching, its body lying held in hands
Making its end, motionless.

A lifeless morning not a human voice is heard
A lifeless morning
Taken in by its absence

Kirk DeDoes

Angel

To my son, Steven Mathew Dirr
I saw an angel tonight.
She was the most beautiful thing I have ever seen.
Her hair so long and spun of gold, her eyes so bright they lit up the night.
Her heart so pure, simple, and true,
She asked me, "Child, what can I do for you?"
I said, "This is the hardest decision I have ever made."
She gently took my hand and held it to her heart.
She said, "Look deep down inside your soul,
For there lies the answer you're searching for."
I said, "I have no soul, I have no faith, I have a decision to make."
She said, "You have faith, you've had it all along;
That's what keeps you strong."
She said, "Keep the faith, don't let go.
God works in ways you'll never know."
She disappeared into the night.
I felt no fear, felt no fright when I saw an angel tonight.
I kept my faith and looked into my soul,
made my decision with the help from above.
She has been there all along; to lose my faith would have been wrong.
I knew everything would be all right because I saw an angel tonight.

Leah J. Landrum

Politicus 1999

Who is this person all tattered and torn?
Discarded by the law, discarded by God?

It is the new prodigal son!
Returning from death from whence he'd come.
It is he whose time is meaningless,
Yet thy shadow sits, watching as all ages around him.

Prometheus bound, feast for the carrion birds.
This is the secret of humanity he claims . . .
ignorance, faithful, blissful, ignorance.

A continent dead . . . this world lost . . . drifting in deceits.
Where, oh, prodigal son, is thy proud father?
The truer question; "Where are thy forefathers?"

A nation lost . . .
the cry of the innocent child.

Bares the forbearance to the destiny at hand
the nation is divided again . . . for sin is so easy a cost to pay.

Camelot brought down to rubble, the golden age tarnished,
democracy crumbles . . .
The long lost dead speak: "Return to that which started the ideal, Faith."

When then the return of thy prodigal son, America?

Clay R. Farebrother

The Master Artist

I stood on the mountain top
And gazed at the scene below.
In awesome wonder I asked,
"Who could have painted it so?"

The rolling hills, the green pastures,
The babbling brook rushing on its way,
Cattle grazing on the hillside,
Deer frolicking in their play.

A weather beaten cottage
Nestled under a clump of trees
Sheltering some simple honest folk
Enjoying the cool summer breeze.

A small white church in the valley,
A steeple with a bell to ring
To bring the folks together
His praises to sing.

From the mountaintop again I ask,
"Who could have painted the scene below?"
The answer comes loud and clear
Only God could have painted it so.

Mary Elizabeth Parker-Seago

Carry On

Nothing will bring back the dead
A hard fact we have to accept.
A heavy load we must carry,
Let's just take it step by step.

Pain from our loss will never leave,
Sweet memories will never die.
Try to be strong and carry on,
For those we love, left alive.

Fate has chosen us,
For this matter we had no say
It's in God's plan, not known by man,
He will comfort us, if we will pray.

No words can describe the loss,
No expressions can reveal the pain.
Rivers of sorrow we cross,
Tears fall like rain.

Memories we cling to,
The rest we let go.
One foot in front of the other,
Down life's road we go.

Mike McCarley

Flowers to Grow

Open me read me
I am a book,
hold me see me
take a look,
through my pages
you will find,
a past a future
to unwind,
the story unfolds
as you read,
understand
the inner need,
for knowledge and wisdom
is beauty within,
a gentle flower
to begin,
a seed planted
branches to extend,
holding a rainbow
colors never end.

Sharon Joy

To My Mother

To my wonderful mother, Catherine Vasco
A mother and daughter relationship is a precious one,
one that cannot be taken for granted, and with all of our ups and downs,
there is no other love that is more enduring than a mother's love.

There have been many peaks and valleys—
maybe more valleys then we'd like to admit—
but there is one thing that I've never forgotten, and
that is your unconditional love for me.

I can now see how much love, caring, disciplining, and
understanding goes into being a mother, and
there were times when I was a difficult child to love.

You have taught me so much about being a daughter, woman, and a mother
that I can only pray that I will utilize everything I have learned.
I now understand that a mother wants to be proud of her child, and I don't
know how I'll handle the challenges, but there is one thing I do know,

And that is that I am so thankful to have a mother like you, and
I pray someday that my son will say the same about me.
You are a strong, caring, and remarkable person, and I am proud to
say you are my mother. With being a mother myself, I see what real love is.

I thank the Lord every day that you are my mother
and that I was given the chance to tell you how much I love you.

Jennifer Staples

True Heroes

Dedicated to the unknown and true heroes
A true hero fights not to break bones,
but fights to break none at all and stands alone.
With a gallant stride, their heads held high,
and a distant look in their eye,
they make those who only catch glimpses of them want to cry.
They show that wisdom and bravery is gained from kindness and loving
and never gained through pushing and shoving.
A true hero fights for people they don't know,
since to them the whole world is their friend,
even those who fight against them.
These heroes don't put their faith in luck
and are, however, so often struck,
but when a hero's blood begins to show
they know in their hearts never to let go, before it is too late.
For that is the course of their unknown fate.
A hero's heart may not be light,
but they know in those warm, embracing hearts that they are fighting for right.
And as the hero lies to die, with his tears the whole world cries,
not for pain or definite sadness, but for infinite gladness.

Claudia Amendola

Happiness

What is happiness? Happiness is what you should feel from day to day.
It's what you should feel instead of sadness.
Happiness should replace your fear and sorrow.
It's the feeling that should be in everyone's heart.

When you find someone you think you've found happiness.
Then they dance on your heart.
You find someone and think you found happiness.
Then they walk away. Then you're alone again.

Everyone thinks they find happiness at one point in time.
Then they wake up.
They feel lonely and down until the right persons come along.
Therefore you ask, what is happiness?

Happiness, happiness, what is happiness?
Happiness is when the person you find makes you feel safe and secure.
They make you laugh and never afraid.
They turn your grey sky blue, and put a smile on your face.
When you find happiness it makes you feel elated.
That's the meaning of happiness.

Kelly Hoadley

Carry Me

Carry me through the first few steps,
So I won't fall.

Comfort me when I'm afraid,
Hold me when I'm sad.

Feed me when I'm hungry,
Change me when I'm soiled.

Embrace me when I'm cold,
And cuddle me and hold.

Tell me everything will be ok,
Just like I did when you,
My child, were young.

Jan E. Gagne

Bliss

At times
I drift on such waves of bliss
I believe myself blessed
by an Angel's kiss
an Angel's touch
I sense them
just out of reach
I see them
just out of sight

And I know
That is when I know
I must believe
what I cannot conceive

And all of this matters!
None of this matters!
Two sides of a coin.

Susanna Boye-Moller

My Love

To Kathy Gregg, my first love
My love is strong my love
is great you are the love of my life
There's not a day there's not a night
that goes by I don't think of you.
As the sun sets and the sun comes up
my love for you is always there

I see you in my mind
I see you in my dreams
I see you all the time
what a beautiful thought that is

I may not hold you in my arms
or kiss your lips when the day comes
all my dreams will come true

Jackie Ray Fennimore

Untitled

Some people ask for wealth untold
Some for the moon
some for diamonds
some for pearls
some a honeymoon

Some I just can't understand
but my wealth is like the land

For like the shining of a diamond
like the setting of the sun
like the bubbling of a brook
you've a love to be won

This love is fine, good and kind
and I find it always on my mind
It's pure and loving, gentle too.
For me, I'm asking God for you.

Nancy R. Smith

Black Man, Black Man

To my mom, whom I love
Black man, black mans what's wrong with you?
You have a good black woman by your side that really loves you.
Together forever is what it should be, but you lie and cheat endlessly.
She takes care of the kids, cooks, and cleans.
But that's not fair to her, if you know what I mean.

Black man, black man, direction is what you need.
You're a father, and a husband, if you know what I mean.
Shape up or ship out and act like a man.
Times are a-wasting, but I know you don't give a damn.

Black man, black man, show your family love.
Hug them and cherish them as if they were a white dove.
Black man, black man, all over the land,
I know you can be kind and sweet, and such a big-hearted man.

Hanna Y. Davis

To Die Is to Gain

When his anger arises, his fist does as well,
If I unveiled the horrible secret, who would I tell?

I sometimes wonder if the pain will ever end,
The right shade of blush will help the bruises blend.

I've heard the promises time and time again,
If you'll forgive me this time, I promise the abuse will end

With each blow to the body, or perhaps to the face,
My identity is no more, it's been completely erased.

I'm afraid to speak out, for retaliation may follow.
You've beat me to a pulp, I'm lifeless, limp, hollow.

At times I feel like a failure, I want to die, end it all right now.
But then I look at my five year-old and I wonder how.

I pray to God these writings do not describe you,
Your life is much too precious to spend it black and blue.

Yvette M. Clemons-Zeigler

Tell Me the Truth

To Jerique Montez Barnes, my grandson
Man, oh, man, oh, man so strong,
Tell me in truth. Just what has gone wrong?
Man, oh, man, oh, man of great strength.
If you don't know the answer, then I will give you a hint.
Look across the fields and the plains not far away,
the oaks, the hickories, and the pines down by the bay.
Look upon the cedars and the magnolias of its beauty and great strength,
and tell me in truth, do you now get the hint?

Roberta Barnes

Legacy

Never a believer,
Yearning for the comforts of faith; respecting others' choices
Epitome of civility,
Living the talk of "family values"; eschewing hypocrisy

Innate analyst,
Outweighing the evidence of facts over faith; remaining agnostic
Perennial researcher,
Extending wealth of knowledge; avoiding rhetoric of "the saved"

Dying with difficulty,
Expecting nothing, hoping against hope for welcoming tunnel of light
Passing eventually,
Becoming a body, flower in hand; creating a void in the hearts of others

Living in perpetuity
Thriving legacy, already bearing familiar fruit; continuing the blueprint
Providing meaning,
Cumulating memories, replacing the void; adding to our collective soul

Christina G. Weaver

Storming Demon

Well, come on ye then
Ye terror dark.
Strike, with thy swiftest speed.

I challenge again
Thy foul cold heart,
And thy boldest, darkest deed.

Yea, I shall meet ye
Out on the shore,
A golden sword to hand.

And ye shall be,
A terror no more
But cast out from the land
H. J. Higbee

Breaking Heart

To Carla, for her loving inspiration
The enduring pain
The unbearable loneliness of soul
The veil of tears that cloud my vision
The portrait of my breaking heart

So, comes this lament
This soulful mourning
The funeral pyre is lit
As the effigy burns
My soul cries out for redemption

All consuming suffering
Is my heart's existence
Degeneration of spirit
Its lonesome wail

So, comes this lament
For love lost
For my breaking heart
Chris Bowers

Secret Feelings

Once was a man that I had love,
But he flew away like a little dove.
I had him once but now he's gone,
he flew into someone else's arms.
Now I am seeing another man,
But I don't know how much longer I can.
When I tell him how I feel,
I'm looking straight into a mirror.
If I could tell him to his face,
I know that he would disappear.
We have become the best of friends,
All my time with him I like to spend.
In my heart I have so much pain,
I want to spill my feelings like the rain.
But I will be happy with him today,
for tomorrow he might go away.
I wish his heart I could set free,
and unlock it with a loving key.
Maybe someday and sometime,
everything will be just fine.
Carlene Young

Memories

As I gaze into the abyss
I think of you and more I miss
All of the love and joy we shared
I realize now that you really cared

I'm sorry that you are out of my life
Now I have to put up with all this strife
Of knowing that you are really gone
But my love for you will always live on . . .
April Petrick

You Are

You are the thoughts in my mind as I sit and meditate.
You are the sound in my ears so small yet so great.
You are the gaze in my eyes staring so far away.
You are the words on my tongue that I'm forming to say.
You are a pleasant aroma that my nose loves to smell.
You are the taste of sweet things, like chocolate and caramel.
You are the touch of silk and satin against my skin.
You are the soft and beautiful notes to a wonderful song.
You are my deepest feelings that come from within.
You are an ocean that flows forever wide, deep, and long.
You're my joy and my laughter, even the tears that I cry.
You're the question, in my head that makes me ask why.
You are the swing of my arms and the sway of my hips.
You are the stride of my legs, even the shape of my lips.
You are my morning, my afternoon, my evening, and my night.
You are my song that I sing and the words that I write.

Yes, all the things you seem to be,
all these things that are so much apart of me.
See you've gained my love and won my heart,
and I hope and pray that what we've put together will never come apart.

Myra McCranie

A Man of Merritt

In memory of my father and my husband
I am sitting down to write this poem about my favorite Dad
Then ponder how silly that sounds, he's the only one I've had.
The debt I owe this man to date is larger than Fort Knox.
I hope they take my credit card at his heavenly mail-box.

Let me tell you of this stoic man with very little to say.
A man of character and principle, who lived life day-to-day.
He taught us by example and did not shoot the breeze,
He showed his love to his family with a gentle little tease.

Dad's life was like a wind-swept prairie in oh, so many ways,
blowing straight-up from North to South and never in a haze.
Things were always black and white with him, never in-between.
A very unique man of Merritt that most have never seen.

Where do I begin to repay his due on all the lesson that he taught?
These words and rhyme seem so cheap for all the things he's bought.
The food, the clothes, the shoes, the car, and least we not forget,
All those spankings that I deserved, but somehow didn't get!

He was husband, dad, grandfather, friend, a trusted confidant.
The funny childhood stories I was told by his sisters, alias, my aunt.
Mom says when he was young, he could work just like the wind,
So he could give us a good life and flash his toothy grin.

Delores Larson

Exile Parents

They took them away when we were searching through its immortality realm,
One two year-old boy and two infant girls eleven and one month.

We were left out in this seldom blissful entity to linger
with the sins of doom,
And our babies were auctioned by the use of an
incentive government financial enticement.

Our mothers and fathers distanced themselves
and no longer were steadfast to our survival,
But conjured emotions to the helpless needs of
the children that they claimed we forgot.

We swear that we'll withdraw from the routine, to love the things
that the drugs view in our minds as non-important events,
"What would it take to get our babies back and felicitate
a family that has never existed?"

"Give up this vile recurring condemned process and effect a paternal image,
Believe it can be and make it so," says the voice of reason.
Tomorrow, for us, seems so real as a good day to concede!

Susan M. Powell

Heartbroken

You're always floating among my mind
Thinking of your eyes so soft
Dreaming of your laughter so kind
Wondering of your thoughts inside
And as I lie hear crying
I think how could this be
After all my work and trying
You're still not here with me
And every step I take each day
And every tear I shed
Shows the pain I've had to pay
Shows the blood I've bled
But all I can say is you hurt me
You left my wounded heart hoping
That one day you would see
You left me here heartbroken
And I can be your lifelong dream
I can take your precious hand
From that fake love of lies and pain
I can love you better then she can

Kari Park

Young Love, Heart Scarred

For dreams of freedom dying here
I look into your eyes
and see all the history you've cried
Those baby blues
they never lie

You say it's all in the past
trying to forget way too fast
Heart becomes burnt
holding on to something that can't last

Where is this life taking me
you say only if I could see
what lay ahead,
what is my destiny.

Questions put before herself
she tries to put his love on a shelf
The surreal pain at the altar
where she knelt

Her lover lay in a casket today
What caused the death, no one can say
Rain driving hard
young love, heart scarred

Edward J. Koch

Tomorrow

Are we destined a tomorrow
just because we had today
No one will ever know
No one can really say
Can we look at the night's sky
and know our future lies ahead
or can another day just pass us by
and we'll discover ourselves dead
Or could we open our minds
and feel that there's no morning
All that we would find
is death without warning
Will tomorrow be talked about
the way yesterday was
or will it be left out
with Armageddon being the cause
Are we going to live another day
of happiness or of sorrow
No one can really say
because we might not have tomorrow

Jahri Gonsalves

The Core of Love

Dedicated to endless devotion . . .
Rhythms of the heartbeat I adore.
The touch, the sounds, the sights of which someday will be no more.
Until that time I'll gaze upon and cherish thee
with all my love through eternity.
Rhythms of the heartbeat I adore.
As day gives way to night, it's in my dreams that I'll keep you in sight.
The pulsations, the angst, the confusion, the fear
are a direct correlation to wanting you near.
Rhythms of the heartbeat I adore.
Though our destiny is uncertain but our feelings are clear
understanding our plight keeps the feelings in flight.
If there's ever a concern or a needing to yearn,
do not distress because . . . Rhythms of the heartbeat I adore.

  Fayton D. Hollington

Colors

First the rising of the sun,
Orange, pink, and lavender slowly peeking one ray after the other
Over the new fresh sprinkled dew of day.

The birds, they echo their chorus joyfully,
Flittering from a quiet black night.

The geese are squawking rudely
As if to purposely waken all from slumber.

The stars begin to fade from sight, the bright orange and golden hues of the full sun
Now appear and melt away the shadowy nightly fears.

The day grows old, the sky is blue. The wind so crisp and the clouds so full,
Each dancing in the white light and blue velvet of the heavens.

The grass so green, the flower so red, and all so beautiful
This rainbow of color to fill our day.

And all at once you hear the hush of nightfall calling all to rest.
Again the colors of orange and lavender, blue and gold
Reappear to bid goodnight. The sun then hides all face from sight.

The birds are hushed, the geese quiet.
The velvet black of night now falls, yet decorated
With a soft diamond glittering of stars.

Once again, all is resting in this cocoon, of the neverending prism of colors.

  Lisa A. Martin

All Alone

I sit in my room for hours and hours just thinking about you and the times we had.
The things we used to do, whether it was talking on the phone or watching a movie together.
Even though we'd had our fights, we'd always forgive each other.
Through thick and thin, you stuck by my side, and I always stood by yours.

But, now you're gone. I can't see how you could leave me, and not say goodbye.
We'd made a promise not to leave each other no matter what happened in our lives.
But you broke your promise, and left me by myself, standing cold in the rain.
I call you selfish all the time, and think to myself,
"Maybe, I'm the one who is selfish to want you all to myself."

My mind travels back to the day you left.
You were dressed in a black suit with black shoes and all.
I remember saying, as a tear rolled gently down my cheek,
"Goodbye, My Friend," but you wouldn't return my last farewell.
As you leave from sight, I toss a rose black as night to where you rest.

Now, you're gone far away from me.
You left me all alone in this world with no one to stand by my side.
Then, without a word, silent as the wind, a voice so near that I knew by heart,
whispered in my ear, "Goodbye my Friend," as a last farewell.

Now, as I sit in my room for hours and hours just thinking about you and the times we had,
I know now what I've known all along. I haven't said my "Last Goodbye."
I'll see you again, and we will be by each other's side once again,
up in God's Kingdom, Now and Forever.

  Marquita C. Streeter

Together

To my mother, Genevieve
The stars throughout the heavens
Shine brightly from above;
For they are now the eyes;
Of those we dearly love.

While gentle breezes softly play
Upon a face of tears;
A warming sun will spread its arms,
Drying those in years.

The same gentle breeze now whispers
From lips which speak our name;
And tenderly caresses us
With cool refreshing rain.

As flowers bloom in glory,
As night turns into day;
We see again our loved ones;
They're really not away.

They are seen in all the beauty
Of what is good and kind;
And stay alive within us,
In our hearts and souls and mind.

  Judy A. Miller

Dreamer

For Timothy W. Shaw, Sr.
I know how you feel
when I look into your eyes.

I see your pain
when you don't even cry.

I feel your touch
as I lie all alone.

The place where you lay
is empty and cold.

Your kiss is remembered
like a little child's dream.

As I smile and reminisce
of our very first love scene.

I hear your promise
as you start to walk away.

My heart is now broken,
for you promised to always stay.

  Sheri Carter

Apocalypse Girl

Within the mist where I exist,
I wait to be kissed by an atheist.

Oppressed by the ominous, oncoming fog,
wherein I fear, hides a rabid dog.
She my savior, the animal my killer,
I pray she will love me, if I will her.

Beneath the dark skies I am under,
I act in lightning, I speak in thunder.
From the stars I will plunder,
light and life are torn asunder.

A silver satellite above a cloud,
solid and shining, it is proud.
Falling like a comet from outer space,
I and Lucifer in disgrace.

Elusive object of my affection,
I fear nothing more than her rejection.
Her every movement my seduction,
This sensual girl, is my destruction.

  John Prince

A Tribute: *AuRevoir*, Shining Star

To my mother and grandmother
Diana, Princess of Wales, like a brilliant shooting star!
So bright, so kind, so warm, so real, and so much more, by far!

Now your lights i dimmed to us, and what are we to do?
We can never properly say goodbye and tell you how proud we were of you!

We knew you first as "Lady Di"
then a Princess, a wife, and devoted mother
But most remembered for philanthropy, full of love,
and style, and grace, like no other!

Out hearts and prayers go out to the ones you loved
Especially your sons William and Harry
How fortunate for them to have had you
How sad for you us you could not tarry!

And now you're gone but oh, too soon
Thank you for making our world a nicer place, by far
We'll miss you sweet, Di
AuRevoir to our "Queen of Hearts," our shining star!

J. R. Humphrey

Two White Clouds

For Les, Lisa, Darrin, Shannon, and Ryan
I sat meditating quietly on the hillside by myself,
Drinking in the lovely beauty God had placed there from His wealth.
My senses thrilled with expectation urging me to drink in more
Of the quiet, precious minutes I had waited so long for.

In the stillness of the moment I lay down upon the grass,
And gazed with child-like wonder as the clouds went drifting past.
Two White Clouds so near together, floating, floating, drifting by;
Each one reaching toward the other, high up, high up in the sky,

Closer, nearer, almost touching, drawing closer to embrace;
But, oh! The wind has changed directions, wider, wider grows the space.
The two sad clouds look back with longing as the wind blows each away,
Forever leaving the sweet communion meant for both of them that day.

Then I set myself to thinking 'bout two people whom I know.
Seems the two clouds tell their story. Why, oh why, must this be so?
Two whose souls are tuned together, two whose souls cry out in pain
With the longing for each other, but those winds of life remain

Ever blowing, making slimmer chances that the two shall be
Free to follow where love leads them, free to sail upon their sea.
Like the clouds, they keep on drifting, keeping locked within two hearts
All the longing for each other that Life's Winds have kept apart.

Ruby Roberts Cox

Long Ago Yesterday

Dedicated to Abba Father
Delicately she twines her velvet fingers . . .
beneath falling tangle of long forgotten hunches . . .
Never acknowledging grimy fingerprints bloodied through sidewalk cracks,
dead with life everlasting . . . and nobody cared . . . somebody cared?
Weaving ribbons or scorn in prideful vengeance . . . following each "whoop" with a silent stare
rough, calloused tapestry scorched in torment, frozen beyond reach.
She could not care . . . why should she care?
Dancing, mocking salt-pricked winds scarred the fabric.
Maiming beyond comprehension, surely there was no hope, it would be destroyed.
Tattered and shorn, every step circling nowhere journeying everywhere does somebody care?
Show me who cares. Her bruised and battered stone-cold heart began to ache,
the throbbing was frightening her hand reaches out . . . her velvet gloves are gone!
Ouch! The tapestry burns! The scars, the scars, they should be covered.
She cries out, "Who cares?" Who cares . . . she knows someone is there,
yet she sees no one. She feels the presence, she smells the warmth.
The air rushes, she looks down to see it dripping from her hands,
the balm, it soothes, the scars are barely visible.
Someone cares! Yes, someone cares!
Yesterday just yesterday, but so long ago, so long ago, yesterday.

Laura J. Howe

The Oak Tree

There was a tree. An oak tree,
but it was a friend to me, it spoke to me.
I listened, it told me
things of the past, it told me
about people of the past.
It told me once a great man
sat under it and asked its advice.
It tried to answer, he could not hear.
Another man asked its advice.
It tried to answer, he could not hear.
I asked why they could not hear
and I could. The tree just said
with a sigh, they did not want to.

Amber Fox

A Simple Man

I have a simple family
Who throughout the years
Have gave me simple joy
We have survived our fears

I have a simple house
It has sheltered many
And to speak of simple hate
I don't think I have any

I have a simple job
I attend to every day
And a very simple car
That keeps me on my way

I have a simple garden
It has grown all my foods
I have gave simple company
My ear, during one of their moods

I am a simple man
But I have done great things
I live a simple life
But I have plenty of dreams.

Michele Markham

Connections

A flash of summers past
warmed this wintry day.
Its gentle glow
settled briefly in my soul,
to ease my faltering way.

This Being I am being
longs for Light and Truth and Love.
Always in connection,
Spirit sends the blessing of
the beautiful bare necessity
of a silently eloquent dove.

Robin Hayes

The Journey of a Leaf

Somewhere a leaf breaks off a tree,
It begins to fall and now it's free.
The wind blows more and more,
And now the leaf begins to soar.
Like an eagle it flies on and on,
Like it is running in a marathon.
This feeling may not be known to man,
But we can guess where it might land.
The leaf is moving steady like a tortoise,
It is floating up there way above us.
Now the leaf has had its fun,
And its journey is almost done.
Slowly the wind begins to die down,
And finally the leaf touches the ground.

Thomas S. McLaughlin Jr.

Dream Girl

I'm searching for the love I find to be true
but to be honest sweetheart I can't find you,
I dream about you almost every day and night
it's your love and affection I crave so tight,
the touch of your hand and smile so sweet
makes my heart just skip a beat,
please girl come into my life and set my heart free
it's been locked up and hidden away from me,
lies, broken promises that led to broken hearts and only made me cry, come into my life
and we'll get lost in love while we're suspended in time
as I look deep into your eyes and you tell me you're mine forever
our love forever it will be true, forever dream girl I'll dream about you
I will give you my heart, I'll give you my love,
because you're the Goddess sent from up above
can't you see I need love but not no ordinary love
I need your love, your affection,
so come out of my dreams and walk into my life
be part of my future as you become my wife.

Jack Gresham Jr.

This Too Shall Pass

To Karie and McKayla

Me being a person who always is worrying about something
actually found some words that can give me some comfort: "This too shall pass."
Sounds pretty simple, and it is. Just being able to trust those words is the hard part.
But once you can trust those words,
it just might be one of the best phrases you could have ever learned.
Because, it's right! Every worry, problem, trouble, sadness, and loss shall pass with time.
Every one of them. All it takes is keeping your mind set that it too shall pass.
It might take seconds, minutes, hours, days, or even years.
But once you have overcome that worry, problem, trouble, sadness, or loss
you will have become a little bit stronger of a person.
God did not put us here on Earth to have a free ride at life.
He wants us to have hard times.
He wants to see how you handle them and who you turn to.
Only you can make those decisions. You determine how your life is lived.
If you make yourself miserable, you will be miserable.
If you try your hardest to fight those unwanted times in your life,
I promise your life will be happier.
But always remember that God will be there helping you fight either way.
I do think that things would work out for the better
if you both were fighting for the same thing.
And always remember this too shall pass.

Crystal Smith

Life, Death, and Freedom

For my brother Benjy

There will always be time,
To write and rhyme,
To write poems that capture the essence of life,
Sharp as a knife.

The truth may be frightening,
A circle, the circle of life always tightening,
Around you,
And when it finally squeezes you out of place,
Out of religion, culture, and race,
To exactly where you don't want to be,
You learn to adjust, to truly be free.

You've never felt this freedom before,
It's like freedom but more,
To live by your own standards rather than the standards of other men.

Then the countdown starts at ten,
Nine, eight, seven, six,
And at five you're gone, gone with the wind.

One wishes for immortality,
But you don't need it in this place you've been sucked up into,
You only need the time you've been given, to live in.

Max Kennedy

My Golden Years

I had worked so many hard years,
Through blood and sweat and many tears.
I raised four children on my own;
No one helped, I was all alone.
My husband left me long ago,
So his wild oats he could sow.
I had kerosene lamps,
And I sewed by hand;
Most of our food came from the land.
Just when I thought my days were done,
Out of retirement I had to come.
So, as time marches,
So I find myself in my Golden years
Under McDonald's golden arches.

Mae Palmer

Untitled

Muscles twitch
empty gaze
to an empty space
Floating through passive rivers
with vibrant emotions
to a stagnant state of mind
Throwing things
while I'm unable to grasp
the sour truth

Chasity Collins

Untitled

I talked about the rain
An' varies of things,
But still she did not smile.
I talked about my big ole feet,
That I'd polished my shoes and
They had been neat right 'til
That ole bus had splashed me.
Still she did not smile.
Now, an undertaker is supposed
to be dead serious all the time.
If I saw him laugh, I'd be undone
Because death is absolutely no fun.

Like I saw her teasing with previous
Patron that was just before me,
But for me she did not smile.

Maybe it's not worth writing about,
But I cannot forget it.
I wasn't dressed to the nines,
But neither were the other ones,
But for me she did not smile.

Sharon J. Stamps

Easter

E is for the early morn
   That dawned so bright and clear
A is for the angel who told them
   He is no longer here
S is for the soldiers
   They nailed him on that tree
T is for the many tears
   He shed for you and me
E is for the empty tomb
   The stone was rolled away
R means He has risen
   For He just could not stay

Put them all together
   and they spell Easter
Oh, what a glorious day

Bobbie H. Wooten

Civil Woe

Bitter conflicts besieged the battlefields; guns fired sending clouds of smoke into the air;
soldiers lay helpless, lifeless, bloodstained.
The smell of death lingered, tyrannical heroes cried out in victory,
though none of us would consider it so. Frightening as it was,
a calamitous heave of roguish beings enriched in their own blood-bathed enemy souls—
conscientious soldiers, grieving over the millions of mishaps of heroic deeds,
until they had but tears and whimpers left in them which had
contorted their faces and corrupted their heart like a multitude of magnetic forces.
As if bewitched by a spell, they were cast upon the darkness
like the sincere patriots they had become.
They recoiled from their pestiferous proposition which darkened bitter hearts,
and strained their conscience for years to come;
and tranquilized the extravagant air with heavy darkness.
Portraying the fervent intoxicating evil of audacious aggressive enemies,
the engraved deaths upon the frontier, wherein the bitter conflicts
befuddled the elusive schemes hacking their hearts into opposing sides.
Resigned to wait helplessly for the gluttonous death to creep upon their souls,
as the ebb of life dissuades routine; the world will never surmise
the perspicacious slayer of man!

   Devi Dakin

My First Love

Oh, corridor of shadow light
Please lead me to the place where last I saw him there,
With arms wide open, on bended knee, waiting for my embrace.

My first love
How well I remember your midnight voice that soothes my every fear,
Your strong arms gently enclose me as a harbor in the storm.
I know I am safe.

I hear a voice softly call and for a moment I turn away
I look back, you are gone.
Where are you? Oh, please come back!
Why all this darkness?

I hear my tiny footsteps echo in the shadows. My small frame trembles.
I am desperate to find my prince, he lives here in my castle . . . my world.

I have been looking for so long
I catch a glimpse and as I run, you gently fade away.
The emptiness of your embrace has seeped into my heart,
I fear it will never leave.

Void. It is always here you know.

Through the restlessness of time, my love is never dim.
I pray that love's light will lead us home someday, my first love, my daddy.

   Bonnie Parkman

The Plea

To God, Ed, and Frances, for faith
If I could ride above the waves, I wonder what I'd see,
Will you be there to greet me, above the restless sea?
The winters come, the winters go, as all the seasons change,
but now I stand still on this earth, to raise my lonely plea.

The days are now so empty, my mind is fading fast,
oh, if I could see you, I know I'd get some rest.
My God, my God, please hear me, don't let me sink so low,
that I could not overcome my sinking in the snow.

My lonely heart is breaking 'cause I can't endure the test,
would you please deliver me and bring eternal rest?

Oh, wait! I see the sun is out, and then in a moment,
I begin to hear you shout . . .

My child, my child, I love you, and alas you cannot go,
there are more deeds that you must do and seeds that you must sow.
Don't tarry now, go about my work and do it with a smile,
For there are wondrous things on Earth that are very worthwhile.

The hungry, the homeless, the empty and lost,
I paid the price for these upon that old wooden cross.
Bring these to me, my little child, and I will see you in a little while.

   Barbara A. Madden

Dream Pilot

To Lucinda, my dream pilot
Her shades on, she watches the land
As she passes by,
Her smart brain, with no worries,
Sweetness, she cries.
Everyone sees her and wants to be her,
Jealousy in some.
See her long hair and glazed brown eyes,
She is the one.

Can we take her home with us
And make all peace?
We watch in fear, we watch in love,
Our adoration screams.
We used to be blind to everything,
She lets us see.
She is the woman, she is the man
Who helps us incredibly.

   Angela Swain

Fathers

To my daddy, with love—Valerie
They care,
We share,
We laugh,
We play,
We stay
In their hearts
Forever
Everything we do,
We do it
Together

   Valerie Luv Kopasz

O' Dancing Eyes

Oh, those coal dark dancing eyes.
My, oh, me should I tell you, do I dare,
how they mesmerize glints of light,
sparkling, reach out to me.
As if there were chords, drawing me near
O' dancing eyes, are they true,
can it be light of love, honesty,
is that passion you wear find my heart
O' dancing eyes, tell me we never will part

   Lee Taylor

Inner Peace

To Thomas, visions through his eyes
The phone rings twice
The children are playing,
I pick up the phone
Don't hear what they're saying.

In the back ground I hear
Mom, I painted some trees,
A house, mountains, snow
So peaceful, can you see.

Inner peace is its name
Beautiful, restfulness, no shame
The glory, peace all around
Inner peace, it earned the name

Do you see what I see
Look through the child's eyes,
Find that true inner peace
Before life passes you by.

Enjoy every new day
The rainbow, sun, or moon.
Tomorrow isn't here
Today inner peace, no gloom.

   Tamie Ray

Every Cloud Has a Silver Lining

Every cloud has a silver lining embedded around the edges
And pouring over the sides gleaming so brightly to turn everyone's head.
There is always a brighter tomorrow and a star to make a wish upon.
Every cloud has a silver lining, from the angels flying around.
Caress all kind who fail to notice, to see everything in true color,
Fail to see everything in reality.
With a sweeter coating or silver lining,
life is a little lovelier than the way things seem.
Crazy, crazy poet living a dreamer's dream
and fantasizing about seeing the unseen.
Holy innocence and new beginning create the life we wish to live.
Light as a feather and a cloud still the same.
Lay down your peace all to play the game.
Distinguish the young difference of kindness and kind.
Nothing new to discover, respect and dignity all clustered in one.
The silver lining makes it attractive and gets interest to join.
Spotlight for you, unique to know.
Sweet ancient lullaby—fall into the cloud
for every cloud has a silver lining.

Winkle Scarberry

As I Walk with Thee

To my Heavenly Father Jesus Christ
As I walk with thee I know you hear my plea.
As I walk with thee you always seem to help me.
As I walk with thee you seem to have the most joy for me.
As I walk with thee you always seem to forgive me.
As I walk with thee you always seem to understand me.
As I walk with thee you seem to stay right beside me through thick and thin.
As I walk with thee you always take up for me.
As I walk with thee you're always there to teach me.
As I walk with thee and I reach out my hand you always seem to grab it.
As I walk with thee and I fall you're always there to help me.
As I walk with thee and I feel down you're always there to pick me up,
That is why I intend to walk with thee all my life.

Crystal Deburow

Your Guardian Angel

To a lost soul
I am the smile that you see each day
I am the conscience that guides you in every way
I picked you up when you would fall, I heard your cry when you called
You depended on me to be your guide, to warm your heart at difficult times
Why do you feel you have nothing left?
I'm still here, you're not by yourself
I'm more in a delicate disguise, I come and go by surprise
I listen to all your thoughts and prayers when you feel no one cares
Why feel guilty as you weep? I've come to protect you as you sleep,
Keep faith, pray night and day, as your Guardian Angel, I'm here to stay,
Ask the Lord for health and strength, happiness and joy is what he meant
Life goes on throughout sorrow, to let you know there's hope for tomorrow
Through darkness, trials, pain and fear, I'll be the one to hold your tear
God sent me to be with you, to ease the pain and see you through
Don't forget that it was He, because without him there would be no me.

Teresa Harden

Dream Time

Thinking of the old ways long gone
Who walked across this land—strong, free, proud.
Who can read the skies,
Winds that are forever blowing new life across our beautiful country.
Into the rivers that give the animals life.
Oceans as deep as life is.
Birds from islands untouched.
Sands move and build strange shapes which are warm to the sea.
New dew has touched the ground before the hunters arrive.
Feeling the rays of the day.
To the old ones for I am proud.
Strong, I have found my spirit!
Entering womanhood free and strong, believing in myself.
"Proud," loving my old ones!

Danza Hapke

Inner Pain

There was a little girl
Who's heart was full of pain
Such a sad little girl
Whose life would never be the same

No matter to embrace her
No father on which to lean
Words like honor and respect
Whatever could they mean?

A life so hard
There was no love
Her heart grew cold
Her mind gave up

Now all that's left
Is an empty shell
There is no life
Just a living hell.

Jane Duncan

Think of Me

When you see a dew drop
think of me,

When you see a rain drop
think of me.

When you see a twig on a tree
think of me,

I am only here for a moment
Waiting for thee.

Polly Halverson

The Power of Prayer

When things are really going wrong,
You wish someone would care.
Why not sit down and concentrate
and say a little prayer.

You'll find it will amaze you
how fast things turn around,
And even as He listens there
you'll never hear a sound.

But as each day goes by my friend
you'll notice things have changed,
and all things that had been wrong
have now been rearranged.

Suddenly the world seems right,
You manage now to smile,
And then you come to realize
He's been there all the while.

So call upon the Lord each day,
And thank Him for His grace,
For I am sure He looks on you
And sees your smiling face.

Lois M. Becker

Stained in Blood

The carving on the banister
is a grave reminder
of a past resident
of this shelter
it says simply,
"this place is hell"
for me, hell is where I've already been
it's why I'm here
and I'll bear my own carvings forever

Leigha Conner

Yesterday You

I hear the clock ticking, the sky is dusty blue, and here I sit thinking of the yesterday you,
I remember all the quarrels over things we used to do; the phone would ring, the voice would say,
"I'm sorry, I love you," and here I sit thinking of the yesterday you,
I cannot forget the way you were, the time once past, but today I worry
about the change in you so fast, and here I sit thinking of the yesterday you,
Tomorrow will soon come, its presence I will dread,
my head will hang in sorrow and my eyes will grow red,
my tears will fall slowly and my mind will drift away, and how I will long for yesterday,
Let me tell you something that hurts me so much inside,
this person that I speak of has crushed the love I now hide,
it is not hard to show love to someone who really cares,
but it is impossible to give love to someone who is not there,
The clock is still ticking as time slowly passes by, my tears are still rolling and my heart still cries,
once hurt be careful because when tomorrow comes around
you may cry those same tears for another you have found.
I still remember all the quarrels over things we used to do;
the phone would ring, the voice would say, "I'm sorry, I love you,"
and here I sit thinking of the yesterday you.

Cynthia L. Mancinelli

Night Plea

So, you say you love me . . . like seducing winds
warm with the covert promise of spring, kiss away city smog—
and make an offer of a keyhole view of blue sky, illusive to my tears.

So, you say you love me . . . I wait with fluttering apprehension,
for you to reveal your heart, kept by silky betrayal, like a child
made to wait to tear the cover off of a gift-wrapped, empty box.

I heard you . . . you said you loved me
Strolls up to my ears with low down sweet-talk like a hustler confidante—
Oozing from swamp like eerie beauty, choking my prized remnant of optimism.

I see your lips moving, saying you love me
Lips the glimmer with the dew of shallow, minute-passion.
You could have convinced me into selling my dreams for cheap wares,
weather worn with broken heart's verdigris.
Ugly appeared as art form, I believed you. Thought you were different.

I see your eyes flood with an empty plea
Your hand outstretched, as if to offer—my heart senses another theft.
Compromised, naked naiveté is your trade . . . I believed you.

I heard you say . . . you love me, in the mist of city night, so adept
at dream-jacking. Yeah, yeah, unnh-huh . . . I heard what you said.
Here's your quarter, go away.

Reverdia Trammell

Trial of Love

Trotting through a desert land and having only a clue
Maps are offered, signs are made but can you make it through

You begin your journey in this land being just a boy
Existing in the world of decay your youth hath been destroyed

Matured now in this strange place movements are made with ease
No one to talk to no need to run doing only as you please

Watch yourself something tells you as you move along
The weak could never survive in this place leaving only the strong

But why you? You ask yourself as the path becomes more dreary
Your steps a little cautious now as your thoughts become more weary

I am not the strong you seek, nor am I the brave
Someone reach into me please for my heart you must save

This world has taken my soul and mind and all that I would be
If you could only read my heart my anguish you would see

No hope in sight you're floating away in this endless place
No one to talk to no need to run and not one familiar face

Traveling now with fear of extinction you turn to look ahead
It seems as though your fears have come true and your love is already dead.

Thaddeus Tutsock

Summer Breeze

I feel the beautiful summer breeze
blowing softly through the trees.
The day is hot, the breeze is cool;
Mother Nature is beautiful.
I wish I could live out here
where the air is clean and water clear,
but I must go back to my home
in the city, never alone.

Jessica Bennett

Remember Me Always

Do not forget me;
remember me always.
You are my family,
and I am the one you love.
Once I am long gone,
I want to be remembered.
I want to be remembered
as someone who cared for others,
wanted to help, and I want
to be remembered as a teacher—
not a school teacher,
but a teacher of different things.
Please do not forget me.
Remember me always
as the way I would like to be remembered.

Kelly Cantrell

The Blood Coat

I was drowning in a sea of sin
So deep, and dark, and cold.
All alone in a big bad world, that
Froze my heart to stone.

The numbing feeling of my heart
Made me sick inside;
Then a voice called and said to me;
"For you I came and died."

The sweetness of this voice I heard
warmed me deep within.
He said his blood would cover me
And wash away my sin.

On my knees, he washed me clean
In the blood coat of his love;
And told about my brand new home
He's preparing up above.

Released I felt, sweet peace within;
Warmed the coldness of my heart.
Thank you Jesus for loving me
And forgiving all my sin.

Barbara C. Mallory

The Winds

The winds pushed us together
As forcefully as they drove us,
Down the tortured pathways
Of our lives.

The winds blew or bodies
Into fates of sorrows,
Stabbing at our souls
With memory knives.

The winds stole our innocence
Swirling it away from us until,
A love breeze could retrieve the laughter
With a reminding tickle in the heart.

The winds raged in our minds until
There was nothing left except,
A gentle breath of air that nudged
Love to a start.

Diane Heresco

True Love

And so it happened one night, that Spartacus called,
And the sky rumbled, he's been through the pain that nearly drove him insane
And he felt his life had crumbled.
Now on that very same night, Fantasia saw light,
when she looked up in the sky, she stretched out her hand
And called for her man, and patiently awaited.
Now Spartacus knew, his true love was due,
He just didn't know where she'd be,
So again he called out, in a thunderous shout,
"I've been ready, please send her to me."
Just then, a bright star, which came from afar,
was sent for them both that day.
It danced and it twinkled, and it caught their eye,
So that it can show them the way.
As it started to race, they followed the chase,
that brought them together, in this one place,
They watched as it shined in the eyes of each other,
And realized that they were each other's true lover
Now the fantasy lives, for Spartacus is,
The true love of Fantasia, and she is his.

Susan DiSalvo

When the Gift Given Was Lost

To Ransom, my brother

The pain I can see on your face, the tears I can see in your eyes.
The loss that you can't describe, oh, how I hurt to see you cry.
The death you've died inside.
Nothing in this world could hide how much you hurt.

There's nothing I can say to you,
there's nothing I can do for you.
Oh, how I long to ease the pain.
The heart wrenching pain inside of you.
I can't take it away no matter what I say or do.

The loneliness you're going through.
The loss that makes you feel blue.
The sadness makes you go insane, oh, how I wish you missed the pain.
The love shared, you didn't hide.
I wish you could go back and it was no one who died.

But after the fact you cannot hide just how much it hurts deep inside.
Oh, how I long to ease the pain.
To help you down this winding lane.
To take the pain you hide away.
Oh, how I wish it could be that way,
but when the gift was given it was lost.

Autumn Waddell

My Guardian Angel

For my angel, Virginia Lee Belt

You are my Angel, you pick me up, when I'm feeling down,
You hold my hand, when I stumble in on Shaky ground,
You are my Angel, you wrap your loving wings around me,
when I'm feeling cold, you watch over me,
when I don't know what tomorrow holds,
You are my Angel, you guide and protect me in a world grown cold,
Oh, Lord, what wouldn't I have given for the chance to have known,
My guardian Angel, oh, Lord, how I believe, it's my sister,
living up there in Heaven with thee.
My Guardian Angel, who is watching over me,
Oh, Sis, how I wish you could have met my family,
met my husband, Paul, and got to hold little Zachary
Virginia, I miss you, even though, I never had the chance to know or see,
but there's a place in my heart, that only you can hold.
My Guardian Angel, who is watching over me,
Oh, how I miss my Angel, and that chance to see, and have that big sister,
That ever sister without, should never be,
My loving Guardian Angel, Virginia,
who I never had the chance to know or see,
But I feel her love and presence, right here on Earth with me.

Diana L. Littlejohn

The Journey Home

Dedicated to John Robert Dalton

A summer night a silent song
A silver memory of times long gone
A hollow pain that grips the heart
A shattered soul that can't restart
A frozen dream built in the mind
A ghostly dream in a ghostly bind
A hidden shadow that feeds on pain
A time-worn feeling an ancient stain
A noble thought lost in the dark
A golden arrow that missed its mark
A stolen kiss a worthless rhyme
An endless game that swallows time
A troubled silence that offers hope
A cherished goal on a slippery slope
A smoky stairway that just goes down
A rainbow joy that's never found
A poor man that enjoys a throne
A tender spot in a wall of stone
A truth outlasts the journey home
A diamond glows its beauty known

Darryl Essex Williams

The Gift

I gathered all the Angels
I could find this time of year
And asked if they could help me
Spread blessings, joy, and cheer

I made a special list
And assigned one to each of you
I gave each one strict orders
On exactly what to do

With her hand upon your head
She'll bless the coming year
And fill your heart with joy
And spread angelic cheer

Your Angel is close by
She's watching from above
Waiting for the perfect time
To bring this gift of love

May your days be merry
May this Christmas be the best
May you grow and prosper
Now that you've been blessed

Norma A. Butler

Age

Gaze at age upon us now,
What became of youth?
Observe the aged brow,
See time in all its truth.

A tale of time that can't erase
The thinning of your hair.
Trace the lines upon your face,
When no one else is there.
Aging blurs the visions sight,
When danger enters near.
Causing victims in their plight,
If people cannot hear.
Senility is the bane in life,
The calm before the storm.
Disease of age in man and wife,
Forgetfulness a thorn.
When illness enters your domain,
Age must bear your ills.
Dark despair a cold disdain,
When poverty is their fill.

Fred Salerno Sands

Song of Myself

To my little sister, Nicole Smith
I see myself in the mirror, I see the stars in my eyes
I see and hear and feel my mother, I see a young, beautiful,
and confused girl

I feel that I am a girl, I feel that I have much to learn
I feel that I need to know what is important to me,
I feel I will some day understand

I am woman, I am smart, I am strong, I am loved
I am important, I am bold, I am the ruler of my soul
and I will always be in control

No one knows me the way I do, no one can copy me
No one knows my feelings, no one needs to

Upon a magic carpet I start my journey out of Ohio to place with beautiful
colors animals and trees over waterfalls and along fields of wildflowers

Butterflies mingle with the bees and a polar bear talking with a spider
makes no matter a circle of life where all is peaceful; all live in happiness
        Jennifer A. Smith

Untitled

Darling,
Twenty-five years have gone by
since first we wed, joined together by God.
Now as we face the future ahead,
I, as your husband and you as my wife,
We shall walk arm in arm through the golden years of our life.

As we walk down life's path,
we will help each other,
should either of us stumble or fall.
And we will hold onto each other until we reach that fork in the road.

As we stroll along we shall pause and embrace,
And I will kiss you lovely face,
And as we hold each other so,
We'll vow our true love whispering, darling,
I love you so.
        Edward Moro

Visions of Our Soul

As the Artist searches through colors
for inspiration to transpose the empty canvas,
the Writer scrolls through words,
interpreting thought for the unscored parchment.

This enactment of self creativity illuminates the visions of our soul,
and shall remain aside of ego and its uncertainty,
only to gain the fulfillment of our accomplishments,
and the empowerment of achievement.
        Dana Dix

Ships at Sea

We were lost like ships at sea, our missions were unknown
Our destinations were uncharted, we each sailed alone.
We were drifting farther apart as each day passed us by,
Life is like the sea—some days rough with waves o' so high.
It took us too long to weather out the storm
It's up to us to never drift apart again,
And up to God to protect us from all harm.
Friends come and go and it's sad, sometimes our children seem to forget,
But family is forever and forever hasn't caught up with us yet.
We forget too soon when we leave home the loved ones left behind,
But deep inside they worry for you each day
And tears keep track of time.
And every visit is so important for the time that you are there
There's happiness and laughter just knowing you still care.
So if life gets to be a burden too much for you to bear,
Just call the ones that love you, and the burden we shall share.
        Gary Hayes

Snow

Snow, snow! Glorious snow!
You can sift it through your hands,
You can sift it through your toes.
Grass may be green and sand may be grand,
But we're just crazy about snow!
        Natalie Carrozza

Who Am I

The sun will always stay in the sky
It will never leave nor die.

You can love a special thing 'til the end
But there is no better love
Than the love of your family and friends

In our hearts for torch of memory
Burns unflickering, bright and true

Its light is sweet for it is fed
On love and tender thoughts of you

Whatever your race may be
Is surely kin to me.

So others then may see
In what we strive to be

Dare to stand alone
Dare to make it known

They give volume to one's voice
Make a humble heart rejoice

Redeemed by the blood of the lamb
His child, and forever I am!
        Thaddeus A. Fletcher

Who Am I?

Who am I, is what I'd like to know
Who am I going to meet
and where I'm going to go.
What is my destiny?
What I'm going to do? Where I am going
To be and if I'll get the flew.
Who am I is what I'd like to know!
Who I'm going to meet and where
I'm going to go.
Where will I work and
If I'll meet the one or if I'll be a jerk.
Who am I is what I'd like to know.
Who I'm going to meet
and where I'm going to go.
        Randy Beeson

I Cry

Sometimes I sit and think of you,
And I begin to cry,
I call to my Saviour, "Oh, my Lord,
Why did he have to die?"

The pain in my heart is an awful thing
I don't think it will ever go away,
There's no one to bring me the joy you did,
There's no one to take your place.

I long to hear your familiar voice,
I long to see your loving face,
There's no one to bring me the joy you did,
There's no one to take your place.

I pray one day we'll be together again,
For I love you with all my heart,
I pray to God for comfort and strength,
Until we're no longer apart.
        Shelia J. Taylor

A Cold Christmas Night

It was a very cold Christmas night,
and all the animals came out to see us freeze with delight!

Doug and I walked hand in hand,
to warm ourselves through the winter maze!

We laughed so hard to see the humming bird sing,
the snakes crawl, the dragon spit his fire,
the woodpecker peck at the trees,
bears roar, tigers run and the spider went up to the ladder to sleep.

The elephants are so gracious and grand, that we were in awe!
And to our amazement, the butterflies left their cocoon,
and came out to gaze, just to fly away to the moon.
And suddenly it seem like spring!

We saw the snowman, so happy and tall,
he led us to the iced carved deer, that would not fall.

We warmed ourselves by the marshmallow's hot fire,
feeling so sad, 'cause it was time to say goodnight
to all the animals who came out on a cold Christmas night!

Theresa D. Medici

Bedtime Thoughts

When I open my eyes, there is nothing new to see
The same four walls staring back at me
When I look in the mirror, there is no one there
My face is transparent, my soul is bare

Where am I hiding? Where can I be?
The desperate need to find myself is only killing me
Where did my innocence go? Will it ever return?
The angel that I once was has forever crashed and burned

I felt like it was stolen, when I was the one who gave it away
And from that day forward all direction went astray
How can worries of a future so bright
Make the present too unbearable, too anguished to fight?

Staring back at me is a lonely star
Who needs a new galaxy to shine her spirits on
How I long to breathe one breath free from consequence
And how I long to meet the one who of it can make any sense

Please just give me a sign that this is all worth it someday
And that I will meet my angel, my star, my innocence . . . again . . .
For the first time

Amy Elizabeth Rasch

Run-Away

To Yvette Johnson
Do you still think about the times we spent together,
When I held onto you, oh, so tightly
As you held onto me
Nothing between us but the night's cool whisper,
And it's been such a long time,
Since I looked into your blue eyes and said I love you
You know, I haven't felt that good in a while,
Let's run away, in each other's kiss
Venture off once again, to the majestic land that only exists in our dreams
Nothing or no one, will ever come between us again
Perfect, it will be; this time I promise
Because no one ever loved me like you
No one ever does things the way you do
It seems no one says words as sweetly, as you,
I've never come close to feeling this before, never loved anyone
Until you,
Even now, I know we can still make it
Because you still have, "that magic"
You might not believe it,
"But you're still the one"

Michael Escalante

Vivid Emotions

When you look into my eyes
What do you see?
Is it a beautiful rainbow,
Or a raging storm?

When you hold my hand
What do you feel?
The warmth of a sunset,
Or the sting of a thorn?

When I talk to you
What do you hear?
Words of confusion,
Or a beautiful love song?

Walk with me
And see the rainbow.
Feel the sunset
And sing my song.

Kalyna Kotenko

God's Gift

To my exceptional wife, Jennifer
As beautiful as one of God's creations,
Such as the Rose,
It doesn't hold a torch to your beauty.

Frank C. Maio

Learning to Be Alone

My nose is tight to the window;
My face is streaked with tears.
Since mommy went to the store,
It seems just years and years.

I watch and wait, and wait and watch
'Til finally I see
My mother walking up the road.
She gaily waves to me.

How glad I am she's coming back.
Of course she said she would
And told me not to be afraid,
To act like a man should.

Now that she's near, I must not cry.
I'll try to hold my own
And say to mommy when she's here,
I've learned to stay alone.

Perhaps next time she leaves the yard,
Staying by myself won't seem so hard.

Eleanor Thurston Hall

His Voice

For Mom and Mum with love
I heard a voice the other day
and knew not whence it came,
a voice as pure as driven snow,
calling out my name.

And from the depths of deep despair
and self inflicted pain,
I heard the voice call once again,
and knew from whence it came.

"Believe," it said, "in your own worth,
keep forgiveness in your heart;
let go of the past you cannot change,
and the pain will soon depart.

Give thanks for every new dawn
and for the cleansing rains;
yesterdays are gone forever,
tomorrow still remains."

Patti M. Albaugh

"Honey, I Never Done You Wrong"

To a very special friend, Brenda
On this Wednesday morning, September's Day of 1998
I parked my car in front of a gift shop in Downtown Princeton.
I got out of my car, to walk around to the front of it.
I heard a sound that got my attention.
Just in time to turn around and look up.
"While you were on my mind."
You are the only sunshine I have in my life.
Oh, how could you take that away from me?
Honey, an Angel pulled me back by my shoulders, and that was you.
A car was coming fast—a Beckley Driver, I did not see.
Oh, I would have been killed if your Angel hands had not been there for me.
So I thank God for those beautiful Angel hands of yours that saved my unhappy life.
The spirit of life was on my mind, and it said to my heart,
"You will love me again,"
and that is the reason for me to be standing here for you.
Your spirit Angel was by my side, and I thank you for that blessed day.
Baby, you are why I'm alive, and do you really care for me?
Then come back to me, because
"I have never done you wrong, Honey, Baby of Mine."

Jack Murphy

Daybreak on my Harbor

If it weren't for you I wouldn't feel this way and that you know,
When the days are long and when the days are short,
With or without you they still go;
The way you acted decides their flow.
Regardless, the way I feel for you is immense,
The love I have for you is more than intense,
So why is it that you talked me into this?
Why so soon are we parting with regret and a single kiss?

Seasons may come and seasons may go,
Being without you makes me feel nothing but sorrow.
Knowing that you are so near, that every word I speak you hear.
Why is it that love is blind?
How can it leave one so mortified?
Even though that is not the way to express the desirable pangs of passion
Yet; no matter how much you give or get, it still leads to unsatisfaction.

You are like the fruit of the beautiful Garden of Eden.
One taste of you leaves me feeling scolded and beaten.
Loving you is difficult yet surreal,
I am sorry that you will never understand how I feel.

Courtney Dyan Frail

Always Remember I Love You

As we race down the long long road of life
I will always love you my children and my darling wife
As we stroll hand in hand through the beautiful trees
Our Lord in Heaven has not given us any guarantees
There are things I have done I cannot change although I have wanted to
But please: Always remember I love you

Our life on this Earth may be short or it may be long
But while we are here we must be very, very strong
As we sit here side by side and look up into the clear blue sky
We know that someday we will be up there You and I
When my race with life on this Earth is through
Always remember I love you

When we were young sometimes time seemed to just stand still
Now we are older time passes by so swiftly against our will
If sometime in the future I should become very weak
And if I should get so ill that I cannot speak
Even though I cannot say it I hope that you will
Always remember I love you

Thomas F. Louk

Forbidden Ground

Stately, Cypress tree.
Black water, reflecting all.
Velvety, gently swaying, Spanish moss.
Raindrops fall, tapping the earth's floor.
All is lost in the surroundings.
Adding to the stillness that is.
Forbidden ground . . . swampland.

Shelby J. Lavoie

The Star

The star, the star, bearing its light,
It sits over Bethlehem,
The star, no other so bright.
It plays a role in Jesus birth,
Part of a story,
Known all over the Earth.
To the Son of God this star will lead
Staring at this wondrous sight,
The Magic of the East proceed.
Not only kings did it call,
With God's confounding grace,
It called unto all.
Come see what God has done,
To all the Earth,
He has given His only Son.
Throughout the land people saw,
This sign from God,
Leaving them in great awe.
The Star!

Lou DeStefano

The Trial of a President

How we will remember you
The trials and tribulations you had
Most of the country knew
You and your family were sad

How brave and steadfast you stood
Your duties, you carried on
Doing the very best you could
Battling impeachment to end your turn

Oh, president, our president
God knows you are flesh and blood
Our sins are God forgiven
No one on this earth is so good

Now that your hearing have ended
The senators you now face
The slander will someday be mended
Although not done in good taste.

Helene L. Thomas

My Afro-Latin Love

My Afro-Latin love
Place no one above her
My Afro-Latin love
Place no one above her
Her eyes shine like the midnight stars
Skin as soft as velvet
Arms that hold me tight at night
Makes my life worth living
Always want her close to me
Swear my life to her
Death will not take me away
Always be her lover
Always love my Afro love
Place no one above her
Place no one above her
Place no one above her

Billy Massi Slade

I Pledge to the Earth

To the Room II, Suva Elementary School
I pledge allegiance to the Earth and to keep it clean,
but if you pollute, you're really, really mean.

I pledge to make the world a cleaner place for kids like me to play.
I promise to keep the ocean clean and not pollute the bay.

I know I can and that's because I pledge to recycle,
reduce, and reuse every single day.
　　　Christopher D. Eastridge

The Enemy Within

It moves silently like a cat stalking its prey, leaving the victim
oblivious to the beast about to attack. You can't see it, there are no
visible signs, but it's there lurking waiting to ravage your body,
hopefully leaving your soul intact. Next comes a feeling of helplessness as
you sit and watch as your best friend, once vibrant and full of life, falls
apart before your eyes. Sitting, listening, offering support anyway you
can, praying every day that you won't have to say goodbye. Life was so rich
and full, we had it all. Everything was falling into place for her and me;
nothing to worry about; our lives were carefree. One moment, one call that
changes it all, and leaves you asking, why me? It changes your life, your
thoughts and your views, you suddenly realize how much you have to lose.
The little things that were once taken for granted, sunrises, sunsets, in
your memory are implanted. You muddle through one day at a time. Learning
as you go, not knowing what's in store for tomorrow, looking for good times
not dwelling on sorrow. It has always been just her and me, preparing
ourselves for all that would be. We have laughed through the good times,
and cried through the sad, always remembering the fun that we had. The
tides are turning and it sometimes looks grim, but my mother, my friend, I
know we can win. Together we will fight the enemy within!
　　　Jo Ann Kryzyzek

Image of an Outlaw:　The Revelation

Bald bold beautiful
Sensual seductive smooth
Image of an Outlaw (the Countess of Plano's Outlaw)
His flame lights her heart and fires her soul,
The missing piece of her puzzle, the half that made her whole.
He is her world her everything her king
His melodious voice and caressing words hold her close, his laugh his touch
His smile, the balms that soothe her soul, her Outlaw in shining armor
Her charming prince her soulmate
Image of an Outlaw
Her angel in disguise, he's most generous passionate kind
His hypnotic eyes sparkle with his undying love
He is her present, her future, the keeper of her heart
He is the man she wants to grow old with
The man with whom she wants to breathe her last breath,
He is the love of her life the heart of her heart her destiny,
He is the Image of an Outlaw, her Outlaw
Now . . . Tomorrow . . . Forever.
　　　ChaKira N. Bell

Not Meant to Be . . .

Can one explain how we have met, the path that led to where we are,
I only know this chance we took each day endears me to your heart.

You, whom I've grown so much to love, are my hope to ever remain with me.
As time grows short for us each day, this love that beckons me,
only deepens and refuses all thought of ceasing.

If only our lives may go on awhile,
so we may one day, one time in this life continue to feel, to touch, to love,
if only as friends, could there finally be a time for us?
The future, so clouded and uncertain still can ensure us a small part
of the love we share in glances, kind words, and touching gestures,
the warmth of passion truly can take us to the height of our love,
maybe never meant to be, but so sure and true to be lasting.

For we have loved and have known it, my heart is your home, my darling,
live there with me, if only in our dreams.
　　　Toni Strzempa

A Bow Hunter's Vow

Here I sit
and I've thought,
the wind I've fought.
I flung an arrow
but yet in vain,
then tonight it started to rain.
The next time I go,
hand on my bow,
that little deer will be no mo'!
　　　Randy Jack Brock

The People of Africa

The people of Africa
The people of the rain
The people of the mountains
The people of the plains.

The people of the meadows
The people of the farms
The people of the animals
The people of the barns.

The people of this country
The people of this land
The people of our culture
The people of the American Clan.

The people of this poem
The people of the day
The people in this world
The people, who pass our way.
　　　Ericka R. Cook

Insight

Looking at you in the day
Offers me no real insight.
Everything is as it should be.
The shades are drawn,
But at night,
When the sun is asleep,
And there is no fear of exposure,
You are revealed.
The light deep within you
Illuminating the things not naturally seen.
Now, there is movement, color, texture.
I want to put my hands on every pattern,
Remembering the way they feel,
The way they smell.
Painting pictures in my mind
That I can take with me during the day,
When the shades are drawn
And everything is as it should be.
　　　Jody Martin

To Say

We are caught up in the everyday,
　　and forget to say
　　　I love you
　　to those most cherished in our hearts.

We are busy at work, at play
　　and forget to say
　　　I am sorry
　　to those we may have hurt.

We are prideful in our ways
　　and forget to say
　　　Lord, forgive me
　　for the wrongs I have done.

It is a brand new day,
　　take the time to say . . .
　　　Dina M. Papas McLean

Life

Life is full of surprises, you never know what'll happen next.
Maybe an elderly woman will be in trouble,
Or the hungry will need more food and help from the more fortunate
Maybe a loved one gets hurt by their loved ones.
Or your friend is a little too lonely for you to leave alone.
Whatever it is, you should help them people,
because you'll really be helping yourself.

Maybe a jock will lose his athletic skills,
Or your best friend gets hurt by the boy she really loved.
You never know who will need your help in a time of need.
So even if you don't like the person, because of skin color or religion
Never judge a book by its cover; reach what's inside and really discover
What that person is really, about.
So don't run away from your problems, face them like you're mature
Be a nice, caring person all of the time,
instead of only when you want something.
Look at life as a treasure and cherish it like a precious jewel.

April Fillinger

My Noah's Ark

For my two beautiful daughters
Lions, giraffes, elephants, monkeys, and bears,
They travel the hallways here, holding hands in pairs.

Hands that are busy, fingers sticky with glue,
Pictures all painted in every bright hue.

The love and the caring on my teacher's face,
I can't think of anywhere I'd rather be than here at this place.

Someday when I'm grown and out there in the world on my own,
I'll look back on the things you have taught me and the love you've shown.

I'll be a better person because of time I spent here,
My Noah's Ark that I'll hold so dear.

Sherry Tellitocci

You Are—My Mother

When I get lonely—I think of you and I'm no longer, 'cause I
know how much you care for me.
When I get sad, I think of you and I'm no longer, 'cause I
know how much I care for you.
When I'm happy, I'm thinking of you, and I'm content, 'cause
you are what I live for.
You are the reason I live, breathe, eat, and drink.
You are the reason I love, care, cherish, and think.
Because you—are my Mother.

I may not be able to see you, but I know that you're there, you're here.
I know that you see me, and when I speak to you, I know that you hear me.
Because you—are my Mother.

I may not be able to touch you, but I can feel your touch.
When I'm sad, lonely or happy, I know that you touch me 'cause I'm uplifted.
My face lights up and your touch brings a smile to my face.
Because you are My Mother!

Joey F. McKee

Untitled

You are the grass tickling me until I laugh
You are like a star looking over me
You are the wind trying to comfort me when I am alone
You are like a tree stretching your arms to shade me from the sun

When you cry, your tears are the rain
When you smile, you are like the sun spreading your joy
When you are tired, you are the darkness letting the world sleep
When you are mad, your voice is the thunder of a storm

You are gone but have come back like the sun
You have left but always come back like birds flying south for winter
You are still here being spread across the earth like flowers in a field
You look over me like a bird watching over its eggs

Alicia Sloma

Suicide

To my good friend Sal Salvadore
My mind aches with the confusion
And the frustration I try to stall
Pent-up anger begins to surface
As hidden tears start to fall

Whatever could possibly go wrong,
has the reassurance I need cannot be found
Continual betrayal of my trust
Even my body is breaking down

Maybe I'm overreacting
As my life again takes a dive
Seeking freedom from the pressure
Wanting no longer to be alive

I kick around the pieces of my life
Found crumpled at my feet
I throw my hands up in surrender
Agonizing my defeat

The gun in my uplifted hand
Is the ticket to set me free
The last prayer ever to leave my lips
Is, "God please forgive me!"

Randy Gayle Hartford

Free Spirit

When my life is over and
God comes to take me home,
He will set my spirit free,
So that it may roam.

Let it soar with eagles,
Watch a sunset on the plains.
Let it play among the children
And frolic in the rain.

God, please don't try to tame it.
Let it go wild and free.
It's the best one that you made,
And you gave it to me.

Ruby Allen

Untitled

Light is the answer to love and compassion
Light eliminates evil.
Light and there is reverence.
Reverence and there is love.
Love and you have everything.
Your heart needs to guide you
And live a life of a multisensory person.
A spiritual being, a reverent being
A being of love and compassion
And insight in tune with the earth's
Natural laws, one in spirit and wholeness.

Nicole Cheek

Good Friday

To my sister, Sandy
As I picture Christ
Upon the cross,
In agony, suffering for all sinners lost,
It causes my eyes to fill with tears,
I weep today, as I have through the years.
Ah! But then! Easter Sunday
I do not mourn for very long,
For in my heart is a joyous song,
Christ conquered death
and lives today,
We will too, if we live his way.

Theresa Stone

When I Walk the Beach at Night . . .

You are all I see when I walk the beach at night.
You beckon me from the ocean,
but no one else can see.
I step closer to the black waves and
feel the cool water crash at my feet.
No one sees you but me.
I come closer and feel the sea soak my white dress
until it clings against my body.
No one sees you but me.
Further and further out I swim
until there is no earth beneath my feet.
You're so close now.
I reach for your outstretched hand
but only water slips through my fingers.
You looked so real this time.
Only blackness I see everywhere I look . . . as if my eyes are closed.
I search the dark on the edge of madness,
not for sand or shore . . .
but for the love I came so close to having . . .
and no one could see it but me.

Lori A. Casebolt

I Once Was a King

I once was a king, I say that indeed,
Just give me five to ten minutes to rest my head
Then come illusions of me living lavish
Away from this world of grief, I live it well
Come inside and you can tell, with famous portraits
Up on my wall and 30 maids to clean the clientele,
Every day friends come over we laugh and chat,
Every day I see different faces, now that's funny,
When I was stranded and alone life wasn't like that,
They don't like mustard, they like Grey Poupon,
Just regular wine couldn't satisfy them, they want Dom Perignon,
I've got exactly 25 driveways with some of the finest cars parked in them,
I put up a humongous golden gate, to keep them safe
because often viewers would stop and stare,
Taking care of my family and at last all the bills are paid,
I finally found something I like, something I wouldn't dare to trade.
Now I'm set, just hand me my crown, dress suit, and nice golden rod,
Over there, hand me that Bible I'm going to church,
No matter how much I get up in life,
I'll never forget about God.

Jerry L. Fisher

No Time

To Brigitte, I've always loved you!
I had my daughter, when I was 16,
I fed, bathed, and watched her,
but I didn't have time for that!

She was one and started to walk, instead of praise
I said, it's about time, you see, I didn't have time for that!

She was talking oh, so very well, instead of listening,
I shut her out, you see, I didn't have time for that,
oh, the questions, the questions,
I gave short answers because I didn't have time for that!

She started pre-school, oh, happy days,
she graduated kindergarten or was it 8th grade?
All of a sudden it was high school, you see, I didn't have time for that!

She asked about boys, asked about love, she asked about becoming a woman,
again short answers. I just didn't have the time for that!

Now she's a woman, more woman than I, no thanks to me, for I had no time,
I missed those years of seeing her grow, I miss those years of hearing her voice,
I missed her then as I am missing her now . . .
'Cause now you see, I have nothing but time.

Victoria D. O'Neal

The Boy on the Neighbor's Roof

"I just want to look at the sky!"
The little boy ran and cried,
Climbing down from neighbor's roof
With people's blame and yells, ran after.

"I just want to look at the sky,
Like the moon seeks the twilight!"
The boy runs and cries.

Gueyer J. Roe

Faith Prevails

When I sit and reminisce
Of sad days and those of happiness,
Life seems like a blooming flower,
Here today but gone tomorrow.
Life's bumpy road is never straight;
We err on turns and make mistakes.
'Tis said, "We are here to be tried."
Misfortune can make a strong man cry.
Tears like rain in life will fall
When sadness strikes like a cannon ball,
Then faith will reign to give courage;
Renewed hopes are given nourish.
The aching heart finds solace in prayer;
God is our salvation—he's everywhere.

Irene Vandemark

Hockey

The boards crackle after the hit;
there is never any time to sit.
Hockey is the game,
and it's not lame.

The shots are too fast!
A lot go past.
The goalies are huge!
I'd rather ride the luge.

But no, this game is great,
so I'll still skate.
I hope I don't end up in the box;
my team's fast as a fox.

The buzzer sounds,
and the huge crowd pounds.

Matthew David

Enya

light headed
the music fills me
swelling into my soul
I eat it and feel full
my arms raise to the beat
freedom

Kate Rooney

I Miss You

I miss you. You say everything is fine,
But I can see some things that are wrong.
It hurts so bad to wait.
Especially when I have to wait so long.

I wait for your return,
But that could be years.
Until I see you again,
There will always be tears.

Wondering if you care about me,
The way I care about you.
I will love you forever.
I hope you love me too.

Danielle Dodson

The President

To me Bill Clinton is a great man
He does things for people no one can
He made a mistake in his life
No one should really care except his wife
He is smart, handsome, and tough too
That he tells the people what to do
No one is perfect in this world today
Maybe someday love, happiness are here to stay
The people don't care what he's done
He is a man of spirit and he's all alone
He's trying to pass new ideas for me and you
If Congress passes them it will be all true
Men, women, children love him as well
But what the White House does it's hard to tell
I like him and honor him in any way
The sex scandal will go, come what may
His family loves him very much
Because Mr. Clinton has that magic touch
God bless him and his family, to that everyone looking says it's true
That Hillary and Bill honest in every way

Don Moriconi

Remembering You . . .

I saw you again after all these years,
and it pained me to see
how much you had changed,
and how much you have remained the same . . .
It brought back
so many painful memories . . .
Memories that I had thought
I had long since locked inside.
I reminded me of what once was . . .
Of the love we had made so long ago.
Reminding me of the most
wonderful period of time in my life . . .
I remember your smile, and that devotion in your eyes
when you looked into mine,
and I remember how much we meant to each other . . .
It seemed like an eternity had gone by, but seeing your handsome face
made all the memories come flooding back . . .
And I remembered you again as if we had parted yesterday,
causing my heart to ache, to bleed,
and shatter in a million pieces . . . all over again . . .

Marianne Stanford

Family's the Reason

To my loving Sister Angie and my darling brother Billy
You never think about how you would feel.
If your parents would die and leave you alone here.
There's only three children from this family of five.
Angie, Tammy, and Billy are still left alive.
You get so lonely for a hug from your mom and dad.
Feeling safe and secure from their love if you are sad.
Asking them questions for their wisdom and grace.
Having their hands wipe tears from your face.
Finding solutions for problems when you think there is none.
Spending quality time with them making memories and sharing love.
It's the simple things in life that we all take with a grain of salt.
Like the love from our parents when it suddenly stops with a halt.
Look at life with your family as the last of their days.
Show them respect and love and pray that God allows them to stay.
Remember everything about your family that you cherish so much.
The love, the words, their face, their touch.
Most of all, remember the parts that made you happy and smile.
Because your family's the reason that makes life worthwhile.

Tammy Jo Hobbs

I Am Dead

To Debra, my murderess
Because I don't have her.

Because I can't tell her.

Because I am afraid.

Because I love her.

Because my soul cries.

Because I am dead.

Michael Ortega

Love

I once loved someone,
But I could never tell him.
But I know I loved him,
And even if I could not tell him,
I knew he would never love me.
So I had to give it up.
I knew if I did not make
My feelings for him go away,
It would ruin my life
Just thinking about him all the time,
When he would never love me
The way I love him.
But now I love him no more.
But I loved someone once.
Love is sad and unpredictable.
It was hard being his friend,
And not able to tell him
I love him.

Shannon Winters

Untitled

In the race of love
A young man loses
His heart to a pretty face

Sgt. Ian Bonnell
USMC

Judgments

If some would assume
What lies in a heart
Never to question
Seek truth from the start
They don't truly care
They don't want to know
Perhaps then they don't
Deserve to be shown.

Angela Parks

Take Control

You looked in my eyes,
I seen your pain,
I wondered why,
You let him in.

He broke your heart,
He hit your face,
He made you cry,
He's in your mind.

You can't let go,
He's in control.
Your life is his,
He own's your soul.

Stand up, and be strong,
You got to hold on,
Don't let him in,
Stop the abuse within.

Ruby Calandrelli

Innocent

For my friend and mentor, Carel

I stand accused of being amused about some of the darnedest matters;
Including, I think, a certain man's chatter of trivial detail including the latter's
Affirmative vow, "I am innocent, dear! You're starting to doubt? You don't trust me, I fear!"
An innocent pretense of virginal white, of an unsullied past as pure as the night!
He wasn't born just yesterday but still maintains in his virtuous way,
Experience he's tasted very little it seems, a definite lapse in his memory of dreams.
Life he's tasted in numerous ways, denies himself as he glides through the days,
And still he affirms he's untouched and chaste; when it comes to intent, no words does he waste!
To maintain his image of fresh driven snow, pure and unblemished all 'round he does go!
You're a natural born flirt and an accomplished tease, as you vie for "your" time with affectionate ease,
You toss caution aside as you search for a way to leave your impressions as you have your say!
And "left-handed" praise you're apt to dish out and deny even knowing what this is about;
But I'm not so sure of your innocent claim; could just be a way to nurture your fame.
"I am so innocent!" You cry with a laugh, while I stammer and stutter and stand the gaff!
You will back off and search for a way to be serious, while I'm left pondering 'bout the words mysterious
You use to covey your "over-used" innocence, proclaimed with a vengeance and lily-white pretense!
You protest over much about your innocent being, leaving me amazed and I find me agreeing;
In order to pamper and tend to your ego as every good woman will have to forego!
She will encourage and conform with obvious delight; only one thing she argues with all of her might;
"You're not an innocent, as you would believe! You've allowed me to know you and you cannot deceive!"

Joyce L. Ryan

The Word

For my wife, Crystal Harrison

Once upon a time there was a bird, a bird that sang a song.
The song was heard for miles around; the melody was soft and the Word was meaningful, soft, and warm.
Have you heard the song? The song that the bird sang?
You should listen to the wind, the wind carried the song that the bird sang; have you seen the wind?
Oh, my! Where have you been? For the wind is everywhere.
Every breath you take you can feel the sadness.
The last time I took a breath, I felt sadness, as I watched a flock of birds fly over.
One of them was hit by a pebble in the sky and I felt the sadness as he fell to the ground.
Did you hear the song the bird sang? Take a breath and come alive, take a breath, take a breath, take a breath.
For the song that the bird sang is in the wind.
The wind is like the Spirit, and the Spirit is within. It is within you and I,
without the wind there wouldn't be the spirit, without the spirit there would not be.
Oh! Oh! Oh! Have you seen the bird that sang the Word? For the Word was in the wind.
You know the wind that was like Spirit that carried the Word into our hearts.
Oh, yes, now I have your attention. Have you seen the wind, the wind that blew the Word that the bird sang?
If it was not for the bird, where would you and I be?
You do remember the Birds and the Bees, don't you?
You remember that dude they called Adam and that chick they called Eve, don't you?
Oh, my! Have you seen the bird that sang The Word?

Rudolph Harrison

"The Emptiness There"

I looked inside my window deep, to life farewell, I beckon to sleep. I had peered into my window deep,
my soul was longing for one to keep, the emptiness was there. "Indeed," I cried, "my window is deep."
The void sneered back, "Your sorrow keep!" No hope was there to stay my grief, my hand I raised to strike my sleep.
I cried aloud, "My world is bleak." My tears flowed out an endless streak. Your face was hid, your voice I heard,
I turned to look, "Who watches my words?" I looked inside my window deep, the emptiness there mocked my grief.
"Again, I say the sorrow keep," the blackness scorned from inside the deep.
Your light appeared tiny and weak, I peered inside my window deep. "Your love is here, your heart I'll keep.
Please, stay thy hand from endless sleep." My shock was great, your voice was heard,
with the peace and softness of a tiny bird. The darkness was enraged at your intrusion, "Harken to me!
She is an illusion." The void held tight in endless cessation, my heart was filled with love's anticipation.
"Behold my light." I heard you say, "My love is great and here you will stay. I'll hold your heart at treasure's lust,
to know my love, this is a must. Trust me, my love, I will be yours and no longer will you hear those awful words."
My tears were gone, my blood flowed hot, the emptiness was there, and I was not.
I looked inside my window shallow, to gloat and say, "You are so hollow, no longer will you hurt my pride,
and with love you will subside." I reached to take your hand so gave, and touched the dirt upon my grave.
"Where is my love? This cannot be." The emptiness was there and now you will see.
I looked into my window deep, the blackness there my soul doth keep.
The void laughed, cried out and said, "You are a fool and I did warn and here you'll stay for me to scorn.
Look here and see you are a fool, your soul lies here in a darkened pool, your love's betrayal was far more cruel.
I sought to take your life and grief, your love gave me your soul to keep. "If you look inside my window deep,
take care my love that I don't speak. Alone I dwell, I know not where, I live inside the emptiness there."

George Krause

Contemplation

I contemplate about love
The love I could give you
The love I want and
The love I need
All I want is to be needed
And all I need is to be loved.

I contemplate about you
The person I want you to be
The person that you are and
The person that you were.
All you are is what I need and
All you were is what I love.

I contemplate about me
The Me that I gave you
The Me that you wanted and
The Me that you said you loved
All I am is what you needed
And all I was, you didn't love . . .

Yvette Chavez

God Thank You for My Friends

The dark clouds rest on the mountains
as the city lights fade away.
It is late at night now
But I still have thoughts from today.

Of being together with all of my friends
and laughing at even the slightest thing.
Oh, but what beautiful memories
Even those tiniest moments can bring.

We all see each other every day.
But each day seems more worth living.
I guess because my wonderful friends
Believe not in taking but giving.

It is time to put my thoughts to rest
as another long day soon ends.
Before I go to sleep I pray . . .
God, thank you for my friends.

Pamela Kuclnski

The Two of Us

The two of us is just you and I
With our hearts we can combine
Combine a love between you and I,
A love that cannot be described
With our hearts we can get through,
Get through all the bad and good
As long as there's just the two of us,
Our love will never turn to dust.

Christina Bailum

to fly

lost . . .
hurt, scared, broken wings
so much pain
wanting to die
longing to fly
not knowing how

lost my way
needing to heal
forgot how to feel
forgot so many things

need . . .
a place to feel
to find my way
to learn so many things
but most of all
to learn how to fly

nina kendrick

Out of the Nest

Little one on a limb
Hanging on for life
Waiting for his mother's call
Breakfast is in sight.

Little one on a limb
Hanging on for life,
Danger lurks beneath you know
In the shadow of the night

Little one on a limb
Hanging on for life
Soon you will be soaring
And be gone out of my sight.

Little one on a limb
never falter, never fear
Spread your wings for flying
God, your Heavenly Father is near

Little one on a limb
Trust in Him today
Let him guide your life
Each step of your way.

Claudette Elam

Life's Interdependency

We are no more than "a"
grain of sand on a beach; but,
we must know that it takes
"a" grain of sand to make up
a Beach!
We are nothing without a
"Higher Power."

Jeanette A. Martin

Our Being

The most precious thing
The Lord blessed us with
Is the breath we breathe
And our children's first kiss

The "special" inner part
That keeps us alive
Is our heart that beats
Which we need to survive

The most deepest love
The Lord provides
Is our significant other
As our souls unite.

The most strongest thing
Our souls can find
Is our strength as a being
And the power of our mind

But, the one thing
We can't see with our eyes
Is our Creator and our faith inside
"Our Being"

Marcella Heinrich

Winter Dance

For Virginia
Beneath a perfumed silver sky
Through groves where starlit shadows lie
In dreams I've dreamt that do not fade
I watched her dancing through a glade
Bright blossoms grow where she had stepped
Fond memories the earth has kept
Despite the frost and winter's chill
The flowers dance there with her still

Robert Fralick

A Holiday Poem

Hot chocolate
On an open fire

Love that warm taste
In a cabin

During cold nights
At the mountains

Yelling happiness to everyone
Saying it is Christmas.

Christopher English

A Father's Hug

A father's hug
Lights the spark
In the forest
Of the heart.

It starts a fire
Where there was death,
And plants a desire
For the best.

It takes the mire
And all the mess
And wipes them clean
And then brings rest.

A father's hug
Brings many healings.
It takes the numb
And brings bright feelings.

So take these hugs
From your father's heart,
And let them heal
Your every part.

Nathan D. Duty

Snow

When winter comes the snow begins to fall
Although the flakes are small
We will have a ball,

There will be no school today
I can ride my sleigh!
Soon the plow will be on its way

We will have a snowball fight,
And make a fort before the night,
Packing all the snow real tight.

When it's time to go inside at night
The snow is really bright
When I am cozy in my bed
My dad will be outside shoveling instead.

Erik Bliss

The Brook's No Longer Merry

The brook's no longer merry
Where we used to run and play.
I have no urge to tarry
Beside the shrunken clay.

This sluggish little stream
Bears oil and waste away.
The happy subject of a dream
Now chokes on factory pay.

No yen have I to linger
At this product of the years.
The brook hears not one singer,
And I'm alone with tears.

David L. Mellett

Jesus Is My Brother

For Michael and Christiana MacDonald

Jesus is my brother,
He is your brother too.
Believe in him.
He'll show you it's true.

Then he'll be by your side,
As you walk down life's path.
He'll protect you from Satan
And his horrible wrath.

Then he'll lead you to Heaven,
To be with our Lord,
Where you'll have a beautiful life,
And you'll receive your reward.

So ask Jesus into your life,
Before it's too late,
And have everlasting life,
Instead of a fiery fate.

Tammy Boyland

Time

For my family and my friends

Time, time, time,
How precious the word
Eternally ours
What evolves from our existence
We cannot deny
We cannot lose foresight
Of time past, lost
We can only reflect
Now, it is precious
The very minute, or second,
Must count
In our deeds
In our consciousness
In our now, in our being
This time is precious
Let's not lose anymore, time
Time is love
Time is relationships
Time is family
Time is love

Teri Lamberth

Gymnastics

Flexible little girls and boys,
All reaching their goals before their eyes,
Touching and pointing their little toes,
Hoping not to break their nose,
Again and again they've got to go,
Wondering if they'll be Olympians, or,
No?

Kasey Stamper

Whispers

I hear you whisper
But I cannot see you
I know you're there
Now I see the glow
Are you my angel
I feel the wind from your wing
I still hear you whispering
Speak to me
I will whisper back
You are my angel
I waited for
Now I can whisper to you
Thank you for being here for me

Donna Blowers

Suicide Pollution

I feel that suicide
is never the solution.
Thinking of killing one's self
is nothing but mind pollution.
You might think your life is bad,
and that suicide is the way.
In my opinion you would be wrong,
and that's just what I would say.
It could be as simple
as a slice of the wrist;
or a jump from a building,
just because you're really pissed.
You can pull out a gun
and put it to your head;
then pull the trigger,
because you wish to be dead.
You should never think of suicide,
'cause there are people who care.
You just have to ask around,
and you'll find out that they are there.

Francis J. Maher

Life

My life is like a never-ending ditch
I try to pull myself out, but I slip
I had never thought I could fall so long
Then suddenly I land on a hard surface
I run and run, but I end up nowhere
Then suddenly everything gets dark
I ask myself is this death?
Is this what death is like?
Then I open my eyes and find out
I am where I want to be

Jennifer Schillinger

Water

The sun rises
steadily revealing the Eagle's flight,
light on the air and soaring,
wind, uplifting spirit clouds
drifting fog receding from around
the bleeding hills of morning.
Water flows freely from the ground
downhill all the way
headwaters encourage the growth of a river
on the shore of valleys descending,
ending abruptly in a pool, controlled.

J. C. Dyer

Blue

With love to my family

Blue is the color of heartbreak and fears,
It feels like the ocean,
It tastes like tears,
It sounds like Louie Armstrong
describing the sky,
It's a slamming door,
an exasperated sigh,
Blue is the color of denim jeans,
and of the Caribbean sea water
of mid summer scenes,
It's a comfortable nap
on satin sheets,
It's a fast Camaro
with bucket seats,
It's the woeful wailing
of a baby's cries,
It's the dazzling sparkle
of Frank Sinatra's eyes,
Though I'll never know if this is true,
Sight is not needed to really see blue.

Maria Calderon

The Lost Ones

For Stephen Roberto Jr., my love

Our hearts were broken
when we lost three
of our dear and loving friends,
and even though they are gone forever,
our love for them never ends.
Sometimes at night,
I will dream about their
afterlife in Heaven with Him.
Then I'll awake and realize
that the ones truly lost
are us,
and not them.

Stephanie Michelle Parks

Pressure

The pressure was ever mounting
Towards that fatal throw.
His hands were numb with sweat,
And the weight began to grow.
His legs felt no support
As he took a look around.
"What if," was the thought
The hesitant competitor found.
He raised the leather ball
Above his shaking head.
The weight was so tremendous
He felt like he was dead.
He cocked with great precision,
And took his daring aim.
He flipped it off his fingers,
And it bounded like a flame.
His heart began to rise
Like a California sun.

Tom Hicks

A Penguin's Day

Penguins, penguins, wobble wobble penguins.
They run, they jump, they swim and play,
They're having fun that cold—cold, wet day.

Tim Kernell

Untitled

When will this dream come to an end
Every night when I die, life comes
And I am there again
With the morning I wake
And the dream cycles again
Full of orange and grey
Surely such misery can't be reality
So I live in the waking dream
And dream in the subconscious reality

James Purcell

Fog

There's been a subtraction of color
For mist has enveloped the land.
All shades of grey have taken over
The seasons are not in command.

There's been a loss now of outline
And distance is nothing but blur.
Trees are but shadows of dark form
And my memory needs a good stir.

There's been an addition of quiet
My mind has captured its song.
All sounds of streets are lost now
This landscape is just newly born.

Alice D. Mertz

Stars

We revolve in circular motions
With the moon controlling our oceans
Yet never shall we touch afar
Those brightly shining colored stars
They fill us with joy and wonder
Never shall we blunder
To think they're actually in reach
Is foolish enough to teach
One to try the impossible
Though it's not plausible
To reach within and seek out answers
Or go out on a limb.

Melissa Foley

A Moment to Cherish

That one moment
It was slow motion
Meeting for the first time
It was magic
My love . . .

That day . . .
Like a written book from Heaven
It happened just then
Our love . . .

We became one
My world had just begun
Cherish the moment
Making a memory

Re-living that one second
Secluded to the world
A paradise . . . my love . . .

Day after day
Watching you loving me
Held within my heart
That first day you came my way

Danielle Green

Jesus Is So Real!

Just open your heart,
and your eyes will see
what God has in store
for them who believe.

By growing and trusting
in God's perfect ways,
mighty miracles he will show you
on those cloudy days.

Great peace and joy
only you would know
as he holds you in his arms;
the devil has to go.

Marion Morrison

Weary Friend

Go ye not, into the night,
Else you will see a horrid sight.

Save thy soul pass you by,
Wonder not of what's inside.

Pass you by this silent tomb,
Or else thy soul will be consumed.

Save thy soul to you I plea,
Pass this place, I beg of thee.

So my friend I say to thee.
Leave this tomb, do not join me.

Bil Hough

Valentine

I would like you to be my Valentine,
I really wish you were mine.
Could you give me a sign,
If you would be mine.
You are just like wine,
You are so very fine
We could go out and dine,
Tonight at nine?

Summer Ann Clayton

Eye of the Beholder

He is an ancient wanderer
Graced with knowledge untold
A mystic journey man
All life before him unfolds

From the beginning of time
He has been made to roam
Watching over this land
With no place to call home

Is it a gift of God
Or some evil curse
To live forever
Made to roam the earth

Look into the eye of the beholder
For the truth of mankind
Every day he shall grow older
And we shall not be far behind.

Timothy David Knight

Just One

If flowers could make wishes
Somehow come true
I'd pick many special bouquets
and send them to you
I would arrange them in many colors
Unique shapes and different smiles
Knowing that over time
They would bring you many smiles
I would include flowers of different blooms
To represents the many reasons
Why true love must be complex
In order to endure the different seasons
and at the center of each bouquet
I would include a very special treat
For there you would find white rose
To make each bouquet complete
Yes, if flowers could somehow grant wishes
How beautiful life would be
Especially, if just may be
One of your wishes was for me

Billy Delgado

Daddy's Love

To Janine, Rob, Mom, and Dad
Waking from a dream
He cries out in the night
Nobody's there to comfort him
He has to live with his fright.

Two years to the day
He sees her lovely smile
Then the memory shifts
All he remembers is the trial

Daddy loved him, or so he said
Hit him often to teach him the way
Mommy loved him, knows it's true
Stopped Daddy's hand two years to the day.

Katie Edwards

Twist

Twist in a bowl of cream,
Twist in the current of a stream,
Twist in an author's voice,
Twist in making the right choice,
Twist in your family's love,
Twist inside nature from above.
If you want to find a Twist
Look around you, there is no mist.

Joelle Te Paske

To Be a Child

Do you know what it's like
To fall into a chair
And with great excitement
Lift into the air?

Have you ever sung
A song that the birds
Envied because
They could not learn the words?

When you relate to your teddy bear
'Bout being happy or blue
When you're done, does he stand up
And talk to you too?

If your answer is yes!
Then you truly are living
But if it's vice versa
Then the gift I am giving

To you is the beauty
That can only be said
In the images found
In a small child's head!

Ariana Lenarsky

See Your Dream

To my children
See your dream
Live it
Go for it
Let go
What you can't see
For you need
It not.

Joyce Crouch

As Restful As It Gets

For my darling man, Lucian Minnick Jr.
Beside the fence
Under the tree
The place where
A country boy should be
Watching sunrise and sunsets
This is as restful as it gets.
Under a warm blanket of snow
Or feeling cool breezes blow
No more problems, no more pain
Now, I feel the gentle rain
My loved ones will miss me
And they will weep
While I am here in peaceful sleep
This is a restful as it gets.
You can see me when you find my star
There I'll look down on you from afar
I'll be your warmth in the summer sun
And watch as you sleep when day is done
This is as restful as it gets
Beside the fence, under the tree.

Delores R. Dyer-Minnick

Somebody Is Everybody

Somebody is everybody 'cause
everybody is nobody
without being somebody.

Everybody is somebody
'cause nobody is somebody
without anybody.

1st there is somebody
2nd there is everybody
3rd there is nobody

Somebody is everybody always

Kea M. Jones

The Friend I Never Had

You're the friend I never had,
The one I've never known.
We've never spoken one word,
Nor shook one hand.
Because you've been so deep,
So deep in my heart,
So now I see the friend I never had was, ME!

Mallory Williams

If I Gave You . . .

If I gave you
A gift of love
I'd give you
My heart
With love in it.
If I gave you
A gift of love
I'd give you
A world
Filled with flowers
And peace.
If I gave you
A gift of love
I'd give you
A box of chocolates
With roses and red hearts
That would fill you up
With joy and happiness.

Amanda D. Ortega

If a Smile Comes Your Way

*For Pastor Gutterridge
and the Single Truth Group*
If a smile comes your way today,
A smile that you cannot explain.
I was thinking of you and smiling too.

Johnny Randell

Tears

I lie here thinking about you,
As the warm, salty tears
Flow down my cheek.

As I slowly fall asleep,
I drown in the sea of darkness.

In my dreams, I'm drowning in the sea.
No one is there to rescue me.

What is going on?
My life is a total mess and now
My dreams turned into nightmares.

Natalia Young

Promise

For Viki Bradford, my forgotten love
In a world of broken dreams,
With shattered lives split at the seams,
Soon the darkness turns to day,
Then the predators become the prey.

Ryan Babcock

Jasper

Why does it have to be you Jasper, why,
You went away unexpectedly never to return.

Jasper
You went away without me
You were suppose to stay with me
You and me were meant to be

We were meant to be together
Never to part
We need to be together
But I cannot make that choice

I want love to lead you back
When you get your wings
Come back to see me,
My love
My Jasper.

Leia Chapas

The Loyal Heart

Look not at race
Nor color of skin,
But look for the heart
That is loyal within.
We all get sick
And we all grow old,
But the heart that is loyal
Will never grow old.

Cynthia Stettinger

Waiting

To Brian, my inspiration
Waiting . . .
He walk in
Gazing . . .
Our eyes meet
Intensity . . .
Hearts beating
Words . . .
Softly spoken
Goodbye . . .
Waiting again

Leigh Ann Mullins

Untitled

Entwined,
In a lovers' embrace
We dance,
Love finds a way
Although the human heart
Breaks again and again.
The human spirit.
Shines in the night,
We dance,
We dance for eternity,
The human soul is immortal
Until the infinite,
To eternity does transcend.

Henry C. Lyko

Someday Love

Someday love
We will meet a long the beach
And fall in love

Someday love
We can watch our children, grow
and hear their laughter down the hall.

Someday love,
We can watch our children have
a family of their own.

Someday love,
we can grow old together
and reminisce about our
good times together

Until then love
I will always keep you
in my dreams

Theresa Pauley

Let Me Be

High in the sky
Don't ask me why
I feel free
So let me be

High in the sky
I knew I could fly
Spreading my wings
Hear me sing

I'll swoop down
Close to the ground
I feel free
So let me be.

Beverly L. Berger

Remember

Remember me when I am gone away,
Gone far away into the silent land,
When you can no more hold me by hand,
Nor I half turn to go, yet turning stay.
Remember me when no more, day by day,
You tell me of our future that you planned,
Only remember me, you understand
It will be late to counsel then or pray
Yet if you should forget me for a while,
And afterwards remember, do not grieve,
For if the darkness and corruption leave,
A vestige of the thoughts that once I had,
Better by far you should forget and smile
Than you should remember and be sad.

Carmen Garcia Lazarte

Sometimes

Across the fields of yesterday,
It oftentimes comes to me,
The good times that we shared as friends,
When we were young and free

Years may come, and years may go,
The friendship's there to stay,
The dearest friends I ever knew,
Were friends of yesterday.

Sometimes, we wander far apart
But memories linger, in the heart,
And to make country ways more fair
Laughter and love was always there
God grant me healthy days to stay
in loving memory of yesterday!

Laura Sue Herrington

Love

If love were a rose bud
all sparkled with dew,
I would have picked it
my darling and sent it to you,
But love is so tender
and sweet to depart,
so all I can give you
is the love of my heart.

Elizabeth Beharry

Expired Grace

Time again repeatedly
Forgive but now forget
The breath of destruction
The tears a flood
A mothers work or a sign of yet
Darkness reaps evil where root rules
It's the coming before being called
Hell perhaps a trial
Or havens of heavenly living
Left to right then closed tight
Interlocking extremities day and night
So many ways but never the path
An expired grace period
Where good is bad

Angela Wilson

Shattered

Crawling inside myself
To outsmart the pain
Balled up in the darkness
Shhh. . . .
Don't even breathe
The spell will be broken
A magical shelter
Built of lies so frail
That they blend with the shadows.

Laura Peet

Evening Tide, Country Side

I travel on, at evening tide.
I see the scenes, the country side
Weary souls, home at last,
Lights come on, shadows cast

I wander as I travel by,
These country roads, the still dark sky,
What life is like for those who dwell
Inside these homes, some strong, some frail
As lights grow dim along my way
If I should speak, what would I say?
I too have known the country side
Where hope and love and peace abide.
Within my soul these memories strong,
Throughout my journey, linger long.

Hazel W. Smith

Love Is a Flame

For George Booth
Gone is the winter of misery it shows.
The spring appears and summertime grows.
Now I feel my soul will shine.
By now I'll have a guy that's mine.
We'll find laughter and love to share.
Only because we both will care.
And as our future life we aim,
Our burning hearts will be a flame.

Frances C. Litten

Once upon Forever

Once upon forever
Where dreams come to life,
A man took a woman
And knew her as his wife.

Love was made and multiplied,
Or so the woman thought.
One heart once free,
Now emotionally caught.

Days into weeks,
Months into years,
A heart reduced to anger,
Another reduced to tears.

Cruel and thoughtless words
At her heart were thrown
But his unrelenting angry fist
Left its mark on bone.

Once upon forever
Where dreams rarely follow
A man took from a woman
Now her heart is hollow

Kayci Hatton

Simplicity of the Mind

A work of art an act of vengeance
A word of hope an angel forgiven
A heart is broken with the blood of a knife
A stab wound evidence concealed
Mind's deadly game happens to all
Thoughts made into reality
Hurts kept secret will surely kill
Life's not a cheap thrill
A breath of cold oh, so old
Smiles of winter's death
Under snow now life never to return
What's done has begun
Clockwise charm of secrets foretold
The birth of a boy the death of a man
A mind jumbled with uncontrolled thoughts
Pain is a memory known no more
Heat is a virtue burning and sweltering
Cold is a stanza of life in the making
Hearts beating with endless might
Love never ends only begins.

Amanda J. Bush

Times of Change

Years ago a child was I,
When moments were rosy and white
And all there was to muse about
Were, with whom to play, and what.
Those thoughts are golden and sweet to me
I'll cherish them all for eternity
Though now must I proceed day to day
Departed from my childlike way.
Today is so unlike the yesteryears
I marvel to come thus far.
The time past has strengthened me,
With a hope no one can mar.
I'll continue to live in the present age
With each reflection gone by.
And clinging to the memories
The morrow shall come, don't sigh!
I'll be ready for whate'er transpires
No matter what life desires.
With a song in my heart I'll endeavor
On to a dawn, that is brighter.

Jennifer C. Rogers

Blue

Blue is as pretty as a sapphire
Blue is as yummy as a blueberry.
Blue is as new as new paint.
Blue is as sour as a Warhead (candy)
Blue is as wavy as the ocean
Blue is as cool as the night sky
Blue is as easy as A-B-C, (simple color)
And now you see what blue can be.

Alison Tray

Forgiven

I look at the sky above
And I see a beautiful white dove
The clouds are so pretty like cotton
And I know God I haven't forgotten
The pretty blue sky
Is never a goodbye
And I never cry
The sunshine is the light
And my heart takes flight
I am blessed on holy Lord
Please take this mighty sword
From the pain of death
So I take a deep breath
Praise the Lord I am forgiven.

Veronica Dahan

Spirit Awakening

For Bob Kalinoski and Roxanne Brocato
Crashing tides,
Body slides
Deep into an unknown abyss.

A struggle to breathe,
The spirit then leaves
Into the land of promise.

Why did he go?
So much life to bestow
On the folks he called family and friend.

His message is clear,
We must love while we're here
Destiny will be ours in the end.

Amy Murphy

My Mentor

My friend, my mentor
What a difference he's made.
He brought me around
He showed me the way

He took the time to care
When no one else would.
He sifted through all the bad
To get to all the good.

He then sat me down
And said, this is the way.
And from that day forward
My life forever changed.

There were times I know
When I made things tough
But he hung in there with me
He never gave up.

So, to you my dear Irish friend
I say thank you and God Bless
May the Lord always keep you
Safe in His nest.

Susan Simmons

Hairy

Because of his thick, long hair
He gets very hot.
Through these hairs lives a tick
With a big, black cooking pot.
During the night he rolls around,
Each night the tick gets madder.
When morning comes this big furry bum
Gets up and around he patters.
He eats his breakfast and goes outside
Around and 'round the bends.
To his surprise he sees a flea
Opposite the house of hens.
He comes back in, the flea on his chin
In place of the last night tick.
This flea and him become great chums
Neither stylin' dudes nor sloppy bums.
And now and then you see him again
The dog, a moonlight howler,
Across the mountains and over the hills
You hear him do his growler: Aaarooo!

Elise Norton

ME

Of all the people in the world
I wish that I could be
Someone I have never met
And only hope to see

I want to change my attitude
My life in every phase
Correct my old identity
And shed this mystic maze

If this I do accomplish
And this other life I lead
I might just discover
This other person's me

Barbara Mason

God's Great Gift

God made the world
Every boy and every girl.
He saw that we had come
To a point that we had done
Awful things to each other
Even to our very own brother.

So He sent to come
His very own son
To come and die for us
Since He loved us so much.
So He showed His love
And became one of us
Even though we didn't deserve all that much.

Andrea M. Ruiz

A Lover's Setting

For Sandra S. Duron,
whose love inspires me
China plates, rims flowered in blue,
Placed on the table, a setting for two
Champagne glasses, pink bubbles of delight,
Candles emitting a soft warm light
Long-stemmed roses in a crystal vase,
Almost as beautiful as my lover's face
Two birds crooning, a lover's call,
As moon beams danced along the wall
My lover and I, in perfect bliss,
As we move nearer, a longing kiss
Music playing soft and slow,
This is the setting all lovers should know.

George A. Calleja

The Riddle

The portrait lives in black and white
It duplicates one mold
But complicates the riddle
That breathes within the pose;

One ribbon crosses at the throat
It hangs against the lace
And decorates the bodice
That binds your breath in gray;

Dark hair pulled taut divides the crown
It parts above the eyes
And represses the majesty
That in your Art survives;

Black eyes discern intruders' gaze
They guard the Sepulchre
And cultivate the budding rose
That struggles to mature;

Still lips protests our scrutiny
They pout with gray repose
And draw descending countenance
That shrouds the Artist's pose.

Patricia Goodwin

My Love

To Youth Village, for encouragement
Flies higher than doves
But is hidden like a treasure trove.

My love
Is never rough;
It stays tender and keeps me tough.

My love
Will never close shut
'Cause my heart can't even be touched.

My love
Sometimes makes me wonder
What I do to make you hurt
'Cause my heart was never rough
And doors never shut
To the ones I've always loved.

Sunda Run

Shattered Glass

My heart is shattered glass
pieced together by countless faces of
rejection in many different times.
Of all the pain of struggle through
the hardest part is losing you.
If only my heart wouldn't break anymore
I'd give a king's ransom.
But alas, my heart is shattered glass.

Carol L. Juge

Dawn Before Dusk

To my mother and two sisters
Dawn before dusk,
Light before night,
I'd rather it be dark,
Than it is to be bright.

Dawn before dusk,
Sun before star.
I'd rather be on the moon,
Than be walking on Mars.

Dawn before dusk,
Day before night,
I'd rather be in a cave
Than be out in daylight.

Kimberly Jo Eichel

One Autumn of Grace

Now in the young September
    We can see the doe-shadowed fawn
Improvising an intricate ballet,
    His personal Ode to the Dawn,
    On the dew-cooled lawn.

Now in the near-by orchard
    We can see him, shy and spotted,
Skillfully ambush an apple,
    One red among the rotted,
    In the time the doe allotted.

Now in the swift-falling dusk
    On the rye, they play tag.
Startled, she signals time
    With a lightning wag
    Of her white tail flag.

Now in the yearling season
    A fawn's heart sings.
After the wooded winter
    And the carefree springs,
    The blue steel rings.

Hilda E. Quy

Love So Love

Love so love how I long.
For the juiciness of your lips.
The warm soft touch of your hands.
My love so love, how can this be?
You are long so long away from me.
To the one I adore.
Let us love again once more.
Let not me go from the grasp of your arms.
Oh, to the one who holds my heart.
Let not my love keep us apart.
So only you kiss my kisses.
Share with me a love so love.
That will mend this, lonely broken heart.

Lisa Ann

Within

Solitude is my angel,
Silence is my fortress
To be alone, a silent war.
The only enemy is me.
There is but one life to lose,
One heart to pierce
No other must bear the blame.
Only one soul must cry for mercy.
If not alone, ask thou not way of me.
But if thou be, must I answer thee?

Eugene Hoffman

The Fall

To what might have been
As summer nights fade
to the autumn of our love
I begin to realize the pain of distance
metaphoric and literal
I need you close to me
but when I say that I love you
you become so vacant
I know that I've lost you
In my insecure prophecies
I predicted this heartache
So to hell with always
and to hell with you and I
but how can I look to
a tomorrow without you
and a winter of darkness?

Paul Carter

A Place Called Home

I remember mama up before daylight
When eggs-n-bacon and homemade bread
Filled the air with delight
I'd pump water and I'd chop wood
When life was simple and times were good

Daddy worked the fields
With two old mules and a plow
I fed the chickens and slopped the hogs
Learned to milk a cow
I'd do my chores hurry off to school
To learn my lessons and the golden rule

And I remember hay rides
Under the harvest moon
I'd hold your hand tight in mine
Oh, how my heart would swoon
Life was easy and free back then
And I want to go there again

To where my memory takes me
A place called home

Russell L. Ferrell

I Guess It Is True

With love to my mom, Irene Britten
I guess it is true,
What people do say,
You get the "ole blues"
At least once a day.

One whole year mom has been gone,
But only in your mind,
It doesn't seem that very long,
She was so loving and very kind.

Some people say I'm crazy,
My dreams I see and talk to her.
Even tho' the dreams are hazy
Oh, God, I know it's her for sure.

Yet she seem so far from me,
I really wonder where she's at,
At times I feel so close indeed,
Just want to reach out for that "ole pat."

There's no more worrying with heart,
Nor sugar, nor cancer,
She says she feels the best she ever had,
Should make me happy for her.

Renee Thelen

Christmas Is Near

For my special daughter, Juliana
Christmas is near
That's when I hear
Bells ringing
People singing
The season is dear

Everyone's jolly
And hangs the holly
Christmas lights
Silent nights
Sally wants a dolly

Christmas is near
Don't shed a tear
Santa's coming
Boys are drumming
In dressed windows we peer

Snowflakes falling
Mommy calling
Everyone bakes
Cookies and cakes
All covered with frosting.

Pat Farley

Locked Away

For Jeremy and Tommy—Bros 4 life
As I look at what my brothers and I share,
The memories seem endless.
The many times we spent together,
Laughing and having fun,
Are countless and unforgettable.

As kids we were inseparable
Disappearing on adventures,
Only the four of us understood,
Meanwhile looking in our hearts.
Each new adventure encountered.

So as I awaken from my thoughts,
I lock them all back up.
I reserve them for another day,
To seize and examine again,
Placing a smile upon my face.

Tommy Andrews

A True Friend

I have a friend
She's there in times of sorrow,
She knows just what to say,
In all the right ways.

She's there to spend happy times,
Every birthday,
Year after year,
In case of any tears!

We have different backgrounds,
But somewhat the same!
She's there to lend support
And always gives you the report

Whether bad or good,
Laugh or cry, she's there!
We're friends forever!
Thanks, God!

Lori Wells

Untitled

Jesus died on the cross.
Why not put him in your heart?
It will not be a loss.

Marjorie Hawkins

The Family Rose

As you journey through life
Take a moment or so,
To notice the roses
And see how they grow.

For they're like a family
That begins at the roots,
To the next generation
Belong the new tiny shoots.

As the shoots grow older
They become sturdy and strong,
And produce a new flower
That won't linger for long.

So why the petals are open
Blooming so big and so bright,
Enjoy the beauty you see
By the sun's shining light.

For time is fast moving
And nothing can stay,
So savor the roses
Before they all fade away.

Lori Rafferty

My Faith

My faith is the stars in the heavens
As countless as waves on the sea,
The glory of a beautiful sunset,
And the world that is ever to be.

My faith is the sands and the ocean,
As old as the beginning of time,
The beauty of lilies and roses,
And the sun that continues to shine.

My faith is the trees so gracious
Of birds that will always sing,
Of his power and glory forever
God, the creator of all things.

Dorothy A. Southworth

Truth

The tears that flow
are never shown because they are hidden
The pain that hurts
is weakness that is forbidden
The anger that builds
is silent but explosive
The love that exists
is overcome with loneliness
The hate that lingers
is seen with a smile
And the pride that prances
sometimes limps in denial

Michael Horton

To My Love

To David McAnnaney
You have brought joy into my life
and love into my heart.
Now that we are together,
I pray we never part.

No words can describe
how much you mean to me.
The kind of love we share
most will never get to see.

God is looking down on us and smiling.
For he knows we are one of a kind
there is denying.

I am in Heaven with you every day.
I know our love is so strong
that it will never fade away.

Stephanie Myers McAnnaney

My Love

I will find her one day if I
have to travel to the sun.
To find her golden hair wrapped up
with me as one. Just to find
ourselves by the burning sea
and whisper to each other we are eternity.

Mike Romig

A Broken Heart

She was a little darling of two or three,
And she'd lost her little puppy.

All the children gathered 'round
As they'd placed it in the ground.

They were sad because it died
And the flowers bowed their heads and cried.

Eunice M. Ingle

Beauty of a Rainbow

Red is for the roses.
Blue is for the sea.
Yellow is for the sunshine.
God gave to you and me.
Orange is for the oranges,
God gave to us to eat.
Green is for the grass,
That we walk on with our feet.

I don't believe the pot of gold
Is really there to see,
But I do believe it's a promise
God gave to you and me.

Nicole Lee

Visions

Waves roll
On the sandy shore
As misty gray clouds lift.
Gulls soar
Through the sunless skies
Their plaintive cries ring . . .

Standing in the shadowed cove
I watch the sky glow warm
As color bursts over the edge
The dawning skies roll.

Clouds once gray
turn blue then white
A hazy pink, mists
And spreads
Now look above at the sky
And see an artist's easel come alive.

Sarita Pillai

Faith in Love

As the morning dew kisses the earth
I am by your side.
Over mountains high as the heavens,
through rivers ten times wide.

After all these years together
Our passion still thrives.
Through tragedy and happiness,
For the rest of our lives.

I'll always be with you
In spirit and heart.
For everyone knows
True lovers never part.

There will always be someone
I can hold on to.
For my darling I know
That someone is you.

Gina Jones

Stormy

To my mother and humane rights
Catch me this very day
'cause I'm so very real.
Although I flood your mind
To you I will appeal.
I'll rain new life on you
And stream new things to see.
When you pass by day by day
In life away from me.
I'll swim along with you
And shield you as you sleep.
And no matter in what storm
I'm always yours to keep!

Roger K. Williams

Friday the Thirteenth

To Mrs. Mary Kirkland, my godmother
Oh, dear! Oh, dear!
Friday the 13th is here!
Here's what happened to me that day.
Here's what I have got to say.
It all started when I went to school.
I was acting all calm and cool.
It took me a while to get a swing.
When I got on the bell ring.
I lost my bookbag on school ground.
I looked for it all around.
When I got in, I found out I was late.
Had a party and didn't get a plate.
Boys held up two fingers on my head behind.
They must thought that I was blind.
My teacher gave me a lot of homework to do.
Math, reading, and language too.
Got punished for something I didn't do.
Burned my finger on a pot too.
That was my awful day.
That's what I have got to say.

Patrice B. Shelton

Still Too Much to Learn

Poor little old man
standing out in the rain
hair all snarled
and eyes bleeding with pain
he hums a song of sadness
for his late wife
she is no longer with us
for drugs have taken her life
he walked by my house
almost every day
he always took the time to greet me
or tip his hat my way
I look at him as a mentor
for making the best of what life dealt
I truly regret not telling him
how I really felt
he now sings with his wife
in the choir above
God bless his soul
for he taught me how to love

Michael P. Malecki

Angel's Voice

To David V. Auer
Talk to me
in an angel's voice
let your soft words
caress my face

Place your hands
on my soul, look inside
let your body feel the pull
leave the world behind

Undress my devil feelings
teach me to feel heavenly things
release the black outside
push your fingers to the soft inside

Look upon my forbidden face
the shattered remnants of a dying race
let go of your consciousness
help to show you want this

You make me see blue
blue in an outside world
hard-boiled and cracked
the devil inside won't be back.

Tim Auer

Ocean to Sea

Ocean to ocean, sea to sea
The sand is hot, that's fine by me.
The clouds are forming up above
And the rain will soon come.
The rain pours, the people leave
And soon deserted it will be.
The sun comes back, the people too
kids play, why don't you.
Ocean to ocean, sea to sea
The sand is hot, that's fine by me.

Jennifer Boaz

Balloons

For my great grandmother, Johanna Reins
We all saw it coming
but we didn't think so soon.
He set her soul free
like a helium balloon.

It soars to the heavens
and doesn't look back.
It reaches the sky
without a split or a crack.

Her soul makes peace
to herself as one.
No more agony or pain
Her suffering is done.

As the balloons goes higher and higher
we wish for one more goodbye.
But all we can do at the moment
is release the tears we cry.

There's not a single tear we cry
that's of sadness or sorrow.
But the tears of joy
and the hope of tomorrow.

Amanda M. Stricklin

A Mother's Love

For Ogie Reed and Kate DeBell
A mother's love, how sweet the name.
What is a mother's love?
A nobly pure and tender flame
Inspired from above.
To bless a heart of earthly mold,
The warmest love that can't grow cold.
This is a mother's love.

Barb Jarman

Angel of Death

The days are bright
the nights are dark.
though everything I see
is but a thought.
The dreams I saw
are now blacked out
for the angel of death
knocked on my door.
What once was
will never be again
for the angel of death
opened my door
for the dreams I have
are what they are,
for what once was
has been taken away
for the angel of death
came in my door.

Evelyn M. Boyd

Titanic

While the sun set on
The night of April 14, 1912
Kids and their parents
Snuggled up in their beds.
Dreaming of the times they had
Of dancing, talking, and touring.
Never before had they thought
of the danger ready to be fed—
Alarms and screaming for hour after hour
Took bravery and courage.
The memory exist now only in our minds
But the experience will last forever!

Amber Clontz

Life

Life is beautiful
Surrounded by love and peace
People live in harmony
Days go by and so does time
As days go by we grow older
And also wiser
And as our time nears
We reflect back to good times
And we see
How beautiful life is
And wish it was not time to leave

Paul A. Lewis

Look at the Stars . . .

To my first love, my inspiration
A celestial eve,
Scattered with fireflies.
Likely to fall from their place
With every blustery gust.
Dancing bright orbs
Make up the Heavens,
Not seeing that they form the skies.
Insignificantly pushing on,
shining, burning with rage.
That even when they're gone,
their memory still burns on.
Eons and eons of passionate light,
Illuminate against the darkness of eternity.

Asad Clinton

Through the Year

I love trees,
I love flowers;
Both are like April showers.
In the month of June, I go in the pool.
In the month of September, I go to school.
My favorite month is December;
That I will remember.
In November is Thanksgiving.
I write poems for a living.
In March is my birthday.
I also like Earth Day.
I am not old;
I am very bold.

Kendell Evelyn

Love Was

For Jimmy, my love
Oh! For the love that was, was once,
I still can't help remembering,
the time you kissed me,
then wept because you had.
Oh! For the love that was,
was once, but now is forever no more.

Sally A. Lukasik

Safely Home

I am home in Heaven, dear ones;
oh, so happy and so bright
There is perfect joy and beauty
In this everlasting light.
All the pain and grief is over,
Every restless tossing passed.
I am now at peace forever;
Did you wonder I so calmly
Trod the valley of the shade?
Oh, but Jesus' love illumined
Every dark and fearful glade,
And he came himself to meet me
In that way so hard to tread,
And with Jesus' arm to lean on,
Could I have one doubt or dread?
Then you must not grieve so surely,
For I love you dearly still.
Try to look beyond Earth a shadow;
Pray to trust our Father's will.
There is work still waiting for you.

Barbara Taffer

The Long Road

Sometimes I just close my eyes,
And let the world fall away.
Sometimes I take off my mask,
And let all the pain come my way
After all I'm only lonely on my inside

Every day I hold it in, hold it down
Sometimes I want to cry in joy
But every second I feel emptiness inside
After all I'm only lonely on my inside

I accepted it long ago
That I would walk this world alone
No arms to hold, no love to let me grow
But my own
After all, I'm only lonely on my inside

Annie Mills

Untitled

As sure as the sky is blue,
my love is true for you.

As sure as the sun shines bright,
it was love at first sight.

As the leaves change their color
for my heart is no other.

I had a dream, I held your hand,
we walked together in the sand.

If you don't deny yourself this one chance,
it will be a great romance!

Jeffrey S. Carden

Sparks

For my soulmate, Rafaelo
To read your thoughts floods
my heart with love.
To hear your voice I am overcome
with waves of emotion.
The anticipation of seeing
your smile stirs a wind of desire within me.
Our embrace sends a tornado
of passion through my body.
Your eyes throw sparks of
intensity, melting my fears,
reassuring me. "I love you."
When we kiss, my soul burns
with ecstasy felt deeply in my heart.
Where the fire of hope roars
for me and you.

Lea Champlin

Inner Child

Who am I? Are you me?
Who is this person that I see?
Don't turn away in disgust.
Look at me! Teach me to trust.

It is not all bad.
In fact, a lot of it is good.
Look again, don't be sad.
Unlock your heart; cherish all that you should.
Look, there's more there than you see
It is kind and gentle; maybe, just maybe.

Look again, don't turn away.
It's ok to run and play.
No more guilt, no more lying,
No more pain, no more crying.
It is time to let it go,
It is time to help it grow.

So look again, yes, it is me.
A wonderful reflection of a soul set free.

Theresa Hymel

Only the Heart Knows

Love can only be felt by the heart
It is something that will never depart.
Its arms can reach out
To comfort in times of doubt.
Its hands can reach out to touch you
And holds you when you're blue.
Love lasts through all the ages
Its wealth can't be measured in wages.
Love can't be bought or sold
Because it is as pure as gold.
Love has a way of sneaking up on you
And when it does, there's nothing you can do.
Only the heart knows true love
Sent from God above.

Theresa Lusk

Untitled

In the lonely cemetery I will soon be laid
it won't be long 'til the grave is made.

In that sweet home where my loved ones wait
is a place for me when I reach the gate.

But as I linger on 'til the sun goes down,
waiting for me is a non-wavering crown.

Lossie Grooms

Truly Yours

It used to be
We knew who we were.
You knew your friends,
your beliefs,
yourself.

Now it is
We know nothing.
No one knows true love,
true faith,
true happiness.

Friends exist only in those who love.
Beliefs exist only in those who have faith.
You truly exist in friendship, love and faith.
You do not know you,
truth,
true existence.

Love.
Have faith.
Be joyful.
Exist.

Jinee Burdg

The Wolves

I hear them now
They are almost upon me
Their bloodthirsty howls echo in the night
Teeth glitter in the shade of moon
Barbaric intelligence lurks in their shining eyes
Assessing me coolly, deciding my worth
How I will appease them, I do not know
I can almost feel their sharpened fangs
Sinking into my flesh
Ripping, tearing, shredding
With not a care for my screams
Suddenly, a lunge!
I hear myself shrieking distantly
Fading, fading, fading with my life's blood
Oh, farewell, cruel and uncaring Pangaea!
I leave thee to thine own devices
Until the mournful cries sound loudly in the night
And the wolves are hungry once again

Nicole Starr Porter

Outlook

Sunrise: Birds sing.
Creatures wake from slumber,
Eat breakfast, rush to work.
Noon: Grass is mowed, plants watered.
Gunslingers have their showdowns.
Creatures eat lunch. Bare flesh is burned.
Sunset: Some creatures sleep, while others stay out.
They dance, drink, talk, rape, kill.
The moon shows its face, and watches, and waits.
Midnight: Creatures dream.
Those still awake watch talk shows, stagger home drunk,
Slink back into the shadows and wait for another victim.
Reality leaves to take a c**p,
And Superstition warms his seat while he's gone.
Lone figures walking down deserted streets,
P*** their pants at the smallest sound.
The moon waits some more.
And then the sun rises again.

Kenneth R. Gerety

Our Secret Fantasy

I'll give you anything, anything your heart desires.
I'll give you a sweet sensation, hot like fire.
I'll give it to you so nice and gentle your body will never tire.
I'll be your only fantasy, with everything required.

My love for you is oh, so strong, it will conquer anything.
I'll give you my all, my heart and soul, I'll give you everything.

I want you to get inside me and know my every move.
I want you to be my keeper, anything done is done for you.
I want you to feel my body, and hold me all the time.
I want to make love to you in a bed of roses with strawberries and wine.
You know I'll only do this for you, if you promise to be mine.

I need you next to me, touching my body right.
All the things you do to me, make me feel so fine.
I want you to know every part of me, you know how it makes me feel.
When I feel your body all over mine, it makes the moment real.

After you are finished and your moment is through.
It then will be my turn to get you in the mood.
I do this to make you feel the pleasures of me loving you.
As the night closes and the pleasures come to an end.
I'll always think of another time when we can do this again.

Alexis Griffin

My Innocence Lost

My childhood taken away from me
My innocence lost
Blew out my spark and left me in the dark
To wander through years of dissemblance and confusion.
I had to live with the vivid and piercing memories
Remembering how your dirty hands felt on my virgin body
You'll never understand what it's like
When you ripped off my angel wings and left me without flight.
The indefinable feeling of loneliness and fears
Seems like no one but me cares
My childhood taken away from me
My innocence lost
I hope and I pray that one day, my soul will no longer ask: "Why me?"

Nicole Hyacinth Roid

The Ascent Beckons

Five blue knolls define the horizon. Each tucked behind each,
The blue backs of a hand of cards.

In the valley a tiny flatbed sounds harsh and then starts,
Loaded with spools of gray hay it begins.
The distance makes rice of the men.

On this hill one Chinese horse empties herself, looks
Toward the motor and returns to the grass.

Wet terns clap the pond for the last mosquitoes,
A constant sewing.

He is dead only five days
And already there are rabbits on the lawn.

Her German woman ties dry dahlias to the lattice.
Inside the cabin his oiled rifle stands by the green door.

As she passes she breathes the scent of the lubricant.
It reminds her of Sundays, stews, and kumiss bread.

The fall sun is low and meddling.
Through the blinds the lint is bright,
The light stripes everything taupe and grey.

The ghost of the German is returning
To hold his woman by the breasts

One last time
Before he ascends to Heaven.

George Handy

Bouncing off the Walls

Bouncing off these walls while lying in this bed
trying not to pay attention to the confusion in my head
sentenced to natural life and really don't know why
without one shred of proof that jury believed a lie
Bouncing off these walls while standing in this cell
a terrible accusation made life a living hell
forced into this environment full of hate death and disease
we have those among us they will never release
Bouncing off these walls while sitting in the hole
a mental torture chamber for the mind about to blow
this was orchestrated so I would take the fall
by some one-eyed mix responsible for it all

Christena Tyson

Hearing Love

To my mother, I love you
I can hear the lovemaking outside and inside.
I can hear it in my house and next door.
I can hear them kissing and hugging and listening to love songs
And watching the people on TV kiss and hug too.
And this is why I tell you making love is a natural thing.

Jessica Reed

A Cold Winter Night

To my family and friends
As cold as Hitler, it blew and through the snow like feathers,
light as air.
As cold as Hitler, people freeze to death
and numb limbs fall off or are amputated.
As cold as Hitler, wish, woo, howl. The wind whips.
As cold as Hitler, bright and brilliant falling snow blinds the eyes.
As cold as Hitler, the snow was an ocean of death.
As cold as Hitler, going insane from starvation or spoiled meat.
As cold as Hitler, the snow and the wind told you what to do
as if controlling the world. Domination.
As cold as Hitler, stabbing knives in the spine, continuous goosebumps.
As cold as Hitler, the smell of rotting flesh in the concentration camps.
As cold as Hitler, the snow covered in blood like a strawberry Slurpee.
As cold as Hitler, as cold as Hitler, as cold as Hitler, as cold as Hitler.

    Trevor Williams

War

As a young man, my friend and I fight for freedom to say we were there,
but as not the movies or books.
We sit there as we did before at school at lunch laughing,
but there were no smiles there behind the piles of sand
as we heard shots rain and the sound of death cries
as we think that this could be the day we die
behind the piles of sand in the war to fight for freedom
and to say we were there, war.

    Jasun Ty Hansen

mother's eye

To Macealah Richardson
Seventeen years, seventeen tears, seventeen reasons to die.
But through her life, she fought her strife, and painfully lived the lies.

Young girl, loved by the world, love deeper than the sea.
Despite all the tears, throughout the years, she had every last reason to be.

Met the wrong man, fell into his trap, fell for his lies and his hate.
Suffered his rage, through every last page, then there was no more to say.

Life in a twist, sliced her wrist, cut away the pain.
As always the same, mother took the blame, dropped to her knees and prayed.

Fighting off the pain, mother reads the note again, seventeen years were gone.
Husband to be, refused to see, emotions in the passing song.

Warm summer's day, as she passed away, Jesus gave her nothing.
Religions lost, burned on the cross, in the summer sky where the birds sing.

Moments past, all tears last, mother thinks to die.
Father in denial, as he dreams of his child, another tear falls from the mother's eye.

Mother in pain, she sees her again, sees the seventeen years.
Picked up a knife, took her life, took away the tears.

Once again, a life has been taken, and so stands another reason to die.
Now there is nothing, but the birds still singing—singing in the summer sky.

    John Freese

Frown

I sit on the cold, hard, wood floor thinking of my past
A pang of energy surges through my body, giving me the strength
I need to move forward, but I let it go
Now it shall never return
A gust of wind brushes against my fragile soul, leaving me torn inside
I hold my future in my palm, but it's rapidly disappearing
And leaving a tear of sorrow in my lonely eyes
The sweet smell of what I once knew is gone
The stench of decaying bones fills
My tiny nose and sends a shiver up my spine
A drop of blood falls from my finger and burns a hole through my heart
The hole in my heart is becoming bigger as I long
For what I once took for granted
Then I open my eyes and take in my surroundings
And pray I shall live just one more day

    Felise Dezen

Passion

Passion stirred by love is everlasting
Nourishment after a period of fasting
Lifting one to heights hitherto unknown
Where sanity and reason to bits are blown.

Passion stirred by lust is fleeting
The coupling of two bodies meeting
An explosion of sexual desire
Quickly extinguishable, like a dying fire.

Passion that is wisely spent
Is surely what the Gods meant
When they decreed, "Man is truly blessed
If by love he is possessed."

    Ruth Stalerman

Justice

Just a toke, just a swallow
Just a tilt, just a shading

A minute lapse in judgment
A non-defining moment

Do not judge, don't extrapolate
And never hold accountable

Just a lie, just a shifting
Just a product of our system

They all do it, who can blame them
And are we any better?

Boys will be . . . boys will be . . .
It's only human nature

Look away, be magnanimous
Forgiveness is a virtue

Just a lark, an indiscretion
Look at the larger picture

Just a symbol, just a leader
Swallow hard, clean the mirror

Who are we . . . who are we . . .
And are we any better?

    Mitchell Danitz

Love's Heartache

Making love
With whispers of the night
Dawn breaking
With the lies of the daylight

Trying
With all my soul to make it last
Lying
With every breath to stop the hurt

Making mistakes
With every heartbreak
Turning away
With just another heartache.

    Jennifer M. Tindall

Life

If we are born,
Why do we die?

If we are sore,
Why do we cry?

If God made tobacco,
Why can't we smoke it?

If God made weed,
Why can't we toke it?

    Jessica Leahy

Ole Man

Ole man was driving down the street one day,
When he suddenly noticed a young girl coming his way.

Ole man said, "Hey, you sweet little thing,
You shoul look good in those tight black jeans."

At first the young girl didn't pay him any mind,
Until she thought for a second and started seeing dollar signs.

The young girl turned around and said, "Hey, can you afford me?"
Ole man shook his head and said, "Yes . . . sa . . . ree. . . ."

The young girl wrote her number and slid it through the window;
Ole man became so excited whereas he started to tremble.

The young girl left and ole man started to pray,
He said, "Thank you, Jesus, for bringing this young thing my way."

Ole man smiled as he made his way home;
He turned on the radio and rocked to blues and love songs.

Aretha Franklin, Johny Taylor, and B. B. King,
All he could think about was his pretty young thing.

Ole man got out the car and creeped into the house,
He pulled off his overalls and laid on the couch.

Ole man closed his eyes and started to dream,
All he could see was his pretty young thing.

Gloria Genell Williams

Monkey in My Pocket

There's a monkey in my pocket. Sometimes he gets out.
He thinks he's so cute and cuddly, he knows everything.
But he's not fooling me—he's only just a rat.
He climbs upon my shoulder then onto my back.
He thinks he's being cunning and no one knows he's there.
He hides in the pantry and sometimes in my truck.
The monkey tells me to do things I would never ever do.
But I listen to him and do exactly what he wants me to.
He thinks my stupid stunts are so very, very cute.
He comes out when I'm bored and have nothing else to do.
He stays with me and plays with me until we are all through.
Then he goes back in my pocket until I think I need him again.
When the monkey's through with me and I am through with him,
I feel so ashamed I don't know what to do.
The monkey doesn't care if I hurt the ones I love and he makes a fool of me.
As long as he's having fun, that's all that matters to him.
If I don't get this monkey out of my pocket and keep him off my back,
I feel he'll soon destroy me and everything I love.

Sandra Sanders

Untitled

The room is dark and quiet
A flame casts a seductive shadow on the wall
As it melts down the hard wax candlestick

A hand reaches out for something, soft and warm
The hands finds a foot
It moves up higher to the thighs
Smooth and sexy

Lips come and give soft, wet kisses
Soothingly around the belly button
Licking and caressing

A hard muscular body slides on top of the soft one
It slides in, it slides out
Noises of pleasure paint the darkness

It slides back in, the flame flickers
It slides out, the flame turns into a fire
Hot and burning, in and out

The flame flickers low
Bodies rest curled against one another
The flame is out
And the room lay dark and quiet once again.

Edward Pare

Lucifer's Gamble

Wash blood away with water
Swallow your fears with wine.
Stare at the sun too long,
And you're surely to go blind.

Kill your next door neighbor,
Rape your daughter dear.
But it doesn't matter much,
Because your time is coming near.

Beat your brother's wife
Make the most of human days!
If only you could know
You'll be suffering in the exact same ways.

It's really not that bad,
And the pain is not too much,
So pack a toothbrush and some clothes
And be careful of what you touch.

Plan this journey wise,
Enjoy the mortal life you dwell.
Who is there to stop you?
You've sold your soul to hell.

Tina Kirkpatrick

Innocence Lost

His arms embrace my soft flesh;
His eyes look into mine.
He kisses every inch of my trembling body.
He presses himself against me.
I am sure of what he wants,
But "No" will not escape my lips.
I am lost in all the emotions
And cannot seem to find my way back.
God! It has happened! My innocence is gone,
And now I am lying here all alone.

Ana Partida

American Ways

As I lie in the great land of the free
I try to find the American dream

Hope and truth are all I ask to find
This great country can't really be this blind

Abortion is considered one way out
Homosexuals are accepted without a doubt

Our girls die in fear of a thing called fat
We use drugs to fill in the empty gap

But if all these things are considered right
Why do our people still cry in the night

Tiffany Moss-Humphres

Long Distance

We live only two-and-a-half hours apart,
But he still knows how to break my heart.
He says that he honestly does care,
But long distance keeps us from being a pair.
When I travel that two-and-a-half hours,
He controls all of my tomorrows.
Trying to figure exactly where we stand,
He says our hearts belong to separate lands.
Yet when I arrive, he never forgets his latex.
His promise of friendship is based on sex.
He knows I love him with my heart and soul;
This knowledge helps him to take control.
Love is supposed to be good, not bad,
Yet my tears aren't of joy but because I'm sad!

Tiffany Clark

The Pain I Love

You said your love would never turn to hate
Now it has and I hate this fate
You made my pain with your words
My blade healed it all, people say that's absurd
You turned your eyes from my shame
Why must you continue this stupid game?
You heard my tears fall to the floor
You twisted my pain a little bit more
You said it felt good to hear me cry
Now even hell passes me by
I fear for my life, but not for my soul
I need you back to make me whole
My scars will never heal and you will never see
How much you really meant to me
You called me a whore, you made me weep
So I cut even more, I cut too deep
As I ran my blade across my flesh
My whole being turned into a bloody mess
Now my soul is lost for eternity
All because you wish you never met me

Annette Nadine Livingston

Cold Winter

Cold murder, cold sweat, cold sinner
Take the sins that I regret
Cold feelings won't stray, it looks
like the cold is here to stay

Strange stranger, I am
I'll take her long before I leave this land.

Young virgin, young blood. Stay distant,
my mind is in the mud.

Bad feelings, new town, I'll make it.
Brighter than a circus clown.
No baggage, on my way
I'll manage, the cold
is here to stay.

Ralph Savino

Secrets

Secret Conversation, Secret Romance
Two people that think alike
The world never to know
Is our only hope in life
Shall we continue, it kinda turns me on
To know when you close your eyes
It is me who is in your thoughts
I won't tell if you don't, please don't ever leave
Alone I cannot be
For in another life, you are my destiny
Secret destiny, secret love, a secret life
That we call our own
To get turned on by your voice
Is a thrill that I wait for
Just once it would be nice
To make love to you under the stars
Or on a rainy night
You're the secret that is in my mind
Never to come out, only in our other life
My secret love, my secret life

Veronica Polzin

Everyday Average Man

I step out the door into the docile wasteland
Filled with joker, trees, and swans.
I picked up the pound of gossip the thirty year-old
Paper boy throws on my doorstep.
The only problem is I forget my robe,
And now the neighbors know I shave my pubes.

Larry L. Bowden

Bitch

Who do these girls think they are?
The things they say and do to me
they just took it a little too far.
Stupidity is envy and jealousy,
They cut me down but,
Then they want to be just like me.
I was there when they needed to talk but,
When I needed them to listen I felt like
I was talking to two rocks.
I tried to like them to be open and cool but,
They just used me and made me look like a fool.
I guess it's useless to be nice,
Because their hearts are as cold as ice.
In my face they act cool towards me,
Behind my back with a knife they stabbed me.

Yvonne Ly

HOW DO I FIND THE WORDS TO SAY?

How do I find the words to say?
It's a shame that things had to go this way,
I used to sit and cry every day,
Wondering how long will it take him to see things my way.
Sometimes I want him to leave, sometimes stay.
Damn, how do I find the words to say?
                                    It's hard.

Alisa Faust

Vitamin AIDS

Introduction, seduction, interruption
You have taken off into a different lifestyle,
Different mindset with Vitamin AIDS
No more tears of glory more like tears of your tragic story
Alienation, interpretation,
The clock is ticking
You plot revenge
For the viral destructor
He didn't make love to you
An act which produces the miracle of life
He chose the sin of murder
The mystery of death

Day Thompson

Dreams Lost

Wearing time like embers of a burned dress
In late June, a hurt, grown child wanders
Harvest of common girl, made into a plain woman
Thoughts of bodies flowing closer
Youth remains unaware of depth of intention, passion, capacity
Leading to misfortunes of home felt touch
Struggling through abusive sleep years later
What is gone, is gone, is gone
Being safe a planned myth
Strangling sanity in black incest of soul
Wanting space to ignite misfortunes
To caress childhood strength of desire,
Expression, but dreams of grandeur lost
Trapped in captivity, with a disheartening secret

Audra L. Albright

Untitled

Witches' brew we have not made,
But we witches shall not fade.
There is a secret that is unknown,
The tales of witches we have sown.
In the night when a full moon is shining,
The evil spells our souls are binding.
In our circle of dreaded deeds,
Everyone will know our needs,
For we are the witches of the winds and the seas,
And we can always do what we please.

Elana Kampff

Tested and Unexpected

True love has grown, when giving to receive.
No worries be your guidance;
His spirit to believe.
Selfless days and sensitive ways;
Heaven's light in truthful rays.
Pleasure and pain, as sure as one;
In spirit's flight through His only Son.
Gift of grace a last surrendering breath,
Promises life . . . when he loves you to death.

Teri Knol

Do Gods Cry?

To my Aunt Mouse
Does the eldest father frown
upon your vicious and scandalous history?
Does the goddess of love mourn
for every child violated or every broken family?

Does the God of war find honor
in using weapons of mass destruction?
Does the Lord of the wild swear revenge
For every creature's extinction?

Does the lady justice get angry
when we forget her right hand bears a sword?
Does the harvest maid get frustrated
when some starve and others have so much more?

Does the green mother shed a tear
when seeing the toxic mess we created?
Does the God of forgiveness scream
when a crime of hate or terror is committed?

Do Gods Cry?

Wayne T. Ballard

Precious Love

In this garden I walk alone seeing flowers all around,
but only one caught my eye and it was love.
I want to feel love, to have its scent
wrapped around me like gossamer wings.
To have it blow over my skin,
in the soft whisper of a breeze and revel in its delight.
I want to be drowned in its depth
and come crashing into you like a wave upon the sand.
As I reach for love and hold it in my hand,
I pray it doesn't fall apart.
This precious and fragile flower, I give to you with all my heart.

Nicole Bennett

The Joys of Dialysis

The alarm clock rings loudly
I get up in a hurry
I shower, have breakfast
And then start to worry.
Have I had too much fluid?
Is my diet OK?
Then quickly I dress
And I'm on my way.
I must stop for gas
Oh, my what a trial it is
On the days that I have
To go for dialysis.

I go into the building
And sit in a chair
And talk with the others
Who also wait there.
The nurse comes to the door
She says, "Hi!" and she smiles at us,
She says, "Come on in, it's time for dialysis."

C. Evans

The Homeless Man

We all have seen the homeless man, out on the many streets.
Their clothes are worn, and tattered, their eyes we never meet
Their pain filled faces, clearly show
A lifetime filled with many blows
They once have worked and loved and played
But fate has made them lose their way
Beware and lend a helping hand
For you could be that homeless man

Mary Ann Leckner

Alone with My Self

For my children, Joshua, Serenity, and Caressa
My lips long to kiss the restless yet gentle breeze,
I feel faint yet calm, my life it seems to seize,
My mind seems to race in an endless turmoil,
When it stops what mood will it spoil;
I sit quietly underneath a tree, and take all of life within,
My body feels as if it has become a piece of the Earth,
is this how it ends; Many thoughts start clouding my mind,
Oh, what adventures will I find;
I day dream for the perfect love to find me,
I'm reaching out but there's no one in the mist to see;
I feel suddenly all alone, my heart feels heavy,
Will no one find the person inside of me, or will
I remain alone on this levee,
I walk along a gently rambling stream,
A brilliance or orange shines behind me and casts a
wondrous glow of a beam;
The sunrise is sinking the day is ending,
A message of calmness and sleep it is sending,
A tear seems to escape and gently roll down my cheek,
I think just what is it that I now seek.

Geneda S. Wallick

Winter!

Cold winter night as the wind brushes against my face.
The redness of my nose starts to shine on to shining.
The chill that crosses my feet as my toes become frozen.
The pure white snow that falls before me is powerful,
how something so beautiful has been created, full of mystery,
not knowing how frozen water could bring
happiness across someone's heart.

The darkness, and the shining of every little
trickle that slowly vanishes with air so fresh,
I feel as my body sits back,
and takes a long lasting breath . . .

Jennifer George

A Juju Be Lullaby

Oh, me, oh, my, I am scatterbrained,
My head is harem-scarem stained.
A patchwork of flap doodle lingering now,
Me woefully starcrossed into a wow!
My nerves be whispering hideous vices,
Me sprinkled with inklings of worn eaten spices.
Oh, heavens to Betsy, solutions still vague,
Of how I can dampen this obnoxious plague . . .
By golly! My balmy, henpecked, and horrible dread,
And my muggy, sluggish shadow has finally fled!
Grizzly gray wretchedness has fallen out the nest,
So suddenly relieved with the promising best.
An astounding allure to delude the despair,
With cataclysmic charisma and comforting care!
A groovy good time to hinder my hurt,
Multitudinous mirth to shampoo the dirt.
Took only a wink, my sorrow went down the sink,
Now my glum is all gleefully tickled in pink!
So you say, lavish luck? Fairy fame? Worldly wealth?
No . . . I just healed up my heart, with the strength in myself.

Erin Tardif

The Heart within a Kiss

The sun falls upon the ripened earth.
The dew drips to the sea.
A wall of silence closes deep inside the heart,
Encaged in a kiss of purity.
Clear as a conscience, but so deep
the feelings roam in a thought of desire.
A touch so near inside this soul of mine.
A word spoken from the mind's eye
Grace the presence of everlasting truth,
For a hope is reborn.
There I trust my soul and self to be taken.
Never forgotten but live still in a kiss from the heavens.

Joanna Fomich

Thank You

Nine months I spent in your womb,
'Til one day I came out into the light,
Not knowing where I was,
Or who you were.
That's the day when life began.

As I slowly started to learn what life meant,
I grew and got older and started to appreciate the true meaning of life,
Not knowing what problems lay ahead
That one day I would have to face.

One day I will be able to know what it is like to create a life.
I will finally realize what it will be like to have a family of my own.
So what I learn from you, I will carry on throughout life.

To the ones I love,
The people who sheltered, fed, and kept me warm,
Thank you for creating me.

Helen Becker

Life's Troubles and Trials

When all around me within,
I stand before a wayward wind.
The wayward wind around me blows,
But nevertheless I'll concur bold.

Though inward strong the wind does blow,
I know that someday I'll onward glow.
Though persecution may arrive,
My inward life does not connive.

Life is a struggle now and then,
I have a hope to live again.
Though earthly task may past me by,
My Savior coming is of nigh.

Life is a rugged raging test,
I am struggling daily to find some rest.
I am feeling the weights of Satan's oppress,
Inclining always to do my best.
Upon this upward hill I climb,
Troubles and trials this way I find.
I know that God is testing me,
By faith I'll gain the victory.

Hayward W. Saunders

My Realization of Changes

To anyone needing to feel love
How do I say goodbye to someone I never really knew?
Someone who unknowingly touched me inside and changed me.
The sadness I feel is not pain, but emptiness—
intolerable emptiness.
I'm lacking something that I almost grasped,
and then suddenly, without warning, it slipped away.
After a while my dreams shatter,
and I realize that I was so vulnerable.
A destructed yet serene closing to a fathomless thing.

Becky Handa

Questions

She looked out the window on that cold winter morning.
She thought of her lover and watched the rain pouring.

He looked at her shadow on the kitchen floor.
He made his decision and smiled once more.

Her mind wandered back to this summer past;
the food, the drinks, the games, what a blast!

Her face grew warm and a smile crossed her lips.
She closed her eyes and remembered his kiss.

He stepped up behind her quickly and silently,
put his arms around her waist and whispered quietly,

"You're the love of my life, my jewel, my treasure.
Will you be my wife, for now and forever?"

Holding the breath he was afraid to release,
his only thought was, "Say yes, please!"

She couldn't believe it, he'd finally asked her!
She turned around and said, "As if you need an answer!"

"Of course I will, we belong together.
If we do things right, it will last forever!"

That was what he needed to hear.
He knew now that he had nothing to fear.

Rebecca A. Walker

What's Love

Is there a God above,
To change this world of hate to love.
Making life a joy to live,
Providing the hearts with a thing called "Forgive,"
Thoughts of others and how they feel,
If prayers help, everyone should kneel.
For it is time for a change to come about,
Stand up, cheer, jump and shout.
Praise the Lord to this very day,
For changes will come but in his own way.
Impatient we are "for time is running out,"
For learning God and what he is about.
Emotions are leading our minds astray,
Let our Father in your life, "He will stay."
And provide you with spiritual needs,
To overcome all the obstacles and bad deeds.
Your days are numbered, so you know not when,
Get your ticket now, don't wait 'til then! (Judgment Day)

John T. Palmer

On the Way to Fame

For Richard, my inspiration
A little girl watched "Miss America" in awe,
A dream of fame in my future I saw.

As I grew older award shows were added.
Fame in my future was the dream that mattered.

I couldn't sing, I couldn't dance,
Acting would be my talent per chance.

On my way to fame
Someone said, "Help" and called my name.

I stopped to smile
And hoped to ease one's burden for a while.
Each time I tried to make my mark
Someone beckoned from the dark.

On my way to fame I touched some hearts and they touched me.
I know my talent that was meant to be.
I try to make the most of every minute
And hope the world is better with me in it.

Joan Druckman

A Ride on the *Titanic*

I got on the big ship with a quiver of my lip.
When the engines started moving, it was very soothing.
After a couple of nights, I turned off the lights.
I felt a jolt in my bed.
My husband said, "We're going down!"
That moment my mind turned around.

I got my stuff, and we ran through the loft.
I hugged my husband goodbye, and gave a sigh.
I stepped into the life boat, and put on my coat.
As I watched the ship sink, to the last life ring.
I felt mad at the loss I had had.

A ship came. I still felt ashamed.
As they lifted us up
And gave us a cup,
I laid down
Until we reached a town.
It was in America,
As I got off, I met my old friend Erica.
I'm lucky to be alive;
I'm sorry, my husband didn't survive.

Kristin Wilson

A Special Friend

To my family and friends
You are a special friend of mine;
We laugh and talk to pass the time.
A better person, you would never find
Than this special friend of mine.

We share our thoughts and ideas, too,
And our secrets are just between me and you.
The ups and downs that we've been through
Have proven our friendship to be true.

You're always around when I'm blue
To pick me up and see me through.
The kind of feelings that we do share
Will show the world that people do care.

For friends like you are far and few,
Like winter rains and morning's dew.
Facing this life alone without you
Would be impossible for me to do.

June Castro

I Am Free

To be able to fly like an eagle,
I would sure like to be.
I would sore high through the sky,
the whole world, for me to see.

Then fences, gates and the razor wire,
by no means, would be, a stop, to me.
Mountains and streams, bogs and mire,
over all of them, I would go; I'd be free!

With my wings stretched out wide,
on thin air, I would ride.
To the arms of my sweetheart, I'd glide,
and by her side, I'd safely abide.

But alas, it cannot be, at least physically.
Only in Jesus, can we really be free,
free of guilt and vengeful thought,
free to hope and dream like I ought.

Free to see, the right from the wrong,
free to live, like I should have all along.
Though still confined, yet in my mind
I'm free, free of the world, I've left behind.

Jack Sapp

A New Millennium

A new Millennium I hear all the time,
They say things must change, I wonder why
Are worldly necessities all they care about?
Isn't caring for others the way it should be?
But things must change they keep on saying.

Computers and money and power, too
Is all I seem to hear.
Whatever happened to care and love?
Aren't they important, too?

But somewhere here, God is here.
I need not worry more.
Peace of mind and of my heart
Will never ever change.

Thank you Lord for all you've done,
and for the future You will guide.
For God knows all, I'll walk beside,
With a Love that will not change.

Lena Osmundson

Where Do We Go From Here?

Was the Lord God inspired to create Heaven and Earth?
Had He planned the design that the cosmos assumed?
He said, "Let there be light!" Was it then, the Big Bang
—the primordial force that burst forth from . . . the source

that swirled worlds into being, set laws and sequences
which Man in his time aimed to tame and command
in pursuit of a life holding more than existence:
sweet sense of invention, discovery, art?

Is intelligent life born to far drifting galaxies,
parsecs removed in time, distance . . . and kind
. . . or is Earth a trial run for God's yet-to-be masterpiece?
Yet-to-be? Out there . . . already become?

Our world *not* the Lord's masterpiece? Wherein our flaws?
Are black holes, as in space, sown, unknown, in our armature,
swallowing light, gorging all in their gravity?
Destruction God's plan? . . . or the plan of God's men?

Miriam Simms Piper

Union Broken

Chastity is mine when you do fade.
Do not leave I imploringly bade.
Death so black, so simple and cold.
Your stare and feet were so bold.
When might you speak again,
tell your heart that I have been driven,
Away on the barren cliffs of solitude.
I never found another to replace your magnificent mood.

Beth Harris

As for Me

To my Nana and Pap
On the day that Christ was born, we celebrate a holiday
Children think it's Santa's day, bringing toys in his sleigh
But as for me, I believe, God's greatest gift is all we need

On the day that Jesus died, we celebrate a holiday
Children think it's the Easter Bunny, bringing baskets full of joy
But as for me, I believe, God's greatest gift has set us free

On the day you first believed, we forget to celebrate
Jesus Christ was shining bright, on that day he gave you light
But as for me, I believe, God's greatest gift will forever be

On this day I'll ask one question, why do we need a holiday
To celebrate salvation? Now I pray that one day
We'll think of Jesus every day, not just on a holiday.

Jennifer Schmidt

Touched by Him

His gentle touch, his warm embrace
His kind, tender, loving face.
His love for God,
His love for me, a love that only we can see.

To live life and share with thee
Special moments yet to be . . .
An open mind and a heart so free, to only ask for eternity.

I ask you to embrace for me, each measure of reality.
Touch my hand and warm my face
I know not of another place, to lift my heart without your grace.

God has given so much to me . . . my memory is now my reality!
I pray for strength and do request my heart remain closed at best
The love we shared will remain with me much longer than even eternity.

His gentle touch, his warm embrace.
Thank you for his kind, tender, loving face!

Linda L. Villarreal

My Baby

To my children, Nicky and Jessica
My baby bringeth laughter to my heart
he brings pleasure from the start

Out of my womb when he was born
straight from there and into my arms

He looked at me with such dismay
probably thinking, it's been a long time, I'd say

The good feelings arose, he was finally here
I began thanking the good Lord that he was so dear.

Robbin Russell

We Three

No sound is as sweet as a new baby's cry.
Or the radiant look in its mother's eye.
For years we gave her pain and sorrow,
Just to watch us grow.
She dried our tears, calmed our fears for her children.
As mothers we three now know.

Over the years, as we three grow, we find joy
And sorrow only a mother could know.
All the hurt and pain, mothers just put away.
Heart to heart it is a mother's loving way
No price is placed on your mother's love, it is
Always warm just like a glove.
It is tenderly yours for all your life long.

Whatever your age, whatever you do, you are
Never too old for me to love you.
You will always hold a special place with her in my heart.
You, your mother, her mother
We three.

Hermella Lane

Special Memories

In memory of my father, Stephen Place
There is a place very special to me.
High on a hill stands a large pine tree.
A beautiful lake is nestled below.
Around the edges pine trees stand in a row.
Wild flowers bloom there under this tree.
Yes! This place is very special to me.
A gentle breeze kisses my cheek
And leaves me breathless unable to speak.
I came fishing here with my Dad.
Now he's gone and left me so sad.
I have precious memories that stay with me.
That's why this place is so special, you see?

Fran Walsh

Daddy

To my father, with love always
Day after day, I prayed to God to help you.
I asked him for a miracle, but he never heard me.
I remember how you looked the pain, the agony.
Walking away that day, I said, "I'll see you tomorrow."
That night in the silence I laid crying and I prayed,
"God please help him or take him from this pain."
Only minutes seemed to pass when I heard the knock on the door.
The voice I knew, the news I knew.
God has answered my prayer.
No more pain, no more fear, the end was here.
I only wish I could have been there
I never got to say goodbye; I never said I loved you.
Why? Daddy, why? Did Jesus hear my cry?
How much I wanted to tell you everything you meant to me.
I thought I had forever, but it should have been yesterday.
I stood beside you to say goodbye and I love you.
Only you couldn't hear me then.
I started to cry and I heard this tiny voice.
She's telling me mommy it's okay! Papa's okay.
Jesus is taking care of him and he's all better now.

Pamela Ann Kegler

Say It Now, You May Not Be Back

Sometimes the prefect thing to say comes to me too late,
the chance goes by, I didn't speak, and now those words must wait.
There are times I know what to say, but verbalize I don't
In hopes the time will come again, but chances are, it won't.

Since all of us are actors, and the world is but our stage.
each day's another chapter, each minute's another page.
When we miss the opportunity to say what is in our heart,
we may have missed the greatest lines ever for our part.

As those perfect words to share come to you, whenever,
write them down or speak you peace, it could be now or never.
Life's too short, we never know if we'll be here tomorrow.
That sentiment you left unsaid could be your biggest sorrow.

As I age I try to tell my family more often
how much they mean, how much they're loved, before I'm in my coffin.
I should have years and years to go to get my thoughts across,
But who knows, it could be tonight when I go meet The Boss.

So when you finally have the chance to express what's on your mind
don't hesitate or put it off, just do it and I think you'll find
my reasoning is obvious, as clear as white from black.
you need to say it now, because you may not be back!

Paul A. Hurdle

Broken Apart

In the blink of an eye, everything was gone.
A special someone I knew so bold and so strong.
He touched me with tenderness and his was so true.
Why couldn't you understand the way I understood you?
I never dreamed about the day that we would actually part.
I loved you more than anything, from the bottom of my heart.
Why did you leave me and leave me in such pain?
Did you actually think you had something to gain?
You left me confused and lost in my feelings.
It would take some time for my heart to start healing.
Yet the pain is still there and it won't go away.
In its place, in my heart it will stay.
I still see your smile and your face in the sun,
I remember the times we used to have fun.
In the strength of your arms, I would lay so happily.
The tenderness of your kiss would come so unexpectedly.
I guess that's why I love you and need you so much.
I really miss your gentle, loving, never-ending touch.

Patricia Skokan

No Words

I wanted to write how I feel.
That's usually what I do.
But, I don't know how I feel.
So there are no words on this paper.

I wanted to tell you that I care.
That's what I figured I say someday.
But I don't know if I do.
So there are no words on this paper.

I wanted to tell you that I would be here for you forever.
That's how I tried to feel.
But, I can't promise that.
So there are no words on this paper.

Erica Corea

Untitled

When these roses disappear
I'm going to press each petal against
Every wound someone else left me
When the tide washes in
It's going to bear my pot of gold
Cool autumn nights
The Flyers are playing
Everything about this man is like lighting a fire
I can't take my eyes off him
Golden and sparkling brown
My long sought after sine qua non
Can I put my bags down
And come into your arms
In the distance I hear the whistle blowing
You don't have to wait for me
I've already arrived

Susan Haines

It's All around Us

I look out of my window and take a big sigh
A canvas of color, an array for the eye
Clouds of white, pink, and gray, make me take a moment to pray
It is so quiet, but what do I hear?
The wind chimes singing, taking away all fear.
The trees sway as the chimes play its song
Thank you God for letting me belong
To take a moment to stop and look
All of creation has become my book
A book of wonder, something to treasure
It's all around me to give me pleasure
So take the time to spend a moment
To look and hear, can be your atonement.
Thank you God for letting me be
A small part of the picture and that moment to see.

Marion Mazzoli

Love in Question

His beautiful lips brushed hers with such passion
and gentleness that her body weakened.
His voice lulled her into a state of serenity.
She longed for his constant affection.
She abstained herself from giving it to him,
being in fear that it was not what he wanted.
She didn't want to smother him, causing his absence.
His eyes entranced her, every time she thought of him she smiled.
Will he break her heart or won't he?
She lives in constant agonizing wonder.
She of course desires the latter.
She doesn't want to be separate from him.
Waves of wonder still brush her thoughts
as to how she caught his eye or peeked his interest.
She is living for the moment,
bathing in his presence.

Jennifer Whitis

The Special Person You Are

For Sandi Grote, my mom
There's not many people in the world who touch
people's lives in a special way.

But you are not those people.
You are to me someone special.

I sit and ask myself, why do you do the things
you do? I never get any answers.
Maybe it's just who you are.

Mom, you are special to me, because you showed
me things I could not see. Your wisdom guides
me down roads that are unbearable by myself.
You love is like arms stretched wide-open
always waiting for a hug. Your knowledge provided
a new way of looking at myself and my situations.
I hope that when I began to walk on my own,
That you will be there to walk with me.

If there is anything that must be said about you,
The only answer that comes to mind is,
you are a very, very special person to me.

John Scales

Comparison

To Mother, whose love still blooms
As I gaze at the rose
In the early morning sun
I think of her
My one and only true love

As the morning sunbeams tenderly caress the rose
Reflecting its deep scarlet hue
My mind is now joyfully alive
By warm, glowing thoughts of her

For is not a rose
But nature's revealed image of a woman's heart
With each petal tenderly placed
And ever so perfectly layered
Nestled snugly
Encircled in a wondrous natural bosom

And her loving heart, like the glorious rose
In the splendid morning sun
Is a striking portrait of Heaven itself

The rose, her heart
When both are touched with love
One is truly blessed.

Edward R. Hendricks

Shower Scene

step in wash out
twenty hours of pure hell
down the drain
over the metal grate
water enters the openings
cleanses the dirt in my pores
that i carry on my skin
watch the mud excise itself
shaky hands push against the tile
steam saturates the chamber
delusions flash in my face
vengeance erupts in my moist body
drops of scorching water fear for their lives
as they hang off of my swollen lips
streams, rivers, slither down my back
and attack my legs as they form a puddle around my toes
and find a better place
as they race to the lead pipes
dry myself with the towels of pity
as another long and hard day comes to an end

Christina Riordan

Meaning Of

To William, Sammy, Gina, Timothy, and Therron
To feel within is a full thought on, life
Life itself is the true reality of life . . . of love
Love and life . . .
A meaning, without . . .
Both, means of one without . . .
Means lost.

Theresa Tyson

An Angel in the Park

As I passed through the park last night,
Men, women, and children, what a sight!
Scattered in sleeping bags, along the ground,
Cardboard boxes, no food to be found.

Sorrowful faces, smudged with dirt.
A baby's cry of hunger or hurt.
Shopping carts filled with all they possess,
Reminiscing of love or a simple caress.

Each one a parcel to his own,
"Do not enter here!" was the tone.
"Whatever I have must last me tonight,
Tomorrow may bring me joy and delight."

If I could just help one of these poor,
With food or shelter or perhaps more.
Maybe I can with a little prayer,
Watch over them all, I know you care.

Anita M. Pastier

Who Am I Really?

Who am I really?
Am I just a young girl with an epiphany?
Or am I just someone craving for attention?
Whoever I am, I know that deep inside of me,
I'm still young and beautiful;
And nothing can ever change that about me.

Maybe I'm a bad girl, maybe I am good;
Who knows who I really am?
Only the one who made me would.
Why is it so hard to find out?
How can it be?
That I'm a girl with only one mind,
Full of thoughts and dreams.
Do I have emotional feelings
That can be hurt very easily?
Or are they just hidden deep inside of me?
And finally,
Do I respect myself enough
To know just who I can really be?

Jonnique Adjmul

A Tear

The prettiest thing I've ever seen in this life
Is something that comes from inside.
As we sat with one another and spent a moment
In time talking about how things have come to pass,
I saw a tear roll down your face
And yes to me that was a beautiful sight.
For in that few minutes I saw all the love
And emotions deep inside, it was a tear from within.
It was heart sent and that's what makes it real.
For the first time I came to realize
A person can see all things on the outside
But being able to vision one's
Inner feelings is what counts in this life.
Even that of a small tear. I now know the power of love
As I turned and walked away I felt a tear
Roll down my face that very same day.

Chris Wilson

My Will Is My Way

My will is my way.
It can't be changed to another day
Or hour, and you can't change it.
It's going to stay the same each and every day.
My will is to go to school.
I think school is no game because if you think
It is, you will have to sit and take the pain.
So don't try to change my will in any way
Because it's going to stay the same each and every day.

Porscha Rush

I Am What I Want to Be

To Alex and Simon, with love
A silent drop in a sea of ocean's
Blanket on your snowy shoulder
And fruit to your naked heart.
Immaculate joy to my priceless treasure
And fuel to the mankind.
I am the seed of the earth and the chant of Eve.
The wine that gushes through your veins
And the coal which ignited your cravings I want to be.
The streams of laughs that revive your glance
A branch where the haggard reposes
And indulges in reveries.
I am the steady rock, anchor to the drowned and lost.
The flute to enchant your memories and hymn to the past
The thirst for the unveiled truth and tree,
Bent by ageless storms flapping of exhaustless wings
And the warmth of the ripe wheat.
I'm wisdom and wishes and comfort and morning and peace.
I'm yesterday and today and tomorrow.
And no one will ever despise me,
For I am what I want to be.

Lucia Gorea

The Moon

Tonight the moon is a sliver of a fingernail,

Tomorrow the moon will be a chipped
Sand dollar lying in the sand.

The next night it will be a full moon
Like a sugar cookie floating in the sky.

Diana Kowalski

Our God

Our God is the Truth most definitely,
He is Creator of all things, including
You and me

He is a God of Love,
A God of Judgment too!
He is as soft as a dove
and as sweet as the Lamb
Run to Him, Run to Him,
He will take care of You!

Come, come and I will give thee rest
all those who are tired of
the sinner's nest.
Open your heart, invite Me in,
that I might do My work in you,
throughout and through in.

I am Your Father, you are
My children, for you no longer
have to roam,
Come to Me! Come to Me!
Come back to Me so that I can take you Home.

Nikesha Hill

The Christmas Mouse

Dedicated to Daniel Corbin
The little mouse came out of his hole.
He could not believe what his eyes did behold.
There stood a tree right in the floor.
How could it get there, he wanted to know?
He knew a tree could not in the floor grow.
God must have put it there, he thought.
I wonder if some cheese he brought.
He jumped on a branch, he wanted to explore.
As a Christmas ball fell and hit the floor.
He jumped down and ran to his hole.
I've had enough for today, he said as he jumped into bed.
I'll go out tomorrow and then I'll explore.
To see how that tree got up through the floor.

Olive Corbin

Life in a Day

She looks at me and smiles and says, "Good morning."
The sunshine, like bright daisies, floods the room.
     The day is new.

She wonders to herself, "Where has the time flown?
What have I done?"   The sun has passed its peak.
     The day is short.

She shuts her eyes in long and dreamless slumber.
"If I should die before I wake, what shall I waken to?"
     The day is through.

Joan Blanchette

A Promise of Fatherhood

To Samantha Rose Marlowe
To my unborn child, I give you these promises of fatherhood.
As your father I promise to teach you about
The Lord and hope you follow his word
I promise to let you grow as an individual
No matter what roads you take
I promise to be patient with you and teach you
Patience, love, compassion, tenderness, forgiveness
And understanding
I promise not only to be your father, but to be
A best friend, a shoulder to cry on a listener
To talk to, a buddy to play with.
I promise to shelter you from harm whenever I can
I promise to raise you the best way I can
And hope you understand, but most of all
I promise you that I will love and care
for you with all my heart.

Dave Marlowe Jr.

A Moment of Wisdom

Are you sure you know the time and the place?
Are you sure you know the way and the where?
Are you sure you know the when and the how?
Then if you know all of these, you know the wisdom of
The universe, the race of human, and the beasts that roam,
But best of all, you know that you among all, are the wisest.

But then in thinking that you knew all there was,
That you knew the time, place, where and when,
You lost the wisdom of humility and placed yourself
Among the stars of the night and the sun of the day.
And when you sought how, you found that your
Shallow wisdom had no foundation, that it was but
A fleeting shadow across your life and you must
Return again to being but a simple human,
Alas, not a wise, universal, all knowing, being.

But, do not be saddened by this return to humanity.
For in the realization of the fact that you did not know all.
You actually grew in wisdom.

C. Clewley

Like Rivers and Streams

Like rivers and streams, and the immaculate sun,
I have to complain of all but one.
One so dear and true to surprise,
the love will shine forth and light up the skies.
Of one I say so far and so few,
put away pride and let beauty shine through.
Your smile is different and words are insane,
to cast away hate and cleanse like the rain.
Your eyes are oceans, so clear and so calm,
you've entered my world, so quote like the psalm.
You managed to break in and steal my heart,
so keep it my dear and freshly we'll start.
For new beginnings are better than life,
an old way of loving and warding off strife.
We'll make it together you've nothing to fear,
thankful we'll be by each passing year.
And the day I quit loving without asking why,
is the day I look up and my body should die.
But still I'll come back to say it's all right,
with you vast in my arms, I will hold you all night.

Diana Nilsson

Loving You

To Warren, love of my life
Your smile lights up the entire room,
I'm never cold since we embraced.
My heart skips beats when you are in sight,
I feel like I'm in Heaven every time I see your face.
I never knew how much I loved you,
now that I love you with all my heart.
But the pain I feel is overwhelming,
every time that we are part.
No matter where you go,
no matter what you do, I'll still hold you close to me
Nothing can keep me from loving you.
I would climb the highest mountain, swim the ocean blue,
cross the largest dessert, just to be with you.
For you I would die, for you I would live,
for you I would lie, for you I would give.
You are the only one on this earth,
that means this much to me.
So I think we should love each other,
and together forever, we should be.

Anna C. Perkins

When Hope Is Lost

To my children, whom I love
I looked at me in the looking glass
I saw many people from my past,
black, white, brown, yellow, and red
Tortured souls, with eyes that said,
I'm lost, I'm hurt, I'm empty and dead

Their faces were lined with sweat and tears
In the droop of their shoulders, I saw the years
of oppression, pain, hunger, and inequality
Their wounds lay open and bare for all to see
The silently screamed, please! please! help me!

My hope is lost and will is gone
I have no strength or desire to carry on
I have come to the end of my journey here
There is no reason now to fear

Lay me now, where I can rest
Place some flowers upon my chest
I await the angel, to climb the stair
I know that Jesus will be waiting there
With outstretched arms, at Heaven's gate
To welcome me and reward my wait.

Evelyn L. Sutton

Veteran's Day Poem

Life is precious, life is sweet.
But you risked yours when the other countries we beat.

God gave you the courage to fight for us,
And today we're given a chance to thank you very much.

You had to leave your family, and all the people you love.
But you are here with us today, by power of the Lord above.

I love you for your courage, and your ability to be strong.
We hate that you had to do this, because fighting is so wrong.

I am just so very grateful that you are here with us today.
And we know because of you, democracy's here to stay.

Jenn Bickford

Sad Weather

I remember fog clouding up the once clear air,
like the tears that clouded the eyes of those who were there.
A dark coldness weighed upon the day
like the grief that weighed upon my heart
when I watched your spirit fly away.
The mist that surrounded your eternal bed was heavy with moisture,
as if tears from a weeping sky were suspended in the air,
while the frigid breeze carried a melancholy murmur.
Sorrow seemed to cast a shadow across the sky,
and the sun's rays seem to be dulled by gloom.
I never knew how much I could cry.
An atmosphere of grief settled around the damp earth where you laid;
I remembered the ruby smile, the raven ringlets,
and the glistening eyes that you once had,
and on your funeral day, I could see why the weather was so sad.

Yen Lam

War

Bullets flew, people died, death falls among us.
As the unknown soldier lay in pain
he lay there in the mud and rain.
Thinking back at the days were gone,
he started to sing a mellow song.
As he hears the people scream,
he lay there weeping in gleam.
All he thought was pain, pain in the poring rain.
He got scared screamed but not heard,
He looked up to see a couple of birds.
He feel asleep to only realize he is going to die.
He asked himself why?
I do this for my country in honor of my name
This is not fake, neither a game.
I lay hear in sorrow feeling sorry for myself
Nothing but pain in the poring rain.
Nothing to earn nothing to gain.

Stephen Phillips

Dad

In memory of my father
Years seem to have a way of slipping through our fingers.
The things we long to say, more silent they may linger.
When words we should be sharing, instead of words unspoken,
Like spirits in a dark room that search for light unbroken.

Our time is running out as panic fills my heart.
How can I say the things I feel before our time to part?
Please! Wait! One more minute, I can't let go just yet,
For down my cheek rolls all those things I haven't told you yet.

Thank you for that open ear that always was around,
And for your mind so open wide that always could be found.
I thank you Dad for your heart so big in truth it only lays.
A heart that's loved and cared so much I've known for all my days.
Just one more thing before you go, please don't ever you forget,
Are all those words I've left unsaid I haven't told you yet!

Kathy Semer

Take My Pain

To all this has touched
Walking down the path of pain,
I look beside me and see again,
The caring face of One who knows,
Every wound that I try not to show.
I cover my pain with a mountain of pride,
His caring hand, I deny.

I'm late to realize, I'd turned away,
From the only hand, that could but save,
My dying spirit, too crushed to survive,
But with His help, would be made live.

Swimming around in a pool of sorrow,
I search for the wall of hope tomorrow.
I realize I must make a decision,
Hang on to the pain, and stay in my prison,
Or let go and draw near,
Breaking from all fear,
To the face of One I'd rejected before.
Lord, I need You now, and forevermore!
I now surrender my hands of pain, and gloves of pride,
At the feet of One, from whom I can never hide.

Sophia S. Williams

The Promise

I want to take you to places you've never been
Show you what it's like to ride the color of the wind
Wrap you in a world of love that only my heart can bring
Surround you with security that will make your heart sing
I want to do things with you that you have never done
Walk with you down paths that neither of us has won
Make your whole body tingle with just one glance
I will do things to you never read in any romance
I want to wrap my fingers all through your hair
I'll show how much love two hearts can share
So, this is "The Promise"
From me to you
I will always love and care for only you.

Wanona S. Feller

The Reading Land of Oz

A lion, a tiger,   a bear, and a cat,
            One read this and
                              The
                              Other
                                 Read
                                    That

        The lion's book was torn
        The tiger's book had
          a horn
                The bear had a
            book on cats
        and   the   cat   had
            a book on
            bats
everyone was enjoying it but
        there was one problem
    The cat couldn't read and
        The bear couldn't read the word
                    CAT!

Lindsay Ross

The Beauty and the Beast

The young lady said, "Look at the beauty I behold,
And look at you, old man, so ugly and old."
The old man said, "There are pretty lines on your face,
But my soul is a beauty that no lines can erase."

Jessica L. Moss

Broken Branches, Scattered Dreams

I am a tree. Majestically, my strong branches
support hopes and fears, like so many leaves.
I am complete. Swiftly comes the savage storm,
severing my branches, scattering my leaves.
I am in pain. Beseechingly, I cry for my lost limbs,
as the wind whips mercilessly.
I am broken. Mournfully, I seek my missing branches,
To find them claimed by earth beneath.
I am alone. Slowly my wounds are covered over by time,
but I will never forget.
I am tired. Wearily, I gaze down and behold flowers,
alive in the ground beneath.
I am confused. Suddenly I understand
that my broken branches have become new earth.
I am amazed. Gratefully, I observe the wonder of new life,
brought forth from shattered dreams.
I am a tree. I am complete.

Tiffany Searing

The Prayer of the Common Man on Christmas Eve

I give thanks to you O Lord this Christmas Eve.
For you gave strength; that no child will go
hungry in my land this night.
I give thanks to you O Lord, that the anticipation
of joy and happiness of the morning,
which will be found under the tree of my child
dances in his dreams,
As he is safe, healthy, loved and warmly
snuggled in his bed.
I give thanks to thee O Lord,
that the memories of the past are filled with
the knowledge of a peaceful, hard working people,
and the kindness and gentleness that is ours
during this time of the year.
O Lord, but most of all, I am thankful
that the Hope for the world is born
does live has secured the certainly
of our future. Amen.

Jack De Young

Mother

Oh, Mother of mine
I loved you so,
I want the whole world to know,
How wonderful you are,
Sacrificing, you would go without
So I could have some things to rave about.
A jolly good sport with all classes of people
In spiritual growth you could tower a steeple,
If my life could be a bit like yours,
I am sure it would all ring true!

Laverna Drella

Grandpa

His hair was gray, his eyes were blue.
His favorite words were "I love you,"
And every little once in a while,
You could look at him and see the prettiest smile.
He always treated me kind and tender,
And his love I'll always remember,
For this man is my grandpa,
An undying part of me.
So I wrote these words for all to see
How much my grandpa means to me.
He was always a young boy's friend,
Even until the very end.
Now up in Heaven is where he will be,
And I hope he still remembers me.
We all love and miss you very much.

Joseph Hudson

A Winner!

I'm a winner, not a pinner or a sinner.
I'm a winner, not a ninner, minner or finner.
I'm a winner, not a loser or a noser.
I chose to be.
I'm a winner. This is my choice, you see.
No half stepping on the move, whole stepping second to none.
I'm a winner! You can't touch this!!!
I can't lose with the stuff I use from God's
Hope chest of life.
I am a winner!!!

Jean Poole

Words from a Burning Cloud

I was created by man.
To summon nations to peace.
Yet all I know is death.
I ride upon a boiling cloud,
And fire is my breath.
The sky is split with a blast of my voice.
The darkness of night flashes day.
Like a thief, I steal the flesh from your bones,
As your armies and fleets fall away.
Though I smite the earth with thunderous force,
My inferno does not pass.
Your once great cities lie void as deserts,
And the sand becomes as glass.
So guard the keys that set me free,
And teach prevention well.
True peace to the nations will come through Christ.
To summon me,
Brings hell!

Tim Bright

Answered Prayer

Kimba
Mostly every night, child, I sit down to pray
for with him beside me my prayers are easier to say.
No matter the thoughts or, even the words unspoken,
His love for you and I can never be broken.
Whether days are bad or good enough to share
His love being whole and immense he has plenty to spare.
For there is nothing that can be wrought by the God, Almighty,
Because He is all knowing and father to many.
So if ever you need, answered, a prayer or two
call to him, he shall always be there to help you.
For there is nothing he hasn't heard before,
especially when He counsels countless numbers
as they enter through His door.
And because his bond within each of us cannot be severed,
His name, always, shall be by one and all revered.

Kim A. Harned

Ode to a Lost Love

Can you by searching find out God,
It's more than difficult, it's more than hard,
Can you imagine just how I feel,
Can you believe it's love and it is real,
As real as the tears I shed now and then,
When I think of you and what could have been,
I never knew how to love in vain,
'Til I loved you, lost, you, and felt the pain,
The pain I've seen through the tears of time,
The pain of knowing you'll never be mine,
I told you I loved you and told you again,
I'm sorry, it's my fault we can only be friends,
Oh! How I loved you . . . did you ever know,
What joy you brought me, you thrilled my soul,
If ever you'll love me I'll never know,
But I'm not afraid this time to tell you so.

Ernest R. Wallace

In My Window

As I sit beneath my windowsill,
I try to grasp the way I feel.
My emotions are scattered, here and there,
With not a soul around to whom I can share.
To be alone, with no one around,
Extreme emptiness is all I have found.
Why am I alone, without a friend
And a broken soul I cannot mend?
There are people outside my window now.
I want to talk to them, but I don't know how.
On my window I knock night and day,
But only silence is what I say.
No words or sounds come out of me;
Just a shadow of a person is all they see.
Will I ever be noticed by the people outside,
Or behind my window will I forever hide?
Only time will tell, whatever may be,
So in my window I sit 'til they notice me!

Lynnette Anderson

The Sadness That Overwhelms Us

The sadness that overwhelms us without warning,
a gray ambush springing from God knows where.
This bitterness that rises, absurd,
in the midst of serenity,
like a dark stain spreading
from the entrails of a star.
There has been no reason to suppress our smile,
no previous disturbance in the coordinates of equilibrium.
Yet we find ourselves, of a sudden,
the unsuspecting recipients of calamity,
stalked in a tangle of seismic fissures.
Anguish cringes at the end of the hall.

Angel Cuadra

A Husband's Love

To Ken and Marguerite Shippee's endless love
God made us to be together forever
God gave us a life he gave us a home
God gave us this bond that would always be shown.
Then the children came the years flew by
As we watched them all grow in the blink of an eye.
Generations were made by our children all grown
As we watched them all follow the traits of our own.
Those times had past us now it's been 55 years
When we made those vows through laughter and tears
I left you now to be in my father God's place
It's funny I know you remember my face.
Remember me and the love that we shared
Pass on all our memories, our love, and our cares
Please don't be sad, sorry, or blue
Always remember that I'll forever love you.
I will protect you and guide you through all of my care
Until that day we rejoin again in Heaven forever to share.

Dale L. Acker

Be

We cannot be unless beyond is known.
But there, can be uncertainty.
We can't be objective, unless it is all clear.
But everything can be questionable?
Can the doubt be fairly answerable?
Can fair be enough anymore?
Can the nature of it all be so significant,
that practical understanding has no place?
Can we be without measures?
Can we be human anymore, without the state
of fault tapping in?
Why can't we just be, what we see there, can be?

Barbara Park

April in England

In memory of Miss O'Neil, my tutor in Nice, France
Come to England in April
Full pockets or on the dole
Come where waits your Joel.

Come to England in April
I'll introduce you to my favorite troll
He'll steal your heart, he'll claim your soul.

Come to England when it is spring
I'll be waiting with a wedding ring
Come on birdy be on the wing.

Jane Pierritz

Ode to Elvis

In the light mist on an August morn
Two souls united at this break of dawn
In meditation spirit would ride above the land
It sought divine purpose, its part amongst man
A white horse would come in a field of light
Tapping its hooves, saying it's time to take flight
Mounting with trust white beauty knew the way
Giving it full rein as the white mane swayed
Soon beauty danced on the sacred ground neighing
Above a stairway master's love stood waiting
One gaze one turn master guided in a lighted corridor
Eye filling beauty enhanced as master unlocked a door

Crossing the threshold I walked in alone
One with a jewel white coat sang a special tone
Standing tall with a familiar crooked grin
A friend of old took hold as a oneness of a twin
It was no beginning for it knew no end
Time, space couldn't separated these friends
Years of service to awaken for this soul
One light brother of many within the divine whole

A. M. George

Choices

We all start our lives the same way on this earth
Fathered by man and a woman gives birth
But from that moment on your destiny's your own
Your parents can guide you just 'til you're grown
Then your own mind kicks in and decides what you'll do
The choices you make are all up to you
You can ask for some guidance as you go along
But you'll know in the end that you have to be strong
And stand on your own feet, decide what to do
Because your life is special and belongs to only you

Peggy L. Parrish

Daddy

For my father, Jesse Franklin Williard
My daddy is a wonderful man who has a heart of gold
His generosity, love, and understanding
grow bigger as he grows old

He enjoys talking and laughing
with whomever he happens to meet
And words of wisdom and inspiration
he is always there to greet

He heads for the mountains, which is now where he calls home
With family, friends, or his God, he never walks alone

You see this man is quite unique, in his way he shows
To walk with God each day that passes your blessings are bestowed

He has taught me many things and always lends a hand
And when things are difficult he encourages me and understands

A star can shine no brighter than my Daddy does to me
In my eyes and others' too, no greater a man can be.

Carolyn Williard Beck

Untitled

When I see you
you always seem to be busy
surrounded in your own little pile of machinery
too old for toys but too young to fade away behind the wrinkles

When I see you walking down the street
I see worn-out boots
torn clothing and always a warm smile

When I hear your voice
I hear a familiar deep scruffy tone
I hear hard times and quiet times also
When I hear of you, I stand up.

Annette M. Summit

The Journey

The glistening of helmets, the excitement and thrills,
The sound of large engines as oncoming speed builds,
With wondrous anticipation of this nights long journey,
We reflect on our past with compassion and yearning.
As I climb inside this cabin so small,
I learn to appreciate the insignificant and all.
For as I experience this, the greatest of times,
I can't help but wonder about continued peace of mind.
The emptiness, beauty, and vastness of space,
Presents the loneliness, and fear which I must now face.
Looking back at the earth suspended below,
Reminds me how little I must now know.
As we continue our journey through the heavens so vast,
I begin to remember the sad memories of past.
With silence, prayer, and so much concern,
I remember the seven who did not return.

Richard Quiggle

More Than a Pet

There is this loving couple, named Sill,
Who lived in a new neighborhood, on Woodhill.
A more beautiful couple you won't find.
Their love for animals, is a love entwined
Their dog for many years, dated back to Egyptian time
Took sick and was very ill
No medicine would help, nor any pill.
Their little dog has long since gone
Left the Sills sad and drawn.
Many tears were shed and a broken heart
Cry no more, dear people, your pet is on the brink of a new start.
She no doubt is in Heaven now.
She looked around and barked to herself and said, "Wow!"
Sought the Lord, and jumped on his lap
Curled up and took a long dog nap.
Probably nibbling on his toes
Or playing fetch with someone she knows.
A large white puffy cloud for her bed
Looks down on two loving people, she'll never forget.

Mildred Jasinski

Another Time

To my inspiration, my grandmother
I looked into your eyes, it seemed so long ago
Another life, perhaps, another you, someone I hardly know
And in those eyes I found all that I had longed to see
Another life, perhaps, another you, and definitely another me
The bluest stars of hope just captured me away
Another life, perhaps, another you, and regretfully another day
They reach into my heart and took from me my soul
Another life, perhaps, another you, someone I hardly know
And took me to a place, I'd always longed to be
Another life, perhaps, another you, and definitely another me
But now the dream has faded and in my heart you'll stay
Another life, perhaps, another you, and regretfully another day.

Michelle Simms

Into the Shadow of Beijing

It is May and a soft field of green begins its song.
Hearts join pride, fists. They climb like new shoots.
Chu Ping proffers whispers in the people's hall.

June arrives melodic, a rose to China's lips
sweet as dreams, as poppies, as emerald fields,
Pure as lilt, a new song, freedom, freedom.

The turn is expected, like late marsh, like rotting flesh
Folding clouds gray; summer's tune rolled under.
Moon and poppies slow their sway.
Children of a thousand prayers fall into shadow.
Fear turns to tear thick as blood against the wall . . .

Arms outstretched, Wang Wei Lin defies the monolith.
He shares vision the world to see, shares dreams.
My God! free now to sing China Shall be free.

It is the fourth of June and aging Mandarin
Can hear the screams of Wang's soul rising.
This new shadow, this eclipse, this rising fist,
Like clouds over promised suns,
Over promised sons . . . what better death than this?

essell

Intelligent Young Man

I am an intelligent, young man who's lost in the world.
I wonder if I'm ever going to be someone special to everyone else.
I hear sirens behind me, wondering if I'm to be harassed again.
I see people looking into my eyes, stereotyping me as a thug.
I want to be an individual like everybody else.
I am an intelligent, young man who's lost in the world.

I pretend I'm a square so nobody dislikes me.
I feel happiness when my mom smiles and gives me a hug.
I touch my heart, hoping God will allow me to fix my sins.
I worry if drugs will really ruin my life.
I cry when I let friends and family down because of ignorance.
I am an intelligent, young man who's lost in the world.

I understand when I make mistakes and let my mom down.
I say, "Sorry," and try to do better next time.
I dream I'd still be famous and amount to something extraordinary.
I try to quit, but I guess it's about will power.
I hope I'm strong enough to get away from it.
I am an intelligent, young man who's lost in the world.

Davin K. Stevenson

Friction

Starry days and sunny nights,
The light of darkness blinked the sight.

A cold desert and warm, dry snow,
The smile of sadness won't ever go.

Change of constant and the end of eternity,
Blank thoughts confuse all the certainty.

Laughter of pain and tears of joy,
Aggressive anger turns light and coy.

The end of the beginning, the past of the present,
Broken love hurts, mended hate doesn't.

The birth of dead and the flaw in perfection,
Little boys torment to show affection.

The rough surface of smooth and the texture of flat,
The throne of good is where evil sat.

A lawless government and a non-melodic song,
A cold sweat breaks when the heat is strong.

The rich are poor, the poor have wealth,
The meaning of life contradicts itself.

Heidi Blair

A Place Called Home

Submerged 7 a.m., Tuesday morning
A phone rings, a child's voice is search of its mother
a cold wet dawn drenches a young girl
aimlessly she wanders alone somewhere
she remembers confounded ruffled
unafraid in smoke-filled room
crawling to gain control amidst laughter
a finger running over
deadened gums
a mirror
an unclosed bottle
an eve gathering of friends
recollecting a New Year.

Kathleen Lux

Lady of Grace

For my breeze of dances
A bright crystal smile shines into me
With brilliant light. Curves of radiance
From the sun's silhouette pierce me with passion.
Waves of silk flow down her back
Like a waterfall down a beautifully crafted mountain side.
The most delicate strokes
From the steadiest hand with the finest brush
From the greatest artist could do no justice
For her gracious lips that allow the sweetest
Voice I've ever heard pass through.
Look into her eyes and you'll see everything
You've ever known to be beautiful magnified
To an infinite amount of flawlessness.
An angel in my eye.
She dances with a swan as doves pass
in her honor and sing her song.

Todd Frederick Gorena

Imagination

I imagine myself to a mysterious place
where I don't recognize anyone's face
Flowers appear every way that I turn
But then everything begins to burn
I come back to reality where life isn't fair
And my daddy is beating me and pulling my hair
I yell, "Daddy, no!" but the belt snaps against my back
It whips me hard, it always happens like that
I try to scream but no sound comes out
I don't understand what it's all about
My daddy drinks then blames everything on me
But I never do anything wrong, why can't he just see
My eyes are dry and I can't cry anymore
So I go back to my mysterious place where I don't feel sore
I fly on my cloud across the sky
I'm safe for now, I'm flying high

Tierra Peters

Dreams

As we enter a world we are able to see things no one else is seeing
Exploring on our journey as if
we are Christopher Columbus sailing the high seas.
What are these happenings that occur in the night?
Are they signs letting us know what's going to happen the next day,
Or just figments of our imagination?
Whatever they are they can come at many different times and places.
Have you ever wondered about where they're coming from,
Or why this certain dream is in your mind?
Nightmares, la-la land, the lair of the big bad wolf,
many different illusions,
We enter a world unknown to everyone.
Then you awaken to the known world,
Leaving the unknown one behind
Until once again a dream becomes your reality.

Samantha L. Guyan

Baby

Little baby in my belly,
You are precious and so full of life.
As I feel your kicks and movements,
I realize that there is a little angel growing within me.
Then one day you will come into this world.
To your parents' eyes you are a miracle come true.
Your early life will be filled with toys.
You will grow up,
And your life will begin to blossom.
Toys will be a thing of the past,
And your future will be filled with decisions.
But never forget,
As the years go by,
You will still be your parents' little baby.

Nathalie Mutafoglu

My Best Friend

I've got a black and white cat, and he is my best friend.
I like to dress him up and we play pretend.
He looks so silly when he wears my mom's hats.
But he thinks he is a really cool cat.
I tell him that it's time for tea,
But he just sits there and looks at me.
Sometimes he is not very much fun,
When I want to play and he just runs.
"Come here little kitty and do what I say,
Or you'll have time out for one whole day."
He looks up at me and blinks his eyes.
Wraps his tail around me and gives me a sigh.
When it's time for bed and we snuggle in,
I know that he really is my best friend.

Karen Richelieu

As I Cried

To my family, with love
As I discovered a great illness in my body,
That threatened my life,
My very being of who I am,
I cried out to God to perform one more miracle.

As I went through the months ahead—
Some good, some bad—
I realized that death could be waiting.
I cried out again, God where are you?

As I waited for the answer, did I desire one?
I thought, we are all going to die;
I will just get to Heaven before you.
I cried out again; God said, "It's not your time,
You'll have to wait."

Linda Taylor

Thanksgiving

It's autumn now and harvest time,
The fields are ready to glean!
The bustling wind sweepings the leaves,
Mother Earth. is winter clean!

All is ready for the Big Feast Day,
I polished all the silver!
Hungry relatives are on the way,
Good grief! I start to shiver!

Thank you Lord, for everything,
The succulent turkey treat.
The Cinnamon-y pumpkin pies I baked
My kids can't wait to eat!

But I'll be thankful, more, I will,
When the platter's clean and dry,
And night creeps in, they've had their fill,
So I can wave, bye-bye!

Jo Anne R. Portelle

Suburban Nightlife

To my loving family and God
Darkness;
Towering reflection of trees
Looking up and away.
Bright stars against a blanket of peace,
Overshadowed by gleaming streetlights.

Mystery;
Dog's barking, magnified by nature singing
and celebrating solitude.
The stillness of man and his raging torment.

Solitude;
Dew falling softly without visibility,
upon fine grass and pavement,
While a cool, moist breeze slowly falling.

Man;
In the distance he still roams, not so softly.
A whistle, thunder of tracks, a train
Rumbling louder and louder.
Vibrating as the horn sounds;
Reminding man still roams in Suburban Nightlife.

Christopher J. Schoate

The Rose

Oh! What mysteries await me
To love and enjoy life
As it is meant to be

Fulfill my dreams
And energies, I implore you
Let me be your slave

To spend but one night
Amongst the beauty you possess
For I will be enchanted with your loveliness.

Lois B. Ringkamp

Untitled

Mama,
Brightly shining for me
A beacon of love and hope
Never failing,
Never lacking,
And I wonder,
How was I so blessed?
Never taking for granted the gift of you
The beauty of your heart,
The pureness of your soul.
My love for you is absolute,
All encompassing and true.
I am so proud of you
Your compassion overwhelming,
Your kindness second to none
All the good in me comes from you
You taught me how to be a man, how to be a person
The epitome of a mother,
I love you;
I love you.

Timothy L. Redus

Angel with God

For Joe, Jeff, Jim, and Mar
He took her from us at such a tender age
The flame within our hearts burn deeply for her return
Yet we all blamed him for we knew not his purpose
Until we realized that he'll return
Her so near because his purpose was
so dear and that was to become an angel with God

Janet Walker

For Mickey

I had a piece of God, I held it in my hands
It lifted all my spirits, it seemed to understand

It didn't have a purpose, the kind that we know of
Its purpose was to love me and for me to return love

I graciously accepted its complicated ways
for the rewards were worth the efforts that now consumed my days

It filled my heart with life I thought was long since lost
I gave it all my love no matter what the cost

Then one day it left me for somewhere up above
Spread its wings and flew away in spirit and in love

And even though the pain is great, at least I had the chance,
To know a piece of God and to hold it in my hands.

Cathie Marie Anzalone

Over in the Sky

Over in the sky are clouds of whiteness,
Over in the sky is a beautiful rainbow,
Up in the sky are our God and Jesus in Heaven.
Up in the sky is a bird flying,
In the sky are pictures of our lost family.
Up above the clouds is our God of hope,
In the lower part of clouds are ourselves.

Amber Keech

Second Time Around

Mothers again for the second time around
My mind is clear, yet I am worn down
I do my best to keep up with the times
But then I remember it is the second time around
I get up early and stay up late
And have seen so many of my friends
Go on through that Pearly Gate
With pains in my body I still love and contemplate
because the only thing I don't want to do is hate
One day I will be going through those Pearly Gates
My children, my children, please have patience and wait
because God wants you to love and not to hate
So while I am here, I will braid the girls hair
and keep them all clean and their minds clear
I will teach them how to read and write
Then one day they will be strong and bright
And when they are grown and on their own
the children will remember that they are not alone
For God is always by their side
to love them and keep them and to guide.

Doris J. Roberts

Chucky and Clyde

Chucky, do you know the truth?
The way Clyde feels inside for you?
Chucky, do you even care,
The way Clyde feels when you are there?
Clyde tries to be strong, so as not to get hurt
But once in a while, Chucky, Clyde slips on your shirt.
Next, Clyde climbs into bed and closes her eyes.
Memories race through her head, as she tries not to cry.
The best times she had, in her twenty four years,
Ended when you left and drowned in her tears.
But now you've come back, and Clyde is confused.
She still wants Chucky's love, but fears being used.
For now no one knows just what will happen.
When Chucky's around, Clyde will be so happy.
Until Chucky goes, Clyde's feelings won't show.
But when Chucky is gone, and Clyde hears the door
I can almost guarantee that the tears will then pour.

Ellen Parker DeShaw

Towards the Future

Unwritten as it may be, the future is open to me
Many roads yet untaken, many yet to be explored.
These things that yet to have a name, remain the nameless
Until the time comes and all is revealed.
And what is revealed is the past.
A past that I had helped to write.

Schuyler R. Thorpe

My Best Friend

Whatever else that I may be,
I am his friend, don't you see?
He's been here with me since my birth,
More than anyone, he knows my worth.
Through all my life journeys, far and wide,
He's always been right here by my side.
At times when I've felt lost and scared,
His loving comfort, he's always shared.
Sometimes I think I can't get through the day,
Then he reminds me to work, but also to play.
My friend is so loving and so caring too,
He always forgives me, whatever I do.
He's taught me such kindness, so let me teach,
All the friends that I can reach.
I've had many friends along the way,
But he's the friend who chose to stay.
If I follow my heart and I do my best,
My wonderful friend will do the rest.
When my journey is over, and come to an end,
I'll rejoice in Heaven with my best friend.

Mary Lou Rich

Squirrel on a Fence

As a baton orchestra, a little stick began
Not to act with consent, as the bee forethought.
As a wafer holder, he sat on this fence
In the part that persecuted him most.
As a performer, he sat backwards to me
On this fence to spin his tail around.
As a perfectionist, he was determined
to fly and brought a friend.
I watched as the incompetent to
See what was stone sober.
I learned to sleep before seeing a
predator on a date.

Dalia Rosas

Truth

Through the hardships and all the trials of life,
To overcome and go beyond, is our everyday strife.
We continue to wallow in our repetitive mistakes,
In our ignorance we realize not, the closeness of our fate.

Wasted is our time, we of simple minds,
Weakness of the flesh, to this earth our hearts do bind.
Greed, selfishness, and to be the golden rule,
Never a second thought to the effects of what we do.

On and on, round and round the earth does revolve,
To awake day after day, to the problems we cannot seem to solve.
All that exist, heard constantly with their complaints,
Whining and crying, held back by their own restraints.

When shall we realize it will all remain the same,
Until we ourselves, are willing to take the blame.
Unless we open our eyes to all that we ignore,
We'll continue to be deprived of the things that make life soar.

It will take more than one to put it into effect,
Only with unity, will the accomplishment reflect.

Vicki L. Bruner

Dances with Leaves

The wind dances with autumn's lissome leaves.
A balmy breeze partners with them from tree
to ground for a slow southern waltz.
A wandering wisp sweeps them up to their toes
in the precision pirouette of ballet.
A gay gust whirls and twirls them along fence lines
in tempos of a jaunty jitterbug.
A zany zephyr moves them across fields in a candid country cadence.
A carefree current whips them into the gyrations
of a buffoonish break dance.
Autumn colors descend, dancing in such rhythmic patterns
that it takes away the sadness of the bare, bleak
branches of winter's approach.

Gale Jackson

Smoke and Mist

To my sons, Phil and Todd Groves
Your music is a sorcerer's song
vapors in a thinning air,

The lyrics not your heart's own voice,
but sinewy web, a lion's lair.

My heart fears windswept words,
formed and forged by sea and fog,

It yearns for Gibraltar's rock,
cleansed pyramids, a prince, not frog.

Games and pretense have no lure,
wintry posing cannot cure,

An angel's quest from high above
to grant my wish, a soulmate, love.

The belltones to my hymn of prayer
are not frail notes, by spiders kissed,

Are not false lines from vultures' throats,
is not a song of smoke and mist.

Sunny Kreis

Green Bay Packers

Packers are number one
because they know how it's done

Their quarterback is Brett Favre
I have know idea if he likes to carve

A wide receiver named Robert Brooks
I wonder if he likes books

A running back named Edgar Bennet
Maybe someday he'll be in the Senate

That's my poem on the Packers
Their nickname I bet could be the "Smackers."

Paul Seaver

Grandfather

Grandpa is someone who really cares,
He always loves sitting in his favorite chair.

With the blue in his eyes and the gray in his hair,
He gives us his love there's nothing to compare.

He's travelled the world from sea to sea,
He'll tell us a story so we can see.

Then comes a joke with a wink and a smile,
It makes us laugh for quite a long while.

Now he's headed for his twilight years,
It's our turn to soothe his fears.

We'll show him our love hope and pride,
And we'll always be right by his side.

Jack Babcock

A Mother's Goodbye

When the time comes to tell your son goodbye
Have a smile on your face and keep your eyes dry.
Try to make him forget, try to make him feel good
And you might even laugh, if laugh you could.

Tell him to never give up, to be a man 'til the end,
And if he fails at a thing, to try it again.
Start him off on his way with a song in his heart,
For there's no better way than a singing start.

Tell him that you're proud, he's privileged to go
And be sure that your love and your proudness will show.
And when he's gone over there to fight,
He'll remember the way you looked that night.

He'll remember the things you said to him then
And he'll repeat them over and over again.
"Have courage my son, keep an iron-bound will,
And if you ever feel licked, keep fighting still."

So all of you mothers, when your sons have to go
Though you're sad in your hearts, just don't let it show.
Have a smile on your face and keep your eyes dry;
Start him off happy, when you tell him goodbye.

Charles A. Miller

A Day in the Life

Tick, it's early yet
A slow breeze blows through the neighborhood.
Tick, there's a girl jogging—pretty
And two kid's playing
Tick, tick, bark, bark
"Hey, give that back!"
Tick, tick, tick, Mrs. Andersen takes out the trash.
Tick, tick, a mailman walks distractedly, waves.
Tick
Tick
Tick, leaves . . .
Tick, falling.
Tick, tick, tick, a shadow is suddenly thrown across her eyes
Her reverie turns to fear until she sees
Tick, it is only the sun near to setting
That hides behind the sash.
Tick
Tick, and here she sits
Tick, waiting
Tick, still.

Karen Jellander

Song to My Father, Song of Faith

To Charles and Ruby Griffin
Upon my knees I do solemnly pray.
That the God of light does show me the way.
My relation of person with him is great.
For he is the author of life, and I wake.
He brings the true joy ending all pain.
He gives the true blessing, sun, wind, rain,
And the good earth upon which I fall to my knees.
Lifting my heart that my God may be pleased.
All that is needed in him I find.
All that is needed in him I find.

My God, before you I in humbleness pray.
Guide me safely upon my life's way.
He listens. He smiles. He sheds his light.
Filling my heart and soul with delight.
Gracing me. Making my inner being swell.
He teaches me life's love that all things I do well.
All that is needed in him I find.
Peace, joy and comfort.
For my body, spirit, mind!

Reginald Anthony Griffin

Untitled

Upon the beautiful ground
There lies a beautiful corpse.
He did not make a sound
When he died the night before.

From the body his life was torn
As the knife brought wonderful pain.
For thirty dollars, nothing more,
An honest man lies dead in the rain.

The lifeless flesh bakes in the sun
As there arises a delightful stench.
The essence of that someone
His soul has not been spent.

For the owner of that flesh
Eternal bliss can now be seen.
On the ground there lies a lifeless mess
While in Heaven there lives a beautiful being.

Nick Husbands

Untitled

Rest, ye soldier of the Lord
For you, warfare has ended!
The place in the hearts of those you touched
Is caught in time suspended.
Thy maker, the Redeemer, the Holy one
Has revealed through you His power,
To endure, we have, and cried all night
But now, for you, joy this hour.
Our walk on Earth is but a vapor
Our steps ordered may be few,
But God assures through Jesus the Christ
Eternal life that is new!

Johnny L. York

Untitled Musing #4

In my life I've done all I thought I could
I tried to be loyal, true to my friends
And I swear my intentions were good
She swore her heart was an empty space
The goodness that used to shine there had gone out
But my heart never shone in the first place
I know I didn't follow through with what I said I would
Promises were broken, reckless vows spoken
But I swear my intentions were good
I tried, but I couldn't stay firm where I stood
I compromised morals, I washed with the tide
All alone, I claimed immortality, and all alone, I lied
I turned my back on old beliefs, I'm sure my mother cried
I only walked through doors that I could see were open wide
So cover my shameful face in my coffin when I've died
Let no one look 'neath the black velvet hood
And tell my loved ones when they come to my graveside
I swear . . . my intentions were good

T. I. Kelsey

Open Your Heart

Dedicated to my gift from God—Matthew
The day you left me my world came to an end,
This broken heart will never mend.

Days and years they all passed by,
Not looking back I wondered why.

As time went by from boy to man,
You said I was never there to lend a hand.

You shut me out I asked you why?
There's never an answer, there's no reply.

In your heart one day you'll see,
I've always been there, open up to me.

Barbara A. Ruslander

Now You Don't Remember Me

To my loving mom
From what they say, Alzheimer's Disease will take you away.
No, not quickly; just a bit every day.
As the months slowly pass
We all wonder how long this agony will last.
We look into your "vague eyes"
The memories are fading, and we wonder why, oh, why?
All the familiar faces are scary—like unfamiliar places.
The memories left just scattered traces.
Your gentle touch, quick wit and loving care
are no longer there.
Along with the good time we used to share.
The joy of your grandchildren's treasures
Are no longer their grandmother's proud pleasures.
Mom, do you remember your wedding day?
Or what games your kids used to play?
Now, you sit with nothing to say.
You used to give your love so free
Singing as I sat on your knee.
Always there, I knew you'd be
You were always there for me, now you don't remember me.

Mary Ellen Strang

Light Our Way—A Prayer

In tribute to William Wordsworth
"We walked along, while bright and red
uprose the morning sun," slowly
unforming night's shadows into
hues of early dawn. Lovers strolling

hand in hand, our half-sunlit faces
bearing childish grins as we joyfully
exchange loving glances and
whisper fairy-like whims. How

lovely to be born again with each
new day, love renewed with the
quickening sunlight rushing in. As
all Earth's creatures blossom in the midst of
the sun's majestic rays—a lineless

backdrop with no hatred or violence
skewing eternal space. Upward,
to the rising sun, we turn, receiving
creation's protective cover, drinking
in the answers to every spoken and
unspoken holy prayer, we are blessed with
love's simple gift of being aware.

Michelle K. Moan

God's Painting

It was warm and lovely on an early Spring Day
When a regal butterfly flew past my way.
One wonders if she possibly knew
That those lovely wings with which she flew,
Were given to her by a Creator who cares
For even the creatures who fly through the air.

The sun was warming the earth beneath
Awakening it from its winter sleep.
The crocus and wild onions had pushed through the ground.
Soft green moss on all the rocks could be found.

The trees and bushes were groaning within
As new life in them was about to begin.
The birds were lifting their voices high while
Silent clouds drifted slowly by,
Both seeming to sense that Spring was nigh.

New Life! New Hope!
Affirmed once again
As God paints His picture
of the Resurrection.

Patsy J. Danec

Fortune, Fate, and Fool

Fortune smiles, once again the world can be yours, Fool.
Fate cuts in 'tis true, my friend.
Though, you must choose which way you'll go.
With one of us you could ride there.
But, what then, would you know?
And one of us will care enough.
To teach you lessons as you go.

Fortune never does smile down.
Where Fate must sometimes go.
Fortune lingers tempting Fool.
Where Fate cannot follow.

Fortune, Fate, life's calling Fool
It's time for him to go
Choose now, Fool.
Whose path you'll take.
Whose ways you will follow?
Fortune's waiting at the gate to take you to the top.
Or, will you tempt the hands of Fate?
Living your life at every stop?

Terri L. Reh

HOME WITHOUT FATHER

In Memory of Grady Kelly (September 9, 1908–December 30, 1998)
Our home departed with father today
As angels made ready and guided the way

No longer a home but now a plain house
For all that remains his broken heart spouse

Dear father now living in Heaven's fair land
No longer we kiss him or hold his frail hand

Taken for granted and thank you's not spoken
We now can't repay with gifts or a token

The absence of father remains evermore
'Til we reunite on Heaven's bright shore

The sick bed no longer a prisoner can hold
For now he is walking on streets paved with gold

A mansion, the city, a river of life
All that is missing is family and wife

No longer living with dread and great fears
He'll never be lonesome or shed my tears

There Grannie Charlton and Granddad Kristal and so many more
All waited to greet him and open the door

Still the same house, just not the same home
A house without father, could never be home.

Roger Kelly

Brown-Eyed Girl

I am a brown-eyed girl who is tired and scared.
I wonder how long the treatment will last.
I hear the treatments drip into my line.
I see myself in my dreams growing up.
I want to go home from the hospital now.
I am a brown-eyed girl who is tired and scared.

I pretend to be flying in the clouds.
I feel the pain being taken a flight.
I touch my mind with my soul.
I worry that I may die.
I cry when I get the medicine.
I am a brown-eyed girl who is tired and scared.

I understand what I am going through.
I say, let the sickness be gone.
I dream of when there is a one time cure.
I try to think good thoughts.
I hope time will pass by quick.
I am a brown-eyed girl who is tired and scared.

Catherine Pecore

God's Little Angels

God's little angels bring so much joy to us
Their precious love surrounds us
By their magic angel dust
The smiles and the laughter and their
Playful tenderness
Gives hopes and dreams and memories
For our own existence
The innocence on their faces as learn
Our lives through them
We guide their paths to our Heavenly Father
So they will soon know him
A mother's love is a special bond that keeps
Them safe at night
Their halos shine throughout the world and
The love will keep it bright

Saundra Crawley

Colby

Who is this sweet infant with a cheek at my breast?
As his mother, I feel I should know best.
As I watch in amazement and smell his sweet breath.
I think he must be an angel, a gift, not a test.

I thank the Lord dearly for blessing my soul,
Allowing a baby so healthy and whole
Into my life to have and to hold.
This boy is more precious than silver and gold.

Jennifer Johnson

Suddenly I Turn Around and . . .

Suddenly I turn around and the things I want just can't be found.
It doesn't have to bring me down, make me upset, or frown.
I'm talking about someone you see, who is very special to me.
He is my companion, my friend, even though he's gone,
I will love him to the way beyond.
This whole story is about my grandpa, he played with me every day,
Even though he had the last word to say.
He was always around to play hide and seek,
He was the one who hid, just like one big kid.
He always played Rummy and Othello, he was always my best fellow.
I was his only one girl, both my cousins are boys,
So, no matter, he always assembled our toys.

Oh, forget about lunch, had to wait for grandma to come home,
Although he loved us a whole bunch.
When there was no more gum, grandpa would go out to buy us some.
He always said, cartoon time in the morning,
Grown up time at night, he loved making us movies,
Which made everything alright.
These are the memories, those were the days,
I will never forget his loving ways.

B. Ferrantelli

Anastasia's Apparition

A silent vessel walks alone
down a crowded street.
With hands bound behind her
she walks along pondering of her existence,
wondering what it would be like to experience
life through the eyes of another.
Her seemingly dark gaze is known
to hold back oceans of pain.
Still she remains strong.
She knows me by name and sees through my heart
as if it were an open diary.
In passing she whispers stories that captive the imagination
sending me spinning and wanting more.
Yet she disappears among the world's patrons
just as my heart falls in love.

Rodney Jenkins

Echoes in the Night

Yes, yes, I hear them small voices, echoes in the night.
They sing, they shout, voices all about, a scene I've seen,
But only in my dreams.

Yes, yes, I see them, small shadows, the echoes of the night.
A mist of white, a peaceful tranquil light, a voice I hear
Echoes envelop the night.

It's warm, I run, but never do I fall?
I'm safe, secure, the echoes voice endures, I'm once again,
Directed to the light, I turn, I breathe, my heart is beating light.
Again, they come the echoes in the night.

I dream, I wonder, how can these things be?
I'm amazed as I gaze, a world within my dreams.
They sing, they shout, voices all about.

It's time at last my life has come to pass.
The echoes which I've heard, were the echoes of my past.

But wait! I can still hear them, the cling,
The clang, the gates of closing cells.
I hear the keys, they're rattling ever so light,
For me to hear once more,
"The echoes of the night."

Felix Feliciano

The Children Disagree

It's useless to discuss societies mistrust of each of us
It terrible the way things sometimes bring
the bad outcome of a human being
You know what I mean!
It's not a good parable to say this life has been bearable
by most of the kids in the world
Children, no family, no help
Walking around with tight curls
Whites and blacks growing up to learn to hate each race
Even though they know everybody is going at the same pace
Not taking time to look at their own face

To say our life has been nothing but cherries and roses
And me, myself, have posed nice posses
That would be a lie, time after time
I mentally die, not physically

Self denied and denial can go so far
so tell me, what is America about
"The Land of the Free"

I believe the Children disagree!

Amanda Brooks

Untitled

To Shea and Miyo Chan—Love, Dad
The way the night skies seemingly
Come alive, to dance and sing as they fill
to overflow with the northern lights, moves me.

The way a small child laughs hysterically
as they discover the joys of life in the most simple things,
yet, hidden from my blind eyes, stirs wonder in me.

The way a song make me laugh or cry, strengthens me.
The way a scent brings fond memories
of a distant time and place, warms me.

The way a tide slowly wears away the shore
and at the same time builds all new,
more fertile ground, gives me hope.
The way you look at me, hold me,
speak to me, share your dreams with me,
Sing to me, cry with me, laugh with me, live with me, love me . . .

Everything you are to me, completes me.
Thank you for showing me the way.

Todd S. Braniff

Art in the Park: A July Fourth Celebration

Along the banks of the Trinity we sit and wait, laughing patiently
Anxious for bombs bursting air.
Children smile and wave their red white and blue enthusiasm,
Not knowing the depth and meaning, who really does?
The symphony sings the pride of the people.
This is America.
Coming together in designer cut-offs,
Laughing and singing pride or indifference.
The round bellied bearded man canoeing
With his lady fair has the right idea.
Or the man on the bike, peddling the small child on the back.
Or maybe I, sitting alone, together with the crowd
Absorbing the laughter and infantile cries
Becoming one with America.

Sherrie Baggott

Soul Sisters

For Pam, Deb, Bev, Peg, and Sonja
Soul sisters
We were told not to talk
For 17, 21, 14 years
We came together to share our stories
We talked, we shared, we told our stories
Together now, we're soul sisters
Bound together by our stories
Who have experienced our experiences
Who have cried our tears
Who have known the anguish of loved ones, unknown
Lost to us in eternity forever gone
To one day meet again soul sisters
We are now bound together

Shari Skramstad

The Challenge!

Oh, Jesus, let me walk with thee,
If not beside, then close in line,
Teach me to follow, prompt me to pray,
Help me to shoulder my cross day by day
Give me a vision, with a purpose to serve,
Let me feel I'm an instrument for good in this world,
Grant me wisdom of choice as I wend my way,
Up the path that's narrow, not the world's high way.
Give me strength to suffer if the need must be.
Give me patience to fear, and humility,
Let me live in deeds instead of years,
Remove from my heart all doubts and fear,
Call to me, master, as I follow through,
To that goal of perfection, which my master is you!

Edna Holt

Before

With all my uncertainty of life, all my sharp corners,
Thou still had a love for me.

With a rebuking heart, I foolishly stumbled on, all too selfish
to turn to thee, but thou still had love, a love for me?

Something so utterly beyond my comprehension draws forth
from mind, a want, a desire, what should I say?

A feeling of unworthiness, a frightening sense of guilt

Crushed beneath this morbid heart all true conceptions were
laid to rest in the back of my mind.

I lay dormant in the hardened shell foolishly stumbling on
all too selfish to turn to thee, but thou still had a love for me.

Now I no more stumble but crawl, with a strong will to
stand and with this love thou has for me,
I'll use as a key to set myself free.

Sabrina Marie Galloway

Our Love

It seems as though I've known you for years,
But alas I have known you for days.
I realized I have been foolish to care,
But not foolish to love.
Although we are so far apart,
But so close together,
Our love for one another is not the same.
For my love is for you and yours for me.
Our love together is our love for one another.
When you fail to love; you fail to live.

Our love is like a rose
Strong at times and weak at others.
Our love is like a book
Long and short, but were together at last.
Our love is like our friends: kind and caring
But painful and hurting too.
As for you and me we are just two lovers lost at sea.
As for me and you we are forever found and never lost.
But as for her, she will never exist
And him the same.

Michelle Haislip

Here I Am, with the Fruit of . . .

To Mom, for being there always
Here I am, with the fruit of my day's work.
With the fruit of my sacrificed womb.
With the fruit that I gave birth to
In order to feed my family-clan.

Here I am, with dust on my surface and dust on my hands.
Here I am, giving birth to this gracious and fruitful land.
Here I am, standing on my ancestral given land.
Here I am, growing hairs of vegetables upon the land.

Here he comes, his name is devastation,
He dressed me with desolation.
I ache in pain, with industrial chemical exploitation.

Do you know who I am?
Do you know where I am?
Do you know where I stand?

Here I am, I'm in your face!
I'm under your feet!
I'm behind you and all around you!

I'm so old, older than the dinosaurs!
Older than Adam the first man!

Do you still not know who I am?

Almond Pedro Nunez

It's Something Wrong

He came into my life
Like a dream, it's seemed
With time it changed, the nightmare it would be
it's something wrong
Cruel and hateful, that he was to me
I longed for love, I never received
Thirsty each day for tender kind treatments
His every breath of harsh words beat upon me
No passion, no love and affection ever shown,
would be it's something wrong
Like a child, I felt no hate, yet my love was still strong
I have often wondered, why, why me
I gave my all, and all to express my love
But it never did any good
It's something wrong
All, I have ever wanted is to love and be loved
Can you imagine, the pain, hurt and agony
I was put through
I want it to be known, yes
It was something wrong.

Mattie Mitchell

Sparrows of Sorrow

No greater pain,
Than the pain of sorrow.
People scorched and slain,
Having nothing to borrow and no one to blame.

Travelling through the treacherous seas of sorrow,
Make way,
A sparrow,
A sparrow of pain that will carry you away.

A hopeless venture in life,
Never to be surpassed,
By the limitations of a man's life
Render yourself on an overpass.

Sorrow knows no end.
It's blind and affects everyone
Luring you in its den.
You are the one.

A victim overcome by sadness and regret
A pawn, in debt,
Sorrow still never gone.

Donald L. Sewell

Upon a November Night

To God

Upon a November night, as I stood there waiting
In my own little world, as I stood there praying

A breeze is slightly blowing, dragging leaves along
Out of nowhere He appears, asking, me, "What's wrong?"

My problems, my fears, I continue to tell Him about it all
And I know that He's there to catch me whenever I might fall

At the dock that night, a night like no other
I wonder to myself if to Him and I am a bother?

As my tears are falling, as I pray for forgiveness
He tells, so ever gently, that I am off His sin list

That day that He went to the cross,
He tells me, His voice so soft,

He loves us so very much
That He would've gone just for one of us.

Just for me, or just for you
There's nothing that He wouldn't do.

As I cry, on this November night
And confess everything in His sight

My problems, my fears, He takes them all away
And He tells me that it'll be all right, everything will be okay.

Jesus, I love You, and I'll worship you every day
Because I know the price, for us, that You had to pay.

Amanda Cowder

The Legacy

For Craig and my children

I have often contemplated how my life will be perceived,
When my time on earth is ended and my soul has taken leave.

I will never cure an illness, never save the world from war.
I will never achieve greatness. I am me and nothing more.

Then I look upon my children and I see reflected there,
Morality and goodness, a sense of righteousness they share.

The bonding of a family I have worked so hard to teach.
A loving, giving, sharing until nothing can impeach.

Then suddenly I realize my legacy on earth,
Began back many years ago, the day that I gave birth.

Janet B. Barron

For Baby

To Dalton Marshall Dekilder, my angel

As you swim inside my womb,
Earth awaits you, sun, stars and the moon.

At this time you're very tiny, very small,
I promise to care for you as if you're big and tall.

For each day you grow, body, heart, and soul.
You're becoming our child, complete and whole.

On that special day that you are born
Trumpets playing, bells a-ringing, they will sound a special horn.

Now comes the time to bring you home.
Tender love and care, you will never be alone.

Soon you will be, here to see,
Life will be very happy with Daddy and me.
Love, Mommy

K. Carter

Golden Dreams of Golden Wings

In loving memory of Pablo Rodriguez

It was a garden of beauty and a fountain of youth
A vision of my beloved one
In the distance I saw his smile shine so bright
On the face of my grandfather the most precious sight

Arms reaching out to hold me like before
And wishes that it would last forever more
Then I woke from my peaceful sleep
Remembering a dream, that only my heart will keep

The warmth of the sunlight on my face
And the memory of his gentle embrace
In my mind I hear the Angels sing
And see the glitter, of his golden wings

Lori Edna Urquidez

The Master Shepherd

Who is the one that trains the wild geese
in perfect formation for their flight?
What makes the grass green, the berries so red
With rays from the same sunlight?
The waves with perfect timing
Lap and curl and return to sea—
Never late, never early, as is supposed to be.
One never sees this trainer but feels the wisdom grow;
One has to want to need him,
Then he will make it so.
What makes the hush before daylight
to let the needs be known?
A direct line to power, on a royal telephone,
He that keepeth Israel neither slumbers nor sleeps.
I wait for the sound of the staff and the Rod,
for he is my shepherd,
This shepherd, my God.
He keepeth my soul, he keepeth his sheep.

Arlie B. Russell

Between Us

I have no sacrifices in the sea than
tears, fetters and bones:
memories so fresh and persistent like shadows.

I have no ties with the sea than
treaties that came with it:
Trick-hooks so binding and fatal like sin.

You are soft, cold, blue,
white and consuming like the sea
I am difficult, sweating, black,
colourful and fruitful like the earth

P. Emeka Aroh

Searching

To my dear friend, John Amos
We escape reality
Searching to find a paradise
hidden deep within the corners of our mind

Always knowing but never admitting we would never find
Mesmerized into a sea of unchanging tides
swallowed by our dreams whipped into a whirlpool of madness

Taken by the wailing of chanting voices
as Mariah beckons us on sanity tugs of our freedom

As the ocean caresses the shores
we caress our ancestry never to escape
the eternal form of being

   Rhonda Arnold

Cloud Paintings in the Sky

As a child, in years gone past,
I used to lie upon the grass,
Gazing up into the sky,
Watching fleecy clouds go drifting by.

What lovely patterns they often drew,
Of common things, which I knew,
Like fluffy lambs or a great white mare,
Or, an all white Santa, with flowing beard and hair.

It brings my day dreams to an end,
When mother calls, "Supper time, you children come in"
Dad waits at the table, to say the grace,
After each one has settled into their place.

Then bath time ends a busy day,
To await the morning, again to go out to play.
O' for the carefree childhood, of years gone past,
When I used to lay and daydream on the grass!

   Foye A. Graves

Daydream

I often daydream, down yonder by the stream
I often wonder will my daydreams ever come true,
like when the skies are gay and blue.
I often wonder will they be exciting and fun.
Or will they be like an adventure
And when I have my daydreams I hope
they are colorful and be more than one
Or should I daydream as it should be in a picture.
I do often daydream down yonder by the stream
I do wonder will they be colorful and ever come true
like when the skies are gay and blue!

   Joyce L. McKnight

An Ending

When I think of death, I think of the end—
death of a marriage,
death of a friend,
and a life full of miscarriage.
My friend's death is the beginning,
and my marriage is the end of that tale—
one that started with punishing
and was marred by fear and worry to no one's avail,
that I would never feel
so enlightened, again.
It took three years to peel
away the skin of angry flesh
to discover the wound of that day was still fresh,
and what I needed to uncover
was buried so deep
that it was time again to mourn,
so I could reap
the inherent spirit of a newborn.

   Loretta Gibson

Untitled

The first moment I saw your soft hazel eyes,
my heart swirled for you.
You are the needle in the haystack that is so seldom found.
Your love is forever held in my soul,
and our lives are wrapped within each other's arms.
For the so many golden moments shared,
full of loving memories.
I think to how it began.
It was those soft hazel eyes.

   Lisa F. Keehner

Wishes

I'd like to slide down the curve of the rainbow,
Play tag with a playful breeze,
Chase recalcitrant sunbeams,
And swing in the tops of the trees.

I want to move like an inchworm
To measure a flower stem
And create for myself from dewdrops
A magnificent diadem.

I'd like to sail down from the treetops
On a red maple leaf in the fall
To land on a cushion of velvety moss
And listen to songbird's call.

What fun it would be at some sunrise
To ride a pink cloud in the sky,
Or to steal a fluttering wind blown ride
On the wings of a butterfly.

In my fancies and in my daydreams
I'd love to do all of these things;
But unfortunately God in his wisdom
Failed to provide me with wings.

   Alda Becker

Ode to Love

To Terrell, with love
Lying close to you; Never having to say
let go . . . I already have.

Omitting my insecurities;
obligating myself to total commitment.

Viewing life over the shoulder of my lover.
Vexing him only a little;
'cause I'm slow, to open—to be free.

Exaltation, elevation, exasperation, emancipation.
Finally drained from my natural "Love High."
Now, I'm free—to be me.

   Felecia R. Davis

Once a Friend

Once I knew you, but now you're gone.
I may not find out where you went,
But maybe that's how it is to be.
Maybe we are to grow apart to grow together.
Everything seems to always be perfect,
But no one's perfect.
It must be a disguise.
I've tried ever so hard to be your friend.
I promised to stay by your side 'til the end,
But we were to end up splitting,
You going your way, me going mine.
Once a friend,
Ended up to be nothing,
In the end.

   Francesca Montelione

A World in Need of Love

Vacant homes, empty hearts, and a desperate cry for love
A hungry child cries out, "But I'm the child of God above!"

There are single mothers, young frightened fathers
And old canned food goods for those who patiently stood.

There's a bench to rest a tired soul
Where a burning spirit has taken a toll.

Even the sun times is used as a blanket and sheet
By a man with card boards on his frostbitten feet.

There's a lonely man at a table set for many
A man willing to share his last penny.

Now, I ask, "Is it so much to give to those who have none?"
Just once, we should take away a desperate man's bullet
And throw away his gun.

What will it take for you to give love to the lonely,
Food to the hungry and the warmth of your heart to all mankind?

I ask you again, "Is there a greater gift than love
for an empty soul to find?

Mechelle Hughes

Problems Shared

For the relatives of the Porcher family
I know your pains, I know your sorrows,
But more importantly God knows all your problems
and He will solve them.
For all the strength that we will receive,
God supplies it and let's us borrow.
We've been this way just a short time ago,
We pulled together as a unit and God helped us through it.
During our grief we'll shed some tears,
While we shed tears today of sorrow,
Let joy be our tears of tomorrow.

Coyell S. Talbert

Untitled

To my soulmate, Ilse
On the threshold of a new century and millennium,
Our Media's count-down has begun,
Mankind foresee, what could happen,
They fear, well doomsday could be near,
Nothing will happen, just have faith,
Spaceship "Earth" keeps turning on its course,
Among the stars in timeless Universe,
The human race, better get wise,
Step into a new Era, hope for the best,
Let's working together with peace in mind,
No wars, no rebellion, no hunger, no strife,
Nations "On-Line," global connections,
People to people, problems resolved,
Mankind able to create a new "Eden"
Tending our garden and feed Mankind.

William Seeger

A Man with No Name

A man with no name sits paled with sadness
Not really thinking but deep in thought
A blank and distant stare

In stillness waits for that which he knows not
with anxious anticipation

Looking back on things that have slipped away
Expecting greater things to come

Knowing this time to let them go
would be inexcusable
A lesson not well learned
And unto himself a sin.

Robert Bowers

Hole in My Heart

There is a big hole in my heart,
It has been there since the day you decided to part.
I know things didn't go well for you and I,
But I will keep the memories until I die.
I will never forget the first time you called me princess,
Nor how our relationship ended in such a mess.
I will always have the memory of our shooting star,
And for you to hold me once more I would run near or far.
This hole in my heart has your name on it,
For you my love won't change one single bit.
I will love you even though we are apart,
You have left me with this hole in my heart.

Alison Lake

If I Sit in the Rain

If I sit in the rain,
I can believe that I do not cry.
It is the raindrops
that streak my face,
it is the thunder
that makes my heart pound heavily within my chest.
It is the weight of the clouds,
that bears down my shoulders.
It is the sky,
that reflects the greyness within my eyes.
It is the cold and damp
which makes me curl
into a shivering ball.
It is only the rain,
not losing you.

Friday, September 20, 1991
Deborah Christenson

To Mother with Love

A mother's love is given,
'Tis never bought or sold,
Her loving care and warm embrace
Consoles us, young or old.

I asked, "Mother dear, what can I do,
To brighten up your day?"
She smiled and joyfully replied,
"Just write me a poem today."

So I wrote a loving poem for my widowed Mother,
Praising her courage facing life
While keeping her family together
Through hard times and in strife.

That was my final Mother's Day poem,
For her there will never be another,
Time and life pass by very fast, they do not last.
Thank God! That poem pleased my Mother.

Alexandra M. Magoulakis

My Proposal

I admire your honesty and respect.
In my proposal, I would like to add your intellect.
You are the center of my heart;
You are the beauty of art.
I love to hold and caress you
Like a mother does her newborn baby.
You are the greatest;
You are the best.
Will you marry me?
Now you know who I am and who I want;
My anger and jealousy I will not flaunt.
If I can not be with you
I am your king and you are my queen
We shall live together in majesty

Eric Hooker

Listen My Child

To Carla, my wonderful daughter
The "Fashion Strut" was planned
Sellers eager, tickets printed
Date, time, and place secured
A moneymaker, they said.

The Pastor preached
Tithing, faith, trust, and love
Believe in God's Holy Word
And never, never, never doubt
That's all we need, he said.

The congregation nodded in agreement
Offering was taken, benediction given
Amen, amen, amen was sung
Before heading to the vestibule
Let's sell, sell, sell, the "strutters" said.

That Sunday morning there were some that heard
And there were some that did hear
There were some that bought
And there were some that bought not
My dear child, which one were you, God asks.

Nancy L. Williams

Born Again

Born in flesh but hungry for more,
sought out all the ways to satisfy my core;
All chances I gave to new fads and new games,
leaving me empty left cold in the haze.

Satan had lied to me every which way,
and run me in circles lost day by day;
for the cares of this world think not of your peace,
and I found myself fallen, desperate and least.

But during my sorrow God showed me a new light,
Jesus Christ, his Messiah, came in his might;
to perfectly pay the price for my sin,
and if asked in my heart, life I would win.

A life full of God who cares for my hurts,
a life full of power leading me through his word;
born again of his spirit in a twinkling of an eye,
a daughter and a priest, set apart, of his kind.

"Come into my heart I give you my life,"
I said to my God who bared all of my strife;
And in me he birthed a brand new breath,
Free from the chains of sin and death.

Dianne Brummett

Poetic Books

To angels, Ivy and Marlie
Banners in the park
Look and see,
Your favorite books in poetry!
Banners everywhere,
Now let's see
There's Arthur and Corduroy
Near the Giving Tree.
The Velveteen Rabbit
has a smile on his face
Because he's sitting near Amazing Grace!
We're are real excited and happy to see,
Frog and Toad Together, reading Jumanji!
The weather man predicted, if rain falls,
It could also be Cloudy with a Chance of Meatballs!
That sounds great, said a crawly creature,
I'm the Very Hungry Caterpillar.
More characters come to enjoy the fun,
There's Amelia Bedelia saying, "My work is all done."
Dr. Seuss has arrived and Alexander too,
They are reading this poem, just like you!

Joycelyn Carpenter

Pick Up

She first caught my eye in a rough part of town.
I'm afraid she was dirty and rather run down.
She stood in a doorway, flirtatious and sly,
Then accosted me boldly as I tried to go by.
When I thrust her aside, she let our a squeal,
"What's the matter? Don't cost much! A drink! A meal!"
That night, I confess, she slept in my bed.
She kissed me, caressed me, and quite turned my head.
Since then, she has shared both my heart and my home,
Has managed my life in my heart she has grown.
Yes, willful she is often horrid it's true.
She's demanding, she's moody, and so greedy, too.
But she's tender, devoted and bright as they come,
Full of ginger, vivacious, good Lord is she fun!
Oh, I know I'm her captive, possessed by her, lost.
But man's a weak vessel and passion's his boss.
Disgusted, my friends say I'm mad and all that.
But I'll not give her up. Not Suzy, my cat!

Ronald Bennett

There's Something Special

Dedicated to Derek Jeter of the Yankees
There's something special about love songs
Its words so hypnotizing and very sweet
Remembering it so deeply, the enchanting beat
Reminding you of your first love, when they broke your heart
Telling you, you have been a better person since you've been apart

There's something special about memories
Remembering your good times and your bad
Describing them so vividly that it makes you glad
It's not just your beautiful gift but precious treasure
Filling your thoughts, with times of fun and pleasure

There's something special about Valentine's Day
A time to give gratitude to a person you care for
Trying every day to give them love, support, and more
Sharing the special feelings you have had together
Hoping that the love in your hearts will last forever

There's something special about family
Your parents are there to guide you on your way
Always willing to listen to what you have to say
They'll always think of you wherever you go
When you need a place to stay, you can always come home

Kimberly Guzman

Granddaughter

To Scott and Family, precious gifts
When you were born I just wanted to hold you right away.
A new little person, so pink and precious,
you stole my heart away.
Somehow you knew I loved you, right from the start.
We seemed so close, and always have,
It helps now that we're apart.

Remember how you'd touch and smell the flowers
when we'd walk along the way?
Sometimes you picked one for mommy
and took it home to her that day.

In your little red wagon I'd roll you along,
and often we would sing a song.
Watch the soft fluffy clouds slowly floating by
And when the rainbow balloons came over,
you'd want to reach up to the sky.

When Daddy's work took you away
I first thought my heart would break.
Then I began to look forward to the trips I would take.
Don't grow up too fast or reach too far
For a while at least, I'd like to keep you as you are!

Patricia J. Apple

Remember the 25 Years

Do you remember the time,
oh, yes, and do you remember the time.
Remembering the times with you, I sure do.
do you remember the day we got married
or the time we just went away, I sure do.
How about in times of hardship or mistrust.
times when things just didn't work out,
where love was just all that mattered,
because we're together, I sure do
the fire that will never burn out,
the flame of life in both of us together, we will live forever.
Remember the times, for they don't always work out right.
When I am with you though, things are always right.
For now it's our silver but the memories will last 'til the gold.
For the years we've been together,
we'll never forget what's been foretold.

Nathan Kirst

In the Country

The grapes hang heavy upon the vine
Purple masses 'midst brown crackling leaves.
Wind whistles up the hill, invigorating as wine
And scatters afar the forgotten sheaves
Of wheat, sown early last spring.

The restless black sheep on the hill, bleat loud.
While the white turkeys huddle to keep themselves warm
Heads raised to the sky and the big black cloud
Fearful of the approaching storm.

The little creatures flee, hunting a warmer nest.
A squirrel's in the cellar, a mouse in the cupboard.
The shutters nailed fast, wood in the chest,
And the bed is made with a warm comforter
For a good night's rest.

Winter's coming, it sings through the air
Bringing new surprises each day to see,
And the still white beauty everywhere
Of frosted earth and icy silvered tree.

Teola Fuller

It

Is it there,
Or is it not,
For it has become
what not has taught.
Through it will be that
And that will be all again it,
Thus it will be as such,
as all beings see fit.
Realization as is, will strike
That it is what you want it to be,
It becomes the you, like or dislike.
And on and on, it goes for you to see,
whether it is not,
And not, it is there,
It is one unending cycle we all seek and sought.

Anne Wachera Thoithi

Untitled

I am a mirror.
Absorbing colours, expressions, and light.
Everything that sees me becomes me.
Reflection, than, is interaction.
Baring, slightly jocund, upon those capable of seeing.
Their reflection puts forth new light unto themselves.
An inception possible by only me.
Engrossed by a ceaseless light,
Creating each moment a new, more beautiful self.
'Til either is broken.

Monika McDowell

Treasures

God has given us all so much
To feel, to smell, to see and touch

From the sun that shines to the moon that glows
He controls the winds and sends the snows

The rivers that run into the sea
To the tireless work of a single bee

The color and smell of a beautiful rose
To the delicate sight of a babies toes

From birds that soar all through the sky
To the mountains standing broad and high

From the running and jumping of puppies at play
To a colorful sunset at the end of the day

The clouds that bring the rains that fall
To the miracle of life he gave us all

Each of these things are here for our pleasure
Every last one is a God given treasure

Allen Liner

The Window

When I look to the window, a child's reflection looks back at me.
With hollow eyes, she seems to be searching for something.
Her soul, once soft in nature, now hardened
with rejection and nights of endless tears.
Her hollow eyes bearing deep into me,
begging me for something I do not understand.
I cannot look away. I am drawn to the reflection in the window.
My eyes locked to hers, trying to find an answer
to her presence but to no avail.
The phone breaks the strain, but I know that next time
I look to the window, she will still be there.

Amy L. Keyes

Lost Leaf

So far from where it was,
trying to figure what it does,
traveling from the wind,
making a crackle sound,

As I look and find a special leaf,
more detail than you could believe,
the sun was right, a clear blue sky,
seeing birds fly, and the same time I sighed.

Chipped and crackled, and discolored,
dry against my moist hand, others didn't
understand, why I liked that leaf,
ugly and gross in their minds, beauty is deep,
different from others, ones you find in gutters,
that's why I love that leaf so.

Evan K. Goian

The Journey

Life is a journey
Constantly weaving its way through unknown territory
Experiences, hardships, and fulfillments await
as destiny seduces personal aspirations
Feelings of tension and desperation
as we are swept away by the waves of uncertainty
Forever persevering, and maintaining hope
that seemingly unattainable goals
set upon the highest of peaks will soon be in reach.
Desire and motivation engaged in an eternal struggle
with knowledge and wisdom.
The victor is neither and the result, reality.

Yisrael Glassberg

My Willow Haven

Finally I sit here alone, just nature and me,
Waiting on the first light to show through the trees.
Pure and untouched is the cool, crisp morning,
The beauty as seen with a new day dawning.

My thoughts being rapid and troubled from the day before,
Lose their significance, like a leaf falling to the woods floor.
As the breeze bends a tree, I shiver a might,
The black fades to gray, no more the dark night.

An early morning fog gently embraces the pines,
Giving an air of mystical lure to all it can find.
A drop of dew forms and slides down a needle,
Like a true master would play an old antique fiddle.

Here, left alone, I wish words could explain,
But they get lost like a drop in a puddle of rain.
For such wonder and beauty are hard to describe don't you see,
You have to experience it, touch it, see it to believe.

For when cares get too heavy, I have a place to retreat,
I come to these woods, find a stand, have a seat.
Here worries aren't important, the clock's broke for a time,
For God smiles on this place, this haven of mine.

Darlene Davis

Grandmamma's Room

I remember great times we had in this room.
As a child I would play under the table.
Windows were covered with thick brocade.
I loved the tablecloths you crocheted,
The table now holds only dust.
The windows dirt, the air musk.

All the furniture has gone to other kin
But I have what can't be given away
You gave me confident pride
You made me believe the world was mine.
You encouraged me to try.

Now vacant windows stare back at me
The room is dull yellows and grays
Like rotten fruit the goodness has gone.

In a minute I'll close the door on this part of my life
But I'll take what is left, the tables and the chair.
And most importantly what you taught me
To be strong and stand tall, don't worry at all.
Life is an adventure, meet it with arms open wide
And lock the door as you come inside.

Janis Suggs Dyson

Love Affair

Looking down the path my vision was clear,
I thought for a moment Edwaldo was near,
When I felt the gust of wind through my hair,
I thought of me and Edwaldo's love affair.

Memories of me and him together made my heart sore,
It brought such deep pain to my core,
Again I felt the gust of wind through my hair,
I thought of me and Edwaldo's love affair.

I loved him like there was no more,
My heart still drips of pain like never before,
As the wind arises and blows through my hair,
I think of me and Edwaldo's love affair.

As I think of Edwaldo with his new love affair,
I wonder if it feels the gust of wind through his hair,
As I lay at night and cry to sleep,
I wonder if the feels my pain so deep.

As I look out my window the sky is clear,
I know now that my death is near,
As I drink the poison without care,
I think of me and Edwaldo's love affair.

Stefanie Gabriele

A Soldier's Prayer

For Guapa

Shall these forces respite
then I, enamored, fisted, steadfast,
mounting strong and vengeance pure
and temper scolding in lament of reason,
shall I strike with purpose the firmer,
avenging that death perhaps with my own.

Brandishing weapons of fairness may I embolden
to partake these great ranks
and die as a dog, shoulder to shoulder
among these new friends.

It is wicked to think such unfavorable things
should retire unchallenged lest
the company of men worthless except
their honor and invaluable intention,
bear down on the throat of the darkest foe.

So bedeck these locks in the wet red shame of my enemy.
Permit this humble sacrifice
in this damned hour,
atop this holy ground,
permit me this and so, die in peace.

James Dyson

The Weaver

she weaves alone
ageless face patient
deft fingers flickering
surrounded by skeins of thread
of good and evil, sorrow, joy

plaited into the tapestry that flows around her
endless to the eye
hues fountaining up from nowhere
twisting, turning, intertwining
fading into nothingness again

lives are patterns, shades and tints
traced from birth to death
playing themselves out
onto the loom
under skimming hands

she who sees everything
a witness of souls
she who holds the essence of being
a weaver of life
a silent observer

Sonie Kamata

Custer's Last Stand

The picture upon the wall tells it all,
The fight of Custer's last battle galore
And of all the tears that went with the bloody gore,
Of the brave and fighting men
And of a terrible battle that they didn't win.
The sight of the many men lying on the battlefield
And of the many souls who were killed.
As the brave and sorry men in their bloody coats of blue
Not knowing if the battle was through
There was nowhere for them to go as their blood ran red in the snow
The enemy whirled and twirled their axes high
With shrill yells that reached the sky.
They were as ready as could be, but Custer his enemies did not see.
As the brave and sorry men flew in their bloody coats of blue,
In memory we still see them in the wood where not a single one stood
They lie bloody in the snow, lying side by side in a row.
The living and the dead the cold snow their only bed
The call came loud and clear as the victor sent up his howling cheer
This was Custer's last stand when he lost every brave man

Sadie White

Nova

there's a sick emptiness in the pit of my gut
as i think back to what is to blame
for so long now my actions are rusted memories
i don't remember a thing
i just don't know the answers to everyone's inquiries,
that must make me a lesser being
what could have been? this thought gnaws at my brain
speak up? this only throws me deeper into this rut
who wants to listen to this troubled child?
The chains anchoring my body are beginning to tighten,
now they mold into my wrists,
a steady stream runs across my palm then trickles off my
outstretched fingers on its way to the soil below
just as the flame of life flares at its brink, my soul dims
to its former state of luminosity only to flicker and die,
leaving behind the pain that was once unbearable
along with the nourishment that i never had
nothing's left to corrupt, living only seemed a poison,
now i leave something that won't be missed . . .

Joshua Bailey

Mama's Boy

To my family and the strugglers
Just like the feeling, of relief and triumph
that Mama had, when giving birth to you

The warmth of love, that glowed around her
as she cradled you, for the first time

She fought her way through, a tunnel filled with darkness
just to give her son, the life he deserved

Like a scared child, you clung tight to her dress
desperate for her guidance, through this strange new world

With greatest care, she tucked you in every night
making sure you were never too hot and never too cold

She cleaned your wounds, whenever you fell down
and baked you a fresh apple pie as a cure for your sadness

Now that you're a man, and Mama's let go of your hand
You manage to keep her words of wisdom, in the back of your mind

You swallowed your fears, and took on the world alone
standing on your own two feet, you became a soldier

At times you may find, your knees becoming weak
from leaping over all of the obstacles, that crosses your path

And tears of anger, strive to come into light
you keep your head up high, determined for survival.

Darlene Jones

From We to Me

To Paul and our wonderful family
I oft look back in my mind and see,
just how good life used to be.

It was always us always we
How comforting that was to me.

My life then was so complete,
I was always happy, so upbeat.

Then suddenly, I lost my spouse,
and for the first time was alone in our house.

I now find myself on family leaning,
to try to give my life more meaning.

Their love for me is so sincere,
that finally, I have no fear.

And now I look ahead and see
There's still a life out there for me.

Dorothy M. Bachman

Children; Bewildered and Lost

We gather wealth and lose our girls and boys,
what's happening to our children today?
Working Mothers have gone away.
Mothers busy from day to day,
working, laboring for tomorrows pay.

Tender Mother's touch has disappeared,
we leave our children with fear.
Her tender care, no longer there,
our children left in others' care.
Holding the key to an empty house,
roaming the streets, looking for love.

Yesterday her love was near,
her gentle hand was here to lead.
The look in her eyes, with love was filled,
her tender heart, no longer here.
So I look to bond with strangers near,
Mother gathered worldly wealth and lost her children dear.

Emily Peaden Daniel

Butterfly Garden

For my biggest inspiration, my husband, Rob
Way up high in the sky so bright
Are the great wonders of butterfly's in flight.

As the flowers start blooming, March, April, and May
Start all the great wonders of butterflies at play.

The cocoon starts the process and with a gentle push
Becomes the great wonders of the butterfly bush.

Daisies, lilies, merrybells, carnations
And the great wonders of butterflies and impatiens.

LaDina Neiger

To a Princess

Your smile to me is like a blossoming rose
A beauty which could not be described in prose
You bring warmth, happiness and love into my life
Words can't describe the beauty of nature
Experience it to appreciate its complete rapture.
This is how I feel about you my dear,
That's why my love for you is so sincere.
I can't explain my reverence for you
You're the world to me and God knows it's true.
You're wonderful, you're marvelous, you're simply adorable.
That's why I find you to be so lovable
Eight years of marriage is simply great
I have love, a friend and a true soul mate.
So fortunate am I to have married you
This I promise will always be true.
So Happy Anniversary to you, my love
You're just like an angel from Heaven above!

Fredric T. Krell

Thoughts

What to think when day is done.
Did my day have any fun?

When walking through my garden still,
Did the flowers hold their scented thrill?
Did my doggy friends come seeking me,
Or do they wish they could run free?
The birds watching me, chirping, on the fence,
Bird seed on a rope, does this make sense
The house is quiet, the chores are through.
Did I stop to think of you?
Yes, dear Lord, my thoughts did roam
To all your children in your home.

Ann Erickson

Texas Pride

Armadillos in the garden rooting up the plants,
Blue skies over bonnets blue, cactus blossoms catching dew,
Dust devils twirling around, Easter fires burning down,
Friendship and frontier history, Fiesta,
God and German traditions,
Horned toad, hail, and heat lightning,
Ice cream made at home,
Jackrabbits, jumping, roaming,
Knowing neighbors near and far,
Longhorns huge and lean,
Mockingbirds and monuments, never letting go,
Open spaces spreading out, pride and persistence,
Quarterhorses smooth and strong, rodeos galore,
Star of flag and soul,
Trust, tumbleweed, and taco,
Undying symbol of courage,
Vitality, verbena, and variety,
White deer, wildlife of scrub and pine,
Xylophone and drum of U. of T.,
Yellow rose of lore, zest of those who love her.

Barbara Ruth Faules

Creator

Creator creating the Creation
After the creation then there began birth
After the birth there was a birth of another creation, which
Formed an after birth
Then there became you and I
Creating Harmony and loving kindness

After the Metamorphosis we became Barbaric Losing all spirituality;
Telepathic, Kinetic, transitory sensory perception
Aka; the Ability to condense thoughts from one to another
With knowing ones movements
Transmitting from ones own Alpha and Omega Brain waves

We separated, causing—disconnection from our unique oneness
We became confused, Chaotic, Annihilating everything in our paths
We destroyed our place of Inhabitance, our land, our earth
We became to be known as beings of color, devoid of perceiving the
God—qualities in our individual selves

We became inhumane Gods whom emptied our minds
Choosing the evil pathway to glory fighting amongst ourselves
We are unique, you and I
We are the Alpha and the Omega.

Darryl T. Williams

Ode to Home

Home
a quiet place,
tranquil
haven of peace.
Resting, shared laughter
lying in front of fires
sitting on the front porch with friends.
A place of security
a place where time was shared
with gone relatives,
friends that have moved on
times that are bad.
Home
home is a place that I can run away to
home is where I relax,
sitting on window seats
watching the rain
drinking hot chocolate with melted marshmallows
or just reading a book.
Home.

Mariah Robinson

Carol

In memory of Carol Ihns
She touched all of our lives in such a grand way!
Forever in our hearts her spirit will stay.
To most of us, she was "Mom," and to every other
Person she was a friend
A classy, sparkly, charming, wonderful lady to the end.
The time we had with her won't ever be enough,
Which will make letting go of the pain really tough.
But go on with our lives and be the best that we can be,
Is what from the heavens she would want to see.
So think about Carol in all that we do,
And make her proud that she was a part of our lives too!

Kimberly Peterson

Father

In memory of Papa Staiano, 1946–1993
Sometimes I wonder why it had to be you,
Oh, God please give me a clue.
It's not the same without you around,
I find it so hard to keep my feet on the ground.
You taught me to love,
To live and to care;
Anything I do,
Anyplace I go,
I wish you were there.
Being without you isn't so great,
I'm not sure if I should love or hate.
Sometimes I wish I could just give up this fight,
And start all over with you and life a new life.
I know that I can't so I stop pretending,
But at the same time I'm not comprehending.
I know that when it's my turn things will change,
So all I look forward to is being together again.

Patricia Stottlar

Prime Rose

Dedicated to possessions of Melancholy Mortal Trauma
Sitting, staying, empty for memory I remember.
Pondering silence, this coldly dismal December.
As the decrepit rose, reminiscing another time,
Once, when a life was still sublime.

Innocence is conceived and beauty is born.
To be plucked, trampled, worn and torn.
Prime rose grows steady in its withering delay,
Realizing nature had written this tragic play.

The will is lessened in decision to live.
Thorns protruding in venom shall not forgive.
Prime rose is young still, though no longer mine,
Still do I witness its steady decline.

Once the first pedals rot autumn and wind,
Prime knows the rose of times is left behind.

Joseph Root

Untitled

I want to fall in love again
I want the laughter, joy, and sweet pain
I love the roller-coaster ride, a million words cannot describe
This feeling that I have inside when I'm in love again
I blossom like a rose in spring, my ESP would then kick in
I see the world through colored lens
Oh, what a sight when I'm in love
My senses soar beyond the sky
Through fluffy clouds that carry me from dawn to dusk
And then into the starry night, such a wonder to behold
When I fall in love again
The sight, the sound, the smell of you
The sheer intensity of you, gives way to the melting you
Like one and one makes two
When I'm in love
One and one makes one

Diana Simmons-Martin

Adolescence

I'm afraid to become the person that as a child
I could only pretend to be.

I'm scared of a time when I'll have more important things
to worry about then just the monster under my bed.

I'm terrified to have to be the one with all the answers
to the questions I used to ask.

I'm down-hearted, to think that there will be a day
when I'll need to step out of my fantasy world
and start being true to life.

I'm worried to think that the heaviness
of the world will soon lie on my shoulders.

I'm troubled that the day will come
when I won't just want to pretend to be beautiful anymore.

I'm fearful that I can't get back
what I let get away . . . my childhood.

Emily Jensen

Mobile Home Parking Garage, 1999

January in tin can alley, fought the urge to
press a brown dust jacket from a cold stained glass
window outside are charcoal   fingered speedbumps and
dirty slush tracks held fast to a frozen road.
My room is the coldest one here and my skull is
still hurting upon awakening, the heavy evening dies slow
in a drunken coma while a pale light recedes from my waxy skin.
Say goodbye to the sun as it slides its way down the backdrop
a bloated bleeding liver exploded in the sky
Say goodbye to another sun as it follows a diseased cycle
born each day through the generations to circle an alien planet.
I wish Dad was still alive, but anyway,
like I was saying, I've been waiting for your call
So let's
    get
        drunk!

Billy McAfee

Erudition

Erudition is the breath that feeds our souls,
The essence, the very core of our being.
It's perceptive, intuitive and insightful
humble, civil and polite.
It's egotistical, arrogant and disdainful
conceited, contemptuous and rude.
It's challenging, illuminating and delightful
enlightening, proud and noble.
It keeps you wanting more.

Victoria Herbst

Clouds

Past my window, blue-gray clouds
shaped like whales
drift by as evening crests and somber notes
from Mozart's Requiem
sound in my inmost thoughts.

My dear, I did not give you permission to go
but you choose to close the door between us
by logical deduction.
Whales, whistling to each other at the ocean floor,
are not so hard of heart.

Have you ever plumbed the waters of love?
I did not think that grief at fifty
was so steep and so dangerous.

But how would you know if you have always
stayed on the shore,
wading in sunny warm pools—shunning the ocean's depth?

Carol J. Ward

Tenderness

To Adrian, the love of my life
Soft as the morning dew
Subtle as the early breeze
That makes a feather writhe in a graceful mode
To finally rest atop a freshly drenched meadow
Bursting with excitement to greet the coming of a new day.
The makings of a new bloom creeping slowly to open up
To the warmth of the sun
Filling the air with its sweet fragrance.
Butterflies a-fleeting from one to next
Leaving sweet kisses on each bloom
Joyously sprinkling the seed of new beginnings
For another wondrous life.
Then the ebb of day starts drawing near its end
And dusk spreads a blanket of darkness over the earth
As if in concentration to get one into deep slumber
With the hopes of dreaming sweet dreams
Of once a happy fulfilling experience!

Necita P. Palen

What Do We Have Here?

This woman that I am stands for everything in this whole world.
She has a will so strong that man always wants to challenge it,
But can never accept it.

She has emotions like the ocean,
But would swim 'til she drowned to save another,
Never stopping to save herself.

She'll get lost on the beach with no one in sight,
And stay lost in her thoughts on purpose
As she soaks up the sun and breathes in deeply the salt air.

She has the spirit of a wild horse,
The sharp sensitivity of an eagle,
And the moral soul of her native ancestors.

A heart that longs to be free,
But not alone.

She wants to experience the world,
At the same time that she wants to grow strong roots.

A pinch of her is satin and curls,
A stitch of her is leather and lace,
Yet everyone could posses these qualities,
But no one could ever take her place.

Shayla Dowell

My Very First Flame

Should I lose you again, from my thoughts, from my dreams,
My memories of you make you real—so it seems.
Should I lose you again, the pain I could bear,
For I've learned to endure, the many years you weren't here.

Not a day passes, I don't think your name.
My greatest desire is that you could do the same.
I wish you were here, right where you belong,
Though I have to remember that you're really gone.

I look at your picture, the way you were then,
Your brown wavy hair, your strong chiseled chin,
Your beautiful eyes, your wonderful smile,
Your devilish ways, but that was your style.

Our short time together those many years ago,
Was so very special, I wish you could know.
At times I feel your presence, so vital and strong,
I reach out to touch you, then realize you're gone.

It took you from me, the disease with no name,
It was hard to lose you, my very first flame.
God had a better plan for your life and mine,
But our paths may cross again at a future time.

Janet Nickerson

Hold On

For my mother, my grandmother, and Jesus Christ
When things in life don't go as planned . . .
Don't be afraid, just hold on to the Lord's hand.

Some people may turn their backs and leave you astray,
but hold on to the Lord for he will not go away.

There may be a time in life where you feel alone . . .
and you have no place to call your own,
But hold on, hold on, hold on tight . . .
For the Lord will embrace you with all his might.

Take the Lord in what you're going through,
For if you hold on to him, he will hold on to you!

Tyeisha Felton

Us

The sun is up, the night is gone,
Hoping to write you a lovely song.
Holding this feeling, so deep inside,
Wishing you were here now, at my side.

Being with you is where I want to be
Spending each day so happily.
While watching the birds up in the air,
Their flying together, is like a love affair.

Back on the ground where we've been found,
With dancing sun shining all around.
I'm squinting my eyes, so I may see
All of your beauty in front of me

I'm reaching out to grasp your love
Thinking you're an angel from high above.
So now at least I'm beginning to see.
That you were honestly made for me.

Holding your hand in the warm sunlight
Knowing how you make my day so bright.
Me holding you, and holding so tight,
Letting you know, it'll be all right.

Jerry Robb

Your Looking Glass

Fate the tireless weaver, her unfolding cloth is made
She decrees youth and vigor bloom, then quickly fade

Some may look to your visage and still be blind
Though beneath your mantle there is gentleness to find

For I do not count your manly worth and treasures
By outward vanity and shallow earthly measures

But rather my heart and mind do choose to see
The depth and dignity of your soul's noble purity

Years may fade my Adonis once so proud and fair
Yet to me your glory is always still lingering there

I see in you a beauty that will never pass
So let my eyes be your looking glass

Sue G. Mahurin

The Threshold of Affection

I welcome you to my place inside . . .
So warm and deep, where emotions hide.
Some doors are always open.
Others are locked and only you hold the key.
Come step into my heart, and experience this reality.
Explore my emotions and feelings deep inside.
The way that I feel for you, I can no longer hide.
My love for you grows stronger, every moment day by day.
If you'll love, trust, and believe in me,
Forever by your side I will stay.

Joseph Vincent Levra

A Morning Walk

In tribute to William Wordsworth
"We walked along, while bright and red
Uprose the morning sun"

We saw it evolve before our amazed eyes
As it came out of the darkness.

We strolled through the gloomy,
Dreary early morning.

We waited for nature's creation
To reveal itself before us.

We watched in silence, as misty, foggy dew
Rose from the cool moist ground.

We were in awe, as the air began to clear
Leaving the sparkling world before us.

We shared the moment, nearly speechless,
As nature revealed the beauty of the day.

We finally spoke in fascination
Knowing we shared this event of expectation.

We basked in the warmth of the light
Feeling a part of the universe.

We moved through the brightness of the day
Enjoying the beauty of the world.

Marlene Gartz

Song

Have you ever heard a song that makes you cry?
Every time you hear it—it's like hearing your life,
Only the music isn't a lie.
The song that sings the truth
Is the song that blows your mind aloof.
Have you ever heard a song that makes you cry,
And every time you hear it
You feel your eyes will never again be dry?
You wonder, can I get through this?
And that one song that represents your life's one promise,
The song that holds all your emotions
In one bottle of tearful water—
Is the song that lets them drop out
And you feel—among things—a martyr.
So you have your choice of the door,
Or listening to the song puddle your emotions on the floor.
That song that makes you cry
That sings the truth
That makes you wonder if your eyes will ever again be dry,
Is the song that you know isn't a lie.

Davelyn Norstedt

My Wind

Mirror image of me some have said
That smile, those eyes
She is my miracle baby.

Young and innocent, I love her this way,
She listens, she respects all that I say.

Wealthy in heart, body, mind and soul,
My priceless child means more to me
Than a pot of gold.

Inseparable we are in my heart, work or play
Instant contact we have all day.

Neighborly to all she may see
My angel is color blind
She makes me proud to be her mommy.
Dear to all, my first baby
I pray that her life will be blessed eternally.

Gwendolyn Johnson Simpson

Beyond Limits

God is the most important being.
Daily we praise Him and all through the night He is seeing . . .
Watching, and lovingly He places us in the palm of His hand,
Whispering, "I love you" and carefully sets us back on His land.
We feel we've been touched by His presence
And know that we'll always need His guidance
For living life without Him would make no sense.

Through our times of trials and hardship . . .
God is all knowing and loving and able to equip.
We accept His strength, and welcome his wonderful encouragement.
Nothing else can truly help, for there is no supplement
For God; His being takes us beyond and above
What our dreams and expectations limit us and we feel His love.
His arms wrap around us and carry us as wings of a dove.

Yvonne Bissonnette

A Daughter's Thank You

You carried me through nine months of pain.
You even gave me my name.
You raised me from an infant.
Your arms were never distant.
You raised me from a toddler, even when I was bad;
You didn't stay mad.
You raised me from a kid,
And I thank you for everything you did.
Now that I'm a teen, you're doing the best you can do,
And I just wanted to say I love you.
When I am an adult, it will be my turn to take care of you.
I promise I will do the best job I can do,
And one day I hope to be just like you.

Otelia Hawkins

"Freedom"

Freedom is a precious thing,
But drugs have stolen mine away.
Once I was happy with friends and a wife;
Now I'm in prison and have no life.
When the doors swing shut and the freedom is gone,
I wonder, how did I go so wrong?
My eyes are misty as I sit in my cell.
Lord knows I'm sorry I have failed,
to keep the freedom that was precious to me.
Five months more to sit in my cell.
When I am free, I can say
Don't go astray or you will pay
With your freedom being taken away.

Golda Baird

My Girl

She came to me as a surprise.
Now, she is the twinkle of my eye.
Watching her grow more and more,
I wonder what I'd done before.
I was letting my life waste away.
It's because of her, I'm here today.
With her big blue eyes so bright,
She's bringing me back to life.
I anxiously wait to see her walk.
I'll cry the day she begins to talk.
When she turns to me with her beautiful smile,
I know I'll walk with her every mile.
One day she'll do great things
Be a doctor, a lawyer, a teacher, or simply sing.
She'll change the world that's for apart
Bring them together with her heart.
When my life nears its end,
I'll wish I could live it with her again.
But when I do leave God's great Earth,
At least I'll know I gave her birth.

Joyce Brumbalow

My Very Best Friend

For my mother, Arlene—I hope she reads my poem up in Heaven.
She was my best friend, but she didn't know
Because I felt funny telling her so

And now it's too late
She got sick and died
My heart's broken in two and I cried and I cried

She took care of me well
She always was there
She gave up her life but she didn't care

She lived for her family
She gave all that she had
Why did she die and make me so sad?

She's been gone a year
I still miss her so
Who is this person?
Do you want to know?

For she is my mother
Who I'll love 'til the end
My strength and my life
My very best friend.

Carol Guidice

Staring

Staring, staring, nothing's there.
Not a movement in the air.
Silence, silence, nothing moving.
Without a worry or a care.
Softly, softly, tiptoe down,
to wake the sleeping infant with that gentle frown.

Jennifer L. Witthuhn

One Day I Woke Up

Dedicated to children with unique disabilities
One day I woke up and I saw
The beautiful person that was inside of me!
All because I saw an angel in front of my eyes,
In the beautiful blue sky,
That was there every single day,
I just never saw it until today,
From all the crying I did yesterday!

Now because of an angel that dried up my eyes,
I see rainbows after the rain,
Instead of the tears that used to cloud up my eyes,
With the bright yellow sun,
To show me what a good job I have done,
Showing everyone their is a bright sun in everyone,
Know matter what you think God has done to me,
I have found the miracles in thee!

Rhonda De Pietto Ocasio

In Betwixt and Between

I'm like a sky full of dreams,
An art gallery it seems.
I'll take you to far places,
The plains of wide open spaces.
A top mountains so high
That you can touch the sky.
I'll make you a queen
Or I'll make you a king.
In betwixt and between a criminal or a cop.
I can also make you a mystery writer at the top.
I've canvasses many with artist's conception.
And factories like Wonka's,
Full of confections.
Sewed and bounded or folded and glued,
I can go most anywhere with you.

Jamie Bernoi

Girl in the Cocoon

Wishing years away, decades at a time
Her youth once had song, a definite rhyme
Our girl lost direction, she knew only "down"
So she dressed herself up in a chrysalis gown

One may not help her out, she's much too elusive
But beware the caged cat, claws and anger effusive
Fitted with daggers and well-rehearsed armor
She's built up such defense so nothing will harm her

Weapons aimed at herself, with most perfect guide
Shoot excuses, mental morphine, echo hollow inside
The worn face in the mirror, the voice in the head
Dulled to latent autism, injected by dread

She was once a Beautiful Butterfly
Since crawled back into the cocoon

Sad eyes seem older
So unwise and colder

The Season of Emergence is past
Beautiful Butterfly finishes last

Stephen J. Gooby

Reflection on Teaching Style

It all started years ago early in the fall
Reading, writing, and arithmetic
was all in a day's routine.
"Round Robin" reading was the style.

Detailed lesson plans, charts and colorful
commercial bulletin boards adorned the small room.
Then came labeled grouping, red birds,
blue birds and yellow birds, too.
Instead of birds, numerics were used, I, II, III
and Johnny was IV.
Traditional programs, tested and tried
were on and off like a merry-go-round ride.
Teachers felt not in control, helpless
and not to mention frustrated.

Out of no where, there came a small we cry,
A different style of teaching had just arrived.
I want to be creative, to create my own style.
I want to do my own thinking to survive.
I am a part of this process too, I yelled.
My imagination is bursting inside.

Anniebelle McIntosh

A Mother's Musings

I wish you could have been there
When the seeds of doubt were sown,
When the burning, loyal passion
Shook from fear it had never known.

I wish you could have been there
Those months of agony without end,
To hear the wailing into the pillow
Night after night, needing her best friend.

I wish you could have been there
To see the pallor of her face,
To watch her ghost-like movement
As she fought to keep up the pace.

I wish you could have been there
The second time you gave her hope
O, lying, conniving personification of betrayal,
You must have felt quite giddy at the success of your little joke.

I wish you could have been there
That day she came to know
The love she once had cherished was lost
But her soul was once again whole.

Sherry Jackson Wolfson

To My Mother

You have created something that before your touch did not exist
I have become the daughter of a daughter of a daughter
Since the beginning of time you, Mother have given
form to my energy, and a name to my purpose
In my hands, from my eyes, throughout my body
carries the lines, sheds the tears and flows the blood
of countless souls before and after this one
With our lives we do in fact become
the children and grandchildren of something invisible
Nothing more than what we can hold,
in our mouths, on our shoulders, under our feet
It's nothing empty, it's everything full
What I taste, what I feel, how I speak, how I look,
has all been passed on through you
The seeds I learn and grown from,
all planted by my mother, her mother, her mother
You have created something that, before your touch, did not exist
I have become the daughter of a daughter, of a daughter

Lisa Marie Bloodgood

Me

These flowers are like me.
They go through their cycles like I do.
They start out fresh and innocent like a child.
They represent the happiness and beauty of my life.
When the flower opens up, it represents me
opening up to Christ and to other people around me.

But then comes the weeds
representing the temptations and sorrows of my life.
The weeds are soon stamped out and the beauty returns.
The flower dies, but its beauty was never really lost
Because next year it will burst forth while with new life
As God intended for all of us to shine forth.

Debra Dealba

Winter

When autumn leaves are blown away and there is frost on your window,
Then you know it is winter.

When soft, little purring kittens are curled up by the fireplace,
Then you know it is winter.

When a swift north wind is howling and it chills all your thoughts,
Then you know it is winter.

When all the sweet, little children are fast asleep dreaming,
Then you know it is winter.

When lacy flakes of winter snow fall gently on the ground,
Then you know it is winter.

When grownups are sipping hot cider warmed by a large blazing fire,
Then you know it is winter.

When everyone is out skiing high up on the icy cold mountains,
Then you know it is winter.

When families are waiting for Santa to squeeeeeze down the chimney,
Then you know it is winter.

Annelie Sauer

The Dreamer

I dreamed you were near me, holding me tight
I dreamed you loving me was your heart's delight
I dreamed you were dreaming of me
I dreamed we were in love eternally
I dreamed of you through loving eyes
I dreamed our love would never die
I dreamed we were together once again
Then I dreamed we were in a place where dreams never end.

April R. Mixon

If I Had One Wish

If I had one wish, what would it be?
Would it be something for you or something for me?
Maybe for fame or for good health
I might even wish for great wealth!

Take your time and think it through,
Think about others, what would they do?
Do you think you would wish for world peace?
Or maybe to sit down to a wonderful feast.

Let me think now, what would I wish for?
Maybe for two or three wishes you know more,
No, I'd not be greedy, I'd wish from my heart
I'd take my time and try to be smart.

What to wish for, world peace, no more wars
Let's see now, no hunger, wealth, behind every door,
No pain or sickness, wouldn't that be great?
Or to know the future, not leaving it to fate.

I know, I'll wish for God's will to be done
That we'd all do His will, yes, everyone!
If that wish came true, how great the world would be
Heaven on Earth, for you and for me.

Marie Gama

Empty

To my best friend, Denae

Every time I see the chair there without you taking up its space,
tears form and roll down my face.
This place is not real to me without you by my side,
for now I do not walk with pride in my stride.
I cannot hold my head up to greet a stranger,
instead I hang my head to my feet.
At night when I pull the covers close
I think of the times I miss most.
My wishes of you coming back are a familiar call of pain I send.
Maybe the hope I will mend.
Please don't forget about me now, because to me
you're the only friend there will ever be.

Alicia Srda

What If . . .

What if green was really yellow, and red really white?
Would the sky be blue today, and black still, tonight?
What if rain was not rain, and snow not really snow,
Would the seasons still be there, and would the wind still blow?
What if trees were called birds, and grass really sand?
Would everything still be the same, all across the land?
What if words did not exist, and books also gone?
Would anyone be writing now, where letters don't belong?
What if you did not exist, and were no longer here?
I would be sad indeed, and shed for you a tear.
What if it is not that way, and will never be?
Will Earth stay the way it is, for all eternity?

Alexia Blanton

A Knight in Armor

To Jack; you are the wind beneath my wings.

A knight in armor he is no more
But he still slays dragons by the score.
The dragons of hunger, of fear, and of cold
Braver is he than the knight of old.
No longer do Indians roam the plains
No fear of scalping or burning remains
But he still stands tall at the door of his home
Though wild animals have long since ceased to roam
To banish, not wolves, or Indians, or bears
But to shoulder instead his family's cares.

Joyce D. Klosky (deceased)

Blue Crystal

To Patricia M. Price

Washed up on the beach, a small blue crystal
Held it in my hand, and it started to tingle
Quiver and shake, try as I might
Couldn't release it, its grip on me so tight

I remember back when I was five
Riding my bike by the river so wide
I saw that blue crystal way back then
Reached out to grab it, but it sank in the sand

Twenty years later, who would have known
That small blue crystal would find its way home
I didn't know what all this meant at the time
That this small blue crystal was a friend of mine

At times when life seemed the darkest
It was then that my friend glowed the brightest
She showed me the way, light from the dark
My little blue crystal buried deep in my heart

Look into yourself and see the beauty
Of the little blue crystal that glows so brightly
You need not look far, in each and every one of us
The crystal is there it's just been forgotten

Don P. Price

Never Say Goodbye, Daddy

To my dad, Allen Manrow

My heart soars with newfound pores
As my dreams form
My thoughts are wild as when I was a child
Waiting to see what life has brought me

A passion so strong there is no wrong
As long as I know you and I
Will never really have to say goodbye
You, Daddy, have shown me a love that goes far above

Letting me dream and have fantasies
Guiding me to a future that I will only succeed
You taught me to triumph
Over the bad times and the rough

You taught me to hold my head high
These characteristics I will carry mightily
As you, Daddy, can smile proudly
As you have touched me tenderly guiding me to the best me possibly

So Daddy, remember that yes my passions are strong
Thanks to all that you taught me about right and wrong
And Daddy, remember all the times that were you and I
And we will never really have to say goodbye

Diane Manrow

What If

Are we really what we appear to be
Is there a greater power that we just can't see
What if the earth is a grain of sand
What if everyone's destiny was already planned
What if the world was to end tomorrow
Would anyone feel any sorrow
Would it be a blessing in disguise
Would anything hear our muffled cries
What if everything just ceased to exist
Would we as the human race be missed
The world would end any day
Why would you have any desire to stay
If you would leave this God forsaken place
Without worrying about being a disgrace
Would you go or would you stay
In hopes of dying before Judgment Day
The choice would be completely up to you
And then somebody dares to ask what if it came true?

Jennifer Hartley

A New Day

The sun is rising, a new day begins.
Yesterday is now in the past.

Some events will be forgotten,
some in memory will forever last.

Planning for the day is merely guessing;
if worked out as planned, it is a blessing.

Some good things or bad happen unexpected;
having just a good day has not been perfected.

A hope or a dream might be there at the start;
will it fill the whole day, or just be a part?

Some put off 'til tomorrow what they should do today:
That's crowding two days into one, shouldn't do it that way!

Each day has a purpose, how it will end we're not certain,
but at the end of the day, like the end of a play,
we bring down the curtain.

Roy L. Gurriell

Untitled

To my boyfriend, Jesse W. Marshik
I love you more than words could say
I love you more every day
But only time could tell how long our love would stay.
I could only wish 'til our dying day
My love for you I can't explain
My life will never be the same
I love you more than you'll ever know,
But I guess it's time to let you go.
And even though you made me cry
And even though you said goodbye.
My love for you will never die.

Kathleen Pusztai

For a Friend

We followed our heart, left our homes to serve you.
A long and tiring journey we have come,
Accomplishing things we never thought we could to be with you.
For a friend, what can we not do?

Your beauty, clothed in shimmering blue, red, and white calls us.
Fifty sparks from your brilliant eyes invite us,
Your warm heart flowing enticingly seven times,
Your peace like clear spring from six channels,
Those stars fifty, turn diamond at your touch.

Emotions shared at first meet we savor
As we look forward to the harmony of an abiding friendship.
For a friend, what can we not do?

Troubled and confused, your word by our side,
Be the shoulder we rest on?
Yet, we hope to share the dreams
Of those who already know your friendship.
For a friend, what can we not do?

Dash not our hopes and drown not the love that drew us to you.
Our request be the gift of friendship to treasure a lifetime.

What can we not do for you, America?

Chiweta A. Onianwa

If My Dad Was Here

If my dad was here my eyes wouldn't tear,
Sometimes I feel he is so near, but also so far away
I miss the way we used to play,
But I know we will be together someday,
In the palace of Heaven.
I've been missing him since I was seven.

John Questel

Untitled

For Jenny, my daughter and best friend
I hate the cold! I really do.
I find it most displeasing!
While others grouse about the heat,
I find my troubles easing.
Arthritis pain and sinusitis disappear
when the weather's warm but winter
they come racing back just like a Voodoo charm,
I hate the heavy clothing to ward off winter's chill.
Give me a ticket to a tropical isle and
I would be there still.
A Jimmy Buffet style of life would suit me to a T.
With rum, calypso music, and a cottage by the sea.
Snow and ice should be abolished, they really are a crime
and that is why they've dubbed me, "Susie Summertime."
If summer could be all the year,
I would be in clover but I am sure when I get there
is the day Hell freezes over.

Susan C. Thompson

Untitled

The urgent desire to find myself within
(amid the chaos of my world)
comes from years of confusion.
Consistently stifled by societal standards
Beauty, Intelligence, Creativity
still I want for answers and definition.

Time ticks swiftly
while I lose myself
to other wasteful tasks.

Questioning constantly—
Who am I? What is my life path? Where am I going?
I search my world
to find the answers
ossified deep within my soul.

Karen Capria

As Time Goes By . . .

To Wendie Simone, love always
As time goes by, changes are made
Birth of a new life, death of an unwilling soul
From sunrise to sunset, day to day
New adventures and mysteries unfold

As time goes by, we try to overcome
The difficult struggles of life
From sunrise to sunset, when the day is done
Our destined hope turns to endless strife

As time goes by, we ultimately conquer
Our desperate efforts to achieve
From sunrise to sunset, while in slumber
We are deep in thought, in dream

M. Murdock

Later Dad

To Edmund Stanley Falkowski, my dad
When I was young, I thought I knew
and didn't want any criticism, lessons, or philosophy from you!
Other things I said I would prefer to do,
The time I chose to not spend with you!
I have come to see now what I can't re-do:
The many things we will never do,
Your grandkids that you never knew,
Your point of view I did not see.
I do now as my daughter does the same with me!
30 years, it seems just flew, since you passed,
so sorry Dad, I miss you!

John Falkowski

The Beautiful

The trees, the trees, the beautiful trees,
that in the fall shed their leaves,
Then in the Spring they grow again.

The leaves, the leaves, the beautiful leaves,
that in the fall travel through the sky and fly, and fly and fly.
They look so nice especially in Spring time.
The grass, the grass, the beautiful grass,
Where in the spring summer and fall, people lay and relax.
But like all things it doesn't last in the cold, cold, Winter mass.
The birds, the birds, the beautiful birds
that all the time go chirp, chirp, chirp.
But in the fall, they travel south day in and day out,
And come back after there is no doubt of cold or drought.

Emmanuel Rivera

Telisa's Sierra

She waited a long time
for this special morn,
when little Sierra
was finally born.

A promise from, God above
to fill her heart and life with love.

The promise was so hard to hold
because it was given, so long ago.
But a vision was given
so beautiful and clear.
God said don't worry, she's still up here.
I haven't forgotten what your heart cries for,
a beautiful child for you to adore.

Like a breeze from the mountains
God's timing was right.
Sierra came home
to start her new life.

Martha Brown

Life

What is life?

To me, it is a long stream of events
where you meet many people and find many places to see.
Sometimes you try to live in the past,
which we all know simply won't last.
Sometimes we like to jump ahead,
which wears us out, and then we have trouble getting out of bed.

First comes childhood, then the teens,
which is usually when we make those terrible scenes.

Soon you're an adult and it is not your fault,
but you say you grew up too fast.
Then you start to wonder just how long you are going to last.

Now you're a senior and you realize you are leaner
and not quite as healthy anymore.

Then as you die, you sit back and sigh
and hope you made a difference in someone's life.

Mike Joslin

Children of God

Children are from God, one and all;
We should love him big and small.

He's always watching us from above;
To see if we're being worthy of his love;

We his children also need to understand;
He needs us to love and protect his creatures and this land;

We are of different colors you see;
But to God he loves us all equally.

Cynthia J. Russo

The Heart and the Feather

Happy the heart that glides so high
And now a feather in the sky;
Lifted by winds on Eagles' wings
Toward his God to sing.

Glad be that heart not near an ounce
No deadly beast could pounce;
A life in BOTTOMLESS LOVING
Whose angels to Heaven are shoving!

Sing all the choir in vibes above
The anthem of this wondrous love;
With ties to bind this Heart no more
It asks to seek—then knocks the Door . . .

Whose knock doth crack the door so wide
That it greets this FEATHER-HEART from the sky;
Who takes its place about the nest
In Mansions of God's Treasure Chest.

Brian Levens

Untitled

How does one first begin to plan
the artistic future of the land

To dream, design, develop and begin
in hopes of coming to the ultimate end

A vision you must first have in mind
and all the necessities you must find

Tolling without a care
Not caring about the wear

Body and spirit both in demand
But what hopes and visions we know will be grand

The earth beneath your feet, the sky above
Part of what God has given us in his wonderful love

And as we finish our job of labor
We can now sit back and savor

Love, peace, tranquility, beauty and God's pardon
In our wonderful backyard garden.

Sandra L. Lodato

Hands

The hands are always warm when it's cold,
The hands are so frail and so old,
They are soft and pale,
Like the skin of a baby whale.

They write a letter to a friend,
Or hold the book read to me from beginning to end.
They wipe away my tears, when I get hurt,
And mend a hole in my shirt.

I love these hands with all my heart,
With these hands I dare not part,
These hands are like no others,
You see, these hands are my mother's.

Richelle Russell

Her

Knowing that you like her and always thinking so,
today will be the day when you will let her know
all the love you have inside the only thing you can't let go.
Knowing now you love her and knowing she loves him,
always keeping you remembered and never letting in.
And then you finally realize the love you have inside
is all the love you kept for her it never did subside.
Then she finally realized the love she built inside
she gave it all to you when she began to cry.

Jason Laflamme

My Dearest Wade

For my late husband, Wade
Memories of you will never fade, and if they start to slip away,
All I have to do is look at our children
And they will remind me of the love we made.

We had our share of laughter and tears,
and through the years, I have heard a many "I love you, dear."

They said our love would never last,
That we got married way too fast.
We were given six months. It was fifteen years.
That was something that made you proud;
You were still married to the same ole gal.

It may have been longer, only the Lord needed you more.
My loss is now Heaven's gain.
At least I know you're not in any pain.

Instead of the clothes you had on when we laid you in the ground,
you now wear a robe and a crown.
You have seen the face of the man who saved you by his grace;
you heard his voice when he said, "My child, welcome home."
I know you're in a better place; however, I still miss you so.
You were my biggest baby, and I was your Lady.
I love you, Wade,
Melody Worley

A Simple Request

Oh, how cruel fate can be
When in the hands of a child we leave it
For this child, with his eyes he cannot look
But with his heart he does see
His arrows fly, their mark they hit
With this pen, the names he does write in his book
So sweet child, I beg you to gaze upon me
And with my hope, never will I quit
For with another I wish to lie by that brook.
David J. Cornelius

The Father I Never Had

You're my father by definition,
But not in my heart,
For a true father is there through everything,
Right from the start.

Mom is both Mom and Dad to me,
She has been there through all of this.
From the first day of school,
To first dates, first crushes, first kiss.

What did I do to deserve this?
Was I that bad
For you to just walk away
And not be my dad?

The next time I see,
Do not expect me to call you Dad.
For I will call you by your first name,
Because you are the father I never had.
Rhonda Switer

My Cat

My cat's as curious as a mouse but he does not live in the house.
His hair is gray and soft and he has a bed above the loft.
He won't count to eat until he hears the squeak of the side door.
He is my pet and he likes my net.
He loves to play with me and chase butterfly and dragonflies
He is a high climber and is a good prey diver.
For a fat cat he can still fit in my dad's hat.
He is in love and as sweet as a dove.
Sharon Beaulieu

The Broken Heart

The flower grows,
rising up from the ground.
Its virgin leaves feeling the warmth
of sunlight.
Its petals open,
the eyes of the rose
seeing the world
for the first time.
Its stem,
legs standing strong.
Its thorns,
a shield for protection.
An alien figure appears blocking the sunlight.
A careless foot comes down.
The shadow moves on leaving behind
the broken rose.
The rose survives, begins to recover
rising up into the arms of the sun.
Like a broken heart
who finds love again.
Ashley Wetherbee

Only a Girl

To Violetta Judson, my reason to live
Only a girl of twelve years old,
I've watched you grow so tall and bold.
It seems like only yesterday I bandaged your knees
and kissed the tears away.

So many memories we've made together,
talking and laughing 'til midnight hours.
You loved to play games, and videos we watched,
chatting and shopping 'til we almost dropped

You shared all your dreams and some of your goals;
the sky was the limit of what your future could hold.
Music you loved and the violin you played;
whether raining or sunshine, you practiced each day.

A young lady now as you're turning thirteen,
laying aside lacy dresses in exchange for blue jeans.

Many more birthdays will come and go,
and like a flower in bloom, your petals unfold.
My sweet little violet, you'll always be,
a bright little blossom for the world to see.

I love you,
—Aunt Kathy
Katherine Judson

Dove Beyond the Sea?

To beloved Paul—deceased July 1998
In the quiet of the night my husband
You slipped away from me silent and alone
That fateful night God took you home
Your life was tired and weary
More than your weak heart could bear
Is that why He came and took you there
On the night you left me my love
I imagine he recreated you into a beautiful dove
Circling the universe at peace.
While on Earth, I grieve, hoping for some release
I loved you with all my heart and soul
Will I ever again feel whole.
But, as sure as day time follows night
And sunshine follows rain
We will someday be together again
'Til then my love keep a spot reserved for me
Way out there beyond the sea
Where we can soar together for all eternity
Sylvia Kochanski

A Packet of Ten

A packet of ten tissues
Stuffed in my coat pocket.
The first went to waste
When a sudden wind caught it.
One wipes a spill I made with my tea.
The next pulls the stinger
Left by an angry bee.
Another cleans my glasses so I can see clearly.
Two more pad my shoulder while I care for
The son I love dearly.
Two I give out to strangers throughout the day.
One dabs at ink that, despite my efforts,
Intends to stay.
The last soaks up my mournful tears
At the passing of a friend.
It looks like it's time for
A new packet of ten.

Gary R. Gowers

Rainbow

Red and green, blue and yellow, orange and pink.
All the colors that make me happy.
And when I look up in sky,
I see many butterflies flying by.

Bob Carr

The Purity of the Rose

You are the gentleness, the tenderness and the softness,
You are the fragrance of a rose.
You are the Jazz Melody,
That is so pure, it softens the senses.
You are the perfect sunset,
That stretches across the horizon.
You are the purity of the rose.

You are the serenity of flight,
That is the bald eagle floating on the wind.
You are my Montana Breeze,
The mountain air glistening through Aspen leaves
On an Autumn Countryside.
You are the enchantment that dreams are made of,
You are the purity of the rose.

You are a gift from God.
You are the one beauty that many, only dream of.
You are to me, the most beautiful woman I have ever known.
Your radiance glows whenever I'm around you.
You are life, you are happiness,
You are the purity of the rose.

Dennis E. Connor

Depression

You're smiling, but with dead eyes I see.
You see no reason to exist, no reason to be.

If I could carry some of that pain for you, I would.
Why the dark cloud is upon you cannot be understood.

We can't ask why, look ahead, please believe.
This dark cloud has knocked us to our knees.
It's time we stand, do it! Believe.

Don't look back on what it's taken away.
All you can do is look ahead,
Live for today.

If you can't live for you right now, live for me.
Someday you'll be back. You will believe. You will be.

You will smile again and you will laugh.
The sun will come, that cloud will pass.

Stacie Gifford

Is There Anybody Out There That Isn't Taken?

To my mom
Ever since I remember,
I have been searching for that special someone
It all started in high school
Every time I asked someone I thought looked pretty
She turned me down
Now that I am older
I sometimes think there isn't going to be
A special person for me
Then there are times I think about this
And I can't stop thinking about it
All I want is someone to do things with
Someone to talk to
Someone to laugh with
All I really want is somebody to share the rest of my life

Jason Lavake

Untitled

The spring, with its warm weather and soft air,
With the rain and wind, the daffodils bend
Perhaps a mother will sit in her chair
Upon her porch as she watches the end
Of her babies' lives as the adults' begin.
She knows they'll do well, but still she worries
That her babies, now grown, will never come in
From the raging storm of life and its furies.
She wishes they could know of life's sorrows,
And the pain one must endure to survive,
But she knows she can't warn them of tomorrow.
At least not enough to save them from their lives.
    To be a mother, what strength one must possess,
    To deal with all the heartbreak, joy, and stress.

Katie Fedigan Linton

Need

For my soulmate, Jerry
I need someone to love me
As I am with all my good and bad
Take me as I am for I shall try and do the same
With all your good and bad
'Cause you're still the very best part of me.

Marthalyn Dale Smith

Untitled

Love is the answer, no matter the question
And when love is in question, let me make a confession
You can't question it, and be in it
And can't be in it, unless you believe in it.

Love is being completely truthful and
the way she makes you feel is completely sootheful
To describe it like on anchor a light as a feather,
ensures you'll be forever together.

Love is looking in me and knowing you need no other
looking to the future, I'm the father, you're the mother
but how is it that I know I love you so much?
It's the feeling I feel within every touch.

So when we look at each other at the very same time,
and know that our words would perfectly rhyme.
But stop short to see that my gaze is reflected,
and words are so simple, they should be neglected.

So don't be afraid of this love we've made,
and the passion between us, don't let that fade.
Always know that you and me will always have the best fun
because love is the answer, no matter the question.

Luke Adkins

The Waiting Room

I want to hear my daughter laugh again, and then again.
A gentle sound of loving raindrops.
To hear this once more, will be an answered prayer.
I cannot remain still, clenching.
Ballerina in a music box. A perpetual existence
Grace captured in pink, the rhythm of her life.
From day care to intensive care
Four years old to ninety-four. A child's play ground.
A simple little sand box in the park,
Dangerously close to the intersection
Intersection of my life. Red lights, green lights.
Who pays attention anymore?
Enclosed in a wooden tomb.
Ballerina in a music box.
No more waiting. Time to rejoice.
Bright eyes looking at me.
Tiny trusting arms grab my neck.
Keep the ballerina in the box.
My baby is coming home.

Tracy Schneider

Untitled

Again I trusted him, believed in him,
gave him my heart and soul.
And again he has let me down, disappointing me,
tearing me down, wearing me out.
My broken heart bleeds throughout my body,
my veins, along my bones and through my muscles.
My soul is no longer here;
it has drained out through the slit
I made for its escape.

Daniela Rusnak

Untitled

As all Christmas go
The stockings are hung, and the children go to bed.
Then in a flash, Santa arrives on his sled!
This Christmas Eve won't be a kick,
Because of the weather, Santa is sick!
They've got the toys ready, then they heard the news.
Now at the toy shop, the elves got the blues.
Who will replace Santa and deliver the toys?
Who will do it for the good girls and boys?
When 12 o'clock struck, the head elf had an idea:
He'd hire a duck from Lake Animonapia!
When he got to the lake, everyone was there,
But he needed a duck who was special and rare.
Out the corner of his eye, he saw a faint glimmer,
Then out of the bushes came a shimmering male swimmer!
From his high arched neck to the tip of his tail,
He was graceful as ever, he couldn't fail!
Soon on to the sled the duck did go,
And off into the night, in the midnight snow,
From rooftop to rooftop did they stop.

Jessica Chan

Forgotten Never

One year ago today, we laid you down to rest.
God took our only mother, he takes only the best.
We miss you more than ever, the tears we try to hide;
The pain we feel is heartache, the loneliness inside.
We know that you are up there, watching from above,
Knowing that you're kept alive, in our hearts with love.
The holidays were lonely, your birthday just another day;
The tears just kept on falling, nothing we could do or say.
We just want you to know you will live on within us forever;
You may be gone, yes that's true, but forgotten never!

With lots of love to you, Mom.
—Dave, Deb, Michele, Lyn, and Dianna

Lyn M. Simmons

For Anyone I Ever Hurt

No matter how hard I try,
I'll always be a failure in your eyes.

I'll never measure up to what you want,
And I know you're ashamed of what you got.

I know your feelings for me you try to hide on the inside,
But I can see them all in your eyes.

It hurts me to know I'm such a disappointment,
All I ever wanted is just one compliment.

I can hear your hate for me in your voice,
But it seems like this road I'm on now is my only choice.

You can't see me accomplishing anything,
Because even I lost all my dreams.

There's no point in me saying I'm sorry,
All I wanted was for you not to worry.

All I wanted is someone to show some interest in me,
But I guess that's never the way it's going to be.

Laura Tank

Thinking of You

Today I sit here thinking of you, Dad,
wondering if you're happy or sad.
I wonder if you're alone,
or if you share happiness with a loved one.

Happiness is slow coming my way,
missing you more every day.
Every day goes by with this hurt in my heart;
you left me, they said it was time to part.

Dad, I'll try and be strong,
knowing on Earth is where I belong.
I'll give Mom an extra hug and kiss,
telling my family how much they're missed.

Dad, I'll love you to my dying day,
making sure I'll visit your grave.
The family will be strong, and try not to be blue,
but today I'll sit here "Thinking of You."

Carolyn S. Hartl

Lost Son

For my long lost son, who's an adoptee
In 1967 I gave birth to my son;
that same year, I lost him. I was 21.
The love I carry deep in my heart
with hopes someday we can make a new start.
My search, my search will not be in vain;
It's a way of releasing all the heartache and pain.
February twenty-first your big day was;
I know God sent you from up above.
I never got to hold you, dear;
Adopted parents raised you through the years.

Nancy Avevitt Campbell

One Nation

Thousands of years of pain and frustration
Dealing with the hardship of segregation
Living each day fearing annihilation
Forced to do works of different variation
Put together by a while organization
Wondering at times what's vacation
Is this life or a violation
Can't confirm because of our lack of education
Lacking the rights to visitation
Never giving up because of our determination
Waiting go the day of conformation
That black and white can live as one nation

Desmond Walsh

Remember My Tear Drops

To the memories of Marva Buford
Tell me, my friends, what do I do when my soul cries?
Do I look to the heavens and glorious skies?

Should I tell the stories of me and my life,
of jealousy and my fear of returning to poverty?

What's next in the life that I live, trying to live positive
and trying to forget all the hurt I feel.

Will they remember me and my name
or will they forget the tears that I shed?
As I walk through the cemetery with all the dead
that know not of what has been said . . .
Remember me.

SN Carlos D. Buford

Awakened Too Soon

In the bleakest hours after midnight
when Morpheus rules the slumbering world,
six-legged nymphs explore the pungent, rotting earth,
and creatures furry scurry far and wide,
greeny-gold eyes aglow.
I awaken from my dreamy daze,
warm and supple, cozy in my soft, woolly cocoon.
From across the fields a whistle pierces
the quiet, dusky stillness,
and the clattering of steel rails
fades into the meekest, shuffling crawl.
My buzzing head sinks back into the feathers and lace
of the peaceful illusions I embrace until the dawn
comes to shatter the starried purple darkness.

Joelle Steele

Ghetto Victim's Crowd

Don't crowd around me now, whispering and pushing,
gawking and gazing at the reality of looking
at stab wounds and gunshot holes piercing through
my very soul, as I wait for death to take its toll.

I tried with all my might; I didn't go down without a fight.
My life flashed before my eyes; I screamed and I ran
to You! I cried, but instead, you turned your head,;
my life meant nothing to you, and now I'm dead.

So don't crowd around me now; you didn't before.
When I needed you most, you chose to ignore.

Delisa E. Young

Zachary

Little boy with your big brown eyes,
What do you see?
How many times must I hear your cries?
Why does it have to be?

You seem so full of life just now,
Running and playing and having such fun.
I silently pray and make a vow
To let you be and watch you run.

A "defective heart" was all that they said
The doctors don't know the whys.
The nights you labored to breathe in your bed,
Your wonderful mothers sighs.

How long will you live?
No one will say.
The tears that we shed, the prayers that we give,
To implore God to give you just one more day.

Will he, dear Zach give you one more day?
One day more on this Earth?
If he'd let me, I'd give mine away
Big brown eyes, you're what life is worth.

Dixine Woyach

Problems? Solutions?

Suicide, matricide, homicide, genocide
Annihilation of a nation.

Alcoholic, crack addicted, disease afflicted
Defecate on a race
Who's to blame? Always the same gunmaker, law breakers.

Sirens blaring, ambulance waiting, mother's wailing
Funeral homes, cemetery's sons, no longer mother's own
Persecution is not an illusion
Police brutality is reality
Jail cell? Does it ring a bell?

Exploitation, depression, deprivation, desperation
Enough protest, off with their heads
Children having children, abortion is not the option
Education, identification, liberation from oppression
Bright minds, always survive.

"A dream deferred," Brother Langston said,
Or by any means necessary, as my main man,
Malcolm X unapologetically expressed.

Juan Sanchez

Grief

The sword went deep. It pierced into my soul.
I fell to earth but feathers stopped my fall.
I landed softly. Why I do not know,
But that I landed on my all in all.

So hard my rock that diamond turn to dust.
So soft my rock in him alone I trust.
He lifted me and placed me near His throne.
Said, Do not fear. Your child has come home.

In my keeping, there 'til you arrive.
In my house, your child is still alive.
I know your hopes and dreams are dashed to earth
Yet always it's my purpose that comes first.

His life is hidden now in the depth of me,
But soon not through a vale you'll see.
Like sunset colors fading into blue,
You'll know the whole when Heaven is in view.

Iona M. Butts

Unspoken Words

For my secret love
My feelings soar to heights unknown, much to my regret,
for there can be no love for me, upon my heart its etched.
Words of pain and loneliness, tear open wounds anew,
because I know there can never be a time for me and you.

Unquenched fires of burning heat, longings running wild,
the growing ache inside my heart consumes me all the while.
Empty arms, no tender kisses, only hunger lingers, because of love
that cannot be, it slips right through my fingers.
I long to feel your loving touch, your kisses warm and tender,
but you will never ever know, my broken heart surrenders!

Patricia M. Foster

Ambiguities

anonymous associations artfully accompanying
meanings made murky, misleading.
being, becoming bashfully betrayed,
incoherent invitations insistently inane,
greedy, grasping, grabbing, gripping,
uniting underneath universal ubiquities.
inconsistent, inadequate, incomplete images
traveling, touring, twisting, turning
inside. incredible illusions internally,
externally exiled. everything equivocal.
suggesting synergistic sensitivity, susceptibility.

T. Charlene Witten

A One-Night Stand

If my heart were a daisy
Used for he loves me, loves me not
It would have no petals left
It would be the stem that love forgot

We were all alone together, in the darkness of the night
You kissed me very sweetly and then turned out the light
We talked about forever and making this our home
But in the light of day, I found myself alone

The petals were my feelings
Blown away upon the wind
And the warmth of the sun
Brought your feelings to an end

If my heart were a daisy
Used for he loves me, loves me not
It would have no petals left
If would be the stem that love forgot.

Ruth Barbour

Into Town

For my dearest Judy May
Around the mountain
And over the hill and down
The path to the mill.
Across the bridge into
Town where I find a bench.
And I sit down
And watch the people
Walk into town.
Some with smile and some with frown.
But I like the people and I like the town
but most of all I love the old bench where
I sit down and watch the people walk into town.

George F. Carter

The Old House

As I sat in a corner in a nook of the house
I felt the strong presence of those long before
Who danced and cavorted on wide polished floors.
The young and the old ones who sat by the fire,
The brides and the grooms in their elegant attire.
What says this old house to those who would listen?
"Make music, make love," and again I will glisten.
"The two who have come here arouse in my pleasure,
and I in return shall care for my treasures."

Fay Miller

Sun

Radiant you are, in your marvelous way,
Warm, and glorious, I respectfully say.
Lovely and bright, a gift from above,
To fill our lives with beauty and love.
Blessed are those whom you have graced,
Who will run to the end a soldier's race.

No one could prepare me, for what laid ahead.
For in a dream I saw, what I must now dread.
All through the night, oh, how I cried.
Tears and loneliness, hurt, confusion, and surprise;
When I awakened that morning, and found you were gone,
Remembering our journey, before you were born.

A lifetime of pain, was all that was left,
Hoping and praying, that you are at rest.
Longing to see your face again, 'cause I miss you,
My joy, my pride, my friend.
Perseverance emerged, and humility begun,
the race to be won, was for my beautiful sleeping son.

Aretha S. Roach

Miracle in Recovery

For Frank, Adrian, Ofelia, and Adam
I was amazed to see that recovery wasn't only staying clean.
Recovery is changing, growing, and maturing.

I realized I was clean for five months and I would lose focus.
I knew there was something wrong.

How could I stay strong?
I took a good look at myself
and started to read the N.A. book.

While I was reading, I was experiencing . . .
Everything I didn't apply is something I apply.
Living life on life terms is better than getting stoned.

Staying drug free, it's just a breeze. I'm so pleased.

I have to say I am surprised. I am amazed.
I finally found the pieces to this maze.

Nancy Torres

My Family

A field of an array of beautiful flowers.
Orange and yellow leaves that blow in the wind.
Stars that lighten the darkest skies.
White, puffy clouds that fill the bluest heavens.
Big smiles on children's faces.
Dreams that seem never ending.
Happiness that has no end.
Hopes and wishes that come true out of nowhere.
Love that goes on forever.
All of these things express
the way I see my family.
My family is the core of my soul.

Sandy Helms

The Old and Tattered Book, Bible

My Savior is the author of an old and tattered book,
he's begging each and every one just to take a look.
That is why I come to you with my heart so full of love,
waiting on my savior, the one who sits above.
You might ask, who is this Savior that you are talking about?
Well, when I give the answer, you will jump and shout.
Why worry about things on Earth, when there's much more to see?
Worry about going to Heaven to see Jesus, that's the key.
He'll welcome you with open arms and hold your little hand,
Though your feet are weary that you can barely stand,
Jesus will pick you up and carry you through this land,
and that is why you only see one footprint, in the sand.

Laura R. McNeil

Raindrops

Raindrops will fall against the window . . .
While you are alone, thinking of the person . . .
That was once in your life.

You try to understand the reasons why the
way you feel inside, and why that person is gone.

Is it loneliness or a broken heart
because they are not there . . .
Or are you mad at yourself because
you could have changed things.

You don't realize what you have 'til it's gone . . .
Then sometimes it is too late.

While alone . . . it may not be the raindrops,
on the window that you will hear . . .

It could be your own teardrops falling.

Robert Fuentes

A Bright Summer Day

Through times we have walked side by side
Caring and sharing, nothing to hide
Good times and bad times, our love stays the same
Running wild and free, unable to tame

A long restless summer, and an old photograph
My memories of you, keep coming back
Oh, how I long for your tenderness
Never did I think it would all end like this

Like a bird in the wind, a rock on the trail
Will things stay the same? Only time will tell
a fish in the ocean, the moon on the sea
there's a place in the clouds for you and for me

As I sit and stare out this old windowpane
It seems to me now that nothing's the same
The sky has turned a cold, dark gray
Never again will I see that bright day.
Oh, never again will I see that bright day.

Alicia Marie Labani

Unavowed

Oh, for the joys of today to last for eternity,
But gone with the winds of tomorrow, now the sadness of yesterday.
Love me for now, for tomorrow belongs not to you and I,
But place within your heart for eternity, the love I so freely give.
The love I feel for you grows stronger with each passing day;
Though the distance between us gets longer,
I hold the closeness of you to me.
I can feel your heart beating beneath my touch,
And within that heart beats a love I wish the world could know.
Your smile makes a warmness cover me I have never known;
Your touch uncovers passion hidden deep inside.
Though no-one may ever know,
the love we have for each other will go on for eternity.

Nancy Wilson

A Kind Thought

To the love of my life, Mr. Fletcher Craig
When the time comes for us to part,
Do not weep, for I'll be there in thought.
Think of the happy times we shared,
And not the bad times that were there.

For we were only meant to share the time given to us,
No more and no less, as the years passed on,
So as we part into a world of no return,
I seek only to know that you were as happy as I.

So weep no more, my love,
for our love will never die,
But only part into eternity,
To last for all time to come.

Cornelia Osgood

What Is Life

Should we know who we are or at least who we want to be?
Is time the only hope for the things we long to see?
Does God plan our lives and the paths we choose to lead?
Or did we just multiply from an ongoing plentiful seed?
Are all our questions answered when our life comes to its end
Or did we miss the secret when we lost a loved one or friend
If we all are loved and watched over by the Lord.
Why must we be cut by a painful repeating sword?
Is it to make us strong and tell us who we are?
Or are the most important things in life all about a scar?
I hope one day I can answer these questions and learn what's true
And maybe understand which life belongs to who.

Terri Williams

Mister Pretender

Mister Pretender, your lips too good to be true.
Kiss me once, kiss me twice. Oh, how nice.
I think, I skip, roo, and love you.
You are my shining knight.

Your hair's is so fair, and red.
Your body is like a jaguar.
Your soft brown eyes say, better get ready
For my touch of my love to set you on fire.

You walk as you are on the moon.
You speak as an angelic choir.
My heart say, I'll be there soon.
You are my desire.

Love me sweet, love me tender, I want you.
Under your magical spill, I surrender.
Juba-Juba means, I love you.
Mister Pretender, you are to be remembered.

Diana L. Boyd

Happy Mother's Day

Your day comes only but once a year,
Which isn't really fair
Because everything you do for me
Is so beyond compare.

You make my bed and fix my meals.
There's nothing you can't do.
You sacrifice all you have for me
To show you love me too.

There's not much I can do in return
For all you've done for me;
At least not yet, because of my age.
But a time will come, you'll see.

I'll make you proud to say, "He's my son."
I'll try with all my heart
To do what you want me to do
And from your ways never to depart.

Your day comes only but once a year;
It's not fair to me or to you
'Cause you deserve all the riches in the world
And some day, you'll get them, too.

Jamison K. Francis

How the West Began

From the hills of Oklahoma
To the plains of Colorado
People risk their lives to follow
And find the Buffalo wallow.

Acres of Buffalo grass and sod
Their only hope was trust in God.
Raising their families without a doctor,
Using horses and mules instead of a tractor.

No telephone or washing machine
No electric lights were ever seen.
The kerosene lantern and a small cook stove
The old dugout their place of abode.

Milk and butter came from the cow.
A few old hens and maybe a sow.
Bacon and eggs were not on the menu.
Pie and cake were just not for you.

Water was hauled from the neighborhood windmill
No lakes, no rivers, no spring, no hill.
Prairie chicken and rabbit were the meat of the day.
Only the bravest were able to stay.

Nellie Burr

Untitled

In this short period of time,
You sparked a vital nerve in my mind,
Captivating my inner essence.
As our two souls intertwine,
We connect at a slow pace,
Allowing no mistakes to enter,
Similar to Father Time and Mother Nature.
Me and you be flowing into zones unknown,
Trying to find love and happiness and making it our home.
I represent the king in the modern-day illusion;
You're my precious queen,
The strong backbone to our foundation.
Together nothing can touch or penetrate what we're creating,
Both searching for love
Seeking God's highest elevation.
As one, we're the manifestation of the universe
Here on Earth, continuing our survival in life.
Through rebirth, I know what love is!

Ernest E. Coles II

Silence

She walked not swiftly upon my conversation.
Trod down on it like it wasn't there.
No words I spoke to her were heard.
'Twas like I wasn't there.
I didn't mean to be so silent.
I thought my words were true and clear.
But fell not they upon their mark.
My words she didn't hear.

John J. O'Rourke Jr.

Untitled

Have you ever seen a tiny church so small,
Yes a one room school house on city ground.

There on a busy corner with modern cars
Buzzing all around.

It served us well, when shorted, but Larry entered first.
We were busy with new house things,
And did not go at first, but go to did not thirst.

It was he who got the going,
A little child shall lead them and this he did.

Howard Handyside

The Darkest Time

For my family, with love
One cross and two on a lonely distant hill,
attended by millions who grieved, one killed.

They crowded the streets for one man to see
and grasped when burden brought him to knee.

"Oh, God, Save thy son!" cried one in prayer.
Then fell to the ground with tears of despair.

With crown of thorns and lashed between two,
he saw not the heavens nor the ones that slew.

The heavens grew darker, the death angel flew;
The heavens began weeping as a soft breeze blew.

Then a voice was heard and the clouds withdrew,
a voice so powerful, and the sun shone through.

"He hath sacrificed to save all men!"
The voice was heard, then spoke once again.

"But he hath not died on this lonely hill,
but shall live on 'til all life is still."

Billy G. Lewis Jr.

Wonders

How can people with scar-ridden and broken dreams
Expect to know true, is in their next chance's heart beams?
Will the walls go away, and leave them standing alone?
Will they bust open the silence, with long sought-after tones?

Will they know they live up to, what their life desires?
Will their fears allow the rekindling of fires
With only a kiss or a touch of hand?
Will they know they are loved, more than beaches have sand?

Does life ever give such a sought-after wish?
They fear that their past will rid them of this.
Will they be able, to honor this love
And put aside the fears, in the questions above?

I think they will know soon after they first meet,
As sure as God sits on his heavenly seat.
They will say, "This is the one I'll spend life with 'til death,"
And they will cherish each other 'til their last sighing breath.

Mike Compton

Prayer for Yanka Milosz

Ancient, as the velvet of the robes
Adorned by the men of God in the temples:
Lost during the winter war; The men sit:
Engulfed in the spirit of spring:
Old and young, and forever returned
By a Father who understands eternity.
The dance changes:
Changes with the music and the seasons
and the dancers:
Changes with the will of God
and changes with wantonness, but forever:
Changes. O Holy Father, maker of my mother:
Keeper of my brother, friend of my child:
Walk with me now in this long evening of earthly grief,
before the river flows to darkness and time, alone, changes.
Changes to light.

Melanie Farmer

Fear Not, Be Calm

It is dark here yet light is all around
Enclosed in fear while space is profound
Even with a map I am still but lost
Rich enough yet too poor to pay the cost
Smothered in warmth but still as cold as ice
Covered in love and so full of despise
Crowded by people yet feeling alone
Places to live without having a home
On firm, solid ground yet trembling, shaking
Deaf with sound, knowing the truth but faking
Too strong and smart to ask for help with hope
Fear of the past, unable to cope
Often I still speak with a silent voice
Sure of the future but with doubt in choice
When will all the loneliness go away?
When will someone come speak to me and say?
Fear not, Be calm, help is on the way.

Aaron M. Chelikowsky

Worlds in Water

When you journey into the water,
you begin to step into a whole new world.
You see things that you wouldn't know existed.
You see things that make you wonder,
why hasn't anyone seen this splunder.
The scene before your eyes just amazes you
to so that you hate to leave such a splendid and wonderful place,
But alas it is time to go.
As you leave you think, will I ever see it again?

Daniel Hammett

Lost Child

In loving memory of Michael
We've gotta find a way, to save our children,
and teach them that life, can be good.
It must be something wrong, with the way we're living,
because it all just ends up in blood.

The Lord gave us the gift of life,
but evil forces will destroy it twice.
A child hasn't got a chance today,
when drugs and violence tries to make them pay.

I've tried the best that I could,
to teach him to be a man, the way that he should.
But that old devil, he came knocking at the door,
now my lost child, is here no more.

So my children remember, that you are our future,
be strong enough to lead the way.
You've got to walk the straight and narrow, or,
there's a price you'll pay one day.

Eleanor Branch McConico

The Special Someone

The days are so hot, and nights so cold
Thinking of your hugs, the warmth they hold
Seeing you smile, bring joy to my heart
Dreaming of days we'll never be apart

You hold a touch, no women could give
Makes every day brighter, more life to live
Just being around you, which is no nice to be
I pray to God, wishing you were with me

I think of you, all day all night
Looking at your pictures, that beautiful sight
I wish you were close, to hold me so near
I have feelings, for you, only you my dear

I know with your situation, it can really be hard
One day you will gamble and flip the right card
If it's not with me, I will be sad and blue
You will always know, I've fallen for you

I wanted you to know, even so far apart
I will cherish your friendship, with all my heart
I think of you always, in dreams and in mind
What ever you decide, happiness you will find

Larry Bardroff

What Used to Be

I often wonder where all the old feelings have gone to
The way I felt every time you called or came near me
I used to look across a crowded room and fantasize
Now I don't even bother to see if you're still there
You don't touch me the same anymore
You kiss me goodbye, at times you forget
I feel lonely even though you are with me
Don't get me wrong, I do love you
It's just not the same anymore
I often wonder where all the old feelings have gone to
We used to be in love, now we love each other
Oh, yes, there is a difference
It's the feeling it brings to you
We very rarely talk about what's important to us
Only what we need to do
You bought me a dog
At least I have something to talk to
It doesn't watch television like you do
Please don't get me wrong, I really do love you still
I just often wonder, that's all.

Jill M. Littrell

Untitled

Alone and waiting.
Don't know what I'm waiting for just sitting, kicking, and twirling.
My foot stops, not letting my leg go straight out.
I try this process again. Kick . . . thump . . . kick . . . thump.
Don't know what it is, so I don't care . . . darkness.
I awake and see some sort of sight. What is that?
I squirm towards this strange light.
When I get right up to it, something pushes me,
Moving without having to struggle.
I feel cold hands on my back.
I feel for the first time how it is to be pulled.
Suddenly everything feels so different.
I feel something wet is on my cheek.
For the first time I hear a loud noise. In a rhythm. Crying.
I feel my mouth open.
Every time I feel my mouth open, that noise happens, that cry.
I feel another thing new. I can breathe on my own.
Oh, I know this is the beginning of a whole new, wonderful world.
I feel warmth in this big lady's arms.
I am born.

Cassandra Forsyth

Need You Near

My bright little doll so far away from me
Only my mind can bring you near.
I want so much to hold you close.
I think of the good times so often we shared
Frolicking carefree on into the mystic night
Those times seem so very distant now and almost forgotten.
But, I struggle to keep them from misbegotten,
I wish so much that you could be here,
To hold you softly so close and so near.
You always help me to get through anything.
If you could be here my heart would sing,
My psyche would smile from Ego to Id,
If only your shining face would shine within.
This place seems forsaken by God at times.
The talk that I hear is both distant and near.
It all serves to remind me that you are not here.
I wish so strong things could be much different
I revel in the thoughts that Heaven could be sent.
My sweet child of Christ, I will wed you one day
But alas, my dear, for now, you are too far away.

John Gordon Ryon

The Prayer of the Evergreens

One cold and snow-covered night in mid-December,
When the nut and fruit trees were in their slumber,
Stripped of their foliage and fruit,
The wind that blew was a brute.

"Dear God," prayed the evergreen,
"There are no nuts or fruit to be seen.
Make us bare—the harvest they need.
They're weak—need nourishment for feed."

The Lord heard and quickly resounded,
"Bear you a harvest," in a loud voice he responded.
Then lo and behold, nuts and fruit they bore,
Figs and dates and peanuts—galore!

The people gathered all, much they stored.
Then sang and danced, thanking the Lord.
They were happy; they continued to pray,
Laughingly, joyfully gay.

Ignatius Pantano

Extinct

To my loving family
Plant a tree and watch it grow,
When they disappear it hurts us so.
We can't go back to the past you know,
When they were a dime a dozen to go.
The need to nurture and protect and sew,
Because our lives around them flow.
Our need is high and supply is low,
The upcoming extinction of even the crow.
We dig and build and move and mow,
We rock this Earth from head to toe.
Our candle soon may right out blow,
And the sun will no longer glow.
We can't just watch the status quo,
We must react right now, or woe!
We'll be a universal planet in tow.
We can't keep going like this, oh, no!
This planet with trees is our friend not our foe.
We must plant them now, all over and in a row.
We must hasten and hurry and not be slow.
Plant that tree NOW and watch US grow!

Gayle Little

Mitzi

She was a joy a blessing to my heart;
She was true happiness right from the start.
As I think of her now as the years go by,
Remembering my Mitzi, I laugh and I cry.
Through it all she was a pal and friend,
And I will never forget her 'til my journey's end.
My wonderful Mitzi who is now in bliss;
She is the dog I will always miss.
If there is a Heaven—and I know there is—
Then she is with God, and now she's his.

Barbara Crowther

Jami and I

Jami and I,
are two birds in the sky.
We fly so very high in the big, bright, beautiful sky.
We have big beautiful feathers,
as we fly so very high.
We live in a big brown Oak Tree,
with beautiful leaves.
Leaves that are blinding to the naked eye,
they sway way up high in the sky.
They are as green as the ocean's seas.
We can see the seas way down below,
as we fly so very high,
in the bright blue sky.
When we fly so very low,
we can touch the seas way down below.
Sometimes we wonder how high we can fly,
up in the big beautiful sky.
Jami and I,
are just two birds in the sky.

Justin Hughes

My Life

Sometimes my life is like a vessel on a raging sea.
The waves enclose me,
As steel bars imprison a criminal.
Often during the storm you will find me in my cabin
speaking to my Master.
Yet, oft my life is a solitary ship on a calm sea.
In spite of the stillness of the wind,
I still manage to raise my eyes to the heavens.
Their beauty consumes me,
and I take time to thank my Father.

John Forrest Douglas

The Game

Plastic soldiers march on the floor
Off to fight a terrible war.

The green troops charge, the gray side falls.
Guns splatter bullets on the walls.

Tanks move in. Jet fighters zoom.
Dropping bombs all over the room.

All the soldiers are dead but two.
The game is over, the war is through.

The plastic soldiers are put away,
What other game is there to play.

Danny Shervin

Autumn Leaves

Early in fall when the warm summer days are few,
The leaves hand their luscious green pigment
To Mother Earth piece by piece.
And in return, they receive bright colors,
Such as apricot, crimson, and dandelion.
Then they surrender their lives to Mother Earth
And flutter to the hard, cold earth,
Floating back and forth like a ship
When the current is rough.
Then they lay and hug the ground
Until the wind decides to sweep up their lifeless
Bodies into its arms and take them
Away to an unknown destination.

Rachel Trinen

Addictive Conversation

Each silent splinter in the skin of the city
Drawing forth the blood of our mouths,
Carrying the precious juice
Through black veins

Drawing for the blood of our mouths
Never ending streams bubbling from our lips
Through black veins
Words course overhead, unseen

Never ending streams bubbling from our lips
Feeding hungry ears
Words course overhead, unseen
Wooden needles feeding our addiction

Feeding hungry ears
Each silent splinter in the skin of the city
Wooden needles feeding our addiction
Carrying the precious juice.

Amanda L. Lashmit

Untitled

Magic carpet ride,
Head ready to fly,
Party all night and all day,
Friends grew up and apart.
And flew away,
Leaving you behind to pick up their mess.

You lose your mind, and your voice,
from laughing, crying, screaming
Just to get someone's anyone's help or attention.
But no one hears you, so you're still all alone.

All alone in darkness, no air, no air, nothing.
Help me! Help me! Help me! Help me!
I'm drowning in my own problems and pity;
I need someone to vent on, but no one is here anymore.
They all left me behind.

Therese Garrett

Ode to Words

Words sing; they lift the heart
"I love you!" "It's not malignant" "I see land" "You passed!"

Words soothe, better than oil on troubled waters
"There, there" "I'll see what I can do"
"Let's sit down and talk about this"

Words divide; left from right, black from white, wrong from right
"Private: Members Only" "NIMBY" "Tuition $20,000 a year"

Words hurt; it isn't true
That only sticks and stones can break your bones
"Get lost!" "I hate you!" "What a dumb question!"

Words kill:
Pax Romana, Deutschland über Alles, Ethnic Cleansing,
Pre-emptive Strikes

Words heal:
"This is for you" "I've changed my mind"
"I'm sorry" "I do love you"

Barbara C. Bowen

Hail to the Champs

For my darling granddaughter, Sara Sather
As time goes by I'll always remember
The football team that plays in Denver
They won in the east, won in the west
Proving beyond doubt they were simply the best
Winning twice was their goal
This they did in the Super Bowl
Denver Broncos is the name
The quarterback destined for the Hall of Fame
After all this I just want to say
You go your way, I'll go Elway

Melvin Sather

Cup o' Java

Java brewing in a coffee pot
Oh, such sweet Aroma filling the air
Sip it in the morning with toast
Gulp it with a Danish
Drink it steaming hot espresso
Or cold frappe
Gotta have it night or day
Try to creamy latte
Or simply have cappuccino
Taste a cup with hazelnut, cream de cocoa, tiramisu
Just to name a few
Drink it here
Drink it there
Drink it in my easy chair
Take some when you're on the run
Please don't spill
It's not much fun
Brew some when you have a crowd
Even if you just have a few
But the best cup o' Java is sipping dreaming all alone

Mary Anne Cockman

Planet Earth, 21st Century

To every existing being on Earth
As the 21st Century approaches we're reminded
what kind of world we live in. Poverty, homelessness,
abuse, crime, and most of all neglect. But there is an
answer—togetherness, which can bring forth love, which will
not be overshadowed by hate and bigotry, but resolve with the
willingness to forgive and the ability to understand.
Only then would there be peace on the planet we call Earth.

Donald Lee

The Sea of Urban Squall

A sea of homes, aligned in a slips
In the harbor of the urban sun.
A briefcase in hand, a baby at my breast,
I face the squall of the urban storms,
Without a net.

As waves overtake my ship
On the way to tow the corporate lies,
I fear I will lose my way
In the urban squall

Waves are getting higher,
No safe captain to guide me to a safe harbor,
Urchins in tow we limp to a harbor of safety.

At sunset on the urban ship,
The waves subsides, but not the squall
In my heart, alone on the sea,
The squall overtake me,
I drown in the night.

Romy Crowton

Jason Andrew Paugh, My Dad!

My Dad is a loveable, big man
When he calls me his "Baby Grace Ann" . . .
I used to sit upon his knee
The biggest bear hugs he gave to me!

My Mom is a "Good-hearted woman"
She's in love with a "Good-timin' man" . . .
Fifty years since they first married
So much love they have carried!

To Dad, we're the family of "The Mules"
To Mom, we're merely her "Precious Jewels" . . .
We're Charlotte, Bill, and Grace
Greatly know as taking first place!

In the army, Dad served our country well
This family has "Travel stories" to tell . . .
This man with the strong hands is "Big Bruiser"
He can build anything from table to cruiser!

There could never be a kinder, more understanding man
Even if I searched over this whole country land . . .
As my "Daddy," the light of my life, my "Father"
He is the reason I can say, "Dad, I love you like no other!"

Grace Ann Fogarty

Babies Having Babies

Two junior high school pre-teenage girls
were conversing at lunch to get acquainted.

A was a long-term resident of the rural school,
while B just moved there from a nearby city.

A: Do you use drugs?
B: Oh, heavens, I just say no!

A: Do you have a driver's license?
B: Oh, no, I'm too young.

A: Do you drink alcohol?
B: Oh, no, I'm too young.

A: Do you smoke?
B: Oh, no, I'm too young.

A: Do you use contraception?
B: Oh, no, I'm too young.

A: Do you plan to attend the Spring Dance activities?
B: Oh, no, that's the week of my EDC!

A: Do you have Welfare/Medicaid? WIC yet?
A: Do you have alternate schooling plans yet?
A: Do you have prenatal care, vitamins, and folate yet?
A: Do you have alternate life plans yet???

Art Schipul, M.D.

Please Remember

For my mother and my son Stephen
Forgive me if I don't always have the time to spend with you;
I really would love to but, I've got things to do.

I hope you know I love you and my time away from you
Is not what I want, and I really miss you too.

Don't hold it against me if I'm not here when you come or call;
Just listen for my heart—I left it here for you all.

Don't worry if you see me cry or brush away a tear;
Just know I'm holding very close the things to me that's dear.

If you speak and I don't answer, don't let your anger fall;
It really matters what you say, however big or small.

Sometimes I may seem far away when you look at me,
But I'm just recalling memories I wish that you could see.

So find peace in knowing that when I'm not around,
Wherever you might have to be, to me is precious ground.

   Patsy Brown

Hero

Cold sweat drips from my brow
running from the trouble that lingers behind me
as I turn to see how far I am ahead
I can feel the hot air from its breath on my neck
it seems no matter how fast I move
the less of my trouble does not appear,
but just gains in strength.
As I reach the pit of self weakness
my body seems to be weakened by my flight
years of punishment come to me at once
joined by thoughts of things I could have done better.
The ground breaks beneath my feet
plunging me to a death I don't know of
Before I can blink my eyes
I'm standing on the other side
of this horrible calamity
How did this happen
who came to the aid of my useless self
At that moment like an eagle gliding in the air
I saw my hero a pure light—an angel in flight.

   Jeremy Cohick

Untitled

Oh, sweet baby we miss you so,
If only you really would know.
Awaiting your birth was great joy,
We prayed for a healthy little boy.
But luck seems to vanish when you need it so,
If there is a reason, "Dear God you must know."
You suffered so much of your short life down here,
On a Sunday God called you, He wanted you near.
He took you to Heaven, where angels met you,
And put some wings on you and made you one too.
He said, "No more suffering for you my dear boy"
"But glorious happiness and eternal joy"
Oh, dear baby we miss you so much,
Your soft little hands we can't touch.
The precious sweet smile on your face,
That nothing in our minds can erase.
Your pretty blue eyes that were shining so bright,
Were the prettiest blue that we saw every night.
We miss you so much since the day you did part,
Ask Jesus to keep us all close to your heart.

   Dula M. Ackermann

The Beauty Lies Within

For Sherry, my vision
"Your vision is lovely," the voices, they say;
'tis that which ushers thy passion in.
"Not to disagree," I softly reply,
"but you look too shallow in view; for beauty abounds,
and cannot arouse, if it rests at the level of skin."

"Then intelligence and wit," they counter with glee,
"her laughter, her charm brought you in."
"Persistent you are," I say with a smile and a sigh.
"You discern well, but there is something you miss;
it's not seen, it's not spoken, it's not touched,
yet there is meaning in this."

"Well, what can it be," they query at last,
"you exasperate us, what makes those feelings begin?"
"I'm sorry," I say, "but I can scarcely describe
the beauty that has captured my soul;
For it's all that you say but in much greater depth,
it's her spirit, the beauty lies within."

   Dale P. Aho

Alone

I'm waiting for Eastern wind
To bring fragrance and beauty of yourself
From distance of eternity
To love you more than anyone else.

I'm waiting, for your coming
While dearly I cry our ill fate
Breaking and making
Our lives separate!

I'm waiting for your meeting
While spring breeze every night
Shaking peach flower and candle light
From scene of dreaming.

I'm sitting in a state of fading
My heart sadly tied, my body almost died
Somewhere you're going: Nirvana or Paradise
Leaving me suffering misery of human life.

Oh, dear! Outside night breeze in the air I hear
Half moon in the sky I see
Inside here, loneliness all my life I bear
By separation between you and me!

   Paul P. Vu (a.k.a. Vu-Anh-Phuong)

The Light's Savior

To my sister, Helena Leach
The night stirs and the wind rustles.
But the questions still remains,
Where is the light?

In the preceding hours the sun supplied the rays of life.
So, what of the moon and the stars.
Where have they all gone?

Have the gods grown tiresome of this mortal's privilege?
A privilege that breeds good deeds and growth.

In a time where Mother Nature is aged and powerless,
A hero must emerge.

Who will save the light?
I must know.
Is there no one that can help?
If only a glimpse of hope would step out to fight for the light.

People need light
Wait, is that the answer.
It couldn't be that easy, but it is.

Humanity is the light.

   Floyd Glasco

The Missing Puzzle Piece

Faith is how I received Christ as my personal Savior.
He doesn't owe any of us a favor.
He gives us a chance out of love, to go live with him
In the heavens above. It's our choice, to be cast into the
Lake of fire, one little drop of water being our desire;
Or to walk the streets of gold, to live in a place of beauty
Almost too much for your eyes to behold.
God loves you and I both. That's why he sent his one and
Only son to die for our sins. I've made my decision,
Have you made yours? I know where I'm going if God were
To come back this very second. Ask God into your heart today.
He will never depart from you, He will live in your heart
And stay. It will change your life, and for the better;
I guarantee. You thought you were missing something,
Not sure what it is. Get God in your life, have faith in
Him, ask Him into your heart. You will soon find out
He was the missing puzzle piece all along.

Katie Bailock

Open Your Eyes

Open your eyes to God
And you will see that he does love you.
And that you will always have a friend
That will love and care for you even 'til the end.
God gave you two eyes so open them to see him
It will be the best thing that you have done.
Because God does love you and he will always be
Your friend!
When you need someone to talk to
God is always there.
He is always sitting and waiting
Just to hear your prayers.
So just open your eyes that God gave you
And you will see that he will always be there
Because God does care.

Christopher W. Bender

Perfection

Perfection, the goal as the bloom comes to life
ever bigger and brighter the flower
The gardener strives for perfection
As she nurtures and waters each hour
But what if results fall short of the goal
If the bloom is less big or less bright
Can the gardener find as she searches her soul
That satisfaction began when she dug the first hole.

Ruth Silverberg

Little Boy and His Grandpa

For my grandparents—I love you all!
Little boy and his grandpa fishing by the sea
Cloudless blue sky as far as the eye can see
True to his word, with eyes alight
Grandpa with his special boy in sight

Little boy fell on the sand
Grandpa picked him up and kissed his little hand
Grandpa threw him in the air
A couple strolling by stop to stare

Grandpa caught the little boy with a hug
Little boy crawled up Grandpa's neck all snug
Grandpa putting down little boy
Grandpa picking up his little toy

Hand in hand, they walk away
The couple over heard the Grandpa say
Remember when I am gone away
You will always have our special day

Jodi Christensen

A Tale of Eternity

In tribute to William Wordsworth
"We walked along,
While bright and red uprose the morning sun,"
Releasing rays of brilliance,
Penetrating deep into the soul of night,
Driving it farther away with every passing breath;
The diamonds slowly vanished from the fading darkness;
Fading away unto the horizon,
Surrendering the shadows,
To the light of day:

With the magical slumber of darkness released,
The day had won its domain:

Soon, so soon,
The day will pass that same horizon,
Hunting night with endless vigilance,
Until one day the two shall meet;
And nothing more will be:

For the time when our night and day finally greet,
Shall be the end of all eternity.

Jeremiah Stacey

I Could, and Would

For Tami, I love you
I could and would, treat you like a queen
You mean that much to me

I could and would, write you the ultimate love song
You mean that much to me.

I could and would, have you as my best friend
You mean that much to me.

I could and would, shower you with love and affection
You mean that much to me.

I could and would, have no other love
You mean that much to me.

I could and would, give you my full attention, always
You mean that much to me.

I could and would, give you room to breathe
You mean that much to me.

I could and would, have you as my love, forever
You mean that much to me.

I could and would, will love you, always forever!
You mean that much to me.

Michael E. Baumann

Let Me Be Free

Let me be free . . .
That I can be free from pain and sorrow.
That I can see love like it was
Between us, and no one else.

Let me be free . . .
That I can enjoy life and live like a person,
And not someone full of thoughts and memories.

Let me be free . . .
That I can live as one,
Not like a person full of imagination of hope,
And laughter, sorrow and pain.

Let me be free . . .
That I can share my loving thoughts, to you,
The one who means the most to me.

Let me be free from pain, from sorrow.
Let me be free.

Frances Fantasia

Granddaughter

For Alexus Reneé, whom I love
I'll always remember the day you were born,
The tears I shed left me torn.
You made your mark upon my heart,
I knew with great certainty we'd never part.
Our dear precious babe, I'll always be near,
To help meet your needs and gently calm your fear.
They say don't expect too much from this grandchild of mine,
But we'll prove them wrong, your light will shine.
Your smile, your coos, your hand reaching out,
It makes me so happy I just want to shout.
Thank you, Lord Jesus, for this gift from above,
My anger replaced with kindness and love.
Send an angel or two, with a harp in their hand;
May they sing their sweet music as they take a stand.
Their wings are out stretched as if to take flight,
But I know in my heart, they protect her each night.

   Judy Bender

Goodbye from Lil' Bit

To my brother Ed, Big Bit
Thank you for the laughter
And your understanding ways,
And thank you very, very much
For sharing these final days.

I needed this time to say goodbye,
Though it's very hard to do,
I just had to say, "You're finally safe,"
And prove these words are true!

I'll always remember this time we have,
The smiles and tears we're sharing.,
And I'll never regret the pain of today,
For it's worth the love and caring!

You've been much more than a brother to me,
Just like my twin, it's true.
For you've always understood my soul,
I'm just a Lil' Bit of you.

May these final days be filled with peace,
May love and joy surround you
And when Jesus takes you home to him,
Just remember, your Lil' Bit loves you!

   Loretta S. Priestley

Time No More

It used to be time for everything
Time to look out at the rain,
While sitting by your windowpane.

Time to wonder what to do with your day,
Knowing whatever it will be, you will have time to play.

Time to have fun with your family and friends
And never thinking about how your day will end.

But time has changed, time is no more
You now have to wonder if you will return home safe
From the corner store.

The corner where you used to play
Is now the corner for the dealers to stand each day.

The window shades are always pulled down
Because you don't want to see the people hanging around.

In the house is now where you have to play
Because being out in the streets,
One way or another somehow you will pay.

Time no more is what I say,
Now is now and this is the new day.
No hopes, no dreams, time no more for anything.

   Consuelo J. Harris

Death

One way or another you will die
You may fall or get stabbed in the eye.

You may choke
You may get your neck broke

You can run, you can hide
but you might fall and get stabbed through your side

You can try and kiss death
but it might not like your breath

So in conclusion there is nowhere to hide from death.

   Nick Leonhard

Love's Philosophy

The fountains mingle with the river
and the rivers with the ocean,
the winds of heaven mix forever with a sweet emotion,
Nothing in the world is single, all things by
A law divine in one spirit meet and mingle.
Why not I with thine?

See the mountains kiss high heaven
and the waves clasp one another, no sister flower
Would be forgiven if it disdained its brother,
And the sunlight clasps the earth and the moonbeams
Kiss the sea, what is all this sweet work worth
If thou kiss not me?

   Joseph W. Stasic

The Sunflower

To Jaime with love
I was walking in the country one night bright sunny afternoon
Standing alone in the meadow, a young sunflower ready to bloom

It gave off this warm feeling face became all flush
What was it about this sunflower my heart pounding, what a rush

I dug it up so careful almost blinded by the sun
Caressing it so gently could this flower be the one

Taking this sunflower everywhere people looked at me so strange
But nothing seemed to matter knowing the sunflower was in range

The summer was ending quickly I knew the time was near
That I would have to let her go this sunflower I loved so dear

Would I dwell about a sunflower that came into my heart
Or remember all the good times before we had to part

Thinking about the summer something came into my mind
Taking pictures of this sunflower in all her beauty and sunshine

They brought back many memories of all the places we had been
My emotions just ran wild face smiling once again

   Michael Stratton

Untitled

For Carol, thinking of you always
Love's light burns brighter than any candle
Or star could ever burn, burning through
The fog of confusion and doubt.

Love's wind is a gentle breeze that calms
The harsh waves of hardship and sorrow.

Love's river flows over the ever expanding sea of time.
Love's mantel is strong and sturdy
To withstand the weight of life's unexpected burdens.

So let me be your mantel to rest upon
While flowing down the gentle river with the wind
To steer us, and the light to guide us.

   Michael T. Schmandt Jr.

Show Me the Way

Show me the way to my Jesus,
Show me the way to my Lord,
As I go through trial and tribulation,
And through the devil's stumbling blocks I fjord.

Help me see the light of my Jesus,
Help me see the light of the lamb,
When in my darkest hours and troubles
Illuminated by him, I know I am

Bring up my burdened soul with the Holy Spirit.
Help my countenance stand for Jesus in the storm.
Keep me strong and sturdy against Satan's
Cold I must fear it
And stand to see and feel the light of
Jesus in it I am forever warm.

Stephen A. Newbern

The Light from the Other Side

For my husband—you've come a long way!
I feel the light from the other side,
But darkness seeps in, not to be denied.
Pills and booze were my only crutch.
Because my life was not meaning very much.
Loneliness and rejection always brought me to tears.
Dying on the street and alone very much were my fears.
The reflection of my life was getting clearer and clearer,
Every time that I look at myself in the mirror,
It burns inside, and I cried and cried,
As I look back at my life as if I'd already died.
As I floated over my body waiting for death,
I saw nothing but darkness as I took my last breath.
Suddenly, a tunnel of light brought me my mom.
She said, "Son, it's not your time," bringing me total calm.

Sheri Anderson

A True Friend

A friend is a guiding light in the midst of a storm,
A gentle candle in the darkness of this dreary life.
She is an assuring fire that keeps you warm,
And a comfort in times of strife.

She is someone you can run to,
When all you can do is cry,
When your world is crashing down on you,
She'll be there to wipe your eyes.

When no one seems to care,
When sadness burdens your mind,
A true friend will always be there,
And in her, a solace you will find.

Sarah Rodrigues

When I Think of You

When I think of you
I seem to feel
The inertia of love profound
Its waves are intense,
They are crashing on my heart,
And my thoughts of you are beginning to drown
I feel upon me, in every way,
A sense of simple peace
It surrounds me
And encases my heart and soul
I pray it will never cease
I have for you
A simple thought,
A simple hope or wish.
I'd like for us forever
To love and be together,
Lifelong friends in happiness.

Tiffany Dodge

One Little Flower

A lover had vanished, left his sweetheart in pain,
Her teardrops were falling like showers of rain,
She wanted something her time to impart,
So a garden of roses she chose for her heart.

The dew drops they nestled among the flowers in bed,
Jack Frost came a-nippin', and they withered instead,
But one little flower Jack Frost didn't see,
And that one little flower set her broken heart at east.

One little flower, one little flower,
One little flower . . . set her broken heart at ease!

Sonya Mosley

Time on My Hands

Sometimes when I look at the hands of a clock,
I wonder if I hear the tick or the tock.

Around and around, my life going fast,
Accented visions of a long ago past.

In retrospect, I can hear the beat,
And know that time does not retreat.

Is time the prisoner of my life,
I always thought it was my wife.

If the hands of time, my warden to be,
What measure of tempo will set me free.

Hold a large clock up in front of you,
This will surely obstruct your view.

Please use this time to think a spell,
Correct answers can free you from hell.

Accent on stress, its cause or reason,
Can make you last for many a season.

Emphasis on time, its length of duration,
Can give your outlook a new creation.

What I am trying to say, is don't waste time,
The more the loss, the bigger the crime.

Ken Pia Sr.

Days

Mothers days, brothers day, father's day too!
There's a day for everyone even me and you
People around the world are having their day
Maybe it's about play!
I'd like to have a party
Or a parade on my special day
Or I could lay down and rest in the shade
It'd be fun to eat a hot dog
And a bun in the sun
Or play in the rain a very fun game
Everyone can have their own day
In any way they please even with cheese!
So remember have your day anyway!

Stephanie Figueroa

The Chair

It's covered in corduroy, faded blue and gray,
with ragged seams and raw patches where cats'
claws have ravaged its façade.

It stands alone in the corner,
out of place, out of touch, never out of mind.
I still see his body in its cushioned softness,
his contours seared within its frame.
A simple recliner, fifteen years old,
an eyesore, a tormenting treasure.
Throw it out, my mind demands, throw it out.
Never! Never! The heart replies tragically . . .
It's all I have left.

Joli Barham

Love

To Michael McGowan and Oliver Vincelette
Love goes by second by second
Second by second a love is born
Born from the light in your eyes
Eyes that twinkle when I am near
Near to your heart I am
I'm in love or I'm not
Eyes that make me think of all my hopes and dreams
Dreams that I hope to come true
Hopes that nothing goes wrong
Wrong with the love I have for you
You, the light in my night
Night that leads to day
Day that leads to sunshine
That sunshine in the rain.

Amanda Vincelette

Divinity

Truly a work of art, that only God could devise,
Could there be more beauty than this creation,
On Earth, and in Heaven?
So simple, yet elegant,
So delicate, and yet robust,
Each lustrous petal, caressed in the finest of silk,
Colored in the most diverse shades of colors,
Of inimitable qualities,
Its colors so bright, and so bold,
Yet lenient,
Picasso, da Vinci, or even Bounarroti,
Has never sculpted, nor painted a masterpiece as divine as this,
Absolute, pure, and majestic in every way,
What is this, that is so perfect and glorious, you ask?
Why, what else than the flower, of course.

B. J. Min

Growing Old

I am young with selfish desires.
I must learn to love others,
Yet I am still young with selfish desires.
I must learn to give, and yet be strong,
Yet I am still young with selfish desires.
I must learn to trust, yet still be cautious,
Yet I am still young with selfish desires.
I must learn to grow old, yet keep my childishness;
I am now eighty with selfish desires.

Angelia Dalhover

Now You Are Gone

So now you're gone and I'm alone
I want to tell you this, but when I pick up the phone
I can't bring myself to talk
I hang up and begin to sulk.
Do you think about me?
It's all just one big mystery
Is it wrong to say I love you?
Or only to expect you to say it too?
Feelings of loneliness I try to hide
You don't understand what I feel inside.
You're nice to me one day
And the next you push me away.
What the hell am I supposed to do?
I lay awake at night thinking about you.
Dream about us together again
Are you meant to be a lover or friend?
Questions that will be answered in time
But all I can think about is you being mine.
I remember all the times we spent together
Does anything last forever?

Michelle Cavanaugh

I Love You

To David Knight and Antoin Huntley
I love you more today, than yesterday.
More tomorrow than today, whisper, I love you to me.
I hear it everywhere. In the yard, in the garden, in the air.
I love you. Whisper softly I love you.
You are everything to me. Spring, summer, fall, winter.
I wrote you a love poem yesterday.
But you didn't answer to me.
You face was distance.
Then only the wind, whisper your voice.
I love you. One day under a tree.
I gave you my heart. You still have it.
More than before.
More than before, you are everything to me.
More than before to me.
Your pulse beats in mine.
More than before.

Mable Knight

A Cry of a Woman

To Shoshana Shaul, for friendship and inspiration
Cry, woman, cry, for there is no hurray.
Sinking into dark,
Uncontrolling emotions
Can't reach out or point
Beyond any understanding!

Staring the unknown
Abandoned by destiny
Aging without control
Is that hat we become?

Why? Why is this occurring
Waves and shadows control our cells
Crawling into bloody veins
Skin hanging with lines of sorrow.

Cry, woman, cry out, for there is no doubt.
The eyes although weakened don't lie!
Oh, mirror, please be cheatful,
You are my only hope,
Where is my old, blurry, hazy mirror
To stop my agony and to erase a bad dream

Rosa T. Shashua

I Am

To God, who gave me talent
I am very musical and artistic
I wonder what I'm going to be when I grow up
I hear a wonderful orchestra playing
I see Picasso painting a dreamy collage
I want a wonderful future
I am very musical and artistic

I pretend I'm a real musician playing
I feel my paint brush gliding across the page
I touch the keys of a grand piano
I worry about my future job
I cry when I mess up my art work
I am very musical and artistic

I understand that not everyone is good at art and music
I say to myself I can be anything I want to be
I dream of being a musician someday
I try to do the best I can at all my work
I hope that my art will be famous someday
I am very musical and artistic.

Amanda Azan

I Will

Who will always be there for you? I will.
Who will bring you up when you are down? I will.
Who will always care for you and not let you down? I will.
Who said they will love you forever? I did.
Who said they would be by your side forever? I did.

Diane Jaquis

Now Is My Then . . .

I didn't do it then, I guess I couldn't then
life's obstacles interfere with life's reality
First your life, then your kid's lives
Then their school, maybe your school.
Maybe not!
You give love and understanding
and you may get some back
You may get left standing, or you may not
You give clothing, shelter and food
They want more whenever they're in the mood.
Mood . . . what's that? Why can't I have one? Or can I?
Now they're all in school.
They're doing, their stuff, their work
I help when thing's get tough, when
Math is hard and I hear, "Mom I can't read this word!" or can he?
Maybe it's Mom they want near them when they discover
that they too can figure out everything I've talked about.
And I'm near, now my turn is here.
My turn to persevere my turn to write, read and calculate
Now is my then!

Sonia Valentin

Untitled

To my inspiring and loving family
I'd sit to write about my love
The one I knew so vastly of
About the memories we had kept
And of the many times I wept
I'd wish he'd be there by my side
But knew my love he had denied
And all the past that I had told
Had now become a thing of old
I wanted back my heart he took
So while he passed I did not look
I hid and watched him go his way
While praying I'd see him in some future today
I wrote it all down on paper of mine
A hidden emotion in each heart felt line
To think to my love I read each sad poem
To dream of the one who is not my own

Jennifer Goodwin

Color

Color, what shade, what form.
To recognize, to contour.

Color, what shape, what form.
To see it, to be it, to love it, to smile, and laugh with it.

Color, what shape, what form.
White, black, red, yellow.

To combine, to collide, to come together as one.
Color, what shade, what form.

To join in events, happy or sad.
To laugh, smile, be one.

No recognized type, or is there?
In times of events, happy, mostly sad.

We are one, or could there be one.
And others as none, or could one evolve into some.

To live, love, and come together as one color.
Let it be as it was.

Madeline Shorter Hall

Thereafter

For Mother, Ramon, Ové, Rebekah, and Kayla
My dreams are dreams of sad visions
In life I'm scared of bad decisions
I do not want to go, I want to stay
But not forever, when all that's known is gone away

I want to live ten thousands of years
Not by myself in sorrows and tears
I do not want to live all alone
Yet I'm scared to pass away to the unknown

My thoughts are thoughts of thereafter
Thinking of the unknown ceases my laughter
My thoughts of no longer existing are scary
The fear of staying or going is contrary

I wish to be around to see my babies grown
But not to be here, when they are gone I'll moan
I want to see Ramon and Ové smile
While Rebekah comforts and kisses Kayla's child

My prayers are prayers of resting my weary soul
But I'm afraid of reaching destiny's goal
My dreams, my visions, are one of a kind
My Lord, my God, saves my mind

Hugh S. Sabre

Who Am I?

To my sister, Rose Addeo Smith
Who am I? To be blessed with precious life.
What's the reason? When born to eternal strife.

Where days turn to years, amid sadness and sorrow.
When will it end? Not this day or tomorrow.

Why the plight? Struggling amid sweat and tears.
Was it through sin? Among life's gloomy fears.

Were it not for love, and a mothers kiss.
Wondering and remembering, one forever to miss.

With whispers of love, humming old golden tunes,
While guiding my youth, as a flower to bloom.

Working was pain, when many hardships prevailed.
Wishful dreams are nightmares, like a windstorm sail.

War was declared, salvaging my life's treasured dream.
Whenever the victory, home coming could only mean.

Waking to a new life, with wife and children dears.
Whatever the outcome, now are called, our golden years.

Who am I?
I am God's chosen one.
To love Him, honor Him, serve Him, and never to Deny Him.

Orlando Addeo

Debra K

Sometimes when I hold you close to my chest,
Arresting, testing the tantalizing smell of your hair,
And stroking your bare shoulder,
I feel like a thirsty man carrying water in his hands.
The cool liquid seeps through fingers
Not tight enough to keep
What's not near enough to quench.
And I go to hold you so you can't seep through.
With all my strength, what it comes to
Is still, still I thirst for you.
If it were only raw desire,
or the fire in my mindless mind, I'd yell, to hell!
But the tears of my heart and fears of every part of me that wonder,
will our parting, be the last goodbye?
I grow weaker, white as snow and know there'll come a time
that I won't let you go and as you rest against my chest
You . . . you also know.

Bruce J. Stupica

The Travelers

Well here we are, we've come so far
Another orbit, more history written on the script
Time is this abstract measure we seem to remember
Our history a second in the infinite heavens
Spinning on an unknown course the journey never ends for us
A piece in the master plan is our fate
Return to where you came, a knock on Heaven's gate
Are we meant to know the plan, put here to ponder
Figure it all out if you can
A traveler in both time and space, a species on edge, the human race
Who is to blame for the troubles that be
We're all in this together as we seek an everlasting peace
On to distant shores in this vast universe
Moving as a whole all singing the same verse

    Timothy Mayott

One Fine Day

What a beautiful gift I received that day
What a blessing it was to see the way

Life was so full of sorrow and tears
Loneliness and fear were there year after year

Full of sorrow, full of tears
What was there to make of those terrible years?

Then all of a sudden the light showed forth
To show his glory, to show my worth

The reason for living was bigger than Earth
That wonderful day the light showed forth

The feeling of joy, the feeling of peace
That one fine day the sorrow ceased

    Carrie Lynn Cannon

He

When we talk He comforts me,
When we walk He lets me see

The way in which I must go
To be with Him I know.

For there are times that I stray away.
He may say my blood was shed for you to live today.

In Heaven I will always dwell,
Forever is a long time to be in hell.

So my eyes will stay upon Him.
My heart full of love will never dim.

He is my Savior and Lord.
I will fight every battle with His sword.

    Elanna Rasco Davis

A Cry of a Woman

Will ever the world learn
Why can't we discern
Please do not always turn
Course . . . from the Cry of a Woman

Point and case
Di called for help
While the town slept
What a chase
Course . . . it was the Cry of a Woman

Who listened to her plea
'Twas a man of Galilee
He did not flee
But calmed her agony
As the world relives, Love in Paree
Course . . . from that (pause) Cry of a Woman

    Erma Lee Summerset

I Hear Nothing

To my loving mother, Luveria D. Reese
I sit alone in my room
staring at the ceiling.
The noise level is high
with the laughter of children,
radios, animals, and cars passing by
yet "I hear nothing."

The day seemed long and
the night seemed even longer,
Television volume on high.
Children playing, talking loudly,
doors being slammed close yet
"I hear nothing."

Its morning the sun shines in
from both windows directly upon my face.
Telephones ringing, pagers beeping,
school buses riding by yet
"I hear nothing."

I hear nothing not because I am deaf or hard of hearing.
It is because of the mental state of my mind
that blocks off unwanted traffic that "I hear nothing."

    Monica S. Reese

Someone Special to Me

Life goes by quickly, day by day;
Someone special you'll meet along the way.
A person so special it makes you smile,
A person to spend time with and talk awhile.
He has a handsome face, a good heart too,
Add "kissable lips," yeah! That will do!
Someone it seems you've known forever,
To forget this person, I think "never."
He makes me so happy and feel brand new;
To find a person like this is seldom and few.
I'd like to hug him each and every day,
to kiss him and comfort him in every way.
He is so special to me, my special someone;
He's my heart, my soul, my ray of sun.
No matter where my life may lead me,
right by my side, I hope he'll be.
Forever and a day—
in every way!

    Linda Carol Williams

A Brother's Love

You live together watching each other grow.
Down deep in your heart you know love is there, but rarely spoken.
You think of it as a token, yours to hold for one another.
Sometimes you must keep your distance from each other,
for it's not the lack of love, but the lack of communication.
We often try to help with answers or a smile.
But love is there, even though we are not side by side.
Life is too short to fuss and fight,
You never know when it may be your last night.
So give a lot of love to each other,
And when one or the other has passed and gone,
you will have answers to the question often asked.
Do we love each other?

    Berry Soles

Fade Out

Is getting old fading out,
is this what it's all about?
The promise of the spring,
will not be in this life, any more.
Soon I will be of things,
from my children and grandchildren's lore.
And this too, my friend, will fade out. . . .

    Martha Thompson

What Is Love?

To my wonderful husband, Jack Farkas
Love is giving, never expecting anything in return,
Love is trust, which is something you have to earn,
Love is hope, when everything seems to be lost
Love is understanding, and paying the ultimate cost.
Love is faith, that problems will work out
Love is patience, even though all the doubt,
Love is sharing, the precious moments of life,
Love is caring, between a husband and a wife.

Mitzi B. Farkas

Life

Life is very fragile,
Sometimes we just don't see,
That what we take for granted,
Comes with no guarantee.

From the hardened face of a weathered man,
To the soft skin of a newborn baby's hand,
There never is a promise there always is a plan,
Our job is to live life to the fullest that we can.

Before another tomorrow there only lies yesterday,
Never knowing if we are truly here to stay.
Savour all the laughter and memories that you can,
Because you never know when fate will take you by the hand.

Diana Phelps

Lost

To my angel, for inspiring me
I did not know
For I love him so
That he would be
Very different from me.
After all, he was only three.

His world and mine, tho' miles apart
I knew I could reach him through his heart.
Being angry at God, couldn't possibly gain,
So I prayed instead, He'd guide me through my pain.

I've kept journals for years
Now that he's six.
I've learned through him
The world is mixed.

I struggle daily to remain realistic,
You see, my son, Chuck, is autistic.

Laurie Pautsch

Present's Past

For my mother Benedetta Vassallo
With hopeful eyes I stare into presents past.
Hoping for a return of the times where everything
seemed simple and unanalyzed.
Yet as I look back, I realize that all that was past
must somehow fit into my present life.
The past not only holds the key to our future,
but it holds a memory of the person we were once.
Not to lose ourselves in our present jobs and responsibilities,
but to remember who we were and why we were somehow
put into this decision to become the person we are today.
Are we happy? Are we content?
Or are we living just to satisfy someone else's needs?
The answer lies within our soles. Can we change back? No.
We must somehow try to become the best person we can be
without someone else's comments or accusations in hand.
Now is the time to come back to present's past.
For remember that all that is not touched by tears
shall soon be swallowed by a river of them.

Mary Burzynski

This Place

Over the hills and far away
Is there a place by the bay
Where there is no trouble and strife
A place, and a chance for a better life

Maybe somewhere off in the distance
It could be there, we might find for instance
A beautiful place, not too far from God's grace
Not too far off in the wilderness, a way out of the rat race

Is it we might find in this special place
A humble dwelling, where we could just touch base
In this place we could just let our cares fly away
Oh, how I wish I could find this place, even today

Does this place that I speak of really exist
Or is it a dream, clouded in fog and mist
Where else could this place be, that I may never find
Could this place be, existing only in my mind

Or maybe God would grant me at least this one wish
And somehow direct me through this fog and mist
Could it be the only way I may find this place
Is for me to accept, and hold in my heart, God's love and grace.

Wm. L. Ingram III

Life

Life—it's just not what it seems;
it's nothing but a world full of empty dreams.
As reality begins to set in, you suddenly realize
that life is really just a nightmare hidden in disguise,
and the only way the nightmare can end is through death,
for it's finally all over with once you've taken your last breath.

No more heartaches, heartbreaks, no more pain,
no more unanswered questions that drive you completely insane,
no more people telling you who you should be and what you should do,
no more parents who just can't accept you for you,
no more rumors, no more lies,
from people you once called friends and now just despise.

And though death is not the answer nor the way,
it seems to be very tempting on a dark and lonely day
when your heart is just breaking deep down inside,
yet, you have no one to scream out to, no place to run and hide.
So, then you realize once again that life must carry on,
to be who you truly are and still prove them all wrong.

Charity A. Hutchins

Untitled

Writing a poem takes imagination and thought
And sometimes the right words can be caught
People's emotions can run like the wind
And make you cry, frown or even grin
But no matter which style that you choose
Like this contest you hope to win and not lose
So if you think that I've made an impression
I'll be glad to accept a "prize" or that $2,000 collection

Harry Hageman

Hidden Inside

Could the child be me, the one that was hiding before I became "we,"
Those beautiful days when the child had a home
She never imagined her life on her own
The pain of loss, what was, will never be
Life without love couldn't happen to me
She had to grow to face her fears
To find inner courage to face the new years
The pain gave her strength, she started to grow
She discovered the woman she was fearful to know
She found peace and love from deep within
The child became a woman and ready to begin

Theresa A. Deemer

Untitled

The mourning of the helpless people,
The cries of the suffering and the dead.
Children watching with innocent eyes
The oppression and diseases of their country.
In what world can one be wealthy and rich
By denying these people a home.
All that is right has died with the past;
What is left is deceit and fear.
Sadness and hopelessness take over tomorrow;
Crying and tears become an eternal lullaby.
Abuse and yelling become a daily encounter
Love is lost and confidence is shattered.
Justice is now bought with money and jewels
Fairness is buried in gold and silver.
Tomorrow has no one except the few
And even they are losing their hope.
Poverty has crushed the people of today
Fright and hate will crush tomorrow;
But let the weak become strong, and the strong merciful,
The merciful, brave and the brave, hopeful.

Lauren DeHamer

Untitled

On this day a child is born
Here's to hope the world doesn't scorn
For if this happens the child will be forlorn
But with the love of the world and his peers
The child will learn to love and be filled with cheer
So be assured to find someone they'll call dear
A twinkle in the eye and a returned smile
Will ensure the world to endure
For if we continue with acceptance and patience
The world could be delivered from its doom
For no man's perfect, only but in a soul mate's stare
Can we even begin to suggest the idea
That the answer to the world strife
Can be found in the eyes of a person who cares
For today and tomorrow will come and go
If no one tries to reach out
No one would ever really know
That the answer to world success
is not what you can do to change the world
But, what you can do to change yourself.

Arthur Henry Knickerbocker

Untitled

Youth has come, and youth has past
When I was young, I thought they'd last,

As a day they've past me by,
the face in the mirror, is different, I wonder why?

Now as I approach middle age
I now am passing through another stage

Yes, how it felt, to once be young,
When we laughed, and foolish hearts sung.

But today, I see a changing me,
After all, I am older, a free spirit I will always be.

Norman J. Jewell

Visions of Sun

The waves crash softly onto the land,
As grains of sands are brushed from my hand.
The sunwaves caress my hair,
And perfumes fill the air.
The blues of the ocean capture my eye.
As vacationing birds overhead fly.
To a place where rapture runs the sea.
Dreams of the sun, the sand, and me.

Jocelyn Arias

Generation Links

When I grow old and become unable
To do for myself what I'd always been able
Will you come to visit, talk, and spend time
Helping me adjust to that new life of mine
Will you kiss my cheek and your hand smooth my brow
As you tell me you love me, yes, even now
Or will I lie there daily and yearn
For the sight of your face and a show of concern
Will you abandon me in my hour of need
Leave me alone with no will to proceed
Will the bond we have shared see us through one more test
As I make the transition from this life to the next?

E. D. Rodriguez

Pretending to Be

No one knows the real me but me
I try to fulfill the dream they want me to be
A bright smile is painted on my simple face
It takes every breath I have to keep up with the pace
I've kept my feelings hid away for so long
If I ever revealed them, everything would go wrong
Pretending to be is my middle name
No one realizes It's just a continued game
I have so many goals that I wish to achieve
Do you think it is too much to still believe?
If I stopped this act now and let the true me come out
I'm afraid you wouldn't understand what I am all about
So I keep putting up this front that everything is just fine
But inside I often cry because these dreams are not mine
And no one will ever know the true me, but me.

Jessica D. Ruiz

The Jumper

To my grandparents Chuck and Connie
A man atop a building stands
With a small photo in his hands,
A picture of his family
Whom a killer took from he,
He tells himself he has nothing more
To live for in this cruel world,
He prays to God to bless his soul
Then he jumps and plummets to the ground below,
And in his final moments it makes him realize,
That life is much, much more than simple material things
It's the laughter, love, and friendship that give life its meanings,
But it's too late for him he knows
And with him all this knowledge goes,
And when he hits bottom
He sees a flash of light,
Then none but darkness
Now and forever night.

Josh Larson

The Dream

Every day I think about life . . .
And what I want to be, later on in life,
I want to know right now.
I feel alone when there's no one to go to,
When life is really hard.
I do have a dream that keeps me going . . .
Someday I want to achieve that dream.

The dream I hold in my heart keeps me going,
When life is really hard and
There's no one to go to.
My dream is to never be alone . . .
For I have not achieved that dream yet,
Someday I believe I will.

Kristen Reising

Sowing and Reaping

For my late parents, Mr. and Mrs. Joseph and Annie Norville
You have twelve months in 1999
From January to December, to sow good words and deeds
So start now and plant your seeds!
Seeds of encouragement, seeds of joy, seeds of love
Plant all good seeds, and you will reap them all.
sow positive seeds, and you will get positive reaps.
What's your choice, or what do you seek?
Will you get paid, for your daily sowing?
What will your harvest, be showing?
Thank you Lord for the grace, and the harvest.
Thank you Lord for giving us time, to make haste,
before it's too late.
Would Jesus, plant seeds of love, joy and peace?
Of course, he would, because he did it at the feast!
Be ready, be ready. He will come in the night.
So, don't let him catch you off guard and you lose the good fight.
God is love and God is true.
Worship God and he will follow through.
You will receive his promises, that are true
If you are willing to do what he says to do.

Kathleen Massenburg

My Past, My Future

I came in contact today
With an element of my past;
In a century's old Bible it lay,
A relic not expected to last.

In a note to a grandmother dear,
A young girl's thoughts were laid out;
To the receiver it must have been clear
That her darling loved her, no doubt.

To me this letter, now yellowed and old
Has a wondrous message to give;
Her secrets and longing so simply told
Are a treasure to those who now live.

It gives me a feeling of wonder and awe,
This link to so long ago;
And though her face I never saw,
Her sweet nature I'm certain I know.

I got in the mail a sweet letter today,
A young granddaughter poured out her love to me;
I'll keep it forever and in the same way,
For those who come after, a treasure 'twill be.

Lorene A. Roberts

The World Today

For my mother, Dolly Berryman
The world does not run as in my mind
For it is not loving, forgiving or kind.
Our society seems demented and cruel,
No longer does anyone live by the rules.

If people could gain by hurting each other,
They would survive that day and see yet another.
What a mess this world has become
I wonder would anyone sacrifice some?

Something, anything for someone else
Or is the new motto only for one's self?
Can we survive a world like this?
I know I can, but how many will miss?

If people tried just a little more
We probably wouldn't lock our doors.
Well I'm happy to loudly announce,
I can't live by just giving an ounce.

When I give, I give it all,
Fat, skinny, short or tall.
I'm not selfish, I was taught to share.
My life is made of simple care.

Delanne E. Reichard

Hands

Hands are beautiful. Long, slender fingers,
well kept nails broken by garden work.
Fingers caressing harp strings,
guitar strings, heart strings.
Hands of a surgeon, exact hands saving life and terrible tears.
Hands building businesses, families, fortunes.
An artist's hands forging beauty skillfully.
Hands knotted together quietly in prayer.
Hands to put together love,
And laughter, dinners with wine, hands to clasp in love.
Strong hands to hold tight. To lift, to carry, so fine.
Hands to remember. Hands to admire
Or hands to drive nails through.

Marilyn Hartman

Sleepless Nights

Sukh, be compassionate enough to comfort yourself, let love in.
In the darkness of the night,
I lay tossing and turning, crying and yearning.
For you, my heart is still burning.
As visions of our love sweep through my mind,
To the soul they're so unkind; stronger than my will,
They haunt me still. This love I hunger for,
You have locked behind your heart's door.
All say in time this will cease,
And, once again, my heart will know peace.
Yet while the nights feel like years,
My pillow absorbs the countless tears
Streaming from my fears of an endless, lost love,
Of never again fitting with you like a glove.
So once again tonight, my spirit takes to flight
Like a dove in search of its love.
Oh, why do you fight your love taking flight,
To my soul where it longs to go?
For there our love could finally rest
Upon one another's chest.
Your key holder.

Dawn Covell

A Seed

A seed.
Wrapped in a package so compact; perfect without seam showing.
Waiting for its entrance into the world.
The basic elements of sun, earth, and water not yet introduced.
Whether a fragrant flower, the largest of trees, or bread for many.
No one can see the potential, the possibilities, the miracle that lies within.
It patiently sleeps and waits.

A thought. A glimmer of light in a dark place grows.
It, too needs life's basic elements—faith, knowledge, and perseverance.
Whether it is belief in God, a cure for disease or freedom from oppression.
No one can see the potential, the possibilities, the miracle that lies within.
It patiently sleeps and waits.

They both need nurturing and room to grow.
An earthen vessel must spread them to be fruitful.
We can only hope that our seed and thought will land on fertile soil.
Only God can see our potential, our possibilities, and the miracle that we are.

Gerilynn Cedzich

A Tribute

So many times I've needed you, so many times I've cried;
If love alone could have saved you, you never would have died.

In life I loved you dearly, in death I love you still;
In my heart you hold a place no one else can ever fill.

It broke my heart to lose you, but you didn't go alone,
For part of me went with you the day God took you home.

Anthony Ivy

Biographies
of
Poets

ACKER, DALE L.
[b.] Gloversville; [occ.] Coordinator for Central Nursing Service; [hob.] Writing poems, art and crafts, bowling, archery, collect Beanie Babies; [sp.] Frank J. Acker; [ch.] Two; [ed.] Graduate of Shenendehowa High School; [pers.] I thank God for giving me my talent, my family for their love and giving me the strength to carry on my goals.

ADDEO, ORLANDO
[b.] Jersey City, NJ; [occ.] Retired Auto Manager; [hob.] Writing, sports, senior social activities; [memb.] St. Francis Holy Name Society, Knights of Columbus; [sp.] Rosalie Addeo; [ch.] Three; [gch.] Seven; [ed.] Through 11th grade in high school; [hon.] World War II Veteran—4 Oak Leaf Clusters, China-Burma; [awrd.] India Campaign (1943 to 1945), Honorary Discharge as Sgt.; [pers.] Personality! I have lived in Hoboken, NJ all my life, plus serving 25 years as a Hoboken Housing Commissioner—Chairman for ten of those years. My sole purpose is to strive to help those in need achieve better housing and living conditions here in Hoboken, NJ.

ADEBIYI, 'TUNJI-KAZEEM
[pen.] Sharer T.; [b.] November 19, 1970; Osogbo, Nigeria; [p.] Chief Sadiq Adebiyi-Adelabu and Mrs. T.A. Adebiyi; [ed.] OYO State College of Arts and Science in Ile-Ife, Obafemi Awolowo University in Ile-Ife, Nigeria; [occ.] Teaching; [oth.writ.] Several poems and an unpublished play; [pers.] Goodness is godliness.

AKINRO, FRANCIS
[b.] November 15, 1969; [occ.] Engineer, Veteran; [hob.] Ping-pong, entertainment; [memb.] SAE, IMECH, SBBA, All State Motor Club; [ed.] B.Sc.; [awrd.] Busary Scholarship; [pers.] My goal as a writer is to appreciate the labor of my mother at my youthful age.

ALBRIGHT, JONALYN A.
[b.] Anchorage, AK; [occ.] Student; [hob.] Writing and sports; [ed.] Seventh grade homeschooler

ALLEN, HANNAH
[pen.] Kat; [b.] Baltimore, MD; [hob.] Piano, lacrosse, drama, soccer, skiing, snowboarding; [pers.] I have been writing poetry most of my life. I'm crazy about cats and other animals, and I often include them in my work.

ALLGOOD, JENNIFER L.
[b.] Jacksonville, FL; [occ.] Student; [hob.] Writing and reading poetry, swimming and roller-lading; [ed.] Tenth grade at Wilford Academy, a homeschooling agency; [awrd.] More than 200 hours for volunteering at Florida Hospital; [pers.] All people are truly happy when they are understood. To me, poetry is an expression of life. I hope that my poems will help others.

AMENDOLA, CLAUDIA
[ch.] One

ANDERSON, SHERI
[b.] Sioux Rapids, IA; [occ.] Medical Transcriptionist; [hob.] Playing piano, reading, traveling; [sp.] Patrick Stanley; [ed.] Secretarial-Business School, one year of college; [hon.] Honor Roll, National Honor Society; [pers.] I occasionally write for fun. My husband, published last year, is a serious writer. Because of his life, he inspired me to write this poem.

ANDREWS, TOMMY
[pen.] TK 20; [b.] Corning, IA; [hob.] Writing, singing; [ed.] College freshman; [oth. wrks.] "The Outsider" in *Treasured Poems of America* (Fall 1998)

ASKE, JOSELYN
[b.] Portland, OR; [occ.] High school student; [hob.] Drawing and band student; [memb.] Junior National Honor Society; [ed.] Freshman in high school; [hon.] Honor Roll; [awrd.] Eighth grade Student of the Year

BABCOCK, RYAN
[pen.] Leighton; [b.] Grand Rapids, MI; [occ.] Student; [hob.] Rockclimbing, pool competition, photography; [ed.] High school; [awrd.] Award on G.P.A. Improvement; [pers.] A good poet is one who can accurately portray their emotions, not those who strive for perfection.

BAIRD, GOLDA
[b.] MO; [hob.] Art, self-taught artist—oils and acrylic; [memb.] Former member of East Valley Art Guild, Charter, Diamon Barliving; [sp.] William Baird; [ch.] One; [gch.] Two; [ed.] Through eighth grade, Hair Stylist/Modeling School; [awrd.] Two first place, three honorable mention, one Picture of the Month oil painting; [pers.] My grandson Michael was sent to prison for one year for drug addiction. My visit with him inspired me to write "Freedom." They were words from him.

BAKER, CHRISTY
[b.] Sparta, TN; [occ.] Child Care; [hob.] Painting, drawing, writing poems; [ed.] High school diploma; [awrd.] Third place in art show; [pers.] I would like to thank my ninth grade teacher, Mr. Conlie of Cherokee High School for inspiring me to write poetry.

BARAN, PATRYCJA
[b.] Krakow, Poland; [occ.] Student; [hob.] Soccer, softball, reading, bike riding; [ed.] Reinberg Elementary School; [hon.] Math; [awrd.] Honor Roll, Perfect Attendance; [pers.] I would really like to get into my school's soccer and softball team. I really would like to write better stories and poems.

BARKER, JORY ANDREW
[b.] Mercy; [occ.] None; [hob.] Biking, football, fishing, baseball, chess; [pers.] Writing lets me be whoever I want to be and lets me travel wherever I want to go.

BARNES, ROBERTA
[b.] Birmingham, AL; [occ.] Self-employed (Interior Hygienist); [hob.] Collect and restore antiques; [ch.] Three; [gch.] Four; [ed.] Jr. college graduate; [pers.] "Tell Me the Truth" was inspired by the fact that our grand Creator is the answer to all of mankind's problems.

BARRON, JANET
[b.] Providence, RI; [occ.] Teacher-Assistant; [hob.] Aerobics, collecting bears, dolls, antiques; [ch.] Five; [ed.] High school; [oth. wrks.] "I Remember So Well" (*Providence Journal*); [pers.] Working with children in an elementary school in my city inspired me to write children's poetry.

BARTOLO, KRISTINA
[pen.] Kristina; [b.] Sewickley, PA; [occ.] Student; [hob.] Writing, listening to music, clubs, parties, cosmetics, exercise; [ed.] Sophomore in high school; [oth. wrks.] One poem published in *The Amherst Society* this year, and three in *Iliad Press* over the

years; [pers.] So far I have two notebooks filled with poems I wrote. I got the idea to write poetry through listening to song lyrics. Tupac Amaru Shakur was an excellent lyricist, and although some people found his songs offensive, he kept it real and spoke the truth—which is more than most people can say for themselves. So wherever he is now, may he rest in peace.

BASS, GLORIA J.
[b.] Colorado Springs, CO; [occ.] Administrative Professional; [hob.] Camping, hiking, gardening, sewing, arts and crafts; [memb.] International Association for Administrative Professionals; [ed.] San Antonio College (Associate's degree), Customer Service, Certified Professional Secretary; [hon.] Dean's List; [awrd.] Anacacho Chapter, PSI, Secretary of the Year (1997–98); [pers.] God has blessed me with the gift of expression through writing. I have a dream of sharing that gift so others may find Him, and happiness, in my words.

BAUER, SUNY
[pen.] Suny Bauer, Suny Sarang, Sunshine Valley; [b.] Hunterdon, NJ; [occ.] Student; [hob.] Drawing, poetry, writing, swimming, singing, dancing; [ed.] American School; [awrd.] One year ago for math and science; [oth. wrks.] "In My Room," published in *Glistening Stars*; [pers.] I really want to become the biggest writer. When do my inspirations occur? Hearing a song, and boom, or just sitting, and "Where's my pen?"

BECK, CAROLYN WILLIARD
[b.] Winston-Salem, NC; [occ.] Box Office Manager; [hob.] Camping, hiking, gardening, needlework; [memb.] Box Office Management International (BOMI); [pers.] My father taught me to appreciate the outdoors, one of his greatest gifts, which is a constant reminder of the many blessings God had given.

BENDER, JUDY
[b.] Wilton, ND; [occ.] Housewife; [hob.] Reading, gardening, crafts; [sp.] Donald Bender; [ch.] Three; [gch.] Five; [ed.] High school graduate; [pers.] Writing poetry allows me to put thoughts and feelings into words that would be left unsaid. I find it's relaxing to read and write poetry.

BLUE, DOROTHEA
[b.] Bernadot, IL; [occ.] Missionary, Housewife; [hob.] Reading, weaving, crocheting, sewing, making quilts; [memb.] Calvary Assembly of God, OAKS (Older American Knox Co.); [sp.] Rev. A. D. Blue; [ch.] Five; [gch.] Twelve; [ed.] High school, Southwestern Bible College

BORDERS, ANNA
[pen.] Hunter Dawn; [b.] Anniston, AL; [hob.] Reading, being outdoors; [ed.] Graduated from White Plains High School; [hon.] Graduated with Advanced Honors Diploma; [pers.] I've always expressed myself through poetry. Though this poem's inspiration was a devastating experience, I drew strength in my writing, and hope others will too.

BOUCHER, JESSICA
[b.] Weymouth, MA; [hob.] Writing poems, drawing, listening to music, hanging with friends; [sp.] Judy Boucher; [ch.] One; [ed.] Baker School

BRADLEY, ANITA
[b.] Port Caibor, PA; [occ.] Retired teacher; [hob.] Singing, reading, walking; [sp.] Harry; [ch.] Three;

[gch.] Six; [ed.] B.S. and M.A. in Education; [pers.] I seek to write those heart felt thoughts that we all have but seldom say.

BRATCHER, COURTNEY A.
[pen.] Penny Brachman; [b.] Reading, writing; [memb.] National Junior Honor Society, Bridge Builders; [ed.] Tenth grade; [hon.] Principal's List; [pers.] I love to write as a way to relieve stress. I never know what will come out of my stress until I read my work.

BRIDE, MICK
[b.] Lake Charles, LA; [occ.] Legal Consultant, Building Protectant, Sales, Pipefitter; [hob.] Fishing, camping, kids, writing, learning; [memb.] Several trade unions; [ch.] Two; [ed.] L.S.U. '76; [hon.] Some acknowledgements; [awrd.] Recognition by kids; [oth. wrks.] Pieces published in several volumes of The National Library of Poetry, other volumes, out of print prose; [pers.] Educated, unreconstructed hobo—Communication welcome, cannot promise reply, road demands

BROOKS, ISAAC
[pen.] Izeek Cellini; [b.] Killeen, TX; [occ.] Cook and Food Service; [hob.] Drawing and reading; [ed.] Junior at Muskegon High School; [pers.] I don't always do the right thing like arguing and being unreal, but I write poems to feel the way I am supposed to feel.

BROOKS, NATASHA
[b.] Florence, SC; [hob.] Writing poetry, reading novels, sewing, surfing the Internet; [ed.] Graduate of 71st High School, currently taking a secretarial course (ICS); [pers.] My inspiration for this poem is to let people know through God all things are possible, and with him great things shall happen.

BROOKS, RUTH
[pen.] Ruth Thomas; [b.] Washington, PA; [occ.] Home Engineer; [hob.] Writing poetry, playing flute and piccolo; [memb.] Crystal Cathedral, Hummingbird; [sp.] Bernard A. Brooks Jr.; [ch.] Two; [ed.] Clairemont High (1973), Atlantic Schools (1973), Rio Hondo (1999); [hon.] Math, English, Adv. Band; [awrd.] 1st Place L.A. and S.D. Adv. Band ('71) Ruby Pin Atlantic; [oth. wrks.] "Soaring Dreams," "Friends," "Changes," "Color," "Tender Loving Care," "Madonna," "Happy Cake," "People"; [pers.] I write poetry not only to convey a message but hope the reader will use their own imagination and find their own message within the creation.

BROWN, PATSY
[b.] Tarboro, NC; [occ.] Special needs caregiver; [hob.] Bible reading, writing, people; [sp.] Glenn H. Brown; [ch.] One; [ed.] High school graduate with some college; [pers.] This is my first published poem. Please remember, I give God the glory and honor. My talent and caring are my greatest gifts from God, along with my salvation and my family.

BROWN, SARAH
[b.] Washington, DE; [occ.] Social Security; [hob.] Cooking, painting furniture, reading, sewing, library; [memb.] Plymouth Congregational Church; [ch.] Four; [gch.] Ten; [ed.] High school and continuing education; [hon.] From Delta Inc. (Tutoring); [awrd.] From Church; [pers.] I would someday like to write a short story.

BRUEGGEMAN, MICHELLE
[b.] Quincy, IL; [occ.] Student; [hob.] Playing soccer, rollerblading, listening to music; [ed.] 7th Grade student at Quincy Junior High School; [pers.] Anything is possible!

BUCK, PATRICIA
[pen.] Tricia La Rue; [b.] June 13, 1922; Burlington, IA; [occ.] Retired; [memb.] Phi Sigma, Florida Institute of Certified Public Accountants, Rebekahs, church affiliations; [p.] Harry and Helen Shauenberg; [sp.] Glenn Buck; December 29, 1947; [ch.] Pamela; [ed.] Burlington High School, two years of college; [hon.] National Honor Society, American Express Card for Easier Readability Award; [oth. wrks.] English sonnets, special poems for family and friends; [pers.] I have been told that I have a "talent to make things beautiful."

BULLER, MENNO
[b.] Mt. Lake, MN; [occ.] Self-employed; [hob.] Working with wood—draw Precious Moments figures and paint them; [sp.] Rose M. Buller; [ch.] Five; [gch.] Ten; [ed.] 12th grade, 5000 hrs. under G.I. Bill; [pers.] My priorities and goals are—first God, then my wonderful wife and family. I am thankful for good health and the ability to serve.

BURCH, MICHELLE
[b.] Douglas, GA; [hob.] Writing poems, reading books; [memb.] FNA at Jeff Davis High School; [ed.] Tenth grade; [oth. wrks.] "Dreams"; [pers.] I would like to thank God; He gave me this wonderful talent. I like sharing my poems with everyone who will listen. Thank You!

BURNETT, FAY
[pen.] Gretel; [b.] Jamaica, WI; [occ.] Secretary; [hob.] Writing short stories and poems, going to lectures; [memb.] The National Library of Poetry; [ed.] G.E.D. from Briarcliff College; [hon.] Editor's Choice Award from The National Library of Poetry for "Don't Make Me Cry" (1997); [pers.] I want my poems to be a motivating factors in the lives of people; but especially to single parent and my daughter Yolanda.

BURR, NELLIE L.
[b.] Erick, OK; [occ.] Homemaker; [hob.] Oil painting, knitting, crocheting; [memb.] Church, AARP, Senior Center; [ch.] Four; [gch.] Fourteen, 34 great-grands; [ed.] One year of high school; [hob.] Just being a housewife and mother—Pure Country; [awrd.] Pennmanship in school; [pers.] I came to Colorado with my parents at age 2—in 1915. I have written my autobiography and have written numerous pieces of poetry for different occasions.

BUTLER, JUDITH A. C.
[b.] Norfolk, VA; [occ.] Technical Instructor; [hob.] Reading, writing poems, short stories, collecting stamps, coins, softball; [memb.] International Society of Poets, Georgia's Writers Group, retired Military; [sp.] Israel Butler; [ch.] Two; [hon.] Twenty years of dedicated service, three MSM, four AAM, four ARCOM; [awrd.] The Great Beyond, "The Departure," *Blossom in the Dawning*, "Validate My Life," *The Shades of Autumn*, "God Gave Me a Set of Wings"

CABLER, JOHN
[b.] Memphis, TX; [occ.] Maintenance for Delta and Pine Land Co.; [hob.] writing, fishing, electronics; [memb.] NGAT; [sp.] Janice Cabler; [ch.] Three; [ed.] Wayland Baptist College

CALDERON, MARIA
[b.] Manila, Philippines; [occ.] Student; [hob.] Reading, dancing, shopping, being with friends; [ed.] Ninth grade; [hon.] 1996 Suffolk Reading Council Creative Writing and Art Cover Certificate, Elementary Gifted Program; [awrd.] New York State Assembly Certificate of Merit, Spelling Bee Champion at Tamarac Elementary School in 1995–1996; [pers.] My poems are usually based on personal experiences, but "Blue" was actually an assignment: "describe color to a blind person."

CAMPBELL, NANCY
[b.] Renton, WA; [occ.] Writer, president of Adoption Support Group; [hob.] Writing, helping others touched by adoption triangle; [memb.] Soundex Reunion Registry—American Adoption Congress—Idaho Search Support Light; [sp.] Kevin R. Campbell; [ch.] Four; [ch.] Four; [gch.] Seven; [ed.] 12th grade; [oth. wrks.] "My Adopted Son"; [pers.] I love helping elderly and helping people touched by adoption either biological—adoptees or adoptive parents. I've been in search for my biological son, born 2/21/67 at 3:30 p.m. in Lewiston, ID, delivered by Dr. Pierce. My goal as a writer is to let people know of our hearts' hopes and dreams to find those I love like my son. I need others to reach out and help me locate my son.

CARROLL, JANIS MEGGS
[b.] Marshville, NC; [occ.] Retired Educator; [hob.] Reading, writing, walking the beach, trading stocks; [ed.] Wingate College in Wingate, NC, Meredith College in Raleigh, NC, UNC-Chapel Hill in Chapel Hill, NC; [hon.] Past President of The International Council for Exceptional Children, NC Council for Children with Behavioral Disorders, Council for Children with Behavioral Disorders: Indirect Services Award; [pers.] "Mother's Hands" was written for a Thanksgiving Meggs Reunion celebrating the life of my mother who was an unbelievable person of love, strength, and wisdom! Focus on her hands was inspired by the artwork of John Biggers.

CARTER, GEORGE
[b.] Frederick, MD; [hob.] Reading, fishing, listening to good music; [ch.] Three; [gch.] Eight; [ed.] 12th grade; [hon.] Honorable Discharge—USAF

CARTER, PAUL
[b.] Boston, MA; [pers.] Sadness is my everything.

CASTRO, JUNE
[b.] Washington, DC; [occ.] Paraprofessional; [hob.] Gardening and reading; [sp.] Eddie; [ch.] Five; [ed.] Attending St. Mary's College; [pers.] As a mother of five, I find the best way to teach them by example, through them, I can help make a better world.

CHAPMAN, PAULUS
[pen.] Paulus Chapman; [b.] Indianola, MS; [occ.] Mover/Packer; [hob.] Poetry—understanding duties among other people; [memb.] Palm Spring's Air Museum, Riverside County Library; [ch.] One; [ed.] High school; [pers.] The children's endless energy and curiosities help me keep moving and use the blessing sent to keep focus.

CHAVEZ, YVETTE
[b.] Fresno, CA; [occ.] Student; [ed.] Pursuing B.A. and M.A. in English/Literature

CHELIKOWSKY, AARON
[pen.] Aaron Wolfekastle; [b.] Circleville, OH; [occ.] Security Guard; [hob.] Writing, drawing; [memb.] Collegiate Challenge, Pickerington Church of the Nazarene; [ed.] Currently enrolled at Capital University; [awrd.] The Dean's List; [pers.] Poetry has always been my emotional release, my method of expressing emotions that I normally could not. I am thankful to have this gift and pray that I have more opportunities to use it.

CHILDERS, LISA
[b.] Zanesville, OH; [occ.] Housewife; [hob.] Writing poetry, hunting, fishing; [sp.] Craig D. Childers; [ch.] One; [ed.] General Study, Vocational School; [pers.] My goal as a writer mainly is to be noticed.

CHILL, ELLA
[b.] South Shields, England; [occ.] Homemaker; [hob.] Music, reading, photography, painting, travel; [memb.] Clan McNicol; [sp.] Seonard Chill; [ch.] Three; [gch.] Three; [ed.] Halwell School for Girls in Launcesron, Cornwall, UK; [hon.] Prizes for Poetry and Art; [awrd.] World of Poetry's Golden Poet Award (1989); [oth. wrks.] "The Survivors"; [pers.] Live life as one day you will wish you had. I remember that youth, like hope, springs eternal.

CHRISTENSEN, JODI
[b.] Nephi, UT; [occ.] Homemaker; [hob.] Writing poetry, reading, making crafts; [sp.] Mark Christensen; [ch.] Two; [ed.] Graduated from Stevens, Henager College of Business; [hon.] Honor Roll, Outstanding Student of the Month; [awrd.] Placed third in filing competitions; [pers.] Writing poetry means a lot to me and the people around me because by expressing my emotions, it helps them and me.

CLAYTON, SUMMER
[pen.] Yellow Rose of Texas; [b.] Montgomery, AL; [occ.] Student; [hob.] Writing poems and songs, drawing, dance-ballet, tap, jazz; [memb.] Girl Scout Troop #72, Junior; [ed.] Sixth grade; [hon.] A Honor Roll and A–B Honor Roll Student; [awrd.] Second Place Gymnastics Trophy, first place winner from radio station, WXVI's Halloween Contest, Poetry Category; [pers.] I enjoy writing poetry and songs because it relaxes me. I have fun making up my own poems and songs.

CLINTON, ASAD
[b.] Denver, CO; [occ.] Student Athlete; [hob.] Football, basketball, baseball, Jack and Jill of America Inc.; [memb.] Leadership Council, Jack and Jill of America Inc.; [ed.] Senior in high school, (J.K. Mullen); [hon.] Honor Roll all four years at Mullen; [awrd] 1998 Beau, recepient of the Keppa Scholarship; [pers.] The road may lead, I go with love in my heart and victory on my mind. Without love, there's nothing.

COLLEY, ERIN
[b.] June 7, 1983; Brooklyn, NY; [p.] Joseph E. and Joan M. Colley; [ed.] Resurrection School, Fontbonne Hall Academy; [pers.] I enjoy reading poetry, and someday I wish to have my own book of poems published.

COLLIER, PEGGY
[b.] Woodward, OK; [occ.] Owner—Collier Property Mgmt. and Maint. Co.; [hob.] Cross stitching, reading, writing poetry, rafting, hiking; [memb.] Better Business Bureau, Credit Bureau of the High Plains, National Federation of Independent Business, Texas Real Estate Commission, Laureate Eta Tau of Beta Sigma Phi; [sp.] Rodney Collier; [ch.] Two; [ed.] Two-year Secretarial School, Real Estate Licensing Educ. (broker), Four years Bus. Admin. with Marketing Emphasis; [awrd.] Diamond Homer Trophy (Famous Poet Society), Queen of Laureate Eta Tau (1998–1999); [oth. wrks.] "Life," "Faith"; [pers.] Someday I want to be able to write full time and give God the glory—maybe soon; my last child is in high school.

CONNOR, DENNIS
[b.] Denver, CO; [occ.] Wine Specialist, Wine and Spirits Manager; [hob.] Writing, completed first manuscript, fiction, *Vertical Deception*; [memb.] Director/Manager of Wine Club, produce monthly newsletter; [ed.] M.S. in Marketing Management, B.B.A. in Business Management, Minor in Sports Medicine; [pers.] Writing is my life. I am able to express my innermost thoughts and feelings. The purity lies in the hand that creates the beauty.

COWDER, AMANDA
[b.] Tampa, FL; [memb.] Council Member of Youth Alive (Christian Club at my school); [ed.] Junior at Plant City High School; [pers.] My special influences have been my family, friends, church and of course, God. God is the answer to everything.

COX, BRIDGET
[b.] Lithe Springs, GA; [occ.] Student; [hob.] Softball, band, writing; [memb.] 4-H, FHA, Truth (Christian Club), Rocky Branch Baptist Church; [ed.] Seventh grade

CRAWFORD, MELISSA
[b.] Landstuhl, Germany; [hob.] Writing poems, songs, and short stories, listening to music; [ed.] Student at Derby High School; [pers.] My friend Kim and 'N Sync are inspirations because they're always optimistic. My biggest inspiration is my best friend Danal; through him, I learn about myself.

CRAWLEY, SAUNDRA
[b.] Yuba City, CA; [occ.] Financial Advisor; [hob.] Acting, photography, writing; [memb.] Make A Wish Foundation; [sp.] Patrick Crawley; [ch.] Two; [ed.] B.A. in Marketing/Mgmt, Sonoma State University; [hon.] Dean's List; [pers.] "God's Little Angels" was inspired by Cameron and Micaela. I wrote it in hopes that all children will know they are loved and watched over by God.

CRESON, ROLAND, JR.
[pen.] Roland C.; [b.] New Orleans, LA; [occ.] Parish Mechanical Inspector; [hob.] Reading; [ch.] One; [ed.] High school G.E.D., one year at Vo. Tech.; [pers.] "I Wish" originated from an eighth grade English assignment about 30 years ago. My teacher gave me the title; Uncle Joe composed the words. Its meaning I share with many. I thank Uncle Joe for giving my feelings words.

CROSBY, MICHAEL P.
[b.] New Orleans; [occ.] International Traders Import-Export; [hob.] Fishing, writing poems; [memb.] ASTRA; [ch.] One; [gch.] One; [ed.] Eighth grade; [pers.] If you're really interested, I have a few more poems. I wonder if it is really possible to make a living writing poems.

DAVIS, FELECIA R.
[b.] New Iberia, LA; [occ.] Rehabilitation Health Care Worker; [hob.] Reading, writing poetry; [ch.] Two; [ed.] Medical Assistant and Certified Respirative Care; [pers.] My deep admiration for Maya Angelou's work allows the inner me to reach another phase of spiritual growth, and really be set free.

DAVIS, JENNIFER
[b.] Adel, GA; [occ.] Student; [memb.] FCA, Christ Club, Unity Free Will Baptist; [hon.] A/B Student; [awrd.] Language Arts Achiement Award; [pers.] I wrote the poem, "My Friend," because in life you only have one true friend, and that's Jesus. When everyone's against you, he's always there!

DAVIS, NIKOLINA
[b.] Omaha, NE; [occ.] Student; [hob.] Poetry, swimming, singing, dancing; [sp.] Bryan Davis; [ed.] High school diploma, going through college now; [hon.] Creative Writing; [awrd.] Creative Writing, Band, Swimming; [pers.] Your feelings to beliefs are how you make it through life. Don't ignore them; honor them to be creative.

DEBUROW, CRYSTAL
[hob.] Skating, singing, playing basketball; [ed.] St. Maria Goretti High School for girls; [hon.] Second honors; [awrd.] Attendants, cheerleading, honors

DEMMONS, BRANDI
[b.] Dayton, OH; [hob.] Writing poems and songs, singing and talking; [pers.] Writing is something I've always loved to do, and I've found a new goal as a writer: to help people feel new emotions.

DIAZ, CLAUDIO
[b.] Puerto Rico; [occ.] Service Writer; [hob.] Writing poems, lyrics, music, short stories, thoughts of gender living; [memb.] Writer's Guild, Photographer's Guild of America, International Society of Poets; [sp.] Kathleen R. Stewart; [ch.] Three; [gch.] Seven; [ed.] Ben Franklin High School in New York, NY, CCNY—B.A. degree; [oth. wrks.] "Autumn Winter Holidays," "Winter Enters," "Black Crow," and "Country"; [pers.] The call of love is the touch of affection in a different warmth. If you have to lie, keep it inside; it will not hurt anyone, except you.

DOMENECH, ANNA
[b.] Los Angeles, CA; [occ.] Student; [hob.] Drawing, dancing, writing, singing; [ed.] Eagle Rock High School, Pasadena Commuity College; [pers.] I'm 20 years old. My goal is to become a great poet published in many books, and write songs for other people as well as myself.

DRAKEFORD, VIVIAN
[b.] Camden, SC; [occ.] Human Relations Advisor, EED; [hob.] Reading, softball, walking, weight training; [memb.] National Guard Association; [sp.] James H. Drakeford; [ed.] Student at Coker College, Soc. major; [hon.] Dean's List; [awrd.] Letter of Commendation, Superior Physical Fitness; [oth. wrks.] First poem; [pers.] "He that is without sin among you, let him first cast a stone." —St. John 8:9

DRUCKMAN, JOAN
[b.] Boston, MA; [occ.] Math Teacher; [hob.] Drawing, painting, biking, travelling, baking; [sp.] Richard Druckman; [ch.] Three; [gch.] Three; [ed.] Simmons College, B.S.; [oth. wrks.] Food Column, local newspaper, 1981; [pers.] Life is most meaningful when we make a difference in other people's lives. Through my words, I hope to enhance the interpersonal connection.

DYE, MICHELLE
[b.] Albuquerque, NM; [occ.] Student; [hob.] Riding horses; [ed.] Eighth grade student at Coronado High School in Gallina, NM

DYER, J.
[pen.] J. C. Dyer; [b.] Choestoe, GA; [occ.] Sign Painter; [hob.] Play flute, paint, enjoy the outdoors; [oth. wrks.] "The Fire Experiment," "The Homebound Traveler," "Crossroads of Consciousness" —all published and promoted by myself; [pers.] Plant a seed wherever you go; with a prayer and water, it will grow. The world will be full of food for free satisfying the hunger of all in need.

EICHEL, KIMBERLY
[b.] Dover, OH; [occ.] Student; [hob.] Reading, writing, talking online; [ed.] Currently attending Dangaree Intermediate School, fifth grade; [awrd.] Two House of Representatives; [pers.] My goals as a new writer are to write a book and to publish many more poems. I thank my mom for my influences.

ELKIN, ROBERT
[pen.] Bob's Country Copyrights; [b.] North Kenova, OH; [hob.] Country music, writing, performing, fishing, hunting, racing; [memb.] NASCAR, Greenbush racing; [sp.] Frieda Marlene Elkins; [ch.] Nine; [gch.] 17; [ed.] 12th grade, Area Tech., plus three semesters; [hon.] Awards for country songs, achievement awards in music; [awrd.] Harmonious award "Honor" for song "Little Angel Dirty Face"; [oth. wrks.] "Song" Tall Hog at the Trough and Rainy River Blues; [pers.] I set goals for "Country Songs" writing poems, many hits: "I'm Riding Dynamite," "All Your Love," "Heart Beat," "You Can't Lose," "Avst Biddle's Fiddle." I am deeply inspired by country singers of the Outlaws and my Uncle Cliff, my dad and mother, and old Avst Biddle and Friends and family.

ELLIOTT, KEISHA
[pen.] A.K.A. Baby Girl; [b.] North Carolina; [hob.] playing basketball, singing, acting, cooking, talking on the phone, writing poetry; [ed.] High school; [pers.] My dream is that someday a troubled teen will read my poetry and discover that whatever the problem, things will get better. But you just have to hold on.

EVANS, IONE
[b.] Jamaica; [occ.] Security Dispatch Officer; [hob.] Reading, writing, listening to music, observing everyday life; [ch.] One; [ed.] Associate Degree in Early Childhood Education; [hon.] English Honor Society, member since February 1996

EVELYN, KENDELL
[b.] New York; [hob.] Art, martial arts, drawing, writing, sports (football, basketball, baseball); [ed.] Fourth grade; [hon.] Honor Roll—attendance, citizenship; [awrd.] Fifty dollar savings bond, Principal's Award

FALKOWSKI, JOHN
[b.] Lorain, OH; [occ.] Ex-private investigator; [hob.] Target shooting, hunting, fishing, stamps, coins, antiques, fossils; [memb.] NRA Firearms Instructor, APS, and Ocean City Country Coin Club; [sp.] Divorced; [ch.] Three; [ed.] Currently Attending Ocean County College; [pers.] Beware! Quiet times of self reflection can lead to poetry.

FARKAS, RHEA
[pen.] Calamity Jones; [b.] Manhattan, NY; [occ.] Professional Student; [hob.] Writing, art, politics, hiking, communing with friends; [ed.] B.S. Degree at Southern State University in New Haven, CT; [hon.] Magna Cum Laude; [pers.] I have never been run of the mill, which can get in the way of Status Quo Policies. Writing helps me escape while sharing a gift.

FAULES, BARBARA
[b.] Austin, TX; [occ.] Retired Elementary Teacher; [hob.] Reading, gardening; [memb.] National Education Association, Missouri NEA; [sp.] John W. Faules; [ed.] B.A. from Harding University (Searcy, AR), M.A. from University of MO at Kansas City; [hon.] Cum Laude at Harding, Academic Achievement Award at UMKC; [oth. wrks.] "Teacher's Aide: A Dream Come True in School Community"; [pers.] Poetry allows an expression of our deepest feelings while giving others an avenue to share those thoughts and relate it to their common human experience.

FELICIANO, CRIS
[pen.] Cris Pulo; [b.] Philippines; [occ.] TVIS Production/Back-Up; [memb.] Morong Tulay Association, San Francisco Branch, US, Morong Branch, Rizal Philippines; [pers.] I write lines of poetry for my family and friends on whichever register in my heart, and through the ink of any pen.

FELTON, LYEISHA
[b.] Philadelphia, PA; [occ.] Up-and-coming writer; [hob.] Reading and writing poetry, also short stories; [memb.] The Reader's Book Club and BMG Music Club; [ed.] High school graduate; [hon.] Honor Roll in (9th, 10th, 11th grades); [awrd.] Journalism and debating; [oth. wrks.] Some writings published only in the school newspaper; [pers.] I write poems in hopes to reach a person who can get a positive message and apply it with their everyday life.

FENNIMORE, JACKIE
[b.] Carthage, MO; [occ.] Paint and Body Shop; [hob.] Woodwork, writing poems, restoring classic cars; [ch.] Two; [ed.] GED; [pers.] James Fennimore Cooper influenced me as a young child. His ability to relate to the world around him inspired me to write poetry.

FINK, ANGELA
[b.] April 1964; St. Louis, MO; [p.] Robert and Barbara McQuitty; [m.] Robert Fink; [ch.] Kaylee Marie and Nicholas Daniel; [pers.] To Maggie, my first inspiration, and to my babies Kaylee and Nicholas—may you never forget the wonders and happiness of childhood.

FIRMIN, MARJORIE
[b.] San Jose, Costa Rica; [occ.] Teacher, Bilingual English, Spanish; [hob.] Writing, reading, walking, travelling; [sp.] Tommy J. Firmin; [ch.] Three; [ed.] Bachelor of Science in Education; [hon.] Dean's List, Honorary Consult of Costa Rica in Houston, 1985–87; [pers.] Thank you God for teaching me that compassion is more important than success, that forgiveness and tolerance of the differences of your people are key ingredients for achieving true happiness and peace of mind.

FISCHER, MARIE
[b.] Sarasota, FL; [occ.] Student; [hob.] Art, reading, writing poetry, music; [memb.] National Art Honor Society; [ed.] Current Student; [awrd.] Celebration of the Arts in Maryland ('97–'98);

[pers.] I would like to thank my family and my best friend Frank for all of their support in my work. I love you all, thanks!

FISCUS, JULIE
[b.] Bedford, IN; [occ.] Student; [hob.] Traveling and dance; [pers.] I use poetry and writing as a use of therapy. Putting my thoughts on paper relieves a great deal of stress.

FIVIS, NICOLE
[b.] Napa, CA; [occ.] Student; [hob.] Guitar, piano; [pers.] Poetry is a gift. Not only to write it, but to understand it.

FOGLEMAN, RUTH
[b.] Omaha, NE; [occ.] Homemaker; [hob.] Reading, house plants, counted cross-stitch, embroidery, other crafts; [sp.] Rick Fogleman; [awrd.] Silver Poet Award (1986)—World of Poetry, Silver Poet (1990)—World of Poetry, Editor's Choice Award (1998)—The National Library of Poetry; [oth. wrks.] "Life's Funny That Way," "To the Child That Might Have Been," "Where Do They Go," "Parting," "Silly Child," "I've Lost Someone"

FORASTIERE, NOELLE
[b.] Glen Cove Hospital, Long Island; [occ.] Student; [hob.] Writing; [ed.] Staples High School; [pers.] I dream to be a good writer and have people enjoy and be able to relate to what I write.

FREESE, JOHN
[pen.] Attriter; [b.] Riverside, Ca; [occ.] Student; [hob.] Writing, computing, skating; [ed.] Sophomore at Rim High; [hon.] Published poetry from '98 Reflections; [awrd.] 2nd Place '98 Orange County Reflection's Contests; [pers.] Love is an emotion of few words, but with such expression, love needs not be defined.

FRITZ, ANITA
[b.] San Diego, CA; [occ.] Student; [hob.] Gardening, penpals, cartooning, art in general writing, seed swapping; [pers.] I find writing poems is a form of art, music helps me to become creative through pen and paper, as well as on canvas with a brush.

GAITHER, SARAH
[pen.] Sara J—Chaney; [b.] Chicago, IL; [occ.] Student; [hob.] Poetry, singing; [memb.] Club Live School Choir, Youth Power Club; [ed.] Will Rogers Intermediate school—seventh grade

GAMBLE, GLENDA L.
[b.] Santa Maria, CA; [hob.] Love to crochet, embroidery, write stories, love to travel; [ed.] Ernest Righetti High School; [oth. wrks.] *The Great Beyond*, featuring poem, "Freedom," Sound of Poetry, featuring poem "One Day," also have written two manuscripts and would love to see them come to life on the big screen

GASTON, TINA
[b.] Great Falls, MT; [occ.] U.S. Army; [hob.] Writing poetry, lyrics for musical arrangements, listening to Jazz, hugging my daughter; [sp.] David Blaney; [ch.] One; [ed.] 12 1/2 years; [hon.] Poem published in the Poetry Guild, Certificate of Achievement for Creative Writing Skills from Chapel Recording Company; [pers.] Thank God for people like The International Library of Poetry. It allows us ("nobodies") the opportunities to see our hard work appreciated and loved by others. Thank you!

GERETY, KENNETH R.
[b.] May 16, 1998; [memb.] International Society of Poets; [hon.] Editor's Choice Award from the National Library of Poetry's recent contest; [oth. writ.] "I am Shadow," published in *Captured Moments*; [pers.] Write what you know, but at the same time, twist things around. Throw your life into a blender and see what happens.

GERZANICOVA, HANA
[b.] November 5, 1928; Plzen, Czech Republic; [m.] Michael Geozanie; October, 1994 (second marriage); [ch.] Six children, seven grandchildren; [ed.] Ph.D. in Philosophy, diploma in Theology; [occ.] Retired—doing cultural interchanges between Australia and Czech Republic; [memb.] Czech Writer's Union, Australian Writer's Union, International Society of Poets, Czech National Library, Australian National Library, S.V.U., Aubspectrum (Sydney); [hon.] Several poetic rewards; [oth. writ.] Two books of poetry published in the Czech Republic, writing bilingually—Czech and English; [pers.] I want to share beauty with my readers, teach them to see "treasures" in little things, to meditate and be grateful for the gift of life.

GIAMPETRUZZI, MARCO
[b.] Rome, Italy; [occ.] Insurance Claim Manager; [hob.] Antique collecting, sports, writing, cars; [sp.] Aniko; [ch.] 3; [ed.] Nassau Community College Palm Beach Junior College, University of Southern Maine Willsey School of Interior Design; [oth. wrks.] Poems "Escape," "Russian Roullette," "The Plight of One"; [pers.] Life is a cycle of ups and downs. Each life must do its very best to cope with all it is asked to endure.

GLASCO, FLOYD
[b.] Cairo, IL; [occ.] Assistant Manager of Security; [hob.] Baseball, writing; [memb.] International Lion Club; [ed.] One year of college; [awrd.] Various military awards; [pers.] My writing's stem from a literature teacher who kept my interest during H.S.—Sister Helena Leach. From that point on, I've been captivated to write poetry.

GLEESON, KELLIE
[b.] Old Bridge, NJ; [occ.] Student; [hob.] Drama, writing, singing, drums, traveling, watching my favorite baseball team—the Yankees; [memb.] Drama Club, Key Club, Creative writing Club; [ed.] St. John Vianney High School Junior; [hon.] Academic honors; [awrd.] Martial Arts; [oth. wrks.] "The Poet," and "The Longing of the Soul"; [pers.] My inspiration comes from the people and things around me, but I do take aspects of my own life as well. People always tell me to write what I know, but how much could I possibly know at age 16? So I always take it a step farther: Instead of writing what I know, I write from the heart.

GOBLE, JEFF
[b.] Killeen, TX; [occ.] Student; [hob.] Writing, listening to music; [pers.] Some influences of my writing were Jennifer Love Hewitt, who really taught me that you shouldn't care what other people think, and my friend Angela.

GODWIN, WILFORD
[b.] Hot Springs, AR; [occ.] Carpenter, (semi-retired); [hob.] Learning the computer, small gasoline engines; [memb.] Associated Brotherhood of Christians; [sp.] Ella Sue; [ed.] Tenth grade; [oth. wrks.] "Faith" (1998)—

Editor's Choice Award; [pers.] I write only when inspired by the Holy Spirit to do so.

GOODWIN, JENNIFER
[b.] Torrance CA; [occ.] Student; [hob.] Traveling around the world, feeding the homeless, helping my church; [ed.] Calvary Chapel; [pers.] I find all my inspiration in my heart. I write what I feel and I feel very much.

GOREA, LUCIA
[b.] Oradea—Romania; [occ.] English Teacher; [hob.] Translating, travelling, philosophy, anthropology; [sp.] Simon Gorea; [ch.] One; [ed.] Graduated University of Bucharest with M.A. in English; [awrd.] Grand Prize at the National Contest of Translations; [pers.] Poetry allows me to express my inner feelings, my deepest thoughts. It is an open window to the world. I've always admired Frost and Kant.

GORMAN, JOAN
[b.] New Jersey; [occ.] Student; [hob.] Skiing, tennis, soccer, helping others (volunteer at the hospital); [ed.] High school sophomore; [pers.] Writing poems helps me relax and overcome many struggles. I wrote this poem while hospitalized for eating disorders; picturing my secret dollhouse gave me hope.

GRAY, PATRICIA JEAN
[b.] Ardmore, OK; [occ.] Sixth grade student; [hob.] Archerrp, cross-stitch; [hon.] "A" average student; [awrd.] NCAA (Math)

GREEN, DANIELLE
[b.] Staten Island, NY; [occ.] Office Manager, writer; [hob.] Sports, soccer, bowling and softball, art and writing; [memb.] WBA—Women Bowling Association; [ed.] Graduated Drake Business School, Kingsborough Community College; [hon.] Congressional Scholar, Sports Achievement; [awrd.] Dean's List throughout Business School, many awards for soccer; [oth. wrks.] Published in *Famous Poets of 1998* and *Cherished Poems of the Western World*; [pers.] I truly enjoy writing to be an inspiration to everyone who reads my work. I give thanks to my parents and future husband for all the love and support they give to me.

GRIFFIN, ALEXIS
[pen.] Alley G.; [b.] Phoenixville, PA; [occ.] Student; [hob.] Dancing, singing, writing poetry; [ed.] Ninth grade student at Pottstown High School; [awrd.] *Who's Who in American History*; [pers.] Writing poetry is a great way for me to look at my life in a different perspective. Thanks to my family and friends for the inspiration.

GRIFFIN, REGINALD
[b.] March 7, 1950; [occ.] Disabled; [hob.] Cooking, playwriting, community television production; [memb.] Black Screenwriters Association; [ed.] B.A. in Management, Columbia College of Chicago (1983); [hon.] 1st Place, Oral Interpretation, National Association of Dramatic and Speech Art; [awrd.] Broadcasting Award for a technician at Kennedy King College; [oth. wrks.] "The Devil's Game"—stage play, musical comedy; [pers.] Began writing stories and plays for reading 1960, performed as a vocalist and instrumentalist since 1955, performed as an actor and poet

GROH, MARY
[pen.] Mary-Kate Groh; [b.] West Allis, WI; [occ.] Housewife; [hob.] Photography, drawing, gardening,

cooking, enjoying my family; [sp.] David Groh; [ch.] Four; [ed.] High school, Technical College; [awrd.] Semi-finalist in the Open Amateur Photography Contest; [pers.] Thanks to God first and foremost! He has and will remain my greatest inspiration. Because of Him I have my wonderful husband and four children.

GROSS, TARA
[b.] Wilmington, DE; [occ.] Student; [hob.] Acting and writing; [ed.] Eighth grade at Shue Middle School; [oth. wrks.] "Will You Come Back?" in *American Poetry Annual*; [pers.] I've been writing for over three years. I have written over 50 poems. I write from experience, and I've experienced a lot for my age.

GUIDICE, CAROL
[b.] Rochester, NY; [occ.] Teacher Aide; [hob.] Singing, playing piano, drawing, exercising, writing; [ed.] High school; [awrd.] Drawing Award; [pers.] Since I was little, my grandmother I called "Mama" used to write stories. She inspired me to keep writing poems and stories. We're a lot alike. She is why I still write poems.

GUTIERREZ, NINA
[pen.] Neen; [b.] McAllen, TX; [occ.] Student; [hob.] Writing poetry; [pers.] My mom was the person who inspired me to be myself. She always gave me hope and something to look forward to. Thanks, Mom!

GUZMAN, JUSTINE
[pen.] Skylar Camden; [b.] Baylor Hospital; [occ.] Student; [hob.] Rollerblading, reading, hockey, singing; [ed.] St. Thomas, Pirrung Elem., Cannaday Elem.; [hon.] Academic Recognition for reading and writing; [oth. wrks.] "Dark Churches"; [pers.] I think for me Shakespeare was a great influence. His great plays-on-words really inspired me.

HALL, ELEANOR THURSTON
[b.] Weston, MA; [occ.] English Skills Coordinator and Teacher, Teaching Summary: Middle School, Concord, MA: Students 9–12, Manter Hall School, Osterville, Cape Cod; MA Buckingham and Brown and Nichols, Cambridge, MA, Middle and 9–12, Maynard Adult Education Center Maynard Adult Education Center Maynard, MA. Lecturer and workshop leader at many U.S. conferences; [hob.] Reading History, Travel—with slides taken on study tours sometimes used to enlarge students' view of the world; [memb.] Museums of Fine Arts/Science, NE Geological Society, Ma. Audobon Society, Family Counseling Service, MA Coaliton for Adult Ed. Region West, Business/Professional Women's Club; [sp.] Robert G. Hall (deceased); [ch.] One; [gch.] Two; [ed.] Cushing Academy, Boston University, Mass. General Hospital, Harvard School of Education; [hon.] Graduated academic, while working in Boston, took many evening courses, Therapy for Specific Reading difficult, Developing Reading ability in Adults, The International Dyslexia Society presented the annual Samuel T. Orton award given to individuals who make significant contributions to the field of dyslexia; [awrd.] Athletic, Ideal Cushing student, Recognition given to E.T.H. by P. American Sociey Board for her years of service as Ex. Dir. in furthering Inter-American relations; [oth. wrks.] Learning the English Language, Skill Books I, II, referenced to the Gillingham Manuel, with students' and the

teachers' manuals; [pers.] "It is an exciting and rewarding experience to find the resources within one's self to release potential in others."

HAMRIC, HOLLY
[b.] Eschenbach, Germany; [occ.] Student, eighth grade; [hob.] Writing, listen to music; [pers.] I wrote this poem because I hate war. My dad was in the Persian Gulf War. My wish is for world peace.

HANDA, BECKY
[b.] Athens, OH; [occ.] Student; [hob.] Writing, reading, rollerblading, running, listening to music; [ed.] High school sophomore; [pers.] I would like to use this space to thank anyone who has influenced and encouraged me in my writing—especially my father who has loved me, taught me, and encouraged me the most.

HANDY, GEORGE
[b.] Providence, RI; [occ.] Ceramic Artist; [hob.] Figure skating, windsurfing; [memb.] Piedmont Craftsman Southern Highlands Guild; [sp.] Dr. Laurel M. Davis, DVM; [ch.] One; [ed.] B.S. English Education; [hon.] Cum Laude Parker Book Award for Excellence in Creative Writing; [awrd.] Ceramic Work included in Smithsonian Institution permanent collection; [oth. wrks.] Arts Journal—black or white; [pers.] Ceramic sculpture is my second preoccupation. This pursuit of form and color keeps my eyes open, however, the writing process opens all of my senses.

HANN, SARAH
[b.] Bridgton, ME; [occ.] Student; [hob.] Field hockey, tennis, creative writing stories and poems, hiking, outdoor activities; [ed.] Current sophomore at Lake Region High School; [hon.] Lake Region High School's Honor Roll; [awrd.] DAR Essay contest Regional Winner in Brighton, ME (1993–1994); [pers.] I would like to thank two of my English teachers, Mrs. Botka and Mr. Benfield for believing in me and helping me reach my goals. I wouldn't have gotten here without them.

HARDEN, TERESA
[b.] Memphis, TN; [hob.] Reading, writing, singing; [memb.] Southside Boys and Girls Club, THA; [ed.] 12th grade; [hon.] District III Spotlights, Plaque and International Purity Bible Bowl; [awrd.] Principal's List Certificate, Basketball Intramural Trophy; [pers.] The most influential people in my life are my grandmother (Frances Coleman), my aunts (Shelea Shelton, Janice Martin, and Elisia Austin), and my best friends (Lakeesha Luckett, De Marcus Peoples, and Michael Pittman). This is dedicated to my inspiration, Dennis Harris.

HARRINGTON, NATHAN
[pen.] Nathan Harrington; [b.] Watertown, NY; [occ.] Retail merchandise salesman; [hob.] Music, poetry, women, hiking, travelling; [ed.] High school diploma, one year in college; [awrd.] 2nd Runner Up for Best Local Band in Syracuse; [pers.] I'm not writing poetry for money. I hope to use my poetry to send a message to everyone.

HARTLEY, JENNIFER
[b.] Spring TX; [occ.] Student; [hob.] Tennis; [pers.] I didn't start to write poetry until I met Matt Pleasant, so I would like to thank him for getting me started.

HARTMAN, MARILYN D.
[b.] Denver, CO; [occ.] Retired Professor; [hob.] Writing, counselling, fine art, singing, letters; [memb.] National Dem. Party Member, Sierra Club, Handgun Control, etc.; [sp.] James L. Hartman Esq.; [ch.] Three; [gch.] Five; [ed.] Doctor of Eng., Education (EdD.) U.C.L.A. ALUM directory 1999; [hon.] First Eng. Institute—Lorette Hts. Denver, C.U. Creative Writing Grant; [awrd.] National Art Competition: Fourth Place of 115, Two being in 75 chosen; [oth. wrks.] Poetry book and published . . . Special for Meth. Church; [pers.] Sing: Cathedral of the Immaculate Conception, Denver—use the talents God has given you. Develop and expand your abilities. Thank Him for love and compassion. Be a friend of God, humble and in awe of His great love.

HARTMANN, LORRAINE F.
[b.] St. Paul, MN; [occ.] Former Industrial Editor; [hob.] Reading, writing, painting faces, fictioned cowboys, Indians, Mexicans; [pers.] Hope to complete writing book

HARVELL, JESSICA L.
[b.] Cherrypoint, NC; [hob.] Writing, dancing, singing; [ed.] Sophomore at Kaukauna High School; [awrd.] National Honor Society; [oth. wrks.] "Quiet" (*Anthology of Poetry by Young Americans*), "The Wind," "The Rain," "The Journey" (*Iliad Press Anthology*); [pers.] God has had a great impact on my life. I give Him all the credit for poems I write. Readers, always remember Jesus loves you!

HARVEY, JOHN
[b.] Monongahela, PA; [occ.] Production Manager; [hob.] Basebal, hunting, golfing, mountain biking; [memb.] ThetaXi National Fraternity, Fayette County Semi-Pro Baseball; [sp.] Rebecca; [ch.] One; [ed.] B.S. in Industrial Technology, A.S. in Drafting Technology

HAYNES, CANDACE L.
[b.] Pensecola, FL; [occ.] Student; [hob.] Singing, writing, writing poems, drawing; [memb.] Y.M.C.A., Boys and Girl's Clubs; [ed.] Elementary School, Middle School

HELTON, CHRISTINE
[pen.] Baby Lovely; [b.] Honolulu, HI; [hob.] Poetry, swimming, volleyball, shopping; [ed.] Eighth grade at Moanalua Inter.; [awrd.] Swim Team

HENDRICKS, EDWARD R.
[pers.] I send this poem out to God, the creator of romance and a woman's heart. For in love, it's a beautiful as the rose.

HENDRY, MADELYN
[b.] Indianapolis, IN; [occ.] Photographer; [hob.] Snorkeling, golf, travel, gardening; [sp.] Dean Hendry; [ch.] Three; [gch.] Four; [ed.] Winona School of Photography; [oth. wrks.] Words of song, "You Make All My Problems Go Away" on album of "April in Love"; [pers.] I've come to appreciate poetic phrases by reading *The Bible*. There are found the words of Jehovah, the Creator of Pictorial Expression.

HENRICK, JEANNE
[b.] Plattsburg, NY; [occ.] Retired Nurse's Aide; [hob.] Crocheting, cake decorating, gardening; [sp.] Wesley Fowler; [ch.] Two; [gch.] One; [ed.] High school and community college; [hon.]

Volunteer of the Year ('95–'96) for American Cancer Society; [awrd.] Oustanding Achievement from Redding Medical Center; [oth. wrks.] "Peter's Lullaby"

HIDALGO, GIL
[pen.] Sonata; [b.] Queens, NY; [occ.] Artistic Director Rodeo Drive Salon; [hob.] Bass guitar, song writing, play station, working out; [ch.] Two; [ed.] Paramus Catholic Boys High School, Bergen Community College, Parisian Beauty Academy; [oth. wrks.] National Poetry Society, "The Goddess Oaisis"; [pers.] I have always been devoted to the changing of consiousness, and the raising of vibration within society, whether through words, music, or thought. My goal as a writer is to write more fourth-, fifth-, or even sixth-dimentions rather than three-dimentional reality.

HILL, BEVERLY
[b.] Cleveland, OH; [occ.] Teacher; [hob.] Drawing, travelling, reading poetry, writing; [ed.] Capital University—B.A. in Human Service; [pers.] Philippians 4:13, "I can do all things through Christ which strengthenth me." Poetry is a God-given expression of what one feels and has experienced in life.

HILLEY, MARIE
[pen.] Dear M.; [b.] September 18, 1961; [hob.] Poetry, photography, music; [memb.] International Library of Poetry, Greenbeltband Church Word of God; [ed.] High school diploma, June 1979—3 years of college; [awrd.] 19 Editor's Choice for Poetry, 10 Photography, Music, several short stories by DDDD publications; [pers.] I like writing and sharing my poems with others and there's no better way to them to have them published by The National Library of Poetry.

HINES, BRYAN
[b.] Baltimore, MD; [occ.] Welding Inspector; [hob.] Writing, Sports, Music; [memb.] NRA; [ch.] One; [pers.] My favorite poet is Robert Frost, but my inspiration is my daughter, Halle Hines.

HINKSON, CYNTHIA
[b.] October 7, 1945; Trinidad; [p.] Irene Hinkson, Samuel Hinkson; [ed.] University of the West Indies. B.A.—Spanish and French, general honours; [occ.] Retired language teacher of South East Port-of-Spain govt. Sec.; [oth.writ.] Several other poems on varied topics. some were published in the local newpapers, *The Newsday* and *The Guardian*; [pers.] "With God all things are possible."

HOEPRICH, ASHLEY
[b.] Fort Collins, CO; [hob.] Playing, music, writing; [ed.] Middle school; [oth. wrks.] "Ghosts" (I hear them howling in the trees); [pers.] Thanks to my teacher, Mrs. Judy Minger, who introduced me to poetry. She helped me realize I could write.

HOFFMAN, EUGENE
[b.] Houston, TX; [hob.] Writing, hunting, fishing, firearms, the study of scripture; [sp.] Melita; [ch.] Three; [gch.] Four; [ed.] AA (Concordia, Austin—55) 2 1/2 years Univ. of Houston; [oth. wrks.] Newspaper "Loving Steps," "Sound of the Golden Trumpet"; [pers.] To awaken people to the knowledge man is born mortal to immortality and the joy of living a life of kindness and courtesy.

HOOKER, ERIC
[pen.] The Father of Destiny; [b.] Dallas, TX; [occ.] Customer Service Clerk; [hob.] Swimming, singing, writing, and playing baseball; [memb.] St. Andrew Church of God in Christ, Powerhouse Fitness; [ed.] Graduated from Martin High School Class of '98; [awrd.] Principal Award; [pers.] My goal as a writer is to get as much work published as possible, and to inspire people who love each other and are going through a rough time.

HORN, KELLY
[b.] Alabama; [hob.] Horse back riding, singing, writing, and swimming; [memb.] West Blocton High School Band; [ed.] Ninth grade at Blocton High School; [awrd.] Spelling Bee, Principal's Award, Science Fair Award; [pers.] First, I would like to thank my grandfather Jack Penfield for believing that I had a talent. I would also like to thank my inspiration, Lance Bass.

HOSKINS, ROBIN
[b.] Seattle, WA; [occ.] High S=school sophomore; [hob.] Singing, writing, playing the electric guitar; [pers.] My dream in life is to have my band be famous someday. I would love to tour with Pantera, Hole, Marilyn Manson, and Garbage.

HOWE, LAURA
[pen.] Laurel Emerson Lawson; [b.] Peoria, IL; [occ.] Student, parent, writer, decorating; [hob.] Dancing, socializing, hiking, reading, speaking, cooking, gardening, camping; [memb.] American Diabetes Association, (daughter has diabetes); [sp.] Steven R. Howe; [ch.] Two; [ed.] B.A. (last semester) University of Kentucky, Child development; [hon.] Dean's List; [awrd.] Local Running Contest in age category, (two) First Place trophies; [pers.] Writing is a healing tool for yourself and others, like an artist painting a picture, it is from the soul. I love Shakespeare and Dr. Suess.

HUMPHREY, J. R.
[b.] Detroit, MI; [occ.] Interior Designer; [hob.] Art collecting, gardening and crosswords; [memb.] Greenpeace, Humane Society of America; [ed.] Michigan State Univ., NY School of Design; [hon.] In honors English and French in College; [oth. wrks.] Had a bi-weekly column on Interior Design in the Toledo, Ohio paper for one year many years ago; [pers.] Writing poetry is the truest expression of one's soul. I aways admired Frost and cummings but am truly inspired by Rod McKuen's music and poetry.

INGLE, EUNICE
[b.] South Haven, KS; [occ.] Retired Teacher; [hob.] Collecting Christian Steinback Nutcracker (and I golf); [memb.] Methodist Church; [sp.] Kenneth V. Ingle (deceased); [ch.] One; [gch.] Four; [pers.] Remember happiness comes from within us. Our attitude makes a difference in this great world. Do something nice for someone each day—even for yourself.

ISHMAN, DELSHUNDA
[pen.] Shun; [b.] Birmingham, AL; [occ.] School Secretary, Hair Stylist; [hob.] Cooking, writing, reading, working out, shopping, fashion and hair modeling; [memb.] Faith Chapel Christian Center Church; [ed.] High school graduate from Ensley High, Lawson State Community Graduate; [hon.] National Dean's List, License Cosmetologist, First runner-up in the Miss Alabama versus Miss Popularity, Best Evening Wear; [awrd.] Honor Student, A/B Honor Roll, first place in state VICA competition; [oth. wrks.] "Stay Gold" for school yearbook; [pers.] In writing I express my feelings. My influence came from my teacher, and God who gives me this special talent.

JALILI, ALEXANDRIA
[b.] Tulsa, OK; [occ.] Student; [hob.] Swimming, writing poetry, reading; [memb.] American Swimming Team; [ed.] Sixth grade at Central Middle School; [hon.] A and B Honor Roll at school; [awrd.] Prize-winning essay for DARE, third in state for breastroke

JASINSKI, MILDRED
[pen.] Millie Jasinski; [b.] Milwaukee, WI; [occ.] Retired from General Motors; [hob.] Gardening, music, crafts, poetry; [memb.] Visiting Nurse Assoc.; [sp.] Chester; [ch.] Two; [gch.] Six (and nine great-grandchildren); [ed.] Bayview High School; [awrd.] Editor's Choice Award from The National Library of Poetry (1994, 1996); [pers.] Writing poetry, a hobby is an expression of my feelings and thoughts of family and friends. I try to do the best that I can and hope for better tomorrow. My goal is to try to help the elderly in any way that I am able to.

JONES, DARLENE
[pen.] Darlene Jones; [b.] Providence, RI; [occ.] Temporary Employee; [hob.] Writing, travelling, bike riding, and boxing fan; [ed.] Graduated from Mount Pleasant High and RI College with a Bachelor's in Mass Communication; [hon.] Made the Honor Roll in high school (sophomore and junior years); [awrd.] Creative Writing Award, high school and school board, also chosen as one of four winners of the National Annual George Houston Bass Play, Rites Festival at age 17 making me the youngest winner in the history; [pers.] I like boxing because I see life as the challenger and me as the champion. It's all about life, love, and lessons. The struggle continues.

KARNS, GLORIA
[b.] Las Vegas, NV; [occ.] Manager of Dry Cleaners; [hob.] Writing; [ch.] Two; [ed.] High school graduate; [pers.] Through the years I have always written my thoughts and experiences down on paper so that I could release any tension and fears that I might have, so that I could start fresh the next day.

KASSLER, SHIRLEY
[b.] Austin, TX; [occ.] Retired Ins. Clerk; [hob.] Writing, bowling, gardening; [memb.] National Home Gardening Club; [sp.] A. D. Kassler—deceased; [ed.] One year college in Business Office Occ.; [pers.] I'm a firm believer in old time philosophies and Indian remedies. I'm the ninth child of twelve children born to a caring father and loving mother.

KEELEY, KRISTINA
[b.] Mt. Home, ID; [occ.] Sixth grade elementary student; [hob.] Dancing and writing poetry

KELLEY, KAYLEN
[b.] Anchorage, AK; [occ.] Student, Model; [hob.] Writing, speed skating, figure skating, soccer; [ed.] Tenth grade at Lumen Christ High School; [hon.] Statewide Essay Winner ('95, '96, '97, '98); [oth. wrks.] "Popularity, A Teen's View," for *Alaska Star*

KENTON, ODIS, SR.
[b.] Camden, NJ; [occ.] System Safety Engineer; [hob.] Music; [memb.] System Safety Society, (Sr. Member) International Society of Poets, NBCFAE (VP); [ch.] Three; [gch.] One; [ed.] University of the Air Force, Grantham School of Engineering and Rutgers University; [hon.] *Marquis Who's Who* (1981, '82 and '83); [awrd.] Editor's Choice Awards (February 1998) ILP; [oth. wrks.] "Deceive Not Thyself," "What You See is What You Get" (ILP 1998); [pers.] Inspiration, Yahweh Elonim and Yahshwa The Messiah.

KIDD, HEIDI
[b.] Fairfax, VA; [occ.] Student; [hob.] Soccer, write poetry, and write songs, singing; [ed.] Pre-school through ninth grade at Bowdish Jr. High; [pers.] What inspires me to write would be my younger sister, Jeralee; she always believed in me. I want to thank her for all her support. Thank you!

KIMBLE, GLORIA J.
[b.] Bronx, NY; [occ.] Sales Rep; [hob.] Racquetball, reading; [sp.] James W. Kimble; [ch.] Two; [ed.] High school and college classes for improvement; [hon.] "Sales Person of the Year" (13 Branches) High Sales Memorial Day (out of 117 stores); [awrd.] Many awards for high sales, trips—money, recognition and gifts; [pers.] As my first attempt at poetry, this little endeavour has inspired me to take some writing classes. I've always wanted to write a book—who knows!

KIRK, JEANETTE
[b.] Montg., AL; [occ.] Nurse retired; [hob.] Artist, crafts; [memb.] International Society of Poets, Poetry Hall of Fame, Creative Writers; [sp.] Charles Kirk; [ch.] Two; [gch.] Four; [ed.] Two years in college; [hon.] Four Editors Choice Awards from The International Poetry Hall of Fame; [pers.] Writing is one way that God gave me the talent to express myself. Being an artist is another way to see and express.

KLOSKY, JOHN
[pers.] Joyce wrote about 5 or 6 poems in 1954–55. I found them after she died. I did not know about them.

KRAJCOVIC, PETER
[b.] Weirton, WV; [occ.] Auctioneer—Satelitte Installation; [hob.] Writing; [sp.] Rhonda Kay Krajcovic; [ch.] Two; [ed.] Duluth Central High School in Duluth, MN

KRAJEWSKI, LANA
[pen.] Zoe; [b.] Northbrook, IL; [occ.] Student; [hob.] Streetblading, writing, track, volleyball, baseball; [ed.] Eighth grade; [pers.] Since I'm only 13, I have many goals, but most of all, I want to enjoy life and have fun.

KURKOWSKI, JENA
[pen.] Silver Dragon; [b.] Wheeling, WV; [occ.] Student; [hob.] Listening to music, writing, reading, looking for inspiration; [ed.] Currently a junior at Wheeling Park High School; [hon.] Being chosen as a semi-finalist is a real honor.; [pers.] My inspiration are mostly just thoughts with a touch of reality and a lot of experience with the creative world."

LADORE, DANIELLE
[b.] Harrison, NY; [occ.] Student; [hob.] Playing softball, hanging with my friends, shopping, talking on the phone and going on AOL; [ed.] Sixth grade; [hon.] Honor Roll two quarters in a. row; [pers.] I was inspired to write the poem "Why" from my experience of my grandfather dying, and what it was like when he did die.

LAMBERTH, TERI
[b.] St. James, MN; [occ.] Mortgage Banker; [hob.] Love movies, books, baking, sitting at the beach, fishing; [ch.] One; [ed.] Misc. College, Re. Courses and License; [pers.] In the depths of us all, we are dying to express. Do not let time flutter away without doing so.

LAMPE, JESSICA
[b.] St. John's Hospital; [hob.] Writing poems, story writing, drawing; [ed.] Sixth grade; [awrd.] Reading; [pers.] I am eleven years old and in the sixth grade, and my poems that I write are what I feel inside and what I like.

LAWRENCE, BARBARA HUGHES
[pen.] Barbara Hughes Lawrence; [b.] Somerville, MA; [occ.] Retired Medical Field; [hob.] Writing, reading, public speaking; [ch.] Five; [gch.] 13; [ed.] Fisher Jr. College; [pers.] I love nature and the ocean, Millay, Dickinson, Caldwell. I wrote "Storage" in 1948; my husband was killed (Navy). I put it away. Now, it has deeper meaning. I have hopes of finishing my autobiography; I believe survivors should write!

LAWRENCE, K.
[pen.] K. E. Lawrence; [b.] Embudo, NM; [occ.] Retired Registered Nurse, Fledgling writer; [hob.] Collecting rare books, playing musical instruments, painting and drawing; [ch.] One; [ed.] Degree in Nursing plus 400-plus credit hours of Various College Credits (Perennial Student); [hon.] Dean's List in College; [awrd.] Three First Prizes in local Poetry Competitions; [pers.] The power of moves not only mountains, but granite hearts. My daughter, Iris, puts the power in my words.

LAZARTE, CARMEN
[b.] Arequipa, Peru; [occ.] Housewife; [hob.] Travelling, reading, watching TV, sometimes singing; [ed.] Seven years in Hunter College New York; [hon.] "Poet of Merit"—American Poetry Anthology, New York, NY; [awrd.] Honorable Mention; [oth. wrks.] "Perestroika," this poem has fifty-one lines, "That Arquitect," "The Death of a Princess"; [pers.] My life has been developed in a quiet, natural way. My parents' home, it was good enough to give me serenity and happiness in my childhood. Nevertheless, this was broken partially because of my mother's death, when I was only thirteen. At that time, I became a housekeeper for my father and two brothers, my older brother, and the other six years younger than me, for whom I was like a mother. During the time all other girls were enjoying life with their boyfriends, I was at home all the time. My father did not let me go outside with anybody but him, or my older brother. That I did not have sexual life in my youth, I don't care about, but I do care, I don't have any children for my old age. As I never married, I am alone. I was unlucky in love. The man who was my greatest love, married somebody else, because the woman got pregnant by him. He was a doctor, and she was his nurse. She knew what to do, and I did not; why? Because I did not have any experience in my sexual life.

LEE, LEONARD
[pen.] Dori; [b.] Glendale, CA; [occ.] Student; [hob.] Play violin, reading books, biking, magic, basketball, roller blading; [ed.] Sixth grade; [hon.] Played in Honor's Orchestra and Tae-Kwon-Do; [awrd.] Trophies in Tae-Kwon-Do and Violin;

[per.] I was inspired by my mom, Penny Lee's love to write this poem. I was amazed at the feeling and emotion of the art, poetry.

LITTEN, FRANCES
[b.] Niagara Falls, NY; [occ.] Retired Printer and Saleslady; [hob.] Photography, writing and painting; [sp.] Harry Litten; [ch.] One; [gch.] Two; [ed.] Business Courses at "Kelly's Business Institute"; [oth. wrks.] Poems and snapshots in local papers; [pers.] I always wanted to be famous from a song I'd written or a photo I'd painted. But I'm just begining to enter contests.

LITTLE, GAYLE
[b.] Corpus Christi, TX; [occ.] Customer Services Manager; [hob.] Reading, music, writing poetry; [sp.] Marcus; [ch.] One; [ed.] High school diploma; [pers.] For me, writing poetry is a limitless way to express myself and reach out to others at the same time.

LUBAS, LAUREN
[pen.] Lauren Lubas; [b.] McNeil Hospital, IL; [hob.] Listening to music, photography; [ed.] Hampshire High School; [awrd.] Science Fair, Art Award

LUNA, AMY G.
[pen.] Amy G. Luna; [b.] Ft Stockton, TX; [occ.] Homemaker; [hob.] Flower arranger, house decorator; [sp.] John R. Luna; [ch.] Four; [gch.] Seven; [ed.] High school; [pers.] I don't have any special awards or honors. This poem was from my heart. Having my first poem noticed in this way—that's my accomplishment!

LY, YVONNE
[b.] Salisbury; [occ.] Student; [hob.] Music, art and skateboarding/rollerblading; [ed.] High school sophomore; [pers.] Don't hesitate to express any of your emotions, love, anger, or pain in any form of art and to the people around you.

MAIO, FRANK
[b.] Manhattan; [occ.] Jack of all trade, master of none; [hob.] Drawing, bike riding, travel, fishing; [sp.] Jennifer Ann Maio; [ch.] Two; [ed.] East Rockaway High School, graduated; [pers.] Jennifer is the hop in my step, the reason for my smile, and my inspiration. Thank you for unconditional love and devotion. Eternally yours . . .

MALLORY, BARBARA
[b.] Indianapolis, IN; [occ.] Wife, mother, and grandmother; [sp.] Charles; [ch.] Four; [gch.] Ten; [ed.] College; [oth. wrks.] "The Spectator," "I am Barabbas," "He's Coming for His Own"

MATUSZEWSKI, MINDIE
[b.] Green Bay, WI; [hob.] Tennis, writing; [ed.] Freshman in high school; [pers.] The death of my mother, Kathryn influenced me to write "Missing You." It helped me feel better about her passing and let everyone know how I felt.

MCBROOM, LINDA
[pen.] Sharon Behrens; [b.] Dallas, TX; [occ.] Secretary Receptionist; [hob.] Reading, writing, sketching; [sp.] (deceased) Kenneth; [ch.] Two; [gch.] Four; [ed.] Two Years Eastfield Community College; [awrd.] 2nd Place Winner Logo Contest Buckner Baptist Benevolence Credit Union; [oth. wrks.] "Platy," "The Child in Us" (Illustration); [pers.] In God's eyes we are all children, no matter what our age may be. Our

inquisitiveness just takes on a different form of expression as we mature in terms of this life and world's viewpoint.

MCDONALD, DIANE
[b.] Grand Rapids, MI; [occ.] Registered Nurse; [hob.] Very involved with Native American activities; [memb.] Grand Traverse Band Ottawa and Chippewa Indians; [ch.] Two; [ed.] Associate Degree in Nursing; [awrd.] 1997 Nursing Award; [pers.] My spiritual journey began three years ago when I met my friend, a traditional native American medicine man. I'm native American and Irish. I belong to Grand Traverse Band of Ottawa and Chippewa Indians.

MCGREEVY, SCOTT
[b.] San Francisco, CA; [occ.] Counselor for Disabled Children's Camp; [hob.] Skateboarding, being with my fiancée Amanda, playing football, baseball; [ed.] Ygnacio Valley High School, hoping to go to medical school; [pers.] I plan to get married, go to a good medical school, and become a doctor. After that, I would like to publish a book of poems with my fiancée Amanda.

MCINTOSH, ANNIEBELLE
[b.] Miami, Fl; [occ.] Teacher; [hob.] Travelling, gardening, sewing, arts and crafts; [memb.] Zeta Phi Beta Sorority, Inc., National Sorority of Phi Delta Kappa, Inc., United Teachers of Dade (Steward), Antioch Baptist Church; [ed.] Florida A and M University, B.S. (1962), and M.Ed. (1970) (Elementary Education—University of Florida, Ed.S—Elementary Administration. Certification: Language Arts (Reading K–12), ESOL, General Science 5–9; [hon.] South Florida Youth Association (Youth Tutoring Youth—YTY Project) (1970, 1971, 1972), Miami Dade Community College, ET College (1972), TV Debate Appearance with Mayor Jack Orr, "Overtown Situation"; [awrd.] Booker T. Washington Community School, Association Distinguished Service Award (1973); [oth. wrks.] Dade County Public Schools Invitational Winter Writing Institute (1993); [pers.] Writing is a good form of personal expression. All during my high school years, teachers at BTW stressed atheistic values to students. I learned and built a repertoire of poems by several poets to memorize, recite for the Annual Oratorical School Contest. Participants gained poise and self expression during this activity.

MCKENZIE, JULIANA
[b.] Charleston; [occ.] Student; [hob.] Reading and singing; [memb.] DECA; [ed.] Tenth grade at Andrews High School; [hon.] Honor Roll student; [pers.] Writing poetry is one of my favorite things to do. It helps me to express my feelings. My mother has always supported my writing abilities.

MCKNIGHT, JOYCE
[b.] Dayton, OH; [occ.] Server, Waitress; [hob.] Listening to music, riding bicycle, walking, reading; [ed.] Graduated Meadowdale High School in 1987; [oth. wrks.] This is my first; hopefully there will be others.; [pers.] Poetry is a great gift. I love to write; with God's help and with my family's pride, maybe I can be among the great poets.

MCMAHON, LYNDSEY
[b.] Irvine, Scotland; [occ.] Student; [hob.] Writing and fly fishing; [ed.] Graduated from high school in

'98; [awrd.] Won first prize in Robert Burns Poetry Competition at School; [pers.] Poetry to me is like an escape route from life, where I share my most personal and intimate feeling with the paper.

MECHELS, SALLY
[b.] Atlanta, GA; [hob.] Writing, painting, skiing and hiking; [memb.] Sheridan Fine Arts Club and Sheridan Artists Club Bighorn Audubon Society; [sp.] Jerry; [ch.] 3; [gch.] 5; [ed.] University of Miami; [oth. wrks.] "You Are Now Home," "Where Were You Last Night," "Forever" (all short stories); [pers.] Writing poetry is the most beautiful way to express your inner spirit and soul.

MELVIN, APRIL
[pen.] April Melvin; [occ.] Student; [hob.] Sports, bastketball, softball, track, writing poetry; [ed.] Junior at Xenia Christian High School; [awrd.] Softball MVP ('92, '94, '95)

MENDEZ, MARCELLE
[b.] Honolulu, HI; [occ.] Retired Counselor, AIDS Educator; [hob.] Drumming, singing, songwriting, hiking, swimming, playing guitar, drawing; [memb.] Volunteer for "The Life Foundation" (AIDS Foundation), Active Bahai and selected to Governor's Commission on AIDS (1993); [ch.] One; [ed.] B.A. in Pacific studies from West Oahu in Hawaii; [hon.] College from 1980 to 1993 on the Dean's List, scholarship in 1982; [awrd.] Peace Education in Waianae and nominated as "Outstanding Young Women of America" in 1986; [oth. wrks.] 1971 *High School Writers Anthology*, 1987 *American Poetry Anthology*, 1991 *Westwinds Literary Review—West Oahu*, 1992 and 1993 *Westwinds—West Oahu* and more; [pers.] Life with the absence of fear is my constant inspiration. The expression of authentic self and justice through guidance leads my every breath.

MENZ, THEODORE
[pen.] T. Jay; [b.] Brooklyn; [occ.] Nassau Downs; [hob.] Writing, fishing, chess, war games and various sports; [ed.] Hofstra University; [oth. wrks.] "It's a Beginning"; [pers.] Writing is a great release for the mind and soul. I hope to publish a collection and expand to songwriting.

MERSENSKI, CELESTE
[b.] Great Lakes, IL; [occ.] Student; [hob.] Reading, writing, making music; [ed.] Freshman at Summerville High School

MILES, BUD
[pen.] Bud Warren Miles; [b.] Cincinnati, OH; [occ.] Plumbing Contractor; [hob.] Fishing; [sp.] Tina; [ch.] Five; [gch.] Two; [ed.] High school; [pers.] The loss of my father was losing my best friend, mentor and of course, my father.

MILLARD, KIP
[pen.] Kip; [b.] Crookston, MN; [occ.] Student; [hob.] Billiards, reading, and various forms of visual entertainment; [pers.] I would like to thank my writing teacher, Mr. David Davidson, for showing me that poetry is not "a bunch of wordy drivel."

MILLER, PHILIP
[b.] Du Bais, PA; [occ.] USN Ret., Certified Photogrammetist; [hob.] Travel, camping; [memb.] American Society of Photogrammetry and Remate Sewing; [sp.] Margaret A.; [ch.] One; [pers.] This poem is my only work; it was written in support of my dear wife who was going through some difficult medical problems at the time.

MILLER, RAMONA
[b.] March 19, 1972; Dayton, OH; [occ.] Bartender, full-time college student; [ed.] Sinclair Police Academy, Mercer County Community College; [hon.] Dean's List, Commendation for Outstanding Job Performance and Dedication from the Gratis Police Dept. (May 1996); [pers.] I want to thank my brother Matt for being my best friend, my dad for always being right, and my grandparents for being constantly supportive.

MINCOFF, MELISSA
[b.] Ft. Wayne, IN; [occ.] Student; [hob.] Exercising and enjoying the outdoors; [memb.] Bethlehem Lutheran Church; [ed.] High school, future college goals; [hon.] Battalion Commander, 1998–1999 Concordia JROTC Cadet Battalion; [oth. wrks.] "Love Is" and "Troubled Soul Set Free"; [pers.] The experiences of everyday life inspire me to write. When I begin to write, everything just seems to fit together. Writing poetry is very relaxing.

MOSLEY, MATHEW
[pen.] Raisyn; [b.] New York; [occ.] Consultant; [hob.] Reading, writing; [sp.] Pamela; [ch.] One; [pers.] Though life presents different obstacles, challenges everyday acknowledge none the less, life can be beautiful.

MURDOCK, M.
[b.] Jamaica, West Indies; [hob.] Listening to music, watching television, writing to penpals; [ed.] High School; [pers.] As a writer, I try to be expressive. I've had a lot of experiences as a child growing up. I try to capture such moments on paper.

MURPHY, JACK M.
[b.] Lackie, WV; [occ.] Disabled Vietnam Veteran—United States Marine Corps; [hob.] Writing my feelings down on paper, reading, listening to music, telling stories of my life and making some up for kids; [ch.] Two; [gch.] Two; [ed.] High School Graduate; [hon.] Honorable Discharge from Vietnam; [awrd.] Certificate of Merit for a song, "There's No Love in This Town"; [oth. wrks.] 1973, I wrote "There is No Love in this Town"; [pers.] When you are left all alone, no one there to talk to, it does good to put your thoughts on paper.

MYERS, PAM
[b.] Indiana, Pennsylvania; [hob.] Sewing, reading, crafts, gardening; [ch.] One; [ed.] Homer-Center High School; [awrd.] Won Ribbons at Indiana County Fair, Indiana PA; [oth. wrks.] "Cat," "Hi-ho!," "Four off the Floor"

NAVARNE, TALEAH
[b.] Modesto, CA; [hob.] Rollerblading, snowboarding, swimming, hiking, wakeboarding, cooking; [ed.] American Home Schooling; [pers.] My inspiration was my boyfriend Willie. He made me think and feel like I was good and that my poems were the greatest.

NEGRON, TONY
[pen.] Romeo; [b.] Derby, CT; [occ.] Bus Boy at Carousel Gardens; [hob.] Play basketball, run track, play football and chill with family; [ed.] Sophomore at Seymour High; [pers.] I would like to thank Carley Rivers for my inspiration. I would also like to thank Mrs. Manning for helping me out in school. I would also like to thank Mom, Dad, Gerry, and Giovanni.

NEIGER, LADINA
[b.] Reed City, MI; [occ.] Cook; [hob.] Home decorating and gardening; [sp.] Robert Neiger; [ch.] Five; [ed.] High School; [pers.] As a mother of kids aged 5 to 15, times can be tough. With my husband starting his own business, he has been on the road a lot; with him being gone, my only time to relax is at night, when the kids are in bed and my thoughts just seem to come out and on paper. It is the best way to remember and enjoy them.

NELTE, JEANETTE
[b.] South Africa; [occ.] Accountant; [hob.] Travelling; [ed.] Graduated University of Cape Town; [pers.] Sometimes the mind will wander. Let it stay its satisfaction.

NEUWERTH, MAX
[pen.] M.A.N; [b.] Great Falls, MT; [occ.] Waiter; [hob.] Writing, drawing, hiking, running, aikido, kenpo; [ed.] Havre High School; [awrd.] Won the spelling bee in fifth grade, yippee; [pers.] Power lies within the imagination, and it is infinite.

NEWBOLD, TAMMY
[b.] Canton, OH; [occ.] Student; [hob.] Music, softball, track, collect porcelain teddy bears; [ed.] Jr. High, Bell Herron Middle School (eighth grade); [awrd.] Softball, Girl Scouts, music, basketball; [oth. wrks.] *Anthology of Poetry by Young Americans* ("Hand in Hand"), *Literary Anthology* ("Lost and Found")

NEWMAN-GREGERSON, DIANE M.
[pen.] Diane M. Newman; [b.] March 2, 1948; East Liverpool, OH; [p.] James M. Plecas Jr. and Marjorie Esther Mitterling; [m.] December 13, 1969; [ch.] Valance R. Newman; [ed.] Oceanside High School, Mira Costa College (1967–68), National University in San Diego (Nov. 1991 to Jan. 1995); [occ.] Writer, poet, professional speaker, clairvoyant-psychic on a network in Beverly Hills, CA; [memb.] Head of the Speaker Bureau at United Nations Association Women's Political Caucus, Mission San Lois Rey, my parish; [hon.] Lion's Club Speakers contest in San Clemente, Presidential Scholarship at National University (1991–1994), Editor's Choice Award (1997–1996), Guest Speaker Award by Toastmasters, Spiritasters of San Diego (1996); [oth. writ.] "Val's Angels" published by NLP (December 1996), "The Prophecy of Diane"; [pers.] "Val's Angels" is a poem written by divine inspiration by God in my life. This poem is a true story regarding the very first breath my only son Val took into this world that was marked with pain and fear. Val is truly an angel from God sent to me to aid me in revealing the truth of mysteries of faith through Jesus Christ my Lord and Savior. I believe with all my heart and soul that each and every individual can become anything that they set their minds to, when they have faith in God.

NIGATU, BETH
[b.] Sioux Falls, SD; [occ.] Student; [hob.] Writing poetry, playing tennis, ping-pong and volleyball; [memb.] YMCA, Girl Scouts; [ed.] Eighth grade middle school student; [hon.] English; [pers.] We only have one life so make the best of it. Even during the bad times think of all the greatness surrounding you and smile!

NUNEZ, ALMOND
[pen.] Peter; [b.] Brooklyn, NY; [occ.] Teacher; [hob.] Singing and playing the guitar; [memb.] Member of a Latin American Youth movement dedicated to promote social and spiritual progress for young people in Washington Heights; [ed.] B.Sc. in Elementary Education; [awrd.] Awarded the "Robert Clement Award" at Boricua College for GPA of 4.0 for four years of Academic Excellence; [oth. wrks.] Written movie scripts, short stories, poems, essays, most of which are unpublished; [pers.] We are capable of doing extraordinary good to mankind or we can inflict the human race with astonishing evils.

NUSIO, JEN
[b.] New Hyde Park, NY; [occ.] Student; [hob.] Skiing, snow boarding, dance, cheerleading, basketball; [ed.] Eight years of grammar school; [hon.] Principal's List, Second Honors; [awrd.] Second place in Irish step dancing, Young Poet of 1998 and 1999; [pers.] My parents and teachers influenced me in poetry. When certain occasions arise, I enjoy expressing my feelings in poetry writing.

OKOLO, ZUBIE G.
[pen.] Zubie; [b.] October 17, 1961; Amawbia - Nigeria; [p.] Geoffrey Okoye Okolo, Felicia U. Okolo; [m.] Mrs. Maureen Zubie-Okolo; October 24, 1998; [ed.] Ezike Memorial Primary School in Nibo, Nigeria, Government Secondary School in Owerri, Nigeria; [occ.] Environmental Consultant; [memb.] Nigerian Environmental Society; Full Gospel Businessmen's Fellowship International, Church Council of "Church on the Word"; [oth. wrks.] Several poems, some of which have been published in local newspapers, published speeches and historical accounts, poems include "Changed," "African City Wash," "Today," "Burnt Offering," etc.; [pers.] A man's quintessential achievment can only be made when he is in unity with God through Jesus Christ. I reflect the gifts of God in emotions and nature and I abhor distortions to these. I have been greatly influenced by great African writers and poets.

ONIANWA, CHIWETA
[b.] Nigeria; [occ.] Graphic Artist, Communicator; [hob.] Meeting people, watching movies, painting; [sp.] Amaka L. Onianwa; [ch.] One; [ed.] Graduated Yaba College of Technology and University of Ibadan, Nigeria; [awrd.] Print making award (Usis Lagos); [pers.] Global Communication may be a geodesic dome but words between North and South of our Country could be the dome without the links.

ORR, SHANNON
[b.] Portsmouth, NH; [hob.] Drawing, arts and crafts; [ed.] Ninth Grader at Noble High School in Berwick, ME; [pers.] My mother and father are my inspirations for encouraging me to be the best I can be.

OSGOOD, CORNELIA
[b.] Augusta, GA; [occ.] Legal Secretary; [hob.] Writing, reading, singing, cooking, knitting, jewelry making; [ch.] Three; [gch.] Seven; [ed.] Three years of college, graduate in Computer Networking; [pers.] My goal as a writer is to complete my book I am currently working on and publish it and my book of poems.

OSLIN, JOANNA
[hob.] Sports, reading books, writing

PALEN, NECITA
[pen.] Ching Palen; [b.] Davao City, Philippines; [occ.] Wal-mart Stores, Inc. (Associate); [hob.] Travel, crafting, listening and singing easy-listening music, writing poems; [sp.] Adrian B. Pallen; [ed.] Graduated Far Eastern University— B.S./B.A.; [pers.] The combination of sweet music and personal deep feelings entices my soul to create the beauty of poetry expressing the fulfillment of love and passion.

PARK, BARBARA
[ch.] Two

PARKER, JAMES M., JR.
[b.] July 12, 1980; Chicago, IL; [p.] James Sr. and Kathy; [ed.] First year of college; [occ.] Student; [hon.] National Library of Poetry, Child's Play Touring Theatre; [oth. wrks.] "The Night Is upon Us"—National Library of Poetry, "Child's Play"— Child's Play Touring Theatre; [pers.] Editor of Morton West Creative Paper *The Egg*

PARKER-SEAGO, MARY
[b.] Potecasi, NC; [occ.] Teacher, high school English; [hob.] Travel; [sp.] Stanley Seago; [ch.] Two; [gch.] Four; [ed.] Graduated East Carolina University in Greenville, NC; [pers.] Writing poetry is a means of expressing personal feelings and views concerning life.

PAULEY, THERESA
[b.] Toledo, OH; [occ.] Bus-Aide; [hob.] Poetry, short stories, puzzles; [sp.] Keith R. Pauley; [ch.] Four; [ed.] High School; [pers.] My husband Keith has always been my greatest fan and my inspiration.

PERKINS, ANNA
[b.] Jackson, MS; [hob.] Playing basketball and spending time with my family and friends; [ed.] Tupelo Christian Preparatory School; [pers.] I have been writing ever since I could hold a pencil and won several times in Gumtree and District. Just practice what you enjoy.

PERMISOHN, KRISTY
[b.] Washington, DC; [occ.] Student; [hob.] Music, hockey, swimming, other sports; [ed.] High school, graduated college in May 1999; [pers.] I wrote this poem as a tribute to my mom, for her love, devotion, and as a way of telling her how much I love her. She has enjoyed it, and I hope you will as well!

PERRY, HENRIETTA A.
[b.] Norwich, NY; [occ.] Housewife; [hob.] Like to knit Afghans, play games, write letters; [sp.] Walter— passed away 1997; [ch.] Three; [gch.] Five; [ed.] High school; [oth. wrks.] "My Granddaughter" in another contest in California (1980); [pers.] I was reading a *McCall's* magazine when I read "A Poem Contest"—the snow was falling to the ground when I wrote the poem "Snow Flakes."

PERRY, REBECCA
[b.] Lake City, FL; [hob.] Singing, Writing poetry and studying English Literature; [memb.] Beta Club, Theta Cappa; [ed.] Freshman in college; [hon.] Graduated with Honors, Dean's List; [awrd.] Outstanding Youth Volunteer, High School English Award; [pers.] I am in college now to become an English teacher. I hope to get a Ph.D. in English Literature. Poetry is my soul music.

PHILLIPS, STEPHEN
[b.] Maryland; [occ.] Student; [hob.] Playing basketball and writing poetry; [ed.] Ninth grade; [pers.] My inspiration comes from my father who served in Vietnam.

PIEARCE, CHRIS
[pen.] Joker; [b.] Dallas, TX; [occ.] Student; [hob.] Baseball, basketball; [ed.] 11th grade in high school; [awrd.] Second place for the tenth grade in The Mockingbird Chapter—Poetry Society of Texas

POCIUS, ETHEL M.
[b.] Camden, NJ; [occ.] Retired Clerical for LA County; [hob.] Writing poetry and lyrics, avid crossword fan, love to crochet; [memb.] National Library of Poets, International Society of Poets; [ch.] Two; [gch.] Two; [ed.] High school graduate, some business, some computer programming; [awrd.] PTA Award; [oth. wrks.] Three Editor's Choice Awards by The National Library of Poets; [pers.] I am an amputee confined to a wheelchair, and I thank God for the miracles He has given me. I also thank Him for my wonderful family and so many friends. I think I have truly been blessed!

PORTELLE, JO ANNE
[b.] Boston, MA; [occ.] Real Estate Broker; [hob.] Writing poems, short stories, photography, dramatic reading; [memb.] WA Assoc. of Realtors, Soroptimist; [ch.] Two; [gch.] Three; [ed.] St. Mary's Academy, Boise State University; [hon.] Student Gov't Day, Cando Award Eastern Airlines; [awrd.] Best Dressed—2 times; [pers.] When employed by Eastern Airlines, I traveled around the world and collected many memories which became the subject of my stories and poems. My photography are of these faraway places and the beautiful scenery in WA state.

PRIESTLEY, LORETTA S.
[pen.] Little Bit; [b.] Princeton, NJ; [occ.] Poet, crafts, housewife; [hob.] Crafts, reading; [memb.] First Baptist Church of White Springs; [sp.] William; [awrd.] Editor's Choice Award (Anger); [oth. wrks.] "To Dad," "Anger"; [pers.] I wrote this poem Saturday and read it to Ed Sunday. He died Friday, from hepatitis C. He stayed with me the last year of his life.

PRINCE, JOHN
[b.] Muskegon, MI; [occ.] Full-time philosopher; [memb.] Meatpuppets for Anarchy; [ed.] Graduate of Mona Shores High School (1998); [awrd.] Winner of the 1998 Western Michigan Showcase Literary Arts Award; [oth. wrks.] "Immaculate Perception," Quill Books, "A Time to Be Free"; [pers.] Someday I'll sit on the bright side of the moon and play solitaire, but for now I think I might settle for balancing my checkbook.

PROCTOR, PETER
[pen.] Peter Proctor; [b.] Belfast, N. Ireland; [occ.] Deep-sea-diver and pile driver; [hob.] Surfing, watching babies grow; [memb.] Local 2375 pile-drivers' union, 2A, 6A; [sp.] Annette Amoroso Proctor; [ch.] Four; [ed.] Avtech Institute, College of Oceaneering, Presently studying at Ohio University; [hon.] Summa Cum Laude; [awrd.] Numerous Accolades; [oth. wrks.] "A Quiet Plain"; [pers.] To restore metaphor to English poetry, we must begin by returning to the music of John Geats, and spark a new generation of creative geniuses.

QUESADA, ALMA
[b.] Miami, FL; [occ.] Student at Mims., Work in community service; [hob.] In Fbla/Future Business Leaders of America; [ed.] 6th Grade; [hon.] Honor Rolls at school; [awrd.] Citenzenship Award, Integrity and Honest Award; [pers.] Writing in my point of view is easy. I write from the heart, I write the truth. My inspiration came by a little help of God; He showed me the way and that's how I learned what I wanted to do.

REED, JESSICA
[b.] Cleveland, OH; [hob.] Swimming, playing basketball, writing; [ed.] Woodbury Elementary School, sixth grade; [pers.] I love to write when I'm in school; I can write maybe four stories a day if I tried. I was eleven years old on May 24.

REESE, MONICA
[b.] Atlanta, GA; [occ.] Safety Officer; [hob.] Reading, writing, playing with my children; [ed.] Graduate of Columbia High School, class of 1990; [pers.] Always believe that with God all things are possible and no weapons formed against you shall prosper. My favorite poet is Maya Angelou.

REICH, JAYNE F.
[b.] Bartow, FL; [occ.] Raise money for Dallas Charities (Volunteer) and homemaker; [hob.] Singing, boating, songwriting; [memb.] TACA (The Arts) executive board, Waikiki Yacht Club, Crescent Club, Tower Club Dallas Opera Women's Board, Kidney Foundation Womens Board, Arboretum Womens Board; [sp.] Donald E. Reich; [ch.] One; [ed.] University of GA, Florida Southern College, Cincinnati Conservatory, Soprano Soloist FL, Southern Chorus 1990–1992 Nashville, TN; [awrd.] Several beauty contest winner-upper 10% in music city songwriting—lyrics and music; [oth. wrks.] Wrote Music to Dallas Video "Cry of the City" with Howard Keelns Narrator; [pers.] I aspired to be an opera singer, songwriter but married a wonderful man instead—have continued my writing however, and have chaired many major charity balls in Dallas: The Northwood Ball with Joan Collins, The March of Dimes Gala with Gary Collins, The Greer Garson Gala, Digging for Diamonds honoring Martin Jurow for Parkinson's for Northwood University

RHODES, SUE
[b.] Benson, NC; [occ.] Retired; [hob.] Crafts, Travel, Reading; [ch.] Three; [gch.] Four; [ed.] One year of junior college in Louisburg; [pers.] Writing poetry gives me an inward peace, and it is an expression for me, to leave for my children.

RIGGS, MICHAEL C.
[b.] Des Moines, IA; [occ.] Student, U.S. Marine Corps; [hob.] Camping, hiking, coin collecting; [memb.] Boy Scouts of America; [ed.] Norwalk Public Schools, Des Moines Area Community College; [hon.] Eagle Scout; [awrd.] Track Letter, Meritorious Mast Volunteerism (Marines)

RIGNEY, NAKISHA
[b.] Roanoke, VA; [hob.] Love to write and design fashionable clothing; [ed.] 11th grade, home-schooled; [pers.] As I grow older, I fall to my knees fighting all these troubles, only then realize even the strong struggle! "Sixteen" was written on October 5, 1998 on my 16th birthday.

ROBERTS, DORIS
[pen.] Sis Doris Roberts; [b.] Charleston, SC; [occ.] Nurse; [hob.] Sewing; [memb.] Abyssinian Baptist Church; [sp.] Robert Roberts; [ch.] Six; [gch.] Twelve; [ed.] High School Graduate at Abyssinian Baptist Church; [hon.] Women Day Honor '97; [awrd.] Christian Service Award; [pers.] I began writing at 53 years old. I have written many more, I am praying that one day they will all be published.

ROBERTS, LORENE
[b.] Prince Edward CO, VA; [occ.] Retired high school Eng. Teacher; [hob.] Genealogy, bridge, golf, music; [memb.] James Allen Chapter NSDAR, Elder—Pryor Mem. Presbyterian Church, Crewe Country Club; [ed.] B.A. in English Spanish—Longwood College, M.S. in Education Longwood College; [pers.] "To God Be All Glory" all gifts come from God, and I give thanks to him for everything I am and have.

ROBERTS, RACHEL
[b.] Cross City, FL; [occ.] Retired Business Owner, Operator; [hob.] Creative writing, oil painting, swimming, reading, crosswords; [memb.] Church of Christ; [sp.] Clarence W. Roberts; [ch.] Two; [gch.] Three; [ed.] Dixie Co. High School, some college hours but no degree; [oth. wrks.] Published in local newspapers, Dixie County Advocate; [pers.] Your own innermost thoughts, your deepest feelings, your sense of wonder and curiosity are the quiet sources from whence creativity flows.

RODRIGUEZ, TERESA
[b.] Brigham City, UT; [hob.] Playing sports, writing poetry and hang out with friends; [ed.] Adele C. Young intermediate school (7th grade); [pers.] Being 13 is very hard, and writing poetry has kept me out of some trouble. Plus I enjoy writing it, and it's fun. You should try it.

ROGERS, KATHY
[b.] Baltimore, MD; [occ.] Accounting Manager; [hob.] Crocheting, reading, writing; [sp.] Timothy D. Rogers; [ch.] Three; [ed.] Watterson College; [hon.] Dean's List; [awrd.] Editor's Choice Award for "Awakening" and Honorable mention for "Thanks for Making a Difference"; [oth. wrks.] "Thanksgiving," "Awakening," "Draw Bridges," "Thanks for Making a Difference," "Emor . . . Peace of Mind"; [pers.] Carolyn, thank you for teaching me to "Take Flight." I've loved having you with me on my journey.

ROOT, JOSEPH
[pen.] Anarchraka; [b.] El Paso; [occ.] Thane of Chaos; [hob.] The Arch desires of Thelema and that of the reveler; [pers.] The infinite cosmos reaches only within it's continues of the uncertain and on predictable. An "order" or "progress" is only but the confusion of another conformity.

RUN, SUNDA
[pen.] Kay; [b.] Dallas, TX; [hob.] Poetry, writing, reading, singing; [memb.] Dallas Public Library; [ed.] N. Dallas High School and Townview Academy; [pers.] My goal as a writer is to be like William Shakespeare. If my career as a poet I'll start writing novels and books.

RYAN, JOYCE
[b.] Indiana; [hob.] Sewing, crafts, gardening, writing; [ch.] Seven; [gch.] Fourteen; [ed.] Selected College Classes; [hon.] Dean's List; [pers.] Want to pursue writing! Would want to accomplish this in varied ways, to the best of my ability, considering all phases possible.

SAFFRIN, MARY
[b.] Evanston Hospital; [occ.] Student; [hob.] LaCrosse, poetry; [memb.] President of Sigma Delta Tau Sorority, Girl Scouts, ISP Member; [ed.] Currently at Bradley University; [awrd.] Many from ISP and Poet's Choice Award; [oth. wrks.] Many in International Library of Poetry and other books; [pers.] "What doesn't kill us make us stronger."

SAMPLES, MARCIE
[b.] Detroit, MI; [occ.] Student; [hob.] Skateboarding, drawing, writing, teaching karate; [pers.] Go forward, straight ahead; there are no limits on your life but those barricades you build yourself.

SANDERS, ROBERT
[b.] Belle Chasse, LA; [occ.] Stocker, Bagger; [hob.] Write poems and stories; [ed.] Graduated from Belle Chasse High School (1995), sophomore at Delgado Comm. College; [oth. wrks.] College Literary Magazine; [pers.] The reasons behind my poems, like others', are aspects of my life or a certain time in my life which I had to write down.

SAUNDERS, HAYWARD W.
[b.] Hollywood, FL; [occ.] Maintenance Worker; [hob.] Golf and gardening; [memb.] Church of God—Minister, AF of P&CC, ASN, DNC, NCSSM; [sp.] Cynthia; [ch.] One; [gch.] Three; [ed.] High school senior; [pers.] The Holy Spirit inspired me to write this poem. During my youthful years, my life was filled with sin, guilt, and remorse, but when I accepted Christ as my personal Savior, it brought peace, joy, and comfort to my soul. But still, many times I was saddened by the harsh treatments I received from many—the harrasments, persecutions, rejections— but by the grace of God, I had the strength to endure, and this poem was given to me through inspiration.

SAVINO, RALPH
[b.] Fishkill, NY; [occ.] Acerobatt; [hob.] Waterskiing, lovemaking, drinking, entertaining; [memb.] Local 201 Pipefitters Union; [sp.] Andrea Lee Savino; [ed.] Harvard graduate; [hon.] People's Choice 1990; [awrd.] 1986 Battle of Bands; [oth. wrks.] "Sexmentally Assaulted," the album (1988); [pers.] Music has always been my inspiration as a writer. This dark poem was originally a song describing the cunning effects of a drifter on a small town.

SCHELLING, JOSEPH G.
[pen.] Gilligan Hayseed; [b.] Richmond Heights; [occ.] Mail Room Press Stacker; [hob.] Gardening, fishing, bicycling; [memb.] MO Botanical Gardens; [ed.] Union High, Union MO, St. George Affton, MO; [awrd.] Three Editor's Choice Award; [oth. wrks.] "Your Treasured Heart," "Prayers to the Blessed Mother"

SCHMIDT, JENNIFER
[b.] Hazleton; [occ.] Student; [hob.] Painting, drawing, fishing, tennis; [ed.] Pennsylvania State University; [pers.] To God be the glory! I will forever praise His name, and Jesus is the inspiration in my life.

SCHOATE, CHRISTOPHER
[b.] Cleveland, TN; [hob.] Writing, karate, hiking, kayaking

SCOTT, DOLORITA I.
[pen.] Della; [b.] Panama Canal Zone; [occ.] Housewife; [hob.] Write poems, crochet, and travel;

[sp.] Winston Scott; [ed.] High school; [awrd.] English class; [oth. wrks.] "Our Mother"

SEEGER, WILLIAM
[b.] Salem, Germany; [occ.] Retired Former Int'l. Airfrt. Forw. and U.S. Customs Broker; [hob.] Chess, swimming, walking, reading; [memb.] Lynbrook Massapequa Lodge 822 F and A.M., Steuben Society of America; [ch.] One; [gch.] Two; [ed.] Academy of Advanced Traffic New York, NY 1956–59; [hon.] First prize for essay issued by The Academy; [pers.] To enjoy the autumn of my life in God's shining light and to use me to reflect his love to all people I meet.

SEWELL, DONALD
[b.] Wichita Falls, TX; [occ.] College student; [hob.] Writing; [memb.] Faith Baptist Church of Iowa Park; [ed.] Junior at Midwestern State University

SEXTON, JAMIE
[b.] Arlington, TX; [occ.] Student; [hob.] Writing poetry, listening to music, just having fun; [ed.] High school; [oth. wrks.] Poem "Life" in the *American Poetry Annual*; [pers.] I would like to thank all my family and friends. I would also like to thank Everett Moran; you were my inspiration for this poem.

SHARAPAN, ROCHELLE
[b.] Pittsburgh, PA; [occ.] Teacher; [hob.] Reading, writing, travel, pets; [memb.] Phi Delta Kappa, Pi Lambda Theta, NCSS, now, USHMM, Southern Poverty Law Center; [ed.] Master of Education, currently a doctoral student; [hon.] Phi Delta Kappa, Pi Lambda Theta; [oth. wrks.] Poem published by The National Library of Poetry, 1998; [pers.] Those who care—teach.

SHASHUA, ROSA
[pen.] Shoshi T. Shashua

SHELTON, PATRICE B.
[b.] Baltimore, MD; [hob.] Reading, writing and drawing; [ed.] Student at Elementary School; [hon.] Certificate of special recognition for artistic ability; [awrd.] Academic Achievement for Excellent Spelling; [pers.] I do my hobbies to get my mind off of the sad things. I play the violin for the same reason.

SIGLER, LEIA
[b.] Perry OK; [occ.] Emergency Room Registration; [hob.] Playing pool, writing, drinking tons of coffee; [ed.] High School Graduate; [hon.] *Who's Who Among American High School Students*, [oth. wrks.] "Memories of Grace," "The Love I've Lost"; [pers.] The person who has inspired me the most in my life is Sarah McLachlan. Her beautiful music and lyrics has deeply touched me and I will be eternally grateful to her. She is truly an angel.

SIKORSKI, LAURA
[pen.] Laura Burton; [b.] October 6, 1976; Glenwood Springs, CO; [p.] Julienne and William Sikorski; [m.] Kris Burton; December 14, 1996; [ch.] Kristian James and Brittany Jannell; [ed.] G.E.D. Northwestern, Michigan College; [occ.] Handicap Advocate; [memb.] Homestretch, Affordable Housing Task Force; [hon.] Student Government Association; [pers.] I try to let my life experience, heart and inner truth reflect in my writings. I believe that poetry is the need to share both joy and heartaches.

SIMMONS, AUNEAKA
[pen.] Neaba; [b.] Chicago; [occ.] CNA, Home Health

Aide, Poet; [hob.] Writing, skating, reading, and watching television; [hon.] Certificate for the Year, Student of the Month; [awrd.] Faith, Hope Youth Young Adult Gospel Choir; [oth. wrks.] Church Need letters, "Looking in the Mirror"; [pers.] My goals to be the best writer I can be and motivate others in doing good instead of people putting people down and not understanding you for who you are.

SIZEMORE, ROBERT
[pen.] Lucifer's Magician; [b.] Detroit, MI; [occ.] Penniless Writer; [hob.] Writing, reading, music; [ed.] 11th grade; [pers.] I owe everything to my parents, for holding me up while I chase my lyrical dreams. To my friends and family: "We'll be there soon."

SIZEMORE, SERENA
[b.] Columbus, OH; [occ.] Production Welder; [hob.] Writing, watching my children grow, my pets, spending time with family; [ch.] Three; [ed.] 13 years; [oth. wrks.] "Taller Than I," "Passers By"; [pers.] If a few words from the heart would make the world a better place, then I would give the world all I have.

SKRAMSTAD, SHARI
[pen.] Snair; [b.] Mandan, ND; [occ.] Transportation Specialist; [hob.] Reading, walking, boating, swimming, snowmobiling, creative memories photo album; [sp.] Rusty Skramstad; [ed.] High school graduate, two years of post-secondary education; [pers.] There are so many successful, intelligent, creative people in this world. If I could be one of them, that would be my dream.

SLAVEN, MARY
[pen.] Cricket; [b.] Colorado General; [occ.] Student; [hob.] Reading, writing, pottery, biking, photography, learning about cultures, meeting people; [ed.] Middle school, eighth grade; [awrd.] Award for Peer Helpers (1997), Reading Improvement (1998), Citizenship (1998); [pers.] Special thanks to Nathan, Linda, Jim, Danny, Sharon, and all my family for support. My heroes are everyone I named, Jim Carrey, Jewel, and Mr. Smith.

SMITH, CRYSTAL
[b.] New Albany, IN; [occ.] Dance Instructor; [hob.] Dancing and I love animals; [memb.] 4-H while I was growing up; [sp.] Jason Smith; [ed.] Graduated of New Washington High School; [pers.] Having a baby at the age of fourteen is difficult. That is my sister's life story. Hopefully she found some piece of mind in reading this.

SMITH, DARLENE
[b.] Mobile, AL; [occ.] Housewife; [hob.] Birds, crafts; [memb.] South Alabama Caged Bird Society (SACBS); [sp.] Robert Smith; [ch.] Six; [gch.] Eight; [ed.] One year college; [pers.] As I held Taffy Cat's limp body in my arms, the years came pouring forth. As I was writing, the pictures were drawn.

SMITH, KRISTY
[pen.] Lynn Rose; [b.] Cincinnati, OH: [occ.] Junior in high school; [hob.] Writing, singing, acting, playing piano; [pers.] When I'm older, I want to become an actress and singer, as well as publish some of my romance stories. Rosie O'Donnell and Alanis Morisette are two of my role models. I also like the interesting works of the Beatles—especially my favorite, Paul McCartney.

SODEN MORELAND, CHERYL
[b.] Indianapolis, IN; [occ.] Library Page/Homemaker; [hob.] Reading, writing, gardening, decorating, antique shopping; [sp.] One; [ed.] Attending Indiana University; [hon.] Having 4.0 average; [oth. wrks.] Several essays published in *Indianapolis Star* newspaper, and poems published in Sparrowgrass Poetry Forum's *Poetic Voices of America*; [pers.] Since early childhood, reading others' words and writing my own thoughts and feelings about life in my diaries and journals have helped me to survive.

SOLES, BERRY
[b.] Whiteville, NC; [occ.] Timken Bearing Grinder/Machinist; [hob.] Poems (Fishing-Bass) hunting; [memb.] Timken Bass Fishing Club; [sp.] Opal Ann Soles; [ed.] 11 1/2 Grade; [awrd.] Art, Band Member; [pers.] This poem was written for my dear departed brother whom I loved but didn't say enough and for the hurt and sorrow of my parents.

SPADAVECCHIA, DANIELLE
[occ.] Student; [hob.] Skating, swimming, reading and writing poems; [memb.] Beanie Baby Club; [ed.] Middle School; [hon.] Grand prize (Curad design contest); [awrds.] Choirs, gymnastics; [pers.] When I write, I feel as though I have brought out my real self esteem and shared it with others, and I hope that others will listen and read my feelings.

SPORES, AMANDA
[b.] St. Lukes, Cedar Rapids, IA; [hob.] Writing poems, collecting sports cards, singing; [ch.] One; [ed.] I'm going to Kirkwood for high school diploma; [pers.] I believe if you sit down with a pen and some paper, anything is possible; as long as you believe in yourself, it is possible.

STALERMAN, RUTH
[b.] March 18, 1919; Bronx, NY; [p.] Sam and Minnie Rosson; [m.] Joseph Stalerman; June 5, 1949; [ch.] Helene L. and Enid S.; [ed.] Evander Childs H.S. (1936), Modern Machines Business School; [occ.] Patient Advocate at the White Plains Hospital Center as a volunteer; [memb.] Board of the White Plain Hospital Auxilliary, Jewish War Veterans, WHAW's Brancox 191 (Chaplain); [hon.] Who's Who of American Women (1997–1998 Edition), Who's Who in America (1998 Edition), Who's Who in the East (1999–2000 Edition), Who's Who in the World (1999–2000 Edition); [pers.] My aim in life is to learn something new each day and to help someone each day.

STAPLES, JENNIFER
[b.] Norristown, PA; [occ.] Marketing Associate; [sp.] Michael Staples; [ch.] One; [pers.] My son, Tyler is the inspiration in my life. He adds a whole new perspective.

STASIC, JOSEPH
[pen.] Joseph W. Stasic; [b.] San Antonio, TX; [occ.] Minister; [hob.] Writing, reading, travelling; [ed.] 4 years college at Rhema Bible, Washington University; [awrd.] Flooring Expert Carpet One; [pers.] My inspiration comes from within, and continous studying to help express myself more clearly and to create a personal feeling to the reader and a visual image.

STEELE, BRANDON
[b.] Murrary, KY; [occ.] Student; [hob.] Collecting baseball cards and Volkswagon Beetles; [memb.] 4-

H; [ed.] Seventh grade student Lakewood Elementary School; [awrd.] Baseball, basketball, football, track

STONE, THERESA
[b.] Cicero, IL; [occ.] Housewife; [hob.] Enjoy cooking; [ch.] Three; [gch.] Five; [ed.] Grammar School; [pers.] I send into our local paper my thoughts on what is going on in our world today. I am 82 years old and live in a low-income apartment.

STOTTLAR, PATRICIA
[b.] Fort Garden, GA; [hob.] Making people smile; [ed.] Graduated; [pers.] I wish someday my writings would be recognized and well-known to other people. Special influences came from my family and friends to keep going and never give up.

SWANSON, DARLENE
[pen.] Stone Wolffe; [b.] Massachusetts; [occ.] Homeopathic Healer; [hob.] Medicinal Herbalist; [memb.] Universal Life Church Clery Person, Founder of TOTEM, The Ordained Temple of Earth Mysteries for Pagans; [ed.] Licensed Aesthetician, Licensed Aromatherapist, Certified Herbalist; [hon.] Reverand, High Priestess of Wicca and Strega; [awrd.] Doctor of Divinity; [oth. wrks.] Forthcoming, "Making Sense of Scents" with companion product catalog; [pers.] The only true sacredness of this world is that of the sovereign citizen. "To live your life in the glorious wonder of full bloom every day!"

TALBERT, COYELL
[pen.] La-La; [b.] Sumter, SC; [occ.] Make Brake Boosters; [hob.] Music, drawing, collecting; [sp.] Raven Talbert; [ch.] One; [ed.] Graduated high school

TAUTIMER, REBECCA
[b.] Tucson, AZ; [hob.] Writing stories, poems, and kickboxing; [ed.] Freshman at Tucson High

THOMAS, HELENE L.
[b.] Richmond County; [occ.] Instructor and Program Director—Surgical Technology; [hob.] Reading, cooking, home decorating, travelling; [memb.] Association of Operating Room Nurses; [ed.] Registered Nurse, B.S.N. from CNOR; [hon.] Outstanding College Students of America 1989; [awrd.] Outstanding Persperative Nurse of the Year 1995; [pers.] I wish to thank my pastor, Rev. J. R. Hatney for his spiritual inspiration and influences for my faith and dedication to God.

THOMAS, KATHREN
[b.] Fort Smith; [occ.] Student; [hob.] Writing poems, music; [ed.] Eighth grade at Raymond E. Wells Jr. High; [pers.] The person that inspires me the most is my father. He believes in me no matter how much I make mistakes.

THOMPSON, LINDSAY
[b.] Clinton, IA; [occ.] Student; [hob.] Photography - 4H, Tennis; [memb.] Youth Group at church, 4-H group, Spring Valley; [ed.] Clinton High School; [hon.] 4-H awards in Photography; [oth. wrks.] Photo published in the International Library of Photography (1998); [pers.] I was inspired to write this poem because of my aunt Julie's best friend's death. Renee touched my family's hearts in many ways.

THORPE, SCHUYLER
[b.] January 3, 1974, Anchorage, AK; [occ.] BCTI Student, Writer; [hob.] Collect comics, write stories, novels, poetry, video games; [ed.] High

school, one year of college; [oth. wrks.] "Dream Girl" (poem), Poetry Guild "Thoughts and Dreams Remembered"; [pers.] Writing is a passion that few people understand . . . those that have an incredible gift.

TORRES, NANCY
[b.] Bronx, NY; [occ.] Homemaker; [hob.] Writing poems, music; [ch.] Four; [ed.] G.E.D. Computer training; [hon.] Recited several poems on Public Access TV channel 68 (Bronx Net); [pers.] I wrote the poem while I was in recovery. I was fighting the demon of addiction; I also was fighting to get my children back in my life. I have lots of beautiful poems.

TRAICOFF, DREMA S.
[pen.] Sandy (only in artwork); [b.] Chelyan, WVA; [occ.] Disciple Ministries—minister; [hob.] Sewing, writing; [sp.] Dennis Norman Traicoff; [ch.] Four; [gch.] Nine; [ed.] High School, Business Education; [hon.] Laid up in heaven; [awrd.] Layed up in heaven; [oth. wrks.] "The Cedar Chest," "Satan Can Speak"; [pers.] God has been my influence in life, coming from humble beginnings, a coal miner's daughter out of the hills of West Virginia, settled in Ohio.

TRUEBLOOD, ERIC
[b.] Fontana, CA; [occ.] Student; [hob.] Soccer, skating, church; [memb.] Member of Crossroads Christian Church; [ed.] High school; [hon.] Creative Literary Magazine *CHS* two years published; [awrd.] Biggest Flirt in Jr. High, Honor Roll; [oth. wrks.] "Denver in Fall," "A Shriveled Rose," "That's Life," "How Do You Win a Hopeless Fight," and "Viva Los Star Wars"; [pers.] Do not conform any anger to the pattern of this world, but be transformed by the renewing of your mind.

TYSON, THERESA
[b.] Mobile, AL; [occ.] Farm Girl; [hob.] Writing, drawing, fishing, flowers; [sp.] William; [ch.] Four; [gch.] One; [oth. wrks.] Editorial for *Bonifay Florida*, Editorial for *Selma Times*; [pers.] Life is not forever; slow down and enjoy life, 'cause the only thing that leaves the world when you go, is your soul.

ULM, KRISTYN
[b.] St. Paul, MN; [occ.] Student; [hob.] Skating, writing, drawing; [ed.] Currently in the sixth grade; [pers.] A couple of my special influences were my grandparents, aunts and uncles, and especially my parents and teachers. My goals as a writer are to keep writing and hopefully I will have a book published with all my poetry in it.

VAN DEN BOOM, SEAN
[b.] November 13, 1983; Adrian, MI; [p.] Wayne and Esperanza Van Den Boom; [ed.] Student of Eppler Junior High, will be attending Utica High in fall of '99; [memb.] PGA Tour charter member, various educational programs, inside of school; [hon.] President's Award for Educational Excellence, Citizenship Award, various Honor Roll awards, and other educational awards; [oth. writ.] Several pieces which are yet to be published; [pers.] Many of my writings are from observations in my life. To view the full potential of life, you must look around your world.

VU, PAUL
[pen.] Vu-Anh-Phuong; [b.] Phat-Diem, Ninh-Binh, Viet-Nam; [occ.] Library Media Specialist; [hob.] Music, sports, writing (poems, short stories), travelling; [ch.] Seven; [gch.] Two; [ed.] B.A.

Teach. Credent. U. of Dalat, 18 years as high school principal (1972–1975) in Viet-Nam; [oth. wrks.] Over 200 poems and 10 short stories will be published in the near future; [pers.] Writing is my hobby to express my feelings, memories, as well as philosophical view point about life, death, fortune, happiness, or misery of human destiny.

WACHERLIN, GEORGE
[pen.] Georgie Boy; [b.] Aurora IL; [occ.] Cable Splicer for Ameritech; [hob.] My home, gardening, restoring old cars; [sp.] Mallisia; [ch.] Two; [ed.] Waubonsee Junior College "Harvard by the Highway"; [hon.] The Lions Club of Elburn had two plaques made one made in Braille. These are both hung on the wall at their club so everyone can enjoy them.; [pers.] I have never rhymed two words together until my loving wife passed away, "Went to Heaven." I have now written six poems. I think it is Mallisia's way of keeping in touch with me. "God Bless!"

WALLACE, DIANA
[b.] Van Nuys, CA; [hob.] Writing, track team; [ed.] High school student—freshman; [hon.] Honor Roll; [pers.] My goal is to try my best and never give up as my mom and dad have taught me.

WALLACE, ERNEST
[b.] Chicago, IL; [occ.] Customer Services Supervisor/Com. ED; [hob.] Singing in Choral Groups, playing the piano, and 35mm photography; [memb.] Deacon of First Greater Bethlehem MBC Chicago IL, American Legion Post 118; [sp.] Judy Ann Wallace; [ch.] Three; [ed.] Junior year of College at Northwestern University in Evanston, IL; [hon.] Associate of Arts Degree, Kennedy King College, Chicago with honors; [awrd.] Chosen as one of the outstanding deacons in Chicago, IL/Midwestern Baptist Laymen Fellowship; [oth. wrks.] Written essays for American Legion Post 118 Bulletin; [pers.] I have been given a challenge by one of my English Professors at Northwestern University and that is to master English. He said it's impossible.

WALLICK, GENEDA
[b.] Mexico, MO; [occ.] LPN; [hob.] Writing, reading, walking, watching videos, fishing; [memb.] NFLPN; [ch.] Three; [ed.] One year of college plus studies in Psychology, Death and Dying; [awrd.] Ideal Nurse Award, Humanitarian of the Year Award, Employee of the Year; [pers.] Through life's tragedies and changes and joy there is always reason and purpose keep the faith and appreciate what you have. Look within yourself for strength.

WALMSLEY, TANYA
[b.] Highland Park Hospital; [occ.] Student; [hob.] Collect knives of many sort, coins, and like horseback riding and computers; [ed.] Senior in high school; [pers.] Life is what you make it to be. You wake up in the morning and you choose what mood you want to be in for the rest of the day— either a good or bad mood. I think people should think about that. I choose a good mood.

WALSH, FRAN
[b.] Collbran, CO; [occ.] Retired, 65; [hob.] Arts and crafts, painting, poetry; [ch.] Five; [gch.] Eleven

WARD, CAROL
[b.] New Haven, CT; [occ.] Reference Librarian; [hob.] Music, reading, health advocacy, travel,

hiking; [memb.] Church, great books, DAMS (Dental Analgom Mercury Support Group); [ed.] Douglas College—M.S. in Library Science from SUNY and Albany (graduated 1966); [hon.] Youth Advocacy, 1983; [pers.] I would like to pay tribute to the strong influence and encouragement of my mother, Mary Jane Ward, and my grandmother, Pearl Cooley.

WASHBURN, RUBY FLOWERS

[b.] August 28, 1924; Knightdale, NC; [p.] Daniel and Maggie Flowers; [m.] Seth Washburn; August 20, 1949; [ch.] Christine, Edward, Cozette, and Timothy; [ed.] Wake Forest University graduate; [occ.] Retired School Teacher; [memb.] Maple Springs Baptist Church, several women's groups; [hon.] Valedictorian at high school; [oth. wrks.] Many poems, some published in local newspaper

WATKINS, CURTIS

[pen.] Malcom D. Watson; [b.] Decoy, KY; [occ.] Chengyman; [sp.] Liz Watkins; [ch.] Three; [gch.] Seven; [ed.] B.A. at Anderson University in Anderson, IN; [hon.] Sponsored "Hiding Grace," a Billy Graham film; [oth. wrks.] "Reggie and Me," "The Dogwood Tree"; [pers.] "Angel," my pet for seven years, died on March 28, 1999. I felt very deeply about this loving, all-white feline. It was a sad day, but the children and the grandchildren helped bury her and show respect. For me there is much to write about.

WEIGLE, BECKY

[b.] York Hospital; [hob.] Riding horses, hand crafting things, hunting, working on cars, going to drag races, and line dancing; [ed.] Junior High; [pers.] I can't really say I have and influence to write, I just sat down one day and couldn't stop writing, But I guess you could say Shakespeare had an influence on me.

WHITEHEAD, CRYSTAL

[b.] Savannah, GA; [hob.] Writing, hanging with friends; [ed.] A freshman in high school; [pers.] Being a teenager or being human isn't always easy, so I enjoy writing about it. It makes me feel better.

WHITEMAN, KIMBERLY

[b.] Wyoming County Hospital; [hob.] Volleyball, poems, short stories, reading, painting, drawing, hiking; [memb.] Girl Scouts; [ed.] Warsaw Central School; [hon.] Silver and Gold Award

WILLIAMS, ERIN KRISTEN

[b.] Peru, IN; [occ.] Student; [hob.] Writing, poetry, singing, hanging out with friends; [memb.] N.M. Bible Club, First Assembly Youth Group, Akron Youth Group; [ed.] 11th grade at North Miami High School; [pers.] God is my savior and inspiration. He will never give us anything too hard to handle, but instead, gives us the strength to overcome.

WILLIAMS, GLORIA

[p.] Dodie; [b.] Saginaw, MI; [occ.] Service Rep. for Coca-Cola USA; [hob.] Reading, writing, bowling, exercising, cooking; [ed.] Bachelor of Science from Michigan University, graduate internship at Wayne State University; [pers.] I would like to thank God for blessing me with a special talent. Special thanks also go out to everyone who encouraged and inspired me.

WILLIAMS, ROGER K.

[pen.] Kent Shivers; [b.] Houston, TX, [occ.] Fork-lift Operator, Craftsman, Landscaping; [hob.] Bowling, chess, watching action movies; [ed.] High School at Evan E. Worthing, Class of '75, Houston, TX; [hon.] 1972 Most Outstanding Male of School, Carter G. Woobson, Houston, TX; [pers.] In this, I am inspired through effective cruises in life, deeply by my dearest mother and endured meditation.

WILLIAMS, TOBY

[b.] Ft. Lauderdale, FL: [occ.] Walt Disney World Entertainment; [hob.] Skiing, cooking, always looking for inspiration in TV or stories; [ch.] Two; [ed.] Some college; [awrd.] 15 years Disney (as a character); [pers.] Influences and inspirations, in a full, open-minded life, as a result, have molded my mind to all the possibilities of life. I believe people are always looking to be inspired and see mankinds true potential. I'd like to aid in those expectations.

WILLIAMS, TREVOR

[b.] Columbia, MO; [occ.] Student; [hob.] Fishing, biking, camping; [ed.] Currently in high school; [pers.] The thing that inspires me to write is my moods, good and bad times.

WILLIS, JAMI

[pen.] Yomi; [b.] VA; [hob.] Writing poems, reading talking on phone; [ed.] Windsor High School; [pers.] The thing that inspired me most is my parents for encouraging me.

WILLMAN, DANIEL

[b.] Nelson, New Zealand; [occ.] Tennis Professional; [hob.] Writing, boxing, rugby; [sp.] Elisa; [ed.] College, University of Idaho, B.S.—Sports Medicine; [hon.] Big West All Conference NCAA Tennis, 3 years; [awrd.] Won New Zealand 16's National Singles and Doubles, former NCAA top 20, NZ Open top 8, most important—Husband of the Year Award from my wife; [pers.] My mother's heart shattered that terrible day when her soulmate of 32 years passed away at 53. My words are dedicated to my mother's daily battles for survival and my father's life.

WINBURN, TIFFANY

[pen.] Tiffany Winburn; [ed.] Still in high school; [pers.] My inspirations go out to all my family and friends that gave me my inspirations. The mistakes in my life help me out, give me my thoughts, and that's what I use to write my poems.

WOYACH, DIXINE

[b.] Big Hork, MN; [occ.] Field Rep.; [hob.] Knitting, fishing, boating, music; [memb.] President, Showboat board of Dir; [sp.] Gerald; [ch.] Three; [gch.] Five

YOUNG, NATALIA

[b.] Waikiki, HI; [occ.] Student; [hob.] Singing, writing music and poetry, drawing, acting, dancing; [ed.] Student at Allentown High School; [awrd.] Excellence in Music; [pers.] Never let anyone hold you back from succeeding in your goals and making all your dreams come true. The biggest obstacle is one's self.

YOUNG, SARAH

[b.] Phillipsburg, NJ; [occ.] Student; [hob.] Baking, camping, reading, running; [ed.] Homeschool; [pers.] My dad works hard and I appreciate and love him for it. He is a special Christian influence for me.

ZAMORA, KERENSA

[pen.] Nita Clay; [b.] Benton, IL; [occ.] House Wife, Artist; [hob.] Painting, drawing; [sp.] Gene Zamora Jr.; [ch.] Two; [ed.] Jefferson High School of Cedar Rapids, IA (Class of '91); [awrd.] In painting: Best of Division, First and Second Place awards; [pers.] I'm an artist, and this is the first poem I've ever written. I just wanted to put in writing what I put on canvas.

Index
of
Poets

Index

A

Acevedo, Judy 78
Acker, Dale L. 191
Ackermann, Dula M. 225
Acosta, Shirley 62
Adamiak, Nadia 121
Adams, A. Perry 110
Adams, Jessica Lynne 49
Adams, Lauren 56
Adas, Jen 76
Addeo, Orlando 230
Adebiyi, 'Tunji Kazeem 132
Adjmul, Jonnique 187
Adkins, Luke 216
Aho, Dale P. 225
Akinro, Francis 146
Akootchook, Annie 28
Alabi, Roslyn C. 100
Albaugh, Patti M. 162
Albright, Audra L. 181
Albright, Jonalyn A. 28
Allen, Amanda Jo 12
Allen, Hannah 110
Allen, Ruby 165
Allensworth, Mary Rozanna 83
Allgood, Jennifer Lynn 25
Amendola, Claudia 151
Amerski, Audrey 140
Ancheta, Johnson 30
Anderson, Eleanore E. 88
Anderson, Jessica 87
Anderson, Lynnette 191
Anderson, Priscilla 34
Anderson, Renita A. 87
Anderson, Sheri 228
Andrews, Chris 137
Andrews, Tommy 175
Angel, Stephanie Files 146
Angles, Jenna 40
Ann, Lisa 174
Anthony, Rosemarie 129
Anzalone, Cathie Marie 194
Appiah, Nina Y. 106
Apple, Patricia J. 203
Appleby, Brenda 126
Arbour, Stephanie 134
Arendas, Jessica 65
Arias, Jocelyn 233
Armstrong, Marcus 136
Arnold, Rhonda 201
Aroh, P. Emeka 200
Arsovska, Jana 38
Arwine, Jamie 65
Aske, Joselyn 19
Assent, Erna 135
Atkinson, Cynthia 89
Atkinson, Maxine 129
Auer, Tim 176
Avestisova, Yelena 48
Axelrad, Gabrielle 44
Ayze, Audrey 28
Azan, Amanda 229

B

Babcock, Jack 195
Babcock, Ryan 172
Bachman, Dorothy M. 206
Baggott, Sherrie 199
Bailey, Joshua 206
Bailey, Montie Ruth 112
Bailey, Opal Marie 15
Bailock, Katie 226
Bailum, Christina 169
Baird, Golda 210
Baird, Helen E. 118
Ball, Ashley N. 109
Ballard, Wayne T. 182
Bannister, Ariana 113
Banovic, Yvonne 20
Baran, Patrycja 57
Barber, Kelly 54
Barbour, Ruth 219
Bardroff, Larry 222
Barham, Joli 228
Barker, Jory Andrew 125
Barker, Mi Wha M. 94
Barnes, Roberta 152
Barnhill, Kristy 32
Baronne, A. J. 131
Barron, Janet B. 200
Bartlett, Brendan 112
Bartolo, Kristina 79
Bass, Gloria J. 89
Bastani, Yolanda Paredes 104
Bastyr, Susan 111
Bauccio, Susanne E. 88
Bauer, Suny 62
Baughman, Amy 80
Baumann, Michael E. 226
Baumer, Lauren 33
Bay, Laura 15
Beaty, Orren, Jr. 142
Beaulieu, Sharon 215
Beck, Carolyn Williard 191
Becker, Alda 201
Becker, Helen 183
Becker, Lois M. 158
Becker, Trisha 33
Bedore, Sandra 56
Beerman, Amanda M. 61
Beeson, Randy 161
Beharry, Elizabeth 173
Belay, Sarah 57
Bell, ChaKira N. 164
Bell, Jean 3
Bender, Christopher W. 226
Bender, Judy 227
Bennett, Jessica 159
Bennett, Nicole 182
Bennett, Ronald 203
Bentivegna, Pamela 7
Berbes, Stephen 118
Berg, Lauren Alexis 17
Berger, Beverly L. 172
Berke, Jessica 53
Bernock, Katy 58
Bernoi, Jamie 210
Berry, Kristie 5
Berry, Linda 99
Bickford, Jenn 189
Bickford, Michelle 30
Billett, Darlene 83
Bishop, Joanie LeCoq 149
Bissonnette, Yvonne 210

Black, Tina 117
Blaho, Danny 145
Blair, Cynthia 115
Blair, Heidi 192
Blakeney, Doralene 148
Blanchette, Joan 188
Blankenship, Dyann 141
Blanton, Alexia 212
Bliss, Erik 169
Bloodgood, Lisa Marie 211
Bloomfield, Rebecca Rosado 93
Bloss, Stephanie Amanda 55
Blowers, Donna 170
Blue, Dorothea E. 110
Boaz, Jennifer 176
Boles, David L. 137
Bomhoff, Alexandra 58
Bonnell, Sgt. Ian 167
Bordeaux, Patricia 53
Borders, Anna Dawn 10
Borger, Sophia Simmons 84
borra-Española, Seurinane Sean 109
Bose, Krishna 5
Boucher, Jessica 42
Bouvier, Ellen 134
Bowden, Larry L. 181
Bowen, Barbara C. 224
Bowers, Chris 152
Bowers, Robert 202
Bowman, Jeanine 85
Bowyer, Florence G. 102
Boyd, Diana L. 220
Boyd, Evelyn M. 176
Boye-Moller, Susanna 151
Boyland, Tammy 170
Boyle, Dessa 17
Boyle, Mary 112
Bracamonte, Vanessa 8
Brachman, Penny 62
Bradley, Anita 109
Bradshaw, Christi 28
Bragdon, Tonya M. 74
Braniff, Todd S. 198
Brannom, Lorie Michelle 133
Brantley, Jessica 73
Bratcher, Staci Ranae 70
Braun, Jenn 75
Bravar, Sandy 24
Breed, Stephanie 71
Bregman, Harriet 94
Brennan, Lori 18
Brent, Pamela ("Pamelot") 111
Bride, Mick 144
Bridges, Michael 132
Brierley, Samantha 79
Bright, Tim 190
Brim, Metokie E. 83
Bristol, Robin 64
Brita, Steven 5
Brock, Randy Jack 164
Brodsky, Alexandra 139
Brooke, Georgie 124
Brooks, Amanda 198
Brooks, Isaac 92
Brooks, Nadia M. 115
Brooks, Natasha Y. 121
Brown, David W. 98
Brown, Martha 214
Brown, Maurice L. 137
Brown, Nicole 63
Brown, Patsy 225
Brown, Sarah 93
Brueggeman, Michelle 40

Brumbalow, Joyce 210
Brummett, Dianne 203
Bruner, Vicki L. 195
Bruno, Kim 51
Buch, Ingrid 90
Buchholz, Jennifer 35
Buck, Patricia 119
Buckley, Karen McCoy 101
Budniewski, Michelle 43
Buechler, Shanna 56
Buechler, SN Carlos D. 218
Buford, Menno L. 146
Buller, Menno L. 146
Bullinger, Nancy 134
Bult, Lisa 50
Bumgarner, Beverly A. 89
Burch, Michelle 69
Burden, Mary 37
Burdett, James, Jr. 101
Burdg, Jinee 177
Burnett, Fay 135
Burns, Alisha 55
Burns, Tracy 90
Buron, Derrick 85
Burr, Nellie 220
Burt, Jeb 103
Burton, Laura 88
Burzynski, Mary 232
Bush, Amanda J. 173
Butler, J. A. C. 136
Butler, Norma A. 160
Butts, Iona M. 218
Buyers, Candice Farley 71
Byrne, Cara 112

C

Cabler, John 141
Cacciamani, Kelly 71
Calandrelli, Ruby 167
Calderon, Maria 170
Calleja, George A. 174
Camp, Jason 34
Campbell, Beverly 19
Campbell, Nancy Avevitt 217
Canada, Bettye J. G. 116
Cannon, Carrie Lynn 231
Cantrell, Kelly 159
Cape, Tina M. 123
Caplan, Jonet 111
Capria, Karen 213
Carasotti, Georgeann 125
Carden, Jeffrey S. 177
Carlson, June M. 142
Carlson, Sarah 24
Carney, John T. 9
Carpenter, Joycelyn 203
Carr, Bob 216
Carroll, Katie 57
Carrozza, Natalie 161
Carry, Anna 21
Carson-Owens, Samisha 45
Carswell, Dorothy 128
Carte, Cassie 26
Carter, George F. 219
Carter, K. 200
Carter, Lela L. 82
Carter, Paul 174
Carter, Sheri 154
Carty, Valerie Y. 41
Casebolt, Lori A. 166
Cashman, Casey Elizabeth 16
Castro, June 184
Catanzaro, Danielle M. 122

Catloth, Kate R. 140
Cavanaugh, Michelle 229
Cedzich, Gerilynn 234
Chamberlain, Courtney 37
Chamblin, Gypsy 21
Champ, Anna 70
Champion, Jessica 77
Champlin, Lea 177
Chan, Jessica 217
Chapas, Leia 172
Chapman, Paulus 139
Chartrand, Carol M. 105
Chaves, Elizabeth G. 143
Chavez, Yvette 169
Cheek, Nicole 165
Chelikowsky, Aaron M. 221
Chen, Teresa 11
Chenoweth, Nicole 56
Cherkin, Marnina 67
Chiang, Iris 54
Childers, Lisa 144
Chill, Ella 142
Choate, Crystal A. 55
Christensen, Jodi 226
Christensen, Sara 41
Christenson, Deborah 202
Chubbs, Christina 131
Clapp, Allison 32
Clare, Doug 107
Clarett, Betty 27
Clark, Leann 35
Clark, Leora 51
Clark, Tiffany 180
Clavey, Heather 41
Clay, Ronnie L. 96
Clayton, Summer Ann 171
Clemons-Zeigler, Yvette M. 152
Clewley, C. 188
Clifford, Gloria J. 115
Clinton, Asad 177
Clinton, Donald H. 59
Clontz, Amber 177
Cloobeck, Melinda 116
Coats, Michelle Ilene 61
Cockman, Mary Anne 224
Cockrum, Christopher 106
Cohen, Catherine B. 3
Cohick, Jeremy 225
Cole, Jennifer 29
Coles, Ernest E., II 221
Collar, Jake 138
Colley, Erin 127
Collier, Peggy 131
Collins, Barbara 131
Collins, Chasity 156
Collison-Jones, D. J. 119
Colquitt, Anthony 31
Compton, Michael E. 120
Compton, Mike 221
Conner, Leigha 158
Connor, Dennis E. 216
Cook, Bobbi 52
Cook, Ericka R. 164
Cooks, Chandra 122
Cooper, Mark 114
Corbin, Olive 188
Corea, Erica 186
Corey, Jacqueline 40
Cornelius, David J. 215
Covell, Dawn 234
Covert, Faye L. 105
Coward, Michelle 60
Cowder, Amanda 200

Cox, Bridget 32
Crawford, Melissa 40
Crawley, Saundra 198
Cremens, Jodi 56
Creson, Roland, Jr. 113
Crone, Telsa Michelle 122
Cronin, Mary J. 126
Crosby, Michael P. 109
Crouch, Joyce 171
Crowther, Barbara 223
Crowton, Romy 224
Croy, Stephanie 22
Cruson, Larry W. 149
Cuadra, Angel 191
Culajay, Juan F. 102
Cunningham, Andrea 70
Curry, Lauren 16
Curtis, Nicky 47

D

Dahan, Veronica 173
Dahlke, Joan M. 10
Dakin, Devi 157
D'Alessandro, Ann 99
Dalhover, Angelia 229
Danec, Patsy J. 197
Daniel, Emily Peaden 206
Daniel, La Donna 72
Danitz, Mitchell 179
Danson, Angela 141
Dass, Maria 87
Dauch, Jennifer A. 98
David, Matthew 166
Davis, Brooke L. 111
Davis, Carson 119
Davis, Darlene 205
Davis, Elanna Rasco 231
Davis, Ernest L. 126
Davis, Felecia R. 201
Davis, Geoffrey 4
Davis, Hanna Y. 152
Davis, Harold 92
Davis, Jennifer 62
Davis, Linden 16
Davis, Nikolina 147
Day, Rachel 15
De Backer, Elaine 7
De Martino, Jessica 148
De Young, Jack 190
Dealba, Debra 211
Deburow, Crystal 158
DeClouette, Markia 38
DeDoes, Kirk 150
Dee Ross, Helen T. 43
Deemer, Theresa A. 232
Defever, Susanna Mason 8
DeHamer, Lauren 233
Deibler, Linda 120
Deimling, Rita 120
Delgado, Billy 171
DeMarrias, Trisha 51
Demmons, Brandi A. 67
Dempsey, Florence E. 116
Dennis, Virginia 105
DeNye, Michelle Grant 121
Deppe, Nichole 81
DeSena, Philip 96
DeShaw, Ellen Parker 194
DeStefano, Lou 163
Detton, Jessica R. 67
Devanath, Anindita 4
Dezen, Felise 179

Di Chiaro, Nicole 49
Diaz, Claudio R. 118
Dillard, Charlotte 122
Dillard, Haley 64
Dillingham, Suzanne Lynn 115
Din, Celia 93
DiSalvo, Susan 160
Ditman, Henry M. 118
Dix, Dana 161
Dobson, Joseph 84
Dobson, Joseph 124
Dodge, Tiffany 228
Dodson, Danielle 166
Dolan, Kelly 70
Dolan, Kirren 73
Dombrosky, Lisa M. 20
Domenech, Anna 37
Dorsey, Chris 45
Doss, Lt. Col. Robert K. 119
Douglas, John Forrest 223
Dowell, Shayla 208
Doyle, Brenna 26
Drakeford, Vivian S. 88
Drella, Laverna 190
Dreveniak, Rachel 70
Druckman, Joan 183
Duncan, Jane 158
Dunnington, Crystal 30
Duran, Michelle 28
Duty, Nathan D. 169
Duva, Jennifer J. 58
Dwyer, Jen 96
Dye, Michelle 61
Dyer, J. C. 170
Dyer-Minnick, Delores R. 171
Dykes, Dr. Ray Francis 128
Dyson, James 205
Dyson, Janis Suggs 205

E

Eastridge, Christopher D. 164
Eckols, Donna 14
Edwards, Katie 171
Eggen, Serianna 59
Eichel, Kimberly Jo 174
Eicke, Annabelle 71
Eide, Karen 54
Elam, Claudette 169
Elkin, Robert L. 135
Elliott, Keisha 49
Ellison, Amber 74
Ellison, Stephanie Rose 59
English, Christopher 169
Engmann, Katie 34
Ensworth, M. Therese 110
Erickson, Ann 206
Escalante, Michael 162
Eson, Jessica 67
Espenschied, Johnny L. 124
Estrada, Oswaldo, Jr. 110
Ethington, Lula 111
Evans, C. 182
Evans, Ione 147
Evans, Tiffany L. 20
Evelyn, Kendell 177

F

Fabian, Heather 41
Falcon, Cassie 38
Falkowski, John 213

Fantasia, Frances 226
Farebrother, Clay R. 150
Farkas, Mitzi B. 232
Farkas, Rhea C. 125
Farley, Pat 175
Farmer, Melanie 221
Fatland, Jessica 71
Faules, Barbara Ruth 207
Faust, Alisa 181
Fearrington, J. 134
Feinstein, Osvaldo Néstor 117
Feliciano, Cris S. 114
Feliciano, Felix 198
Feller, Wanona S. 189
Felton, Tyeisha 209
Fennimore, Jackie Ray 151
Ferguson, Gwendolyn 110
Ferrantelli, B. 198
Ferrell, Russell L. 175
Fevold, Shelby L. 53
Field, Edmund 100
Figueroa, Stephanie 228
Fillinger, April 165
Filomeno, Jessica 44
Fink, Angie 127
Finkelman, Sol 59
Firmin, Marjorie R. 107
Fischer, Marie 138
Fiscus, Julie 35
Fish, Markie 33
Fisher, Catherine 9
Fisher, Jerry L. 166
Fisher, Kia 22
Fivis, Nicole Cain 70
Flaherty, Amy Marie 69
Fletcher, Thaddeus A. 161
Fleureton, Margaret 122
Flick, Lindsay 91
Flores, Rebecca 63
Foate, Wayne R. 115
Fogarty, Grace Ann 224
Fogleman, Ruth E. 87
Foley, Melissa 171
Fomich, Joanna 183
Fontana, Nichole 24
Forastiere, Noelle 21
Foreman, Carol 6
Forsyth, Cassandra 222
Fortin, Rejeanne 100
Foster, Ginger 117
Foster, Jennifer 78
Foster, Patricia M. 218
Foust, Garrett 48
Fox, Amber 155
Foy, Karrianne 56
Frail, Courtney Dyan 163
Fralick, Robert 169
Francis, Anika 137
Francis, Jamison K. 220
franick, bekah k. 11
Franks, William J. 119
Fratello, Stephen 50
Frater, Stefanie L. 66
Freeborn, Jenny 142
Freeman, Virginia 105
Freese, John 179
Fritz, Anita 106
Frost, Miranda Tela 53
Frye, Lee Ann 79
Frye, Ronald 145
Fuentes, Robert 219
Fuller, Teola 204
Fultz, Lacey 62

G

Gabriele, Stefanie 205
Gagne, Jan E. 151
Gaither, Sarah 35
Galland, Loretta 119
Gallaway, Amanda 18
Galloway, Sabrina Marie 199
Galvan, Minerva 56
Galvan, Rosa Maria 30
Gama, Marie 212
Gamache, Michelle 68
Gamble, Glenda L. 128
Gannon, Kailie 63
Gantt, Romica 128
Ganz, Yaakov 129
Garcia, Angela 9
Garcia, Miriam P. 137
Garcia, Stephanie 15
Gardner, Mariana Zavati 96
Garrett, Gene 89
Garrett, Therese 223
Gartz, Marlene 209
Garza, Ashley 36
Garza, Marissa 68
Gaston, Tina 23
Gatian, Rebecca 7
Geiser, Paula Lampman 142
George, A. M. 191
George, Jennifer 182
Gerbus, Jackie 111
Gerety, Kenneth R. 178
Germine, Laura 108
Gerzanicova, Hana 126
Giampetruzzi, Marco 83
Gibson, Loretta 201
Gibson, Mary 126
Gifford, Stacie 216
Glasco, Floyd 225
Glassberg, Yisrael 204
Gleeson, Kellie 80
Glensky, Cindy 128
Goble, Jeff 73
Godwin, Wilford Robert 85
Goian, Evan K. 204
Golden, Rachel 68
Gomez, Cynthia 66
Gong, Vanessa 55
Gonsalves, Jahri 153
Gonzales, Pete 138
Gonzalez, Amelia 80
Gonzalez, Mary Y. 108
Gooby, Stephen J. 211
Goodwin, Jennifer 230
Goodwin, Patricia 174
Goral, Patti 27
Gorea, Lucia 187
Gorena, Todd Frederick 193
Gorman, Joan 34
Gottesman, Steven J. 141
Gowers, Gary R. 216
Grady, Christina 57
Grant, Jenna 31
Grantham, Henry 123
Grauert, Ruth E. 9
Graves, Foye A. 201
Gray, Connie L. 90
Gray, Jonathan R. 148
Gray, Patricia J. 94
Green, Danielle 171
Green, Kodi 80
Green, Stephanie 93

Gresham, Jack, Jr. 156
Grey, Sarah 130
Gribble, Doris Lee 120
Grice, J. 97
Griep, Heather 72
Griese, Justina 19
Griffin, Alexis 178
Griffin, Donna J. 14
Griffin, Reginald Anthony 196
Grillo, Doris Marie 122
Grimes, Bridgette 69
Groh, Mary Kate 105
Grooms, Lossie 177
Gross 53
Gross, Tara 59
Gross, Tracey 63
Grubb, Serena Marie 143
Grubham, Katie 43
Grueber, Laurel E. 28
Gruenwald, Miriam 114
Guidice, Carol 210
Guido, Diana 68
Guillory, Becki 116
Gurriell, Roy L. 213
Gutierrez, Nina D. 81
Guyan, Samantha L. 193
Guzman, Beatriz 23
Guzman, Justine 37
Guzman, Kimberly 203

H

Hageman, Harry 232
Haines, Susan 186
Haislip, Michelle 199
Hale, Jennifer 113
Hall, Eleanor Thurston 162
Hall, Madeline Shorter 230
Hallman, Brenda 27
Halloway, Amanda 21
Halpin, Amanda 34
Halverson, Polly 158
Hamby, Kim 43
Hamilton, Jack A. 143
Hamm, Jessica 63
Hammett, Daniel 221
Hamric, Holly 44
Handa, Becky 183
Handford, Michael 8
Handy, George 178
Handyside, Howard 221
Hann, Sarah 81
Hansen, Jasun Ty 179
Hansen-Solum, Nicole I. 67
Hapke, Danza 158
Harden, Teresa 158
Hare, Chris 127
Hargrove, Maurice 144
Harklerode, Allison 32
Harmon, Lea Anne 26
Harned, Kim A. 190
Harper, Melanie S. 145
Harrington, Nathan 113
Harris, Beth 184
Harris, Consuelo J. 227
Harris, Cristy Diane 27
Harrison, Rudolph 168
Hart, Peggy J. 118
Hart, Vicki 15
Hartford, Randy Gayle 165
Hartl, Carolyn S. 217
Hartley, Jennifer 212
Hartman, Marilyn 234

Hartmann, Lorraine Foss 57
Hartwick, Jessica S. 22
Harvell, Jessica 22
Harvey, John B. 111
Harvey, Tawana 64
Hatton, Kayci 173
Hauck, Kayla 46
Hawkins, Amy 13
Hawkins, LayKisha 114
Hawkins, Marjorie 175
Hawkins, Martina 65
Hawkins, Otelia 210
Hayes, Gary 161
Hayes, Robin 155
Haygood, Jeremy 107
Hayman, Sarah Catherine 26
Haynes, Candace 41
Hayward, Christia 122
Haywood, Gloria 114
Healey, Marilyn 108
Hedrick, Lindsey 61
Heggan, Margaret 77
Heid, Mary 11
Heim, Eileen Mary Theresa 13
Hein, Elizabeth 7
Heinrich, Maroella 169
Helmrich, Ashley 60
Helms, Sandy 219
Helton, Christine 46
Helton, Grace 87
Hemken, Mary Jo 116
Henderson, Aaron Da'Mar 116
Henderson, James William, Jr. 101
Hendricks, Edward R. 186
Hendry, Madelyn 104
Henrich, Richard 127
Henrick, Jeanne 115
Hepa, John W. 123
Herbst, Victoria 208
Heresco, Diane 159
Herrington, Laura Sue 172
Hertzberg, Matt 117
Heye, Claudia 40
Hicks, Tom 170
Hidalgo, Gil 128
Higbee, H. J. 152
Higginbotham, Troy 126
Hiles, Michael 4
Hill, Beverly 140
Hill, Constance Mutka 104
Hill, Lindsay 50
Hill, Nikesha 187
Hilley, Marie 127
Hines, Bryan S. 92
Hinkley, Talia 32
Hinkson, Cynthia 129
Hlady, Jarret Quinn 119
Hlas, William A. 109
Ho, Nam 103
Hoadley, Kelly 151
Hobbs, Tammy Jo 167
Hodson, Ida Rose 117
Hoeprich, Ashley 71
Hoerner, Amanda 76
Hoffa, Thomas 81
Hoffman, Brandy 72
Hoffman, Eugene 174
Hohrman, Deanna 58
Holbrook, Pamela 47
Holbrook, Sarah Mae 58
Holbrooks, Bobby L. 90
Hollingsworth, Dianne E. 6
Hollington, Fayton D. 154

Holmes, Joan Worth 110
Holmes, Shelly 112
Holt, Edna 199
Hood, Kathrine M. 135
Hood, Rhonda Lee 30
Hooker, Eric 202
Hooper, Michelle D. 125
Hope, Allegra 35
Hoppe, William M. 95
Hopper, Jami 60
Hopson, Debbie 29
Horn, Kelly 64
Horton, Michael 175
Hoskins, Robin 17
Hough, Bil 171
House, Elise 9
House, Sandy I. 92
Howe, Laura J. 155
Howells, Marriane 52
Howrey, Brenda S. 100
Hudnall, Ariel 71
Hudson, Joseph 190
Huedepohl, Misti 7
Hughes, Justin 223
Hughes, Mechelle 202
Hughes, Sara 25
Hugues, Ben 103
Humphrey, J. R. 155
Hunwardsen, Jerry 146
Hurdle, Paul A. 185
Hurst, Katie 18
Hurst, Susan 12
Hurt, Chenika 78
Husbands, Nick 196
Huston, Krystal 78
Hutchins, Charity A. 232
Hutchinson, Ashley 66
Hutchinson, Kara Ann 50
Hymel, Theresa 177

I

Ingle, Eunice M. 175
Ingram, Wm. L., III 232
Irons, Emily 42
Ishman, Delshunda L. 47
Isley, Stephanie M. 35
Ivery-Lucas, Gloria 149
Ivy, Anthony 234

J

Jackson, Amanda 32
Jackson, Gale 195
Jackson, Lindsay 64
Jackson, Peaches 23
Jackson, Raymond C. 94
Jacobovitch, Sandy 69
Jalili, Alexandra 36
James, Connie 81
James, Melissa 55
Jamison, Bianca 39
Jankowski, Laura 141
Jaquis, Diane 230
Jarman, Barb 176
Jasinski, Mildred 192
Jaskiewicz, Samantha 17
Jellander, Karen 196
Jena 21
Jenkins, Rodney 198
Jennings, Amanda 28
Jensen, Emily 208
Jensen, Lindsay 20

Jewell, Norman J. 233
Jiron, Desiree Nichole 58
Johnson, Amanda 64
Johnson, Amanda Jean 19
Johnson, Elizabeth 100
Johnson, Jaya 16
Johnson, Jennifer 198
Johnson, Lynetta M. 84
Johnson, Mark E. 98
Johnston, Nicole 22
Jones, Darlene 206
Jones, Dennis M. 125
Jones, Donald R. 99
Jones, Gina 176
Jones, Kea M. 172
Jones, Olander G. 80
Jorgensen, Sharlee 32
Joseph, Ashley 54
Joslin, Mike 214
Joy, Sharon 150
Judson, Katherine 215
Juge, Carol L. 174
Julbe, Deanna 138

K

Kaiser, Susan A. 3
Kalyvas, Catlyn 132
Kamata, Sonie 205
Kampff, Elana 181
Kareiva, Frank 83
Kassler, Shirley G. 143
Kat 16
Kathol, Brea 30
Kazee, Tyler Seth 74
Keebler, Rebecca 98
Keech, Amber 194
Keehner, Lisa F. 201
Keeley, Kristina 21
Kegler, Pamela Ann 185
Keith, Tim C. 46
Kelchner, Kathryn 4
Kelley, Kaylen 133
Kelley, Louise 107
Kelley, Michelle 133
Kelly, Roger 197
Kelly, Susan 98
Kelsey, T. I. 196
Kendhammer, Lisa 45
kendrick, nina 169
Kennedy, Max 156
Kennington, Marry 83
Kenton, Odis W., Sr. 133
Kenwin, Kathleen 144
Kerby, Janelle 65
Kermode, Kelly 20
Kern, Kristina A. 62
Kernell, Tim 170
Ketchum, Kara 34
Keyes, Amy L. 204
Kidd, Denise 53
Kidd, Heidi 35
Kilburn, Janice 111
Killian, Brett E. 123
Kilpatrick, Tina 56
Kindred, Jodi 27
King, Marty 86
Kinney, Patrick 139
Kinsey, Martie 146
Kirchner, Theresa 114
Kirk, Jeanette 121
Kirkpatrick, Tina 180
Kirst, Nathan 204

Klausner, Jeri 78
Klein, Rachael 77
Kline, Harry S. 8
Kloppenborg, Calie 29
Klosky, Joyce D. 212
kms 7
Kneitel, Karin 95
Knickerbocker, Arthur Henry 233
Knight, Mable 229
Knight, Timothy David 171
Knodel, Joyce L. 120
Knol, Teri 182
Koch, Edward J. 153
Koch, Glen V. 95
Koch, John 130
Kochanski, Sylvia 215
Koegler, Chrysstina M. 115
Koelsch, Kristen 54
Kohl, Mira 79
Kopasz, Valerie Luv 157
Kopet, Roger Scot 101
Kopplin, Kay 136
Kotenko, Kalyna 162
Kovich, Rachel Lee 53
Kowalski, Diana 187
Krajcovic, Peter 109
Krajewski, Lana 47
Krause, George 168
Kreis, Sunny 195
Krell, Fredric T. 206
Krohnfeldt, Jinny 3
Krueger, Lisa 22
Kryzyzek, Jo Ann 164
Kucinski, Pamela 169
Kuhn, Pauline B. 130
Kumarasamy, Anicham 45
Kundrat, Albert 149
Kuniewicz, Gina 12

L

Labani, Alicia Marie 220
LaBree, Jon 3
Lacad, Marion 84
Lack, Leah 72
Lackner, Jessica 61
LaDore, Danielle 24
Laflamme, Jason 214
LaFountain, Renee N. 109
Lake, Alison 202
Lam, Yen 189
Lamberson, Sally 110
Lambert, Darlane 114
Lamberth, Teri 170
Lamont, Joseph 146
Lampe, Jessica 42
Lamporte, Joan 91
Landreth, Deloyed Charles 140
Landrum, Leah J. 150
Lane, Hermella 185
Lanter, Donna 97
Larson, Delores 153
Larson, Josh 233
Lasher, Sylvia E. 96
Lashmit, Amanda L. 223
Lavake, Jason 216
LaValley, M. 134
Lavoie, Shelby J. 163
Law, Talitha Jo 33
Lawrence, Barbara 102
Lawrence, K. E. 109
Lawrence, Katie P. 37
Lawson, Christy 76

Lazarte, Carmen Garcia 172
Le, TuCuong 25
Leach, Kim 23
Leahy, Jessica 179
Leary, David Ray, II 109
Lecey, Barbara M. 117
Leckner, Mary Ann 182
Lee, Donald 224
Lee, Leonard 142
Lee, Nicole 176
Lee, Patricia 114
Leffler, Ravani Jewett 131
Lemke, Linsay 80
Lenarsky, Ariana 171
Lentz, Kathryn J. 113
Lenz, Megan M. 61
Leonhard, Nick 227
Levens, Brian 214
Levin, Erica 117
Levra, Joseph Vincent 209
Lewandowski, Christine 6
Lewis, Bernice 147
Lewis, Billy G., Jr. 221
Lewis, Earlene 91
Lewis, Paul A. 177
Lightfoot, Susan 12
Lindgreen, Jennifer 69
Liner, Allen 204
Link, Helen L. 86
Linton, Katie Fedigan 216
Linzalone, Debbie 15
Litten, Frances C. 173
Little, Gayle 223
Littlejohn, Diana L. 160
Littrell, Jill M. 222
Livingston, Annette Nadine 181
Lodato, Sandra L. 214
Logan, Sarai 12
Logsdon, Amber Elizabeth 42
Long, Heather 86
Long, Megan 68
Lort, Kristin 23
Louk, Thomas F. 163
Lovisone, Tiffany 80
Lowder, Vicky M. 138
Lowe, Crystal 58
Lubas, Lauren 19
Lucas, Naomi 111
Lukasik, Sally A. 177
Luna, Amy G. 140
Lusk, Theresa 177
Lux, Kathleen 193
Ly, Yvonne 181
Lyko, Henry C. 172

M

M., Josh 103
Mack, David L. 121
MacLaren, Ashley 68
Madden, Barbara A. 157
Magallanes, Kristina 65
Magoulakis, Alexandra M. 202
Maher, Francis J. 170
Mahone, Lena P. 117
Mahurin, Sue G. 209
Maine, Wendell 111
Maio, Frank C. 162
Malecki, Michael P. 176
Mallory, Barbara C. 159
Mancinelli, Cynthia L. 159
Manrow, Diane 212
Marcella, Samantha 49

Markham, Michele 155
Marlowe, Dave, Jr. 188
Marshall, Diandra 72
Marshall, Josh 57
Martens, Brad Coyote 120
Martin, Amanda 73
Martin, Jeanette A. 169
Martin, Jody 164
Martin, Lisa A. 154
Martin, Scott 111
Mason, Barbara 174
Mason, Martha 125
Massenburg, Kathleen 234
Mathews, Vanessa 43
Matthews, Jennifer 45
Matuszewski, Mindie 47
Mauck, Kayla 27
Mayfield, Sebrina 49
Mayott, Timothy 231
Mazzoli, Marion 186
Mazzotta, Bruno 133
McAfee, Billy 208
McAnnaney, Stephanie Myers 175
McAtee, Emily 24
McBean, Kateri 14
McBroom, Linda Behrens 92
McCabe, Carissa 75
McCaffrey, Alyssa 40
McCain, Heather 116
McCain, Kenneth 123
McCarley, Mike 150
Mcclellan, Robert 11
McColl, Sara 146
McConico, Eleanor Branch 222
McCranie, Myra 153
McDonald, Candyse J. 19
McDonald, Diane Marie 112
McDowell, Monika 204
McFarland, James E. 105
McFarland, Katherine 44
McGee, Michelle 101
McGreevy, Scott 41
McGrew, Daina 26
McGuinness, Elizabeth 136
McIntosh, Anniebelle 211
McKee, Joey F. 165
McKenzie, Juliana 54
McKinney, Jessica 70
McKnight, Joyce L. 201
McLaughlin, Thomas S., Jr. 155
McMahon, Lyndsey 37
McMillioan, Marian 116
McNeil, Laura R. 219
Mcsherry, Brian 5
Mechels, Sally E. 97
Medeiros, Kellie 107
Medici, Theresa D. 162
Meggs Carroll, Janis 100
Mellett, David L. 169
Melvin, April 73
Menchinella, Carla 17
Mendez, Marcelle A. 113
Menz, Theodore 108
Meredith, Dana 59
Merrill, Mary Louise 98
Mersenski, Celeste 53
Mertz, Alice D. 170
Mickschl, Karen 75
Middleton, Danielle 31
Miles, Bud 101
Miles, Morgan 69
Millard, Kip 148
Miller, Charles A. 196

Miller, Esther 39
Miller, Fay 219
Miller, Judy A. 154
Miller, Maria 3
Miller, Missy 44
Miller, Patricia Carolyn 84
Miller, Philip R. 15
Miller, Ramona 87
Mills, Annie 177
Milyavskaya, Lana 31
Min, B. J. 229
Minchew, Laura Susan 102
Minchew, Stacy 65
Mincoff, Melissa 21
Misch, Robert A. 84
Mitchell, Mattie 199
Mixon, April R. 211
Mixon, Melissa R. 132
Moan, Michelle K. 197
Mongilardi, Raoul Peter 99
Monpas, Nicole Marie 16
Montelione, Francesca 201
Moody, Irma A. 118
Moore, Antoinette 132
Moore, Doreen 78
Moore, Mark 103
Moore, Stacy 38
Moraca, Christine L. 124
Moriarity, Jessica 25
Moriconi, Don 167
Morina, Nicholas 109
Moro, Edward 161
Morrison, Ina Walters 14
Morrison, Marion 171
Morrison, Ross E. 112
Mosing, Renee 45
Mosley, Matthew 108
Mosley, Sonya 228
Moss, Jessica L. 189
Moss, Lilly 66
Moss-Humphres, Tiffany 180
Mudrinich, Ashley 135
Muench, Ryan 26
Mulac, Brandee 44
Muller, Jana 59
Mullins, Joy 47
Mullins, Leigh Ann 172
Murdock, M. 213
Murphy, Amy 173
Murphy, Hortense M. 117
Murphy, Jack 163
Murphy, Jennifer 55
Musser, Annie 38
Mutafoglu, Nathalie 193
Myers, Pam 93
Myers, Stephanie 37

N

Nair, Sangeeta 12
Napier, Mariah 24
Natali, Jennifer 56
Navarne, Taleah 58
Navarrete, Monica 135
Naylor, Melanie Susan 65
Naylor, Terry 106
Neal, Debra 146
Nealon, Linda Kay 6
Negless, Sara A. 33
Negron, Tony 33
Neiger, LaDina 206
Nelson, Barbara L. 110
Nelte, Jeanette 117

Nesbitt, Robert E. L., Jr., M.D. 94
Neuwerth, Max 145
Newbern, Stephen A. 228
Newbold, Tammy 47
Newman-Gregerson, Diane M. 144
Nguyen, Nha X. 59
Nichols, Aletha 116
Nickerson, Janet 208
Nicks, Jessica 112
Nigatu, Beth 45
Nilsson, Diana 188
Norstedt, Davelyn 209
Norton, Elise 174
Norton, Kellijo 56
Nowadzky, Roger A. 81
Noyes, Lenda 13
Nunez, Almond Pedro 199
Nusio, Jen 51
Nutick, Rebecca 54

O

Obercian, Olivia 39
Ocasio, Rhonda De Pietto 210
O'Donnell, Courtney 10
O'Donnell, Darlene 104
Okolo, Zubie 131
Oliver, Rachel D. 37
O'Neal, Victoria D. 166
Onianwa, Chiweta A. 213
Oppriecht, Elizabeth 8
Orefice-Jones, Denise T. 42
O'Rourke, John J., Jr. 221
Orr, Shannon 79
Ortega, Amanda D. 172
Ortega, Michael 167
Osbourne, Jessica 60
Osburn, Elizabeth 137
Osgood, Cornelia 220
Oslin, Joanna 36
Osmundson, Lena 184
Ott, Helen M. 136

P

Page, Donna 148
Pait, Martha S. 14
Palen, Necita P. 208
Palmer, John T. 183
Palmer, Mae 156
Pantano, Ignatius 222
Papas McLean, Dina M. 164
Pardee, Joyce 93
Pare, Edward 180
Paris, Jananya 46
Park, Barbara 191
Park, Kari 153
Park, Kristoffer 97
Parker, Amanda 86
Parker, Heather 133
Parker, James M., Jr. 90
Parker-Seago, Mary Elizabeth 150
Parkman, Bonnie 157
Parks, Angela 167
Parks, Stephanie Michelle 170
Parmentier, Dawn 69
Parrish, Peggy L. 191
Partida, Ana 180
Partridge, Jacqueline 48
Passmore, Jennifer J. 74
Pastier, Anita M. 187
Pauley, Theresa 172
Paulo, Terri-Lei L. 68

Paulson, Dorothy A. 89
Pautsch, Laurie 232
Pecore, Catherine 197
Peet, Laura 173
Peloquin, John 8
Penwell, Kristen 115
Pepin, Kristen 39
Perez, Eduardo 138
Perez, Gloribelle Janisse 53
Perez, Patricia 76
Perkins, Anna C. 188
Perline, Jenna 40
Permisohn, Kristy 107
Perona, Lauren J. 128
Perry, Henrietta A. 111
Perry, Jeffrey 143
Perry, Jessica 15
Perry, Rebecca 112
Persico, Heather 49
Peters, Tierra 193
Peterson, Charlene 105
Peterson, Jillian 55
Peterson, Kimberly 207
Petrick, April 152
Pettyjohn, Mellissa 76
Petzold, Lindsey 52
Phelan, Edward 5
Phelps, Diana 232
Phillips, Stephen 189
Phillips, Terrie 55
Pia, Ken, Sr. 228
Piazza, Shellise 8
Picazo, Gustavo 112
Piearce, Chris 116
Pierritz, Jane 191
Pillai, Sarita 176
Pilley, Amanda 53
Pinske, Jessica 18
Piper, Miriam Simms 184
Pirtle, Tina 58
Pizarro, Jessica 29
Plikaytis, Staci 54
Pocius, Ethel M. 82
Poet 109
Polzin, Veronica 181
Poole, Jean 190
Portelle, Jo Anne R. 193
Porter, Nicole Starr 178
Potisek, Deborah 65
Poulter, Scott L. ("essell") 192
Powell, Amanda 58
Powell, Susan M. 153
Poxson, Emily 137
Pratt, Amy 66
Preston, Kimberly 33
Prete, Alyssa 75
Price, Don P. 212
Priestley, Loretta S. 227
Prince, John 154
Proctor, Peter 135
Prol, Shanna 66
Pruitt, Sue 106
Pugsley, Misty 115
Purcell, James 170
Pusztai, Kathleen 213

Q

Quackenbush, Erin 54
Quesada, Alma 36
Questel, John 213
Quiggle, Richard 192
Quintana, Angela 48

Quintana, Jessica Y. 54
Quy, Hilda E. 174

R

Race, Shaina L. 34
Rafferty, Lori 175
Raichert, Jayme 64
Ramsden, Melissa 74
Randell, Johnny 172
Rangel, Diana 22
Rasch, Amy Elizabeth 162
Rase, Jessica 54
Ray, Tamie 157
Redus, Timothy L. 194
Reed, Gladys 82
Reed, Jessica 178
Reed, Quinta 49
Reese, Monica S. 231
Reh, Terri L. 197
Reich, Jayne 132
Reichard, Delanne E. 234
Reinke, Megan 77
Reising, Kristen 233
Reno, Charles E. 14
Reph, Tabatha 63
Reyna, Glenda J. 147
Rhodes, Sue 143
Rhodes, Summer 26
Rice, Linda 73
Rich, Mary Lou 195
Richelieu, Karen 193
Riggs, Michael C. 145
Rigney, Nakisha 38
Riley, Linda C. 101
Rindell, Suzanne 12
Ringkamp, Lois B. 194
Riordan, Christina 186
Rivera, Emmanuel 214
Roach, Aretha S. 219
Robb, Jerry 209
Robbins, Danielle 70
Robbins, Jennifer 19
Roberts, Brett 5
Roberts Cox, Ruby 155
Roberts, Doris J. 194
Roberts, Lorene A. 234
Roberts, Rachel Hilliard 102
Robins, Aisha Claire 9
Robinson, Amy 38
Robinson, Dorothy Sharples 83
Robinson, Mariah 207
Robinson, Melinda S. 52
Robles, Adelina 113
Roche, Stephen 4
Rochet, Jacinda 123
Rochet, Jaime Humberto, Jr. 92
Rodrigues, Sarah 228
Rodriguez, E. D. 233
Rodriguez, Teresa 18
Roe, Gueyer J. 166
Rofrits, Shelly 17
Rogers, Jennifer C. 173
Rogers, Kathy 16
Roid, Nicole Hyacinth 178
Rojanasupya, Bethany 52
Rojas, Elizabeth 57
Romig, Mike 175
Rondeau, Susan 86
Rooney, Kate 166
Roop, Stephanie 107
Root, Joseph 207
Rosas, Dalia 195

Rose, Cassandra 41
Rose, Charlene 77
Rosen, Jessica 76
Ross, Kim 6
Ross, Lindsay 189
Roszell, Rayona 113
Roth, Sara 93
Rothenberger, Joshua 1
Roy, Danielle 20
Ruetz, Kimberly 95
Ruiz, Andrea M. 174
Ruiz, Jessica D. 233
Run, Sunda 174
Rush, Porscha 187
Ruslander, Barbara A. 196
Rusnak, Daniela 217
Rusnak, Miro 147
Russ, John Cory 139
Russell, Arlie B. 200
Russell, Lou 55
Russell, Richelle 214
Russell, Robbin 185
Russo, Cynthia J. 214
Rutherford, Kristen 60
Rutherford, Michelle 54
Ryan, Joyce L. 168
Ryan, Peter 145
Ryon, John Gordon 222

S

S., Danielle 17
Sabre, Hugh S. 230
Saffrin, Mary 118
Saheb, Rashaan A. 4
Samens, Stephanie 46
Samples, Marcie 68
Sanchez, Juan 218
Sanders, Clara L. 37
Sanders, Robert 126
Sanders, Sandra 180
Sanders, Shelley Williams 129
Sands, Fred Salerno 160
Sannes, Dorothy 91
Sapp, Jack 184
Sardella, Rebecca 129
Sather, Melvin 224
Sauer, Annelie 211
Saunders, Hayward W. 183
Savino, Ralph 181
Scafidi, Joe 139
Scales, John 186
Scarberry, Winkle 158
Schaaf, Danette M. 103
Schelling, Joseph G. 95
Schelling, Joseph G. 96
Schillinger, Jennifer 170
Schipul, Art, M.D. 224
Schmandt, Michael T., Jr. 227
Schmidt, Jennifer 184
Schmitt, Shirley M. 113
Schneider, Elizabeth 59
Schneider, Tracy 217
Schoate, Christopher J. 194
Schuerman, Amber 44
Schulte, Leah 46
Schwarzer, Edward 99
Schwotzer, Peter D. 120
Scott, Dolorita 104
Scott, Emily M. 141
Sczygielski, Jeanette 130
Searing, Tiffany 190
Seaver, Paul 195

Seay, Betty Jane Smith 113
Seeger, William 202
Segers, Mark Alan 121
Semer, Kathy 189
Semmler, Sharon 115
Session, Carmen 21
Sewell, Donald L. 200
Sexton, Jamie 30
Sharapan, Rochelle 85
Shashua, Rosa T. 229
Shawley, Katrina 16
Sheldon, Kathleen 10
Shelton, Patrice B. 176
Sheridan, Christie 33
Shervin, Danny 223
Shimel, Danielle 23
Shine, Ashley 25
Shoemaker, Erin L. 27
Shoumaker, Mary 84
Sigler, Leia 42
Sills, Promise 71
Silverberg, Ruth 226
Simmons, Auneaka 28
Simmons, Lyn M. 217
Simmons, Susan 173
Simmons-Martin, Diana 207
Simms, Michelle 192
Simpson, Francie 100
Simpson, Gwendolyn Johnson 209
Sino, Mary Ann 87
Sitar, Danel 6
Sizemore, Robert 57
Sizemore, Serena L. 78
Skizas, Michael Ann 51
Skokan, Patricia 185
Skramstad, Shari 199
Slade, Billy Massi 163
Slaven, Mary 52
Sloma, Alicia 165
Smith, Carrie J. 138
Smith, Crystal 156
Smith, Darlene 139
Smith, Hazel W. 173
Smith, Janice J. 133
Smith, Jen Lynn 3
Smith, Jennifer A. 161
Smith, Kristine H. 127
Smith, Kristy Lynn 146
Smith, Maria A. 127
Smith, Marthalyn Dale 216
Smith, Meghan E. 55
Smith, Nancy R. 151
Smith, Nyisha N. 29
Smith, Phillip A. 147
Smith, Richard E. 97
Smyth, Aury E. 18
Soden Moreland, Cheryl 140
Soles, Berry 231
Solomon, Michele 11
Sonnier, Lois B. 29
Sorrells, Juton 74
Southworth, Dorothy A. 175
Sparks, Kellie 49
Spaulding, Brian 41
Speck, Gina Marie 130
Spector, Mel 125
Splittgerber, Matthew B. 112
Spores, Amanda 31
Srda, Alicia 212
Stacey, Jeremiah 226
Stacy, Jennifer 77
Stalerman, Ruth 179
Stamper, Kasey 170

Stamps, Sharon J. 156
Stanford, Marianne 167
Stanley, Cristina M. 74
Stanley, Melissa 46
Stanton, Shannon 31
Staples, Jennifer 151
Starks, Evelyn Lea 114
Starr, Melody 50
Starr, Stacey 10
Stasic, Joseph W. 227
Staudenmier, Trenda 114
Steege, Elizabeth A. 110
Steele, Brandon 45
Steele, Joelle 218
Stefan, A. 7
Stefanile, Lawrence V. 59
Stepan, Jeri 106
Stephens, Shakila 142
Stephens, Shannon N. 75
Stepke, David G. 139
Sterling, Virtré 74
Stermer, Alice D. 89
Stettinger, Cynthia 172
Stevenson, Davin K. 192
Stewart, Mattie M. 86
Stewart, Michael J., Jr. 147
Stickney, Erick L. 102
Stoltman, Amanda 18
Stoltzfus, Siobohn 53
Stolz, Carol K. 85
Stone, Theresa 165
Story, Brian R. 91
Stottlar, Patricia 207
Stoudt, Kenneth K. 142
Strahan, Tina 53
Strakhov, Liza 80
Strang, Mary Ellen 197
Strange, Charity 61
Stratton, Michael 227
Straubhaar, Chris 41
Streeter, Marquita C. 154
Strickland, Nina 32
Strickler, K. 53
Stricklin, Amanda M. 176
Strzempa, Toni 164
Stupica, Bruce J. 230
Sullivan, Nicole 79
Summerset, Erma Lee 231
Summit, Annette M. 192
Surdo, Ellen Ward 94
Suri, Sheri 25
Sutton, Evelyn L. 188
Swain, Angela 157
Swain, Samantha 50
Swamy, Ursula 88
Swanner, Martha A. 123
Swanson, Darlene 113
Switer, Rhonda 215
Sydlansky, Laurel A. 143
Szewczyk, Zuzanna 20
Szurgot, Cheryl A. 108

T

Taffer, Barbara 177
Tafoya, Gilbert P. 114
Talbert, Coyell S. 202
Tamayo, Joanne J. 93
Tank, Laura 217
Tarantino, Jennifer 60
Tardif, Erin 182
Tarshik, Zhanna 58
Tautimer, Rebecca 76

Taylor, Bobbie R. 75
Taylor Carmo, Kimberly 59
Taylor Carmo, Kimberly 82
Taylor, Lee 157
Taylor, Linda 193
Taylor, Shelia J. 161
Te Paske, Joelle 171
Tellitocci, Sherry 165
Terry, Peter 85
Thelen, Renee 175
Thoithi, Anne Wachera 204
Thomas, Catherine L. 148
Thomas, Helene L. 163
Thomas, Kathren 36
Thomas, Robert 88
Thomas, Ruth 134
Thompson, Day 181
Thompson, Heather 67
Thompson, Lindsay 36
Thompson, Martha 231
Thompson, Michelle 134
Thompson, Stephanie 61
Thompson, Susan C. 213
Thomson, Ashley 42
Thorpe, Schuyler R. 195
Timm, Dawn 25
Tindall, Jennifer M. 179
Tkach, Kristina 48
Toppings, Sandra 19
Torres, Melissa D. 66
Torres, Nancy 219
Torres, Sarah 39
Tracey, Teagin 79
Traicoff, Drema 90
Trammell, Reverdia 159
Tray, Alison 173
Treadway, Dee 11
Trenner, Jeff 10
Treon, Kheonna Corene 75
Trinen, Rachel 223
True, Jillian 110
Trueblood, Eric A. 48
Tuccillo, Joseph 124
Tucker, Amber 63
Turner, Agnes L. 104
Turner, Marghuerita 129
Tutsock, Thaddeus 159
Tyson, Christena 178
Tyson, Theresa 187

U

Ulm, Kristyn L. 23
Ultican, Crystal 57
Upshaw, Meghan 27
Urquidez, Lori Edna 200
Utomo, Ruslina 50

V

Valentin, Sonia 230
Valverde, Kari 51
Van Den Boom, Sean 108
Vandemark, Irene 166
Vanderhoff, Heather 46
Vargas, Kristina 22
Velasquez, Jenna 23
Vennera, Dominic 55
Vidergar, Frances 115
Villarreal, Linda L. 185
Vincelette, Amanda 229
Virzi, Paul 4
Voelker, Robert 131

Volkert, Shawn W. 17
von Wellsheim, Sarah 72
Voskuhl, Tristan E. 61
Vu, Paul P. 225

W

Wacherlin, George L. 136
Waddell, Autumn 160
Wade, Jeanette 72
Wade, Valerie 149
Wahlberg, Kathy 113
Walker, Brandon 106
Walker, Breanne 56
Walker, Janet 194
Walker, Rebecca A. 183
Walker, Rev. Theodore 81
Wall, Krista M. 40
Wallace, Diana 31
Wallace, Ernest R. 190
Waller, Samantha 69
Wallick, Geneda S. 182
Walmsley, Tanya 34
Walsh, Desmond 217
Walsh, Fran 185
Walsh, Isabella 145
Walters, Donald 95
Walton, Jesse A. 92
Walton, Lindsay 36
Wamsley, Alice 140
Ward, Carol J. 208
Washburn, Ruby Flowers 91
Washington, Flossie M. 106
Wasson, Kimberly 98
Watkins, Curtis D. 124
Watkins, Jeanne 117
Watkins, Loma 132
Watkins, Patricia Ann 130
Watson, Barbara J. 87
Weaver, Christina G. 152
Webb, Deborah J. 81
Webster, Jean Howard 85
Webster, Michael J. 85
Wegman, Linda Jean 127
Wegner, Alyssa 64
Weidinger, Sarah 73
Weigle, Becky 21
Weinmeister, Jennifer 63
Weiss, Lizzy 43
Welch, Whitney 24
Wellman, Katie 41
Wells, Jennifer 73
Wells, Lori 175
Wellstein, Nicole J. 43
Welsh, Amanda Katherine 53
Welsh, Stacey 42
Wendt, Julie A. 133
Wessel, Amy 56
Wessler, Dominique 57
West, Tanya 25
Wetherbee, Ashley 215
Wheatley, Jennifer 72
Whitaker, LaTarsha 149
White, Corrie M. 135
White, Sadie 205
Whitehead, Crystal H. 49
Whiteman, Amber 57
Whiteman, Kimberly 26
Whitis, Jennifer 186
Whitmarsh, Sheana 67
Whitt, Heather 79
Wilborn, Melissa 30
Wilborns, Sylvia L. 86

Wileczek, Iza 62
Willbanks, Maria 52
Williams, Cecil 5
Williams, Darryl Essex 160
Williams, Darryl T. 207
Williams, Eileen Linda 82
Williams, Erin 18
Williams, Gloria Genell 180
Williams, Justin D. E. 109
Williams, Kenneth D. 99
Williams, Linda Carol 231
Williams, Mallory 172
Williams, Melinda M. 6
Williams, Nancy L. 203
Williams, Roger K. 176
Williams, Sophia S. 189
Williams, Terri 220
Williams, Toby 97
Williams, Trevor 179
Williams, Wesley 141
Willis, Jami 20
Willman, Daniel 136
Wilson, Angela 173
Wilson, Beverly 67
Wilson, Brian 10
Wilson, Chris 187
Wilson, Kristin 184
Wilson, Nancy 220
Wilson, Nancy L. 91
Wilson, Sherry L. 139
Winburn, Tiffany 39
Wine, Mary E. 55
Winters, Shannon 167
Wisdom, Michelle 75
Witten, T. Charlene 218
Witthuhn, Jennifer L. 210
Wolf, Tina 29
Wolfe, Casey L. 43
Wolfson, Sherry Jackson 211
Wong, Debbie 24
Woods, Trista Faith 36
Woodworth, Hope 77
Wooten, Bobbie H. 156
Worley, Melody 215
Woyach, Dixine 218
Wright, Evelyn 82
Wright, James 14
Wright, Megan 128
Wright, Tamika L. 63
Wynn, Miracle M. 90

X

Xiong, Cheryl 29
Xiong, Wei Wei 39

Y

Yaccarino, Frank 86
Yaccarino, Frank 94
Yang, Kyung 103
Yeager, Casey 144
York, Johnny L. 196
Yother, Amber 55
Young, Carlene 152
Young, Delisa E. 218
Young, Natalia 172
Young, Sarah 88

Z

Zamora, Kerensa Lee 99
Zanikos, Anacaonia 48

Zimmerman, Yolanda 46
Zmuda, Mary Ann 130
Zona, Candess 66
Zook, Mei-lan 39
Zumbrink, David A. 103